1.50

THE JACKSONIANS

By LEONARD D. WHITE

THE FEDERALISTS

THE JEFFERSONIANS

THE JACKSONIANS

THE *Jacksonians*

A STUDY IN ADMINISTRATIVE HISTORY

1829-1861

by Leonard D. White
UNIVERSITY OF CHICAGO

THE MACMILLAN COMPANY
NEW YORK
1954

PRINTED IN THE UNITED STATES OF AMERICA

First Printing

TO

JOHN MERRIMAN GAUS

Friend and fellow worker
in the field of public
administration

PREFACE

The present volume, successor of *The Federalists* and *The Jeffersonians,* concerns a period of administrative history of major importance. The inauguration of Andrew Jackson as President of the United States coincided almost precisely with the construction of the first steam railroads and with the opening of the industrial revolution in the United States. Before the outbreak of the Civil War, the economic and social life of the American people had been transformed by the growth of manufacturing, the rise of cities, and the activities of corporations.

The political life of the Americans was also transformed. Manhood suffrage rapidly became the rule, democratic dogmas overwhelmed Federalist and Jeffersonian ideas of a governing elite, and the mass political party replaced the congressional caucus as the means of selecting candidates for the White House. Where the people could—in the states and localities—they insisted upon electing their officials; where they could not—as in the federal government—they achieved somewhat the same purpose by the rule of rotation.

The thirty-two years from Jackson to Lincoln were full of constitutional debate, party conflict, and sectional strife, comprising an era of tension that overshadowed the steady normal operations of government. Despite the resounding party and sectional battles, there was a remarkable stability in the structure of government and at the same time a profound change in its quality and its standards. The external forms would have seemed familiar to Alexander Hamilton, but the spirit would have been strange and forbidding. Democracy and the political party had seized upon the administrative system, for better or for worse.

From the political point of view the Jacksonian period may be said to have terminated by 1845. From the administrative point of view, it continued in substance, whether Democrats or Whigs were in office, until it was broken off abruptly by the secession of the southern states. From 1861 to 1869 administrative history was primarily the record of war and military government. As reconstruction gradually came to an end, the excesses of Jacksonian democracy flourished, but forces were at work that would soon require a new philosophy and new machinery for carrying forward the collective business of the people.

During the thirty-two years covered by this volume the American people turned to their state and municipal governments for assistance in the novel problems caused by bank failures, railroad impositions, insurance agent frauds, and immigrant paupers, or by the need for municipal services in water supply, sewage disposal, vaccination, public health, police and fire protection, and the education of children. While the national government hardly did more for citizens in 1860 than it was doing in 1800, the states and their subdivisions were actively pushing into new fields, unhampered by the constitutional doubts of statesmen on the national scene although restrained in some measure by the dominant philosophy of laissez faire. The administrative history of the states and cities, therefore, becomes now a matter of much importance to a full understanding of the overall system that served the needs of the American people. Indeed the reader of de Tocqueville will be constantly impressed by his preoccupation with states and localities rather than with the nation.

In his Inaugural Address on March 4, 1841, President William Henry Harrison remarked, "Upward of half a century has elapsed since the adoption of the present form of government. It would be an object more highly desirable than the curiosity of speculative statesmen if its precise situation could be ascertained, a fair exhibit made of the operations of each of its departments, of the powers which they respectively claim and exercise, of the collisions which have occurred between them or between the whole Government and those of the States or either of them." Daniel Webster privately hoped to pursue this task, but the burden of office became an insuperable barrier.

More than a century has come and gone since Harrison proposed an administrative history, and Webster yearned to undertake it. Meanwhile the materials for such an enterprise have accumulated at an alarming rate. As long ago as 1839 Secretary of the Navy James K. Paulding complained that "the great increase of public records and documents renders all reference to the past more embarrassing." Neither fire, flood, nor pillage have stopped the accumulation, and war merely accelerates the process. The hazards of writing history consequently mount in something like geometrical progression.

This study, like its predecessors, is based principally on the source materials in the public documents, collected letters, and the manuscript treasures of the National Archives. In large measure the participants in the great administrative events and trends of these decades have been allowed to speak for themselves, since my interest is as much in the changing climate of opinion and theory as it is in the facts of the administrative world.

In the preface to his *History of the Navy of the United States of America* James Fenimore Cooper wrote in 1839, "The first, and great desideratum of history, is truth; the second, just reflections on it." The documentary record has provided me, I hope, with substantially the truth; the reflections on it are principally those of contemporaries, not those of the author.

It is a temptation to quote another preface, written by William M. Gouge (a minor character who appears in the pages that follow) in his *Fiscal History of Texas*. Apologizing for his subject he wrote, "If the book is not as amusing as the last new novel, the writer cannot help it. He has done the best he could, in the short time allowed him, with the dry and stubborn materials he had to handle. He comforts himself with the hope that, as he does not write for boarding-school misses, such dryness as necessarily arises from the nature of the subject will be pardoned." I cannot plead the quality of my material, which is full of movement and of human interest despite its formidable encasement in thousands of dusty volumes.

For the convenience of the lay reader I have inserted at the end of the book a *List of Important Characters* which may be helpful for quick reference. Many of the men who played a useful, or at times a spectacular, if not useful role in the domestic affairs of the nation from 1829 to 1861 are now unknown. Some deserve a better fate.

My indebtedness for aid runs in many directions. To the National Archives it is particularly heavy. To the Library of Congress, the University of Chicago Library, the Baker Library at

Dartmouth College, the Hoover Library at Stanford University, and the library of the New Hampshire State Historical Society it is also great. Various chapters of the book have been read by my colleagues, C. Herman Pritchett, Earl J. Hamilton, W. T. Hutchinson, and Robert A. Horn. The University of Chicago, the Public Administration Clearing House, and the Rockefeller Foundation have made financial contributions without which the work could not have been done.

Finally I must again record my cumulative debt to Jean Schneider for her skill in locating material, her perceptiveness as a critic of the art of writing, and her care in preparing the manuscript for the press. My friends are charged with such excellence as the book may have; the author may be properly charged with its inadequacies.

Leonard D. White

June 30, 1953

CONTENTS

THE JACKSONIANS

CHAPTER ONE

The State of the Nation and Its Administrative System

Andrew Jackson left the Hermitage for his inauguration as President of the United States on January 18, 1829. The day before, Daniel Webster had written: "Nobody knows what he will do when he does come. . . . My opinion is, that when he comes he will bring a breeze with him." [1] Never was Webster more successful in prophecy. But over the horizon were more winds than any man could foresee, blowing in storm after storm from the south and southwest that were one day to burst into the bitter gales of civil war.

I

Many thoughtful persons were apprehensive at the prospect of a President with the reputation of Andrew Jackson. He was himself aware of this and in 1824 had written his old friend, John Coffee, "Great pains had been taken to represent me as a savage disposition; who allways carried a scalping knife in one hand, and a tomahawk in the other, allways ready to knock down, and scalp any and every person who differed with me in opinion. . . ." [2] Even Martin Van Buren, before he knew Jackson, had his own doubts. "Of his habitual self-control . . ." he wrote in a characteristically cautious phrase, "many of his warmest

1 *The Writings and Speeches of Daniel Webster* (National ed., 18 vols., Boston: Little, Brown, and Company, 1903), XVII, 467 (Jan. 17, 1829).

2 *Correspondence of Andrew Jackson* (John Spencer Bassett, ed., 7 vols., Washington, D.C.: Carnegie Institution of Washington, 1926–35), III, 256 (June 18, 1824).

supporters were not without lively apprehension—a portion anxiously distrustful." [3] Political opponents who flocked into the Whig party were less restrained. John Quincy Adams called Jackson "a barbarian who could not write a sentence of grammar and hardly could spell his own name." [4] Henry Clay was more vehement—"he is ignorant, passionate, hypocritical, corrupt, and easily swayed by the base men who surround him. . . ." [5]

Jackson made a deliberate effort to counteract the "savage" stereotype that his enemies had circulated. His bearing during his second brief service in the Senate (1823–25) combined urbanity, courtesy, and the social skills of a gentleman and convinced those who saw him in Washington that his character had been misunderstood. Webster wrote his brother Ezekiel that "General Jackson's manners are more presidential than those of any of the candidates. He is grave, mild, and reserved." [6] Mrs. Webster was his supporter in preference to either Henry Clay, John Quincy Adams, or William H. Crawford. Both before and after he became President, however, Jackson was capable of hot indignation and was not averse to bearing down his critics by simulated rage. Controversy, indeed, buoyed his spirits. At the height of the struggle over the Bank he wrote Colonel Anthony Butler that recent events had given him an excitement far better for his recovery than all the stimulating medicines of the medical faculty.[7] Few if any of his Cabinet members were fully at ease in his presence.

The day-by-day business of administration is not conducted, however, by convulsions of temper, and in his normal administrative contacts Jackson was patient and considerate with his immediate associates, although unyielding at moments of decision. Martin Van Buren was qualified to speak of these matters, even though his testimony may disclose some partiality. In his *Autobiography* he recalled Jackson in these words.

3 *The Autobiography of Martin Van Buren* (John C. Fitzpatrick, ed.), American Historical Association, *Annual Report, 1918,* II, 267.

4 *Memoirs of John Quincy Adams* (Charles Francis Adams, ed., 12 vols., Philadelphia: J. B. Lippincott, 1874–77), VIII, 546 (June 18, 1833).

5 *The Works of Henry Clay* (Calvin Colton, ed., 6 vols., New York: A. S. Barnes and Burr, 1857), IV, 368–69 (August 2, 1833).

6 Webster, *Writings and Speeches* (National ed.), XVII, 346 (Feb. 22, 1824).

7 Jackson, *Correspondence,* V, 213 (Oct. 1, 1833).

Although firm to the last degree in the execution of his resolution when once formed, I never knew a man more free from conceit, or one to whom it was to a greater extent a pleasure, as well as a recognized duty, to listen patiently to what might be said to him upon any subject under consideration until the time for action had arrived. Akin to his disposition in this regard was his readiness to acknowledge error whenever an occasion to do so was presented and a willingness to give full credit to his co-actors on important occasions without ever pausing to consider how much of the merit he awarded was at the expense of that due to himself. . . .[8]

Jackson drew his general political views from Thomas Jefferson. His Republican antecedents led him to a strict construction of federal powers, to reliance on the states, and to a guarded use of authority found in the Constitution. He accepted without question the general opinion of his day, that matters went well when the government left people alone. Like Jefferson, he favored frugality and economy in governmental operations, and ranked high among his duties the final discharge of the public debt.

Jackson's administrative experience before he became President had been military in nature. He was accustomed to the art of command, not the art of leadership of Congress or a Cabinet. Nevertheless, he fitted readily and easily into the pattern of civil administration. Both his military experience and his own dominant personality, however, inspired him to take the responsibility for the decisions that had to be made by the Chief Executive. Webster was wholly and entirely wrong when he concluded in 1829, that "Genl. J. has not character enough to conduct his measures by his own strength. Somebody must and will lead him." [9]

Jackson's tastes and interests were political, not administrative. He bore the heavy load of office routine patiently and with fortitude, but thought of no way to reduce it. An endless stream of petty matters came into the White House in accordance with the practices of earlier Presidents and department heads. All of them, Jackson included, were anxious to insure the integrity and correctness of action taken by subordinates. Department heads

8 Van Buren, *Autobiography*, p. 312.

9 Webster, *Writings and Speeches* (National ed.), XVI, 188 (Feb. 23, 1829).

played safe. In Jackson's case it must be added that he had little confidence in some of his Cabinet members, and that he liked power and the sense of personal participation. Although Jackson handled much departmental detail, there is considerable evidence that he lacked adequate means of knowing what was going on in the offices or, if he knew, that he was reluctant to interfere. Department heads brought him the cases on which they needed his help or prior approval. They were unlikely to bring him the cases they preferred to keep in the departmental closet, and Jackson was consequently ignorant of circumstances that he would not have tolerated.

Jackson's loyalty to his friends was not always conducive to success in administration, particularly since this loyalty sometimes obscured his judgment in making appointments and refusing to make removals. He appointed Samuel Swartwout collector of the port of New York although Van Buren warned him against this choice. He put Major John H. Eaton in the Cabinet despite his knowledge of disquieting rumors about the Major's earlier relations with Peggy Timberlake, now his wife, and wrecked his Cabinet as a consequence. He endured William T. Barry as Postmaster General long after his incompetence had been exposed. Even a President as independent and forthright as Andrew Jackson did not have a free hand in picking executive heads and subordinate officers, and some of his mistakes may be charged to force of circumstances and pressure of party. Some of his mistakes were his own; and his greatest successes—such as Martin Van Buren and Amos Kendall—were often happy chances. He knew neither man personally when he decided to appoint him. In building his civil administration Jackson tended to judge men by their political faith and personal loyalty, not by their executive talent.

The consequences of the Jacksonian era (1829–61) upon administration were manifold, but to an intelligent and informed observer like Amos Kendall the net result of thirty-years development must have seemed a substantial retrogression. The deterioration is often charged against Jackson, as the originator of the spoils system. Such a conclusion would be unjust. Jackson did introduce *rotation* into the federal system for reasons which carried weight in the light of the situation that had grown up in the first forty years of national experience. He did not introduce the spoils system. His personal standards of integrity were fastidious, and he insisted upon a high level of honesty and propriety in the public service. He was betrayed by some officials, and his views of official conduct were undermined by a general decline in business morality. But Jackson would have been as violent an enemy of "honest graft," favoritism, waste, misuse of public funds for party purposes, and outright embezzlement as any of his contemporaries, Whig or Democrat. The idea of rotation was a rational remedy in 1829 for an admitted problem of superannuation, but the cure introduced evils of greater proportion. Jackson may well be criticized for failing to see the consequences of the theory of rotation which were obvious both to intelligent friends and enemies. He can hardly be criticized for the purposes he sought to achieve—to destroy the idea of property in office, to cut down an officeholding class, and to give all citizens an equal opportunity to enjoy the privilege of participating in the task of self-government.

Jackson took the administrative system as he found it, changed its leadership, made some improvements, and accepted the responsibility for operating it. He did not advance the art of administration or go beyond the precepts of morality and common sense. He wrote and thought in terms of individuals. His letters and writings betray only rarely a sense of administration as a process that could be described in general terms.

On a broader scene, Jackson holds a secure place in history for his devotion to democratic ideals, for his defense and development of executive power and his concept of the President as a direct representative of the people, and for his support of the Union against nullification. Masses of people believed he was their friend—the "monstrous crowd of people" that Webster observed at the inauguration ceremonies on March 4, 1829, seemed really to think that the country had been rescued from dreadful danger.[10] When, eight years later, Jackson stood on the rear platform of the railroad car on his way again to the Hermitage, no sound came from the multitude that bade him farewell. Emotions were too deep for expression.

10 *Ibid.*, XVII, 473 (March 4, 1829).

II

The party of Andrew Jackson was destined to guide the affairs of the Republic for the next thirty-two years, excepting only the two administrations of Harrison and Tyler, and of Taylor and Fillmore—and Tyler was an old-school Democrat holding office for nearly four years of a presumably Whig administration. The policy positions of the Democrats were such as to discourage the development or expansion of the national administrative system. The Jackson wing of the old Jeffersonian Republican party was devoted to laissez faire, and the defeat of John Quincy Adams in 1828 marked the climax of his effort to use national power and resources for what he conceived to be national purposes.

President Van Buren stated the underlying Democratic philosophy clearly and unequivocally in his message to Congress in 1837. "All communities," he declared, "are apt to look to government for too much. . . . But this ought not to be. The framers of our excellent Constitution and the people who approved it with calm and sagacious deliberation acted at the time on a sounder principle. They wisely judged that the less government interferes with private pursuits the better for the general prosperity. . . . its real duty . . . is . . . to leave every citizen and every interest to reap under its benign protection the rewards of virtue, industry, and prudence." [11]

Policy followed this philosophy consistently. Jackson withdrew the federal government from the field of internal improvements on Monroe's doctrine of strict construction and on policy grounds as well. Naval policy was against expansion, and the conservative views of naval officers delayed the transition from sail to steam. Military policy favored a small standing army, just enough to police the frontiers. Fiscal policy centered on the discharge of the federal debt, accomplished momentarily in 1836, and on holding down expenditures to the bare minimum. Administrative policy favored parsimony at every point except where the political machine was gathering in the sinews of war—an expanding area that was to produce many a scandal.

[11] James D. Richardson, *A Compilation of the Messages and Papers of the Presidents, 1789–1910* (11 vols., New York: Bureau of National Literature, 1911), III, 344 (Sept. 4, 1837).

At many points the policy positions of the Whigs contradicted those of the Democrats. The central core of the new Whig party comprised the Adams-Clay wing of the Republican party, known for a few years as the National Republicans. Like the Democratic party, this was not a sectional group; it had strong representation in the South, the West, and the East, although the center of gravity of the new combination tended to be in the latter section.

The Whigs, reflecting Henry Clay's ideas, had a positive program for the federal government. It included the free exercise of national power by rechartering the Second Bank of the United States, by favoring a protective tariff, and by advocating internal improvements under the authority of the federal government. These policies, known collectively as the "American plan," rested on a liberal construction of the Constitution, Hamiltonian in its origin. However, as a party of opposition to Andrew Jackson, the Whigs were driven to resist the growth of executive power and to magnify the role of Congress. At times they appeared almost to endorse an American equivalent of the English responsible cabinet system. They carried only two elections and were unable to put their policies into operation. They were, however, an active and powerful opposition until their collapse in 1856.

The changes in the administrative system that developed during the Jacksonian years were much less the consequence of bold innovation and pioneering in new fields of governmental activity, much more the result of changes in magnitude, in complexity, and in the influence of external forces, principally the political party. Mere magnitude was quietly but certainly affecting the administrative services, although its influence was a silent one. Secretary of the Navy James K. Paulding wrote in 1839: "The rapid growth of the country produces a corresponding accession to the duties of every department of Government and every public servant. The multiplication and complexity of laws involving new powers, new restraints, and new duties, call for additional labor and circumspection. The great increase of public records and documents renders all reference to the past more embarrassing; and the frequent calls of Congress imposing a necessity for researches, which comprehend the history and transactions of the department from its first organization, all contribute to render the duties of every officer and every clerk more difficult, complicated, and laborious." [12]

The country was bigger in every dimension in 1860 than in 1830, and these dimensions were relevant to the public business. The most dramatic index of magnitude was geographical. As a consequence of the War with Mexico the westward boundary was carried in one surge to the Pacific. The contemporary settlement of the Oregon question fixed the northern boundary and set the United States firmly on the western coast from San Diego to the Straits of Juan de Fuca. The Great Lakes, only recently on the untracked frontier, became the center of new enterprise. "The harbors of the lakes," said the chief of the topographical engineers in 1839, "are seaports, crowded with vessels of all sizes and of all kinds, and their beautiful waters are whitened with many a sail, and teeming with prolific steam. One universal aspect of enterprise, of wealth, and of activity presents itself. . . ." [13]

New states were being admitted in pairs, north and south: Arkansas (1836) and Michigan (1837); Florida and Texas (1845); Iowa (1846) and Wisconsin (1848); but then the movement of events and population brought four northern and western states into the Union in succession: California (1850), Minnesota (1858), Oregon (1859), and Kansas (1861). The political center of gravity was marching west, and as territorial governments were set up and land opened to settlement and mails brought to the edge of civilization, the administrative system expanded over the Mississippi and in the 1850's across the Rocky Mountains.

The physical character of the country was changing, too, as civilization took its westward way. The herds of buffalo that were once found on the shore of Lake Erie receded across the Mississippi toward the Rocky Mountains, and the trappers followed the beaver to the waters of the Columbia.[14] Still in 1835 Philip Hone, the conservative Whig merchant of New York, saw a flight of wild pigeons not far up the Hudson River: "The

12 House Doc. 39, 26th Cong., 1st sess., p. 7 (Dec. 30, 1839).

13 House Doc. 2, 26th Cong., 1st sess., pp. 634–35 (Dec. 30, 1839).

14 *North American Review*, XXX (1830), 65–66.

air was filled with them; their undulation was like the long waves of the ocean in a calm, and the fluttering of their wings made a noise like the crackling of fire among dry leaves or thorns." [15]

Governmental expenditures, excluding debt retirement, grew even more rapidly than population despite the frugal intentions of the Jacksonians. While the number of persons was somewhat better than doubling, federal expenditures more than quadrupled, rising from $15.1 million in 1830 to $63.1 million in 1860.[16] Thus was well fulfilled the prediction of Senator Thomas H. Benton that the patronage of the United States, based in the early years on an expenditure of $2 million and on $20 million when he spoke in 1826, would rise in the days of men then living to $50 million a year.

Increase in expenditures was not caused primarily by new functions of the general government. They included principally the lifesaving service, the inspection of steamboat boilers on vessels engaged in interstate commerce and the inspection of imported drugs, a naval observatory and a naval academy, and the collection of some meager agricultural statistics.

The expansion of governmental functions from 1829 to 1861 affected primarily the states and cities. They now became the busy workshops of administration. New York and Pennsylvania had already launched great public improvements before Jackson came to power, and for two decades the states directly and indirectly engaged in various public works programs, mainly building canals and assisting the construction of railroads with the aid of federal land grants. Help was given to farmers by state support of fairs, premiums, and prizes, and demonstration of good farm practice. Institutional care for the insane and the handicapped was expanded and improved. Most significant of the future, Massachusetts established the first state bank commission in 1838. Government thus entered the complex field of the regulation of business. By 1860 the states had begun to curb the excesses of insurance companies and railroads, as well as banks.

15 *The Diary of Philip Hone, 1828–1851* (Allan Nevins, ed., New York: Dodd, Mead and Co., 1936), pp. 181–82 (Nov. 4, 1835).

16 U.S. Bureau of the Census, *Historical Statistics of the United States, 1789–1945* (Washington: Government Printing Office, 1949), p. 300.

Cities were driven into the basic municipal functions: maintenance of law and order and protection of property against fire, as publicly supported police and fire departments gradually took the place of night watches and society-minded volunteer fire departments; paving and lighting of streets and building of sidewalks; supply of water through a central system of water mains and engineering works; minimum protection of public health by vaccination, quarantine, and the disposal of sewage and refuse; and regard for public safety and welfare by licensing some activities and occupations. All of these were inescapable if cities were to exist.

Beyond these essential housekeeping and regulatory functions, cities and towns, under the inspiration and example of Horace Mann, took up the education of children through the primary and grammar schools. An optimistic confidence in the wisdom of public opinion was tempered by a realization that men had to be informed, and that the capacity to read was essential to this end. Workingmen began to organize, politically and in unions, and demanded means of educating their children. A labor convention in Boston in 1833 resolved that no person would receive their votes "but such as are known to be openly and decidedly favorable to a system of general education, by means of manual labor schools, supported at public expense, and open alike to the children of the poor as well as to the rich. . . ."[17] This resolution was symptomatic of the future, as Americans came to realize that government could make positive constructive contributions to the needs of people, and was not necessarily either a threat to liberty or a drain on the nation's resources.

These fascinating aspects of the American administrative system, so important to a full understanding of its history, lie beyond the scope of this volume.

[17] *Niles Register*, XLV, 147 (Nov. 2, 1833). In 1838 Marcius Willson published his *Treatise on Civil Polity and Political Economy . . . for the Use of Schools,* designed in the words of the author "to increase the intelligence and excite the patriotism of his fellow-citizens, and prove an efficient auxiliary in the cause of common education."

III

The most important influence upon the administrative system during the years from Jackson to Lincoln was the wide enfranchisement of adult male citizens and their organization into a national party system, accompanied by a surge of democratic sentiment that fanned an already active desire for office. Alexis de Tocqueville declared in 1835 that "the political activity which pervades the United States must be seen in order to be understood. No sooner do you set foot upon American ground, than you are stunned by a kind of tumult . . . almost the only pleasure which an American knows is to take a part in the government, and to discuss its measures." [18]

National party organization was hardly known before the 1830's, although both Federalist and Republican parties existed and strong party organizations became well established in some states, notably New York. The origin of the national party structure began with the end of the congressional caucus in 1824. Its collapse left a vacuum in the institutional arrangements for reaching a party agreement on the choice of a candidate for the presidency. In 1828 the vacuum was filled, after a fashion, by state legislatures, state nominating conventions, and party conferences. The new machinery, the national nominating convention, originated with the anti-Masonic party in 1831, was tried out in 1832 by the Democratic party and accepted in 1836 and subsequently by both Whigs and Democrats. It became the focal point, once every four years, for intense activity leading to the party nomination for the presidency. For nearly twenty years, however, there was no permanent continuing party headship. In 1848 the national party committee was established by the Democrats but it did little except to call succeeding national conventions.

The machinery of the national party was therefore undeveloped, but paradoxically national elections and issues dominated the local organizations where the real strength of the party machine lay. This consequence came about as a result of the

18 Alexis de Tocqueville, *Democracy in America* (Henry Reeve translation, 2d ed., 2 vols., Cambridge, Mass.: Sever and Francis, 1863), I, 318, 319.

mutual needs of Presidents desiring reelection and of local machines needing resources to pay their workers.

Through the election of 1824, a candidate for the presidency had had to deal merely with the handful of leading party members already assembled in Congress; after 1832, a candidate *or a President desiring to succeed himself* had to deal with the delegates of a national convention—or more precisely with the state conventions and party factions that controlled the selection of the delegates. Every President from Jackson to Buchanan who survived his term desired to succeed himself, with the single exception of James K. Polk. Most Presidents therefore had to negotiate with the state and big city party organizations, and win support from them and their often disputing factions.

Presidents desiring a second term, now forced to deal with party and factional organizations, possessed large resources for the support of the machines on which their personal fate was dependent. These assets were adventitiously multiplied by the democratic idea of rotation that Jackson had announced in his first annual message, a doctrine highly congenial to the democratic climate of the time. It also was in accord with the mounting passion for officeholding that inspired Americans to endless effort and trouble.

By the 1840's the movement for universal manhood suffrage had run its course. A new political force was thus introduced and a novel practical party obligation—the task of organizing a mass electorate and directing it toward the polls with correct ideas at the recurring crises of state and national elections. This proved to be a task of great magnitude and difficulty, characteristics which fostered the rapid growth of party machines, unparalleled party activity, and a type of practical party politician that, although not hitherto unknown, seemed now ubiquitous. It also proved to be a task requiring large resources for the payment of party workers, and for the first time raised the problem of the proper sources of party funds.

Thus the necessities of Presidents both to attain their personal ambitions and to nourish the strength of their parties, the requirements of party machines for the sinews of war, the doctrine that citizens generally should have a turn at the business of government, and the anxiety of thousands of citizens for the privilege of office, all conspired to build a national-state-local party organization, geared to success in winning the great political prize, the White House and control of Congress. These forces also conspired to break down the stable, permanent, politically inactive type of career system that had grown up during the first four decades of the Republic.

These two effects were to be observed in the active participation in, if not indeed domination of, the state machines by three powerful sets of federal officials stationed in the field—the collectors of customs, the postmasters, and the district attorneys. The collectors and the district attorneys had gradually been acquiring political overtones during the 1820's. In the next decade all three groups became highly active politicians, intermediaries between national and state and local interests, sometimes ground between them, and sometimes ruthlessly driving the state or local machines for national purposes. The collector of the port of New York, Cornelius P. Van Ness, wrote Secretary of War William L. Marcy in 1845, "I am sure you perfectly understand the bearing which the management of the Custom House has had, for the last 10 or 15 years, upon our City elections; which is, that when well managed we have gained, otherwise, lost." [19] Federal office could be used to win state or local elections; and state and local machines were the organizational key to success in the national elections.

Jackson's early views on party appeared to be drawn directly from Washington's farewell address. In 1816 he wrote President-elect Monroe, "Now is the time to exterminate the *monster* called party spirit. By selecting characters most conspicuous for their probity, virtue, capacity and firmness, without any regard to party, you will go far to, if not entirely, eradicate those feelings which, on former occasions, threw so many obstacles in the way of government. . . ." [20] After some years of experience as Presi-

19 Library of Congress, William L. Marcy Papers, Vol. 10, No. 34,411 (April 10, 1845). Cf. Buchanan's comments: "it is quite necessary that all the Federal officers in Philadelphia should be a unit in action. Without this, they neutralize the administration and leave it powerless." *The Works of James Buchanan* (John Bassett Moore, ed., 12 vols., Philadelphia: J. B. Lippincott, 1908–11), XI, 513 (Feb. 15, 1858).

20 James Parton, *Life of Andrew Jackson* (3 vols., New York: Mason Brothers, 1860), II, 361 (Nov. 12, 1816).

dent, he changed his view, now recognizing the necessity of party support. "It is certain," he wrote, "that whichever party makes the President, must give direction to his administration. . . . No one can carry on this Govt. without support, and the Head of it must rely for support on the party by whose suffrages he is elected. . . . I have long believed, that it was only by preserving the identity of the Republican party as embodied and characterized by the principles introduced by Mr. Jefferson that the original rights of the states and the people could be maintained as contemplated by the Constitution. I have labored to reconstruct this great Party and bring the popular power to bear with full influence upon the Government, by securing its permanent ascendancy. . . ." [21]

The necessity of party was reluctantly recognized also by Daniel Webster, but not its consequences for the disruption of administration. "The existence of parties in popular Governments is not to be avoided," he declared, "and, if they are formed on constitutional questions, or in regard to great measures of public policy, and do not run to excessive length, it may be admitted that, on the whole, they do no great harm. But the patronage of office, the power of bestowing place and emoluments, create parties, not upon any principle, or any measure, but upon the single ground of personal interest. Under the direct influence of this motive, they form round a leader, and they go for 'the spoils of victory.' " [22] For better or for worse the political party was here to stay, and the country threw itself joyfully into the excitement of political campaigns. The consequences for the public service became a secondary consideration to the play of mass democratic participation in the business of government.

IV

The immediate result of these developments was to politicize the public service. Yet, as subsequent pages will demonstrate, important sections of the public service were undisturbed, retaining the older qualities of permanent tenure, expertness, and

21 Jackson, *Correspondence,* V, 338, 339 (April 24, 1835). It was in this letter that Jackson declared, "It is as true in politics as morals, that those who are not for us are against us."

22 *Register of Debates,* 23d Cong., 2d sess., p. 459 (Feb. 16, 1835).

quasi-professional devotion that make a career service. Middle management, by and large, was spared the impact of rotation, and enough of the rank and file were continued by Democrats and Whigs alike to permit the public business to be transacted. Indeed in 1853 the reaction to the confusion and waste of rotation had become so great as to persuade Congress to reinstate by law a genuine career service among the departmental clerks. Pressure from beyond the walls of the citadel was, however, too great. The doctrine of rotation progressively prevailed over earlier concepts of stability. Buchanan finally rotated *Pierce* Democrats out of office to make room for *Buchanan* Democrats.

The spirit and quality of the public service deteriorated under the impact of these new conditions. Its quality and strength had come from the class of gentlemen who, from 1789 to 1829, had accepted the duty of government. The moral tone of society, business, and government, on the whole, had been remarkably high during the first forty years of the Republic. The extension of manhood suffrage threw into the arena of public affairs new segments of the population, and cultivated a new type of political manager, not accustomed to the restraints and understandings of earlier years. Speculative opportunities in private enterprise offered enormous prizes to the skillful or the lucky, and in the hot pursuit of these prizes misrepresentation, disregard of the law, and corruption began to invade the business world on an alarming scale.

The tone of politics, which had begun to show signs of wear in the 1820's, deteriorated steadily. Drunkenness ruined many promising careers, violence was common even in congressional circles, gambling was general, and the level of political discourse —despite the eloquence of Webster and Clay and the close reasoning of Calhoun—fell to mediocrity as both Whigs and Democrats sought victory by avoiding issues and men of conviction. Irresponsible attacks on officials by members of Congress under cover of congressional immunity became so common as to cause the *Charleston Mercury* to declare that no one was safe, that men of sensitive and elevated character were being driven out of public life, leaving only the callous and unprincipled to possess public honors.[23] Under circumstances such as these it was

23 Quoted in *National Intelligencer,* Jan. 29, 1853.

inevitable that the moral standards of officeholders would be affected.

A reckless disposition to use small appointments in customhouses and post offices to pay political debts or to get political work done at election time appeared, especially in the larger cities. Personal friends, relatives, and party hacks multiplied on the public pay rolls. Control of the field services was lax, and abuses were reasonably free from detection. Discipline was often slack, and subordinates followed their own preferences as to work and absence. Some dramatic cases of embezzlement occurred in high office. The moral standards of the old Republicans were undermined as a new class of men swept in and out of office.

While it is therefore necessary to record deterioration, it is also necessary to hold a true balance in assessing these years. Many men in public life spoke out against the trends they observed. The personal standards of official morality of every President were high. A code of ethics promulgated by Amos Kendall for his clerks in the fourth auditor's office was as rigid as that practiced by Federalist and Republican heads of departments. Outside the larger cities earlier patterns of behavior were likely to prevail. The South tended to maintain higher standards than the North or the West.

If it be true that never before in the history of the Republic had any public officer so betrayed his trust as Samuel Swartwout, it is also true that the combination of administrative and scientific capacities of Alexander D. Bache in the Coast Survey had never been equaled in earlier times. George Bancroft was a diligent and efficient collector of the customs in Boston, a bold Secretary of the Navy, and an able diplomat in London and Berlin as well as a famous historian. Horatio King, first assistant postmaster general, had an impressive career in the post office from 1839 to 1861, from Van Buren to Lincoln. And it must be remembered that Senator Marcy, when he became Secretary of State, introduced a plan for apprentice consular agents selected on the basis of merit.

The history of Jacksonian administration is, therefore, not a simple tale of rotation, spoils, confusion, and deterioration. There was deterioration in moral standards and in the efficiency of the great departments, on the whole. But there was progress as well. A huge experiment in the education of citizens in democracy by direct participation in officeholding, local, state and federal, was in full motion. Public functions expanded in cities and states. Moreover, there were sufficient examples of high-minded public service to demonstrate that Federalist ideals, conserved by Republican Presidents, had not disappeared from the administrative tradition.

V

The buoyant optimism of the 1820's carried forward into the 1830's, but was badly shaken by the panic of 1837 and the following years of depression, and almost silenced by the slavery agitation of the 1850's. In 1829 the editor of the *North American Review* could declare that the delicate experiment of 1789 had succeeded "beyond the expectations of the most sanguine." [24] In the same year editor Niles pointed out that the moral power of the American system rested not upon mercenary bayonets, but upon freedom of sentiment.[25] Van Buren told his fellow citizens in 1838, "It was reserved for the American Union to test the advantages of a government entirely dependent on the continual exercise of the popular will, and our experience has shown that it is as beneficent in practice as it is just in theory. . . . the intelligence, prudence, and patriotism of the people have kept pace with this augmented responsibility." [26] Polk reiterated these sentiments in 1847. "After an existence of near three-fourths of a century as a free and independent Republic," he declared, "the problem no longer remains to be solved whether man is capable of self-government." [27]

The editor of the *Missouri Republican* asked triumphantly in 1831, "Where is 'the west,' " and suggested that St. Louis might be the future capital of the country. "Space," he wrote, "seems about to be annihilated. . . ." [28] Caleb Cushing visited the coal mines of Pennsylvania in 1836, "a few years ago one of the most desert regions of the United States," and found there a vast business that had created an inexhaustible store of wealth

24 *North American Review,* XXIX (1829), 280.
25 *Niles Register,* XXXVI, 17 (March 7, 1829).
26 Richardson, *Messages,* III, 484 (Dec. 3, 1838).
27 *Ibid.,* IV, 532 (Dec. 7, 1847).
28 Quoted in *Niles Register,* XLI, 267 (Dec. 10, 1831).

and opened a new commerce and a new bond of fraternity to the whole Union. He left the scene "with a strong and abiding sense of the energy and spirit of our people, with renewed admiration of the resources and destinies of our country, and with deep-felt gratitude to that bountiful Providence which bestowed upon us this our happy land." [29]

"America has no Past, but she has a Future," wrote the historian John Lothrop Motley.[30] As travelers climbed off the lumbering stagecoaches into the railroad cars they could fervently join in this sense of achievement and optimism, even as they brushed cinders and soot from their garments. As one of them said, "We may sigh that we are born fifty years too soon." [31]

Unhappily the travelers in the railroad cars could not brush aside the moral, economic, and sectional problems of slavery as readily as they could shake off the soot and cinders of the locomotives that carried them hither and yon at such unprecedented speed. A sense of doom gradually darkened the satisfactions of what once seemed the inevitable march of progress.

The years of the Jacksonians, from 1829 to 1861, were years of almost uninterrupted excitement, tension, crisis, and apprehension. Nullification in South Carolina, the battle against the Second Bank of the United States, the resolution censuring Jackson and its final erasure from the Senate journal, the panic of 1837, the ostracism of John Tyler by the Whigs who had elected him Vice President, the controversy with Great Britain over Oregon, the War with Mexico, the problem of slavery in the newly acquired territories leading to the Compromise of 1850, the moral and administrative crisis precipitated by the Fugitive Slave Act, "bleeding Kansas," the panic of 1857, John Brown's raid—all these events gave neither the politicians nor the people any peace. It was not surprising that statesmen begged the country to be quiet after Henry Clay's last compromise. But peace was not to come by exhortation.

In these years of turmoil and anxiety the administrative system, described by President Tyler as "the complex, but at the

29 *North American Review,* XLII (1836), 241–42.

30 *Ibid.,* LXIX (1849), 495.

31 *Ibid.,* L (1840), 42.

same time beautiful, machinery of our system of government,"[32] went steadily on its way, carrying on the business of the American people as best it could. To its successes and failures, to the storms that beat upon it, to the personalities who protected and at times betrayed it, the following pages are devoted.

32 Richardson, *Messages,* IV, 270 (December, 1843).

CHAPTER TWO

The Presidency

During the thirty-two years following the election of Andrew Jackson, the presidential office fluctuated violently in influence and power. It seemed to many contemporaries at the close of eight years of "King Andrew" that the power of the Chief Executive could hardly be restrained,[1] but Van Buren's succeeding four years were one long stalemate between Congress and the White House, and his Whig successor, William Henry Harrison, was committed to executive surrender to the legislative branch. The surrender was avoided by Harrison's death, but John Tyler destroyed his influence over either Congress or his own party by his vetoes of two Bank bills and a tariff bill. The presidential decline from 1837 to 1845 was swift and extreme.

Events, however, again reversed the trend. Polk was an active, powerful, and stubborn man who knew what he wanted from Congress and who, with infinite trouble, forced Congress to follow his leadership. In his success Polk demonstrated a capacity for positive executive achievement that equaled if, indeed, it did not exceed, that of Andrew Jackson. The War with Mexico over, slavery dominated the years until the outbreak of the Civil War. The times were not conducive to executive leadership, however urgent was its need. The death of Zachary Taylor in 1850

1 This was the normal view of the Whigs, well expressed in 1833 by Henry Clay: "Are we not governed now, and have we not been for some time past, pretty much by the will of one man? And do not large masses of the people, perhaps a majority, seem disposed to follow him wherever he leads, through all his inconsistencies? . . . If that single man were an enlightened philosopher, and a true patriot, the popular sanction which is given to all his acts, however inconsistent or extravagant, might find some justification." Henry Clay, *Works,* IV, 368–69 (August 2, 1833).

opened ten years of weakness in the presidential office. Fillmore, long active in New York politics and in Congress, lacked executive experience and was almost immediately faced with negotiations looking toward a second term; Pierce was a weak personality involved in details and dependent upon friendship; Buchanan, an indecisive politician busy building a personal machine on patronage and contracts in order to succeed himself.

It is therefore impossible to discern a clear trend in the executive office of the general government during these years. The record is one of fluctuation from one extreme to another. Personality seemed to play a role outweighing in importance whatever influence underlying conditions may have brought to bear.

These, too, were ambiguous. The emerging changes in the economic order called for strong government and executive leadership, but they bore their natural fruit only two generations later. The restless uneasiness of the South within the federal Union called for strength in the executive branch, and strength was forthcoming in the nullification crisis of 1832–33, but lacking later. The baffling problem of the extension of slavery seemed insoluble, and the politicians of both major parties instinctively avoided taking positions on this issue, hoping that the Fates would some day clear the way to a solution. This did not facilitate energetic leadership in the White House; nor did executive preoccupation with patronage—recognized as a curse by Polk and as an opportunity by Buchanan, but in either case obscuring the position of the President as a leader of the nation. Only two Presidents during the course of thirty-two years deserve to be remembered as effective leaders of their time—Jackson and Polk; and they are probably the only ones who, waiving the external forces that would aid or handicap them, had the personal power to dominate the public scene.

To state this conclusion does not, however, imply that Congress made good the deficiencies of executive leadership. Such a redress of balance had occurred once, when Henry Clay and his friends in the House of Representatives seized control of affairs from the indecisive hands of James Madison. It did not happen again. When Presidents were weak, Congress was also weak or divided, and stalemate and drift were the outcome. The record of the years from 1829 to 1861 sustained the thesis advanced by Henry Jones Ford: "It is the rule of our politics that no vexed question is settled except by executive policy." [2]

Executive initiative in policy matters had become so widely accepted and had been found such a convenience to Congress that few members complained in principle on this score. Old Republican fears had been well resolved. Echoes of the past, however, continued to whisper in the corridors of the Capitol. As late as 1842 Henry Clay asserted in the Senate: "On principle, certainly, the executive ought to have no agency in the formation of laws. Laws were the will of the nation authoritatively expressed. The carrying of those laws into effect was the duty which ought to be assigned to the executive, and this ought to be his sole duty, for it was an axiom in all free governments that the three great departments, legislative, executive, and judicial, should ever be kept separate and distinct." [3] Neither Whigs nor Democrats, however, were ready to accept such executive abnegation.

While the course of executive power was thus uncertain, four notable contributions were made to its foundations, all of which can be laid to events occurring in Jackson's administration. They were (1) the Jackson-Polk theory that the President was a direct representative of the people, as truly as Congress; (2) the extension of the veto power to include mere differences of opinion concerning the expediency of legislation; (3) the unrestrained use of the removal power; and (4) leadership of the political party, based on mass participation and organized for national action. The consequences of these innovations were vast, even though they were not always apparent. They tended to make the presidential office what the framers had broadly intended, but within a structure of party organization that they had not imagined. Great as these influences were, they were balanced to a degree by the doctrine of the supremacy of law, energetically supported by Jackson himself, by the doctrine of strict construction of executive powers, and by the general fear of uncontrolled discretion in the hands of executive officers. They were also contradicted by the Whig theory of executive power.

2 Henry Jones Ford, *The Rise and Growth of American Politics* (New York: Macmillan Co., 1898), p. 283.

3 Henry Clay, *Works,* VI, 309 (Jan. 24, 1842).

THE DOCTRINE OF DIRECT REPRESENTATION

The novel theory that the President was a direct representative of the people was stated in Jackson's "Protest" in order to differentiate his office from that of the heads of departments: "The President," he declared, "is the direct representative of the American people, but the Secretaries are not." [4] He did not then develop this idea beyond pointing out that heads of departments became responsible to the people only because they were subordinate to the President.

In his first annual message, however, Jackson had recommended the direct election of the President so that "as few impediments as possible should exist to the free operation of the public will." [5] This proposal was designed primarily to prevent a recurrence of the events of 1825 when Congress in joint session elected John Quincy Adams as President in the face of Jackson's plurality both in the popular vote and in the electoral college. It fitted perfectly, however, with the doctrine that the President was the direct representative of the people. Jackson repeated his recommendation in subsequent messages but neither Congress nor the country was interested in such an amendment to the Constitution.

The idea that the President was an immediate and direct representative of the people was, however, his settled conviction. He construed the election of 1832, which had been fought over the Bank in large measure, as a mandate from the people in support of his policy. Jackson's view was widely accepted both by his friends and political opponents. *Niles Register* reluctantly agreed that the President had "cast himself upon the support of the *people* against the acts of both houses of *congress,*" and had been sustained.[6] Privately both Henry Clay and Nicholas Biddle recognized that Jackson's reelection would amount to "something like a popular ratification" of the President's policy.[7]

The concept took hold rapidly. By 1841 Charles Francis Adams observed with concern that the democratic element was gaining

4 Richardson, *Messages,* III, 90 (April 15, 1834).

5 *Ibid.,* II, 448 (Dec. 8, 1829).

6 *Niles Register,* XLIII, 177 (Nov. 17, 1832).

7 *The Correspondence of Nicholas Biddle Dealing with National Affairs, 1807–1844* (Reginald C. McGrane, ed., Boston: Houghton Mifflin, 1919), pp. 113, 118–19.

strength through the election of the President. In a prophetic passage he wrote of the presidency:

> . . . . To that every other part of the system is now made in a great measure subordinate. And, instead of being regarded as the mere Executive head, charged with the duty of carrying into effect the laws, the President is looked to, by the great body of the people, as a person whose abstract sentiments upon every subject of public interest ought to be declared and made the subject of rigid examination. Should the practice of cross-questioning every candidate for the office become settled, the time will not be far distant when they will take the field in person, and solicit the people's votes. This can hardly fail to be attended with serious consequences to the Constitution, for it will have the effect of drawing the Executive and the people into a close union at the expense of the other departments of the government, as well as of consolidating the power of the national chief magistrate at the expense of that of the States.[8]

In 1848 President Polk developed the idea of direct representation in his defense of the veto power. He informed Congress:

> The people, by the Constitution, have commanded the President, as much as they have commanded the legislative branch of the Government, to execute their will. . . .
>
> If it be said that the Representatives in the popular branch of Congress are chosen directly by the people, it is answered, the people elect the President. If both Houses represent the States and the people, so does the President. The President represents in the executive department the whole people of the United States, as each member of the legislative department represents portions of them. . . .
>
> In the exercise of the power of the veto the President is responsible not only to an enlightened public opinion, but to the people of the whole Union, who elected him, as the representatives in the legislative branches who differ with him in opinion are responsible to the people of particular States or districts, who compose their respective constituencies. . . .[9]

The abandonment of the congressional caucus and the establishment of the national nominating convention also aided powerfully the idea that the President was a direct representa-

8 *North American Review,* LIII (1841), 77.

9 Richardson, *Messages,* IV, 664–65 (Dec. 5, 1848).

tive of the whole country. The delegates to the national convention were selected by party conventions in the states, which in turn were built on local urban and rural organizations of party members. Granting that delegates were not always speaking for the rank and file, they could nevertheless claim a democratic foundation that made their choice an act of the people—a national, not a sectional preference; a representative, not an oligarchical choice. Neither Jackson nor Polk put this claim into words, but it was quietly influential through the following decades.

It could hardly be argued that this was the intention of the framers of the Constitution. While Jefferson was not averse to assuming the role of executive leadership of an irresolute Congress, he did so not in the character of a direct representative of the people but as the head of a coordinate branch of the government. Polk's bold declaration was not contrary to the spirit nor yet was it found in the letter of the Constitution. Its actuality depended not on the constitutional formula but on the march of events and the quality of statesmen. Much water was to run under the bridge before Polk's propositions could be accepted as a description of accepted dogma, but nevertheless he spoke correctly in the terms of the future. The ultimate consequences for enlarging executive powers were great.

The decline of Congress. The position of the President as spokesman of the people was strengthened by the progressive deterioration of the manners and morals of Congressmen. The quality of Representatives seemed to sink as the full effects of manhood suffrage were felt. De Tocquevile commented on the "vulgar demeanor" of the House of Representatives and added, "Its members are almost all obscure individuals, whose names bring no associations to mind." [10] Politicians, in the sense of successful manipulators of caucus and convention, replaced the men of property and standing who had on the whole dominated the scene before 1829. Drunkenness was more common, partisanship more unreasonable, debate more personal, and corruption more widely suspected. Petty misrepresentations were made on the travel allowance of members. In 1833 Niles asked, "If . . . Mr. Grundy [is] required to return the excess into the treasury,

10 De Tocqueville, *Democracy in America* (1863 ed.), I, 259.

what will happen to Mr. Benton, also a member of the senate, who received pay for a *supposed* journey from Washington city to St. Louis, and back again, between 12 o'clock in the night of the 3d March, and 12 o'clock M. on the 4th of the same month?" [11] Champagne was available in the Senators' cloakroom and the story is told that it was charged as stationery against the Senate contingent fund. President pro tem Mangum thought this arrangement incongruous, and had it charged to the fuel account.[12]

Francis Bowen expressed a contemporary judgment in the *North American Review* in 1850.

> We complain, then, that both houses of Congress have been virtually transformed into noisy and quarrelsome debating clubs, to the almost entire neglect of their proper business of legislation.
>
> . . . . Furious menaces and bellowing exaggeration take the place of calm and dignified debate; the halls of the capitol often present scenes which would disgrace a bear-garden; and Congress attains the unenviable fame of being the most helpless, disorderly, and inefficient legislative body which can be found in the civilized world.[13]

This opinion was confirmed from within by Robert Toombs, a member of the House from Georgia. Writing privately to a friend, he declared: "The present Congress furnishes the worst specimens of legislators I have ever seen here, especially from the North on both sides. There is a large infusion of successful jobbers, lucky serving-men, parishless parsons and itinerant lecturers among them who are not only without wisdom or knowledge but have bad manners and therefore we can have but little hope of good legislation. With a large number of them their position is chiefly valued for the facilities it gives them for a successful foray upon the national treasury." [14]

Congress suffered from poor organization as well as bad manners. The standing committees impaired the unity of the House particularly, and also the capacity of the party to execute what-

11 *Niles Register,* XLV, 210 (Nov. 30, 1833).

12 T. N. Parmelee, "Recollections of an Old Stager," *Harper's New Monthly Magazine,* XLV (1872), 603.

13 *North American Review,* LXXI (1850), 224, 264.

14 Ulrich Bonnell Phillips, ed., *The Correspondence of Robert Toombs, Alexander H. Stephens, and Howell Cobb,* American Historical Association, *Annual Report, 1911,* II, 188 (March 22, 1850).

ever policy it might have; the seniority rule was a handicap; the power of the Speaker, for the election of whom some bitter battles were fought, was excessive; and the coordination of committees and the executive branch was at times inadequate.[15]

The lobby, which is dealt with later, was also conducive to the decline of congressional morality. Corruption was exceptional, but enough was known to cause mistrust. In 1853 members of Congress were forbidden by law to take compensation, directly or indirectly, for prosecuting any claim against the government, and penalties were provided for bribing or attempting to bribe them.[16] In 1857 four members were recommended by a select committee for expulsion from the House.[17] It was doubtless these revelations that impelled Francis Wharton to declare that politicians were publicly bought and sold "at the Washington brokers' board . . . like fancy railroad stock or copper-mine shares. . . ."[18]

Although both the House and Senate contained many men of character and responsibility, including such notable figures as Webster, Clay, and Calhoun, the prestige of the representative body fell. Its decline facilitated the idea that the President, too, could speak for the people. This novel idea was, and was to be, a strong buttress to the presidential office.

The Whigs and the doctrine of direct representation. A bold assertion that the President represented the people as directly as Congress could not fail to stir opposition from the Whigs, notwithstanding their ideological inheritance from the Federalists and Alexander Hamilton. Webster was their principal spokesman.

> . . . . The President [he stated] declares that he is "responsible for the entire action of the executive department." Responsible? What does he mean by being "responsible"? Does he mean legal responsibility? Certainly not. No such thing. Legal responsibility signifies liability to punishment for misconduct or maladministration. But the Protest does not mean that the President is liable to be impeached and punished if a secretary of state should commit treason, if a col-

15 Allan Nevins, *Ordeal of the Union* (2 vols., New York: Charles Scribner's Sons, 1947), I, 170.

16 10 Stat. 170 (Feb. 26, 1853).

17 House Report 243, 34th Cong., 3d sess. (Feb. 19, 1857).

18 *North American Review,* LXXXVII (1858), 119.

lector of the customs should be guilty of bribery, or if a treasurer should embezzle the public money. It does not mean, and cannot mean, that he should be answerable for any such crime or such delinquency. What, then, is its notion of that *responsibility* which it says the President is under for all officers, and which authorizes him to consider all officers as his own personal agents? Sir, it is merely responsibility to public opinion. It is a liability to be blamed; it is the chance of becoming unpopular, the danger of losing a reëlection. Nothing else is meant in the world. It is the hazard of failing in any attempt or enterprise of ambition. This is all the responsibility to which the doctrines of the Protest hold the President subject.[19]

Specifically as to the doctrine of direct representation Webster continued: "Connected, Sir, with the idea of this airy and unreal responsibility to the public is another sentiment, which of late we hear frequently expressed; and that is, *that the President is the direct representative of the American people.* This is declared in the Protest in so many words. . . . Now, Sir, this is not the language of the Constitution. The Constitution nowhere calls him the representative of the American people; still less, their direct representative. It could not do so with the least propriety." [20] The Whigs thus stood on a reading of the Constitution, old Republican in its origin, that prescribed executive responsibility to Congress, but not to the people.

THE VETO POWER

Federalists and Jeffersonians had agreed that the power to negative laws was justified on grounds of unconstitutionality and to protect the executive branch against legislative encroachment. Washington had faced the question whether he was justified in using the veto power on grounds of expediency, but had declined to take this position. His successors had used this authority sparingly, and primarily for reasons of alleged unconstitutionality of bills presented to them for signature.[21] In forty years there had been only nine vetoes, some of which turned on questions of constitutionality and only three of which concerned

19 Webster, *Writings and Speeches* (National ed.), VII, 137–38 (May 7, 1834).

20 *Ibid.*, VII, 144.

21 Edward Campbell Mason, *The Veto Power: Its Origin, Development and Function in the Government of the United States, 1789–1889* (Boston: Ginn and Co., 1890); *passim,* list of vetoes, pp. 142–207.

large matters of public policy. As John Quincy Adams observed at the close of Jackson's first Congress, "The Presidential veto has hitherto been exercised with great reserve." [22]

Jackson vetoed twelve bills, put to use the pocket veto, and killed the recharter of the Bank of the United States in a resounding exercise of this executive authority. In addition he legitimized the veto as a means of defeating bills on grounds of expediency, thus asserting the weight of the presidential office as the substantial equivalent of two-thirds of both Houses of Congress.

His course in this respect, as in others, was cautious. He put his first veto, the Maysville Turnpike bill, primarily on constitutional grounds, but did not fail to add his views on the inexpediency of the proposal.[23] On vetoing a rivers and harbors bill, he informed Congress of his objections to governmental subscriptions to the stock of private companies on the grounds of "the impropriety as well as inexpediency of such investments." [24] The veto of the bill to renew the charter of the Bank of the United States rested on grounds both of constitutionality and expediency, but policy was the controlling consideration.

In his second annual message Jackson notified Congress that he would use his own judgment on the wisdom of their enactments. The language was conciliatory, but its import clear. "It is due to candor," he declared, "as well as to my own feelings, that I should express the reluctance and anxiety which I must at all times experience in exercising the undoubted right of the Executive to withhold his assent from bills on other grounds than their constitutionality. That this right should not be exercised on slight occasions all will admit. It is only in matters of deep interest, when the principle involved may be justly regarded as next in importance to infractions of the Constitution itself, that such a step can be expected to meet with the approbation of the people." [25]

Jackson's views were adopted by other Presidents. John Tyler's second bank veto rested on "constitutional and other

22 Adams, *Memoirs,* VIII, 230 (June 6, 1830).
23 Richardson, *Messages,* II, 483 ff. (May 27, 1830).
24 *Ibid.,* II, 509 (Dec. 6, 1830).
25 *Ibid.,* II, 512 (Dec. 6, 1830).

grounds." [26] James K. Polk vetoed a rivers and harbors bill on strict and exclusive grounds of expediency.[27] Franklin Pierce vetoed a bill making appropriations for an ocean mail subsidy as violating "the soundest principles of public policy." [28] James Buchanan vetoed a private act satisfying a claim which had been rejected by the Post Office Department and the Court of Claims, in an amount over three times that originally requested, obviously mistrusting the judgment if not the integrity of Congress.[29] No constitutional question was even remotely involved.

The Whigs, however, were so indignant at presidential vetoes on other grounds than constitutional doubts that they started a move to impeach President Tyler, led by no less a person than John Quincy Adams. Tyler defended himself vigorously, although the House refused to accept his vindicating message.[30] The impeachment proceedings were not pushed.

The influence of the presidency was again greatly increased by this reading of its constitutional powers, a reading that had not been pressed by the Virginia-Massachusetts line of Presidents. The veto power now operated upon policy not merely subsequent to congressional action and under cover of a constitutional doubt, but prospectively as Congressmen weighed the probability of a veto even as they debated the issue. The influence was negative from one point of view, but its consequences might turn out to be positive in nature. Moreover it tended to support the idea that the President could speak for the people, as well as Congress, and could ask the people to make the final decision. De Tocqueville, observing America in Jackson's first administration, sensed this connection between the President and the ultimate source of power. "The veto," he wrote, "is, moreover, a sort of appeal to the people. The executive power . . . adopts this means of pleading its cause and stating its motives." [31]

The Whigs on the veto power. The pocket veto was the first innovation to meet with Whig criticism. Webster attacked it in 1832 before the National Republican Convention at Worcester,

26 *Ibid.*, IV, 71 (Sept. 9, 1841).
27 *Ibid.*, IV, 460–66 (August 3, 1846).
28 *Ibid.*, V, 325 (March 3, 1855).
29 *Ibid.*, V, 607–8 (April 17, 1860).
30 *Ibid.*, IV, 190 (August 30, 1842).
31 De Tocqueville, *Democracy in America* (1863 ed.), I, 153.

calling it "the silent veto" and "a great practical augmentation" of the President's power. Its tendency, Webster argued, was "to turn that which the Constitution intended only as an extraordinary remedy for extraordinary cases into a common means of making executive discretion paramount to the discretion of Congress, in the enactment of laws." [32] Henry Clay developed this theme in a Senate report in 1834 with reference to a bill defeated by a pocket veto at the *expiration,* not the *adjournment,* of Congress. "By retaining this bill, and not returning it to the Congress which passed it, the qualified veto of the President was converted, in effect, into an absolute veto." [33]

However this might be, the Whigs could do not much more than promise to restrain the executive power when it should fall into their hands. This vow they took. Harrison echoed their convictions in his inaugural address: "it is preposterous to suppose," he declared, "that the President . . . could better understand the wants and wishes of the people than their own immediate representatives." [34] On the other hand their "accidental" President, Tyler, proved as insistent on the use of the veto as his great Democratic predecessor. Two vetoes of bank bills on grounds of unconstitutionality and two vetoes of tariff measures on grounds of public policy drove the Whigs to recommend a constitutional amendment restricting the President's powers in this respect.

The Whigs were unable to attack the constitutionality of Tyler's vetoes, nor could they suggest corruption in his motives. They were forced to take either the relatively vague ground that Adams took—an "abusive exercise of the constitutional power" which had "struck with apoplexy" congressional capacity to enact laws essential to the welfare of the people,[35] or the principal ground assumed by Clay, that the executive branch possessing the veto improperly outweighed the responsibility of the two Houses to enact legislation.[36]

Since Clay's exposition was the most elaborate put forward by the Whigs, its main arguments will be stated. The veto power

32 Webster, *Writings and Speeches* (National ed.), II, 117, 118 (Oct. 12, 1832).
33 Senate Doc. 323, 23d Cong., 1st sess., pp. 1–2 (May 2, 1834).
34 Richardson, *Messages,* IV, 10 (March 4, 1841).
35 *Congressional Globe,* 27th Cong., 2d sess., pp. 894–96 (August 16, 1842).
36 *Ibid.,* pp. 164–66 (Jan. 24, 1842).

was conferred, according to Clay, primarily to protect the executive against legislative encroachments, secondarily to protect the country against crude and hasty legislation. Clay did not deny the virtue of these objects, but drew the conclusion that the protection afforded was much too great. Taking Congress as it then stood, the weight of the executive veto was equal to that of the votes of nine Senators and forty Representatives. Clay argued that such a veto was in effect absolute, and, indeed, when he spoke no bill had yet been reenacted over the President's objection. Clay went beyond this and declared that the mere threat to use the veto was as effective as its exercise. He appealed to states' rights sentiment by arguing that the state that held the presidency far outweighed the others; and sought to assuage southern fears by declaring that the veto power was not necessary to protect minorities. He proposed to reduce the weight of the executive by requiring only a majority of the whole number of Representatives and Senators to override a veto, instead of two-thirds.

Buchanan made the Democratic reply.[37] He declared that the veto was a "mere appeal by the President of the people's choice from the decision of Congress to the people themselves," that the President was directly responsible to the people, and did in fact more nearly represent a majority of the whole people of the United States than any other branch of the government. "The fallacy of the Senator's argument," Buchanan continued, "from beginning to end, consists in the assumption that Congress, in every situation and under every circumstance, truly represent the deliberate will of the people. The framers of the Constitution believed it might be otherwise; and therefore they imposed the restriction of the qualified veto of the President upon the legislative action of Congress."[38] Buchanan reminded the Senate also that of all executive powers, this was the one least to be dreaded. It created nothing, it changed no law, it destroyed no existing institution. "It is a mere power to arrest hasty and inconsiderate changes, until the voice of the people . . . shall be heard. . . . The veto power is every thing when sustained by public opinion; but nothing without it."[39]

37 Buchanan, *Works,* V, 98–139 (Feb. 2, 1842).
38 *Ibid.,* V, 116.
39 *Ibid.,* V, 138.

The view of the Democratic party prevailed. Although Polk felt called upon to offer a further defense of the veto power in his fourth annual address, the decision was quietly taken at the end of the Clay-Buchanan debate in 1842. Clay's proposal slumbered.

THE REMOVAL POWER

None of Jackson's predecessors had used the power to remove subordinate officers and employees for other reasons than well-justified cause, excepting Jefferson's removals in 1801 and 1802 to secure a party balance. Both Monroe and Adams deliberately refused to take advantage of the Tenure of Office Act of 1820 in order to appoint their friends to vacancies. Jackson and every one of his successors to 1861 reversed this rule and deliberately removed or sanctioned the removal of hundreds, indeed thousands, of subordinates for personal and partisan reasons. The Whigs and some conservative Democrats fought this innovation both on grounds of constitutionality and expediency, but in vain. To the constitutional argument against such free use of the removal power, Jackson's friends said flatly that the issue was settled; Webster himself had said it for them, indeed, better than they, although he proposed to reopen what he believed to be an erroneous interpretation of the Constitution: an interpretation, he admitted, "settled by construction; settled by precedent; settled by the practice of the Government; and settled by statute." [40] To the argument of expediency the Democrats replied that removal to encourage rotation was the essence of the American theory of democracy.

The scale and consequences of such an application of the removal power on the public service are dealt with elsewhere.[41] Here it is relevant only to note that the power of the presidential office was thus expanded to proportions hitherto unknown or unthought of, that it was directly felt in every part of the country, and that it necessarily increased, year by year, as the country grew and officeholding multiplied. The President naturally did

40 *Register of Debates,* 23d Cong., 2d sess., p. 462 (Feb. 16, 1835). When later the Whigs were in control, Webster reiterated this view, as having become "the legal construction of the Constitution." *Congressional Globe,* 31st Cong., 1st sess., p. 1126 (June 4, 1850).

41 See below, chs. 16–17.

not make all the appointments personally that rotation in office provided, but he selected many, was consulted on many more, and his voice was decisive wherever it was heard. No single change in the practical operation of the executive branch gave Presidents greater power than this, for the capacity to remove could be used to induce almost universal compliance among officeholders, either by its exercise or by mere threat or expectation of its use.

The most spectacular case of the exercise of the removal power occurred when Jackson replaced William J. Duane as Secretary of the Treasury. The removal was significant not only in itself, but because it asserted the power of the President to remove a Cabinet member for failure to follow the President's wishes in a decision confided by law specifically to the Secretary, not to the Chief Executive. Its sequel, the condemnation of Congress and the subsequent expungement of the vote of censure, marked a dramatic triumph of the executive over the legislative branch.

The setting for this exciting episode goes back to 1816 when Congress established the Second Bank of the United States, granting a charter to expire twenty years hence. In 1832 Congress, led by Clay, passed legislation to recharter the Bank at once. Jackson vetoed the bill, and went to the country in the presidential election of 1832 on this and other issues. His crushing defeat of Clay convinced him of popular support and early in his second term, anticipating the termination of the Bank, he decided to remove the deposits of government funds, transferring them to state banks.

The President, however, did not possess the power to remove the deposits. Congress had carefully vested this authority in the Secretary of the Treasury, in precise language: "the deposits of the money of the United States . . . shall be made in said bank or branches thereof, unless the Secretary of the Treasury shall at any time otherwise order and direct. . . ." [42]

Jackson's then Secretary of the Treasury, Louis McLane, was

42 3 Stat. 266, sec. 16 (April 10, 1816). The only authority vested in the President was to appoint five government directors of the Bank, with the advice and consent of the Senate, and to remove them; and to initiate legal proceedings if satisfied that the charter had been violated. *Ibid.*, secs. 8, 23.

opposed to the removal of the deposits and the President took occasion to transfer him to the State Department. His successor, William J. Duane, took the oath of office June 1, 1833, and in an interview with Jackson on June third immediately expressed doubt about the legality or wisdom of removal and suggested a congressional inquiry. Jackson demurred. He had no intention of bringing Congress into the situation.

The issue between Jackson and the Secretary of the Treasury was soon joined in a rapid sequence of letters and interviews. On the surface the question seemed to be whether the President could require the Secretary of the Treasury to exercise a discretionary authority vested in him by law as the President desired, even against the Secretary's judgment. In fact Jackson never claimed such an authority. He contented himself with urging Duane to recognize the correctness of his views, but denied that he intended to interfere with Duane's independent judgment. The real issue was whether a President was justified in removing a Secretary of the Treasury for exercising his statutory judgment contrary to the judgment of the Chief Executive.

A brief and partial summary of the Jackson-Duane exchange of opinions will illuminate the problem. During his trip to New England, Jackson wrote the Secretary of the Treasury a long exposition of his views, containing the following passage.

> In making to you, my dear Sir, this frank and explicit avowal of my opinions and feelings, it is not my intention to interfere with the independent exercise of the discretion committed to you by law over the subject. I have thought it, however, due to you, under the circumstances, to place before you, with this restriction, my sentiments upon the subject, to the end that you may upon my responsibility allow them to enter into your decision upon the subject, and into my future exposition of it as far as you may deem it proper.[43]

This declaration seemed to recognize Duane's responsibility for the ultimate decision on removal, and Duane so understood it. There ensued a long exchange of letters, many conferences, and

[43] Jackson, *Correspondence,* V, 111–13 (June 26, 1833). The complete exchange of letters between Jackson and Duane, and the latter's account of successive meetings between them is found in William J. Duane, *Narrative and Correspondence Concerning the Removal of the Deposites. . . .* (Philadelphia, 1838).

mounting tension as the Secretary of the Treasury steadily refused to follow Jackson's policy. Duane insisted that the decision was his and that he was duty bound to exercise his own judgment. His analysis moreover forced him to the conclusion that the removal of deposits was not urgent, that the state banks were unsafe, and that it was due to Congress to give its members an opportunity to discuss the proper agency for holding public funds. At the same time Duane agreed with Jackson that the United States Bank should not secure another charter, and that some other means of handling government money had to be found.

In the course of the discussion, Duane on his side made an important concession. He wrote to the President, "when the moment for decision, after inquiry and discussion, shall arrive, I will concur with you, or retire." [44] This declaration seemed to recognize the authority of the President to make the final decision in fact, if not in law, and Jackson so understood it.

For reasons which are not too clear Duane changed his mind on his duty to retire. After two Cabinet meetings Jackson read to the Cabinet the famous "Paper" in which he reaffirmed his intention to cause the removal of the deposits, and stated again his understanding of his position and that of the Secretary of the Treasury.

> . . . . Viewing it as a question of transcendent importance, both in the principles and consequences it involves, the President could not, in justice to the responsibility which he owes to the country, refrain from pressing upon the Secretary of the Treasury his view of the considerations which impel to immediate action. Upon him has been devolved by the Constitution and the suffrages of the American people the duty of superintending the operation of the Executive Departments of the Government and seeing that the laws are faithfully executed. In the performance of this high trust it is his undoubted right to express to those whom the laws and his own choice have made his associates in the administration of the Government his opinion of their duties under circumstances as they arise. It is this right which he now exercises. Far be it from him to expect or require that any member of the Cabinet should at his request, order, or dictation do any act which he believes unlawful or in his conscience condemns. . . .

44 *Ibid.*, p. 90 (July 22, 1833).

The President again repeats that he begs the Cabinet to consider the proposed measure as his own, in the support of which he shall require no one of them to make a sacrifice of opinion or principle.[45]

As the Cabinet retired, Duane asked Jackson whether he understood the President as *directing* him to remove the deposits. Jackson, according to Duane's account, replied that such was his desire, but upon the President's responsibility. Three days later Duane told the President he would not remove the deposits, in a conversation which was "long and occasionally animated," and in which Jackson sought to avoid a break. "A secretary, sir," said Jackson, "is merely an executive agent, a subordinate, and you may say so in self-defence." To which Duane replied, "In this particular case, congress confers a discretionary power, and requires reasons if I exercise it. Surely this contemplates responsibility on my part." [46] Here was the heart of the matter. On September 23, 1833, Jackson solved the problem by summarily removing Duane. To Van Buren he wrote, "In his appointment I surely caught a tarter in disguise, but I have got rid of him." [47] Taney became Secretary of the Treasury, and the deposits were removed.

Jackson defended the removal of Duane in his "Protest" to the Senate, stating again his conception of the relations between Presidents and heads of departments.

Thus was it settled by the Constitution, the laws, and the whole practice of the Government that the entire executive power is vested in the President of the United States; that as incident to that power the right of appointing and removing those officers who are to aid him in the execution of the laws, with such restrictions only as the Constitution prescribes, is vested in the President; that the Secretary of the Treasury is one of those officers; that the custody of the public property and money is an Executive function which, in relation to the money, has always been exercised through the Secretary of the Treasury and his subordinates; that in the performance of these duties he is subject to the supervision and control of the President, and in all important measures having relation to them consults the Chief Magistrate and obtains his approval and sanction; that the law

45 Richardson, *Messages,* III, 18–19 (Sept. 18, 1833).
46 Duane, *op. cit.,* pp. 102–3 (Sept. 21, 1833).
47 Jackson, *Correspondence,* V, 207 (Sept. 23, 1833).

establishing the bank did not, as it could not, change the relation between the President and the Secretary—did not release the former from his obligation to see the law faithfully executed nor the latter from the President's supervision and control.[48]

The ambiguous position of the Secretary of the Treasury, growing out of the organic act of 1789, was thus brought to an end. Whatever responsibility to Congress the Secretary may have had by the terms of the act of 1789 or the Second Bank Act, it was clear that he had a more immediate and direct responsibility to the President, and that duties enjoined upon him by law had to be exercised within the framework of presidential policy.

This view of the position of a department head was denied a few years later by the Supreme Court of the United States, in *Kendall* v. *Stokes*. In this case the Supreme Court took a position substantially the same as that which Duane had assumed. Amos Kendall, then Postmaster General, had refused to pay Stokes, a postal contractor, a sum of money alleged to be due under an earlier decision of his predecessor, Major Barry. Congress thereupon directed the solicitor of the Treasury to settle the claim and ordered Kendall to pay the amount fixed by him. Both Kendall and Jackson believed the claim fraudulent but Kendall reluctantly credited Stokes with part of the sum determined by the solicitor.

Stokes thereupon sued Kendall for the balance. Kendall sought to avoid payment by arguing that he was subject only to the direction and control of the President, with respect to the execution of the duty imposed upon him by law to satisfy Stokes's claim—that is, that process against him, as head of a department, would not lie in the courts to compel observance even of a mandatory act of Congress contrary to the orders of the Chief Execu-

48 Richardson, *Messages,* III, 85 (April 15, 1834). Cf. a strong defense of Jackson's position by Hugh Lawson White: "the framers of the Constitution intended that the executive power should be vested in one head, who would be bound not only to discharge, faithfully, all his *own personal duties,* but likewise should be clothed with the necessary powers to *compel* the inferior officers in the *executive* department, to perform theirs likewise. . . . When they conscientiously disagree, one must yield, or retire, and that should be the subordinate; otherwise we have no executive government, of any practical utility." *A Memoir of Hugh Lawson White* (Nancy N. Scott, ed., Philadelphia: J. B. Lippincott, 1856), p. 138 (March 24, 1834).

tive. The Supreme Court declined to approve this argument: "It would be vesting in the president a dispensing power, which has no countenance for its support, in any part of the constitution; and is asserting a principle, which, if carried out in its results, to all cases falling within it, would be clothing the president with a power entirely to control the legislation of congress, and paralyze the administration of justice." The Court admitted that there were certain political duties vested in subordinate officers to be exercised under the control of the President, but declared that "it would be an alarming doctrine, that congress cannot impose upon any executive officer any duty they may think proper, which is not repugnant to any rights secured and protected by the constitution; and in such cases, the duty and responsibility grow out of and are subject to the control of the law, and not to the direction of the president." [49]

This decision stated the constitutional authority of Congress to vest powers directly in the heads of departments, but it did not affect the power of the President to control the discretion of the head of a department by his removal. Subsequent light was thrown on the issue by a well-known opinion of Attorney General Caleb Cushing. To one of the weakest Presidents, Pierce, Cushing addressed one of the strongest expositions of executive power. "I hold," wrote the Attorney General, "that no Head of Department can lawfully perform an *official* act against the will of the President; and that will is by the Constitution to govern the performance of all such acts. If it were not thus, Congress might by statute so divide and transfer the executive power as utterly to subvert the Government. . . ." [50]

No department head other than Duane put presidential authority to the acid test. Cabinet members took the less distressing path of resigning either when they lost the confidence of the President or, as in the case of Tyler, when the President lost the confidence of his Cabinet. The dramatic removal of Duane, however, remained as precedent, forming a clearer reading of

49 12 Peters 613, 610 (Jan. 1838). The Circuit Court had held that the President, under the clause requiring him to see that the law is faithfully executed, had "no other control over the office [i.e., the head of a department] than to see that he acts honestly, with proper motives. . . ."

50 7 *Official Opinions of the Attorneys General of the United States* 453, 469–70 (August 31, 1855).

executive authority in the field of administration than had yet been achieved.

Whig views on the removal power. The Whigs fought the Democrats both on the unrestricted right of removal, and on the implied authority to control the discretion of a department head in decisions confided by law specifically to him. Senator Livingston declared that Jackson's removals had "made the land pale," and the Whigs worked out a novel doctrine for the control of this executive power. Their first move was a resolution sponsored by Senator Ewing, alleging that the practice of removing public officers for any other reason than securing the faithful execution of the laws was hostile to the spirit of the Constitution, prejudicial to the public service, and dangerous to the liberties of the people; and expressing the opinion that the Senate should not confirm an appointment unless the prior incumbent was removed for sufficient cause.[51]

The ultimate Whig position was more precisely stated in a series of resolutions offered by Henry Clay in 1834. Since they covered the ground on which opposition to Jackson's removal policy was destined to rest, they deserve quotation.

1. *Resolved,* That the Constitution of the United States does not vest in the President power to remove, at his pleasure, officers under the Government of the United States, whose offices have been established by law.
2. *Resolved,* That, in all cases of offices created by law, the tenure of holding which is not prescribed by the Constitution, Congress is authorized by the Constitution to prescribe the tenure, terms, and conditions, on which they are to be holden.
3. *Resolved,* That the Committee on the Judiciary be instructed to inquire into the expediency of providing by law that, in all instances of appointment to office by the President, by and with the advice and consent of the Senate, other than diplomatic appointments, the power of removal shall be exercised only in concurrence with the Senate; and, when the Senate is not in session, that the President may suspend any such officer, communicating his reasons for the suspension to the Senate at its first succeeding session; and, if the Senate concur with him, the officer shall be re-

[51] Senate Doc. 41, 22d Cong., 1st sess. (Jan. 26, 1832). Calhoun also entered the lists against Jackson with a committee report that was a curious mixture of fact and fancy. Senate Doc. 108, 23d Cong., 2d sess. (Feb. 9, 1835).

moved, but if it do not concur with him, the officer shall be restored to office.[52]

The precise issues that fell under discussion were (1) the repeal of the first two sections of the Tenure of Office Act of 1820 specifying fixed four-year terms of office for most officers handling money, and (2) a limitation of the President's power to remove, in the following language: "in all nominations made by the President, to fill vacancies occasioned by removal from office, the fact of removal shall be stated to the Senate at the same time that the nomination is made, with a statement of the reasons for such removal." [53] This language, while not specifically asserting the prerogative of the Senate to judge of the propriety of the reasons, left no doubt that such was the purpose and would be the consequence.

In challenging the constitutional power of the President to remove, the Whigs had to controvert Madison's reading of the removal power set forth in 1789. They boldly undertook the task. Webster, Clay, White, Calhoun, and Ewing joined to argue that the original decision of 1789 was an error, however well established by subsequent practice.[54] They asserted that the power to remove was neither a specifically delegated power, nor an inherent part of the executive power, and was therefore subject to regulation by act of Congress. Senator Ewing put this position in a single powerful sentence, "It appears to me clear, Mr. President, that the constitution does not confer on the President alone the power of removal, that it is a mere matter of legislative provision, subject to be vested, modified, changed, or taken away by the Legislature at their will; and, if it is not regulated at all by law, it vests in the President and Senate as part of the appointing power."

At the conclusion of the Senate debate the bill to repeal the first and second sections of the Tenure of Office Act and to re-

52 Senate Doc. 155, 23d Cong., 1st sess. (March 7, 1834).

53 *Register of Debates,* 23d Cong., 2d sess., p. 479 (Feb. 16, 1835). The full text of the Whig proposal is reprinted in Senate Doc. 399, 28th Cong., 1st sess., p. 86.

54 *Register of Debates,* 23d Cong., 2d sess.; Webster, pp. 458–70; Clay, pp. 514–23; White, pp. 483–91; Calhoun, pp. 553–63; Ewing, pp. 440–47. They were answered by Charles Francis Adams in *An Appeal from the New to the Old Whigs* under the pseudonym, A Whig of the Old School (Boston: Russell, Odiorne, and Company, 1835).

quire the President to submit the reasons for making removals was passed by a vote of 31 to 16.[55] It went to the House, but Jackson's friends never reported it out of committee.

The consequences of Whig success in requiring the reasons for removal would have been beyond calculation. No President could have removed a district attorney, a collector of customs, a federal marshal, or any other officer appointed with the consent of the Senate without in effect securing consent to the removal. This consent would have gravitated into the personal possession of the Senator or Representative from the state or district concerned. The unity and energy of the executive branch would have been gravely impaired, if not destroyed. The center of gravity of the constitutional system would have been cut loose from its established location, and hardly to the benefit of responsible administration.[56]

The Whigs were even more perplexed in finding a solution to the problem of curbing presidential authority over the decisions of a department head on matters confided to him by law, despite the support they had received from the Supreme Court in *Kendall* v. *Stokes*. The competence of Congress to vest independent authority in the hands of the Secretary of the Treasury was stated and defended by Daniel Webster in his reply to Jackson's "Protest." Webster drew a distinction between the power to remove, which he admitted in this debate, and the power to direct a Secretary in the performance of duties prescribed by statute, which he denied. "The law," he declared, "charges the officer, whoever he may be, with the performance of certain duties. The President, with the consent of the Senate, appoints an individual to be such an officer; and this individual he may remove, if he so please; but, until he is removed, he is the officer, and remains charged with the duties of his station, duties which nobody else can perform, and for the neglect or violation of which he is liable to be impeached." [57] Webster argued that the

55 *Register of Debates,* 23d Cong., 2d sess., pp. 446–47 (Feb. 14, 1835).

56 These consequences were ably stated by a House select committee reporting against a proposed Whig amendment to the Constitution in support of their doctrine. This Democratic committee had no hesitation in quoting Alexander Hamilton in support of its position. This document deserves not to be lost from sight. House Report 296, 24th Cong., 2d sess. (Feb. 28, 1837).

57 Webster, *Writings and Speeches* (National ed.), VII, 107 (May 7, 1834).

discretion over the deposits was "the Secretary's own personal discretion," that Congress had intended it to be thus, and that "the interposition of the authority of another" was an assumption of power.[58] He denied Jackson's position that the President was responsible "for the entire action of the executive department," and, without fully stating his view, argued that subordinate executive officers could be vested with independent authority and thus become "agents of the law," not of the President.[59]

The specific Whig reaction to Jackson's removal of the deposits from the United States Bank was to demand "the separation of the purse from the sword." This war cry was reduced to particulars. In his inaugural address, Tyler solemnly proposed to save the liberty of the people by protecting the public funds from the executive branch.

> . . . . I deem it of the most essential importance that a complete separation should take place between the sword and the purse. No matter where or how the public moneys shall be deposited, so long as the President can exert the power of appointing and removing at his pleasure the agents selected for their custody the Commander in Chief of the Army and Navy is in fact the treasurer. A permanent and radical change should therefore be decreed.[60]

The plan was reduced to the form of a bill and presented to Congress in December 1841. It provided for an independent Board of Exchequer of five, the majority of which, appointed by the President with the advice and consent of the Senate, were to be removed only for physical inability, incompetency, or neglect or violation of duty, with reasons laid before the Senate. The Exchequer Board was to become the sole agency to receive, hold, and disburse all public money—"safe from Executive control." [61]

Such a scheme outdid Jefferson, who had no intention of turning over to Congress the central agency of administration and finance. It can hardly be understood except in the light of the

58 *Ibid.,* VII, 109.

59 *Ibid.,* VII, 136.

60 Richardson, *Messages,* IV, 37–38 (April 9, 1841). His program was set out in greater detail in his message of Dec. 7, 1841, *ibid.,* IV, 84–85, and followed up in his second annual message, to no avail. *Ibid.,* IV, 204–6 (Dec. 6, 1842).

61 House Doc. 20, 27th Cong., 2d sess., pp. 6, 13–14 (Dec. 21, 1841).

fear created by recollections of a strong-minded and hot-headed general seated in the White House for eight years, engaged in one conflict after another with Congress, and generally successful in imposing his will. Other issues pushed aside one so academic in nature. No President followed Tyler's lead.[62]

The conflict between Democratic and Whig concepts of executive power was epitomized in the Resolution of Censure offered by Henry Clay and approved by the Senate on March 28, 1834. This resolution condemned Jackson's course in removing the government deposits from the Bank of the United States—"*Resolved,* That the President, in the late Executive proceedings in relation to the public revenue, has assumed upon himself authority and power not conferred by the constitution and laws, but in derogation of both." [63] Jackson responded by presenting a "Protest" which the Senate declined to receive.[64] Senator Benton promptly gave notice of a resolution to expunge the censure, and by persistent work in succeeding elections to the Senate commanded the necessary majority in 1837. The Resolution of Censure was formally expunged on January 16, 1837.[65] Thus Jackson earned a personal triumph, and thus symbolically his reading of executive powers gained political confirmation. "Never before and never since," wrote Corwin, "has the Senate so abased itself before a President." [66]

THE PRESIDENT AS PARTY LEADER

A political party might theoretically be held together by the common views of its members on public policy. Daniel Webster expounded this doctrine in the passage already quoted. Presidents and party leaders, in this view, would be primarily concerned with announcing, defending, and putting into effect the policies on which they agreed. Such a course, however logical, was never attained, but Federalist and Republican Presidents

62 In 1841 Congressman Millard Fillmore was committed to "the separation of the purse and the sword from the hands of the executive." *Millard Fillmore Papers* (Frank H. Severance, ed., 2 vols., Buffalo: Buffalo Historical Society, 1907), II, 225 (Sept. 23, 1841). As President he forgot the issue.

63 *Senate Journal,* 23d Cong., 1st sess., p. 197.

64 Richardson, *Messages,* III, 69 (April 15, 1834).

65 *Senate Journal,* 24th Cong., 2d sess., pp. 123–24.

66 Edward S. Corwin, *The President: Office and Powers* (New York: New York University Press, 1940), p. 267.

alike tended to pursue this mode of conduct. As noticed in the previous chapter, they had no nationally organized parties to be concerned about.

This view of the nature and function of party did not adequately describe the activities of parties in the states prior to 1829, and failed entirely to explain their efforts from 1829 to 1861. The nearer object came to be to win elections and to enjoy the fruits of victory in the shape of offices, contracts, and other perquisites, although some devotion to principle might usually be discerned by careful observers.

To win victory, a party operating on a national scale became essential. Both parties lacked effective national organization. The President and his advisers became the natural party leaders, so far as central leadership could be maintained. The qualification is important, because both parties were rent by feuds; state organizations were difficult and sometimes impossible to control; and ambitious personalities within the party, and occasionally within the government, resisted the influence of the Chief Executive in party maneuvers.

Nevertheless the President could not be ignored. He usually sought to dominate the party to secure his legislative program and to bring about his renomination—or to weaken his competitors. Factions in the state organizations sought to strengthen themselves by winning presidential support and the nomination of their friends to federal office in the locality. A President was thus bound to the party which by its efforts had placed him in the White House, and the separate party machines were equally bound to him. The more forward frontline fighters were not reluctant to remind Presidents of their duty.

The relation of the President to his party was emphasized by his opportunity to support the party press, a matter which is dealt with later. Here it is enough to state that by the appointment of editors to office, by the selection of newspapers for official notices, and by the award of printing contracts to the party press, a President could mobilize great resources to support his partisans and to facilitate his renomination.

Party leadership by the President was informal and did not become institutionalized. It was nevertheless a source of added power and influence, since both sides were bound by the strongest of incentives, self-interest and mutual expectations of reward for services rendered. The Whigs severely criticized this increase of executive influence. When, however, they took possession of the White House, they followed Jackson's precedent.

TWO THEORIES OF THE PRESIDENCY

As the natural successors of the National Republicans, the school of Henry Clay, John Q. Adams, the young Calhoun, Rush, and others, the Whigs should have been the foremost defenders of strong executive power. As the party of opposition to Jackson, they were forced into the position of weakening the executive branch, and they took their task so seriously that they outdid the most timorous Republicans of earlier years.

Ardent Whigs, however, were not the only ones to be alarmed at the apparent extension of executive authority. A conservative wing of the Democratic party, of whom Hugh Lawson White was an exceptionally thoughtful member, was also disturbed. Although White supported Jackson in the removal of Duane and in most other matters connected with the United States Bank, he stood squarely on the necessity of curbing the power of the Chief Executive. He wrote:

> No matter who is President of the United States, I firmly believe executive power ought to be limited within the *narrowest* limits compatible with an administration of the government; otherwise all *efficient agency of the people,* in their own affairs, will soon be lost. If the executive power and patronage be left as they now are, and we should ever have a popular Chief Magistrate willing, from any motive, to lend his influence, and to use his patronage for the purpose of designating and electing his successor, then will this tremendous power be felt. . . .
>
> I was born under a king, but raised and educated in a Republic. To secure to our posterity the same freedom for which our fathers toiled, it is essential that executive favor and patronage should be limited by law; otherwise the day may not be remote when we will have in fact a monarchy, and it the more odious because a deceptive form of a republic may be continued.[67]

Whig doctrine concerning the presidency was spelled out in detail in Harrison's inaugural address, prepared, strangest of

67 White, *Memoir,* pp. 179–80 (Sept. 17, 1835).

all, with the active assistance of Daniel Webster, who still had his eye on the high office whose powers were now so ruthlessly to be curtailed.[68] Harrison solemnly declared that the concentration of power in executive hands was a clear trend toward despotism and announced his determination to arrest this tendency. To this end he made specific assurances and offered specific reforms. He pledged himself to one term only. He promised caution in the use of the veto power. He declared that the framers of the Constitution committed a great error in not making the head of the Treasury Department "entirely independent of the Executive." He accepted the Clay-Calhoun doctrine that a President should communicate the reasons for making removals, at least of the Secretary of the Treasury. He confessed that the power to recommend measures was not intended to make the President the source of legislation, and in particular asserted that he should "never be looked to for schemes of finance." The mode of keeping the public revenue should be prescribed by Congress, "and the further removed it may be from the control of the Executive the more wholesome the arrangement. . . ." He finally assured Congress that all the influence he possessed would be exerted to prevent the formation of an executive party in the legislative halls.[69] Apparently the Whigs intended to reduce the President to a mere figurehead, for Harrison was momentarily forced to yield his will to a majority vote in his Cabinet. Whether a government could be successfully maintained on these principles was not put to the test, for Harrison died after exactly one month in the White House.

Evidence was already beginning to appear even within this brief interval that the Whig doctrine would not work. Harrison quickly showed unorthodox signs of independence. He put Henry Clay in his place when Clay tried to push him, and resisted party leaders clamoring for patronage. At a Cabinet meeting, so the story is told, Webster informed the President that the Cabinet had decided on James Wilson to be governor of Iowa. Harrison wrote a few words on a slip of paper and asked Webster to read them aloud: "William Henry Harrison, President of the United States." The President then rose to his feet and said,

68 Clay probably assisted Webster, and he, too, still aspired to the presidency.
69 Richardson, *Messages,* IV, 5–21 (March 4, 1841).

"And William Henry Harrison, President of the United States, tells you, gentlemen, that, by ——, John Chambers shall be Governor of Iowa." [70]

The same contradictory evidence recurred when the second Whig President, Zachary Taylor, entered the White House in 1849. In cautious phrases at the close of his first annual message he rejected the idea that the President was the direct representative of the people and declared himself against "every claim or tendency of one coordinate branch to encroachment upon another." The executive, he said, had authority to recommend but not to dictate to Congress, and having spoken should not interpose until Congress had enacted legislation for his signature. The veto power he thought was an extreme measure.[71] All this hardly bespoke the energy and direction of a Hamiltonian or a Jacksonian Chief Executive, but before Taylor's death he had found that he could not follow the self-effacing precedents of Madison. His stubborn independence on the proposed terms of the slavery compromise in 1850 threatened a major crisis, but the crisis did not deter him. Hearing of threats of secession, he offered to take the field and hang the offenders. He died before the crisis matured. Fillmore repeated Whig assurances in favor of restraint on executive power.[72]

The undercurrent fear of executive power that ran through Whig doctrine came to the surface in John J. Crittenden's remarks on an innocent bill introduced by a fellow Whig Senator, Richard H. Bayard, to provide a guard for the public buildings "against the torch of the incendiary." Crittenden warned that such a force might be turned into a political guard for the Executive whose full development might overshadow the liberties of the people. Reminding his fellow Senators that the Roman consular guard consisted originally of but thirty men, he begged them to legislate cautiously in these portentous matters.[73] The bill was postponed.

The force of events and the strength of personality of two Democratic Presidents, Jackson and Polk, set precedents that

70 Parmelee, "Recollections of an Old Stager," *Harper's New Monthly Magazine,* XLVII (1873), 754.

71 Richardson, *Messages,* V, 23–24 (Dec. 4, 1849).

72 *Ibid.,* V, 79 (Dec. 2, 1850).

73 *Congressional Globe,* 27th Cong., 2d sess., p. 854 (August 6, 1842).

were destined to make the office of Chief Executive one of power and influence—Whig opposition notwithstanding. Hamilton's doctrines of energy and unity, which were also Jefferson's guide to action if not to theory, were reaffirmed, although not consistently put into practice. The formal constitutional position of the Chief Executive was not changed by the Democrats, but they were responsible for precedents that gave vigor and power to an office destined for national leadership. The idea that the President was a direct representative of the people and represented all the people more certainly than Congress was a never-ending source of strength; the idea that the President's view of public policy ought to prevail against that of Congress through the veto power brought him influence both positive and negative upon the coordinate branch; the doctrine that Congress could not place executive authority in a department head safe from presidential dictation, although disputed by Congress and denied by the Supreme Court, nevertheless prevailed in practice and confirmed the unity of the executive branch while strengthening it internally and externally; the free use of the removal power and the unblushing appointment of party supporters to the vacancies thus opened up created a form of power that reached into every section and that could be understood by every citizen; and the emerging role of the President as the leader of the party in power concentrated all these trends toward eminently practical purposes. It was not surprising that the conservative wing of the old Republican party was disturbed, nor that the Whigs raised the cry of executive usurpation.[74]

[74] On one point the Whigs were needlessly alarmed, viz., the selection by an outgoing President of his successor. They recognized correctly that Jackson picked Van Buren to follow him in the White House (Van Buren, *Autobiography*, pp. 505–6) and predicted the end of the Republic. The precedent has been repeated only rarely.

CHAPTER THREE

The President as Commander in Chief

James K. Polk was the second American President to wield power as commander in chief in wartime. James Madison during the War of 1812 had done little to reveal the actual authority that lay concealed in the title. Abraham Lincoln pushed the constitutional power of the commander in chief to its outer limits, but problems of this order did not arise in the War with Mexico. Polk gave the country its first demonstration of the *administrative* capacities of the presidency as a war agency. He proved that a President could run a war.

Polk became Chief Executive on March 4, 1845, after a long public career in his native state and in Congress. On May 11, 1846, Congress declared that a state of war with Mexico existed. The northern Mexican provinces were occupied as far south as Monterrey by October 1846; Vera Cruz was taken in March 1847; Mexico City fell in September 1847; and ratifications of the treaty of peace were exchanged on May 30, 1848. Polk therefore operated for about two years as commander in chief during war. What he did in this capacity is the subject matter of the present chapter.

Polk's activities during these years were profoundly affected by his concept of himself in the role of President. When he was about to set out for Washington in February 1845, he let it be known that he intended to be *the President.* When war broke out he made it equally clear that he intended to be *the commander in chief.* He told his land office commissioner, James

Shields, who was ambitious for military glory, that he hoped his friends in Congress would allow him to conduct the War with Mexico as he thought proper.[1] The President, Polk declared, was held responsible for the conduct of the war; he intended to be responsible, and he exercised that responsibility to the limit of his endurance.[2] He determined the general strategy of military and naval operations; he chose commanding officers; he gave personal attention to supply problems; he energized so far as he could the General Staff; he controlled the military and naval estimates; and he used the Cabinet as a major coordinating agency for the conduct of the campaign. He told the Secretaries of War and Navy to give their personal attention to all matters, even of detail, and to advise him promptly of every important step that was to be taken. The President was the center on which all else depended; Hamilton's doctrine of the unity of the executive power was seldom more truly exemplified.

Among the principal civilians with whom Polk was in constant touch were the Secretaries of the War, Navy, and Treasury Departments. William L. Marcy, Secretary of War, was a Brown University graduate who had studied law and engaged professionally in politics. He had held municipal and state offices in New York before going to the Senate in 1831, where he coined the famous phrase, "to the victors belong the spoils." He resigned his seat to become governor of New York (1833–39). He was Polk's Secretary of War and Pierce's Secretary of State. He was a genial, honest politician with a lively sense of humor and a fondness for desultory reading.

George Bancroft, Polk's first Secretary of the Navy, was a Harvard man, with graduate training in philosophy and religion in Berlin, an unsuccessful Unitarian clergyman, an unsuccessful schoolmaster, a highly successful Massachusetts machine politician, and a rising historian in 1845 when he took over the navy on his way to his first diplomatic mission in Great

1 *The Diary of James K. Polk During His Presidency, 1845 to 1849* (4 vols., Milo Milton Quaife, ed., Chicago: A. C. McClurg and Co., 1910), I, 427–28 (May 25, 1846). Shields went out to Illinois and became brigadier general of Illinois volunteers, was badly wounded at Cerro Gordo, but survived to serve a term in the U.S. Senate (1849–55) and to fight in the Civil War as a brigadier general of volunteers. See William Henry Condon, *Life of Major-General James Shields* (Chicago: Blakely Printing Co., 1900); *Dictionary of American Biography*, XVII, 106.

2 Polk, *Diary*, II, 355–56 (Jan. 25, 1847).

Britain. His successor, John Y. Mason, was a lawyer who had been active in Virginia politics, had served six years in Congress and about seven as a federal district judge before entering Tyler's Cabinet and then Polk's. The Secretary of Treasury, Robert J. Walker, a Mississippi lawyer best known as a land speculator and as an advocate of a tariff for revenue only, had served ten years in the Senate before taking his Cabinet post.

On the military side, General Zachary Taylor was a farmer's son who began a forty years' career in the army in 1808 with a lieutenant's commission. Until the Mexican War his experience had been limited to fighting Indians before, during, and after the War of 1812. He had made an excellent record in such small-scale engagements. General Winfield Scott also joined the army before the War of 1812, and, although not a West Pointer, revealed a greater professional interest in the military art than most of his contemporaries. He became known later as a quarrelsome letter writer, much too greatly impressed with his own dignity and rights. General Thomas S. Jesup, the quartermaster general, had been one of Calhoun's able young men during the eight years of his administration of the War Department when army management had been carried to such a high level.

DETERMINATION OF GENERAL STRATEGY

President Polk took immediate responsibility for making the fundamental decision whether to wage a war on foreign territory with the regular army, or with the army supplemented by volunteers.[3] Here he made his principal mistakes. Instead of asking Congress for authority to recruit men to fill up existing regiments and add new regiments to the regular army, he requested authority to call for volunteers. He compounded this mistake by fixing the term of enlistment at twelve months *or* for the war, which was construed to give the volunteers an option to withdraw at the end of one year's service. So many took advantage of this option while General Scott's army was before Mexico City that military operations were halted for months.

In the broad field of overall strategy Polk promptly took the

[3] The course of events as seen by General Winfield Scott is ably described by Major Charles Winslow Elliott, *Winfield Scott: the Soldier and the Man* (New York: Macmillan, 1937).

lead. The general movements of the war were simple. The northern provinces of Mexico, south and west of Texas, were to be seized and held, and California was to be taken by sea and by land. If these movements failed to produce peace, an invasion of Mexico from Vera Cruz was to drive on Mexico City. Geography suggested these grand outlines, and the Cabinet concurred with Polk in settling upon them nearly a year before hostilities broke out.[4] The navy was to blockade most Mexican ports, and to transport men and supplies.

War once declared, Polk wasted no time in determining the precise course of the campaign. On the evening of May 14, 1846, Secretary of War William L. Marcy and General Winfield Scott came to the White House. "I gave it as my opinion that the first movement should be to march a competent force into the Northern Provinces," the President notified his advisers. Marcy and Scott concurred.[5] Two days later the President presented a more detailed plan of operations to the Cabinet. "My plan was to march an army of 2000 men on Santa Fé & near 4000 on Chihuahua . . . leaving Gen'l Scott to occupy the country on the lower Del Norte and in the interior." [6] In early June the expedition against California was agreed upon in Cabinet, and an order to Colonel Philip Kearny read by Marcy. Polk rewrote it.[7] In July Polk drafted instructions to Taylor in relation to the manner of conducting the war, depending on Colonel Benton for a part but himself preparing, as he said, the most important section. The instructions took the form of a letter from the Secretary of War to Taylor; Polk showed Marcy the text, and "the Secretary of War approved it." [8] In short, the President participated actively in every major decision regarding the military strategy of the war, initiated some of them, and at times presented a well-defined plan of operations. As will be seen later, he also directed a multitude of details.

4 Polk, *Diary*, I, 9–10 (August 29, 1845); *ibid.*, I, 12 (August 30, 1845).

5 *Ibid.*, I, 400 (May 14, 1846).

6 *Ibid.*, I, 403–4 (May 16, 1846).

7 *Ibid.*, I, 443 (June 2, 1846).

8 *Ibid.*, II, 16–17 (July 8, 1846). The instructions, under date of July 9, 1846, are found in House Ex. Doc. 60, 30th Cong., 1st sess., pp. 155–58. They are of primary importance, stressing the desirability of conciliating the Mexican people, keeping open a channel of communication with the Mexican army, and encouraging a separatist movement in the northern provinces.

THE COMMANDING OFFICERS

A crucial aspect of military affairs is the choice of the high command. The President personally selected the commanding officers, so far as he had freedom of action, and tried unsuccessfully to maneuver both Taylor and Scott into a secondary position. Here he encountered some of his principal frustrations.

At the outbreak of war, Winfield Scott and Zachary Taylor were the senior general officers. Polk almost immediately lost confidence in Scott and eventually in Taylor. Some of the considerations that entered into the assignment of commanding generals may be illustrated by a view of the case of General Scott. Immediately after war broke out Scott was informed that he would be sent to Mexico with the volunteers "to reinforce Taylor"—and also by virtue of rank to supersede him in command. According to Scott, Democratic Congressmen went to the White House predicting that his anticipated success at the front would "prostrate the Democratic party in 1848." To prevent this, the House Democrats entered a bill to authorize the President to appoint two major generals and four brigadier generals, all presumably Democrats and designed to supersede Scott and other Whig generals. Scott saw the bill, at once "smelt a rat" and promptly told Marcy that he saw the trick. Believing, as he said, that he was a stronger man than any of his *"entrappers,"* he "flung, the next day, the 21st, a letter into the teeth of the poor Secretary (the mere tool in the hands of party) . . ." [9]

In the course of the letter he declared that he did not desire to place himself in the most perilous of all positions: *"a fire upon my rear, from Washington, and the fire, in front, from the Mexicans."* [10] This was strong language for a military man to use in addressing a Secretary of War and, by implication, a President of the United States. This letter sufficiently demonstrated Scott's bad feelings. Polk concluded, "His bitter hostility towards the administration is such that I could not trust him. . . . Gen'l Scott's partisan feelings must not interfere with the public service

9 Scott to R. P. Netcher (June 5, 1846), in Ann Mary Butler Coleman, ed., *The Life of John J. Crittenden* (2 vols., Philadelphia: J. B. Lippincott, 1871), I, 244–46.

10 Senate Doc. 378, 29th Cong., 1st sess., p. 5 (May 21, 1846).

if another suitable commanding officer can be had." [11] Much to Scott's dismay and surprise, he was ordered to remain in Washington.[12]

In due course of time Polk had to find a commander of the expedition against Vera Cruz. His dislike of Scott had not diminished and by this time he had also lost confidence in Taylor.[13] He turned to his Cabinet for help, but all "were at a loss to designate who should be the chief in command." [14] Bitter necessity finally forced Polk to give the command to Scott.

The problem of selecting the field generals was complicated on account of the political connections of both Taylor and Scott. Polk hoped to avoid winning the war with victorious Whig generals who might easily defeat a quarrelsome Democratic party in the 1848 election. But no general officer of the regular army was an avowed Democrat. Scott was a convinced Whig, and had been and was a receptive candidate for his party nomination. Taylor became a hopeful candidate during the course of the Mexican War.

Polk made an extraordinary maneuver to extricate himself from this difficulty by proposing to revive the rank of lieutenant general, last held by General Washington, with the intention of appointing to this office, as supreme commander, Senator Thomas

11 Polk, *Diary,* I, 415–16 (May 21, 1846).

12 *Ibid.,* I, 424 (May 25, 1846). Marcy's reply to Scott's accusations was thought so important that Polk called a special meeting of the Cabinet to consider and approve it. Scott was *persona non grata* whether in Washington or elsewhere. Just before the episode related above, Polk had discovered that Scott intended not to go to the front until September 1846. The President told Marcy that Scott would proceed "very soon" or be superseded in his command. Marcy replied that Scott was embarrassing him by his schemes, constantly talking and not acting. Polk told Marcy "to issue his orders and cause them to be obeyed." *Ibid.,* I, 407–8 (May 19, 1846). Held in Washington by the Cabinet decision of May 25, he continued, according to Polk, to be a problem. "Gen'l Scott is of no aid to the Department, but his presence at Washington is constantly embarrassing to the Secretary of War. I will observe his course, and if necessary will order him to some other post." *Ibid.,* II, 151 (Sept. 22, 1846).

13 Polk wrote in his diary, "He is evidently a weak man and has been made giddy with the idea of the Presidency. . . . I am now satisfied that he is a narrow minded, bigotted partisan, without resources and wholly unqualified for the command he holds." *Ibid.,* II, 249–50 (Nov. 21, 1846). The break became complete when a critical letter from Taylor to General Gaines (then in disgrace) was published with Gaines' connivance. *Ibid.,* II, 353–55 (Jan. 25, 1847).

14 *Ibid.,* II, 236 (Nov. 14, 1846).

H. Benton. Benton was willing, but the Senate was not. The scheme did Polk little credit. Major Elliott condemned it in a passage from his biography of Scott: "Nothing in Polk's clumsy direction of the war illustrates more graphically his utter ignorance of the history, the principles, and the necessities of warfare than this readiness to place in command of his armies the arrogant and self-confident civilian politician." [15] Senator Benton had held a militia commission, but his military experience was so inferior to his political availability that his senatorial colleagues put an end to this expedient. Much against his will Polk had to deal with two commanding generals he did not trust—feelings that came to be reciprocated on their part.

The President was active in selecting officers for lesser posts. He commissioned his former law partner, Gideon J. Pillow, as general, assigned him to Taylor, and used him as a confidential source of information. Polk himself proposed Patterson, Pillow, and Shields for the Tampico expedition.[16] He decided to appoint personally the officers of a newly authorized regiment of riflemen and, with Marcy, agreed that "a portion of the officers should be Whigs." He spent hours examining the papers and recommendations of applicants.[17] Later he spent more time with Marcy in arranging the nominations of officers under the Ten Regiment Bill. On this occasion he sought "in vain to turn over the horde of applicants to the Secretary of War, that I might have his Report upon their respective merits." For more than a week he spent three or four hours a day hearing claims for commissions. "I have pushed them off and fought them with both hands like a man fighting fire, and endeavored to drive them to the Secretary of War. . . . It has all been in vain." [18] The President had brought all this on himself. Marcy wrote a member of Congress who was trying to get a commission for a constituent, "it is proper to say what I presume you are not

15 Elliott, *Winfield Scott,* p. 437.

16 Polk, *Diary,* II, 148–49 (Sept. 21, 1846).

17 *Ibid.,* I, 412–13 (May 21, 1846). He appointed Colonel Clarkson, a Whig, to the office of paymaster at the request of Whig Senators Crittenden and Morehead. "I was gratified myself that I had it in my power promptly to meet the wishes of these gentlemen, and thus to prove to them that I was not proscriptive in my appointments." *Ibid.,* II, 6 (July 2, 1846).

18 *Ibid.,* II, 382–83 (Feb. 19, 1847).

ignorant of, that the selections are not made by the War Department, but by the President himself." [19]

In 1847 Polk decided to appoint a few noncommissioned officers who had distinguished themselves in battle to vacant second lieutenancies. The army preferred West Point men, and the adjutant general stubbornly delayed furnishing the list of vacancies, a mild form of sabotage. Marcy could not get the list. Polk sent for the adjutant general, who started to debate the issue with him. Polk was much vexed and told the reluctant adjutant general that he, Polk, was commander in chief, and ordered him to produce the list. "I repeated to him," he wrote in his diary, "that he must regard what I said as a military order & that I would expect it to be promptly obeyed." [20]

Polk kept his hand on the field commanders as well. General Scott detached Colonel William S. Harney from his regimental command, an act which the President described in his diary as arbitrary and tyrannical conduct. Polk ordered Harney to be restored. Marcy, however, agreed with Scott and delayed writing to him. Polk learned of the postponement and told Marcy if he was unwilling to write the letter that he, the President, would. Marcy promptly yielded.[21]

THE SUPPLY OPERATIONS

Another major administrative problem in the conduct of war is supply and transportation. Polk had a shrewd common-sense grasp of the problems involved in maintaining an army in the field, and more capacity for forward planning than some of his staff officers. His diary contains many records of conferences with General Jesup, the quartermaster general, and other supply officers, and we may guess that the "details" he was constantly concerned with were primarily matters of supply. A few specific examples will illustrate his constant preoccupation with such arrangements, and with energizing subordinate military and naval officers.

Early in the course of the war, Polk asked Marcy to bring to

19 Library of Congress, William L. Marcy, Private Letter Book, 1845–1849, pp. 20–21 (Sept. 2, 1845).

20 Polk, *Diary*, III, 31 (May 19, 1847).

21 *Ibid.*, II, 384–86 (Feb. 20, 1847).

the White House General Gibson, the commissary general of subsistence, and General Jesup. Polk had "a full interview" with both officers, telling them that he wished ample provision made for the army but no wasteful expenditure, and that he would hold each of them responsible for any failure. This was the first of many direct contacts between the President and the supply services during the war. Summer vacations took Marcy out of Washington, war or no war, and Polk then in effect became acting head of the department. Thus he recorded in his diary in September 1847, "During the absence of the Secretary of War much of my time is occupied with the details of the War Department connected with the Mexican War. I saw the adj't Gen'l & the Quarter master Gen'l to-day & conferred with them, and gave directions in reference [to] many of these details." [22]

Procrastination was an evil that Polk was constantly fighting. The ship *Lexington* was scheduled to sail from New York with troops but sat in harbor. Polk learned of this and asked the Secretary of the Navy for an explanation. Bancroft cleared himself by stating he had sent orders by mail to the *Lexington*'s commanding officer who was in nearby Virginia and simultaneous orders to New York that as soon as the troops were on board, the ship should sail with another officer, if necessary. No one knew where the negligent commander was. Polk ordered the ship to sail instantly, and the Secretary to court-martial any officer who had been guilty of unreasonable delay.[23]

A year later Polk was still having trouble in getting troops out of New York. A regiment under Colonel Stephenson was to proceed by sea to California. After repeated conversations with the Secretary of War, Polk learned that the delay was caused by lack of transports. He then sent for Jesup, who could give no satisfactory explanation beyond saying that orders had been issued to engage the vessels. Polk retorted that he thought there had been culpable delay, and ordered Jesup to see that the transports were procured.[24] Two weeks later Colonel Stephenson was still in Washington. Polk exploded; Stephenson gave some unsatisfactory explanations, and Polk told him that if further delay

22 *Ibid.*, III, 158–59 (Sept. 3, 1847).

23 *Ibid.*, I, 14–15 (Sept. 2, 1845).

24 *Ibid.*, II, 103–4 (August 29, 1846); II, 117–18 (Sept. 5, 1846).

occurred, the negligent officers would be arrested and tried.[25]

The matter of army transport in Mexico was much on Polk's mind. In early autumn, 1846, he called in Jesup and asked why baggage wagons were being used by Taylor's army instead of mules. Jesup promptly gave "his decided opinion that baggage wagons should be dispensed with and mules employed. . . ." Polk then asked Jesup and Marcy, who was present, why mules had not already been provided. Jesup was evasive: "he had received no communication from Gen'l Taylor or the War Department on the subject. . . ." Marcy apparently was silent. The purchase of wagons went on just the same.[26]

Polk came back again to the issue of mules *vs.* wagons in the following spring, asking Marcy to come in with the acting quartermaster general, Colonel Stanton. The President roundly condemned the purchase and use of "miles of wagons" but declined to issue a positive order forbidding them. He then opened up on the purchase of 1,000 horses in Ohio to be transported to Mexico to mount the Third Dragoons, and the purchase of mules in the states. "I expressed the opinion strongly that this was great folly." Stanton could find no satisfactory explanation for failure to buy horses and mules in Mexico at one-fourth the price, except that he thought American specimens were larger and better. The President was "much vexed at the extravagance & stupidity of purchasing these animals in the U.S." [27]

MILITARY ENERGY

Indeed, Polk was deeply dissatisfied with the lack of energy on the part of the military establishment. He found two reasons for failure to perform—superannuation and political unreliability. On the score of old age, well before the war he remarked that many of the army and navy officers had become so fond of their ease and comfort that it was necessary they should be taught their duty by enforcing rigid discipline.[28] Early in the war he

25 *Ibid.*, II, 146–47 (Sept. 20, 1846).

26 *Ibid.*, II, 118 (Sept. 5, 1846). Polk had received a tip from an informant in New Orleans, *ibid.*, II, 86–87. Jesup might have recalled that he had been given specific instructions by General Scott on May 15, 1846, to investigate the relative value of wagons or pack mules. House Ex. Doc. 60, 30th Cong., 1st sess., p. 546.

27 Polk, *Diary*, II, 430–41 (March 20, 1847).

28 *Ibid.*, I, 14–15 (Sept. 2, 1845).

told General Jesup that many of the officers of the regular army had become gentlemen of entirely too much leisure, "and that some of them required to have a coal of fire put on their backs to make them move promptly." [29] In the spring of 1847 he repeated these sentiments: "The truth is that the old army officers have become so in the habit of enjoying their ease, sitting in parlours and on carpeted floors, that most of them have no energy. . . ." [30] He had no easy way of getting rid of deadwood, since the army had no retirement system. The consequence was precisely the same as that which had undermined the army in the early years of the War of 1812; command by men in some cases far beyond their prime, bereft of energy and drive, and unable to stand the rigors of field campaigns.

The army tradition of 1846, at least as understood by Marcy, forbade a drastic solution of the problem by removal of officers at the head of the military bureaus. The Secretary of War disclaimed any personal responsibility for failures of supply. The law, he explained, had assigned the heads of the various military branches, meaning presumably by virtue of the seniority rule. "These could not be changed by me nor could I make them over. Instructions, admonitions &c. cannot give appropriate qualifications when nature has denied them." [31]

There was another limitation inherent in the situation. If it was out of the tradition to remove a quartermaster general, it was also difficult to appoint competent understudies for them. Many persons applied to both Marcy and Polk for military commissions, and some of them might have been useful in supply operations. Marcy explained his dilemma to his friend Wetmore: "I have to scold not a little at the Q.M. Department, & if I overrule them in the selection of subordinates they naturally say things would go better if you would give us the officers we ask for." [32] Civilian heads could go only so far.

On the score of political infidelity, Polk was equally dissatisfied. By September 1846, he reached the conclusion that several

29 *Ibid.*, II, 117 (Sept. 5, 1846).

30 *Ibid.*, II, 431 (March 20, 1847); cf. *ibid.*, II, 439 (March 24, 1847); *ibid.*, III, 24 (May 13, 1847).

31 Library of Congress, William L. Marcy Papers, Vol. 12, No. 34,862 (Nov. 8, 1846).

32 *Ibid.*, Vol. 12, No. 34,911 (Dec. 25, 1846).

of the officers in Marcy's immediate entourage were "politically opposed to the administration," an opinion shared by Marcy.[33] In 1847 Polk put down in his diary: "The Subordinate officers at the head of the different bureau[s] in the War Department are generally Federalists, and many of them are indifferent. . . . They take no sort of responsibility on themselves, and this renders it necessary that the Secretary of War & myself should look after them, even in the performance of the ordinary routine of details in their offices." [34]

Polk probably exaggerated the influence of politics on the bureau heads in the War Department. Their antecedents might have been "Federalist" and some of them might have been Whigs, but they were also professional soldiers. The supply services were faulty, but it is probable that the cause lay in the system and in poor judgment rather than in the deliberate intention of politically minded regular army officers to discredit the administration by risking loss of the war.

THE PRESIDENT AND WAR FINANCE

Congress accepted the recommendations coming from Polk and the Treasury for financing military operations. Indeed, after a warm battle in which the President had to exert all his influence, Congress agreed with Polk's bold proposal to reduce the tariff in 1846 when revenue needs were great and unpredictable.

The major precedent established by Polk in the field of finance was to reverse the historic practice by which the President had had no responsibility for the departmental estimates. This matter is dealt with at a later point.[35] Here it needs to be recorded that for the first time the President insisted upon reviewing the estimates and controlling them. Polk was his own budget officer, and he acted with his customary vigor to overcome the resistance of the army officers against cuts in their figures.

The nature of Polk's fiscal preoccupations can be appreciated by events which came to his attention in the week from August 18, 1847, to August 25. On August 18 he learned that his plan to call out 6,000 more volunteers might be foreclosed for lack

33 Polk, *Diary,* II, 151 (Sept. 22, 1846); II, 154 (Sept. 24, 1846).

34 *Ibid.,* III, 26 (May 14, 1847).

35 See below, ch. 4.

of available funds. This struck him with great astonishment. He sent for Treasury officers and Cabinet members, and directed the quartermaster general, Jesup, to be ordered back from New York by telegraph. None of Jesup's clerks could explain the deficiency nor indeed could Jesup when he reported on the 21st.

On August 25 Jesup finally made a confidential report to Polk, the nature of which, as the President said, nearly made him sick. It appeared that on June 17 the chief clerk of the Treasury Department called on Jesup in company with Mr. Corcoran, of the banking house of Corcoran and Riggs, and asked Jesup to requisition $2,000,000 on quartermaster funds to be transferred to New Orleans. Jesup did not then need the money at New Orleans, but nevertheless he drew the requisition. Corcoran and Riggs became the transfer agents. On July 27, $400,000 had been paid over to the quartermaster in New Orleans, but at the end of August the bankers still held the balance. Jesup admitted that he understood the money was used by them for stock speculation.

Polk was greatly upset and condemned the whole transaction. He had no satisfactory explanation from Secretary of the Treasury Walker, nor indeed from any source. The whole episode confirmed his intention to watch every department to the limit of his capacity.[36]

THE PROBLEM OF COORDINATION

One of the universal problems of administration is the proper coordination of various elements in a complex program. The problem is particularly acute in wartime, when military strategy, foreign relations, state and federal relations, internal politics, finance, contracts, transportation, and personal ambitions intermingle. Polk used the Cabinet effectively as a major coordinating body. Indeed in his day, it was the only instrument of top coordination directly available to him, since no one had thought of the multiple agencies later invented for this purpose.

The Cabinet considered every important aspect of the contest with Mexico, and some that were merely incidental. General strategy, basic orders to naval commanders and army generals, circulars of information to consuls abroad, selection of commanding officers, commercial regulations in captured ports were

36 Polk, *Diary*, III, 125–47, *passim* (August 1847).

among the general problems that Polk put to his Cabinet colleagues. The decision to hold Taylor's forces at Monterrey and to strike the main blow at Mexico City through Vera Cruz came up for Cabinet discussion and approval. It had obvious political as well as military implications and Polk put every member of the Cabinet on record. The letter of instructions to Taylor "was fully considered paragraph by paragraph, and after undergoing various modifications was unanimously agreed to. It was a matter of so much importance that I was particular to take the opinion of each member of the Cabinet individually. . . . The subject was under consideration for more than two hours." [37]

The coordination of naval and military movements gave rise to one embarrassing moment for Secretary of the Navy John Y. Mason. He was discovered in Cabinet session to be unaware of the date of the attack on Vera Cruz and had failed to order supporting naval vessels to the scene. Polk was greatly disturbed and said that he "had taken it for granted that they [i.e., Marcy in the War Department and Mason in the Navy] were constantly in conference with each other, and that each understood the movements & operations" of the other. Marcy lamely remarked that "he had supposed that the Secretary of the Navy knew all about it." The mortified Mason deserted the Cabinet meeting to issue the necessary orders.[38]

The load of day-by-day business was, however, transacted not by the Cabinet, but by Polk and Marcy, and to a lesser degree by Polk and Bancroft or Mason. The President became the coordinator in chief. It had been understood from the days of Washington that the President gave personal and immediate direction to the conduct of foreign affairs, but Treasury, War, and Navy had been left pretty much in the hands of their respective heads, and the Post Office Department had been unusually free from presidential attention. Now both War and Navy were forced into the position that the State Department had historically occupied.

In the case of the War Department, this consequence followed both from the vigor of Polk and the inadequacy of Secretary Marcy. Their relations are not unfairly illustrated by the re-

[37] *Ibid.*, II, 204 (Oct. 22, 1846).
[38] *Ibid.*, II, 388 (Feb. 20, 1847).

peated, and apparently customary, ritual in which Marcy brought dispatches to the White House, and, seated before the President, read them aloud to the Commander in Chief.[39] Marcy was not equal to his task, if Polk can be trusted. He was "overwhelmed with his labours and responsibilities," and so greatly oppressed with the duties of his office that Polk aided him by giving all the attention to them that his time would permit.[40] He seized the initiative in fact on many matters that Marcy might have been expected to handle in the first instance. Thus it was Polk and Benton who drafted Taylor's general instructions, not Marcy.[41] It was Polk who saw the prospects of obtaining revenue by raising the blockade on captured ports and Marcy who "concurred in this opinion." [42] It was Marcy who finally confessed his inability to control the quartermaster general's department and who asked Polk to call in its two principal officers.[43]

The Navy Department gave Polk much less concern. The two men who served at its head during the Mexican War were competent executives, and the Navy Department appeared much more in control of its affairs than the War Department. Its task was relatively simple.

THE PRESIDENT AS COMMANDER IN CHIEF

Despite all the trouble that Polk encountered, despite all the shortcomings of organization, manpower, and system that are inevitable in any administrative structure, the army marched to the field, was supplied, fought a numerically superior enemy, won a series of victories, and conquered a peace. Taken in the large this was a remarkable exploit by a commander in chief who had never donned a uniform, backed by a civilian Cabinet composed of lawyer-politicians and a historian at the head of the Navy Department (Bancroft), and of whom only one (Marcy) had had the benefit even of elementary military lessons learned

39 Examples recur in the diary from September 15, 1846 (*ibid.*, II, 139), to May 18, 1847 (*ibid.*, III, 29–30), sometimes before the President, sometimes before the Cabinet.

40 *Ibid.*, II, 150 (Sept. 22, 1846); *ibid.*, III, 24 (May 13, 1847).

41 *Ibid.*, II, 16–17 (July 8, 1846).

42 *Ibid.*, II, 420–21 (March 12, 1847).

43 *Ibid.*, III, 80 (July 10, 1847).

in a state militia. Their sense of overall strategy was sound, and although Polk misdirected the expedition against Chihuahua [44] he was not only steadily thinking ahead of events, but was reaching decisions that were generally correct in view of the objects he set for the country.

Thoughtful persons who reflected upon the administrative lessons of the war as peace came in 1848 could have found some assurance in certain broad observations. It was clear the Congress had not run the war. Polk had denied the military aspirations of most Congressmen. He had taken the lead in war legislation and finance. He had governed the size and disposition of the armed forces. He had formulated the terms of peace. At the same time Congress had a veto power which occasionally it used, notably in the refusal of its leaders even to consider replacing Taylor and Scott.

It had been demonstrated that a civilian commander in chief could—and did—function effectively as the single center for direction, authorization, coordination, and in lesser degree for control of a large military and naval effort. All lines concentrated in the White House, and the Chief Executive required every matter of consequence to be brought to him for approval. Thus was achieved a genuine unity of command that was not only unchallenged by either civil or military branches, but that succeeded in keeping in coordination the various movements in the field.

There were limits, nevertheless, to the personal capacity of even such a hard-working commander in chief as Polk. They included the universal limits of time and knowledge. Apart from the fact that Presidents commanded no more hours in the day than clerks, it was also true that the Commander in Chief learned about many matters too late to enable him to have any influence. Polk frequently complained about the handicaps due to lack of information. The army apparently had almost no prior knowledge of Mexican terrain. The campaign against Vera Cruz was launched on the basis of sketch maps made in the White House

44 After a long march the initial expedition against this city was abandoned. Later it was taken, almost by accident. See Oliver Lyman Spaulding, *The United States Army in War and Peace* (New York: G. P. Putnam's Sons, 1937), pp. 190–91, 197–98.

by a former United States consul at that city whom Polk located in Boston.

There were limits also due to the capacity of the army to resist presidential suggestions, short of orders, for the conduct of the campaign. The classic case was that of the army mules. The Commander in Chief declined to take the responsibility of issuing a positive order on the subject,[45] and wagons continued to be used.

Another old lesson was confirmed by the Mexican War—that personal and political ambitions and considerations were not driven from the field by union to win a war with a foreign power. Polk was a Democrat, as well as commander in chief, and most of the top military posts at his disposal went to fellow partisans. Taylor and Scott, Wool and others were Whigs, but as regular army officers the President could do nothing about them. The volunteer regiments, however, fought principally with Democratic officers.

Some administrative problems arose for which no answer was found. The monopoly of officer posts in the regular army, held by West Pointers, was not broken by Polk's single breach of the works. The disposal of superannuated army officers defied solution. The development of a *system* for army-navy coordination was not achieved. The failure to maintain an adequate medical corps was a constant drain on the effectiveness of the army. The means of energizing an organization like the regular army—an organization with a permanent corps of officers, with a marked professional solidarity, and with a rigid system of seniority—were not readily to be found.

While these and other administrative problems remained unsolved, one major administrative question had been answered. A President could also be a commander in chief. A President could run a war.

[45] Polk, *Diary*, II, 429–30 (March 20, 1847).

CHAPTER FOUR

The President and the Administrative System

Forty years of consistent experience had confirmed the precedents established by Washington with regard to the relation of Presidents to department heads and the daily business of administration. The unity of the executive branch was explicit; the heads of departments were assistants to the President and took their directions from him; the Cabinet had become a well-recognized institution but not a competitor for power. The Treasury Department held a vague position suggesting an undefined degree of independence flowing from Hamilton's practice. Nevertheless, in the realm of administration the central responsibility of the Chief Executive remained unimpaired.

Precedent suggested, however, that the presidency would be what Chief Executives could make it, despite accepted doctrines of unity, internal responsibility, and executive leadership of Congress. It was far different under Madison than under his great predecessor, and, as John Q. Adams was to discover, far different when a President's friends commanded a majority in Congress than when his critics were in control. Notwithstanding Whig opinions to the contrary while they were in opposition, Presidents continued to maintain their administrative position intact from Jackson to Lincoln. Indeed the considerations that have already been set forth strengthened the President as he dealt with administration no less than when he dealt with Congress.

As Chief Executive, the President had to deal with three principal and separate branches of administration—the foreign service, the armed forces, and the civil service. Every President tended to be his own Secretary of State, so far as major issues or bothersome problems were concerned. Webster had a relatively free hand in the negotiations over the Maine boundary, but Buchanan had little while serving as Secretary of State under Polk, and when he became President, allowed little to Secretary Cass. The relations of Chief Executives to the army and the navy suggested that in times of peace the armed forces drifted along in a settled routine while the principal attention of Presidents was devoted to foreign affairs, internal politics, and civil administration. During the Mexican War, however, President Polk was an active and energetic commander in chief.

In the pages that follow Presidents may be seen as they worked at their incessant tasks of making decisions on administrative detail, of acting as the chief personnel officer of the government, and, in the case of Polk, as the chief budget officer as well, and of supervising departmental policies. This was done with practically no personal assistance except from members of the President's family until 1857. The relations between the President and the heads of departments are examined in the following chapter.

PRESIDENTS AND DEPARTMENTAL BUSINESS

Federalist and Republican tradition alike had imposed burdens on Presidents for the day-by-day conduct of the public business. Congress tended to place the power of decision on matters large and small in the hands of the Chief Executive, or to require his approval of acts of department heads.[1] They, in turn, tended to defer to Presidents in departmental affairs, and for their part the Secretaries accepted a heavy load of routine business as a duty of their office. The relatively limited scale of operations allowed the system to work, although at heavy cost of time and effort by responsible officials whose resources might have been devoted profitably to larger matters. These early precedents were carried into and through the Jacksonian period. The in-

1 A careful analysis of legislation during Jackson's administration revealed approximately eighty enactments that designated the official to authorize an expenditure. Twenty-two designated the President, the remainder a department head. Albert Somit, "The Political and Administrative Ideas of Andrew Jackson," unpublished doctoral dissertation, University of Chicago, 1947, p. 139.

creasing volume of business called for better technical means of disposing of it that were slow to emerge; meanwhile Presidents manfully read reports, held conferences, studied individual cases, gave directions, and signed a staggering number of documents.

James K. Polk was one of the most diligent and faithful of Presidents and in his diary has left an extraordinary record of his daily preoccupation with current business.[2] He devoted himself to detail not only by preference, but on grounds of principle, and great was his satisfaction when he could record at the end of an evening's labor that he had cleared his table. In the hot summer of 1848 most of the Cabinet members fled Washington. Polk remained and became in effect the acting head of every department whose Secretary was absent. In late September he wrote in his diary, "I have conducted the Government without their aid. Indeed, I have become so familiar with the duties and workings of the Government, not only upon general principles, but in most of its minute details, that I find but little difficulty in doing this. I have made myself acquainted with the duties of the subordinate officers, and have probably given more attention to details than any of my predecessors." [3] That Polk was acting on principle in deciding on details is obvious from the passage in his diary that follows.

> . . . . The public have no idea of the constant accumulation of business requiring the President's attention. No President who performs his duty faithfully and conscientiously can have any leisure. If he entrusts the details and smaller matters to subordinates constant errors will occur. I prefer to supervise the whole operations of the Government myself rather than entrust the public business to subordinates, and this makes my duties very great.[4]

2 He had the benefit of an invaluable contact man with Congress, the Postmaster General, Cave Johnson. For an account of his varied services to the President, see Dorothy Ganfield Fowler, *The Cabinet Politician: the Postmasters General, 1829–1909* (New York: Columbia University Press, 1943), pp. 60–62.

3 Polk, *Diary,* IV, 130–31 (Sept. 23, 1848).

4 *Ibid.,* IV, 261 (Dec. 29, 1848). Polk transacted much business directly with subordinate officers. There are not infrequent references to this during the last two years of his term such as, "Several of the Heads of Bureau and other public officers also called on business" (*ibid.,* III, 51, June 7, 1847); "I saw some of the subordinate officers, and transacted business with them" (*ibid.,* III, 115, August 10, 1847); "I saw also the commissioner of Public Lands and other subordinate officers on busi-

Such a task wore him down and he died shortly after leaving the White House. Buchanan declared that Polk was the "most laborious man" he had ever known, "and in the brief period of four years had assumed the appearance of an old man." [5]

Pierce was fond of detail and encouraged department heads to bring matters to the White House. In contrast to other Chief Executives, he frequently visited the various offices and talked with bureau chiefs and clerks. "The PRESIDENT," reported the *National Intelligencer,* "visited some of the Departments this morning in his usual quiet and unceremonious way." [6] Nichols suggests that he undoubtedly "spent long hours and wasted a great deal of time in pleasant puttering around." [7]

Other Presidents than Polk operated on his principles. Indeed law and practice condemned Chief Executives to be in fact the "city managers" of the federal government, although no present city manager in a large town would bother with the detail that Presidents handled. Presidents were operating executives in the strict sense of the term, dealing with the business of every agency as it was brought to them. Polk, in the language of Representative Vinton, was converted into "a sort of supervisor of roads"; even the common laborers "were in the habit of running off to the President of the United States, besieging him day after day about the little affairs of the streets, grounds, and roads of this city." [8] Fillmore had to approve a plan to supply the New York Navy Yard with water from a spring,[9] and to settle a quarrel over the assignment of officers' rooms on a public vessel on Lake Erie.[10]

Such miscellaneous and unrelated items of business could be illustrated a thousand times. They fell into no categories and were subject to no general rules. Other matters, equally petty, fell into broad classes, and to some extent could be dealt

ness" (*ibid.*, IV, 151, Oct. 9, 1848). His direct contact with the military bureaus has already been noted.

5 "Selected Letters from the Donelson Papers," *Tennessee Historical Magazine,* III (1917), 267 (June 29, 1849).

6 *National Intelligencer,* July 30, 1853.

7 Roy Franklin Nichols, *Franklin Pierce: Young Hickory of the Granite Hills* (Philadelphia: University of Pennsylvania Press, 1931), p. 381.

8 *Congressional Globe,* 30th Cong., 2d sess., p. 515 (Feb. 12, 1849).

9 *Fillmore Papers,* I, 332–33 (Sept. 11, 1850).

10 *Ibid.,* I, 332 (August 2, 1850).

with by analogy to practice in the agencies or in the accounting offices. Thus Presidents were regularly called upon to approve unusual expenditures. Jackson had to authorize a payment of nearly $3,000 to the U.S. consul at Isle de France for safekeeping American sailors charged with mutiny; [11] and every request for extra compensation to district attorneys in his time was sent to him for approval.[12] Presidents were also often called on to locate public buildings. The whole Cabinet participated in locating the Smithsonian Institution; Jackson had to approve the relocation of a customhouse in St. Marks,[13] and Buchanan was called in to locate the federal courthouse in Baltimore.[14] Presidents were expected to assign new activities authorized by Congress, whose official status was not designated by law. Thus Jackson was requested to place the disbursing agent for the Potomac Bridge construction in the Treasury,[15] and Van Buren had to decide who should purchase a fire engine authorized by Congress.[16]

Presidents listened to all sorts of complaints from citizens. A resident of Memphis, Tennessee, called with a letter from his Congressman complaining about delay in construction of the Memphis Navy Yard. Polk immediately sent for Bancroft and demanded action. At four o'clock the Secretary of the Navy came back to report that he had conferred with the proper bureau chief and that orders would be issued forthwith.[17]

Presidents were also greatly encumbered by the democratic dogma that they had a duty to see anyone who appeared at the White House—a view that was also held by John Adams, but in a day when not everyone understood that he had a democratic right to call. Beginning with Jackson, the White House was

11 National Archives, Treasury Department, Miscellaneous Letters to the President, Set A, p. 31 (Nov. 4, 1835).

12 National Archives, Treasury Department, Letters to Cabinet and Bureaus, Set B, No. 1, p. 227 (May 25, 1835).

13 Treasury Department, Miscellaneous Letters to the President, Set A, p. 26 (July 20, 1835).

14 George Ticknor Curtis, *Life of James Buchanan* (2 vols., New York: Harper and Brothers, 1883), II, 242 (May 14, 1859).

15 Treasury Department, Miscellaneous Letters to the President, Set A, pp. 24–25 (April 8, 1835).

16 *Ibid.*, p. 53.

17 Polk, *Diary*, I, 303–4 (March 26, 1846).

thronged with visitors. A good description of what was probably a characteristic scene was written by Gideon Welles, who came to see President Taylor in 1849. He found sixty or seventy persons assembled, some on the White House portico, some in the hall, some in the oval room and the east room. Welles found that most had called as a matter of ceremony, but there were anxious expectants and agents intriguing for their clients. "Knots gathered in corners," some conversing freely but others in earnest whispers.[18]

These examples illustrate to what an astonishing degree the Chief Executive participated in the multifarious daily events occurring within the administrative system. Much, of course, was settled below in accordance with established practice, but cases still piled high on presidential desks.

PRESIDENTS AND PERSONNEL ADMINISTRATION

In substance the President was the chief personnel officer of the government during the Jacksonian period. There was, in fact, no alternative. All the difficult matters involving the approximately fifty thousand officers and employees tended to come to the President's desk, especially when the problem involved political considerations. The Chief Executive was consequently busily engaged in appointments and less frequently in removals, in cases of discipline, and by law in the review of the decisions of military and naval court-martials. No other officer of the government had a responsibility for personnel matters of a service-wide nature, and indeed the public service had hardly acquired a sense of corporate unity. It remained still a body of departmental clerks and agents, responsible to the individual Cabinet members. The President was the single official having some responsibility for the whole service.

Appointments required the most attention. To understand the responsibility of the Chief Executive for making appointments it is useful to differentiate several classes, in descending order of importance. Class one included officers requiring sen-

18 Holman Hamilton, *Zachary Taylor: Soldier in the White House* (Indianapolis: Bobbs-Merrill, 1951), p. 219. Harrison's encounter with a mob of office seekers is related elsewhere. Polk's diary is full of complaint about time wasted in meeting visitors.

atorial confirmation, and these invariably secured the personal attention of the President. Here were found heads of departments, the chief accounting officers, territorial governors, ministers and consuls, the judges of the federal courts, and such lesser officers as postmasters in the larger cities, collectors of customs, district attorneys, land agents, and others. In 1849 these officers were reported to number 929.[19]

Class two included officers appointed by the heads of departments, such as chief clerks, clerks and messengers, subordinate fiscal officers, and numerous field agents. Presidents were often consulted in the higher levels of this class, sometimes but not usually in the lower. Self protection drove them to approve Van Buren's policy of declaring that the heads of departments were responsible for their subordinate clerks.

Class three comprised subordinate field employees, the minor customs officers being a good case. Here appointment was made by the collector, subject to approval by the Secretary of the Treasury. Formally the latter took no initiative, but in the larger customhouses there is evidence of prior consultation. Usually a President would not be informed of such nominations, but where factional feeling ran high, the Chief Executive might participate personally in making up the list of appraisers and assistant appraisers. For example, Marcy, Walker, and Polk spent four hours with the collector of the port of New York deciding on three appraisers and three assistant appraisers. The collector was allowed to make his own choice of customhouse auditor.[20] Polk controlled the appointment of navy pursers, and in at least one case participated in the appointment of an Indian subagent.[21] Taylor was consulted on the appointment of a post-office agent.[22] Fillmore, on the other hand, made it "an invariable rule not to interfere with the appointments of the Heads of Departments." [23]

Class four comprised rank-and-file employees in the field offices appointed on the authority of the agent in charge. In the rare

19 Hamilton, *Taylor: Soldier in the White House*, p. 204.

20 Library of Congress, Marcy Papers, Vol. 10, No. 34,436 (May 12, 1845); Vol. 10, No. 34,438 (May 14, 1845); Vol. 10, No. 34,456 (May 22, 1845).

21 *Ibid.*, Vol. 11, No. 34,581 (March 9, 1846); Vol. 10, No. 34,446 (May 19, 1845).

22 Ann M. B. Coleman, ed., *Life of Crittenden*, I, 346 (July 14, 1849).

23 *Fillmore Papers*, I, 333 (Oct. 7, 1850).

case of political controversy the choice might be referred to Washington, but normally the matter was closed on the spot.

Presidents, therefore, were involved in the selection process, directly or indirectly, at many points. For top appointments they were their own personnel officers; for intermediate appointments and many lesser ones they were consulted and their preferences were directly controlling. The task was time-consuming and often disagreeable, but it was too important to be ignored. Richard Cobden had an evening of gossip in the White House with his old friend James Buchanan, who "spoke of the unpleasant task which every President has to undergo of dispensing the patronage—he having upwards of 20,000 places directly & indirectly to fill up." [24] Every President complained, but none found a remedy.

Disciplinary problems were often brought to the White House for advice or for decision. A clerk in the register's office made an error which led to charges against the register. Jackson allowed that the mistake was excusable, but warned him "that in future heads of bureau will be held responsible for like errors." [25] Persistent delinquents in accounts were regularly called to the President's attention when departmental pressure brought no results. The records of defaulters were frequently sent up for instructions. Polk's directions were crisp: "I ordered him to be removed instantly. . . . In less than three hours after the case was reported to me the removal was made, a commission issued for his successor, signed, and the orders issued to the U.S. Attorney for the District of Ohio to prosecute criminally the defaulting Receiver." [26]

The newly appointed postmaster of New York City, Robert H. Morris, failed to give bond and answered the Postmaster General evasively. Polk told the Postmaster General to inform Morris that if he did not give bond immediately, he would be removed. This brought Morris to the White House. Polk told him that it was useless to talk further on the subject and that if the bond was not executed on the next day, "I would certainly remove

[24] *The American Diaries of Richard Cobden* (Elizabeth Hoon Cawley, ed., Princeton: Princeton University Press, 1952), p. 179 (April 29, 1859).

[25] Treasury Department, Letters to Cabinet and Bureaus, Set B, No. 1, p. 181 (Jan. 20, 1835).

[26] Polk, *Diary,* III 59–60 (June 12, 1847).

him." Morris was a leading Democrat but Polk would not trifle with the requirements of the law.[27]

To what an extent it came to be recognized that the President *ought* to deal personally and directly with appointments and personnel matters was unconsciously revealed in a letter from a still obscure Whig politician and lawyer, Abraham Lincoln. Lincoln objected to Taylor's policy of throwing responsibility for making appointments on the departments. "This," he said, "must be arrested, or it will damn us all. . . . The appointments need be no better . . . but the public must . . . understand . . . they are the President's appointments." [28]

From the days of Washington, every President had as a matter of course attended personally to the appointments requiring confirmation, and had given occasional thought to lesser appointments such as the officers in command of revenue service cutters. The change that occurred after 1829 arose because offices, great and small, became pawns in the play of politics. An administration measure might be defeated, a state might be lost, a renomination to the presidency denied because of mistakes in the selection of a collector or naval officer, a postmaster, or an officer among the Mexican War volunteers. Presidents became personnel officers in precarious times, but they assumed this function along with their historic tasks.

PRESIDENTS AND DEPARTMENTAL REPORTS

The annual departmental reports to Congress came to be a standard means of inviting attention to proposals for policy changes and administrative needs as well as a yearly review of achievements. Presidential messages were based in part on them. The regular Cabinet discussion of the annual message served to bring unity of opinion and consistency of policy between the Chief Executive on the one hand and reports of the bureau chiefs and department heads on the other. Polk laid a vigorous hand on the departmental reports and took pains to see that no policy variations crept into them.

At a Cabinet meeting on October 25, 1845, he asked the heads of departments to have their annual reports laid before him on

27 *Ibid.*, I, 405–6 (May 18, 1846).

28 Quoted in Hamilton, *Taylor: Soldier in the White House*, p. 217.

November 15 or sooner, and informed them that he "wished to examine them fully and minutely before they were communicated to Congress." [29] He required the Secretaries to read their reports verbatim, sometimes in the presence of the Cabinet, sometimes before himself alone,[30] as he required Marcy to read military dispatches during the Mexican War.

The special historic position of the Secretary of the Treasury was not forgotten, but Polk imposed the same requirement on him as on the others. Secretary Walker read a controversial paragraph of his annual report to the President and Cabinet in 1847. "I finally said to Mr. Walker," Polk recorded, "that by law he made his Report to Congress and not to the President, but, though this was so, the country would hold the President responsible for it. . . . I thought if he took up the subject in a finance Report it would place me in a very embarrassing condition; that I would be charged with holding one policy in the message and causing my Secretary of the Treasury to hold another in his Report. . . ." [31] Walker agreed to delete the offensive paragraph. A couple of weeks earlier he had read the tariff sections of his annual report which Polk thought "speculative, and perhaps too highly wrought. I suppose he will revise it." [32]

No evidence has been noted to suggest that Taylor and Fillmore, Pierce or Buchanan pursued the schoolmaster tactics of Polk by requiring their department heads to sit before the presidential desk and read. On the other hand, the annual message of the President to Congress continued, of necessity, to rest on the reports of the respective departments and on the needs of the public service revealed in them. It may be assumed that the annual reports went to the White House before or as they went to Congress, but no conclusions can be drawn from direct evidence concerning the extent to which they were reviewed and revised. Normal expectations of official subordination would preclude any significant divergences in executive policy.

29 Polk, *Diary*, I, 73. He repeated his orders on November 1, *ibid.*, I, 85.
30 *Ibid.*, I, 103 (Nov. 27, 1845); III, 231–32 (Nov. 26, 1847).
31 *Ibid.*, III, 241–42 (Dec. 7, 1847).
32 *Ibid.*, III, 229 (Nov. 23, 1847).

PRESIDENTS AND THE ESTIMATES

The annual estimates of expenditure originated in the various bureaus, offices, and establishments of the departments, and with field officers such as the Indian agents and the surveyors of public lands. There is some evidence to indicate that the department heads reviewed these estimates before incorporating them in the figures sent to the Secretary of the Treasury. Practice apparently varied, but tended to be more demanding in time of financial stringency. Some examples follow. In 1838 Secretary of War Joel R. Poinsett sent the bureau estimates directly to the Ways and Means Committee to allow the committee to see the reductions he had made by comparing them with the general estimate that had been forwarded by the Treasury.[33] In 1847 Alexander D. Bache, superintendent of the Coast Survey, stated that the estimates for field work were founded "on a close control of expenditures." [34] Secretary of War John B. Floyd cut the army estimates to a point where a Senate committee felt obliged to restore some of the funds requested for fortifications. The army had proposed approximately $1,900,000; Floyd reduced it to less than $700,000; the committee recommended about $1,200,000.[35]

The evidence at hand does not suggest a systematic departmental review of the original bureau estimates, and it is certain that no Secretary possessed staff aides to assist him in this duty. No law required the department heads to review the estimates and except during the Polk administration they were apparently not under executive pressure in this respect. Most Secretaries were in accord with their bureau chiefs in believing that larger appropriations were needed even to carry on work already well established; and reduction of the bureau estimates by them would doubtless have seemed in many cases akin to administrative treason.

The responsibility of the Treasury Department with respect to the estimates was limited to that of collecting them into a single document and transmitting them to Congress. Secretary

33 House Doc. 38, 25th Cong., 3d sess., p. 1 (Dec. 15, 1838).

34 House Ex. Doc. 2, 30th Cong., 1st sess., p. 192 (Oct. 25, 1847).

35 *Jefferson Davis, Constitutionalist: His Letters, Papers and Speeches* (Rowland Dunbar, ed., 10 vols., Jackson: Mississippi Department of Archives and History, 1923), IV, 436–37 (June 2, 1860).

Levi Woodbury expressly rejected any responsibility for the amounts or objects of expenditure in his annual report of 1839. "The various items of new appropriations asked for are, as usual, in the amounts requested by the different departments having charge of the different subjects. If any omissions or miscalculations occur in them, they must, therefore, happen from inadvertence by those officers best acquainted with the business within their own peculiar province." [36] The clerical task of calling for the estimates and arranging them for transmission was performed by the register of the Treasury. It followed, consequently, that Congress did not receive an executive budget, but only the collected departmental estimates based upon bureau and field figures that might or might not have been reviewed.

A Chief Executive who intends to be influential in administration must exercise control over the estimates of the subordinate agencies. In the organic Treasury Act of 1789 Congress had made it the duty of the Secretary of the Treasury, not the President, to prepare and report estimates of expenditures. Hamilton set the precedent of not even consulting the President, a remarkable arrangement that prevailed for decades. Monroe had complained about the neglect of the Chief Executive when Crawford kept him in ignorance of his financial plans for the fiscal year 1821, and John Q. Adams thought the practice quite inconsistent with the spirit of the Constitution.[37] Adams had Rush submit to him the annual report of the Treasury Department [38] but no evidence has been discovered that he also saw the departmental estimates.

Money was easy while Jackson was President; revenues regularly exceeded expenditures, the debt was steadily reduced and eventually extinguished, and there was hardly any occasion for Jackson to be concerned about reviewing estimates, which in any event did not equal anticipated revenue. No evidence in fact has been met with to show that Jackson ever dealt with the annual estimates.

Van Buren on the other hand had a difficult financial problem

36 House Doc. 3, 26th Cong., 1st sess., p. 7 (Dec. 30, 1839).

37 Leonard D. White, *The Jeffersonians: a Study in Administrative History, 1801–1829* (New York: Macmillan, 1951), pp. 68–69.

38 Adams, *Memoirs*, VII, 82, 347.

during the whole of his administration as revenues dried up after the panic of 1837. A full account of Treasury efforts to reduce expenditures and of the influence of the President on estimates cannot yet be written. A significant letter from Secretary of the Treasury Woodbury to the President in 1839 suggests that Woodbury was at least asking for help in squeezing the departmental figures.[39] He presented a financial picture to the President as "a general guide in relation to the estimates for 1840" which were in preparation. He recalled that the estimates for 1839 had been reduced some eight or ten millions below actual expenditures in 1838 and went on to say, "it will be prudent in the opinion of this department to diminish them, so as to make expenditures in 1840 at least five million below the actual expenditures in 1839." After going on record against a new issue of Treasury notes, he allowed that he was unable "to understand the details of the present expenses of each department and to judge which will best bear any reduction and how much." He nevertheless made some suggestions—that the civil list could least of all bear any reductions, that the War Department could be reduced from about fifteen million to nine or ten, and the Navy to about five. These remarks, quite modern in their tone, were forced by an extremely tight financial situation and were not typical of better times.

Polk was faced with a similar financial problem, since, although collections were good, he needed large sums to conduct the Mexican War. Furthermore, like the old Republicans, he had an inbred taste for economy and a hatred of public debt. He promptly began to bring pressure to bear on the departments to hold down their estimates, and waged a four-year war on this front.

At a Cabinet meeting in the autumn of 1845, Polk told the department heads that he wanted the estimates to be made on the most economical scale, and that "they must give vigilant attention to the estimates and Reports prepared by the several Heads of Bureau" since they were generally favorable to large expenditures.[40] In 1846 the War Department was called upon

39 National Archives, U.S. Treasury, Miscellaneous Letters to the President, Set A, p. 133 (Oct. 21, 1839).

40 Polk, *Diary*, I, 48 (Sept. 30, 1845).

for estimates in case of a rupture with Great Britain. Polk advised Marcy to cut down the bureau estimates: "He said he would do so and *submit to me* his answer to the call before he sent it to the Committee." [41] Consideration of the regular estimates for 1847–48 came up in the Cabinet in November 1846. The War Department had estimated for 15,000 regular troops and 25,000 volunteers, involving expenditures of 20 million dollars beyond peacetime levels. Buchanan thought such expenditures would alarm the country and affect adversely the public credit; he consequently proposed a smaller force, merely adequate to hold the northern Mexican provinces already seized. Others talked about a war of invasion, and a contingent estimate was finally agreed upon.[42]

In September 1847 Polk directed the Secretaries of War and Navy to make their 1848 estimates on the basis of the armed forces then employed.[43] When the War Department estimates came in, consternation reigned. Including a deficit for 1847, they amounted to nearly sixty million. Polk expressed astonishment at the amount, and said there must certainly be some mistake. Marcy confessed that he had not revised the bureau estimates. Polk told him to do so, and if possible to reduce them.[44] Marcy came back privately a few days later, said that he agreed reductions should be made, but tacitly admitted he could not control his bureau chiefs. "He suggested," said Polk, "that I should see and converse with the Heads of Bureau who had prepared the estimates." Polk immediately accepted this invitation, and within an hour the paymaster general and the commissary general had called. ". . . I held separate conversations with each. The result of which was that they were satisfied that some reductions could be safely made." [45] The next day the quartermaster general called and reported that he had already reduced his estimates nearly seven million. The President ended his day's work by observing, "I think it probable that the estimates may now be brought down to a reasonable amount." [46] The House

41 *Ibid.*, I, 314–15 (March 31, 1846). Italics are author's.
42 *Ibid.*, II, 219–21 (Nov. 7, 1846).
43 *Ibid.*, III, 178–79 (Sept. 21, 1847).
44 *Ibid.*, III, 212–13 (Nov. 6, 1847).
45 *Ibid.*, III, 218–19 (Nov. 10, 1847).
46 *Ibid.*, III, 219–20 (Nov. 11, 1847).

Ways and Means Committee helped the good work when they came to examine the estimates. Two of its members conferred with the Secretary of the Navy, the Secretary of the Treasury, and the President in his office. At the end of the conference the Secretary of the Navy agreed to reduce his estimate by $1,500,000 below the figure that had passed the President.[47]

Peace had returned when the estimates for 1849, under discussion in the autumn of 1848, came before Polk. He took an early occasion to inform the Treasury that he wanted to begin payment on the public debt, implying that the estimates should be made with this in view.[48] He directed his Cabinet to reduce their requests to "the absolute necessities" of the public service, and entered some remarks in his diary that showed him to be well aware of the "custom" of budget making as it then operated. "It has heretofore, I learn, been the habit of the Heads of Bureaus of the Diffe[re]nt Departments who have been charged with the duty of preparing these estimates to make them larger than is necessary, calculating that they will be cut down and reduced by Congress. This is wrong." [49] He continued his indictment of bureau chiefs a few days later, referring to their large and sometimes extravagant figures. "They do this for two reasons, first, because they suppose their own consequence depends somewhat on the sums they may [have] to disburse in their respective branches of the service during the year; and secondly, because they say their estimates may be cut down by Congress. These Bureau officers are, moreover, generally Federalists, and in favour of large expenditures." [50] "My secretaries," he wrote, "have a constant struggle with the Heads of Bureau[s], who are charged with preparing the detailed estimates, to keep down the expenditures to a reasonable point." [51]

Marcy again told the President he was having much trouble with his bureau chiefs, but he did not require Polk to put the screws on them personally. The same end was achieved; Marcy came in with the figures he had secured from the various army

47 *Ibid.*, III, 312 (Jan. 24, 1848).

48 *Ibid.*, IV, 162–63 (Oct. 21, 1848).

49 *Ibid.*, IV, 165–66 (Oct. 24, 1848).

50 *Ibid.*, IV, 175 (Oct. 31, 1848). The Democrats were accustomed to calling the Whigs "Federalists," as a term of derogation and reproach.

51 *Ibid.*, IV, 190 (Nov. 11, 1848).

branches, and Polk directed further reductions and the complete elimination of some items.[52] Great was his indignation when he discovered that some river and harbor estimates had been smuggled into the Treasury estimates. Walker had to admit that he had not observed them. Polk had already vetoed a river and harbor bill and directed these estimates to be struck out, in the amount of several hundred thousand dollars.[53] It was evident that the President had to be his own budget officer if he expected any influence to be brought to bear on the bureau estimates.

No evidence has come to view that any of Polk's successors to 1861 followed the precedents that he established. Taylor was wholly unacquainted with such matters. His department heads, moreover, were inexperienced in official business except Ewing who had been in the Treasury for a few months under Tyler. At Taylor's death they went out to permit Fillmore to select another Cabinet, all without experience except Webster, who reoccupied his old post in State. They in turn gave way to a set of Democrats when Pierce came in after a couple of years. These were the precise circumstances, quite apart from the quality of Presidents, to solidify the increasingly powerful position of the bureau chiefs, especially in the armed forces. The precedent established by Polk disappeared from view, and a new start had to be made many decades later on this aspect of presidential power.

THE WHITE HOUSE ESTABLISHMENT

The official life of Presidents was made much more burdensome because Congress allowed them no funds for private secretaries or administrative assistants. Following the precedent established by Washington, some member or members of the President's family usually joined the household and served as a private secretary or, alternatively, was given a departmental clerkship and actually assigned *de facto* to the White House. Major Andrew Jackson Donelson, Mrs. Jackson's nephew, held a clerkship in the General Land Office but served as Jackson's private secretary during most of his administration, being succeeded

52 *Ibid.*, IV, 180–81 (Nov. 6, 1848).
53 *Ibid.*, IV, 190–91 (Nov. 11, 1848).

by Andrew Jackson, Jr.[54] Tyler's private secretary was his son John. Both Polk and Buchanan employed nephews. The White House also possessed a "porter" who, from Polk's diary, would seem to have been occupied in bringing letters to the President, and vainly trying to keep visitors out of his office. In 1833 a clerk had been provided by Congress to sign land patents on behalf of the President.[55] Clerks could be borrowed for long copying jobs, such as making fair copies in duplicate of the President's annual messages, but were not on loan for normal routine. Taylor wrote personal letters in his own hand, and the replies to a multitude of inquiries and invitations were written for him by Colonel William Bliss, his son-in-law.[56]

This anomalous situation was corrected in part in 1857 when Congress finally authorized the President to appoint a private secretary at $2,500 a year; a steward to take charge of the plate and furniture and the White House domestic establishment at $1,200; and a messenger at $900. The President also secured a contingent fund of $750. This, in the language of the appropriation act, was the President's "official household." [57]

The duties of a private secretary were described by Buchanan's nephew, James B. Henry. They began with attendance on the President in his office from eight in the morning until one and after luncheon until five, when Buchanan took his daily hour's walk. Henry had charge of the library fund, the payment of the steward and household staff, and kept the President's private accounts. He organized a set of books in which to record the receipt and disposition of correspondence. "Such letters as the President ought to see I folded and briefed and took them to him every morning at eight o'clock and received his instructions as to the answer I should make." Once a day he sent to each department by messenger a large envelope containing letters for its attention. In addition he had to assist in the arrangements for state dinners to the Supreme Court, the diplomatic corps, and members of Congress.[58]

54 Jackson, *Correspondence,* V, 433, n. 2.

55 4 Stat. 663 (March 2, 1833). Over 20,000 were then awaiting his attention. Senate Doc. 9, 23d Cong., 1st sess., p. 52 (Nov. 30, 1833).

56 Hamilton, *Taylor: Soldier in the White House,* p. 354.

57 11 Stat. 206, sec. 2 (March 3, 1857).

58 Curtis, *Life of Buchanan,* II, 235.

Burdened with an incessant round of duties and harassed by problems large and small, Presidents, as Polk put it, found their exalted position "no bed of roses." [59] After a few months Jackson wrote, "I can with truth say mine is a situation of dignified slavery." [60] Van Buren found the office "one of toilsome and anxious probation." [61] Tyler asked one of his friends, "would you exchange the peace and quiet of your homestead for such an office?" [62] Polk declared he was the hardest working man in the country, and in late 1847 wished that the remainder of his term was over.[63] As his administration drew to an end, he wrote in his diary that his four years had been years "of incessant labour and anxiety and of great responsibility. I am heartily rejoiced that my term is so near its close." [64]

It might be argued that Presidents thus inadequately served were prisoners of the administrative system. Their freedom of action was limited by the collective habit and weight of momentum of the machine itself and by the comparative feebleness of their own means of action. Law and practice had already created an elaborate body of precedent. The routine of the system had become well set. It tended to bury the Chief Executive in detail, and gave him no institutional support for thinking and planning, or for controlling, on a broader scale. With fortitude if not always with patience, Presidents performed their laborious duties, and the machine, now continental in scope, went steadily on its appointed way. The center was without doubt the White House, but the revolutions of the administrative wheels often seemed to derive their sustaining power elsewhere.

59 Polk, *Diary,* III, 162 (Sept. 4, 1847).

60 Jackson, *Correspondence,* IV, 96 (Nov. 30, 1829).

61 Van Buren, *Autobiography,* p. 448.

62 Oliver Perry Chitwood, *John Tyler: Champion of the Old South* (New York: D. Appleton-Century Co., 1939), p. 387.

63 Polk, *Diary,* II, 360 (Jan. 28, 1847); III, 210 (Nov. 2, 1847).

64 *Ibid.,* IV, 331 (Feb. 13, 1849).

CHAPTER FIVE

The Heads of Departments

The Democrats maintained the tradition that heads of departments were assistants to the President.[1] Any doubt about the independent position of the Treasury was dispelled when Jackson removed William Duane. No Secretary from 1829 to 1861 challenged the supremacy of the Chief Executive. The Whigs appeared at times to lean toward a type of cabinet government, but such a theory found lodgment nowhere. The President appointed, the President gave directions, and in case of necessity, he had the undoubted power to remove the department heads.

All this did not require Presidents to be dictators, and none were. A government has to operate by the consent of its principal figures, as well as to be sustained by the consent of its citizens. Every President yielded and compromised on particular matters, postponed and avoided others, and wrestled with his colleagues in the process of finding agreement. Probably every President kept in the Cabinet persons whose resignation would have been welcome. When judgments on individual cases differed, the President's opinion prevailed if he so desired. Thus Polk overruled Bancroft by mitigating a naval court-martial sentence, but took care to tell Bancroft that he meant no disapproval of the Secretary's initial action.[2] When decisions on major policy had to be made, the President in the last analysis made them.

No President, whether Whig or Democrat, really intended to yield his administrative authority. Harrison came nearest to surrender. Tyler, who would have given up the purse, declined to give up the executive office upon invitation of the Cabinet.

1 6 *Opinions of the Attorneys General* 326, 339–44 (March 8, 1854).

2 Polk, *Diary,* I, 42–43 (Sept. 27, 1845).

This remarkable episode was narrated long after the event by Tyler's son and private secretary. At his first Cabinet meeting Webster told Tyler that during Harrison's few weeks in the White House it had been the practice for all matters relating to the administration to be brought before the Cabinet and to be decided by majority vote, the President having one vote. Tyler rose to his feet and told the Cabinet that he would never consent to such dictation. "I, as President, shall be responsible for my administration. I hope to have your hearty co-operation in carrying out its measures. So long as you see fit to do this, I shall be glad to have you with me. When you think otherwise, your resignations will be accepted." [3]

The internal balance in each administration settled generally as events and personalities dictated. Polk drove his Cabinet team with a tighter rein than perhaps any other President from 1829 to 1861, including Jackson. Van Buren stood with Pierce at the opposite extreme, while Buchanan tended to control closely both the State Department and the patronage agencies of the government.

Keeping department heads on duty in Washington was not an unknown problem before the days of the Jacksonians and remained a point too delicate for effective official discipline.[4] Polk tried to anticipate a difficulty that he was cognizant of by issuing a general notice to every man invited to sit in his Cabinet. He wrote:

> I disapprove the practice which has sometimes prevailed, of Cabinet officers absenting themselves for long periods of time from the seat of Government, and leaving the management of their Departments to chief clerks, or other less responsible persons than themselves. I expect myself to remain constantly at Washington, unless it may be that no public duty requires my presence, when I may be occasionally absent, but then only for a short time. It is by conforming to this rule that the President and his Cabinet can have any assurance that abuses will be prevented, and that the subordinate execu-

[3] Interview given by John Tyler, Jr., in 1888, *Lippincott's Monthly Magazine,* XLI, 417–18.

[4] The summer months were trying for Cabinet members who usually took their vacations at this season. Niles noted in July 1830 that Postmaster General Barry and Attorney General Berrien were the only heads of departments at the seat of government. *Niles Register,* XXXVIII, 355 (July 10, 1830).

tive officers connected with them respectively will faithfully perform their duty.[5]

POLICY CONFORMITY

Heads of departments necessarily occupied a dual position. As advisers to the President they were concerned with policy and politics; as heads of operating agencies they were concerned primarily with administration. The mixture of statecraft, politics, and administration in any particular case depended on circumstances and on the taste, talents, and ambition of Cabinet members, as well as their relations to the President. It also depended on the need of Presidents for supporting political strength among the Cabinet members.

Under both Federalist and Republican administrations, the strength that Presidents sought from Cabinet members was primarily derived from sectional representation rather than from party standing. The south, the middle states, New England, and eventually the new states across the mountains were regularly recognized with Cabinet seats. This distribution also roughly recognized the great economic interests—shipping and overseas trade; manufactures, banking, and finance; the plantation slave economy; and the wheat and corn growers of the middle west. The personal political weight of individuals was not overlooked but it was associated with geographical rather than with party or factional considerations.

As parties took shape in the 1830's and fought on fairly even terms for the next two decades, the political importance of each Cabinet member became a primary consideration. The fortunes of the administration, the probability of party success at the next election, the personal fate of a President, turned in constantly greater measure on the appeasement of factions. The choice of Cabinet members consequently became less the personal preference of Presidents, and more the result of the balance of power within the party organization. The controlling consideration was political weight rather than administrative skill. The interests of department heads were inclined in consequence toward politics rather than toward administration, although they had executive responsibilities that could not be avoided.

5 Buchanan, *Works,* VI, 110–11 (Feb. 17, 1845).

Omitting persons who held acting appointments, there were seventy-six men who held Cabinet posts from 1829 to 1861, a few on two different occasions. It is possible to identify only ten who were not active participants in the public affairs of their respective states, and all but twenty had served in Congress before they became heads of departments. The career of James Buchanan is in point. Admitted to the bar in 1812, he was elected to the Pennsylvania House of Representatives in 1814 and 1815, and to Congress from 1821–31; in 1832 he became American minister to Russia; back again in 1834, he was elected to the U.S. Senate where he sat until he became Secretary of State in 1845. Meanwhile he was very active in Pennsylvania politics. John J. Crittenden, a well-known Whig, began his career as attorney general for the Territory of Illinois in 1809. Removing to Kentucky he was promptly elected and reelected to the State House of Representatives. For two years (1817–19) he sat in the U.S. Senate. He was secretary of state in Kentucky in 1834, and became U.S. Attorney General in 1841. Crittenden was not only politically active in his own state but was a leading figure on the national scene.

These and many similar cases illustrate the remarks of Senator James M. Mason of Virginia in the debate on the Interior Department bill. "Why, sir," he declared, "the heads of the departments are not only statesmen, but politicians, a great many of them, and necessarily so. They administer the Government honestly, I have no doubt, and correctly, within the sphere of their appropriate and regular duties. But they do more. They are managing the great political machinery of Government out of doors." [6]

The Gilmer Committee on Retrenchment (1842) stated these various duties in language which could hardly be improved.

The duties of the heads of the Departments, the committee suppose, bear a general analogy to each other, modified by the peculiar objects as well as the peculiar organization of their respective Departments. They all have the same political or cabinet duties to perform. They provide for the appointment of the officers and agents of their Departments, for paying their compensation, for advancing the moneys they require, direct details of service and supply, make con-

[6] *Congressional Globe,* 30th Cong., 2d sess., p. 672 (March 3, 1849).

tracts, and generally superintend the various interests and objects confided to their Departments, leaving the adjustment of the accounts which may grow out of these appointments and advances, contracts and superintendence, to the accounting officers. The duties of the heads of the Departments may be considered as administrative, and should be regarded as essentially and properly separate and distinct from the settlement of accounts.[7]

Spurred on by the need for peace of mind as well as by the requirements for official success, every President sought anxiously to create and maintain unity of policy among his immediate advisers. Much experience had already demonstrated how difficult it was to grasp harmony, especially the stormy years of Monroe's second term when three members of the Cabinet were fighting to succeed him. Presidents continued, nevertheless, to stumble through many a dark swamp in search of this will-o'-the-wisp.

Jackson was greatly upset over the antagonisms that developed around Peggy Eaton and declared that those who could not harmonize had better withdraw.[8] With Van Buren's help, they did. But on matters of policy, Jackson tolerated an unexpected degree of independence. Louis McLane and Lewis Cass did not conceal their opposition to removal of the deposits, and Jackson recognized their right to their opinions.[9] To Van Buren he wrote, "You will find Mr. McLane differs with me, on the Bank, still it is an honest difference of opinion, and in his report he acts fairly, by leaving me free and uncommitted. . . . I like his frankness, and that open candeur with which he acts—he is a fair honorable man, with whom I am much pleased, and will get on with very well." [10] At the end, however, there was only one Bank policy. It was that of Andrew Jackson.

Polk started with the intention of selecting as members of the Cabinet "gentlemen who agree with me in opinion, and who will cordially co-operate with me in carrying out these prin-

7 House Report 741, 27th Cong., 2d sess., p. 7 (May 23, 1842).

8 Jackson, *Correspondence,* IV, 124 (Jan. 29, 1830).

9 Cass determined to resign in 1832 but Jackson dissuaded him. He again offered his resignation in 1835, but Jackson declined to accept it. Frank B. Woodford, *Lewis Cass: The Last Jeffersonian* (New Brunswick: Rutgers University Press, 1950), pp. 178–80.

10 Jackson, *Correspondence,* IV, 379 (Dec. 6, 1831).

ciples and policy." [11] Subsequently he was often irritated with Buchanan but tolerated differences of opinion and an often sulky personality on the part of the Secretary of State, while overriding him at times. The situation was not unknown abroad. Thomas Corwin wrote a friend, "Buchanan is treated as no gentleman would treat a sensible hireling." [12] Not long before Corwin was writing in these terms, Polk was recording in his diary that if his suspicions of political disloyalty were correct, he would act "with promptness and energy towards Mr. Buchanan, whatever the consequences to myself or my administration may be." [13]

One aspect of the problem involved top strategy in recognizing factions within the party at Cabinet level. It could be argued that a desire for harmony and party success would require factions to be represented in the administration. Others took the opposite view. Shortly after Pierce was elected President, Buchanan offered him some advice on this point, ". . . *the cabinet ought to be a unit.* . . . I undertake to predict that whoever may be the President, if he disregards this principle in the formation of his cabinet, he will have committed a fatal mistake. He who attempts to conciliate opposing factions by placing ardent and embittered representatives of each in his cabinet, will discover that he has only infused into these factions new vigor and power for mischief." [14]

Another aspect of the problem was competition among heads of departments for the succession to the White House. Jackson warned Polk specifically on this point, and Polk required a written undertaking from every one of his Cabinet members that, should he seek the presidency, he would resign at once.[15] Polk

11 Buchanan, *Works,* VI, 110. For an interesting example, concerning the appointment of Nathan Clifford as Attorney General in 1846, see Philip Greely Clifford, *Nathan Clifford, Democrat* (New York: G. P. Putnam's Sons, 1922), p. 139.

12 "Selections from the William Greene Papers" (L. Belle Hamlin, ed.), *Quarterly Publication of the Historical and Philosophical Society of Ohio,* XIII (1918), 14 (Jan. 14, 1846).

13 Polk, *Diary,* I, 153 (Jan. 3, 1846).

14 George T. Curtis, *Life of James Buchanan,* II, 72 (Dec. 11, 1852).

15 The matter is referred to in Polk's *Diary,* III, 403 (March 24, 1848). The letter, dated February 17, 1845, is printed in Buchanan, *Works,* VI, 110–11. See also Jackson, *Correspondence,* VI, 331 (Nov. 29, 1844); *ibid.,* VI, 363 (Jan. 15, 1845). Marcy gave a written reply to Polk's letter expressing his "entire approbation."

nevertheless had no doubt that Buchanan had been maneuvering to succeed him almost from the moment he became Secretary of State.[16] The difficulty of enforcing such a pledge as Polk required was doubtless one reason why the attempt was not repeated.

Another means of securing policy agreement that occurred to Presidents was to take pledges on the principal issues before making a Cabinet selection. Jackson tried, through Kendall, to get an expression of opinion from Duane on the Bank issue, but unsuccessfully.[17] The President did not reveal his policy to his prospective Secretary of the Treasury,[18] nor did Duane reveal his views to Jackson and of course did not make a commitment. In the correspondence that grew out of the difference of opinion there is a significant passage in one of Jackson's letters.

> The circumstance of your differing in opinion from me upon this point, and the failure to communicate your views at an earlier period require'd no apology; that I am disappointed in the result, I frankly confess to you, for, as I knew that we agree'd so well in our general opinions in regard to the Bank, I did not, I admit, apprehend so serious a difference of opinion, in the details of our respective duties. Contenting myself with informing you before you entered upon office, on two occasions, that the question of a removal of the deposits was under consideration in my Cabinet—that I had asked their opinions in regard to it respectively; and not apprehending that you would understand me as referring to an appeal to congress upon the subject, I thought it would be more delicate, and respectful to yourself to avoid any thing like a previous stipulation, in relation to the manner in which your official duty should be performed. Not having required explanations from you I do not complain that you did not tender them in advance. . . .[19]

Jackson did not make the same error twice. After dismissing Duane he wrote to Van Buren, "professions will not do to be

---

Library of Congress, William L. Marcy Papers, Vol. 10, No. 34,338 (March 5, 1845). But on the envelope containing Polk's admonition, he wrote "& prescribing rules! to be observed by Cabinet. . . ." *Ibid.*, No. 34,333.

16 Polk, *Diary*, III, 403 (March 24, 1848).

17 *Autobiography of Amos Kendall* (William Stickney, ed., Boston: Lee and Shepard, 1872), pp. 377–78.

18 William J. Duane, *Narrative and Correspondence Concerning Removal of the Deposites*, p. 38 (July 10, 1833).

19 Jackson, *Correspondence*, V, 139–40 (July 17, 1833).

relied upon now a days where the *power* of *the Bank* comes in question—hereafter I will have a Pledge." [20] But no President can exact pledges with respect to an uncertain future, and the hazard of discord was hardly to be eliminated in this way. Presidents doubtless sought by private inquiry to ascertain the views of prospective heads of departments, but men of standing could hardly be expected to sign away their freedom of judgment on issues yet unknown or in process of formulation.[21]

Problems of policy conformity did not usually reach below the Cabinet level, but as the great bureaus were gradually formed, heads tended to fall within this group of officials whose policy views were important. An early case was that of Colonel Thomas L. McKenney, appointed superintendent of Indian trade in 1816 by Madison, and head of the bureau of Indian affairs by Monroe—a warm friend of the Indians. Jackson replaced him. McKenney asked the acting Secretary of War for the reasons and was told, "Why, sir, every body knows your qualifications for the place; but General Jackson has long been satisfied that you are not in harmony with him in his views in regard to the Indians." [22] This was an accurate statement of the situation.

THE PRESIDENT AND THE CABINET

Experience from 1829 to 1861 confirmed that the Cabinet was useful primarily in the field of policy and political management rather than as an instrument of administration. So far as the available evidence goes, matters of administration were

20 *Ibid.*, V, 207 (Sept. 23, 1833).

21 Polk consulted his Cabinet in 1848 on a new Attorney General. "They all expressed an unwillingness to be associated with a Wilmot Proviso man." Polk, *Diary,* III, 431 (April 22, 1848). Pierce was said to have required concurrence in his inaugural address as a *sine qua non* for appointment to the Cabinet. Ulrich B. Phillips, ed., *Correspondence of Toombs, Stephens, and Cobb,* American Historical Association, *Annual Report, 1911,* II, 326 (March 10, 1853). For a case illustrating opposite practice, consider the appointment of Alexander H. H. Stuart as Secretary of the Interior by Fillmore in 1850, Alexander F. Robertson, *Alexander Hugh Holmes Stuart* (Richmond: William Byrd Press, 1925), pp. 51–52. Stuart had no intimation of the appointment when he was awakened at midnight by a messenger who was directed to secure an answer on the spot and return with it posthaste to Washington. The President's letter of invitation was merely an inquiry as to his availability and touched on no question of policy or administration.

22 *North American Review,* LXIII (1846), 482–83.

ordinarily settled between the President and department heads in private conference. Usually only such administrative problems appeared on the Cabinet agenda as involved policy matters, political repercussions, or important personalities. If any exception to this general observation is required, it would have reference to the administration of James K. Polk.[23]

In the realm of policy and politics a President might depend heavily on his Cabinet, as did Pierce, or very little, as did Jackson. He might consult regularly, as did Tyler and Polk, or he might call the Cabinet together only as occasion required. The tendency was definitely toward regular stated meetings, the system vainly urged upon Jefferson by Gallatin. Polk was firm for regular sessions and held nearly four hundred meetings, but his diary indicates that there was little business to transact at some of them and that attendance of department heads was irregular. All great matters of public policy, nevertheless, made their way to Cabinet discussions: the tariff, nullification, the Bank, Oregon and Texas, the conduct of the War with Mexico, and slavery. Many lesser matters were also brought up for notice.

On two brief occasions the Cabinet appeared to have taken over the reins of government. The first of these occurred under Harrison and has already been noted. Whig leaders had picked Harrison's Cabinet and the Cabinet then proceeded to exercise his authority for him.[24] Fate intervened to end this situation after one month. The second occurred at the close of Buchanan's administration, when a Cabinet majority forced its policy on a bewildered Chief Executive.[25] This situation was quickly terminated when Abraham Lincoln became President. The Whigs were committed to a reduction of executive power, but it is impossible to believe that they would have put the presidential office in commission. Experience confirmed the single responsibility for decision in the hands of the President.

Experience also confirmed the proposition that a President

23 In 1848 he recorded, "At each meeting of the Cabinet, I learn from each member what is being done in his particular Department, and especially if any question of doubt or difficulty has arisen." Polk, *Diary,* IV, 131 (Sept. 23, 1848).

24 T. N. Parmelee, "Recollections of an Old Stager," *Harper's New Monthly Magazine,* XLVII (1873), 753.

25 Mary L. Hinsdale, *A History of the President's Cabinet* (Ann Arbor: George Wahr, 1911), p. 168.

was not bound to consult his Cabinet. Thus Jackson vetoed the Maysville Turnpike bill without taking the matter to the Cabinet, although Van Buren participated privately in the decision.[26] Tyler vetoed the fiscal corporation bill without prior consultation, although the bill had been under intense Cabinet consideration for months. Polk vetoed a river and harbor bill without consultation: "I did not consult the Cabinet to ascertain their opinions on the subject. Having made up my mind that I could not sign the Bill under any circumstances, it was unnecessary to consult the Cabinet on the subject." [27]

These were years of violent political controversy and party instability. Cabinets tended to reflect the unsettled state of affairs, although the record of instability was due in part to other considerations. Jackson's Cabinet was formed and reformed, first on the Peggy Eaton affair, then on the removal of deposits from the United States Bank. Jackson had four Secretaries of State, five Secretaries of the Treasury, two Secretaries of War, three Attorneys General, three Secretaries of the Navy, and two Postmasters General. These fluctuations were greater than the country had ever before experienced. Van Buren kept Jackson's Cabinet, and had to make only four replacements. Tyler's Cabinet resigned as a body, with the exception of Webster, in 1841, and in the nearly four years of Tyler's administration there were three Secretaries of State, three in Treasury, three in War, four in Navy, one Postmaster General, and two Attorneys General, not counting acting appointments. Polk held his Cabinet nearly intact for the full four-year period.

In the four years of the Taylor-Fillmore administration there were three Secretaries of State, two in Treasury, two in War, three in Navy, three in Interior, three Postmasters General, and two Attorneys General. Pierce was as successful as Polk in maintaining his Cabinet, but Buchanan's Cabinet fell to pieces in the last months of his administration.

The standing of the Cabinet as an institution of government was adversely affected by these constant interruptions and explosions. It was also undermined by the advent of the "Kitchen Cabinet," a product of Jackson's first term. Jackson's interest

26 Van Buren, *Autobiography*, pp. 319–21.
27 Polk, *Diary*, II, 58 (August 1, 1846).

lay in politics and personality, not in administration, and his inclinations of long standing led him to confide in men who held his personal confidence. Hence arose naturally a group of personal advisers, primarily concerned with patronage and party manipulation. They included Andrew J. Donelson, Jackson's ward and private secretary; Amos Kendall, one-time editor; Duff Green and then Francis P. Blair, also editors; Major William B. Lewis, who lived in the White House; Isaac Hill, another editor and politician from New Hampshire; and later Roger B. Taney.[28] Tyler was almost forced into the same kind of arrangement, deserted as he was by Whigs and Democrats alike. Other Presidents had their personal friends and occasional advisers, but the Kitchen Cabinet as a continuing and active group was associated primarily with Jackson and Tyler.

DEPARTMENT HEADS AND STAFF ASSISTANCE

If Presidents suffered from detail, department heads endured a much heavier trial. They had to bear the brunt of office seekers, from whom there was no escape. They had to deal with members of Congress on matters large and small. They had a mass of official papers on which to make decisions that constantly threatened to overwhelm them. Secretary of the Navy Paulding, interested in literature and the life of a well-to-do gentleman, wrote a friend inviting him to Washington, "if it be only to see a gentleman of leisure metamorphosed into a pack-horse." [29] Secretary of War Poinsett declared that the labor of regulating his office, dispatching the multifarious business constantly before him, and receiving innumerable visits and applications was overwhelming.[30] Jefferson Davis complained privately about "the little carking cares" that beset a Secretary.[31]

The Treasury papers of the 1830's reveal the wide range of matters that required the attention of the Secretary of this de-

28 Hinsdale, *History of the President's Cabinet,* pp. 84–86.

29 William I. Paulding, compiler, *Literary Life of James K. Paulding* (New York: Charles Scribner, 1867), p. 272 (Dec. 24, 1838).

30 "Poinsett-Campbell Correspondence" (Samuel Gaillard Stoney, ed.), *South Carolina Historical and Genealogical Magazine,* XLII (1941), 158 (March 23, 1837).

31 Davis, *Letters, Papers and Speeches,* II, 474 (July 23, 1855). There is a good description of Daniel Webster's official day in the State Department in Charles Lanman, *The Private Life of Daniel Webster* (New York: Harper and Brothers, 1853), pp. 83–84.

partment. On the one hand were great matters of state such as those pertaining to the Bank of the United States, the custody of public funds at a time when in many parts of the country all banks were closed, the framing of legislation for an independent treasury system, and the tariff. On the other were such matters as the appointment, transfer, and promotion of clerks, an increase of pay to the keeper of the Cleveland lighthouse, the use of a room in the State Department building, and the purchase of a dictionary by the first comptroller.[32]

That a department head could no longer personally conduct the business of his agency merely with the assistance of clerks was apparent from the official records of the time. The chairman of the House Ways and Means Committee declared in 1836, "To suppose that the present small number of heads, compared with the numerical size of their offices, can now, as they did in those days, adjust the accounts, keep the public books, prepare exhibits, or even conduct all the correspondence, would argue but a slight acquaintance with the course of the public business." [33] By 1852 the Postmaster General admitted that most of the business of the executive departments and offices had to be performed "without more than very general directions from the heads of departments and bureaus." [34] In the same year the first comptroller stated to Congress that there were more complicated questions of law and fact to be decided in his office than could be properly investigated and decided by himself.[35] The department heads needed help, and the help came principally from the organization of bureaus and the devolution of operating responsibility to their respective heads.[36]

In some degree, however, help came from the establishment of assistant secretaries in Treasury and State, although in practice this innovation proved less useful than might have been anticipated. No exact precedents existed, although the Secretary of War had the General Staff and the Secretary of the Navy had had professional advice from the Board of Navy Commissioners

32 These examples are taken from correspondence in the National Archives, Treasury Department, Letters to Cabinet and Bureaus, Set B, *passim*.

33 House Report 641, 24th Cong., 1st sess., p. 7 (May 10, 1836).

34 Senate Ex. Doc. 69, 32d Cong., 1st sess., p. 12 (May 3, 1852).

35 Senate Ex. Doc. 7, 32d Cong., 2d sess., p. 11 (Nov. 23, 1852).

36 This matter is dealt with below, ch. 27.

until 1842, and the Postmaster General had the equivalent of assistant secretary support in the first, second, and third assistant postmasters general.

In 1848 Secretary of the Treasury Robert J. Walker asked Congress for aid in the management of the department by establishing the office of assistant secretary. He wanted, he said, "a man of great talents and experience . . . who should examine all letters, contracts, and warrants prepared for the signature of the secretary, and perform such other duties not requiring the signature of the secretary, as might conveniently be devolved upon him by the department. To maintain the unity and efficiency of the system, he should be appointed by the secretary, and subject to his direction." [37] Congress enacted legislation establishing the office of assistant secretary of the Treasury, in precise accordance with Walker's proposal.[38]

So far as the record can now be reconstructed, the Treasury on the whole failed to get men "of great talents and experience" as assistant secretaries. Peter G. Washington, who served from 1853 to 1857, was the only one whose record shows an administrative background. He had had long clerical experience, and was sixth auditor from 1845 to 1849. Allen A. Hall, one of his short-term predecessors, was a lawyer-journalist who had enjoyed four years of political reward under Tyler as chargé d'affaires at Venezuela.

In 1846 Buchanan proposed to convert the chief clerk of the State Department into an assistant secretary, to be appointed by the President and Senate, and to be authorized by law to transact all the business of the department, except that purely diplomatic in character, under the general supervision of the Secretary.[39] Congress was indifferent, but finally recognized the need for high-level assistance by establishing the office of assistant secretary in 1853. The duties of the incumbent were such as the Secretary of State should prescribe or as the law might require. In this case confirmation by the Senate was not required.[40]

37 House Ex. Doc. 7, 30th Cong., 2d sess., p. 36 (Dec. 9, 1848).

38 9 Stat. 395, sec. 13 (March 3, 1849).

39 Buchanan, *Works*, VI, 414 (March 16, 1846).

40 10 Stat. 181, 212 (March 3, 1853).

Early appointments were such as to bring experienced men into the department. William Hunter, whose father had been U.S. minister to Brazil, and who had served continuously in the State Department since 1829 as translator, bureau chief, and chief clerk, was offered the assistant secretaryship but declined. A. Dudley Mann, assistant secretary from 1853 to 1855, was educated at West Point, and for a decade before his appointment had been U.S. Consul at Bremen and special agent negotiating commercial treaties with a number of European states.[41] Mann was succeeded for a couple of years by John Addison Thomas of New York. From 1857 to 1860 the office was filled by John Appleton, the main thread of whose career was politics and journalism, but who had had some diplomatic experience in Bolivia and in Great Britain.[42]

The two elder civilian departments thus were organized, as in another form the War Department, the Navy, and Post Office had been organized, to give high-level assistance to the head of the agency. It now became possible for business of a secondary order to be transacted, under only general supervision, by an officer acting for the Secretary. The process of delegation, with power to act, was put in motion.

DEPARTMENTAL PERSONALITIES

The quality of top-level administration under the Jacksonians is suggested in part by the personal background, experience, accomplishments, and interests of the heads of department. The data in the *Dictionary of American Biography* permit some analysis of the characteristics of this group of seventy-six Secretaries. Only ten were born into an urban environment; three in Philadelphia and two in Charleston, South Carolina. Only twelve were born into families that can be definitely classified as well-to-do. Many, however, acquired wealth, and many came from families in comfortable circumstances. Others, a minority, were born to poverty.

The contrast in family background may be illustrated by reference to the early life of Joel R. Poinsett and Tom Corwin.

41 *Dictionary of American Biography,* XII, 239.
42 *Ibid.,* I, 329.

Secretary of War Poinsett was born in Charleston, South Carolina, the son of a wealthy physician. His education was pursued abroad at St. Paul's School in London and at Edinburgh. He traveled more widely than almost any American of his day—England, the Continent, Russia, Cuba, and South America.[43] In contrast Secretary of the Treasury Corwin was born of poor parents on the Kentucky frontier, was self-educated, became a wagoner, studied law, and began his public career as a member of the Kentucky legislature at the age of twenty-seven.[44] He often told Secretary of the Interior Stuart that "the happiest moments of his life had been when the long line of wagons would come to a halt and the drivers would go to the provision box for their bottles and dinner." [45] When he ran for governor of Ohio in 1849 his friends shouted for "Tom Corwin, the wagon-boy." [46] He was not the only Horatio Alger of his time, but not all could poke fun at themselves in the exercise of the power which one day they acquired. In 1851 Corwin wrote a friend, "I do everything in the Treasy but sign Warrants. I have grown quite judicial, I condemn a ship & cargo—value $300,000 & take a segar!!!" [47]

It comes somewhat as a surprise to discover that fifty-one of these seventy-six Secretaries were college men, while ten more attended an academy. Thirteen had only a common-school education. At the other extreme two were educated abroad. In a generation when democracy was on the march, the college-trained man in five cases out of seven won his way to the Cabinet seats. Yale and the University of North Carolina each were represented by seven, Princeton and William and Mary by four, Harvard and Dartmouth by three. One West Pointer, Jefferson Davis, became a Cabinet member. The number of students in all American colleges in 1829 was about 3,400 in a population

43 J. Fred Rippy, *Joel R. Poinsett, Versatile American* (Durham, North Carolina: Duke University Press, 1935).

44 Josiah Morrow, ed., *Life and Speeches of Thomas Corwin* (Cincinnati: W. H. Anderson, 1896).

45 Alexander F. Robertson, *Alexander H. H. Stuart*, pp. 54–55.

46 John Sherman, *Recollections of Forty Years in the House, Senate and Cabinet: an Autobiography* (2 vols., Chicago: Werner Co., 1895), I, 91.

47 "Selections from the William Greene Papers," *Quarterly Publication of the Historical and Philosophical Society of Ohio*, XIII (1918), 37–38.

of about 13,000,000. The proportion of college students native to any state was greatest in Massachusetts—one in 1,300—and generally much less in the southern and western states.[48]

It is also surprising, in an era when agriculture and rural life were still dominant, to discover the near monopoly held by lawyers in these positions. Sixty-eight had been admitted to the bar, and most of them had engaged in the active practice of the law. The remainder, eight, included four businessmen, two professors (Bancroft and Everett, each of whom could be classified with Paulding as a writer), one editor, and an army officer turned planter—Davis. The law had been an important road to public life in earlier years; now it was by far the principal avenue.

Only one head of a department during these thirty-two years could be classified as coming up through the ranks. Horatio King began his public service career as a post office clerk in the General Post Office in 1839, received one promotion after another under successive Whig and Democratic administrations, was first assistant postmaster general from 1854 to 1861, and Postmaster General for a few weeks at the close of Buchanan's administration.[49] King fully justified the recommendation made by the Maine delegation to Postmaster Kendall in 1839:

> If you want as a clerk in your office a gentleman of talent, integrity, and exemplary morals, of unwearied and persevering industry, of regular and economical habits, a good penman and correct draughtsman, a man in whom you may place the most implicit confidence in all situations and under all circumstances, and a Democrat to the core, sound, radical, ardent, and persevering, the undersigned most respectfully present and earnestly recommend as such an individual, Horatio King, Esq., of Maine.
>
> In whatever situation he may be placed, you may rely that his services will be most invaluable.[50]

The level of competence of department heads appears to have declined after John Quincy Adams left the White House. While there were incompetent heads of departments under both Fed-

48 *Niles Register,* XXXVII, 2 (August 29, 1829).

49 Horatio King, *Turning on the Light* (Philadelphia: J. B. Lippincott, 1895).

50 Kendall, *Autobiography,* p. 369.

eralist and Republican Presidents, the general level of executive ability had been good, and in some cases reached great heights, notably in the careers of Alexander Hamilton and Albert Gallatin. From 1829 to 1861 no administrative genius appeared in the federal system, although Amos Kendall, John J. Crittenden, Caleb Cushing, James Guthrie, and Jefferson Davis made excellent executive records.

Only six Secretaries are widely remembered. Two became President, Van Buren and Buchanan; and one became President of the Confederate States, Jefferson Davis. Webster and Calhoun, both Secretaries of State, were great figures of their time, but Webster was not interested in administration and Calhoun's executive achievements already lay far behind him. Taney, whose interim appointment to the Treasury was denied confirmation, became Chief Justice of the Supreme Court.[51] The great majority of Democratic and Whig Cabinet members from 1829 to 1861 are, however, unknown to history, and left few marks on the administrative system. Hardly one of them ever thought of administration in general terms or had a discernible body of administrative principles by which he was influenced. De Tocqueville observed in the early 1830's, speaking of the states as well as the federal government, that the race of American statesmen had evidently dwindled most remarkably in the course of the last fifty years.[52] He would have been disappointed at the course of the next thirty.

A number of circumstances may have been at work to produce this result. The fact that heads of departments had to be chosen for their political weight, irrespective of executive experience or talent, doubtless played its part. The rise of business, bank, insurance, and railroad corporations may have drained executive talent out of the stream of public life. The instability of political life from 1829 to 1861 and the intensity of factional controversy were probably unfavorable factors. The brief tenure of many department heads did not lead to distinction. From

51 Some might wish to include in this list George Bancroft, remembered as an historian rather than as a public figure, and Edward Everett, remembered as an orator rather than as a Cabinet officer.

52 De Tocqueville, *Democracy in America* (1863 ed.), I, 254.

1829 to 1861 only six men held their Cabinet office for more than four years. Twenty-four were mere birds of passage, holding authority for less than one year; and twenty-one more left office after less than two years.

The tastes and interests of these seventy-six Cabinet members, as already noted, were political, not administrative. Their years in public life were spent for the most part in legislative chambers; they fought elections, won and lost and won again; they helped to manage the political organizations, in the big cities with the aid of high federal officeholders, among whom could now be found some "lame-duck" Congressmen; they debated the issues of their day and did the errands of their constituents; and when they found themselves for a few years at the head of a department, they discovered within themselves considerable knowledge of its business. Some, like Robert J. Walker in the field of tariff theory, had capacity for broad generalization; others, like Bancroft, had capacity for the analysis of administrative needs, the imagination to state remedies, and the determination and skill to put them into operation. Many were content to take things as they found them and to devote their energies to the papers that came to their desks, meanwhile keeping warm the connections between their departments and Congress and its committees. All this was essential to the operation of the public service in a democracy.

If department heads were on the whole less able than their Federalist and Republican predecessors, they were nevertheless, with few exceptions, capable men with broad experience in public life, and with a strong desire to leave a record of constructive accomplishment. Edward Livingston, Senator from Louisiana and Secretary of State under Jackson, was admired by de Tocqueville and deeply respected by his contemporaries as a man of integrity and courage. He possessed one of the ablest minds of his time.[53] George Bancroft wrote his Massachusetts friend, Marcus Morton, that he would be governed by two maxims as Secretary of the Navy: "First, regard to the public service; and next to act as if the eye of the whole democracy watched every motion and its ear heard every word I shall utter.

53 William B. Hatcher, *Edward Livingston: Jeffersonian Republican and Jacksonian Democrat* (Louisiana State University Press, 1940), pp. 460–62.

Duty and publicity will be my watchwords. . . ." [54] Attorney General Clifford wrote his wife, "the day is gone before I know it. I can hardly stop to eat or sleep lest something should be neglected. . . ." [55] Most Secretaries could claim that with diligence and good conscience they were serving the Republic, not merely their party or their own personal fortunes.[56]

54 M. A. DeWolfe Howe, *The Life and Letters of George Bancroft* (2 vols., New York: Charles Scribner's Sons, 1908), I, 263 (March 10, 1845).

55 Philip G. Clifford, *Nathan Clifford,* p. 149 (Nov. 21, 1846).

56 Some of the great men in public life were recognized by honorary degrees. Thus Secretary of State Henry Clay received a degree at Harvard; Secretary of State Van Buren at Rutgers; President Jackson at Harvard, much to the disgust of J. Q. Adams; Attorney General Berrien at Princeton; Attorney General Crittenden at Harvard; and others.

CHAPTER SIX

The Struggle for Power: The Control of Appointments

John Adams had declared, many years before the day of Andrew Jackson, that the executive and legislative branches were natural enemies. The early history of the Republic seemed to confirm this doctrine, although the institutional character of the struggle was often obscured and embittered by personal feuds and ambitions. The executive branch tended to dominate under Washington, Adams, and Jefferson; the legislative branch was in the clear ascendancy under Madison, and held its own under Monroe and John Quincy Adams.

Conflict between the two branches mounted to new heights during Jackson's two administrations, and broke out with renewed violence under John Tyler. The net outcome of the three decades 1829–61 was far from clear, since the battle was fought on many fronts and under generals now strong, now weak. What Jackson won for the executive branch was not forgotten, but his successors were unable at times to hold their ground.

Henry Clay believed that the executive power was destined eventually to prevail, and in a sonorous passage predicted the subordination of the legislative branch. "The executive branch of the government," he exclaimed, "was eternally in action; it was ever awake; it never slept; its action was continuous and unceasing, like the tides of some mighty river, which continued flowing and flowing on, swelling, and deepening, and widening, in its onward progress, till it swept away every impediment, and broke down and removed every frail obstacle which might be set up to impede its course." [1] Clay had done and continued to do his best to confound his own prediction. He fought and subdued Madison; he fought Monroe on foreign policy; he fought Jackson; he sought to dominate Harrison; he ruined Tyler; and he was in a deadlock with Taylor when the President's death smoothed the way for his last victory by compromise.

How difficult it is to draw easy generalizations about the drift of executive relations with Congress will be manifest in the pages that follow, in which the rivalry of the two branches in the great arenas of personnel and finance and in some lesser fields will be explored.[2] The story of conflict, however, need not obscure the record of cooperation at many points. It must be understood also as not merely an institutional jealousy, which it was in part, but also as one phase of the party conflict which is an inherent aspect of democratic government. In this chapter the central theme is the control of appointments.[3] As the scene opens, the executive branch possessed it, but Congressmen were covetous.[4]

The Constitution, it may be recalled, provided that top-level officials should be appointed by the President with the advice and consent of the Senate, and that inferior officers might be appointed by the President alone, the heads of departments, or the courts, as Congress should prescribe. These two classes of appointments took form in subsequent legislation, and the Tenure of Office Act of 1820 enlarged the first group by requiring confirmation for most subordinate officials handling public funds. Forty years' practice before Jackson, however, had left the executive branch substantially free from congressional dictation, although Congressmen were recognized as well-qualified sources of information and as entitled to make suggestions of suitable persons for appointment in their states or districts. Their proposals carried weight but were not decisive.

After 1829 the practice of rotation, combined with a larger

1 Clay, *Works*, VI, 309 (Jan. 24, 1842).

2 Conflict over pay policy is discussed in ch. 20.

3 The partisan aspects of the rule of rotation and its effects upon the public service are dealt with in ch. 16.

4 On the subject of this chapter there are excellent secondary references. See a study by Joseph P. Harris, *The Advice and Consent of the Senate* (Berkeley: University of California Press, 1953); Dorothy G. Fowler, *The Cabinet Politician*, and an article by the same author, "Congressional Dictation of Local Appointments,"

number of offices due to the mere physical expansion of the country, greatly increased the number of appointments that had to be made. The number of players in the game consequently increased as the good things to be won multiplied. The organization of two national political parties in the 1830's brought a type of systematic pressure on both the appointing power and Congressmen that had been unknown. Constituents and local machines drove Congressmen to the executive branch for jobs. The halcyon days of relative peace and freedom, not then appreciated by executives who had merely to fill vacancies caused by death or resignation (and Jefferson had remarked that few died and none resigned), were gone forever.

The actors in the play now became principally three: the President and other appointing officers; members of both Houses, especially Senators; and the party organizations, often split into hostile factions. The interplay of these three groups was constant during the Jacksonian period, but it can be illustrated by special notice of the events of Jackson's administration and that of Polk.

JACKSON, THE SENATE, AND THE APPOINTING POWER

Jackson men controlled the House of Representatives by substantial majorities in each of his four Congresses. The Senate was more closely balanced, and party lines did not always hold, notably when Calhoun broke with the President early in his administration. The Senate stood 26 Democrats and 22 anti-Jackson men in the twenty-first Congress (1829–31); 25 Democrats to 21 National Republicans and two others in the twenty-second; 20 Democrats to 20 National Republicans and 8 others in the twenty-third; and 27 Democrats to 25 Whigs in the twenty-fourth. The Senate opposition was therefore as substantial as it was determined.

Jackson promptly ran into trouble in the special session of the Senate, March 4 to March 17, 1829. A considerable number of nominations ranging from department heads to land agents were confirmed by unanimous consent, but three nominations were disputed, and Jackson's nominee for district attorney of Massachusetts was confirmed only by the close vote of 25 to 20.

Journal of Politics, VII (1945), 25–57; Carl Russell Fish, *The Civil Service and the Patronage* (Cambridge: Harvard University Press, 1904).

A flood of appointments came before the Senate at its first regular session, 1829–30. The first rejection of a presidential nominee occurred in February 1830, when Lemuel Williams failed confirmation as collector of customs at New Bedford, Massachusetts.[5] On reconsideration, an adverse vote of 34 to 11 was changed to a favorable vote of 26 to 20. Henry Lee suffered the rare distinction of being unanimously rejected as consul general at Algiers. Samuel Herrick was rejected and then confirmed as district attorney for Ohio. John P. Decatur was rejected, 43 to 1, for collector at Portsmouth, New Hampshire, on the same day that Samuel Swartwout was confirmed for New York. Samuel Cushman was rejected as district attorney of New Hampshire, 36 to 9.

These, and other close votes resulting in confirmation, were climaxed by the rejection of one of Jackson's most ardent supporters, Isaac Hill of New Hampshire, nominated for the prominent post of second comptroller.[6] A whole series of battles now broke out. Jackson's nominee as surveyor and inspector of revenue in the port of New York was rejected, 23 to 25; on reconsideration the Senate was in a tie, 22 to 22, and Calhoun came to the rescue with the vice-presidential vote. He had already saved Amos Kendall for the office of fourth auditor by his casting vote. The nominee for the land office at Tiffin, Ohio, was rejected unanimously, and the nominee for receiver at Cincinnati by an overwhelming majority. Jackson's selection for agent to the Shawnee and Delaware Indians lost, 21 to 23; and when renominated by Jackson lost again, 20 to 21. The great majority of the President's nominations were of course confirmed, but with an impressive number of roll calls, revealing a determined opposition. Toward the close of the first regular session Webster wrote privately that were it not for fear of Jackson's popularity, the Senate would have rejected more than half his nominations.[7]

The twenty-second Congress (1831–33) was also unreliable from Jackson's point of view. Two noteworthy cases occurred—that of Samuel Gwin and of Martin Van Buren. Gwin was a post office clerk in Washington who had secured the President's

5 Data taken from *Senate Executive Journal,* Vol. IV, *passim.*

6 The rejection was received bitterly by Jackson, whose satisfaction was great when Hill was elected a member of the Senate in 1830.

7 Webster, *Writings and Speeches* (National ed.), XVII, 501 (May 9, 1830).

favor and had been given a recess appointment dated October 3, 1831, as register of the land office at Mount Salus, Mississippi. Nominated for a regular appointment, he was rejected by the Senate on December 22, 1831, by a vote of 13 to 25, in the light of a Senate resolution of the previous Congress (February 3, 1831) disapproving appointments of a citizen of one state to an office in another state in which he did not reside. Jackson was not disposed to yield and on June 11, 1832, renominated Gwin. The Senate laid this nomination on the table. Jackson promptly gave Gwin another recess appointment dated July 21, 1832, an act which Senator George Poindexter of Mississippi tried without success to have the Senate declare a palpable violation of the Constitution and a dangerous usurpation of power.[8] On February 19, 1833, Jackson tried again, putting in Gwin's name for the third time. The Senate again rejected him, 19 to 20. Jackson thereupon notified the Senate that he would abstain from any further effort to fill the office, and asserted that the "local residence" requirement was an unconstitutional limitation of his power to nominate.[9] The Senate yielded, rescinded the resolution, and confirmed Gwin on nomination as register of a land office in the northwestern district of Mississippi, while accepting another Jackson nominee to the disputed office at Mount Salus. Jackson, in his words, thus won "a triumph over the factious senate headed by Poindexter." [10] He also succeeded in appointing an agent who was to become a notorious defaulter.[11]

The second case involved a more notable personality and was followed by more spectacular consequences. On January 25, 1832, Martin Van Buren was rejected as minister to Great Britain by an arranged tie that gave Calhoun an opportunity to cast the deciding vote against his rival. It was on this occasion that Calhoun is reported to have exclaimed in exultation, "It

8 *Senate Executive Journal,* IV, 293–94 (Dec. 31, 1832).

9 Richardson, *Messages,* II, 636 (March 2, 1833). The case aroused great interest.

10 Jackson, *Correspondence,* V, 27–28 (March 3, 1833). The bad blood generated by this case was to have fatal consequences. In 1836 Poindexter was alleged to have publicly abused Gwin, who challenged Poindexter. His law partner, Caldwell, took up the challenge and a duel was fought at thirty paces with four pistols. Caldwell was killed and Gwin severely wounded. *Niles Register,* XLIX, 389 (Feb. 6, 1836).

11 Senate Doc. 151, 23d Cong., 2d sess., pp. 4–5 (March 3, 1835).

will kill him, sir, kill him dead. He will never kick sir, never kick." [12] Calhoun's judgment was faulty; Jackson was doubly incensed; Van Buren became his heir apparent and went on to the White House in 1837.

During the twenty-third Congress (1833–35), the Senate and the President again locked horns on appointments in connection with the conflict over the Bank of the United States.[13] The Senate rejected four government directors friendly to Jackson, and on renomination declined again to confirm, even more decisively. It was on this occasion that John Tyler stated the opposition of the Senate to renominations and to executive comments on the reasons of the Senate for refusal to confirm. "The committee," Tyler reported, "do not deny that a right of renomination exists; but they are of opinion that, in very clear and strong cases only should the Senate reverse decisions which it has deliberately formed, and officially communicated to the President." Tyler found no cases of renomination by Washington, Adams, or Jefferson; two by Madison and several by Monroe; none by J. Q. Adams.[14]

Jackson subsequently nominated one of the Bank directors, Henry D. Gilpin, to be governor of the Territory of Michigan, only to incur another rejection. A year later Gilpin was confirmed as U.S. district attorney in Pennsylvania. Jackson also stood by a second Bank nominee, John T. Sullivan, by nominating him as army paymaster, but the Senate refused to confirm. The running battle broke out again when the Senate rejected Martin Gordon as collector of customs for Mississippi. Jackson promptly nominated Gordon's son, who was also rejected. Two years later Gordon senior was confirmed as superintendent of the New Orleans mint, and Gordon junior as naval officer for the district of Mississippi.

This Senate also refused to confirm the Speaker of the House, Andrew Stevenson, as minister to Great Britain, for reasons which revealed an old ground for legislative suspicion of the executive branch. Stevenson was Jackson's choice for the Court

12 Thomas Hart Benton, *Thirty Years' View* (2 vols., New York: D. Appleton, 1854–56), I, 219.

13 See below, ch. 24.

14 This valuable report is in Senate Doc. 333, 23d Cong., 1st sess., pp. 11–14 (May 2, 1834).

of Saint James after Van Buren was rejected and had a private understanding with Jackson that he would go to London as soon as the House committees had been organized. He too was rejected by the Senate and Jackson left the office unoccupied until in 1836 he again proposed Stevenson, now to a friendly Senate. Henry Clay, chairman of the Senate Foreign Relations Committee, made a scathing report recommending a second rejection. After noting the desirability of maintaining the independence of action of each of the three branches of government beyond the influence of the others, he continued, "But, if the head of one of those Departments may, at a critical period, confidentially present, and for a long period of time hold up to the presiding officer of the popular branch of another, the powerful inducement of a splendid foreign mission, is there not imminent danger of undue subserviency. . . ." [15] The Senate declined to accept Clay's argument and now confirmed Stevenson.

The Senate also dealt Jackson other blows during the twenty-third Congress by refusing to confirm Roger B. Taney as Secretary of the Treasury in 1834 and as associate justice of the Supreme Court in 1835. Jackson later nominated Taney as Chief Justice of the Supreme Court and a cooperative Senate confirmed him in 1836. The twenty-fourth Congress (1835–37) saw an end to Jackson's battles over nominations. Only three rejections occurred.

The engagement over presidential offices thus concluded with substantial victory for the Chief Executive. Jackson had more difficulty with the Senate than any of his predecessors and most of his successors, but he succeeded in imposing his will upon a recalcitrant upper House in an impressive number of cases. He declined to yield to the Senate, although in some cases, such as the Bank directors, he found other nominees. If defeated, he bided his time and again offered the same man for the same office or a different one. Negatively, the Senate was unable to protect the public service against Jackson's removals, or to compel Jackson to accept its own choice by successive rejections of the Presi-

15 *Senate Executive Journal,* IV, 515 (March 3, 1836). Clay, with his tongue in his cheek, added for good measure, "Doubtless no personal feelings or wishes to achieve a triumph over the Senate can have prompted the renewal of this nomination." *Ibid.,* IV, 516.

dent's nominees, or to require Jackson to give his reasons for removals for its approval.

Long after he had left the White House, Jackson gave his friend Major William B. Lewis the secret of his strategy in these encounters over appointments. "I could recommend to Mr. Tyler," he wrote, "to do as I did, whenever the Senate rejected a good man, on the ground of his politics, I gave them a hot potatoe, and he will soon bring them to terms, and if not, if they leave the office not filled, the vengeance of the people will fall upon them." [16]

POLK, CONGRESS, AND THE APPOINTING POWER

The return of the Democratic party to power in 1845 was the occasion for renewed pressure on the executive branch. Polk had a hard time between Congressmen's desire for their own appointments, civil and military, their pressure for constituents, and the quarrelsome tactics of factions in New York and Pennsylvania. From the wealth of information in Polk's diary it is possible to reconstruct an account of the struggle for the control of patronage during his administration.

Senators and Representatives were constantly calling at the White House seeking appointments for their friends and constituents. Senator Breese of Illinois was "the most troublesome and inveterate seeker for office for his friends in either House of Congress," always calling at the White House with an axe to grind, and causing Polk to make some bad appointments in the Senator's search for his own political fortune. Senator Benton was also an annoyance, embarrassing Polk by seeking positions for his relatives. He proposed his son-in-law, just married, for a post abroad as chargé d'affaires. This failing, he tried for the postmastership at New Orleans. His son, John Randolph Benton, demanded a lieutenancy in the U.S. Army and became very

16 Jackson, *Correspondence,* VI, 142 (Feb. 28, 1842). The hectic record of Tyler's administration hardly reflects general trends. After being disowned by the Whigs and rejected by the Democrats he had almost no support. During his last two years the Senate rejected four nominations to his Cabinet, four to the Supreme Court, and his choice of minister to France and to Brazil, as well as his nominations to many lesser posts. The Whigs confidently expected that Henry Clay would fill these positions after March 4, 1845, but even when their hopes were dashed, they continued to be obstreperous. The qualifications of nominees were hardly even a secondary consideration.

impertinent when Polk did not immediately consent, finally leaving the President's office "in quite a passion, & very rudely, swearing profanely." Another son-in-law, John C. Frémont, one day to be the first Republican nominee for President, was in the army and the subject of awkward interventions by Benton.[17]

Polk had almost no major battles with the Senate of the order that harassed Jackson. He consulted freely with Senators and Representatives about appointments in their states, and in common with his predecessors sought agreement. Senators had the privilege of direct access to the White House on these matters. For his part, Polk expected support from his party friends in the Senate. He told Senator Lewis Cass bluntly that "the rejection of my prominent nominations by the Senate at the opening of my administration was calculated to weaken my administration before the country, and destroy my power to carry out any of my recommendations of measures before Congress." [18] He sometimes lacked this support, due not to considerations of principle, but to the influence of faction.

The case of Henry Horn, a prominent Pennsylvanian who had once been a government director of the Bank of the United States, provoked a head-on collision between the President and the Senate. It involved a factional fight among the Pennsylvania Democrats to get possession of the patronage of the Philadelphia customhouse. Polk nominated Horn to be collector of customs. The nomination was rejected by the Senate on May 25, 1846, by a combination of the solid Whig vote and three Democratic Senators—Calhoun, Cameron of Pennsylvania, and Westcott of

17 Polk, *Diary,* II, 426 (March 17, 1847); II, 445 (March 29, 1847); III, 13–14 (May 5, 1847); III, 202–4 (Oct. 25, 1847).

18 *Ibid.,* I, 207 (Feb. 2, 1846). Lewis Cass (1782–1866) spent most of his life in the public service, civil and military. At the age of twenty-four he became a member of the Ohio State Legislature, served on active duty with distinction in the War of 1812, was governor of the Territory of Michigan from 1813 to 1831 and Secretary of War under Jackson. In 1836 he became minister to France. In 1845 he was elected to the U.S. Senate and in 1848 was the Democratic candidate for the presidency. He returned to the Senate in 1849 and from 1857 to 1860 was Secretary of State under Buchanan, resigning in protest against the decision not to reinforce the Charleston forts. He wrote numerous essays, and a book entitled, *France, Its King, Court, and Government.* See Frank B. Woodford, *Lewis Cass.*

Florida. Polk suspected connivance on the part of Secretary Buchanan.[19] The Democratic members of the Pennsylvania delegation then held a caucus, and agreed to recommend a political unknown named Eldred. When they came to Polk with their choice he told them bluntly that "no man or his friends who had any agency in Mr. Horn's rejection, should ever profit by it, by having any man whom they preferred appointed to the vacancy which they had created." [20] He promptly renominated Horn, and the Senate promptly rejected him a second time. Over Buchanan's opposition Polk then nominated Colonel James Page. Buchanan asked Polk to consult the Pennsylvania delegation, to which he retorted that his "independence as President of the U.S. required that I should show to Mr. Cameron and others who had made a factious opposition . . . that by their rejection neither they nor their friends should be profited by it." [21] This was Jackson's "hot potato" treatment. Page was confirmed, after Polk's stubborn assertion of presidential independence and determination.

Polk's second general problem vis-à-vis Congress concerned the appointment of members to executive positions. The independence of Congress against executive temptation by hope of office had been an object of concern among the Jeffersonians, and Henry Clay's opposition to the Stevenson appointment, already noted, was in strict accord with older doctrine. Jackson had expressed his own conviction that members of Congress ought not to receive executive appointments, but he made a few such, almost exclusively to Cabinet positions, foreign stations, or territorial judges.[22] The mounting thirst of Congressmen for office gave Polk much embarrassment. The traditional concern about the independence of the legislative branch seemed to vanish before congressional appetite for jobs. "The passion for office among members of Congress," noted Polk in his diary, "is very great, if not absolutely disreputable, and greatly embarrasses the operations of the Government. They create offices by their own

19 For an especially illuminating passage, see Polk, *Diary,* I, 218–19 (Feb. 11, 1846).

20 *Ibid.,* I, 432–33 (May 27, 1846).

21 *Ibid.,* I, 488 (June 25, 1846).

22 House Doc. 76, 22d Cong., 2d sess. (Jan. 11, 1833).

votes and then seek to fill them themselves. I shall refuse to appoint them . . . because their appointment would be most corrupting in its tendency." [23]

Polk was writing with special reference to military commissions, which the Mexican War made plentiful. The day before war with Mexico was declared, Congressman Haralson (a general in the Georgia militia) and Congressman Baker of Illinois made it known to the President that they desired high command in the army of volunteers. "I talked civilly to them," Polk recorded, "but made no promises." [24] General Cass, some of the western members of Congress, and the commissioner of the General Land Office (Judge Shields) all offered to go west and organize the volunteers. Polk discouraged them.[25] An Ohio Congressman, Brinkerhoff, soon appeared and asked to be appointed paymaster. Polk told him that he intended to appoint Congressmen only to such high posts as Cabinet member, minister, or judge of the Supreme Court, following the spirit of the Constitution that prohibited their appointment to any civil office created during their congressional term. Brinkerhoff responded by making a violent attack on the President on the floor of the House. He was joined by another disappointed Congressman, Tibbatts of Kentucky.[26]

Senator Semple of Illinois, a brigadier general of militia, was recommended by his state delegation to command the Illinois brigade. After discovering that Polk had sent in another nomination, Semple quickly withdrew his application, but the President noted that the letter "was not written in good temper." [27] Later Semple caused Polk some very anxious days in the passage of the tariff bill. On the day when Polk was expected to make his nominations for officers of the volunteer force, he had an "unusually large crowd of visitors," among others, members of the delegations from Ohio, Indiana, Illinois, Kentucky, Arkansas, Mississippi, Alabama, Georgia, and Tennessee. Such experiences caused Polk to write in his diary, "The selfishness, and I might add the

23 Polk, *Diary*, I, 483 (June 22, 1846).

24 *Ibid.*, I, 388–89 (May 10, 1846).

25 *Ibid.*, I, 427 (May 25, 1846).

26 *Ibid.*, I, 466–67 (June 12, 1846); I, 497–98 (June 30, 1846).

27 *Ibid.*, I, 482–83 (June 22, 1846); I, 493–94 (June 29, 1846).

corruption of a few members of Congress, if disclosed, would be incredible to the public." [28]

These scenes were repeated in February 1847 when the President had to select officers for ten additional regiments authorized by Congress. Scores of persons called to urge their cases, and many Senators and Representatives. "Members of Congress tell me that they are compelled to come with their constituents to present their claims, and some of the members apologize for troubling me as much as they do." Polk confessed that he could bear this labor with more patience "if members of Congress and others were more candid, and would not, as they do, constantly deceive me about appointments." [29] He declared he had never been so annoyed and wearied in his life.

Polk's experience with the Senate thus conformed to that of Jackson, but without the long series of battles in which the latter had engaged. The net outcome was to preserve executive independence in nominations to presidential offices. A new element, new at least in intensity, arose as members of both Houses sought executive appointments for themselves. Polk resisted these demands on the whole successfully.

THE EXECUTIVE, CONGRESS, AND THE INFERIOR APPOINTMENTS

The conflict between Jackson and the Senate on presidential offices obscured a quite different tendency that was developing with regard to the inferior offices. This countercurrent was quite as important as that which appeared superficially to be the main stream. It indicated a marked increase of influence of Senators and Representatives alike, solidifying their expectations for consultation if not indeed for decision on the smaller field offices.

The evidence is set out in part in the appointment letters of Levi Woodbury, Secretary of the Treasury under both Jackson and Van Buren, to members of Congress. Woodbury had been a member of the Senate before entering the Cabinet, and it was here rather than as a member of the executive branch that he had had his first experience in appointment practice. He proved to be complaisant toward his former colleagues in the Senate and

28 *Ibid.*, I, 492–93 (June 29, 1846); I, 497 (June 30, 1846).
29 *Ibid.*, II, 382, 383 (Feb. 19, 1847).

his fellow Democrats in the House. Woodbury never stated general rules, but the cases recorded a degree of congressional activity that was so novel as to become practically an innovation in kind.[30]

The correspondence demonstrated a tendency for Congressmen to take greater initiative in making recommendations for appointments. The Treasury devised a form letter acknowledging receipt of applications and informing the Senator or Representative that "at the proper time, it shall be respectfully considered." There were other instances, however, where Congressmen intended their protégés to succeed, and some cases in which the whole state delegation acted as a unit.[31] These might lead to protracted negotiations. In a few cases Congressmen went beyond solicitation for office and asked the Treasury to promote an officer, to increase his pay, or to transfer him from an undesirable post.[32] Such requests were regularly denied unless they fell within established procedures.

Secretary Woodbury continued, like his predecessors, to ask Congressmen for information about prospective appointees. It became more customary to ask for the collective opinion of the whole state delegation—in part doubtless a protective device by which the Treasury could hope to escape divisions of opinion among its advisers.[33]

On other occasions Woodbury went beyond this to ask specifically for nominations. Two or three examples will illustrate the case. In 1835 he wrote to Congressman Robert T. Lytle of Ohio, as follows: "The Commission of Mr. Larrabee, the Surveyor of Cincinnati, will shortly expire, & he having declined a reappointment, I must beg the favor that you will name some fit person as a successor." To Senators Benton and Linn of Missouri he wrote that the receiver of public moneys at Augusta had resigned—"Can you recommend a fit person for the successor?" [34] An espe-

30 The letters are in the custody of the National Archives, Treasury Department, Letters and Reports to Congress, Series E, *passim;* cited hereafter as Treasury Letters, Series E.

31 Treasury Letters, Series E, VIII, 299–300 (Feb. 17, 1835).

32 *Ibid.,* VIII, 142 (June 11, 1834); VIII, 189–90 (Dec. 8, 1834); VIII, 405 (Jan. 1836).

33 *Ibid.,* X, 37 (April 9, 1838).

34 *Ibid.,* VIII, 242 (Jan. 17 and 19, 1835).

cially illuminating inquiry of this sort occurred in 1838. "Mr. Woodbury's respects to the delegates in Congress from Alabam [*sic*], & would inform them, that the term of office for Jacob S. Bradford, Register at Mardisville expires on the 14th of June, and the Treasury Department will be happy to submit their wishes or those of any of the Delegation to the President on the subject of Mr. Bradford's re-appointment—or of the nomination of a successor to him, if one be desired." [35]

In a number of other ways the Treasury showed a deference to Congressmen in acting upon appointments in their states or districts. Thus there was no hesitation to grant postponement of decision upon a member's request. The names of persons on the pay roll of a collector's office were furnished with no questions asked about the nature of the Congressman's interest. Members were given free access to all the letters on file with respect to applicants for appointment to designated positions. Congressmen were asked if they had objections to the reappointment of incumbent officers.[36]

Congressmen were also consulted in some instances of pending removal. The case of the Owls Head lighthouse keeper, about to be removed for intemperance, indolence, and inattention, was called to the notice of Senator Ruggles of Maine, together with the name of his proposed replacement.[37] The delinquent brother of Senator Linn, a collector of public money, was a case that peculiarly required consultation on the part of the Treasury. Woodbury was delicate with the Senator and lenient with the collector.[38]

An abundance of examples such as these suggests a change in the character of relationship rather than strange and unknown events. They demonstrate that Congressmen were demanding a greater share in the appointment of the inferior officers. The Constitution and the law were unchanged, but custom was being altered. The Treasury letters from 1829 to 1841 do not, however, lead one to conclude that executive discretion in these appointments had been surrendered. They do demonstrate that

35 *Ibid.*, X, 172 (May 1, 1838).

36 *Ibid.*, VIII, 190 (Dec. 8, 1834); VIII, 257–58 (Jan. 24, 1835); X, 49 (Jan. 31, 1838); VIII, 195–96 (Dec. 16, 1834).

37 *Ibid.*, X, 154 (April 14, 1838).

38 *Ibid.*, VIII, 180 (Oct. 21, 1834). The case is discussed below, ch. 22.

beneath the partisan battle over presidential offices there was ample cooperation between the executive branch and its party friends in Congress by which their mutual interests were advanced.

A moderate statement of the position of Congressmen with respect to appointments was made by Abraham Lincoln in a letter to the Secretary of the Treasury. "Col. E. D. Baker and myself are the only Whig members of congress from Illinois. . . . We have reason to think the whigs of that state hold us responsible, to some extent, for the appointments which may be made of our citizens. . . . I therefore hope I am not obtrusive in saying, in this way, for him and myself, that when a citizen of Illinois is to be appointed in your Department to an office either in or out of the state, we most respectfully ask to be heard."[39] Congressman Lincoln made no distinction between offices high and low, of local or national jurisdiction, but he asked only to be heard. Other Congressmen were less moderate in their demands.

The potential influence of Congressmen over local appointments was magnified in 1853 by the adoption of an apportionment rule for clerical appointments in the Washington offices. This rule, which is described at a later point, was forced on the departments by members as a means of avoiding a general scramble for whatever appointments could be wheedled or coerced from executive officers.[40]

How far the power of Congressmen over inferior appointments in the field establishments was destined to reach by the close of the period is amply revealed by conditions in the New York and other navy yards.[41] Against the resistance of yard commandants but with the connivance of Navy Secretaries, the local members had acquired mastery of the appointing power and used it boldly for electioneering success. Here the victory of Congressmen was for the moment complete.

39 *The Collected Works of Abraham Lincoln* (8 vols., Abraham Lincoln Association, Roy P. Basler, ed., New Brunswick: Rutgers University Press, 1953), II, 32 (March 9, 1849).

40 See below, ch. 21.

41 The evidence is presented below, ch. 11.

THE ROLE OF SENATORIAL COURTESY

The rule of senatorial courtesy, in its strict formulation, permits a Senator of either party (usually the majority party) to rise on the floor of the Senate with respect to a pending presidential nomination to an office usually situated in the Senator's state, and to defeat the nomination by declaring that the person proposed is personally obnoxious to him. He need not give his reasons, and they need not bear on the qualification of the candidate for office. By custom of the Senate, the members support their colleague against the President in the face of this kind of objection, and senatorial courtesy is the sanction whereby a Senator of the same party as the President maintains the right *de facto* to select the persons to be nominated to presidential offices situated in his state. The rule is seldom invoked since some compromise can usually be worked out before reaching such an impasse.

In a more general sense, the term senatorial courtesy refers to the deference given, when vacancies arise, to the opinions of a Senator concerning persons under consideration for inferior federal posts situated in his state, and to the expectation that he shall be consulted with respect to the President's choice of a nominee. Consultation usually implies that the Senator must be satisfied. In the narrow sense of the term, senatorial courtesy is invariably accorded when requested; in the broader sense of the term, it is a description of standard practice, which, however, permits some deviation.[42]

The most careful statement of the role of Senators that has been encountered in this period was written by Jefferson Davis to a Tennessee Congressman whose recommendations for a postmaster had been disregarded, and who was considering resignation in protest.

> . . . . In the remarks to which you refer as made by me in the Senate you will recollect that I stated to Dr. G. that if he objected to the nominee for cause, I might if it was stated, vote against his confirmation, but that I could not do so on the ground that the Senators from the state had not been consulted; and that he denied having any

42 See Joseph P. Harris, "The Courtesy of the Senate," *Political Science Quarterly*, LXVII (1952), 36–63.

objection to the individual and pressed his claim to an advisory power over nominations to be made of the Citizens of the State he represented. Now this you will see is destructive of the division which the Constitution makes, and will strip the Executive of his prerogative of nomination so that in point of fact two members of the Senate would nominate to the Senate in session, the appointments which they might deem it expedient to make—the rule if it is worth anything would have to work both ways, and a State represented by the enemies of the Administration would thus possess the means of paralizing its policy, in a large number, it might be a majority of the states. The Constitution makes it the duty of the Senate to revise the appointing power of the Executive, gives them the power to confirm or reject the nomination. There surely can be no indignity in not asking a Senator to do more than belongs to his office (viz), to give advice before the nomination is made. . . .[43]

The first instance that has come to attention in which a member of Congress sought to defeat a presidential nomination by declaring the nominee personally obnoxious occurred in 1859. Fenner Ferguson, territorial delegate for Nebraska, addressed a letter to Senator R. W. Johnson, chairman of the Committee on Public Lands, protesting the nomination of Peter F. Wilson as receiver of public moneys at Omaha. The terms of his spirited letter are sufficiently significant to deserve quotation in part.

. . . . I, as the Representative of that Territory, take the liberty of entering my *Protest* against his confirmation and for the following reasons—
1st I, together with the Governor, and the late Governor of the territory, have earnestly requested the reappointment of Col. A. R. Gillmore. . . .
2d I have protested against the appointment of said Wilson as being *personally* obnoxious to me for reasons which I will hereinafter state—
3d I have claimed that as the Representative of the Territory some respect should be paid to my wishes in the premises—
4th I have claimed that the appointment belonged to the Territory, and that it was wrong in principle, *to import* a man to hold a local office in Nebraska.[44]

43 Davis, *Letters, Papers and Speeches,* III, 116 (May 9, 1857).

44 National Archives, Congressional Committee Records, Senate 35B–A5 (5). Letter dated March 8, 1859.

The ground on which rested the charge of being personally obnoxious was an allegation that Wilson had abstracted from the official files some derogatory information about Ferguson that had been used against him in the recent election in which Ferguson had been defeated. Wilson's denial of the charge seems convincing, although there is no doubt that the two men were politically at odds with each other. Wilson was unanimously confirmed by the Senate.[45] Ferguson's term had expired on March 3, 1859, and the Senate was obviously not very much impressed by the high tone of a lame-duck territorial delegate.

The classes of positions, appointments to which required senatorial confirmation, were not substantially increased during this period. Confirmation had always been required for judicial appointments, department heads, diplomatic and consular officials, army and navy officers, the principal auditing officials, the commissioners at the head of bureaus, and the principal field agents—the collectors of customs, district attorneys, marshals, mint officials, land agents, Indian agents, and territorial officials. From 1829 to 1861 Congress extended the list of presidential officers to include the assistant secretary of the Treasury Department, the postmasters in the larger cities, the appraisers of merchandise, the superintendent of public printing, the assistant treasurers in the independent treasury system, the naval engineer in chief and chief engineers, the warden of the District of Columbia penitentiary, and the President's secretary to sign land patents.

No clear distinction had yet been made between the patronage status of presidential nominations on the one hand and inferior appointments on the other. The constitutional difference was obvious, but the struggle between Congressmen and the executive over appointments was not fought on constitutional issues. Presidents and department heads resisted the interference of Congressmen in inferior appointments and repeatedly stated the independent ground on which they stood. The course of events, however, ran against them. The visit of two Michigan Congressmen to complain about appointments made by Secretary Marcy became the occasion for a significant entry in President Polk's diary. "It is," he wrote, "one of the many instances

45 *Senate Executive Journal,* XI, 95 (March 9, 1859).

which have occurred in my administration to show the importance which is attached by members of Congress to petty offices. *Indeed many members of Congress assume that they have the right to make appointments, particularly in their own states,* and they often, as in this case, fly into a passion when their wishes are not gratified." [46] This was an assumption that Polk would not accept.[47]

The dominance of Congressmen over inferior appointments in their districts was asserted at the opening of Pierce's administration. Congressman Thomas B. Florence was offended because Quartermaster General Jesup failed to appoint his man to be shoe inspector at the arsenal near Philadelphia, and sent a protest containing the following assertions. "As this Building is within the Territory, which comprises the First Congressional District of Pennsylvania, and the *practice* has been invariably, under every Democratic Administration of the General Government that appointments immediately local, such as this is, should at least *be approved* by the Member of Congress for the time being . . . it is not therefore asking too much of you to inform me at your earliest convenience, the objection you may have entertained, against my written verbal and pressing personal importuning in behalf of William Caslin. . . ." [48] The Congressman also complained directly to Jefferson Davis, Secretary of War, but stated the appointing rule somewhat more cautiously, "The rule under former Democratic Administrations of the General Government, was to give the member of Congress advisatory power at least, in merely local appointments in his District." [49]

The standing of Congressmen in inferior offices in the Post Office was specifically stated in 1861 by Horatio King, replying to an indignant member protesting against the removal of a route agent in his district. King wrote:

46 Polk, *Diary*, IV, 28–29 (July 26, 1848). Underlining author's.

47 Referring to three unreliable Democratic Senators, Hannegan, Semple, and Atchison, Polk wrote, "I have treated them with great civility and have yielded to their wishes about appointments in their respective States until they seem to have come to the conclusion that I must administer the Government precisely as they may direct. In this they will find themselves mistaken." *Ibid.*, I, 486–87 (June 24, 1846).

48 Jefferson Davis, *Letters, Papers and Speeches*, II, 198–99 (April 7, 1853).

49 *Ibid.*, II, 197.

. . . the right which you seem to claim, of controlling the appointments in your district, has no existence in fact. Excepting the comparatively few cases in which the law imposes this duty on the President and Senate, the power of appointing the officers of this Department rests exclusively with the Postmaster-General, who alone is responsible for its proper exercise. By courtesy, the member, when agreeing politically with the administration, is very generally consulted with respect to appointments in his district; but his advice is by no means considered as binding on the Department, nor is the Postmaster-General precluded, even by courtesy, from making removals or appointments on satisfactory information, as in the present instance, exclusively from other reliable sources. When the member is politically opposed to the administration, it is not usual to consult him.[50]

The same opinion was stated by Jefferson Davis with reference to the appointment of cadets to West Point. ". . . the selection of Cadets rests exclusively in the discretion of the President; and their appointment is the exercise of his constitutional power. The so called right of nomination by the representatives in Congress is simply the right which every citizen has to recommend candidates for office, and though their recommendations are uniformly followed, it is not because they are obligatory upon the Department, but because, in addition to the weight due to any recommendation from that source; the representatives possess a special and almost semi-official knowledge of the legal residence and other qualifications of candidates from their districts." [51] Davis' own statement suggests how far custom and Constitution had diverged.

Amidst an almost infinite variety of circumstances, Senators and Representatives and party organizations thus bargained with Presidents and heads of departments over appointment to office, high and low. The most important new element in the process was the impact of the political party, the success of whose local organizations seemed to depend much more on securing office, contracts, and favors for their members than on campaigning over disputed issues of statesmanship. Party pressure was brought to bear on Congressmen and Presidents alike, and factions, it was found, could fight over jobs as fiercely as parties.

50 Horatio King, *Turning on the Light*, p. 50 (Feb. 22, 1861).

51 Davis, *Letters, Papers and Speeches*, II, 355 (May 10, 1854).

The formal position of the Chief Executive as the nominating authority for presidential offices remained unimpaired. The stubborn will of Andrew Jackson maintained established principle and gained many notable personal triumphs. Polk could be equally stubborn and independent, but other Presidents, Tyler excepted, preferred accommodation at most points. Congressmen were numerous, and by a process of attrition, of which Woodbury's record is an example, they won substantial control of local appointments from department heads and the principal field officers. In this aspect of the struggle for power, the legislative branch stood relatively a victor in 1861 even though the executive still held high ground.

CHAPTER SEVEN

The Struggle for Power: Finance

Well after the Jacksonians had left the scene, a House committee looked back over their experience and confirmed another phase of the power struggle, the control of expenditures. "From the time of the first enactment to the present," declared the Committee on Appropriations, "a continual struggle has been going on by the several executive departments with Congress to relieve their departments from this control of public expenditures by Congress, and as constant endeavors by the legislative department to hold the executive to specific expenditures under specific appropriations." [1] It had been a stubborn engagement, involving more issues than that of specific appropriations. The outcome was indecisive, not because Congress failed to write clear instructions to the executive agencies but rather by reason of ingenious construction of bothersome requirements, plain evasion in some cases, and force of circumstances in others, leaving no rational choice to responsible officials but to disobey Congress.[2]

In accordance with British inheritance the Constitution had prescribed that no money should be drawn from the Treasury but with authority of law. Congress thus became the undisputed

1 House Report 14, 40th Cong., 2d sess., p. 2 (Feb. 4, 1868).

2 On the subject matter of this chapter, consult especially Lucius Wilmerding, Jr., *The Spending Power: A History of the Efforts of Congress to Control Expenditures* (New Haven: Yale University Press, 1943); Fred Wilbur Powell, *Control of Federal Expenditures: a Documentary History, 1775–1894* (Washington: Brookings Institution, 1939).

master of the power to appropriate and of the corollary power to impose conditions upon its grants. The normal practice was to specify in detail the purposes or objects for which money could be spent, the amount allowed to each object, and the agency authorized to act.

The Federalists had designed appropriation acts intended to leave much discretion in the heads of departments. The Republicans enacted appropriation bills designed to limit executive discretion to the utmost, and had also put on the books restrictive legislation that was brought to its logical conclusion in the act of 1820. This law, based on the standard practice of specific appropriations except for the armed services, severely limited transfers of funds from one head to another, required unexpended surpluses to revert to the Treasury, and prohibited contracts without authority of law or appropriation.[3] A few years' experience proved that the Republicans were unable to control the application of appropriations by this legislation. The system, on its exposed fronts, broke down in the following decade. Federalist doctrine prevailed in the face of Republican prohibitions. The issue was not merely a party one. It was inherent in the relations existing under any party between the money-raising and the money-spending branches of government. Nor was there any obvious solution of the problem, as became evident with the success now of one branch and now of the other.

THE ESTIMATES

One point of potential control or relative freedom involved the preparation, review, and disposition by Congress of the annual estimates of expenditure. There was a tendency during the Jacksonian years for Congress to become more particular with regard to the form of the estimates, and to require better justification for the amounts requested. A large part of the annual appropriation, however, was fixed and well established, continuing by general consent year after year without much change.

The form of the estimates had been left to the executive departments until 1836, when the Post Office Department was required to submit "specific estimates" of the amount required

[3] 3 Stat. 567 (May 1, 1820).

under twelve stated heads.[4] In 1842 Congress laid down a general obligation upon all departments "to specify, as nearly as may be convenient, the sources from which such estimates are derived, and the calculations upon which they are founded"; to identify the statutory authorization on which they rested; and to discriminate between items that were conjectural in character and those founded upon actual information.[5] These requirements were supplemented in 1844 by more stringent provisions, reflecting the annoyance of Congress at the prevailing looseness of some of the estimates.[6] The departments were now required to give "minute and full explanations" of any material variation from previous estimates and of any new items; and for public works estimates Congress specified a full plan and detailed figures, and a full explanation of any subsequent excess over the original estimate required to complete the work.[7] These requirements were renewed in 1855, with an additional prohibition against resting an estimate merely upon executive "distribution" (presumably interpretation) of the provisions of law.[8]

Congress was obviously intent upon obtaining full information concerning the departmental fiscal plans. On the whole it succeeded. The printed estimates were full of particulars: salaries were enumerated one by one, building estimates included everything from basement to roof, the lighthouse establishment set out the number of linen cleaning cloths and the cost of each, and the superintendent of the Military Academy segregated $45.00 in 1859 for "brooms, brushes, tubs, pails, &c., for policing." [9]

At one crucial point Congress was less than successful, i.e., the estimates for the heavy expenditures for the maintenance of the army and the navy. The quartermaster's department sent in

4 5 Stat. 80, sec. 2 (March 3, 1836).

5 5 Stat. 523, sec. 14 (August 26, 1842).

6 This dissatisfaction was of long standing. See for an example House Report 297, 24th Cong., 1st sess., p. 2 (Feb. 10, 1836).

7 5 Stat. 681, sec. 2 (June 17, 1844).

8 10 Stat. 643, sec. 8 (March 3, 1855).

9 "Letter from the Secretary of the Treasury transmitting Estimates of Appropriations required for . . . the fiscal year ending June 30, 1861," House Ex. Doc. 1, 36th Cong., 1st sess., p. 243 (Sept. 1, 1859).

figures for 1860–61 "for regular supplies" amounting to $1,580,000 (an excess of $140,000 over the previous year) under four heads: fuel, $160,000; forage, $1,400,000; straw, $5,000; and stationery, $15,000. For incidental expenses, the quartermaster asked a single sum of $475,000; for transportation, a single sum of $2,360,000.[10] The Navy Department likewise had succeeded in clinging to some major lump-sum heads. The bureau of construction, equipment, and repair sent in an estimate of over $2,500,000 for construction and repairs; of $840,000 for fuel; and of $300,000 for the purchase of hemp *and other materials* for the navy.[11] These and similar heads had been carried from the time of the Jeffersonians.

If the army and the navy were recalcitrant, in accordance with old tradition, the civil departments bowed to the edict of Congress. Their estimates were in detail, and members could not complain for lack of information.[12] Even the army and navy presented a mass of detailed estimates, notably for personnel and for construction.

From the beginning there had been informal consultation between the Treasury and the departments on the one hand, and the chairmen of the finance committees of the two Houses on the other. During the Jacksonian period these committees became more exacting in their demands for explanation of proposed expenditures, and tended to resort to written as well as informal communication. The process of justification was taking form, although still in an early stage.

The annual reports of the several departments gave Congress a general view of departmental programs and plans, and frequently contained specific requests for remedial legislation or for added resources. They were not adequate to support the exact amounts that appeared in the estimates, and both the House Ways and Means Committee and the Senate Finance Committee required more convincing data and arguments. Thus in 1835 the Ways and Means Committee asked explanations for

10 *Ibid.*, pp. 161–65.

11 *Ibid.*, p. 280; italics are author's.

12 To build a hospital at Key West, Congress was requested to provide, among other materials, one string piece 86 feet, 8 inches by 10 inches, $11.48; eight floor joists, $4.00; three partition doors, $10.00; and four pieces of scantling, $1.18. *Ibid.*, pp. 182–86.

the lighthouse estimates; [13] in 1836 inquiries were made concerning the estimates for fortifications; [14] and in 1841 Chairman Millard Fillmore of the Ways and Means Committee sent a nine-point interrogatory to the commissioner of Indian affairs, concluding "on looking at my red marks you will see many other things on which I desire a brief explanation." [15] Many examples of Fillmore's inquisitions on behalf of the Ways and Means Committee are available in his *Papers.* Thus he asked for the reasons why Secretary of the Navy Abel P. Upshur requested $5,000 for contingent expenses instead of the prevailing sum of $3,000; proposed a ceiling of not over five or six million dollars for naval expenditures for 1842–43 and asked him to reveal the items that could best be cut; and required detailed statements of the amounts estimated for hospital repairs.[16] When Polk was chairman of the Ways and Means Committee he considered it his duty "to have constant intercourse with Executive Department,—in regard to the various appropriations which passed through that committee. . . ." [17]

The correspondence between the financial committees and the departments had a quality often quite modern in its character. In 1842, Congressman Fillmore put the various agencies under strict scrutiny. The head of the Library of Congress explained anxiously why he had proposed to have a floor of hydraulic cement laid, and offered to sell the two carpets then in use (which contained a great quantity of dust), and some old furniture to help offset the expense. The Secretary of the Treasury defended an additional item of $250 for labor because the senior messenger was too disabled by rheumatism to bring up wood and coal from the basement. The Navy bureau of medicine and surgery defended its contingent fund of $450 by calling attention to "what the bureau *saves* the Government," and reminded Fillmore that while enough food was as good as a feast,

13 National Archives, Treasury Department, Letters to Cabinet and Bureaus, Set B, No. 1, p. 177 (Jan. 13, 1835).

14 House Doc. 56, 24th Cong., 2d sess. (Dec. 28, 1836).

15 House Report 75a, 27th Cong., 2d sess., pp. 1–2 (Dec. 31, 1841).

16 *Fillmore Papers,* II, 226 (Jan. 15, 1842); II, 227 (Jan. 19, 1842); II, 236 (April 29, 1842).

17 Joseph H. Parks, ed., "Letters from James K. Polk to Samuel H. Laughlin, 1835–1844," East Tennessee Historical Society, *Publications,* No. 18 (1946), p. 153.

with less than enough a man could not live long. The sixth auditor asked the Ways and Means Committee to reflect on his additional work and his need for a horse in view of the removal of his office from the central Treasury building.[18]

Substantial reductions were made by Congress in the estimates, although the great bulk, including appropriations for officers and clerks, maintenance of public buildings, supplies and materials, foreign service expenditures, and the operating expenses of the army and navy, were usually accepted much as proposed. In 1842, a year of retrenchment, the Ways and Means Committee struck out slightly over $300,000 in an appropriation of over $7,500,000 for civil and diplomatic expenditures.[19] The Committee on Public Buildings and Grounds eliminated all but "a small portion of the sums" requested by the departments and the commissioner of public buildings.[20] After the depression of 1857, John Sherman reported that the Ways and Means Committee had cut down estimates by about $1,230,000.[21]

Notwithstanding these cuts, appropriations normally exceeded estimates, even in hard times. From 1823 to 1837 inclusive the appropriations were regularly one million dollars in excess of estimates, and usually several million.[22] The excess was due in part to various unpredictable items, such as judgments against the United States, refund of duties, claims, treaty awards, and Indian wars; in part to decisions of Congress in favor of public buildings, river and harbor improvements, increased pay to the army and navy, and pensions.[23] Congress intended to force the executive departments to disclose in detail their expenditure plans, but this object had no relation to its own independent program of appropriating public funds for such purposes as it deemed suitable. The deflationary consequences of itemization were more than balanced by the inflationary tendencies of Congressmen.

Consideration of the estimates by the House Ways and Means

18 House Doc. 39, 27th Cong., 3d sess., *passim* (Jan. 4, 1843).

19 House Report 44, 27th Cong., 2d sess., p. 1 (Jan. 25, 1842).

20 House Report 879, 27th Cong., 2d sess., p. 1 (June 21, 1842).

21 Sherman, *Recollections*, I, 184.

22 Senate Doc. 497, 25th Cong., 2d sess., *passim* (June 29, 1838).

23 See Senate Doc. 15, 22d Cong., 2d sess., for a statement of estimates and expenditures for the support of government, 1791–1831.

Committee and the Senate Finance Committee constituted in principle an effective means of congressional control of the executive agencies. It operated as such, but apparently without system or general appreciation of its institutional character. A particular estimate was in view, not a theory of governmental relationships.

LUMP-SUM OR SPECIFIC APPROPRIATION HEADS

The struggle to retain or to restrict executive discretion in expenditures turned on four other major issues: the itemization of *appropriations;* limitation of authority to transfer funds from one appropriation head to another; the control of deficiencies; and the prevention of expenditures or commitments unauthorized by the legislative branch. In addition Congress controlled official discretion by many specific prohibitions as to the use of money.

An obvious way for Congress to control executive agents was to specify in detail the precise amounts and objects of expenditure. Where this procedure was feasible it was followed, notably with respect to appropriations to pay the salaries of executive officers and clerks. Departmental leeway was secured in narrow limits by appropriations for extra clerk hire. Funds for supplies were appropriated in small sums for each office. Appropriations for public buildings, fortifications, and other public works were separately designated, as well as for maintenance of each of the several executive buildings in Washington. The rivers and harbors bill comprised a long list of specific appropriations for particular projects. In these and other enactments, there was no drift away from close itemization during the years from 1830 to 1860.

Itemization of appropriations in the armed services was more difficult. Indeed, the services declared it was impossible, and they succeeded in obtaining from Jackson's day to the end of Buchanan's administration a number of lump-sum appropriations that left them ample freedom of operations. In fact, the form of the military and naval service appropriation act was substantially unchanged. Control by itemization of appropriations thus made little progress in two areas accounting for about one-half of total expenditures.

Amos Kendall, as fourth auditor, proposed a means of avoiding the restrictive effect of itemized appropriations while retaining effective congressional control over naval expenditures. He recommended specific departmental *estimates,* an *appropriation* in gross, and an annual accounting under each head of the estimates. But Congress was not receptive to giving the navy a general fund applicable to all naval purposes, even though it were subsequently informed as to variations in expenditure from the estimates.[24]

Kendall held to his plan, however, and when he drafted the post office reorganization bill of 1836 introduced it into legislation that passed Congress—apparently without any member of Congress being aware of the innovation that they were approving.[25] "The design," according to John Quincy Adams, "was not apparent on the face of the bill—it was disguised under a provision requiring of him specific estimates; and now, in his report, he says his object has been to *substitute* specific accountability instead of specific appropriations."[26]

The Post Office Department estimates for 1838 were submitted under the required headings; the chairman of the House Ways and Means Committee then moved to appropriate a single aggregate sum of $4,694,000; Adams promptly objected. On behalf of the Post Office Department, Representative Charles E. Haynes of Georgia argued that a specific appropriation would endanger the operations of a department "so subject to constant change and extension" and that inconvenience could only be avoided by giving the head of the Post Office a discretionary power "which it would be manifestly improper to confide to any other department of the Government."[27] Adams demanded a roll call, and the motion in favor of a single lump-sum appropriation was lost, 64 to 66. Thus narrowly did an experiment in appropriation procedure fail. Congress in fact gained little

24 Senate Doc. 1, 21st Cong., 1st sess., p. 274 (Nov. 30, 1829).

25 5 Stat. 80 (July 2, 1836). Section two required specific estimates under each of twelve designated heads; section three provided that "the aggregate sum . . . shall be appropriated by law out of the revenue of the Department"; section twelve required the accounts to be kept under the same headings as those specified for the estimates.

26 Adams, *Memoirs,* IX, 514–15 (March 24, 1838).

27 *Congressional Globe,* 25th Cong., 2d sess., pp. 257–58 (March 24, 1838).

beyond a reaffirmation of principle, for the amounts appropriated under the specified headings ranged from $6,000 to $3,400,000, including an item of $40,000 for "miscellaneous." [28]

In 1842 Congress tied down the contingency appropriations, which had long been an object of suspicion among members, by painstakingly specifying for each of thirty-seven agencies and subordinate divisions three or four subitems with a figure attached to each.[29] This was done for the declared purpose of limiting incidental and contingency appropriations to specific objects as far as possible. Congress was pushing Gallatin's theory of legislative supremacy to an extreme point, unmindful of the executive view that it "is impossible to estimate, with minute precision, as to all the various items or heads of expenditures. . . ." [30]

TRANSFERS

The primary escape from a specific appropriation was to transfer sums from one appropriation head to another. Recourse to transfers had been regulated by the act of 1820, and more drastic action was threatened by Congress from time to time in the sense of an absolute prohibition. The act of 1820 specified what transfers the President could make and forbade all others, and ended, it was supposed, the transfer of funds appropriated for the service of one year to that of another.[31]

The tide of executive freedom to transfer funds flowed in and out during the Jacksonian period. In 1834 the President was authorized to transfer naval funds from any branch of the service to any other between the close of the year and the passage of the next year's appropriation act—usually a period of several months.[32] In 1836 the President was authorized to transfer appropriations for fortifications from one to another. In 1838 authority to transfer post office funds was granted to the President.[33] Finally in 1842 general authority was vested in the heads of departments to transfer surpluses from one item to another

28 5 Stat. 223 (April 6, 1838).

29 5 Stat. 523, sec. 22 (August 26, 1842).

30 House Doc. 39, 27th Cong., 3d sess., p. 8 (Dec. 18, 1842).

31 3 Stat. 567 (May 1, 1820).

32 4 Stat. 742 (June 30, 1834).

33 5 Stat. 78 (July 2, 1836); 5 Stat. 216, 223 (April 6, 1838).

in the same department—the appropriation for newspapers excepted.[34]

The Navy Department lost all authority to transfer almost immediately, at the instance of John Quincy Adams.[35] It had indeed been stubborn in refusing to accept congressional efforts to control its expenditures. In 1829 Amos Kendall, fourth auditor, had told Congress that the whole object of specific appropriations had been defeated by irregular and unlawful Navy practices.[36] Now it suffered the consequences. The War Department was curtailed by the army appropriation act of 1852, putting matters back again to the limited authority conveyed by the legislation of 1820.[37] The civil agencies, however, continued to retain the authority granted in 1842 to transfer surpluses from one office to another.

The question arose, what was a surplus? An old enactment had required that any appropriation remaining unexpended after two years should cease and revert to the Treasury surplus fund. This requirement was reenacted in 1852, and the Treasury surplus fund further protected against diversion.[38] It consequently became to the advantage of the departments to prevent their surpluses from capture by the Treasury. This special interest was completely secured by opinions of the Secretary of the Treasury, the first comptroller, and the Attorney General, the net result of which was to read "unexpended" to mean an *unobligated* appropriation and thus to defeat the clear intent of Congress.[39]

Congress finally closed the door to transfers by repealing the general authorization given in 1842 and already withdrawn from the navy and the army.[40] The War Department still retained power to transfer appropriations for subsistence and forage and in the commissary and medical departments, but the discretionary powers of other departments ceased. This drastic

[34] 5 Stat. 523, sec. 23 (August 26, 1842).

[35] 5 Stat. 579, sec. 11 (August 31, 1842); Adams, *Memoirs,* XI, 245 (August 30, 1842). The Navy at this time had lost the confidence of Congress.

[36] Senate Doc. 1, 21st Cong., 1st sess., p. 273 (Nov. 30, 1829).

[37] 10 Stat. 105, sec. 2 (August 31, 1852).

[38] 1 Stat. 433, sec. 16 (March 3, 1795); 10 Stat. 76, sec. 10 (August 31, 1852).

[39] Wilmerding, Jr., *The Spending Power,* pp. 110–14.

[40] 12 Stat. 103, sec. 2 (June 23, 1860).

solution, however, was quickly nullified by the outbreak of the Civil War.

The attempt to operate the government on the basis of specific appropriations and to enforce the terms of the appropriation act by forbidding transfers could hardly succeed. Congress itself vacillated, and the great spending departments—War and Navy—stubbornly resisted, declaring in substance that an army and a navy could not be sustained on such a theory. In effect, Congress concurred, for the basic military and naval appropriation heads remained lump sums. For the rest, the executive branch construed legislative prohibitions with such liberality as to cause the administration of the public business relatively little embarrassment.

DEFICIENCIES

The departments had found one other means of escape from the limitations imposed by Congress, viz., to create deficiencies and then ask Congress for additional money to meet a moral if not a legal obligation. Congress was thus placed in an awkward dilemma, left with no real alternative but to appropriate.

The situation became acute in the 1850's and caused a congressional storm. The deficiency for the fiscal year 1850 was over $2,800,000 and in the succeeding six years fluctuated between $2,500,000 and $5,500,000.[41] Members severely criticized this escape from legislative control in discussing the deficiency appropriation for 1858. "I hold," declared Galusha A. Grow of Pennsylvania, "that the Department is bound to keep within the regular appropriations by Congress. Otherwise, we have no control over the expenses of the Government." [42] Representative Garnett of Virginia called upon Thomas Jefferson in reproving the executive branch.

> It was a cardinal principle taught by the States-rights Republicans of Mr. Jefferson's day, that no money should be drawn from the Treasury except by appropriation by Congress, and no expenditures made except by express legislative sanction. By all the minuteness of specific appropriations Congress was to prescribe not only on what objects money might be expended, but *how much* on each object.

41 Figures from *Congressional Globe,* 35th Cong., 1st sess., p. 1501 (April 6, 1858).
42 *Ibid.,* p. 1495.

. . . But it is vain for us to attempt to limit the expenses of Government, if when, after due consultation with the Executive Departments, we have determined the amount we are willing to sanction, the Executive may exceed the limit as far as it pleases, and call on us to approve the excess, under the name of a deficiency.[43]

Congressman Burnett of Kentucky declared, "there is an evident and growing disposition, on the part of the executive department of the Government, to absorb all the powers of the legislative branch. . . . We find that this system of deficiency bills is rapidly growing; and that, unless it is checked by the legislative department of the Government, there is no telling where it will end." [44]

No one rose to defend the executive branch. An old hand admitted that deficiency bills were an evil, but maintained that it was a necessary one.[45] Impeachment had been suggested as a remedy, but it was clearly not appropriate. Representative Miles Taylor of Louisiana demanded that a special session of Congress be called to consider supplementary funds rather than to leave the executive free.[46] Many years later Congress was ready to send to jail any officer who incurred a deficiency but this remedy, not thought of in the 1850's, likewise proved without value. Deficiencies continued to arise, and Congress continued to appropriate to cover them. To this extent, the executive branch retained considerable freedom of action in following *established lines of expenditure*. It could not go far beyond.

UNAUTHORIZED COMMITMENTS

Deficiencies were normally incurred in the regular course of administration for the purposes or objects that had been already sanctioned by Congress or that were closely related thereto. There was also some complaint that executive agencies made commitments for purposes not authorized by legislation. The point was raised in the perceptive report of Representative Thomas W. Gilmer of Virginia in 1842 for the House Select

43 *Ibid.*, p. 1501.
44 *Ibid.*, p. 1503.
45 *Ibid.*, p. 1496.
46 *Ibid.*, pp. 1504–5.

Committee on Retrenchment, in disapproval of a practice that he declared had long prevailed "and to a pernicious extent."

. . . . Under color of what are termed *regulations,* large amounts of money are often applied to purposes never contemplated by the appropriating power, and numerous offices are sometimes actually created in the same way. It appears, from the testimony submitted, that the accounting officers of the Treasury feel themselves "bound to presume that these regulations are pursuant to law." These are dangerous precedents, and deserve the prompt rebuke of Congress. The peculiar and exclusive prerogatives of the legislative power may be thus assumed by the Executive. The whole revenues of the Government may be misapplied, and all limitations on appropriations set at defiance, if those whose duty it is to see that the disbursements conform to law are at liberty to recognise any other authority as paramount to the expressed commands or prohibitions of the legislative power. Such a recognition of Executive supremacy is fatal to the best-considered checks and balances of our scheme of government. It destroys the equilibrium of the system, and annihilates a power which the people, through their immediate representatives, have always claimed as indispensable to the existence of every representative government.[47]

The nature and effect of the power to make regulations that would support expenditures appeared in testimony given by the second auditor, William B. Lewis, before the Gilmer Committee.

Q. If the Secretary of War should insist on the payment of salary . . . would you feel bound to allow the claim if no law existed for its allowance?
A. No, not unless it was authorized either by law or regulation. . . .
Q. Do you consider such regulations binding on you officially?
A. Where they do not conflict with positive acts of Congress or decisions of the Supreme Court of the United States, I do.[48]

The committee roundly condemned this practice of expenditure based on regulation, but the passing years showed no trend away from such executive discretion. Administrative necessities prevailed, not over law, but in the interstices of law.

47 House Report 741, 27th Cong., 2d sess., pp. 17–18 (May 23, 1842).
48 *Ibid.,* pp. 53–54.

The Committee on Public Expenditures also discovered what it thought a dangerous situation in the revenue cutter service. "This is," the committee reported, "a naval force springing up amongst us, controlled by the Secretary of the Treasury, accountable to no one but him, extended at will by him, supported by him out of the revenue before it gets into the Treasury, and may cost the country whatever he shall direct. He appropriates and pays, without the sanction of Congress, and even without its knowledge. The country knows nothing of the expenditure, unless called for by either House. The collectors of the ports pay the expenses of this Treasury navy, and the Secretary of the Treasury approves or rejects the expenditures. The crews, ships, and boats, are subject to their order, for pleasure, interest, or public service." [49]

Another aspect of the same problem was the conclusion of contracts in advance of appropriations, "thus," as John Sherman argued in the House, "compelling Congress to sanction them or violate the public faith." [50] This was a difficult issue, since the army and navy supply agencies were practically compelled to contract ahead of appropriations. In 1860 Congress forbade any contract unless already authorized by law or by an appropriation adequate to its purpose, army and navy supply contracts excepted.[51]

CONGRESSIONAL CONTROL BY SPECIFIC DIRECTION OR PROHIBITION

The twin powers of legislation and appropriation endowed Congress with authority to control the conduct of administration to a theoretically extreme degree. Specific statutory direction of work to be done was the usual procedure for public works projects, such as river and harbor improvements and fortifications. The ordinary flow of work through the departments and agencies was not, however, specified by legislation, but left to executive direction within broad statutory assignments of functions.

Careful members of Congress were alert to refrain from mak-

49 House Report 756, 27th Cong., 2d sess., p. 6 (May 25, 1842).
50 Sherman, *Recollections,* I, 155.
51 12 Stat. 91, sec. 3 (June 23, 1860).

ing administrative decisions for the executive. Thus by way of illustration, Senator Lewis Cass protested against a bill to require the navy to install a specified type of condenser in its vessels. He declared:

I repeat, this is a question of administration. Why should you legislate as to a particular condenser any more than a particular boiler, or the breech of a musket, or the size of a cannon, or any other improvement that may take place in any measure required in the operations of the Government? . . . If the Executive wants authority to do this, I am perfectly willing to vote an appropriation, to be placed at the control of the Navy Department, to enable them to put the best condenser in the vessels of the Navy of the United States. That is all that can be properly required.[52]

Occasional exceptions modified the normal balance between the executive and legislative branches. Thus in 1839 the War Department complained that Congress, in addition to specifying particular public works, also stated in the appropriation act that the work was to be performed "agreeably to the plan and estimate made by Hartman Bache, of the engineering corps." Congress was justified, the Department agreed, in requiring a plan and estimate, but to incorporate them in the appropriation act rendered it impossible to modify the plan in the light of further information or experience.[53] Appropriations for extra clerk hire, tied to a particular office, also gave trouble. The commissioner of the General Land Office asked Congress to avoid this restriction and said frankly that the extra clerks were used in fact where the need was greatest.[54]

Occasionally Presidents had to remind Congress that the legislative branch did not possess the executive power. In 1860 the Washington aqueduct was in process of construction. In the sundry civil appropriation act for 1860–61 a rider was inserted terminating the office of engineer of the Potomac waterworks and specifying that its duties be discharged by the chief engineer, Captain Montgomery C. Meigs, an officer in the corps of engineers. The effect of this proviso was to assign an army

52 *Congressional Globe,* 32d Cong., 1st sess., p. 2448 (August 30, 1852).

53 5 Stat. 183 (March 3, 1837); House Doc. 2, 26th Cong., 1st sess., p. 48 (Nov. 30, 1839).

54 House Doc. 5, 24th Cong., 1st sess., p. 2 (Dec. 5, 1835).

officer to a particular duty by statute. Buchanan told Congress that if this was the necessary interpretation of the clause, he would have vetoed it without hesitation as an encroachment on the executive power. He rejected this as an "impossible" interpretation and told Congress that he did not consider himself bound by it. "How demoralizing," said Buchanan, "[would be] its effect upon the *morale* of the army, if it should become a precedent for future legislation. Officers might then be found, instead of performing their appropriate duties, besieging the halls of Congress for the purpose of obtaining special and choice places by legislative enactment." [55]

Positive directions on particular cases were less common than general or special *prohibitions.* Consider for example the reforming act of 1842, encompassing a number of small matters that had been accumulating on the congressional docket. It repeated rules against extra allowances and strictly limited the appointment of extra clerks; it forbade every department except State to spend more than one hundred dollars for newspapers and denied the use of contingent funds to purchase books, periodicals, pictures, or engravings except by the written order of the head of the department; it required a detailed report of expenditures from contingency funds; it set the maximum salary of the dragoman at Constantinople; and it forbade any expenditures for commissions of inquiry (except courts-martial or naval courts of inquiry) unless specifically appropriated for by Congress.[56] This action against executive commissions of inquiry followed promptly after Tyler had appointed three persons as a commission to report on the degree of skill, fidelity, and economy with which public works in Washington were being constructed.[57]

A similar stringent ban directed against the commissioner of the patent office through the Secretary of the Interior occurred in 1859. The commissioner had called an agricultural conference in Washington in 1858, defraying the expenses out of such funds as were available. Congress indignantly reprimanded such an excursion into a governmental field occupied by the states

55 House Ex. Doc. 101, 36th Cong., 1st sess., p. 2 (June 25, 1860).
56 5 Stat. 523 (August 26, 1842).
57 Webster, *Writings and Speeches* (National ed.), XII, 216–17 (March 27, 1841).

by providing in the next appropriation act that no part of it should be used to defray the expenses "of any body of men or delegates assembled in Washington or elsewhere as an agricultural congress, or advisory board on agriculture, convened under the orders of the Secretary of the Interior, or any other person under any name or for any pretended object whatever." [58] Such a prohibition, had it become set in the law, would have made impossible the use of consultants or advisers for any purpose.

Congress was thus engaged, during the Jacksonian years, in a long battle to realize its full control of federal expenditures. Its principle of action was prescribed in the Constitution and was stated forcefully by Representative John Sherman. "The theory of our government," he declared, "is, that a specific sum shall be appropriated by a *law* originating in this House, for a specific purpose, and within a given fiscal year. It is the duty of the executive to use that sum, and no more, especially for that purpose, and no other, and within the time fixed." [59] Congress never succeeded in making such a rigid interpretation of the Constitution a reality. It did not appropriate specific sums for the armed services; it regularly held appropriations open for two years; it did not punish executives for using more money than had been appropriated nor for requiring more time than had been planned.

The executive branch, on its side, found means, where necessary or useful, to avoid or to evade many of the fiscal limitations that Congress deemed it proper to impose. It drew the teeth out of some requirements by interpretation, it pleaded necessity in other cases, it confused Congress by its accounts, it made commitments that Congress had to honor, and it spent more than Congress had appropriated. In all of this there was a ready acquiescence on the part of individual Congressmen or party factions that wanted some particular payment made or task undertaken. The interests of the Congressmen were often different from and contrary to the interests of Congress. So also the interests of administration were often contrary to the requirements of an appropriation act.

58 11 Stat. 427 (March 3, 1859).
59 Sherman, *Recollections,* I, 155.

Nevertheless, the basic theory of the Constitution and of the organic legislation was not challenged. It was agreed by heads of departments, bureau chiefs, and accounting officers alike that money could be drawn from the Treasury only with the authority of law. The issue was to harmonize administrative efficiency with the terms of appropriation acts.

CHAPTER EIGHT

Congress and Administration

The relations between Congress and the executive agencies were not confined to the struggle for power that has been described in previous chapters. In the day-by-day activities of individual Congressmen and in the work of the House and Senate committees there were endless contacts between the two branches marked normally by cooperation and mutual accommodation. Although it was true that the executive branch was dependent on the legislative in ways fundamental, it was also true that Congressmen were dependent on the executive departments. A number of these points of mutual accommodation remain to be explored: the dependence of Congressmen on the executive departments to take care of the problems of their constituents, and to furnish information on all sorts of matters as well as drafts of bills; the duty of Congress to investigate the operations of the public agencies to expose misfeasance and promote efficiency; the obligation of Congress to avoid executive waste and extravagance; and the transfer from Congress to a new agency of the responsibility for settling claims having only a moral, not a legal foundation. The interplay of Congressmen and the executive departments in making appointments has already been considered; and other examples of congressional-executive relationships will appear in the chapters that follow. The whole administrative process, indeed, was influenced by the common interest of both the legislative and executive branches in its conduct and its consequences. Constitutional doctrines of separation of powers faded before the necessities of government and the opportunities of Congressmen.

CONSTITUENT BUSINESS

We may begin by observing that Congressmen were more and more oppressed by "constituent business," i.e., performing errands and transacting private affairs for their constituents. This phase of a Congressman's duty was not unknown in earlier years, but with a new spirit of democracy and a much enlarged body of voters it moved into new dimensions. The great were burdened as well as the humble, as the experience of John Quincy Adams and James K. Polk makes perfectly evident.

Adams, as is well known, sat in the House of Representatives from 1831 until his death in 1848. His diary is full of records of calls upon the various departments on behalf of his constituents. Thus, by way of example, he went to the Secretary of War to correct the date of the pension certificate of Asa Lapham; he obtained for an antiquarian a copy of the certificate of discharge of a Revolutionary War soldier named Oliver; he conferred with the Secretary of the Treasury about the reappointment of the collector at Plymouth; and left with the Postmaster General "nine several letters of application for post-offices or mail agencies" while on his way to the Secretary of State to urge "the Rev. Charles Sewell's claim to a devise in Germany. I mentioned to him the names and claims of Hodgson, Homer, Todson, and Offley." [1]

Representative James K. Polk was as methodical as Adams, and fortunately he preserved the record of his work for his constituents during the 1831–32 session.[2] Most of the help he was asked to give concerned pension claims, the establishment of post offices, and land claims. A great variety of constituent business pressed upon him, however; a claim for property destroyed by Indians and a request for information about bidding on an Indian contract; an appointment as midshipman, and the transmission of letters for an appointment at West Point; a claim for extra services in the War of 1812; a search for a letter in the dead-letter office, and so on.

1 Adams, *Memoirs,* IX, 219 (March 11, 1835); IX, 227 (March 30, 1835); X, 108 (March 25, 1839); X, 423–24 (Feb. 16, 1841); X, 465 (April 19, 1841).

2 "James K. Polk and his Constituents, 1831–1832," in *American Historical Review,* XXVIII (1922–23), 68–77. Papers of public men are full of this sort of activity. For another example, see *Fillmore Papers, passim.*

Treasury letters to Congressmen also revealed a wide variety and a large number of cases in which constituents asked help from their Representatives.[3] Merchants and shipowners sought help in getting remission of fines and forfeitures; army officers sought transfer from one post to another; a claimant for land asked to be heard by the General Land Office; a bondsman desired release from his obligation; a New York Congressman urged the Treasury to procure marble or granite for the New York customhouse in his own state—and doubtless for one of his enterprising constituents.

The drain on the time of department heads and clerks in providing answers to such requests, in addition to the formal demands for reports and information for committees, was heavy. Secretary Poinsett wrote a friend, "When congress is not here I can despatch my business at the office; but during the session I am obliged to bring it home; for it rarely happens that from 9 to 2 I am alone five minutes." [4]

EXECUTIVE INFORMATION SERVICE

Much of the business of Congress, as editor Hezekiah Niles observed in 1834, depended materially upon the annual and special reports of the executive agencies.[5] Occasionally a Congressman would resent this, but the old fear of executive domination by means of its reports and recommendations had receded. On technical matters such as patents, Congressmen were particularly dependent on executive advice. Senator Jefferson Davis emphasized the point. "I do not hesitate," he said to one of his colleagues, "to tell him that, unaided by the officers of the bureau, or those equally familiar with it, the Senate is, in my opinion, unable wisely to legislate upon the minute details of patents and the Patent Office. I think it would not detract from the Senate, but be acting the part of prudence, to go to those who have special information before legislating upon such subjects." [6]

3 National Archives, Treasury Department, Letters and Reports to Congress, Series E., *passim*.

4 "Poinsett-Campbell Correspondence," *South Carolina Historical and Genealogical Magazine*, XLII (1941), 166 (Oct. 17, 1837).

5 *Niles Register*, XLVII, 233 (Dec. 13, 1834).

6 Davis, *Letters, Papers and Speeches*, II, 5 (Dec. 19, 1850).

At almost any point of legislative business, whether technical or not, the executive agencies were likely to be called on for information, and a steady stream of reports went to congressional committees. These were strictly informative in nature, with no suggestion of potential criticism or reproof in the making of the request. The reports formed a normal part of the lawmaking process. The curiosity of Congress not infrequently exceeded the capacity of the departments to satisfy it. Amos Kendall had to tell the House that to comply with a request for information on extra allowances to each naval lieutenant would require an examination of "cart loads of papers," keeping three or four clerks busy for nearly a year. Kendall was not evasive, but the task was too great.[7] Thoughtful members of Congress were appalled at the burden and cost involved in irresponsible requests. "Congress," it was said, "often subjects the Treasury to very large and perfectly useless expense, employing many regular and sometimes extra clerks for weeks and months in preparing what is never applied to any further purpose, except to be printed at an additional expense." [8]

Before the Jacksonian era Congress had established a regular reporting system designed to present important basic data showing trends in the economy and the operations of the administrative system.[9] The reporting system was extended from 1830 to 1860, particularly with reference to financial transactions and establishments. Fiscal reports from the departments, supplementing the annual Treasury reports, were required in 1842. By this enactment each department was required to show expenditures from its contingent fund.[10] Other laws required regular reports of expenditures on buildings and grounds, in each customhouse, on the Coast Survey, and extra allowances to post office contractors.[11]

The basic general requirement of annual reports on contracts

7 House Doc. 132, 22d Cong., 1st sess., p. 3 (Feb. 25, 1832).

8 House Report 741, 27th Cong., 2d sess., pp. 21–22 (May 23, 1842).

9 For a list of the reports to be made to Congress, see House Doc. 1, 23d Cong., 2d sess. (Dec. 1, 1834).

10 5 Stat. 523, sec. 20 (August 26, 1842).

11 6 Stat. 815, sec. 9 (July 21, 1840); 9 Stat. 398, sec. 6 (March 3, 1849); 10 Stat. 189, sec. 2 (March 3, 1853); 5 Stat. 80, sec. 22 (July 2, 1836).

made by the respective departments had been enacted in 1808. It was extended to cover contracts for the transportation of the mail in 1836, and contracts for ocean transportation of the mail in 1845. Congress also required an annual report of any postal contractor guilty of entering a combination to interfere with competitive bidding on mail contracts.[12]

One other subject engaged the attention of Congress: the number, names, and compensation of persons employed by the respective departments. This requirement, originally made in 1818, was extended in 1842.[13] It was specifically applied to each customhouse in 1849 and to the Coast Survey in 1853.[14] The rule of publicity was thus enforced on finance, contracts, and employment; and from time to time Congress required special reports on these and other phases of administrative operations. Each House of Congress also required its clerk to prepare annually a statement of all appropriations, a list of all new offices with the salaries of each, and a statement of all increases in salary.[15]

Congress depended on the departments to draft bills, having no special service of the kind within its own organization. Thus, by way of example, the reorganization of the General Land Office in 1836 was based on a bill drafted by Commissioner Ethan A. Brown.[16] The bill for reorganizing the Navy Department in 1842 was written by Secretary Upshur and submitted with some very sensible recommendations to the House Committee on Naval Affairs.[17] The bill providing for the Department of the Interior was drafted by the Treasury at the request of Chairman Vinton of the Ways and Means Committee. He had no hesitation in informing the House that the bill "with one or two unimportant

[12] 2 Stat. 484 (April 21, 1808); 5 Stat. 80, sec. 22 (July 2, 1836); 5 Stat. 748 (March 3, 1845); 5 Stat. 80, sec. 28.

[13] 3 Stat. 445, sec. 9 (April 20, 1818); 5 Stat. 525 (August 26, 1842).

[14] 9 Stat. 398, sec. 6 (March 3, 1849); 10 Stat. 189, sec. 2 (March 3, 1853).

[15] 5 Stat. 117, sec. 6 (July 4, 1836). The first report of this series is found in Senate Doc. 427, 24th Cong., 1st sess. (July 11, 1836). In 1842, a year of retrenchment, only three salary increases were recorded: the assistant librarian of the Library of Congress from $800 to $1,150; the library messenger from $300 to $700; and a clerk in the office of the Secretary of the Navy, from $800 to $1,000. Senate Doc. 444, 27th Cong., 2d sess., p. 47 (Oct. 10, 1842).

[16] Senate Doc. 216, 24th Cong., 1st sess., pp. 1–2 (March 2, 1836).

[17] House Doc. 167, 27th Cong., 2d sess., pp. 1–2 (March 7, 1842).

alterations made by the Committee of Ways and Means . . . was the bill as it came from the hands of the Secretary of the Treasury." [18]

In 1858 Congress requested the Secretary of the Treasury to report a plan (already recommended by him) for reducing the expense of collecting the revenue.[19] Howell Cobb drafted a bill including such radical changes that it found less than the necessary support in Congress. It eliminated 41 ports of entry and 21 ports of delivery, reduced the number of employees, discontinued contracts for rent of customhouses as rapidly as possible, and transferred the revenue cutter service to the navy.[20] Irrespective of the fate of particular proposals, the fears of timid Jeffersonians about executive domination of Congress through departmental reports had obviously evaporated.

CONGRESSIONAL INVESTIGATIONS

From the beginning to the end of the Jacksonian period, Congress was busy investigating the executive branch. Reports of investigating committees were often partisan affairs and their conclusions have to be read with caution. On the other hand much of the evidence they heard and much of the information they gathered was reliable and is useful in reconstructing the administrative history of these three decades.[21]

The several committees on expenditures in the departments, set up in the House of Representatives by the Jeffersonians, were inactive during the Jacksonian period, having been crowded out by the Committee on Ways and Means and by the committees on substantive legislation. They were useful havens to which the Speaker could assign members with whose unfitness as legislators he had been impressed.[22] The Committee on Public Expenditures was also inactive except for one burst of energy during the 27th Congress (1841–43). These were the years of conflict between President Tyler and Congress, and also years during

18 *Congressional Globe,* 30th Cong., 2d sess., p. 514 (Feb. 12, 1849).

19 11 Stat. 337 (June 14, 1858).

20 House Ex. Doc. 55, 35th Cong., 2d sess. (Jan. 15, 1859).

21 On this subject see Lauros G. McConachie, *Congressional Committees* (New York: Thomas Y. Crowell, 1898); and Marshall Edward Dimock, *Congressional Investigating Committees* (Baltimore: Johns Hopkins Press, 1929).

22 L. G. McConachie, *op. cit.,* p. 234.

which retrenchment and reform were lively issues. At this time the Committee on Public Expenditures looked into matters general and particular, producing reports on the executive departments, the New York customhouse, the reduction of salaries, contracts for mail bags, Indian affairs, and public buildings. On the other hand the standing Committee on Expenditures in Public Buildings was constantly active. Expenditures on the Capitol Building, the Executive Mansion, the departmental buildings, and some structures in the field were investigated, often with devastating results.

Other investigations were made by the regular standing committees and by select committees. The latter tended to deal with particular scandals, such as the management of the New York customhouse. Some of the principal cases are noted in the following paragraphs.

A full-scale investigation of the post office was made in 1834–35 by both the Senate and the House. Its findings resulted in a post-office reorganization and a new head of the department. A House inquiry of 1836 proposed reorganization of the customs service in general accordance with a plan already recommended by Secretary of the Treasury Woodbury. No change was forthcoming. In his 1836 annual message, Jackson asserted that the Executive departments were well managed, in a passage that gave the Whigs an opportunity to set up a select committee to make an examination of the record. The report was a partisan document of defense by the committee majority and of condemnation by the minority. Samuel Swartwout's embezzlements in the New York customhouse resulted in an extensive House investigation in which the principal facts were laid bare but without agreement on responsibility. This customhouse had to be investigated again in 1842.

A much more constructive investigation was made in 1842 by the House Select Committee on Retrenchment, Thomas W. Gilmer, chairman. This report led to negligible results, caught as it was in the battle between Tyler and the Whig party. In 1850 a partisan investigation was made of patronage and party activity under Polk, resulting in commendable resolutions that squared neither with Whig nor Democratic practice.

Other investigations ran through the years. The record of

this period ended with two legislative revelations: the ruin of the Brooklyn Navy Yard by the New York politicians, and the political abuse of appointments and contracts under Buchanan, with his connivance if not at his direction. The subject matter of most of these investigations is dealt with at the proper place in subsequent chapters.

One problem of general and continuing significance arose concerning the proper scope of legislative investigations. It was called to mind by John Quincy Adams in the course of the Bank investigation of 1832, instituted to inspect the books and proceedings of the Bank in order to ascertain whether the charter had been violated. Adams argued that the only persons whose conduct was in question were the president and directors of the Bank and that "the first principle of national justice" denied the committee any right to look into the conduct of others. The committee took the opposite view.[23]

That Congress performed a useful function in the course of its many investigations of the executive departments cannot be doubted. They were usually too late to remedy the evil that brought select committees successively into being. They succeeded, however, in turning the spotlight of publicity on evildoing and in arousing indignation over official abuses. The tide was not running toward reform or high standards during these years, and the positive achievements of committee reports were at times discouraging. Nevertheless, some able men in Congress participated in these inquiries, notably Senator George Poindexter of Mississippi and Representative Thomas W. Gilmer of Virginia, and they found in their reports a useful forum to urge a better public service and an end to corruption.

Poindexter had had a long public career in the Territory and State of Mississippi, was a member of the House of Representatives from 1817 to 1819, governor of Mississippi, 1819–21, and a member of the Senate from 1830 to 1835. He had a moody and variable temper and became an unrelenting enemy of Andrew Jackson. In the state election of 1835 he ran for reelection as a Whig but was defeated by Robert J. Walker and withdrew from public life.[24] Thomas W. Gilmer was a strong states' rights

23 House Report 460, 22d Cong., 1st sess., p. 409 (May 14, 1832).

24 *Dictionary of American Biography*, XV, 29.

Virginian, who deserted Jackson in 1833 and joined the Whig party. He was governor of Virginia in 1840 and entered Congress in 1841 where his devotion to economy and old Republican ideals earned him the nickname of "Retrenchment Gilmer." The report of the committee of which he was chairman in 1842 is one of the ablest of the whole period. He became Secretary of the Navy in 1844 and was killed within two weeks by the explosion on the *U.S.S. Princeton*.[25]

CONGRESS AND RETRENCHMENT

Congress discovered again in 1842 how difficult it was to reduce establishments and expenditures.[26] The Gilmer Select Committee on Retrenchment reported ruefully that they had met a want of cooperation and had failed to secure from the departments "any suggestions favorable to a general or systematic reform of those abuses already much complained of. . . ." [27] The committee had invited suggestions from the heads of departments concerning reduction of expenditures and staffs, improvements in the mode of transacting the public business, and ways by which "the aid of the Legislative department of the Government can be of service in rendering the Executive agents more efficient." [28] The response was a general request for more clerks.

Otherwise the departments replied with monotonous uniformity that all was well and that no retrenchment was possible. Secretary of the Navy Upshur stated that he did not know any way to reduce the expenses of his Department. "Its duties are daily *increasing,* and there is now neither room enough nor labor enough to conduct it properly. The Government loses, *by want of proper expenditure upon this Department,* much more than it could hope to save by any possible curtailment of its present inadequate means." [29] The first auditor reported that no reduction of clerks could be made in his office, "compatible with the proper despatch of business and the true in-

25 *Ibid.*, VII, 308.

26 For its initial experience from 1818 to 1820, see White, *The Jeffersonians,* pp. 119–25.

27 House Report 741, 27th Cong., 2d sess., p. 1 (May 23, 1842).

28 *Ibid.*, p. 31.

29 *Ibid.*, pp. 31–32.

terests of the country." [30] The commissioner of the General Land Office denied that his force was disproportionate to its labors. "These statements," he wrote, "are made with no view to invest this branch of the public service with a fictitious consequence, or to make a parade of services. . . . I have, however, always regarded it as true economy to do, as soon as practicable, what was necessary to be done, and for that purpose to employ the necessary force to do it in a reasonable time, and do it well." [31]

The Gilmer Committee was not to be stopped by lack of executive cooperation and boldly proposed to eliminate the second and third auditors, the Board of Navy Commissioners, the commissary general of purchases, and the solicitor and the recorder of the General Land Office; and in addition to reduce the number of clerks across the board.[32] The Navy was already anxious to eliminate the Board of Navy Commissioners, and this was done. The commissioner of the General Land Office had no use for the solicitor, and his office was abolished in 1844. Most other items of retrenchment failed.

Congress was constantly frustrated, in fact, in seeking to reduce operating expenses by any substantial amount. Another attempt was made after the depression of 1857 but without substantial results. The possibility of bludgeoning the executive departments into admissions that they had unnecessary clerks did not exist. Congress itself lacked the will to reduce expenditures by cuts in substantive programs. Senator Jefferson Davis, who had recently retired as head of the War Department, spoke bluntly but with good sense to his economy-minded colleagues. "Much more frequently have I seen recommendations from Executive Departments to change the service so as to promote economy, than I have seen votes in Congress to sustain the recommendations." [33] Referring to a proposal to reduce drastically the size of the army, he replied, "This is not economy; it is not retrenchment; it is declamation. . . ." [34] Declining to agree that $50,000,000 was needed for the year's expenditures,

30 *Ibid.*, p. 140.

31 *Ibid.*, pp. 159–60.

32 *Ibid.*, p. 28 (May 23, 1842).

33 Davis, *Letters, Papers and Speeches,* III, 250–51 (May 25, 1858).

34 *Ibid.*, III, 536 (Feb. 12, 1859).

he continued, "I trust a less sum will suffice; but if more is required to perform the duties of the Government, and to maintain its honorable obligations, I am prepared to maintain it. . . ." [35]

Senator Davis could have found many examples of unaccepted retrenchment offers from the executive departments to support his statement. The reports of Secretary of the Treasury Levi Woodbury during the depression years following 1837 were full of advice to Congress on this point, and the respective departments in fact substantially reduced their requests. "The true question," said Woodbury, "in respect to expenditures, is, not how large burdens can be borne, but how much can be dispensed with. It is not what is splendid, but what is useful and necessary." [36] To make the issue specific, Woodbury pointed to expenditures for the navy, pensions, Indian disbursements, "and a class consisting of lighthouses, fortifications, roads, and improvements in harbors and rivers." [37] Rather than expose the Treasury to bankruptcy, Woodbury would have reduced the compensation of all civil and military officers, executive, legislative, and judicial. In this case, as in others, Congress was not prepared for retrenchment on such a scale.

In fact, in this particular emergency Congress found an easier solution by authorizing the President to postpone expenditures under certain appropriation heads for the army and for fortifications, in an overall amount of nearly $2,200,000. The pressure of local interests was apparent in the latter case by the very awkward proviso that any order of postponement was to be made alike applicable to each fortification—so far as a due regard to the public interests would permit.[38]

Congress, in short, had no suitable agency to guide it in a retrenchment program. There was without doubt much waste and extravagance in contracts for supplies and printing, but these were perquisites that few Congressmen cared to disturb, or indeed even to look into. There was little superfluous employment in the civilian offices, many of which were lamentably

35 *Ibid.*, III, 537 (Feb. 12, 1859).

36 House Doc. 3, 26th Cong., 1st sess., p. 8 (Dec. 3, 1839).

37 *Ibid.*, p. 9.

38 5 Stat. 404 (July 20, 1840); 5 Stat. 407 (July 21, 1840). For results, see report submitted by Van Buren in House Doc. 30, 26th Cong., 2d sess. (Dec. 23, 1840).

understaffed; and the surplusage, mostly in the customhouses and navy yards, was again an asset that Congressmen did not care to disturb. Congress had no means of intelligent inquiry into procedures, the organization of bureaus, the location of field offices, or the due responsibility of subordinate officers, all of which were potential subjects of improvement. As to the reduction of substantive programs—the construction of fortifications, the building of naval vessels, the size of the armed forces, and the like—the issue involved a political decision, and no administrative inquiry was likely to be of assistance. Retrenchment in fact was not in the order of the day.

THE RULE OF PARSIMONY

Former attitudes about public expenditures, dominant especially among the old Republicans, persisted during the Jacksonian years. Spending the taxpayers' money was tinged with a sense of sin, and the less that could be spent the better, except where some local or party benefit was apparent. The Jeffersonians, unhampered by party considerations, were able to harmonize their predilections with their practice; as John Quincy Adams said, "Jonathan lives snug." The Jacksonians inherited the old tradition, and applied it with a will at least to the departmental establishments.

Thrifty Congressman Francis O. J. Smith of Maine raised the doctrine of parsimony to a high and general level of discourse in a report from the Ways and Means Committee in 1836. "Heedless and useless or unavailable expenditure of the public treasury, are alike to be avoided in all legislation. . . . Every Government, like every individual, has a moral being superior to its physical composition; and its moral being, like that of an individual, is susceptible of acquiring habits of lavish expenditure and extravagance in its operations. These habits, by a long course of perseverance, become incurable, and induce, ultimately . . . every species of peculation and corruption among the persons brought within the influence of the Government thus demoralized." Smith resolved to save society by reducing the rivers and harbors appropriations, not an auspicious opening.[39]

39 House Report 297, 24th Cong., 1st sess., pp. 1–2 (Feb. 10, 1836).

If there is a single theme that runs through departmental correspondence with Congress, it is the constant appeal for enough clerks to carry on the ever-mounting volume of business. Congress was consistently reluctant to yield to this perpetual clamor, and the conduct of the public business suffered by delay, at times so great as to amount to a denial of the just rights and expectations of citizens. Secretary Paulding told Congress that the criticisms of the Navy Department—at a low point in its history—originated more from a deficiency of clerks than from any defect in its organization.[40] Surgeon General Lawson of the army indignantly informed Congress that the business of his office could not be well done, or done at all, with his single clerk. "I am willing, and so is the clerk, to do all that other men can do. I am ready to undertake whatever man can accomplish; but I cannot perform impracticabilities, and one of these is, to keep pace, with one clerk, with the continually increasing business of the Medical Department of the army." [41]

Unwillingness to allow enough clerks was duplicated by reluctance to pay adequate salaries. The evidence on this subject is collected elsewhere.[42] Suffice it to say here that there was constant complaint by the heads of departments as well as clerks that salaries were wholly insufficient to support a family, that families tended to be large, and that many clerks died in office after long years of service leaving their dependents without resources.

Parsimony was also largely responsible for the failure of Congress to authorize new bureaus or agencies long after the need for them had become apparent. The debate concerning the establishment of the Department of the Interior, noted below, illustrates the point.[43] The tenor of the argument is suggested by the remarks of Senator Allen of Ohio. "Sir," he said, "I remember full well, some years ago, when the proposition to have a clerk, or half a dozen clerks, added to one of the departments, would occasion debate for a week, during the administrations of Jackson and Van Buren. Such propositions never failed to be

40 House Doc. 39, 26th Cong., 1st sess., p. 7 (Dec. 30, 1839).

41 Senate Doc. 1, 25th Cong., 3d sess., p. 146 (Nov. 10, 1838).

42 See ch. 20.

43 See ch. 26.

denounced as seeking to plunder the treasury . . . the whole country [was] called to reprobate the tendency in the Executive to augment its power, and pander to its own appetite." [44]

The establishment of the Lighthouse Board, a reform greatly needed to improve the lighthouse service, was fought by the economy wing of Congress, a member of which promptly said, I told you so, when its first appropriation came due. "I predicted," said Representative James Brooks, "at the last session of Congress, that this Light-House Board which was going to cost nothing, would crop out in all of the appropriation bills. While we refused to create an Agricultural Bureau because of its expense, we established this Light-House Board, which is likely to increase the expenses of the Government to a far greater extent." [45]

Congress pinched pennies also in providing quarters for the conduct of official business. In 1853 the War Department's office building could accommodate less than half its bureaus; the clerk occupied with the interests of agriculture was housed in the cellar of the Patent Office building; the Post Office Department experienced great difficulty in finding quarters in the larger cities, but Congress had allowed it to own only a few local post office buildings; in 1853 eight or nine General Land Office clerks had to be crowded into rooms built for two; and, as noted elsewhere, the field agents of the General Land Office had to provide their own offices.[46]

The rule of parsimony, thus cherished by Congressmen, hampered the proper conduct of administrative work. Congress, at this point, was a drag upon the executive branch, and sometimes added insult to injury by loud denunciation of the supposedly excessive number of clerks and the extravagant habits of departments. The normal habits of departments were "to do, as soon as practicable, what was necessary to be done, and for that purpose to employ the necessary force to do it in a reasonable time, and do it well." Congress could not quarrel with such administrative doctrine, but it failed to authorize the necessary manpower to make it effective.

44 *Congressional Globe,* 30th Cong., 2d sess., p. 679 (March 3, 1849).
45 *Ibid.,* 32d Cong., 2d sess., p. 656 (Feb. 16, 1853).
46 Allan Nevins, *Ordeal of the Union,* I, 161–62.

THE SETTLEMENT OF CLAIMS

The respective duties of Congress and executive agencies in the settlement of claims arising from the daily business of government were in controversy almost from the foundation of the Republic. They were finally clarified and settled in 1855 by the establishment of the Court of Claims. The subject is of considerable importance in relation to the balance between the legislative and executive branches, as well as from other points of view, and the subject matter of the claims themselves furnishes a fascinating record of the grass-roots operation of the administrative system.[47]

Claims against the government having a legal foundation normally went to the Treasury accounting offices and were there finally settled. Private land claims in territory acquired by purchase or conquest were so complicated that they were heard and adjudicated by special tribunals established by Congress, as, for example, the commission to determine private land claims in California.[48]

Some claims had no legal foundation but rested upon equity; these were usually the hard cases where a sense of fairness and justice dictated relief but where the strict rules of accounting officers prevented the normal process of settlement. There was an almost infinite variety of such cases. Thus a poor woman, unable to provide recognizance for her appearance as a government witness in a case to which she was not a party, was confined in jail until the date of trial, and could not even be paid witness fees for this period of incarceration.[49] Contractors on certain army fortifications lost a large sum when work was suspended because Congress refused further appropriations. The only relief was from Congress itself.[50] A sailing master going to Madeira on his first trip overseas failed to secure a "Mediterranean passport," not understanding it was necessary for any for-

47 See for early cases *American State Papers: Claims,* and for subsequent cases the reports of House and Senate committees in the public document series.

48 9 Stat. 631 (March 3, 1851).

49 *American State Papers: Claims,* p. 263 (March 31, 1802). It was not until 1826 that Congress finally passed a law to correct such a situation. 4 Stat. 174 (May 20, 1826).

50 House Report 69, 18th Cong., 2d sess. (Feb. 16, 1825).

eign port beyond the West Indies. He incurred a penalty of $200, which the House Committee on Commerce suggested be refunded.

To consider such equitable cases the House of Representatives set up a Committee on Claims in 1794. Its business became so time-consuming and so complex that other committees of the same sort were required: a Committee on Public Lands (1805), a Committee on Pensions and Revolutionary Claims (1813), a Committee on Private Land Claims (1816), a Committee on Revolutionary Pensions (1825), and a Committee on Invalid Pensions (1831). The Senate also had committees to deal with claims, and disappointed applicants might go from one to the other House. Service on these committees was arduous and unpopular, and the results were extremely unsatisfactory.

Cases originated upon presentation to the House or Senate by a member, and were referred to the appropriate committee. The committee sought information from the executive agencies, sometimes held hearings, and studied the files. Reports went on the calendar, but there was no certainty that even if favorable they would be considered. If reached, a report usually was approved, but it then had to await action by the other House. Many claims never reached even the stage of a committee report for mere lack of time.

Apart from the inordinate delay there were many other grounds of criticism. The business of Congress was cluttered up with matters of no general importance; there were no recognized standards of judgment; precedents were not followed; a disappointed claimant could renew his plea before a new committee of the next Congress; the procedure was costly to the claimant; and the public interest was often lost from sight. In 1832 Adams recorded in his diary that this kind of private business ought to be excluded from Congress. "One-half of the time of Congress is consumed by it, and there is no common rule of justice for any two of the cases decided. A deliberative assembly is the worst of all tribunals for the administration of justice." [51] Despite these glaring faults the monetary volume of claims finally authorized by Congress was considerable. In five years, 1834 to 1838 inclusive, private claims in the amount

51 Adams, *Memoirs,* VIII, 480 (Feb. 23, 1832).

of $1,581,776.88 made their tedious way through both Houses.[52] This figure enforced the need for a better method.

Members of Congress serving on claims committees were strong in their condemnation of the procedure, but for years Congress was unable to agree on any alternative.[53] Some proposed to soften the rules of the accounting officers, but this was believed too risky. Others proposed to turn the cases over to the courts, but their procedures seemed not to promise a satisfactory solution. In 1828 the Senate Committee on Private Land Claims recommended an administrative tribunal.[54] Ten years later the same recommendation was again presented to Congress in an able report from the House Committee on Claims.[55] Congress remained indifferent.

Matters did not improve. Another decade passed and another able House committee report condemned the prevailing practice and urged a board of claims commissioners.[56] The chairman of the Claims Committee, John A. Rockwell, made an indignant exposure of "a system of unparalleled injustice, and wholly discreditable to any civilized nation." Honest citizens with claims about whose justification there was no question but whose payment was barred by auditors' rules were sent to Congress where interminable delay might result in eventual refusal of Congress to act. Even if a bill finally squeaked through, the claimant was denied interest on his judgment. The system was equally defective, in the opinion of the committee, from the point of view of protecting the rights of the government.[57] Still Congress took no action.

President Fillmore raised the problem again in his annual message of 1850 but without response.[58] In 1855 Congress finally

52 Senate Doc. 32, 25th Cong., 3d sess., p. 31 (Dec. 27, 1838). Cf. another compilation covering the years 1836–1841, in Senate Ex. Doc. 387, 27th Cong., 2d sess., p. 1 (August 2, 1842).

53 For an intelligent commentary, see House Report 100, 17th Cong., 1st sess. (April 27, 1822).

54 Senate Doc. 22, 20th Cong., 1st sess., p. 5 (Jan. 9, 1828).

55 House Report 730, 25th Cong., 2d sess. (March 28, 1838).

56 House Report 498, 30th Cong., 1st sess. (April 26, 1848).

57 *Ibid.*, pp. 2–7. The committee collected some interesting reports of claims procedure in other countries, an early example of seeking a solution of American problems by the methods of comparative government. *Ibid.*, pp. 23–28.

58 Richardson, *Messages*, V, 91–92 (Dec. 2, 1850).

established the Court of Claims.[59] This body was not a part of the judicial system, nor was it under the jurisdiction of the executive branch. In essence, it was a hearing body authorized to formulate a decision on specified claims cases for presentation to Congress for final action. In this respect it was expected to serve as a substitute for the various claims committees of the House and Senate. The Court consisted of three judges appointed by the President and confirmed by the Senate, holding office during good behavior. It received cases directly by petition from claimants or by reference from Congress. Government interests were represented by a solicitor appointed for this duty alone. The Court was permitted to call on the departments for documents and evidence.

Although the organic act authorized the court to hear and determine claims, in fact it was required to report all its decisions, favorable or adverse to the claimant, to Congress.[60] Both classes of cases went on the congressional calendar and were kept there, even from one Congress to another, until finally dealt with. Favorable decisions by the Court of Claims were accompanied by bills, the enactment of which would satisfy the claims. Adverse decisions approved by Congress were conclusive, thus putting an end to repeated hearings on the same case. Nothing was said in the act concerning the legal or equitable principles on which the court was to act; it was merely given authority to establish its own rules and regulations.

The high hopes of relieving Congress and providing speedy justice to claimants through this new agency were not immediately fulfilled, owing to an excessive caution on the part of the House Committee on Claims. It was supposed that this committee would accept the determinations of the Court of Claims without a reexamination of the evidence, but the committee resolutely refused to abandon its own responsibility. It decided to study the proceedings and determination of the court and to reach its own independent conclusions. Claimants were thus

59 10 Stat. 612 (Feb. 24, 1855). The informing discussion of this measure in the Senate is printed in the *Congressional Globe,* 33d Cong., 2d sess., pp. 70–74 (Dec. 18, 1854); and pp. 105–114 (Dec. 21, 1854).

60 Two volumes of cases were reported to the House of Representatives, 34th Cong., 1st sess. (1855–56). The first case involved the claim of a purser that had been pending since 1815.

forced to try their cases twice, and neither Congress nor claimants obtained relief. Furthermore, favorable reports were often not agreed to or acted upon by Congress, and were finally lost altogether.[61]

This stupid perversion of the intent of the law, superficially justified by sending the whole record of each case to Congress, was terminated in 1863.[62] Henceforth the judgment of the Court of Claims was final, was certified to either a district or circuit court, and was enforceable as any other decision of such court. Appeal was allowed to the Supreme Court, but no reference to Congress was permitted. The problem of equitable claims was thus finally settled, not by extending the jurisdiction of the Treasury accounting officers nor by establishing an executive commission responsible to the President, but by creating a legislative court. Congress rid itself of a crushing burden, but without running any risk of increasing executive power.

Congress failed to do justice to the administrative services at many points. It seemed to be more interested in reducing expenditures, in tracking down wrongdoing, in guarding against the possibility of error, in asserting its own special interests than in facilitating the conduct of the public business. Members easily worked themselves into a passion when their individual requests were denied by the executive branch, but were slow in responding to obvious needs of both the civil and military branches. Members were devoted to the needs of their constituents and to their own fence-building for reelection rather than to developing a competent and trustworthy administrative organization. Additional evidence of congressional delay and failure appears in subsequent pages.

At the same time Congress was active and useful in performing its proper function of inquiry and supervision of the administrative machine. From time to time it enacted constructive

61 William A. Richardson, *History, Jurisdiction, and Practice of the Court of Claims (United States)* (Washington: Government Printing Office, 1885), pp. 8–9. The House Judiciary Committee, reviewing the first five years' experience, declared, "The Court of Claims, with its present powers, is conceded to be comparatively useless," and recommended that all claims in law or equity not settled by the accounting officers be determined by the judicial courts. House Report 513, 36th Cong., 1st sess. (May 18, 1860). Quotation from page 4.

62 12 Stat. 765 (March 8, 1863).

legislation, and it must be agreed that many of its restrictive laws were designed to remedy errors or faults that came to public attention. On the whole, however, the record of Congress in the field of administration was a record characterized by delay, indifference, partisanship, and reluctance to provide the resources for effective work.

CHAPTER NINE

The Treasury and Customs Administration

The early role of the Treasury Department as the dynamic center of the administrative system under Alexander Hamilton and Albert Gallatin had faded away with lesser men in the face of competition from the War Department under John C. Calhoun. It was this agency which became responsible for the internal improvements and public works activities of the 1820's, and its large-scale civilian operations, its technical engineering skills, and its contacts with private canal and railroad enterprises thrust it into the focus of public interest and approval.

The situation shifted again after 1830, now in favor of the Treasury. The Jacksonians opposed national support of internal improvements and many of the new issues were of a nature that required Treasury initiative and leadership. Some of them, moreover, were highly controversial, and it was Treasury, not War, that stood in the center of debate and argumentation. Thus the problem of renewing the charter of the Bank of the United States and of withdrawing government deposits was primarily a Treasury affair. The disposal of the surplus revenue during the mid-1830's involved a political decision in which the Secretary of the Treasury was active, and the technical aspects of which were fiscal in nature. The tariff was a political issue, but among the departments it was the Treasury that was primarily concerned. Deficit financing after the panic of 1837, and war financing during the Mexican War were Treasury responsibilities. The Secretary of the Treasury was regularly a close adviser to the President. Moreover, the Treasury was one of the large patronage agencies, and the Secretary of the Treasury was often a leading figure in the disposition of offices and contracts, and in the political storms that gathered around these matters.

While the Treasury Department thus resumed the leading role in the official family that Hamilton and Gallatin had won for it, nevertheless it did not become a central agency of administration. Indeed, there was none such. The Treasury had no authority to revise the expenditure estimates of its sister departments, and the settlement of accounts was a legal and arithmetical procedure, in no wise an efficiency audit. The Treasury had not recovered the purchasing authority which Hamilton had wrested from his unwilling colleagues, and which had been lost under John Adams. There was no administrative center for personnel operations; each department hired and fired on its own responsibility. The Treasury had no sense of obligation for administrative operations, government-wide in nature; it had no doctrine of sound administrative practice; and it had no means of impressing its views on other departments or agencies.

The priority of the Treasury, so far as it existed, was in policy making.[1] In the hands of the ablest Secretaries, such as Robert J. Walker or James Guthrie, the Treasury approached the role so brilliantly stated by Henry Adams in his *Life of Albert Gallatin*. "In governments, as in households, he who holds the purse holds the power. The Treasury is the natural point of control to be occupied by any statesman who aims at organization or reform, and conversely no organization or reform is likely to succeed that does not begin with and is not guided by the Treasury. The highest type of practical statesmanship must always take this direction." [2] Henry Adams admitted that most financial ministers had not so understood their duties, and argued that they did not leave great reputations behind them. On the American stage he found only two who had the breadth of mind

[1] The incidental central banking functions of the Treasury are described in Esther Rogoff Taus, *Central Banking Functions of the United States Treasury, 1789–1941* (New York: Columbia University Press, 1943), chs. 1–3.

[2] Henry Adams, *The Life of Albert Gallatin* (Philadelphia: J. B. Lippincott and Co., 1879), p. 267.

to grapple with the machine of government as a whole—Hamilton and Gallatin. Most Secretaries were content to restrain themselves within their obvious departmental duties.

The internal structure of the Treasury Department remained in broad outline much the same during the Jacksonian years.[3] It was simplified and strengthened in 1849 when the Interior Department was established, by transferring to it the General Land Office and the supervision of the accounts of marshals and clerks of courts. By the same statute the office of assistant secretary of the Treasury was established.[4] The Department was conceived as built around the related functions of finance and commerce, and in the latter field it retained the revenue cutter service (Coast Guard), the Coast Survey, the mint, weights and measures, the marine hospitals, and the lighthouse system. Not only were the basic functions and organization substantially unchanged, the organic administrative statutes relating to the collection of customs, procedure against delinquent agents, fiscal and other reports, and the like were not greatly altered, although subject to improvement from time to time.

THE ACCOUNTING OFFICES

The system of accountability set up by Hamilton and expanded by Congress in 1817 stood intact during the Jacksonian years despite some adjustments to volume of business.[5] The number of auditors was increased from five to six, the responsibility for pursuing delinquent fiscal officers was given to the Treasury solicitor (established in 1830), and the accounting supervision of the collectors of customs was turned over to the commissioner of customs in 1849. These were changes of detail, not of system.

Fiscal reporting by departmental officers became much more prompt and reliable. The Navy announced that it had disbursed between three and four million dollars in 1833 without a single

3 For a contemporary account of its evolution, organization, and proposed reorganization, see House Report 81, 25th Cong., 2d sess. (Dec. 22, 1837).

4 9 Stat. 395, sec. 13 (March 3, 1849). See Secretary Robert J. Walker's recommendations for this Treasury reorganization in House Ex. Doc. 7, 30th Cong., 2d sess., pp. 35–36 (Dec. 9, 1848).

5 For a brief but excellent contemporary account of procedure, see Senate Doc. 1, 25th Cong., 2d sess., pp. 710–11 (Nov. 8, 1837).

instance of loss.[6] The army paymaster general stated in 1835 that accountability might be considered "as perfect as it can well be made." [7] Amos Kendall reported, after he had restored order in the Post Office, that the accounts of postmasters were rendered with admirable promptitude.[8] President Tyler told Congress in 1844 that during the preceding four years over $120 million had been collected and disbursed "without the loss by default of any amount worthy of serious commentary." [9] This excellent record of promptness and fidelity was marred by some exceptional cases of fraud, and by a general letdown in the land offices during the 1830's.[10] The record as a whole was, however, good; accountability had been generally achieved and had become habitual.

The auditors' and comptrollers' offices tended to become bottlenecks, and there was considerable complaint of long-standing unsettled accounts. Major Crosman informed Senator Robert M. T. Hunter in 1852 that he had had accounts waiting three years for settlement and in the name of his brother officers asked for "radical reforms." [11] Relief came in the person of the vigorous Secretary Guthrie, who drove the accounting officers relentlessly until they had cleaned up their arrearages. Institutional reform, however, was not to be had.

The relations between the Secretary of the Treasury and the accounting officers was the subject of some concern, particularly to the latter. The Federalists had established the rule that the *expediency* of an outlay was decided by the heads of de-

6 Senate Doc. 1, 23d Cong., 1st sess., p. 39 (Nov. 30, 1833).

7 Senate Doc. 1, 24th Cong., 1st sess., p. 88 (Nov. 30, 1835).

8 Senate Doc. 1, 24th Cong., 2d sess., p. 541 (Dec. 5, 1836).

9 Richardson, *Messages,* IV, 351 (Dec. 3, 1844).

10 Cf. the following passage from the report of the second comptroller. "But yet, with all these guards around the Treasury, flagrant cases of frauo do occasionally come to the knowledge of those who have the settlement of the public accounts; such as cases of forgery, by which claims utterly groundless are exhibited, apparently well supported by unquestionable proof; charges, supported by vouchers improperly obtained, in which the price of the article purchased is grossly inflamed, or even, in some instances, by vouchers for articles never in fact purchased; and some cases have been detected where officers, upon their official certificates, have drawn pay twice for the same service." Senate Doc. 1, 25th Cong., 2d sess., p. 167 (Nov. 8, 1837).

11 *Correspondence of Robert M. T. Hunter, 1826–1876* (Charles Henry Ambler, ed.), American Historical Association, *Annual Report, 1916,* II, 143–44 (May 21, 1852).

partments, its legality by the comptroller. In principle, the latter's decision was final and conclusive, but the lines of differentiation were not always easy to discern. The issue arose early in Van Buren's administration.

A disappointed claimant asked Secretary of the Treasury Woodbury to reexamine his case. Woodbury requested the first auditor for information. In complying with this request, the first auditor took occasion to instruct Woodbury.

> . . . I deem it my duty respectfully to remark, lest the making of this report should be construed into an admission on my part of the right of the Secretary, in *ordinary matters* of account, to direct the Auditor what he shall allow and what he shall disallow, that such is not my understanding of the law and organization of the department. The law undoubtedly makes it the duty of the Auditor, in the settlement of accounts, to act upon his own judgment and responsibility in the construction of the law and the facts of the case, and has provided a court of revision in the Comptroller to correct his errors of judgment and of fact, and to whom the law expressly says an appeal may be made. There are, however, special cases that no doubt form an exception to the general rule, when the ultimate decision is placed by special legislation, or the very nature of the case itself, under the direction of the Secretary. In ordinary cases, however, falling within the general provisions of the law establishing the accounting offices of the department, I regard the decision of the Comptroller in the construction of the laws relating to accounts as having the same force and obligation upon the Auditor as the decision of a superior court has upon an inferior one.
>
> I shall always, however, feel it to be my duty to give respectful consideration to any opinion that the Secretary may deem it his duty to give in relation to any matter connected with the department, and will always be happy to correct any error when convinced that I am in the wrong. And in questions involving the construction of laws relative to the settlement of accounts, where doubts exist, I shall feel it my duty to yield to the opinion of the Attorney General, as the law officer of the Government.[12]

In replying to his correspondent a week later Woodbury accepted this position. ". . . after the final decision of the Comptroller," he wrote, "a formal appeal may be made to the head of the department [i.e., to the Secretary of the Treasury] only for

[12] Senate Doc. 265, 25th Cong., 3d sess., pp. 8–9 (May 31, 1837).

the purpose of showing that the law and evidence have been departed from in the case, in such a manner as indicates misconduct, which should be reported to the President for the removal of the officer, if he declines correcting any manifest error. Beyond that the head of the department has, by the decision of the Attorney General, no right to examine and reverse the decisions of the Auditors and Comptrollers, and direct different ones upon mere matters of account." [13]

The accounting officers remained touchy, nevertheless. The first comptroller, George Wolf, protested a request of Woodbury for the reasons underlying disallowance of an item in a current account. Woodbury wrote a tart reply, stating the President wished the information in order to consider what steps if any should be taken to modify the law to prevent allowance of such claims in future, "or adopt any other course which he may deem appropriate." Woodbury again disavowed any intention of interfering with the settlement of accounts.[14]

By delegation from the Secretary of the Treasury both the first comptroller and the fifth auditor had duties not concerned with the settlement of accounts. The former was in immediate charge of the customs service, the latter the official head of the lighthouse service until 1852. Examination of the manuscript records of the Treasury Department during the 1830's demonstrates that in these areas the first comptroller and the fifth auditor operated as other bureau chiefs subject to instructions and control by the Secretary of the Treasury. It was Woodbury, not the accounting officers, who construed the meaning of the customs laws and who issued directions on lighthouse administration.

Moreover with respect to all accounting offices the Secretary was responsible for management operations. The appointment, transfer, and promotion of clerks in the comptrollers' and auditors' offices required the approval of the Secretary. The Secretary did not hesitate to call attention to errors and to order them to

13 *Ibid.*, p. 9 (June 7, 1837). The opinions of the Attorneys General had not been clear until Taney settled the issue in 1832. Berrien had left authority with the President to alter a "final" settlement. 2 *Opinions of the Attorneys General* 303 (Dec. 4, 1829). Taney's contrary opinion, that the decision of the comptroller was conclusive upon the executive branch, followed in 1832. 2 *ibid.* 508 (April 5, 1832).

14 National Archives, Treasury Department, Letters to Cabinet and Bureaus, Set B, No. 2, pp. 8–9 (Oct. 10, 1837).

be corrected. The Secretary gave many specific directions on business going through the accounting offices—requiring an alphabetical list of debtors on customhouse bonds, notifying securities of neglect by their principals, refusing allowances on expense accounts, waiving appropriation warrants in certain cases prior to settlement, fixing the methods of calculating compensation of customs officers, requiring individual reports on the salaries of court officials, and fixing procedure when issuing warrants out of the regular routine.[15] In short, except for the single operation of settling accounts, the auditors and comptrollers had no more independence than a collector of customs or the Treasury solicitor.

This dual relationship persisted despite criticism by the Treasury and by some members of Congress. The Gilmer Select Committee on Retrenchment put the case for reform in convincing terms.

> The union of administrative and accounting duties, in the hands of the First Comptroller, the committee regard as peculiarly objectionable. As the final judge in matters of account, he was designed to be independent of the Secretary; but, in superintending the customs, he appears to be entirely subject to his control. The tendency of this submission in one part of his duties is but too well calculated to impair his independence in the other; and it is probable that, in the practical operations of his office, the distinction between his two classes of duty is apt to be overlooked. The general tendency of the system has doubtless been to give a prevailing influence, touching even upon accounts, to the administrative branches of the Departments over the accounting. The higher salary of the Secretary, his political position and connexions, and his access to the President, contribute to this influence, and doubtless to disincline the accounting offices to resist his authority, whenever he is inclined to assume the responsibility of decision. This office should be restored to what it was, or was intended to be—the final umpire in matters of account—and should be freed from the administrative duties in connexion with the customs.[16]

The incongruity of these functions of the first comptroller was not corrected, despite the case for transfer elsewhere of his duties as immediate head of the customs service. The fifth auditor

15 *Ibid., passim.*

16 House Report 741, 27th Cong., 2d sess., p. 11 (May 23, 1842).

eventually lost supervision of the lighthouse service to a special board.

THE CUSTOMS SERVICE

Among the various divisions of the Treasury Department the customs service had always been the largest and most significant. Through the collectors of customs the Treasury touched the commercial and maritime interests of the country, always influential; in customs dues the general government found by far the greatest share of its revenue; and as the doctrine of rotation took hold, it was the customs service that opened rich resources to the political parties.

By 1858 the customs service stretched from Frenchman's Bay in Maine to San Francisco, California. There were then 152 ports of entry and collectors. The offices varied greatly in size and activity. At one extreme were small customhouses such as that at Richmond, Virginia, with a staff of six persons, including the collector; or the establishment at Havre de Grace, Maryland, with a single officer, the surveyor. Many such small offices had been eliminated, but local influence, exerted through a Congressman, had saved some. At the other extreme stood such offices as San Francisco with a staff of 127, Philadelphia with a force of 189, and New York with a pay roll of 861 officers and employees.[17] The port of New York in fact collected normally about two-thirds of the whole customs revenue.

The system of headquarters control of the customhouses was well developed from one point of view, and very inadequately from another. The formal auditing system was complete on its surface—regular and frequent reports of collections, expenditures, and importers' bonds were received in Washington, and balances ascertained. The interpretation of the tariff acts was supposed to be unified by instructions from the first comptroller, and the collectors were accustomed to ask for guidance on difficult or controverted cases. The machinery for action against delinquent collectors through the courts was formally complete. Experience over many years had solidified practice and made most of it routine. The fatal inadequacy of the system lay in the fact that until 1854 the Treasury had no inspection system to

17 House Ex. Doc. 3, 35th Cong., 2d sess., pp. 240–59 (Nov. 22, 1858).

ensure that the collectors' reports were an accurate reflection of the money actually collected. As the event was to prove, the auditing control also was weak, particularly when it was reduced to the sketchy routine that gradually developed. The second inadequacy of the control system grew out of the political invasion of the customhouses by strong local party machines that were impressed more by the necessity of carrying elections than by the formalities of customs collection.

The law made the Secretary of the Treasury responsible for the customs service, and until 1792 Hamilton personally discharged this duty. He then delegated to the comptroller (eventually the first comptroller) responsibility for "all matters arising out of the laws which respect the laying or collecting" of the customs.[18] The comptroller thus became the Treasury agent for interpreting the tariff acts and instructing the collectors. In this operation he consulted the Secretary of the Treasury when necessary, and in the 1830's such consultation was frequent.

In 1834 Secretary Woodbury proposed a reorganization to consolidate the settlement of accounts in a single comptroller, and to place the superintendence of the customs in the hands of the second comptroller under the new title of commissioner of customs.[19] The object was to secure a more energetic supervision over the collectors and the collection of the revenue. The program was not accepted by Congress. Years later an officer designated commissioner of the customs was established by Congress, upon whom were devolved the accounting duties of the first comptroller relating to receipts from customs and collectors' accounts.[20] The office, having nothing to do with the administration of the customs service or the interpretation of the laws relating to duties, failed to measure up to Woodbury's earlier hopes.[21]

That change was needed was certified both by the laxness of Treasury control apparent in the defalcations of Samuel Swartwout, collector of the port of New York from 1830 to 1837, and

18 Circular of Oct. 25, 1792, reprinted in House Report 740, 24th Cong., 1st sess., p. 16 (June 7, 1836).

19 *Ibid.*, p. 31 (Dec. 5, 1834).

20 9 Stat. 395, sec. 12 (March 3, 1849).

21 Laurence F. Schmeckebier, *The Customs Service: Its History, Activities and Organization* (Baltimore: Johns Hopkins Press, 1924), p. 16.

by the defiance of Jesse Hoyt during Van Buren's administration. The almost total neglect of a real examination of collectors' accounts was revealed when the Swartwout affair was investigated.[22] The Whig majority of the House investigating committee reported that the duties of the first comptroller had been so administered that no means existed to detect either fraud or error in the collectors' accounts, apart from arithmetical computation. "The office, as administered, has been only in contemplation of law, and not in the execution of it, any check whatever upon either the First Auditor or collectors. In a word, the certificate of the Comptroller has been a fancy affair throughout. . . ." [23] Although the Democratic minority of the House committee sought to excuse the first comptroller and first auditor, the finding of the majority was confirmed in substance by the new occupant of the comptroller's office, James N. Barker.[24]

Swartwout's successor, Jesse Hoyt, freely denied Treasury control. A House committee reported in 1839 that he had violated the instructions of the Treasury Department, had put at defiance the duties assigned to him, had repudiated the official decision of the Attorney General, and was guilty of the illegal retention and use of the public money. The tone of Hoyt's correspondence may be caught from one of his letters to the comptroller: "I write now to say, peremptorily, that I will not pass the money I receive under protest to the credit of the United States until Congress makes provision for my protection." [25] It may well have been Hoyt's contumacy that prompted Congress to put in statutory language the historic and undoubted obligation of collectors to obey Treasury instructions: "the decision of the Secretary of the Treasury shall be conclusive and binding upon all such collectors and other officers of the customs." [26]

The basic difficulty in Treasury control of its field agents was the lack of an inspection system. The fault had been recognized in 1836. The House Committee on Commerce then argued strongly for "personal examination" by "a competent agent"

22 See below, ch. 22.

23 House Report 313, 25th Cong., 3d sess., p. 53 (Feb. 27, 1839).

24 House Doc. 13, 25th Cong., 3d sess., p. 99 (Dec. 1, 1838).

25 House Report 313, 25th Cong., 3d sess., p. 121. Letter dated Feb. 1, 1839.

26 5 Stat. 548, sec. 24 (August 30, 1842).

to produce uniformity of action, to detect unworthy officials, to eliminate unnecessary employees, to prevent "undue preference to one merchant over another," or the acceptance of presents. The inspector, the committee argued, could also look into the public storehouses, the lighthouses, and marine hospitals.[27] Congress was not moved to action and the Treasury remained bereft of direct personal contact with the collectors until 1851, when four general appraisers assumed their duties. Their assignment, however, was primarily concerned with the valuation of imports, not with the efficiency of the customs staff.[28]

In 1854, without specific statutory authority, Secretary James Guthrie introduced an efficiency inspection for the first time. The collectors' offices were visited by William M. Gouge, an old hand at field inspections in the General Land Office, "to ascertain how their books and accounts were kept, and, by personal inspection, how the official corps discharged their duties." [29] Guthrie declared that errors and omissions had thus been corrected, and that greater vigilance and a more faithful application of the revenue laws had resulted.[30] Gouge also inspected the field offices of the independent treasury system,[31] and the marine hospitals.[32]

Most collectors were responsive, of course, to Treasury instructions. Few were in a position to defy the Treasury as did

27 House Report 740, 24th Cong., 1st sess., p. 7 (June 7, 1836).

28 A furor over "secret inspectors" arising in 1847 concerned local agents appointed by the collector to detect smuggling. They were not supervisory agents responsible to the Secretary. House Doc. 80, 29th Cong., 2d sess., pp. 1–8 (Feb. 5, 1847). They gave obvious opportunities to pay political debts and in 1853 Secretary Guthrie discharged all of them, 42 in number. They had been appointed during the preceding Whig administration, the last one on Feb. 25, 1853, with an advance payment of $1,000. Senate Ex. Doc. 2, 33d Cong., 1st sess., pp. 112–13.

29 William M. Gouge (1796–1863) was known as a writer on financial subjects, the author of *A Short History of Money and Banking in the United States* (1833, 2d ed. 1835; reprinted in London under the title, *The Curse of Paper-Money and Banking*); *The Fiscal History of Texas* (1852); and other works. From 1834 to 1841 he was a clerk in the Treasury Department and cooperated in writing many official reports. His contribution to administration developed from his employment at various intervals as inspector of field services, especially his examination of the subtreasuries, Senate Ex. Doc. 2, 33d Cong., 2d sess., pp. 255–75 (May 26, 1854). *Dictionary of American Biography*, VII, 444.

30 Senate Ex. Doc. 2, 33d Cong., 2d sess., p. 13 (Dec. 4, 1854).

31 *Ibid.*, p. 14.

32 Senate Ex. Doc. 2, 34th Cong., 1st sess., p. 25 (Dec. 3, 1855).

Jesse Hoyt. The general problem was not, however, how to put a few powerful figures under control, but how to secure uniformity, impartiality, and correctness throughout the service. Instructions were useful to this end, but by themselves inadequate. The customs service until 1851 remained a loose-jointed organization, with wide latitude for varied if not inconsistent application of the tariff acts.

POLITICS IN THE CUSTOMS SERVICE

There had been signs of party interference in the subordinate staffs of the customhouses in Baltimore, Philadelphia, and New York during the administration of John Quincy Adams. He resisted this tendency and resolutely refused to profit by it in the campaign of 1828. The trend was accelerated when Jackson became President and within a decade the customhouse staffs became deeply involved in Whig and Democratic politics.

The problem was less in the small customhouses than in their giant relatives, but the experience of Salem, Massachusetts, suggested that the same influences were widely at work. The collector at this quiet and pleasant port was General James Miller, a hero of the War of 1812 whose portrait still hangs in the corridors of the Capitol building in Concord, New Hampshire. General Miller, a Jacksonian Democrat, became collector of the port of Salem in 1824 and resigned his office in 1849—in favor of his son—when the Whig candidate for the presidency, General Taylor, defeated the Democratic standard bearer, Lewis Cass. The Whigs of Salem promptly petitioned Taylor to oust the younger Miller, and complained that during General Miller's long tenure, the customhouse had become the "confluence and receptacle of the most active and obnoxious leaders" of the Democratic party. They declared that the Salem community, decidedly Whig, had "become prejudiced, and even incensed, against the political partisans entrenched within its walls." [33]

President Taylor quickly did his duty to the Salem Whigs. Out with the younger Miller went also Nathaniel Hawthorne, who had earlier served an unhappy apprenticeship as a measurer in the Boston customhouse; an experience that he had called "a

33 Winfield S. Nevins, "Nathaniel Hawthorne's Removal from the Salem Custom House," in Essex Institute, *Historical Collections*, LIII (1917), 111.

very grievous thraldom." [34] The business of the Salem establishment, according to Hawthorne, was not discharged by the collector, General Miller, who had long been incapacitated, but by that indispensable person, the old-timer, who outlived every change of administration. Let Hawthorne tell the tale.

. . . . There was one man, especially, the observation of whose character gave me a new idea of talent. His gifts were emphatically those of a man of business; prompt, acute, clear-minded; with an eye that saw through all perplexities, and a faculty of arrangement that made them vanish, as by the waving of an enchanter's wand. Bred up from boyhood in the Custom House, it was his proper field of activity; and the many intricacies of business, so harassing to the interloper, presented themselves before him with the regularity of a perfectly comprehended system. In my contemplation, he stood as the ideal of his class. He was, indeed, the Custom House in himself, or, at all events, the mainspring that kept its variously revolving wheels in motion; for, in an institution like this, where its officers are appointed to subserve their own profit and convenience, and seldom with a leading reference to their fitness for the duty to be performed, they must perforce seek elsewhere the dexterity which is not in them. Thus, by an inevitable necessity, as a magnet attracts steel-filings, so did our man of business draw to himself the difficulties which everybody met with. With an easy condescension, and kind forbearance towards our stupidity,—which, to his order of mind, must have seemed little short of crime,—would he forthwith, by the merest touch of his finger, make the incomprehensible as clear as daylight. The merchants valued him not less than we, his esoteric friends. His integrity was perfect: it was a law of nature with him, rather than a choice or a principle; nor can it be otherwise than the main condition of an intellect so remarkably clear and accurate as his, to be honest and regular in the administration of affairs.[35]

Although such men could be found in customhouses nearly everywhere, as the years went by the pressure for political appointments became nearly irresistible. The demand was greatest in the big cities, where the voting power of the new mass electorate was concentrated. The port of New York revealed in

34 Nathaniel Hawthorne, *Passages from the American Note-Books* (Boston: Houghton Mifflin and Co., 1896), p. 215 (March 15, 1840).

35 Nathaniel Hawthorne, "The Custom House." Introductory to *The Scarlet Letter* (1850) as reprinted in 1949 (New York: Farrar, Strauss, 1949), pp. 21–22.

sharp outline the decline of the customhouses in the great centers. The office of collector of the port became one of the principal prizes in the patronage lottery. Here Jackson made one of his gravest mistakes in the appointment of Samuel Swartwout, and Van Buren committed as great an error in selecting Jesse Hoyt. President Polk had a bitter conflict with Pennsylvania factions in the appointment of the collector of Philadelphia—a battle over the control of the customhouse patronage. George Bancroft became collector of the port of Boston and *ipso facto* head of the Democratic machine in the Bay State.

The sinister consequences of the political character of the collectorship were pointedly revealed in private letters of William L. Marcy at the moment when Polk had to determine who would be collector in New York. The question was an absorbing one, in which the President personally participated. The decision was finally made to keep temporarily Cornelius Van Ness, a Democrat who had been put in by Tyler in 1844. Marcy wrote his New York confidant, General Prosper M. Wetmore, "The keeping in V. N. in whose hands is the almost entire amt of patronage rendered it expedient that there should be an exceedingly honest & vigilant N. officer [i.e., naval officer] & one who would divide the responsibility in case of trouble. Hoffman is a real watch dog—that I had to admit. So far as the money is concerned he will look well to it. This view was considered very important in a certain quarter." [36]

By the end of Buchanan's administration there was evidence that customhouse standards had deteriorated in New York into extensive blackmail of importing merchants, requiring them to pay fictitious charges or wait indefinitely for port services. Twenty-two ship captains finally made a public protest in the *New York Commercial Advertiser,* exposing a situation that was called a picture of "stupidity and corruption." [37]

The collectorships, until 1829 held on substantially permanent tenure, fell almost completely under the system of rotation. The subordinate staff could not escape. When Edward Curtis became the Whig collector of the port of New York in 1841 he

36 Library of Congress, William L. Marcy Papers, Vol. 10, No. 34, 430 (May 3, 1845).

37 *North American Review,* XCI (1860), 449–50.

found seventeen measurers on duty. He discharged them all and appointed fifteen new men.[38] The *New York Herald* described the clamor for appointments. "There was a terrible rush at the Custom House yesterday. . . . The poor devils of locofocos behind their desks eyed the crowd of hungry loafers in front as mice might a cat about to devour them." [39]

The Democrats returned to power in 1853 after a second Whig administration. On April 22 the incoming collector at Philadelphia notified upward of sixty customhouse employees that their services would no longer be required. According to the *Philadelphia Ledger* "the gentlemen who received the notice appear to take the matter good-naturedly" and joined in the speculation about their successors among the hundreds of applicants.[40] By June it was reported that there were 27,000 applicants for about seven hundred subordinate positions in the New York customhouse.[41]

The inevitable end of such transactions appeared in a controversy between Secretary Guthrie and Greene C. Bronson, collector of the port of New York in 1853. Bronson had been chief judge of the New York Court of Appeals, had declined to allow his friends to urge his appointment to the collectorship, but against his preference was put in this office by President Pierce. On October 3, 1853, Guthrie complained that Bronson had not given proper recognition to the Barnburner faction of the local Democracy in the subordinate customhouse appointments and gave orders in the following terms: "Allow me to express the expectation that you will so recognise them in the only way that will carry conviction with it." [42]

Bronson made a prompt and tart reply. He told Guthrie that it was impossible to administer the rule of factional representation and that its necessary consequence would be to weaken,

38 House Report 669, 27th Cong., 2d sess., p. 153 (April 28, 1842).

39 Quoted in Robert Greenhalgh Albion, *The Rise of New York Port, 1815–1860* (New York: Charles Scribner's Sons, 1939), p. 226 (April 1841).

40 *National Intelligencer,* April 30, 1853.

41 *Ibid.,* June 4, 1853.

42 *Ibid.,* Oct. 11, 1853. The *New York Journal of Commerce* commented that, "Hereafter the Government will be chiefly devoted to this important business of peddling out small offices, and quarrelling with such collectors and other chief officers as may not consent to be the convenient tools of the Executive." Quoted in *National Intelligencer,* Oct. 18, 1853.

not to strengthen, the party. He declared that no member of the Cabinet had ever before interfered with the discretion of collectors, marshals, and postmasters having patronage to bestow, and that this was the first example of an order to make a "just distribution" among factions. He denied Guthrie's right to make such a requirement of him and flatly refused to obey.[43] He was instantly removed for this show of independence.[44]

Such a removal was adequate notice to collectors generally that subordinate customs officers were selected by the collector subject to the approval and in accordance with the policy of the Pierce administration. Practice over many years had left the nomination of these customs agents to the collector, but his lists had to be confirmed in Washington. The struggle over such inferior appointments was most acute in Boston, New York, Philadelphia, and Baltimore, and it must not be presumed that the whole customs service was swept in and out of office with a change of administration. In the big ports, however, the trend was in this direction.

THE MERCHANTS AND THE CUSTOMS SERVICE

It was in the midst of such turmoil that the business of entering and clearing ships, the appraisal and classification of goods, and the assessment of duties had to be carried on. The principal technical problem that the customs service dealt with was the appraisal and classification of goods, and this was also the point at which the interests of importers and merchants were most likely to come into conflict with the collectors' staffs.

There was much evidence of the good faith and lawful intentions of the merchants as a body. Secretary Louis McLane declared in 1831, "The punctuality of the American merchant in the payment of duties, in every period of our history, and under the most severe vicissitudes, is deserving of the greatest admiration." [45] There was also much evidence of a lack of common understanding and uniformity of practice among the different customhouses, different rules of appraisal, and the ab-

43 Letter of October 17, 1853, in *National Intelligencer,* Oct. 20, 1853.

44 Letter of removal in *ibid.,* Oct. 25, 1853. John A. Dix, a leading New York Democrat, resigned as assistant treasurer at New York in protest at Bronson's removal.

45 House Doc. 3, 22d Cong., 1st sess., p. 19 (Dec. 7, 1831).

sence of adequate means for an administrative review of collectors' decisions on the classification and appraisal of imports. A House committee report of 1836 presented definite conclusions on these matters.

> . . . a great diversity of opinion prevails among the officers at different places, concerning the powers confided to them by law. . . . there is a great want of uniformity in the manner of making entries and keeping books. . . . there is a great difference in the rates of duty paid at different ports growing out of a great variety of causes, which in no way impeach the character or capacity of the officers of the Department. This may be occasioned by invoices being in foreign currency, the value of which is not fixed by law, and which may be valued differently in different ports of the country, and also in a want of uniformity in the classification of goods, which are free, or subject to different duties as they shall fall into one class or another.[46]

It was also obvious that undervaluation of imports in any port would tend to draw the import trade to that place, and there were hints that this was a factor making for lack of uniformity.

The Treasury thus faced a common administrative problem, to secure consistency and uniformity of action among a number of field offices. The principal means of securing these ends had always been instructions from the Treasury to the collectors, interpreting and applying the terms of the tariff acts. These instructions were often, if not usually, based on requests originating with collectors who found themselves in disagreement with importers. The Treasury, however, had no way of discovering lack of uniformity among the collectors unless and until a case was presented to it, apart from circulating standing instructions as to procedure. There was consequently plenty of room for the variety discovered by the House committee in 1836.

Merchants who suffered by presumed errors of appraisal or classification had no easy remedy. The early tariff laws were silent on any relief from errors on the part of the collector. It was his function "to estimate the duties payable" on imports, and it was apparently the expectation that this would be largely a simple clerical operation based on the invoices showing actual cost.[47] The tariff act of 1799 introduced special appraisers to

46 House Report 740, 24th Cong., 1st sess., p. 1 (June 7, 1836).

47 1 Stat. 36, sec. 5 (July 31, 1789).

deal with two contingencies—the valuation of goods not accompanied by an invoice, or goods damaged during the voyage. The collector in such cases appointed one merchant, the owner or importer another; their appraisal was apparently conclusive.[48] The problem of fraudulent invoices was also dealt with in the same way. A collector suspecting undervaluation of true cost was authorized to appoint one reputable merchant, and the importer one, to ascertain the true value at the time and place of importation.[49]

These *ad hoc* appointments were supplanted in 1818 by two full-time appraisers in each of the large ports—Boston, New York, Philadelphia, Baltimore, and Charleston; elsewhere the old system prevailed. The appraisers' jurisdiction extended to the valuation of such goods as the collector might direct. In each case one official appraiser acted with a second person selected by the owner or importer.[50]

It was not until 1842 that the owner or importer was given the right to have recourse to appraisers to correct an alleged error in valuation running against his interest. In such a case the law now directed the collector to appoint *ad hoc* two discreet and experienced merchants to appraise the goods. In case of disagreement the collector decided, otherwise the valuation of the two discreet merchants was final.[51] The owner or importer prior to 1842 had not been wholly without a remedy against collectors' errors, but his recourse was judicial. By common law principles, the collector who went beyond his legal powers rendered himself personally liable, a liability technically arising under the law of the state in which the port was situated. The action of trover or of assumpsit became the recognized remedy to test the legality of the government's construction of the tariff laws, originating in a state court and then transferred to the United States district court.[52]

By the act of 1842, therefore, the merchants gained an administrative review supplementing their judicial remedy. The

48 1 Stat. 627, sec. 52 (March 2, 1799).

49 *Ibid.*, sec. 66.

50 3 Stat. 433, sec. 9 (April 20, 1818).

51 5 Stat. 548, sec. 17 (August 30, 1842).

52 Ernst Freund, *Administrative Powers over Persons and Property* (Chicago: University of Chicago Press, 1928), pp. 242–43.

problem of lack of uniformity was, however, still untouched. It was attacked in 1851 by the establishment of four general appraisers, appointed by the President with confirmation by the Senate.[53] Under the direction of the Secretary of the Treasury, it was their duty to visit the various ports of entry to ensure the security of the revenue and uniformity in its collection. Wherever practicable, furthermore, one of them served as the official appraiser (with a merchant) to hear merchants' appeals under the act of 1842. The appellate function was obviously an important means of securing uniformity, as the general appraisers went from port to port.[54]

By a long process of gradual evolution, the valuation of imports was thus safeguarded both in the interest of the government and the protection of the importer. The foundation of the system was the discreet merchant appointed *ad hoc,* supplemented in the large ports by professional appraisers, and completed by four general appraisers having both powers of inspection and review upon an importer's appeal. The system was extended in 1864 by allowing an importer's appeal to the Secretary of the Treasury and in 1890 by allowing an appeal to the United States Circuit Court in lieu of the common law action against the collector.[55]

During most of the nineteenth century the principal function of the general government which brought it into administrative contact with private rights of property was the collection of the revenue. The development of procedure in this area therefore possessed a special interest as private and public values came into conflict with each other.

TWO SECRETARIES OF THE TREASURY

Robert J. Walker was certainly one of the most extraordinary persons ever to sit at the head of the Treasury Department. A "mere whiffle of a man," thin, angular, dyspeptic, and so weak in 1847 that Polk feared he might be at the point of death, he was endowed with restless energy, enormous capacity for work,

53 9 Stat. 629 (March 3, 1851).

54 See remarks of Senator Winthrop, *Congressional Globe,* 31st Cong., 2d sess., p. 269 (Jan. 17, 1851), and the remarks of Senator Hunter and Senator Winthrop, *Congressional Globe, Appendix,* 31st Cong., 2d sess., pp. 127–29 (Feb. 4, 1851).

55 13 Stat. 202, sec. 14 (June 30, 1864); 26 Stat. 131, sec. 15 (June 10, 1890).

and a towering ambition. He was trained as a Pennsylvania lawyer. By virtue of marriage into the Bache-Dallas family he became an original Jacksonian before he removed to Missisippi in 1826. In temperament he was a promoter, speculator, and adventurer on a huge scale, said to have been bankrupt much of his life but plunging forward nevertheless with investments in plantations, slaves, and wild lands.[56]

His sense of morals was less exacting than that of the old Federalists and Republicans but was not different from what was generally acceptable in his time. He arranged a ten million dollar loan from the Bank of the United States to the state of Mississippi, a sun which was then loaned to needy planters and others (including himself), and eventually repudiated because it contravened the state constitution. The whole venture was opposed by another Mississippian, Jefferson Davis. During the Civil War, Walker was in Great Britain as a northern agent selling United States securities and undermining the sale of southern government bonds. To this end he convinced the British that repudiation in Mississippi had been the work of Davis himself; and that a similar course could be confidently expected from the Confederate States. While at the head of the Treasury Department, he urged upon the first comptroller the payment of some very dubious claims amounting to $112,000 that he had already failed to push through the Senate. The matter came to Polk's attention from a distressed clerk in the department. Polk instantly forbade payment without a full investigation of what he called "a singular transaction." [57]

As Secretary of the Treasury during Polk's administration Walker was primarily concerned with policy, in harmony with his earlier service in the Senate. He favored free land, a tariff for revenue only, the independent treasury, and above all an expansive imperialism. Quite in harmony with his imaginative and venturesome personality, he vigorously advocated the annexation of Texas and the whole of Oregon, tried to persuade the government to buy Cuba, at one moment expected to acquire Yucatán and probably hoped for the whole of Mexico.

56 William E. Dodd, *Robert J. Walker: Imperialist* (Chicago: Chicago Literary Club, 1914); *Dictionary of American Biography,* XIX, 355.

57 Polk, *Diary,* II, 126–28 (Sept. 9, 10, 1846).

After the Civil War he helped "arrange" the purchase of Alaska and talked about the absorption of Canada.

Within the Treasury Department Walker discharged effectively the major task of financing the War with Mexico, but with a complaisance toward bankers' profits that caused Polk much anguish. Walker had a good sense of organization, and succeeded finally in convincing Congress of the necessity for an assistant secretary of the Treasury, an improvement long overdue. He also induced a reluctant Congress to create the Department of the Interior, thus enabling him to unload some functions unrelated to finance or commerce. He caused the introduction of the warehouse system in the customs service, a means of storing and controlling imports that is still in use. He drove himself and his department so hard in the preparation of the 1847 annual report that he collapsed, and several of his assistants had to take to their beds.

Walker was not a man to undertake the reform of the party system or to alleviate the evil consequences of the aggression of party on administration. He accepted the practice of rotation, notably in the customs service, but did not impose rotation on the accounting services. As an active Mississippi politician for twenty years he knew the advantages of office for party reward.

His contribution lay primarily in his exposition of doctrine. His annual Treasury report for 1845 became a classic of free-trade literature. Much less well known was his vision of an alliance between capital and labor, in a free world market. ". . . when all our capitalists . . . shall find it to be their true interest, in addition to the wages paid to the American workman, to allow him voluntarily, because it augments the profits of capital, a fair interest in those profits, and elevate him to the rank of a partner in the concern, we may then defy all competition." [58]

James Guthrie, Secretary of the Treasury under Franklin Pierce, was a vigorous and effective administrator but, unlike Walker, not concerned with matters beyond his own department. Born in Kentucky in 1792, he practiced law in Louisville and built up a fortune in real estate, banking, and railroads.

58 House Ex. Doc. 6, 30th Cong., 1st sess., p. 24 (Dec. 8, 1847).

For fourteen years a member of the Kentucky legislature, he had held no federal office until his party labors and personal competence were recognized by appointment as Secretary of the Treasury.

In appearance he was uncouth and unprepossessing and was permanently lamed in a personal encounter in his youth. "He was a man of many eccentricities, of a domineering and arrogant personality, and wholly lacking in the usual graces of the politician." [59] He had the great assets, however, of sound judgment and a reputation for absolute honesty and integrity. He put his business experience to work in the Treasury with all the zeal of a ruthless reformer.

In his first annual report (1853) he recorded his improvements. He had eliminated the secret customs inspectors, discharged twenty-seven redundant revenue cutter officers, called in $4,900,000 in the hands of agents for purchase of the debt, for transfer, and other purposes, required monthly instead of quarterly accounts from the collectors and their prompt settlement, initiated a drive on over $100,000,000 of unsettled accounts in the auditors and comptrollers offices, introduced a rule prohibiting reopening a claim once settled, stopped payment on a handsome extra allowance to the collector of the port of New York, and promulgated a businesslike set of office rules.[60] Furthermore he borrowed an army engineer to supervise the construction of Treasury buildings.[61]

Guthrie could be adamant against outside pressure for appointments. A New York delegation from the Chamber of Commerce appeared in his office in May 1853 with a list of nominations for the assay office. They proposed their candidate for superintendent. "That is fixed already," said Guthrie, "and cannot be altered." They then proposed a man for treasurer. That too had been already settled. In despair the delegation urged a man for assayer. Guthrie had settled this matter by transferring a supernumerary from one of the southern mints. "The New Yorkers gave up the contest, convinced that they could do noth-

59 *Dictionary of American Biography*, VIII, 60.

60 Senate Ex. Doc. 2, 33d Cong., 1st sess., pp. 10 *et seq*. (Dec. 6, 1853).

61 House Ex. Doc. 47, 34th Cong., 3d sess., p. 5 (March 4, 1854).

ing with a Secretary who had already fixed every thing, and, besides, was bent on *saving expenses*." [62]

Guthrie did not hesitate to use peremptory language to his staff, or to criticize roundly the unbusinesslike methods of the department. The mass of unsettled accounts implied, he said, looseness and irregularity, and presumed either defects in or an entire want of system, discreditable to the government.[63] At the end of three years the amount unsettled had been reduced to less than $24,000,000, of which about $6,000,000 had been utterly lost.[64]

Promptly upon taking office, Guthrie addressed a circular to the collectors of customs, telling them that they could not "too soon enter upon the task of reforming what has been amiss, and introducing a more energetic, vigilant, and economical system." He declared that it was his aim and wish "to infuse vigilance, fidelity, and economy into the public service" committed to his care, and to supersede all sinecures and persons not fully adapted to their proper employment.[65]

Somewhat later he sent a circular to the heads of the Treasury bureaus setting standards for the behavior of the clerks. No absences were allowed except for sickness on a doctor's certificate. The first indulgence in ardent spirits was punished by removal. Bureau heads were earnestly requested "to promote habits of order and decorum," to repress so far as possible newspaper reading in office hours, and waste of time by frivolous or unnecessary conversation. Every employee was instructed to treat the public with frankness, courtesy, and kindness, but to defend unflinchingly the interests of the government. Guthrie sensed the public relations value of citizen contacts: "thus, by dignity of deportment and an accommodating spirit, [each clerk would] serve to conciliate, within the sphere of his employment, the confidence and respect of the people for the government and institutions of their country." [66]

Both Walker and Guthrie were types substantially unknown

62 *National Intelligencer,* May 7, 1853.

63 Senate Ex. Doc. 2, 33d Cong., 1st sess., p. 120 (Nov. 21, 1853).

64 Senate Ex. Doc. 3, 34th Cong., 3d sess., p. 36 (Dec. 1, 1856).

65 Senate Ex. Doc. 2, 33d Cong., 1st sess., p. 111 (April 1, 1853).

66 *Ibid.,* p. 355 (Oct. 1, 1853).

in the Cabinets of Federalist or Republican Presidents. Walker was an adventurer and a speculator, but nevertheless a man of ideas and a wide-ranging vision of a continent dominated by the United States. Guthrie was an early example of the American businessman, heavily engaged in large-scale enterprises and active in politics who, for a few years, accepted the responsibilities of public office and applied there the business standards to which he owed his private success.

CHAPTER TEN

Management Problems in the War Department

Congressional parsimony and Republican distrust of an armed force kept the army and the War Department in a constant state of frustration from 1829 to 1861, excepting only the years of the Mexican War. The same kind of problems vexed the army as disturbed the navy, although the War Department had the asset of the Military Academy and a professionally trained officer corps. This advantage was achieved by the navy in 1845, but both armed forces had many and similar complaints to make about their organization and resources.

The morale of the army declined during the years from 1829 to 1845, but was restored during the campaigns of the Mexican War. The *Army and Navy Chronicle* spoke in 1837 of "the contempt in which the military service is held by Congress in time of peace—the smallness of pay, and the slowness of promotion." [1] In 1839 it declared, "The military profession in this country has been so poorly encouraged, that but little incentive is held out to devote exclusive attention to it. . . . The distrust of military men, so prevalent among politicians who hold out the idea that they are dangerous to the safety of a republican form of government, it might be supposed would long since have yielded to the light of reason and experience." [2] The army suffered not only from democratic distrust but from the complete absence of any obvious external enemy. An army without a calculable major mission is per se under a grave handicap.

1 *Army and Navy Chronicle,* III, 138 (1837).

2 *Ibid.,* IX, 392 (Dec. 19, 1839).

An army without legislative support also operates under severe limitations. For years prior to 1861 Congress failed to make adequate provision either for the army or for weapons for the militia. The armories were equipped to turn out 40,000 stand of arms a year, but appropriations allowed production of only 18,000. Congress appropriated exactly the same amount for arming the militia in 1860 as it had authorized in 1808, although the population had increased fourfold.[3]

MILITARY POLICY

The military policy of the country from 1829 to 1861 was a projection of that which had obtained in earlier years, i.e., distrust of a standing army, parsimony in military expenditures, and reliance upon the militia or volunteers in an emergency.

In the *North American Review* for 1832 it was written, "A large standing army has no advocates among us, and is wholly adverse to the spirit of our Government and to public sentiment." [4] Twenty years later the Board of Visitors at West Point, an annual committee of inspection, declared, "The militia will constitute the great bulwark of defence; and as in past warfare, so again in that of the future, their strong arms and brave hearts are ample guarantees against entire subjugation." [5] President Polk agreed. "A volunteer force," he told Congress in 1846, "is beyond question more efficient than any other description of citizen soldiers." [6] All this echoed the convictions of that great citizen-soldier Andrew Jackson, who in his first inaugural address asserted that "the bulwark of our defense is the national militia, which in the present state of our intelligence and population must render us invincible." [7] However great were such illusions, it was nevertheless true that the militia was an organization truly democratic in its character, and that a standing army was still the support of monarchy in most parts of the world.

In conformity with these views the United States Army was

[3] A. Howard Meneely, *The War Department, 1861: a Study in Mobilization and Administration* (New York: Columbia University Press, 1928), pp. 49–50.

[4] *North American Review*, XXXIV (1832), p. 257.

[5] Senate Ex. Doc. 1, 32d Cong., 2d sess., p. 169 (June 17, 1852).

[6] Richardson, *Messages*, IV, 443 (May 11, 1846).

[7] *Ibid.*, II, 438 (March 4, 1829).

held at a minimum strength. Its size had been fixed at the close of the War of 1812 at 10,000, but as a consequence of the post-war depression it had been reduced in 1821 to 6,183 officers and men. The Seminole War in Florida caused a temporary increase, but in 1842 on the occasion of the general retrenchment drive it was reduced from something over 12,000 to 8,613 authorized strength. At the close of the Mexican War, President Polk informed members of the Senate Committee on Military Affairs that all the land forces raised to serve during these campaigns should be discharged and that the "old army" with authority to fill each company to one hundred men would be sufficient.[8] Congress reduced the authorized strength to 10,320. On December 11, 1860, the Senate asked its Committee on Military Affairs whether the expenses of the War Department could not be further reduced.[9]

In 1860 the nation was "nearly destitute of military force." The authorized strength of the army had risen to slightly over 18,000 but the returns showed only about 16,000 officers and men in service. The militia were so lacking in instruction and training, with the exception of a few city regiments, that they could hardly be called a military force.[10] Equipment was poor and uncared for. The Indiana militia had been abandoned in 1834 and its arms lost. "An extravagantly fancy uniform for the commanding officer was often sufficient for an entire company. . . ."[11] Congress had never been able to agree on legislation to introduce order, system, and efficiency into these bodies of citizen soldiers, nor had the states responded to their own immediate responsibilities.

Except for a few detachments assigned to man coastal fortifications, and the officers attached to headquarters in Washington, the army was seldom seen by citizens. This was in full harmony with the settled convictions of Albert Gallatin who had said privately that the best place for soldiers was in distant garrisons where few other inhabitants were to be found. "I

8 Polk, *Diary,* III, 495 (June 20, 1848).

9 *Senate Journal,* 36th Cong., 2d sess., p. 37.

10 General Emory Upton, *The Military Policy of the United States* (Third Impression, Senate Doc. 494, 62d Cong., 2d sess., 1912), p. 225. This work was written in 1880.

11 Meneely, *The War Department, 1861,* pp. 23–24.

never want," he said, "to see the face of one in our cities and intermixed with the people." [12] The army was indeed in distant garrisons, scattered along the western and southern frontiers in small posts where the sparse civilian population comprised traders, trappers, and settlers in their small clearings.

Public policy was committed to employment of the militia and volunteers for emergencies rather than to the expansion of the regular army. The legislation of 1821, indeed, gave no authority to the executive to fill up the companies (set at sixty-one men) as a means of increasing military manpower. During the Seminole War in Florida in the late 1830's the militia and volunteers were the principal means of enlarging the armed forces. When the Mexican War broke out, Polk's first move was to call for 50,000 volunteers and to authorize calls on the state militia. The regular army was increased also, but the volunteers and militia outnumbered the regulars.

THE WAR DEPARTMENT, THE COMMANDING GENERAL, AND THE MILITARY BUREAUS

To control and command these scattered detachments and to equip them with arms, supplies, and subsistence were the major peacetime functions of the War Department and the top command—the General Staff and the general field officers. The department also had civilian duties—responsibility for Indian affairs and, until 1849, for the Pension Office. It also included the bounty land office to discharge land claims of former soldiers. The army built forts and constructed roads in addition to keeping the Indians away from the pioneer settlements.[13]

The War Department. The civilian components of the War Department were not impressive. They included the Secretary of War, his chief clerk, and a few clerks working in his office. Other civilian employees worked in the military offices of the General Staff, but they were nothing more than clerks. There was no assistant secretary of War; there were no administrative assistants; there was in fact only a single civilian officer of author-

12 Henry Adams, *Life of Gallatin,* p. 304 (July 7, 1802).

13 The great contribution of the War Department and the Department of the Interior to western roadbuilding is ably described in W. Turrentine Jackson, *Wagon Roads West: A Study of Federal Road Surveys and Construction in the Trans-Mississippi West, 1846–1869* (Berkeley: University of California Press, 1952).

ity, the Secretary himself. The civilian structure was as simple and undeveloped as it had been in the days of Secretary McHenry under Washington and Adams.

The department had twelve Secretaries from 1829 to 1861, a record that compared favorably with other departments. Only Lewis Cass served more than four years (1831–36). He and Marcy had had some early military experience, and Jefferson Davis (1853–57) was a West Point graduate with several years' service in the regular army. During this same period, the army had two commanding generals, Major General Alexander Macomb (1828–41) and Major General Winfield Scott (1841–61). The frequent changes in the office of the Secretary of War during the Harrison-Tyler administration (four Secretaries in four years) prompted Henry Whiting to declare: "Fortunately, the welfare of the army does not depend for its stability upon this high functionary. He may go out and come in with each season; he may be as deciduous as the leaves; and yet the military establishment, and the national defence . . . remain the same. There is a permanency in the command of the army, and in all the subordinate departments connected with its administration, that makes it nearly independent of these fluctuations." [14]

The Secretary in fact found his immediate assistants and advisers in the person of the commanding general and in the General Staff, an institution established during the War of 1812 and brought into full vigor by John C. Calhoun. The General Staff consisted of the heads of the "housekeeping" departments and auxiliary services, such as the adjutant general, inspector general, quartermaster general, commissary general of subsistence, and paymaster general. It did not act as a collective body and was not the equivalent of the General Staff as organized in 1903.

The commanding general. The subordination of the army to the civil authority in the person of the Secretary of War was not disputed, but there was much ambiguity and difference of opinion concerning the relationships of the one to the other, and the proper organization of military leadership.

By a fortunate combination of circumstances, a commanding general was recognized in 1821 by authorization of the rank of

14 *North American Review,* LXI (1845), 321.

major general, in gratitude for the services during the War of 1812 of General Jacob Brown. This gentleman died in 1828, and a movement developed in the Senate to abolish the office, leaving two brigadier generals as the officers with highest rank. Senators argued that the army (then about 6,000 enlisted strength) was overstocked with officers: "there are now, in this mere shadow of an Army, officers enough for one of 50,000 men"; that no inconvenience would ensue; and that retrenchment was due. Senator Nathaniel Macon of North Carolina asserted, indeed, that it was bad to have too many officers. "When war came, the kind of character you want will come out, nor was it necessary to be seeking it out when it was not wanted." [15]

The central issue in the discussion was seized upon by Senator William Henry Harrison, viz., the need for one commanding officer. He succeeded in sending the matter to committee and brought in an able committee report defending the necessity of unified military command. The alternatives, he pointed out, would be either that direct command would be exercised by the President or Secretary of War, or by the staff officers who surrounded him. Any one of these choices, he argued, would be fatal to the energy and effectiveness of the army.[16] The Senate was satisfied and authorized continuance of the rank and office of major general.

Another attack was launched against the office in 1834. Secretary of War Lewis Cass defended it before the House.

> I consider the office of major general essential to the unity of command. He is stationed at this city to superintend and direct those parts of the administration of the army which are strictly military in their character, and which, to be properly conducted, require not only the advantage of military experience, but of a military connexion with the army. If the office of major general should be abolished, and but two brigadier generals retained, they must either remain in command of separate districts, and this department thus be deprived of the assistance and advice of an officer of high rank, in the management of those concerns which peculiarly affect the army, or one of them must be stationed here exercising an authority over the

15 *Register of Debates*, 20th Cong., 1st sess., pp. 372–79 (Feb. 29, 1828).

16 *American State Papers: Military Affairs*, III, 820 (March 19, 1828).

whole service. The latter arrangement would certainly be liable to objection, and would be inconsistent with the established principles of the military service.[17]

Cass apparently convinced Congress that a two-headed army was an error in military organization. The office of major general was continued, and its occupant remained the commanding officer of all the military bodies. This issue was now settled.

The military bureaus. Another difficulty was to persist, the subordination of the staff officers at the head of the great military bureaus to the commanding general and the Secretary of War. This problem reached no crisis, but there were indications that it existed. The rule of seniority brought officers to these positions, and guaranteed them tenure therein, short of a court-martial. They were consequently well placed to develop their own routines and work procedures. Henry Whiting observed that when the bureaus were established during the War of 1812, there was no commanding officer and they were all placed in immediate communication with the Secretary of War. This arrangement was terminated in principle in 1821, but in 1845 Whiting still found it necessary to argue that all the military bureaus should be subordinated to the commanding general.[18] In 1857 Secretary of War Floyd confirmed Whiting's criticism. In his annual report he declared that one of the greatest errors of organization was "the separate, independent character of our staff corps," a status which, he said, "removes them from their proper position as aids or assistants to the commander and constitutes them his equals. . . . He is bound, as they are, by the law, and his construction of it should govern them, not theirs him."[19]

We have already observed the difficulty experienced by Secretary of War Marcy in his dealings with these bureaus. His troubles were compounded by reason of the disfavor into which General Scott fell, both with Marcy and Polk, in the early months of the Mexican War. During the war Polk maintained direct contacts with the heads of the military bureaus. After Scott left Washington to lead the Vera Cruz expedition, there was indeed

17 House Report 46, 23d Cong., 2d sess., p. 4 (Dec. 24, 1834).

18 *North American Review*, LXI (1845), 321–22.

19 Senate Ex. Doc. 11, 35th Cong., 1st sess., p. 9 (Dec. 5, 1857).

no alternative. The commanding general, the symbol of unity of the army and the principal adviser to the civilian authority, was in the field, days or weeks distant by the best means of communication.

When peace returned and General Zachary Taylor became President, another awkward situation developed. Scott and Taylor were political as well as professional rivals and the former (as commanding general) could not endure to live in the same city with his Commander in Chief, the President. He consequently moved his headquarters to Governor's Island in New York harbor and remained there most of the time for ten years.

Feuds and disputations. The War Department and the army were torn by quarrels in circles high and low. In 1839 the Charleston *Patriot* complained: "It is most deplorable to perceive the many quarrels which occur between the officers both in the naval and military service of the United States. . . . They have multiplied of late in the American army and navy to a discreditable, if not an alarming degree. Some remedy must be found for this degeneracy, or the service will become a theatre of wrangling and vituperation. . . ." [20]

Among the leading characters involved in these unfortunate affairs was General Winfield Scott. In addition to high qualities as a military officer and student of the art of warfare, Scott had a sharp temper and a too ready pen and tongue. As a young officer he declared that General James Wilkinson was as great a traitor as Aaron Burr, an indiscretion that cost him a year's suspension from the army. In 1817 he criticized a military order of General Jackson as mutinous, and Jackson in turn called him a hectoring bully. In 1828 he resigned his commission in disgust when Alexander Macomb was preferred as commanding general. His resignation was not accepted, but for some time he and General Macomb were not on friendly terms. In 1837 a court of inquiry set up to inquire into the causes of the Seminole campaign reprimanded both Scott and General Edmund P. Gaines for their intemperate language.[21]

20 Quoted in *Army and Navy Chronicle,* VIII, 156 (March 7, 1839).

21 *Dictionary of American Biography,* XVI, 505; Charles Winslow Elliott, *Winfield Scott,* pp. 325–31.

Scott's most extraordinary quarrel occurred after the Mexican War and involved no less an antagonist than Secretary of War Jefferson Davis. Bad feeling began in 1851 when Davis, then in the Senate, opposed a resolution to grant the rank of lieutenant general to Scott. This step was finally taken in 1855. Scott thereupon claimed back pay of $30,000, and Davis, now Secretary of War, resisted the claim. Davis also opposed some of Scott's claims for transportation and servants, and for a percentage on certain moneys involved in the Mexican campaign. Furthermore he accused Scott of rank insubordination in refusing to observe an order to cancel a leave of absence for General Ethan Allen Hitchcock.

The temper of the two parties can be disclosed only by excerpts from their voluminous correspondence. By 1855 it had descended to extraordinary levels on both sides. On July 25 Davis wrote Scott, "I leave unnoticed the exhibition of peevish temper in your reply. . . ." [22] Scott retorted that Davis seemed to consider it his special mission, by repeated aggressions on Scott's rights and feelings, to goad him into some perilous attitude of official opposition, and to crush him into servile obedience. He asked Davis to show President Pierce the letter.[23] Davis answered the charges in a letter he considered unofficial, whereupon Scott replied that he would treat all of Davis's communications, "whether designed as private and scurrilous, or public missives of arrogance and superciliousness," as equally official.[24]

After further interchange of long arguments tinged with insults, hot war broke out again early in 1856. Davis poured out his indignation over the "gratuitous and monstrous calumnies" that he alleged he had received from Scott, and concluded a lengthy letter by declaring, "Your petulance, characteristic egotism and recklessness of accusation have imposed on me the task of unveiling some of your deformities," adding that Scott's military fame had been "clouded by grovelling vices" and his career marked by "querulousness, insubordination, greed of lucre and want of truth." [25] Scott told Davis that his letter was

22 Davis, *Letters, Papers and Speeches*, II, 475 (July 25, 1855).

23 *Ibid.*, II, 476, 481 (July 30, 1855).

24 *Ibid.*, II, 488 (August 6, 1855).

25 *Ibid.*, III, 1, 10 (Feb. 29, 1856).

merely a new example of "chicanery & tergiversation." [26] After another exchange, Scott declared, "My silence, under the new provocation, has been the result, first, of pity, and next, forgetfulness. Compassion is always due to an enraged imbecile, who lays about him in blows which hurt only himself, or who, at the worst, seeks to stifle his opponent by dint of naughty words." [27]

All of this vituperation was utterly foreign to proper communication between a Secretary of War and a commanding general, and even in the perspective of nearly a century can only cause wonder at the character of the two participants. On the matter of salary claim, Scott apparently was justified by the letter of the law. Pierce sustained this claim although he decided against others.[28] Davis, however, properly accused Scott of insubordination in failing to obey an order to cancel the leave of General Hitchcock.[29] He informed Pierce of Scott's "persistent disobedience," and recommended that his headquarters be removed from Governor's Island to Washington, and that all orders affecting the army generally should be communicated by the War Department (i.e., by Davis) directly through the office of the adjutant general.[30] So wide was the gulf between the Secretary and the commanding general!

Despite much loyal cooperation within officer ranks, it could not be said at any time from 1829 to 1861 that the War Department and the army comprised such a team as that which Calhoun had constructed when he was Secretary of War. These eight years remained as the epitome of good relations between the Secretary of War, the General Staff, and the army. This was due certainly in large measure to Calhoun; but it may have been due in part to the fact that the army appeared to have a significant and large-scale mission: the planning and construction of internal improvements.

ARMY PERSONNEL PROBLEMS

The army was troubled with officer resignations and rank-and-file desertions during most of the Jacksonian years. The

26 *Ibid.*, III, 11 (March 20, 1856).

27 *Ibid.*, III, 36 (May 21, 1856).

28 *Ibid.*, II, 542–44 (Oct. 29, 1855); II, 548 (Nov. 7, 1855); II, 550 (Nov. 12, 1855).

29 *Ibid.*, II, 472–73; 475–76; 508; 509.

30 *Ibid.*, II, 510–11 (Sept. 25, 1855).

causes were varied, but they centered on the unsatisfactory conditions of service offered by the army so far as privates were concerned, and on the lack of prospects for the officers.

Army officers. Until 1838 West Point cadets were conditioned to five years of service, four of which were spent at the academy. Subsequently Congress required an engagement of eight years, including four at the academy. Many officers made military command their career, but others resigned to seek their fortunes in civil life. It was widely argued that such resignations were not necessarily a loss to the country, since West Pointers contributed assets of various kinds to civilian life. The Board of Visitors observed in 1830, in the hyperbole that ran through its subsequent reports as well:

> . . . . We consider, then, that this academy is expected to furnish to the Army a supply of efficient officers; to the militia an intermixture of well trained citizens, qualified, on emergency, to discipline that last and best arm of republics; to internal improvement, a corps of engineers, capable of giving wholesome direction to the spirit of enterprize which pervades our country. It ought to furnish science for exploring the hidden treasures of our mountains, and ameliorating the agriculture of our valleys; nor is it upon inert matter alone that it ought to extend a vivifying influence. Inheriting from our varied ancestry the discordant characteristics of every people on the globe, it yet remains to form a specific and all pervading character for the American nation; nor do we conceive any surer method of stamping upon the yet glowing wax a more majestic form, than by sending into every district young men emphatically the children of our country, trained to the manly exercise of arms, and imbued with the tastes of science and literature; instructed in the principles and action of our political system, and the living exemplar from which sound education may rear the social edifice.[31]

However great these varied services, the loss to the army was nevertheless substantial, because the ablest officers were most likely to resign their commissions.

Resignations were particularly heavy during the 1830's, no less than one hundred and seventeen officers handing in their commissions in 1835 and 1836.[32] The service lost such men as

31 Senate Doc. 1, 21st Cong., 2d sess., p. 115 (June 1830).

32 A list of names and rank is found in House Report 303, 24th Cong., 2d sess., p. 191 (Jan. 2, 1837).

Horace Bliss, a celebrated engineer; W. C. Young, who became a railroad president; R. P. Parrott, an inventor; Alexander D. Bache, one of the most distinguished scientists of his generation; Henry DuPont, who became proprietor of the DuPont powder mills; Jefferson Davis; and men who were later to make their military reputations such as N. B. Buford, Leonidas Polk, Joseph E. Johnston, and George G. Meade.[33]

West Point engineers were much in demand for civilian business. A report in 1848 showed that of approximately 1,350 graduates since 1802, 132 had resigned to become civil engineers or engineers for railroads and canals. West Point graduates were also scattered through other civilian professions and vocations: eighty became lawyers; forty-two became college professors and five, college presidents; seventy-two held elected political offices; and twenty-nine became planters or farmers. Others took up a miscellaneous array of occupations: merchants and manufacturers, authors, clergymen, and physicians.[34]

Three principal causes were at work adverse to the army: unattractive service on the frontier; competition of the emerging business and railroad world; low pay and slow promotion, governed by seniority. The young lieutenant, fresh from West Point with good foundations in engineering, the sciences and mathematics, and warmed by the parade and display of the Military Academy, would probably soon find himself west of the Mississippi on the very edge of civilization. He had nothing to do except command a small detachment to quiet the Indians. It was not surprising that ambitious men resigned, or if they stayed in the army suffered deterioration.[35] Jefferson Davis stood it for seven years and then became a Mississippi planter.

33 William Addleman Ganoe, *The History of the United States Army* (New York: D. Appleton, 1924), p. 179. An official compilation made in 1847 gave the number of cadets received at West Point from 1802 to 1846 inclusive as 3,206. Of these 1,330 graduated, and among this number 597 were then in the regular army of the United States. A small number were serving also with the Mexican War volunteers and the newly organized ten regiments. Senate Ex. Doc. 1, 30th Cong., 1st sess., p. 652 (June 12, 1847).

34 House Ex. Doc. 1, 30th Cong., 2d sess., p. 295 (June 1848).

35 ". . . most of the real service rendered by the army is performed on the frontier, beyond the reach of even the pioneer settler, and . . . consists in a great degree in preserving the peace on the frontier . . . from this fact . . . the army appears to be of but little use." *Army and Navy Chronicle*, III, 334 (1837).

Young officers were also often put on quartermaster duty, for which they secured no training at West Point and which was peculiarly odious to men endowed with martial ardor. To all intents and purposes they became insignificant countinghouse clerks, with the added risk of auditors' disallowances. The *Army and Navy Chronicle* spoke of this as a great evil, both because the work was not well done and because many young officers became disgusted with this form of service.[36]

In the 1838 act to increase the military establishment, Congress made a very modest effort to render the life of an army officer more attractive. It forbade separating an officer from his regiment or company for employment on civil works of internal improvement, and protected him against assignments as acting paymaster or disbursing agent for the Indian department.[37] These provisions eliminated some distasteful civilian duties but hardly reached the heart of the problem.

Promotion was so slow and so firmly anchored to the rule of seniority that young West Point lieutenants had only distant prospects of becoming captains or colonels. Civilian Secretaries assailed the seniority rule but the army resisted change in this respect. Secretary of War Floyd gave Congress a convincing lesson on the point in 1857 but to no immediate end. "All that has been urged in favor of retaining it [i.e., seniority] with us is the danger of political or personal favor governing a selection. There may be danger from this source, but, by the rule of seniority, the *worst* officer of any arm *must,* if he lives, come to be one of the most important and responsible officers under the government—the colonel of a regiment. By selection, it is possible that the very best may not always be chosen, though the chances are in favor of this hypothesis; but certainly the very worst never will be, and this is surely a gain on the present rule." [38]

The army was not an expanding organism, and vacancies occurred principally as senior officers died or resigned. Given the relative proportion of higher commands to lower, the pros-

36 *Ibid.,* VI, 108 (Feb. 15, 1838). "The Auditors, seated in their arm-chairs," said the editor, "hold him accountable to the uttermost farthing, and the last pound of nails."

37 5 Stat. 256, sec. 31 (July 5, 1838).

38 Senate Ex. Doc. 11, 35th Cong., 1st sess., p. 10 (Dec. 5, 1857).

pects in a small and stable force could not be promising. They were worsened by pressure from civilians for commissions in competition with West Point graduates, and were threatened to a degree by demands from the noncommissioned officers. At times there were not enough vacancies in the rank of second lieutenant to absorb all the West Point men,[39] and they were given brevet commissions and assigned to special duty. In the 1850's the balance of vacancies and graduates was about even.

Peacetime appointment of officers from civilian circles was not new to the Jacksonian years, but it caused much disturbance. When new regiments were authorized in 1838, their officers were chosen from civilian circles. Applications were made to the War Department which selected names of persons to appear before an army board in Washington for examination.[40] The procedure was regularized by Secretary of War Joel R. Poinsett in 1839, authorizing an army board to sit annually in September to examine candidates for commissions nominated by the department. Married men were excluded; age limits were set from twenty to twenty-five; sound physical condition and good moral behavior were prerequisites. The examination covered mathematics, geography and popular astronomy, history and the political organization of the government as developed in the Constitution. College graduates were allowed five additional marks above their earned rating.[41]

This was the War Department's response to democratic sentiment. The army was not pleased, however, and the *Army and Navy Chronicle* reprinted a counterargument published in the *New York American*. The article stressed the want of early training and discipline of civilian candidates, their comparative ignorance, the want of harmony with West Point men, and the certainty that appointments would be made from political motives.[42] The situation from the academy point of view grew worse in the 1850's. President Pierce added insult to injury when

39 The House Committee on Military Affairs reported in 1834 that the average number of vacancies in the army for the preceding decade was twenty-five. House Report 466, 23d Cong., 1st sess., p. 13 (May 17, 1834).

40 *Army and Navy Chronicle,* VII, 104 (August 16, 1838).

41 *Ibid.,* X, 313 (May 14, 1840).

42 *Ibid.,* IX, 182 (Sept. 19, 1839).

he filled forty vacancies occurring in 1855 from civil life, none from the academy.[43] General Pierce was not himself a West Pointer.

Pressure upon officer rank from civilians found a counterpart from the noncommissioned officers. Early in 1837 they petitioned Congress to authorize the appointment of some lieutenants from among the sergeants. They declared that the West Point monopoly was "*contrary to the true spirit of our country, and in opposition to all our republican institutions.*" Exclusion from the officer ranks constituted, in their opinion, the cause "for the present abandoned and degraded condition of the American soldiery." [44] By the end of the year the *Army and Navy Chronicle* was able to report, with approval, that a number of such promotions had been made.[45]

In 1847 Congress authorized the President to promote a noncommissioned officer who had distinguished himself in the service to the rank of brevet lieutenant; and to give a private soldier under these circumstances a certificate of merit with two dollars a month pay increase.[46] Army resistance to such an invasion of the officer corps has already been noted. In 1854 Congress gave general authority to the President to grant lieutenant's commissions to meritorious noncommissioned officers found qualified by an army board.[47] The prospects of cadets for the higher life were thus weakened from more than one direction.

The rate of promotion was also retarded because the army did not have a retired list. Since there were no means of separating officers from the service except for serious offenses and a verdict of a court-martial, they remained in service drawing full pay and perquisites, however feeble and incompetent they might have become. In 1839 Congress asked for the War Department's advice on a proposal that officers reaching the age of sixty have the option of retiring on half pay. Major General Macomb thought half pay would not induce retirements, and proposed full pay, their replacements to draw only the pay of their lower

43 Robert M. T. Hunter, *Correspondence,* p. 268. This letter is incorrectly dated 1858.

44 House Doc. 88, 24th Cong., 2d sess., p. 1 (Jan. 16, 1837).

45 *Army and Navy Chronicle,* V, 378 (Dec. 14, 1837).

46 9 Stat. 184, sec. 17 (March 3, 1847).

47 10 Stat. 575 (August 4, 1854).

rank so long as the superannuated officers lived.[48] Nothing came of this proposal.

The need for reform was vigorously stated from the Mexican field by Senator Hunter's cousin, R. S. Garnett. "The army," he wrote, "is almost paralyzed by the imbecility of its old officers . . . Congress could not possibly pass at this time an act which would more essentially benefit the army than that establishing a retired list, and in saying this, I feel safe in adding that it is the uniform opinion of the whole army." [49] However great the need, whether in war or in peace, Congress was not disposed to embark upon a retirement scheme. Jefferson Davis took up the cause again in 1854, but again to no avail.[50]

Pay was also a common topic of complaint and better rates were frequently urged. Congress was reluctant, already impressed with the heavy costs of the military and naval services. In 1842 an infantry second lieutenant was paid $25 a month and four rations; by 1858 his pay had advanced to $45 a month and four rations. Assuming that his probable prospects upon taking his commission as second lieutenant in 1842 were to hold the rank of captain in 1858, he would then be paid $60 a month and four rations.[51]

Enlisted men. The quality of the rank and file of the army was impaired by a number of causes, long at work. When times were good the army had great difficulty in filling its quota, and then only by recruiting drifters, incorrigibles, and "undesirables." When times were bad it was possible to recruit mechanics and farmers, but generally the army service did not appeal to Americans. The state of morale and the symbol of deterioration were evident in the rate of desertion.

Although the offense of desertion from the rank and file was punishable until 1830 by death, the penalty had little consequence. Desertion was a persistent and at times a major problem. The number of deserters in 1826 was 636, in 1829 it had risen to 1,115, and in 1830 to over 1,200.[52] In 1832 and again in 1836 the number was exceptionally high; ordinarily it varied

48 Senate Doc. 49, 26th Cong., 1st sess., pp. 1–2 (Jan. 4, 1840).

49 Robert M. T. Hunter, *Correspondence,* p. 86 (Jan. 30, 1847).

50 Davis, *Letters, Papers and Speeches,* II, 407–8 (Dec. 4, 1854).

51 Data from *Official Register of the United States.*

52 House Doc. 2, 22d Cong., 1st sess., p. 18 (Nov. 21, 1831).

from about 5 per cent of the enlisted force as a minimum to about 20 per cent as a maximum.[53] In 1853 Jefferson Davis calculated the normal turnover in an army of 10,000 men as follows: 1,290 discharges at the end of enlistment; 726 discharges for disability; 330 deaths; and 1,465 desertions. These figures indicated replacement of one-third of the whole army annually.[54] The situation was obviously unsatisfactory.

A first reform was to abolish the death penalty for desertion in time of peace, already a dead letter, and to pardon all deserters.[55] Confinement and hard labor became the substitutes, and, as Secretary Lewis Cass complained, they were not effective. ". . . where a soldier is confined in a guard-house, and his companions stationed to secure him, and with all the facilities of constant communication, we may well doubt whether his situation is so much more unpleasant than theirs. . . ." [56]

Much hard thought was given to find either punishment or reward to cure the evil. At its root was the irresponsible character of many privates. Secretary of War John H. Eaton wrote a masterpiece of understatement when he solemnly informed Congress in 1830, "there is no disguising the fact, that the rank and file . . . are too often without those considerations of high self-respect, which should invariably belong to this important arm of national defence." He declared that men of intemperate habits and dissolute character should no longer be received in the army. To remove "from the public mind the received opinion of inferiority" attached to the army and to give incentive for enlistment to a better class of men, he recommended promotion of the "gallant and faithful soldier" to commissioned rank.[57] This reform was squarely within democratic dogma; indeed Eaton flatly said, "Barriers to advancement should not exist in a country which avers that men are born free and equal." [58] It ran counter, however, to army preference for West Point officer material.[59]

53 Davis, *Letters, Papers and Speeches,* II, 298 (Dec. 1, 1853).

54 *Ibid.,* II, 298–99.

55 4 Stat. 418 (May 29, 1830); see Richardson, *Messages,* II, 499–500 (June 12, 1830) for the pardon.

56 House Doc. 2, 22d Cong., 1st sess., p. 18 (Nov. 21, 1831).

57 Senate Doc. 62, 21st Cong., 1st sess., pp. 1–2 (Feb. 17, 1830).

58 *Ibid.,* p. 3.

59 The army preference was well stated soon after Eaton's proposal in the

Failing in this direction, Eaton then proposed to withhold part of the private's monthly pay until the end of his enlistment, to be forfeited in case of desertion. He eliminated the whiskey ration, but without much confidence in the beneficial results.[60] Sutlers and taverns were too close at hand. A year later Secretary Cass reported that desertions were increasing.[61] Cass asserted that intemperance, the prevalent vice of the army, was responsible for both crimes and desertion, and proposed to find a remedy in the soldier's mental and religious improvement. His moral culture, Cass said, was wholly neglected. The employment of chaplains was his road to reform.[62]

Another attack on the evil was suggested by the House Committee on Military Affairs in 1832, viz., the enlistment of lads from the ages of sixteen to seventeen, organizing schools for their instruction, and after four years of service exempting them from militia duty. General Macomb objected to taking young men at this age since "none but idle, profligate, and incorrigible lads, who could not be controlled by their parents or guardians" would be allowed to enlist, and proposed instead to enlist boys aged not less than twelve nor more than thirteen, for a twelve-year term. With this change Macomb saw much virtue in the plan, notably to "render the rank and file of the army more respectable." [63] The navy tried an experiment of this sort for the same reasons, but without success. The army did not launch its program to recruit innocents at age twelve.

Poor pay, no prospect of a commission, garrison life on the frontier, enforced labor on roadbuilding, a low tradition of morality, and good chances for civilian employment were too great handicaps to be overcome. The army steadily lost large numbers by desertion, the proportion varying with the state of the labor market. The discovery of gold in 1849 was disastrous upon the companies stationed in California.

Congress was not wholly unresponsive to the recommendations of the army and the War Department. In 1838 it directed

---

annual report of the Board of Visitors to West Point, June 16, 1832. House Doc. 2, 22d Cong., 2d sess., p. 119.

60 Senate Doc. 1, 21st Cong., 2d sess., p. 30 (Dec. 1, 1830).

61 House Doc. 2, 22d Cong., 1st sess., p. 17 (Nov. 21, 1831).

62 *Ibid.*, p. 19.

63 House Doc. 16, 22d Cong., 2d sess., pp. 1–3 (February 1832).

that two dollars a month be retained from the private's monthly pay of eight dollars until the expiration of his enlistment. The law substituted coffee and sugar for the whiskey ration, gave a bounty of three months' pay for reenlistment, and offered 160 acres of land for ten years' service. In addition the officers at any post were authorized in their discretion to employ a chaplain.[64] Thus morality and self-interest were put to work to keep the enlisted men at their stations.

WEST POINT

The Military Academy, reluctantly founded by Thomas Jefferson and raised to excellent standards of education and discipline by Major Sylvanus Thayer, passed through a crisis of democratic hostility under the Jacksonians. The record of academy graduates in the Mexican War restored the institution to democratic favor, and it made an essential contribution to the defense of the country throughout the many years when the army was not an object of congressional favor. The program of study was gradually, but cautiously extended; equipment was slowly improved; but problems of instruction and discipline remained.[65]

The course of instruction. The primary object of the Military Academy was to prepare young men for officers' commissions in the regular army, and the course of instruction was duly directed to this purpose. It fell into three grand divisions: military instruction including the French language; scientific instruction; and moral and religious instruction. The latter was a poor third. Military instruction included infantry tactics and formation drill, in which the cadets were spectacularly successful; artillery tactics; engineering, with application to military problems; horsemanship and fencing. Scientific instruction included primarily mathematics, physics and electricity, and chemistry, a broad area then known as natural philosophy. Moral and religious instruction included not only ethics but whatever social science studies the chaplain was prepared to offer in such time as was free.

64 5 Stat. 256, sec. 18 (July 5, 1838).

65 For two contemporary discussions of the Military Academy, see *North American Review,* XXXIV (1832), 246–61; and *ibid.,* LVII (1843), 269–92.

The equipment and facilities for instruction in the military arts improved, as Boards of Visitors suggested one need after another. The library had been neglected, but was slowly built up. No pieces of field artillery were available in earlier years, but were eventually supplied. They were at first dragged from place to place by the cadets, but at the suggestion of the Board cavalry horses were furnished. Cavalry drill then became possible. Swordsmanship was introduced. The laboratories were chronically deficient in "philosophical" apparatus, but additions were made from time to time. New barracks were built, and a building in which cavalry practice could take place. A hotel was even constructed for guests, but put under severe restrictions for cadets.

Instruction in engineering was superior but the social sciences were neglected stepchildren. In the annual report of the Board of Visitors for 1840, the members declared that the duties of the chaplain, who was also professor of ethics and whose department included political science, history, grammar, rhetoric, and geography, were "certainly very onerous." [66] Colonel Joseph G. Totten, chief of the engineer corps, agreed that more time was required for the English and French languages, history, geography, ethics, rhetoric, logic, and international, constitutional, and martial law,[67] and eventually a fifth year of instruction was added. This year, however, was promptly dominated by military studies, not the humanities or the social sciences. As late as 1854 the Board of Visitors deprecated the absence of a course in history, "an evil so glaring and palpable" that the members urged immediate improvement.[68]

The teaching staff in 1859 consisted of eight professors, including the chaplain who was also professor of ethics and English studies; and in addition the commandant of cadets, the sword master, and young military officers assigned to the academy as assistant professors. The professors, who were civilians, held chairs respectively in military and civil engineering, natural and experimental philosophy, mathematics, drawing, French, ethics and English studies, chemistry, and Spanish. The com-

66 Senate Doc. 1, 26th Cong., 2d sess., p. 148 (June 22, 1840).

67 Senate Doc. 1, 29th Cong., 2d sess., p. 135 (June 1846).

68 Senate Ex. Doc. 1, 33d Cong., 2d sess., Part II, p. 130 (June 22, 1854).

mandant of cadets gave instruction in artillery, cavalry, and infantry tactics. There was also an army officer, instructor of ordnance and gunnery.[69]

The assistants were army officers, detailed to West Point for a four-year tour of duty. This service was not popular as a rule. General Thomas S. Jesup spoke warmly against it. "It may truly be said," he declared, "that the spirit of the service is gone, or fast going, when officers of respectable standing can be found ready to abandon the high and honorable duties of their profession to become schoolmasters at West Point. . . . While the Government encourages, or even permits, officers to be so employed, it is impossible that the army can improve." [70] The Board of Visitors, on the other hand, set great value on the contribution these officers made, and urged that the four-year rule be abrogated and appointments be made without term.

The Board of Visitors was chronically alarmed about the moral instruction and behavior of the young cadets, including the use of tobacco and alcohol. Its members were horrified in 1841 upon examining the principal textbook in the study of the French language, a novel "not of the most moral and useful character." They declared firmly that "the youthful imagination is too delicate and too susceptible of wrong impressions to be safely exposed to the exciting scenes frequently introduced into novels of the class to which this work belongs." [71] The Board deplored that these young men had to read such a book aloud in the presence of others, and to commit portions of it to memory. Year after year it impressed upon the commandant and professors the need for safeguarding the morals of these young warriors.

The academic mortality rate among the students was high. A statement made in 1836 showed that four classes with an original average enrollment of one hundred and eleven graduated an average of forty-five.[72] The causes were stated to be mental and physical disability, inadequate preparation, and an indisposition to conform to rules.[73] Discipline was apparently a persistent

69 *Official Register, 1859,* pp. 126–27.
70 *Army and Navy Chronicle,* VI, 138 (March 1, 1838).
71 Senate Doc. 1, 27th Cong., 2d sess., p. 155 (June 21, 1841).
72 Senate Doc. 1, 24th Cong., 2d sess., p. 311 (June 18, 1836).
73 Senate Doc. 1, 27th Cong., 2d sess., p. 159 (June 21, 1841).

problem, magnified because high authority in Washington failed at times to support the commandant. Jackson was a well-known offender in this respect.[74] Van Buren's Secretary of War, Joel R. Poinsett, declared that he found the discipline of the academy "in a state of great decadence," due to the ease with which reinstatements had been secured.[75] The Board of Visitors in the 1850's was still begging the War Department to sustain the commandant, and declared that the reinstatement of a cadet exerted a baneful influence that tended to paralyze and destroy the discipline of the institution.

Some of the trouble obviously lay with the method of selection of cadets. Numbering as a body usually from 225 to 250, they were nominated for the most part by Congressmen, each entitled to one from his district in rotation. A small number were nominated by the President, often from sons of army officers. Polk performed this duty personally.[76] Jefferson Davis defended the rule of congressional nomination: "We do not have with each change of Administration, a change in the political character of the appointments to the academy; they follow still the political sentiment of the district which each one represents in the academy. They thus carry into the Army every variety of opinion and of feeling which exists in the country. . . ." [77] The academy was often praised as a truly national institution, but it was hardly to be expected during years of rampant partisanship that Congressmen would inquire too closely into the qualifications of their nominees.

The democratic attack. Despite its obvious public utility, West Point fell under a determined assault during the years from 1830 to the Mexican War. The attack and defense illuminate the great currents of opinion that prevailed in these years.

Hostilities opened in Tennessee, the home of Andrew Jack-

74 Cf. his letter overruling Major Thayer and reinstating Cadet Hammond, Senate Doc. 1, 24th Cong., 2d sess., pp. 323–24 (Dec. 8, 1835); and Secretary Eaton's warning letter of Nov. 9, 1830, reprinted in *Niles Register,* XXXIX, 232 (Nov. 27, 1830). Thayer resigned, unwilling to continue without proper support. Sidney Forman, *West Point: a History of the United States Military Academy* (New York: Columbia University Press, 1950), p. 51.

75 "Poinsett-Campbell Correspondence," *South Carolina Historical and Genealogical Magazine,* XLII, 164 (August 11, 1837).

76 Polk, *Diary,* I, 239 (Feb. 20, 1846).

77 Davis, *Letters, Papers and Speeches,* III, 560 (Feb. 15, 1859).

son, in 1833, when the state legislature resolved that the Military Academy was inconsistent with republican institutions and dangerous to the principles of free government, and requested the Tennessee delegation in Congress to seek its termination.[78] The Ohio legislature followed in 1834, resolving that the Military Academy was partial in its operations and wholly inconsistent with the spirit and genius of American institutions.[79] The House subsequently set up a select committee whose report was adverse both as to the constitutionality and usefulness of the academy.[80] ". . . if schools may be established by Congress, to educate men for the army, at the public expense," inquired the committee, ". . . may they not, by a most obvious parity of reasoning, be established to educate them upon the like easy terms, for diplomatists, or for heads of departments, or for clerks and accountants?" [81] The committee concluded that "constitutional principles, principles of sound policy, and principles of fiscal economy" were all opposed to West Point, especially because, it was said, the academy was educating more officers than the army needed.[82]

Apart from constitutional objections the report made a slashing attack on the Military Academy. It argued against educating persons not a part of the effective military force; against failing to require a long-term obligation to military service after graduation; and against entering more cadets than could be employed in active service.[83] It criticized the insubordination of the cadets and asserted that for many the academy was merely a chance for a free education.[84] The committee complained particularly about its undemocratic character, since West Point graduates filled all the officer grades in the army, "excluding unqualifiedly all persons above the age of twenty-one years, from entering, as officers, the army of the United States, however pre-eminent they may be in qualifications. . . ." [85]

The committee offered a defensible substitute. Its members

78 House Report 303, 24th Cong., 2d sess., p. 166 (Nov. 26, 1833).
79 Senate Doc. 247, 23d Cong., 1st sess., p. 1 (March 3, 1834).
80 House Report 303, 24th Cong., 2d sess., *passim* (March 1, 1837).
81 *Ibid.*, p. 15.
82 *Ibid.*, p. 16.
83 *Ibid.*, p. 13.
84 *Ibid.*, pp. 20, 24.
85 *Ibid.*, p. 30. This allegation was not strictly accurate.

proposed that basic training in the military arts be taken over by "colleges and other literary seminaries," that this training be required as a prerequisite for officer appointment, and that West Point be transformed into an advanced school of application and practice for officers in active service detailed for this purpose. This plan, the committee argued, would keep "wide open all the grades of office in the army to the free and honorable occupation of all classes of citizens," including the army rank and file.[86]

An independent attack on West Point was launched by a minority of the Board of Visitors in 1840, comprising four members from the west and the south. They criticized congressional nomination of cadets as motivated by politics and favoritism, and urged that the nomination be made by volunteer military companies in the several states and territories. They proposed an entrance age of eighteen, in place of sixteen (originally fourteen). They recommended a change in the course of instruction so that "those in whom the martial spirit predominates should not, with their ripening years, have their ardor quenched by the cold process of mathematical demonstration, nor the minute investigation of scientific studies." [87]

It is difficult to estimate how great was the danger to which West Point was exposed, but it was substantial. Underlying the hostility to it was an old distrust of a standing army and a democratic resentment at what was alleged to be an aristocratical institution. The academy had its defenders, and among them were to be found a solid phalanx in the Board of Visitors, with the exception of the dissenting minority of 1840. Their praise, it must be said, was sometimes too fulsome to be convincing.

The most damaging charge alleged that West Point was "aristocratical in its constitution." The method of appointment obviously had no taint of aristocracy in it, but there was a widespread opinion nevertheless that only the sons of the rich could gain admission. The House Committee on Military Affairs denied the allegation in 1834 and asserted that not more than one-fifteenth of any class could otherwise have received more than a "common English school education" and that even a smaller proportion of officers in service possessed any other means of

86 *Ibid.*, p. 33.

87 Senate Doc. 1, 26th Cong., 2d sess., pp. 149 ff. (June 25, 1840).

support than their regular pay.[88] Colonel Totten fully disposed of this misapprehension in his annual report for 1845, showing by statistical analysis that of 236 cadets who were in attendance in 1845, only twelve had parents "stated to be independent in life." The parents of eight were said to be indigent; of thirty-six in reduced circumstances; and of 164 in moderate circumstances. The largest number came from families on farms or plantations; the next largest in turn from families in which the father was a lawyer or judge, or merchant or mechanic.[89]

Another complaint was not so easily disposed of: the irresponsible behavior of the cadets. The Board of Visitors remarked in 1847 that the government of so large a number of young men was necessarily difficult.[90] The demerit system in effect from 1826 to 1834 classified offenses against the regulations into seven categories, the most serious carrying a weight of ten, the least a weight of one for the first-year men; for upper classmen a "supplement" was added increasing each year. A House select committee compiled the demerits earned year by year from 1826 to 1834 inclusive. The number of demerits began to drop off in 1831, probably a change in faculty attitude rather than an improvement in behavior. Taking 1831 as a sample, 150 cadets earned not more than 50 demerits; 88 earned not more than 100; 34 suffered up to 150, and 16 were even more delinquent. Too much cannot be read into these figures alone, although the House committee presumed that in no other institution of learning could anything be found "that will at all compare with . . . the annual delinquencies and mal-conduct in the academy at West Point. . . . It is seen that scarcely one in twenty escapes the contamination of the evil associations engendered there. . . ." [91] The exaggeration of an unfriendly committee may be discounted, but it was apparent, and indeed inevitable, that a group of energetic lads, each with congressional or executive backing, would hardly be respectful of the regulations.

The hostility to the Military Academy subsided in the face

88 House Report 466, 23d Cong., 1st sess., p. 13 (May 17, 1834).

89 Senate Doc. 1, 29th Cong., 1st sess., p. 271 (Nov. 1, 1845).

90 Senate Ex. Doc. 1, 30th Cong., 1st sess., p. 630 (June 18, 1847).

91 House Report 303, 24th Cong., 2d sess., pp. 23–24 (March 1, 1837).

of the achievements of West Point graduates in the Mexican War. A businessman's opinion was vigorously expressed by Philip Hone, who wrote in his diary in 1847, "It is to be hoped that the senseless clamor of ignorant fools in Congress, who have been placed by constituents as ignorant as themselves in a situation where folly becomes dangerous, and ignorance is supported by power, will now cease to be employed against the noble institution, the military academy of West Point." [92] The Board of Visitors in 1848 expressed "their deliberate and unanimous opinion, that this academy has been of incalculable value to the country, and is fully entitled to the fostering care which has been extended to it by the government." [93] General Scott, himself not a West Pointer, echoed these sentiments: "I give it as my fixed opinion that but for our graduated cadets the war between the United States and Mexico might, and probably would, have lasted some four or five years. . . ." [94] West Point had won its victory.

92 Philip Hone, *Diary* (Nevins ed.), p. 820 (Sept. 28, 1847).

93 House Ex. Doc. 1, 30th Cong., 2d sess., p. 282 (June 1848).

94 Quoted in Upton, *Military Policy of the United States*, p. 222.

CHAPTER ELEVEN

Management Problems in the Navy

John Quincy Adams' prophetic declaration in 1826 "that it was the destiny and duty of these confederated states to become in regular process of time and by no petty advances a great naval power" was denied by Democrats and Whigs alike, as well as by the reluctance of professional navy men to allow steam to replace the winds of Heaven. The navy drifted. Naval policy and naval leadership were vacillating and infirm. The peacetime duties of the navy were chiefly the protection of American commerce and citizens in foreign ports and waters, the suppression of the slave trade, and the conduct of explorations and surveys. The duty of the navy during the Mexican War was to transport and to blockade, tasks the performance of which brought none of the dramatic gun-to-gun victories that stirred admiration for its achievements during the War of 1812. At the close of the conflict with Mexico, Secretary of the Navy John Y. Mason announced that the country could manage with "a few ships of war."

NAVAL POLICY

The policy of the Democrats had steadily favored a small and an inexpensive navy.[1] Jackson declared the bulwark of American defense was the militia and recommended stockpiling materials rather than building ships.[2] Only two capital vessels

[1] See especially Harold and Margaret Sprout, *The Rise of American Naval Power, 1776–1918* (Princeton: Princeton University Press, 1939).

[2] Richardson, *Messages*, II, 459 (Dec. 8, 1829).

were in active service in 1836. Van Buren was indifferent to naval needs during the great depression of 1837–40; Polk put reliance on subsidies to privately built ships that could be converted to war purposes. Secretary of the Navy James C. Dobbin (1853–57) was more energetic and expansion was in the air, but authorization for five shallow-draft steam sloops was all that a Democratic Congress would allow. Buchanan in turn announced a small navy policy.

The Whigs, inheriting the Federalist tradition, might have done more had their administrations not been broken by death and harassed by faction. Secretary Abel P. Upshur recommended, in vain, a sharp increase in naval expenditures. The West was opposed. General Taylor was not a strong navy man, and on naval matters the Taylor-Fillmore administration displayed no energy. In 1853 the United States possessed not one vessel that could have stood up against any first-class European warship.[3]

The small navy policy of the Jacksonian era, the unglamorous tasks to which the navy was assigned, the absence of sustained vigorous civilian leadership, and the loss of morale in the uniformed forces combined to lower the high standing the navy had held from 1816 to 1829. These factors affected disadvantageously the administrative problems that the department encountered. Nevertheless a new form of overhead organization was introduced, long desired by the navy itself; the Naval Academy was established despite congressional indifference; superannuated officers were weeded out by means of the first retirement system to be established in the federal government; and many technological advances were introduced. Other problems defied solution.

That the navy was slipping from the standards reached under John Quincy Adams was apparent from the guarded annual reports of successive Secretaries. More of the truth—with perhaps some exaggeration—appeared in a long series of articles and official investigations.[4] Lieutenant Alexander S. Macken-

[3] Harold and Margaret Sprout, *op. cit.*, p. 138.

[4] The principal contributions were a temperate but critical article by Lieutenant Alexander S. Mackenzie in the *North American Review*, XXX (1830), 360–89; a series of articles in the *Globe*, a semiofficial spokesman of the Jackson and Van Buren administrations, August 1, 2, 1838, reprinted in *Niles Register*, LV, 23–24

zie began the broadsides in 1830 by exposing the needs of the navy—better rank, pay, and prospects for officers, a naval academy, a naval observatory, improved relations between ship captains and junior officers, the abolition of the marine corps, and the abolition of flogging.[5] Lieutenant Matthew F. Maury declared in 1841, "Bad management and injudicious legislation have reduced the Navy to a state of confusion and disorder never before witnessed." [6] In these words he was but repeating the judgment of Commodore John Rodgers a decade earlier. Rodgers told John Quincy Adams that he had been sorely tempted to resign his commission, "so miserably conducted was the administration of the Navy Department." [7]

The general tenor of the complaints against the navy were set forth in the *Globe,* August 1–2, 1838. This presumably friendly newspaper declared that "the general impression is that the discipline and character of the navy are at a very low ebb." "We are assured," said the Globe, "that there is a total want of that *esprit de corps,* without which there can be nothing high or ennobling in the profession of arms. . . . There is a disposition in too many of our young officers, most especially, to decline or (in other terms) to skulk from service; or at least from all service but such as they may be pleased to think agreeable, or worthy of their pretensions, real or imaginary. . . . They seem to think, so we are told, that the motives and feelings which compel a man to handle a spade or shovel for his daily bread, are those which inspire him to wield his sword in the service of his coun-

(Sept. 8, 1838); a series of articles, "Scraps from the Lucky Bag," written by Lieutenant Matthew F. Maury, one of the navy's most brilliant officers, under the pseudonym Harry Bluff, in the *Southern Literary Messenger,* VI (1840), 233, 305, 785; VII (1841), 3–25; the annual reports of Secretaries Upshur, Bancroft, and Dobbin; the report of the House Select Committee on Naval Contracts and Expenditures, House Report 184, 35th Cong., 2d sess. (Feb. 24, 1859); and the report of the Naval Board of Inquiry, House Executive Documents 34 and 71, 36th Cong., 1st sess. (1859).

5 *North American Review,* XXX (1830), 360 ff.

6 *Southern Literary Messenger,* VII (1841), 15.

7 Adams, *Memoirs,* VIII, 354 (April 13, 1831). Some light is thrown on the state of the navy by allegations of Representative Loyall of Virginia in 1835 that the U. S. ship *Enterprise,* bound for New Orleans, was fired upon by a foreign cruiser, and that the officers declined to return the fire "because they had females on board," i.e., wives of members of Congress. *Niles Register,* XLVIII, 38 (March 14, 1835).

try. . . . It is impossible to make heroes out of men who adopt the maxims and principles of cobblers and tinkers." The *Globe* condemned some officers of the navy for "the habit of coming to Washington, and tagging at the heels of members of congress, with the pertinacity of sturdy beggars . . ." and for pushing themselves forward by the aid of personal importunity or extraneous influence.[8] Lieutenant Maury testified to the correctness of this charge: "a cruise of a few months in Washington tells more than a three years cruise at sea in an officer's favor." [9] The naval officers stationed at Pensacola held an indignation meeting after the publication of the "scurrilous articles" in the *Globe* and declared them utterly false and without foundation.[10] Unfortunately the facts hardly sustained their defense, despite the high character and professional skill of many men in naval uniform. "Sam Jones" declared in the *Army and Navy Chronicle,* "To any one who has been at all conversant with the navy for the last twenty years, the great and much to be regretted change that has taken place in its discipline must be apparent. . . ." [11]

The navy was suffering from congressional neglect, from bad management, from indefensible personnel policies, and, as the years went by, from political interference. The story of the struggle for reform, in part successful but hampered by adverse influences, follows.

REORGANIZATION OF THE NAVY DEPARTMENT

A radical reorganization of the department occurred in 1842 under the first Whig administration, although it had been urged for more than a decade by Democratic Secretaries and by the Board of Navy Commissioners.[12] The initial intention of the Board's proposals was to secure greater efficiency by substituting individual for Board responsibility, but this was not enough to

8 Reprinted in *Niles Register,* LV, 23–24 (Sept. 8, 1838). These articles were so persistently ascribed to Secretary of the Navy Paulding that he had to authorize an explicit disclaimer. *Army and Navy Chronicle,* VII, 158 (Sept. 6, 1838), and *ibid.,* VII, 202 (Sept. 27, 1838).

9 *Southern Literary Messenger,* VII (1841), 24.

10 *Niles Register,* LV, 84–85 (Oct. 6, 1838).

11 *Army and Navy Chronicle,* VIII, 72 (Jan. 31, 1839).

12 5 Stat. 579 (August 31, 1842).

get action from Congress. Evidence of waste and extravagance and of abuse in the transfer of naval funds from one appropriation head to another finally brought Congress into agreement with the department, but for different reasons.

At the time of its establishment in 1815, the Board of Navy Commissioners had represented a great advance in departmental organization. It gave the Secretary a body of professional advisers and relieved him of much burden of detail in the construction of ships, the management of the navy yards, and the supply of naval vessels. Naval expansion after 1816 kept the Board ever busier on these managerial functions.

By the end of Adams' administration, experience had suggested that the Board was no longer adequate to the prompt performance of its duties. Jackson proposed to abolish it.[13] Up to a point the Board agreed in its own demise. In an able analysis of its operations, the Navy Commissioners declared that much delay was involved in deciding routine matters by the Board collectively and recommended that most business be allocated to each of the three members respectively for execution.[14] There remained the duty of deciding upon principle and policy, and for this purpose it was proposed to retain the Board. There were, said Commodore John Rodgers, "many, very many cases, of too much importance to the national interest to be committed to any one person, however eminent in his profession, however extensive his experience." But, he added, "the decision of a fundamental principle is one thing; the carrying that principle into effect is another." [15] Congress took no action, and despite repeated requests from the Navy Department the issue drifted under both Jackson and Van Buren.[16] The problem was not a political one, but it fell to a Whig administration to bring about the change in 1842 that Jackson had proposed over a full decade earlier.

The strictly administrative objective of the reorganization

13 Richardson, *Messages,* II, 460 (Dec. 8, 1829).

14 Senate Doc. 1, 21st Cong., 1st sess., pp. 299 ff. (Nov. 23, 1829).

15 *Ibid.,* p. 301.

16 The two major departmental reports were by Secretary Paulding and Secretary Upshur respectively. James K. Paulding's able report is in House Doc. 39, 26th Cong., 1st sess. (Dec. 30, 1839); Upshur's is in House Doc. 167, 27th Cong., 2d sess. (March 7, 1842).

was stated by Secretary Upshur in terms that have a modern tone. "But the great purpose which the Department aims at on this occasion is the introduction of a system of vigilant, intelligent supervision over all its concerns; to guard against all impositions, in whatever form or shape they may be attempted; to check all extravagant expenditures; to secure the faithful and economical application of the means provided for the support of the navy; to establish a strict accountability for all supplies on shore or on ship board; to improve, so far as may be practicable, the energy and efficiency of the navy, and at the same time to diminish its expenses." [17]

The bill to reorganize top-navy management was passed in great haste at the very end of a turbulent session during which the quarrel between President Tyler and the Whigs reached its climax. The Senate barely took time to hear Senator William S. Archer claim an estimated saving of between $600,000 and $800,000; the House heard an attack on navy waste and extravagance, on the high cost of ship construction, and on the irresponsible transfer of money from one object to another, and voted, without any serious debate but by a convincing majority (117 to 35), to terminate the Board of Navy Commissioners. No one came to its defense.

The duties of the Board were now assigned to five bureaus: navy yards and docks; construction, equipment and repair; provisions and clothing; ordnance and hydrography; and medicine and surgery. They stood without substantial change until 1862. The five bureau chiefs were to be appointed, not by the Secretary of the Navy, but by the President with the consent of the Senate. Here lay the seeds of future trouble as the bureaus developed a strong sense of independence, despite the care of Congress to declare that their duties should be performed under the authority of the Secretary.

The bureau chiefs were usually professional naval officers of high rank and appear to have held their positions irrespective of change of administration. President Tyler made one political nomination, former Senator Isaac Hill of New Hampshire, as chief of the bureau of provisions and clothing. The Senate refused to confirm, although the bureau of provisions and clothing

17 *Ibid.*, p. 7.

stood on a different footing from the others, since Congress did not require a uniformed officer at its head. The first incumbent, Charles W. Goldsborough, was a navy clerk who had risen to become secretary of the former Board of Navy Commissioners. After Tyler had been rebuffed in 1844 in attempting to make a political appointment in the person of Isaac Hill, Commodore W. Branford Shubrick took the post. At the outbreak of the Mexican War he applied for sea duty, and at the close of the war became in succession head of the Philadelphia Navy Yard, chief of the bureau of construction, equipment and repair, and from 1852 to 1871 chairman of the Lighthouse Board. After Shubrick went off to the Mexican War, the bureau of provisions and clothing returned to civilian hands with the appointment of Gideon Welles. He was succeeded by navy men, a purser, and then a pay director, Horatio Bridge, who served from 1854 until 1869. The evidence thus clearly indicates that with hardly a variation the bureau chiefs in the Navy Department were professional naval officers holding these positions on a nonpolitical tenure.

The basic pattern of organization established in 1842 thus brought an end to the one important operating board in the early history of the federal administrative system. Its initial virtue, providing professional aid to a lay Secretary, had been outweighed by the delay inherent in three-man consideration of operating detail involving no matter of principle or policy. On policy issues the Board had an undoubted value, and the lack of formal provision for common consideration of policy matters was a weakness of the new arrangement. However this may be, the navy now fell in line with the normal scheme of organization; a political Secretary, aided by a number of bureaus, each directed by a single official.

POLITICS IN THE NAVY YARDS

The remedial powers inherent in a mere change in the form of organization were not so great as either the navy or Congress had hoped. Moreover the pressure of politics on the award of navy contracts, civilian employment, and management in the navy yards grew more and more disturbing. The lid blew off in 1859 when the House received specific allegations of favoritism in bids for boilers and machinery for naval vessels. John Sherman of Ohio became chairman (and a minority member) of a select committee to investigate the charges, the committee comprising two Democrats, two Republicans, and a Whig who joined the Democrats in the majority report.

Both majority and minority reports were scathing indictments of conditions in the navy yards, with special reference to Brooklyn and Philadelphia.[18] The Democratic majority admitted that the testimony proved "glaring abuses" in the Brooklyn Navy Yard, and that the agency for the purchase of coal had been in the hands of a person "wholly inefficient and grossly incompetent." They cleared Secretary Isaac Toucey of any acts that impeached his personal or official integrity, and found that any favors he had granted were not designed to the detriment of the government. The minority, however, thought both Buchanan and Toucey deserved censure.

The hearings disclosed a degree of partisan influence in the Brooklyn Navy Yard that was truly "destructive of discipline, corrupting in its influence, and highly injurious to the public service." Since 1842 or 1843 the master workmen, who controlled *de facto* the appointment of craftsmen and laborers, had been appointed by the two Brooklyn Congressmen. When Buchanan became President, other members from New York City and neighboring districts demanded a share of the master workman patronage, and it was agreed by Toucey to allow a master workman to each district, so far as practicable.[19] However, some districts got as many as three masters, while others had to be content with one.

The majority report admitted that "the system of appointing and retaining men in the yard upon political influence works great evil. Men have been appointed without due regard to their qualifications and retained sometimes after they had shown themselves unworthy. They learned to rely in part upon a strong

18 House Report 184, 35th Cong., 2d sess. (Feb. 24, 1859); majority findings at p. 53, minority findings at p. 89. The report (122 pages) was followed by four supplements dealing respectively with the purchase of coal (138 pages), contracts for live-oak timber (167 pages), contracts for constructing steam machinery (340 pages), and material relating to the management of the navy yards (390 pages).

19 *Ibid.*, p. 5.

friend to retain them, instead of striving to entrench themselves behind meritorious services. This state of things has shown its natural result in producing insubordination, idleness, and a disregard of obligation and duty in general." [20]

A recent member of the House from New York frankly revealed the party stranglehold on the yard. He testified to the effect that "when the whigs formerly had the yard they would, of course, turn out the democrats, every man of them; they would not permit them to work there; and as soon as the democrats got into power again they would turn out the whigs, and so it has been in all the offices in New York, post office, customhouse, &c., and so it is to-day in the appointment of the police; the republicans appoint all republicans; it is very seldom that a democrat can get a place; if he does it is through some extraordinary influence." [21]

The indictment drawn by the House Select Committee, based principally on the situation in the Brooklyn Navy Yard, forced the Navy Department to look into the conditions prevailing in the yards generally. A Naval Board of Inquiry, consisting of five high-ranking naval officers, was appointed by Toucey on April 1, 1859, and proceeded to make a field investigation of each yard. Their report was no more flattering to the management of the department.[22]

The Board of Inquiry asserted: "All the troubles in our navy yards are owing to the system on which they are organized, and not owing to a want of proper administrative talents in the heads of departments." Waiving for the moment the Board's endorsement of the personal qualities of fellow officers, it became clear that the essential fault in the system, as the Board analyzed the situation, was the mixture of civilian and naval responsibility within the yard itself. The commandant could not control the civilian working force or prevent the play of

20 *Ibid.*, p. 6.

21 *Ibid.*, p. 4.

22 The report, dated June 20, 1859, remained confidential for some months but was called for by the House in 1860 and published as House Ex. Doc. 34, 36th Cong., 1st sess., pp. 1–80. The evidence taken by the Board was subsequently called for and printed in full in House Ex. Doc. 71, 36th Cong., 1st sess. (April 16, 1860), pp. 1–316.

politics in its ranks, nor could he restrain the encroachment of civilian influence upon naval officer jurisdiction.

More specifically the Naval Board found that "the authority of the commandant is extremely limited"; that the rank and authority of different officers and civilian heads were not clearly stated or understood; that great abuses occurred by taking on many employees when they were not needed, "to please an outside influence"; that the storekeeper's office was considered a political plum and had "generally been given to some person as a reward for political service"; that there was little control to insure that men remained at work after reporting in the morning; that the naval constructor had assumed the authority to equip as well as to construct vessels, contrary to sound policy; and that many positions in the yards filled by civilians should be occupied by older petty officers.[23]

To cure these evils, the Board proposed one essential reform and a number of corollaries. The essential change was to make the navy yards strictly "military" establishments subject to the exclusive direction of the commandant. "In the government of a navy yard the commandant should be considered in the same position as if in command of a ship; and all persons employed by the government within its walls should be held to the strict observance of the laws of the navy as applied to yards; and no person should ever be employed who sets those laws at defiance, or refuses to subscribe to a strict enforcement of them to the letter." The navy yards, declared the Board, should "be placed at once under strictly military rule, and . . . the commandant alone be held responsible for the faithful performance of the duties of all those under his command."

The primary corollary of this recommendation was that all master workmen be *nominated* by the commandant for approval by the Secretary and that they be required to pass an examination before a yard board touching their moral, physical, and mechanical qualifications. The existing system left these appointments to the Secretary without qualification. A second corollary provided that the power of master workmen to employ men be terminated, and that all men be appointed by the commandant: "and that when any doubt exists as to their ef-

23 House Ex. Doc. 34, 36th Cong., 1st sess., pp. 2–8.

ficiency, or the motive which induces their employment," an inquiry should be made "to rectify any abuses." [24]

A further corollary was designed to clip the wings of the naval constructor (a civilian employee). ". . . he should be entirely relieved from the duty of equipment, which more properly comes within the scope of the duties of a naval officer." The same recommendation was offered with respect to the office of naval storekeeper. "The public property in store should be under the charge of a naval officer already in the receipt of a salary, which would be an economical arrangement, besides strengthening the military organization of the yard." [25]

Before recording the consequences of these professional recommendations, we may return for a moment to the managerial talents of commandants and executive officers. Although the officers of the Naval Board defended them without qualification, they made subsequent remarks that suggested improvement was possible. In the inauguration of the new system, said the Board, "much will depend on the persons appointed to carry it out. . . . *Seniority* does not always insure the proper qualifications for the performance of the duties of commandant. . . ." Again: "The executive officer of a yard is the pivot on which the efficiency of the establishment turns; and if an officer is selected for this important duty without a due regard to qualifications necessary for the position, there can be neither harmony, discipline, efficiency or economy." [26] It is not necessary to read very closely between the lines to suspect that part of the difficulty in the navy yard establishments arose from the lack of management ability of the commandants.[27]

The central recommendation in favor of unity of command in the hands of naval officers responsible for the yards was too strong medicine for Secretary Isaac Toucey, a lifelong Connecticut politician who was then Secretary of the Navy. In 1860 he informed the House, "So far as the report recommended the relinquishment of important powers of the department to its subordinates, or a more complete subjection of the civil to the

24 *Ibid.*, p. 3.

25 *Ibid.*, p. 8.

26 *Ibid.*, pp. 2, 4.

27 In its report on the Norfolk Navy Yard, the Board by implication found both the commandant and executive officer incompetent. *Ibid.*, pp. 30–32.

naval branch of the service, or the transfer of the appointment of master mechanics employed in the construction of ships-of-war to those whose profession it is to navigate them, the department did not concur with it." [28] In other words, the Democratic party did not intend to relinquish the navy yard patronage.

A new set of rules, however, emphasized the sole responsibility of the commandants, even for the acts of those civilians appointed by the Secretary as "a reward for political services." The commanding officer, declared the new instructions, "shall . . . exercise entire control over every department in the navy yard, and will be considered responsible for the due preservation of all buildings and stores contained therein, and of all vessels in ordinary or repairing, and for the judicious application of all labor." [29] He was required to be "particularly careful that none but effective men are employed, and no more than are requisite . . ."; but unfortunately the commandant had little control over those who hired the men and none over the "outside influences" that had already caused scandal. Pressure for further improvement was, however, great and Toucey soon had to yield at a crucial point. The master workmen were subjected to an examination before a board of naval officers whose certificate of qualification became a prerequisite to appointment. The tendency of this rule was to consolidate the authority of the yard commandant and to diminish political interference by local Congressmen.[30]

The great purpose at which Upshur had aimed in 1842 in the reorganization of the department—the introduction of a system of vigilant, intelligent supervision over all its concerns and the improvement of the energy and efficiency of the navy—thus remained in 1860 yet to be achieved. The fault lay deeper than organization.

SHIP CONSTRUCTION AND NAVAL SUPPLY

These were the years of painful transition from sail to steam in the American navy. The sentimental attachment to sailing vessels was profound and for years delayed a full appreciation of

28 House Ex. Doc. 71, 36th Cong., 1st sess., p. 1 (April 16, 1860).
29 *Ibid.*, p. 4.
30 Senate Ex. Doc. 1, 36th Cong., 2d sess., Part III, p. 6 (Dec. 1, 1860).

the coming of a new era of technological progress. Lieutenant Mackenzie wrote in 1830, "We know of no work of art, no production of human genius and human power, that in any manner rivals, or may even be named in comparison with, the sailing ship." [31] Secretary Paulding loved a sailing vessel, too, and wrote a friend in 1839, ". . . I will never consent to let our old ships perish, and transform our Navy into a fleet of sea monsters." [32]

Apart from sentiment there was much skepticism concerning the technical advantages of a steam warship.[33] James Fenimore Cooper flatly denied that steam would supersede older methods of conducting naval warfare. "No vessel," he declared, "can be built of sufficient force and size, to transport a sufficiency of fuel, provisions, munitions of war, and guns, to contend with even a heavy frigate, allowing the last to bring her broadside to bear." Steam batteries for harbor defense he thought practicable, "but it is illusory to suppose that vessels of that description can ever be made to cruise."[34]

Early experience with the side-wheelers *Missouri* and *Mississippi* tended to support these views. "It is found," reported Secretary Upshur, "that the steamships Missouri and Mississippi are unsuited to cruising in time of peace. Their engines consume so much fuel as to add enormously to their expenses; and the necessity that they should return to port after short intervals of time for fresh supplies, renders it impossible to send them on any distant service." [35] The invention of the screw propeller settled the issue of sails *vs.* steam, so far as technology was concerned, but the navy dallied for years without taking advantage of an initial lead.

By 1853, however, Secretary Dobbin told Congress that steam was "unquestionably the great agent to be used on the ocean, as well for purposes of war as of commerce." [36] His immediate

31 *North American Review*, XXX, 360.

32 William I. Paulding, *Literary Life of James K. Paulding*, p. 278.

33 The principal work on this topic is by Frank M. Bennett, *The Steam Navy of the United States* (Pittsburgh: Warren and Co., 1896).

34 J. Fenimore Cooper, *The History of the Navy of the United States of America* (2 vols., Philadelphia: Lea and Blanchard, 1839), I, xxxiii.

35 Senate Doc. 1, 27th Cong., 3d sess., p. 535 (Dec. 1842).

36 Senate Ex. Doc. 1, 33d Cong., 1st sess., Part III, p. 309 (Dec. 5, 1853).

predecessor, Secretary John P. Kennedy, had already taken steps to convince President Pierce, for whom he conducted a presidential party on a tour of a "caloric vessel" moored at Alexandria. The engine was kept in motion during the inspection, to the delight of the distinguished visitors. "We had Mr. President Fillmore and his elect successor, Mr. Pierce, Captain E. [Ericsson] and myself, and Mr. Everett, all riding together up and down on the piston—rather an amusing and rare inauguration of a new invention." The party terminated with a "sumptuous collation, beautifully served" in the ship's saloon.[37] Not all the members of Congress could be introduced to the possibilities of steam by such an admirable public relations program, and sails struggled with steam right down to the Civil War. The navy was also reluctant to experiment with armored vessels, of which not one was built before the Civil War. "The American navy clung tenaciously to its wooden walls." [38]

The *type* of naval construction was a technical problem. The *cost* of ship construction was an administrative problem. The record of the navy in this respect was not reassuring. Lieutenant Maury presented a dramatic indictment of navy costs in his series of papers advocating naval reform. ". . . the cost of work at the public dock-yards," he wrote, "greatly exceeds the cost of similar work at private ship-yards." The cost of construction and equipment of a sloop of war at the Brooklyn Navy Yard was estimated at $85,000. Across the river in New York, packet ships, one-half larger, "fitted and found in the most elegant manner" were built and equipped for $80,000. ". . . the mechanics of our Navy-Yards," declared Maury, "vie with each other in doing little, rather than much. . . . When an officer demands more work of them than is required by their rule of private interest, he does it at his own peril." [39]

Lack of judgment as well as extravagant costs appeared in Maury's indictment. The schooner *Pilot* was built at a navy yard for $33,000 and sold before her first cruise for $3,000. The schooner *Active,* a ship of the same size, was bought to replace

37 Henry T. Tuckerman, *The Life of John Pendleton Kennedy* (New York: G. P. Putnam and Sons, 1871), p. 224 (Feb. 27, 1853).

38 Harold and Margaret Sprout, *Rise of American Naval Power,* p. 149.

39 *Southern Literary Messenger,* VII (1841), 15–16.

the *Pilot;* the *Active* cost $8,000. She was immediately taken to the New York Navy Yard and repaired at the cost of $13,700, then sent to Norfolk for more repairs, and then sold for $4,500. The frigate *United States* was repaired in 1832 at a cost of materials amounting to $141,000, and additional unknown labor costs. In 1834 she was repaired again at a materials cost of $52,-000, and in 1839 at a cost of $75,000. "After having been repaired this last time . . . she was found to be rotten and is now lying at Norfolk unfit for sea." [40]

Secretary Upshur confirmed these charges in his annual report for 1842. "It can not be denied," he wrote, "that our navy has cost much more than it ought to have cost. . . . I have very little doubt that much of the mechanical labor which has been performed at our navy-yards has been too dearly paid for." The high price and indifferent quality of iron and copper he found to have been responsible in part for excessive costs. "In *copper,* the frauds which have been practised upon the Government, have been gross and enormous." Unscrupulous contractors had been hovering around the navy.

Upshur introduced reforms in the method of navy supply. The new bureaus, replacing the old Board of Navy Commissioners, were "diligently and successfully engaged in devising suitable means of guarding against similar impositions for the future." Where possible, supplies were purchased directly instead of through middlemen. Others were subject to rigorous inspection to insure good quality and reasonable prices. The purchase of surgeons' and pursers' supplies had been subject to constant impositions and in many cases to gross frauds. Naval storekeepers were required to account for goods delivered to them, "with a degree of minuteness which promises to guard effectually against any waste or extravagance in the use of them." [41] The remedy failed to live up to this expectation, notwithstanding some improvement.

The revelations of Lieutenant Maury produced some imme-

40 *Ibid.*, VII, 18. As early as 1829 the Board of Navy Commissioners had urged accounts to be kept so as to show the cost of building and repairing ships and the annual cost of maintaining each one in service; but apparently this reform had never been introduced. Senate Doc. 1, 21st Cong., 1st sess., p. 310 (Nov. 23, 1829).

41 Senate Doc. 1, 27th Cong., 3d sess., pp. 551–54 (Dec. 1842).

diate improvements, but the general level of naval preparedness was low. In 1853 Secretary Dobbin had to report that of the seventy vessels then comprising the navy, many were not only unfit for service, but not worth repairing. There were not forty vessels which could be brought into service in ninety days of preparation.[42] The lack of a stable and consistent naval policy, congressional indifference, confusion over the relative merit of sail and steam, and incompetent management doomed the navy to decay.

TWO SECRETARIES OF THE NAVY

Before turning to other phases of navy administration, it is convenient to add a few words on the office of the Secretary, and on two of its most energetic incumbents during these years.

Lieutenant Maury had complained about the quality of the Secretaries of the Navy Department. They were usually selected "from among politicians, who have never made Naval affairs any part of their study. Neither is the selection made on account of any peculiar fitness or qualifications on the part of the incumbent for the duties of his office. . . . The Secretary of the Navy usually comes into office uninformed as to the condition of the Navy, ignorant of its wants and usages, and unacquainted with the official character and standing of most of its officers. Accordingly he goes to work in the dark, and, of course, blunders and mismanagement ensue." [43] Secretary Upshur complained about the multitude of duties imposed upon him, which any one of his clerks could discharge as well as he, and which caused all of his time to be occupied with trifling details.[44]

Maury had a remedy, that all the details of the service "should be entrusted to a sort of Under-Secretary holding the rank of Post Captain . . . [with] precedence over all the others. . . ." [45] The Secretary should be responsible for the general management of the navy and exercise an appellate jurisdiction over the bureau chiefs. The Under Secretary was designed by Maury to be the equivalent of the adjutant general in the army. These

42 Senate Ex. Doc. 1, 33d Cong., 1st sess., Part III, p. 307 (Dec. 5, 1853).

43 *Southern Literary Messenger,* VII (1841), 23–24.

44 Senate Doc. 1, 27th Cong., 2d sess., p. 378 (Dec. 4, 1841).

45 *Southern Literary Messenger,* VII, 24.

specifications were none too precise; but so far as has been noted this is the first occasion on which an office denominated "Under Secretary" was proposed in the American government. The office was not established.

Most Secretaries of the Navy from 1829 to 1861 might privately have endorsed for themselves Paulding's estimate of his own abilities: "I doubt my capacity for the situation." [46] Later Kennedy stated, "I am not much versed in this Executive business, but I suppose I shall learn that as I have done other things, and get on without much trouble." [47] The *Globe* asserted that the complaints against Secretary Mahlon Dickerson "originated in those qualities, which, though they constitute the charm of social life, too often stand arrayed in direct hostility to our public duties. He was too indulgent. . . ." [48]

Secretary George Bancroft had no doubt about his capacity to manage the navy, although he had hoped to receive from President Polk the diplomatic appointment that later became his. Born in 1800 in Worcester, Massachusetts, the son of a clergyman, he graduated from Harvard in 1817, and after another year in Cambridge devoted to theology, he went to Göttingen for his doctor's degree in theology and philosophy.[49] After some unsuccessful experiences as a Harvard tutor and as a clergyman, he founded the Round Hill School for boys at Northampton in 1831. His young charges called him "The Critter," and this school enterprise was no more to his taste than his Harvard tutorship.

Meanwhile he began to dabble in politics and with a shrewd estimate of future trends joined the Democratic party at a time when such a step in Massachusetts promised nothing but social ostracism. By dint of much political speaking and writing he became a leader of the rural Democrats and, in a struggle between this wing and the Boston phalanx that culminated in

46 William I. Paulding, *Literary Life of James K. Paulding*, p. 270 (May 11, 1838).

47 Tuckerman, *Life of John Pendleton Kennedy*, pp. 219–20 (July 20, 1852).

48 Reprinted in *Niles Register*, LV, 23 (Sept. 8, 1838).

49 *Dictionary of American Biography*, I, 564; Russel B. Nye, *George Bancroft: Brahmin Rebel* (New York: Alfred A. Knopf, 1944); William M. Sloane, "George Bancroft—in Society, in Politics, in Letters," *Century Illustrated Monthly Magazine*, XXXIII (1886–87), 473–87.

1837, he suddenly found himself collector of the port of Boston and recognized leader of the party in his state.

Bancroft had already published three volumes of his *History of the United States.* He now combined an energetic and successful administration of the port with close attention to building up the Democratic machine, and wrote when he could on the fourth volume of his *History.* He discovered a marked aptitude for business affairs in both his public and private transactions, as well as a keen sense of the right political connections.

The Whigs removed him from office in 1841 and Bancroft became historian again. In the 1844 Democratic convention he was one of the leading Polk men, and secured a not wholly desired reward as Secretary of the Navy. Although previous Secretaries of the Navy had not been seadogs, the appointment of an historian-politician with a doctor's degree in theology caused the eyebrows of practical men to rise quizzically. Thomas Corwin, with his customary sharp wit, wrote a friend, "Bancroft . . . is said to be an Unfrocked Parson, having graduated in the spiritual mysteries of Unitarianism first, & closed with the propagation of Universal salvation. He is I doubt not learned in the abstract Philosophies of Emmanuel Kant, Spinoza & Schelling, and vulgar prejudice hints that he is therefore totally ignorant of the science of Hallyards Gunwales & Main masts." [50]

This estimate was doubtless correct, so far as it went. It missed the quality of a dynamic and positive personality, and Bancroft's capacity to seize upon the weaknesses of the navy and to proceed to act. Within a brief term of slightly over a year, Bancroft had created a naval academy in the face of congressional opposition, and for a short while had introduced the rule of promotion by merit rather than by seniority. He grasped instantly the central problem of manpower.

His real ambition in the world of affairs was, however, diplomacy, and with delight he accepted an appointment to the Court of St. James in 1846. As he left the American shore he penned a note to his friend Marcy, who wrote General Wetmore, "I got a brief note from Bancroft written just as he sailed. It was writ-

50 "Selections from the Follett Papers" (L. Belle Hamlin, ed.), *Quarterly Publication of the Historical and Philosophical Society of Ohio,* IX (1914), 82 (March 7, 1845).

ten as if he was well charged with exhilerating gass." [51] The rest of his long life was devoted to history and the art of diplomacy.

James C. Dobbin, born in Fayetteville, North Carolina, in 1814, the son of a prosperous merchant, graduated from the University of North Carolina in 1832, studied law and entered upon the successful practice of his profession. He saw service in the state House of Commons and in 1852 was speaker of the House. At the Baltimore convention of 1852 he led the stampede for Pierce and in 1853 became Secretary of the Navy. His biographer writes that "he was not only a man of vision but an able executive as well; clear-headed, practical, tactful, and . . . easily the most popular of the Pierce cabinet." [52]

Dobbin's efforts to improve the navy appear at length in subsequent pages. He had the rare advantage of four full years in office, coupled with an astute recognition of the problems from which the navy was suffering. He was an advocate of steam and urged a substantial increase in the size of the navy. He stood with Bancroft for promotion by merit, as against seniority, and won a major victory in securing an officer retirement system. He took steps to secure a permanent body of seamen and reintroduced a naval apprentice system. His reforms were substantial, but reformers had to fight against strong vested interests and the rising tide of political interference in naval administration.

51 Library of Congress, William L. Marcy Papers, Vol. 12, No. 34, 814 (Oct. 11, 1846).

52 *Dictionary of American Biography*, V, 335.

CHAPTER TWELVE

Personnel Problems in the Navy

The utilization of manpower in the navy was so incompetent from 1829 to 1861 as to multiply the handicaps imposed by mediocre and temporary leadership, faulty organization, management breakdown in the navy yards, and political interference in the employment of civilian personnel. Every rank from the seaman before the mast through the midshipmen to the commodore and captain had its grievances, many of them well justified and recognized by one Secretary after another. Congress realized that the morale of the navy was low, but declined for years to follow the recommendations of the department for reform. Secretary Abel P. Upshur indeed declared in 1842 that for twenty years past the navy had received from the government "little more than a stepmother's care." [1]

Two major reforms were eventually worked out that gave promise of improvement: the foundation of the Naval Academy in 1845 and the retirement system for superannuated or incompetent officers introduced in 1855. A harsh corrective of many years of personnel mismanagement was the outbreak of war in 1861, causing a general shake-up and the emergence of new men in crisis conditions.

The principal causes of discontent among the senior officers turned on rank, promotion, and retirement. The midshipmen became a burden to the navy, because more were appointed than could be utilized. The seamen were so poorly treated that as a

1 Senate Doc. 1, 27th Cong., 3d sess., p. 545.

class they represented the least, not the best qualified of their vocation, and even then were hard to recruit. The reputation of the navy as the scene of action for either officers or men sank to a deplorable level.

SENIOR NAVAL OFFICERS

Rank. The principal complaint of the senior naval officers was the matter of rank. The highest grade allowed by Congress was that of captain, and the number of these on active service was necessarily limited. This grade compared unfavorably with the title of admiral in other navies. James Fenimore Cooper declared that the rank of captain could never "be a sufficient inducement to attract the highest talents, in a country in which every species of preferment is open to competition." The same status (captain) was necessarily held by the commander of a fleet as by the commander of a single vessel of the larger class; "as great an absurdity," said Cooper, "as to pretend to manage ships with no other rank than that of a midshipman." [2] The consequences were bad not merely for the senior officers, but for the navy as well.

Discipline suffered. Lieutenant Mackenzie wrote, "It does not require any familiarity with discipline either ashore or afloat, to conceive how different may be the tardy and reluctant compliance conceded by one captain to another, temporarily placed over him, but hereafter to become his equal, from his unhesitating and earnest obedience yielded to a General or an Admiral." [3] Lieutenant Maury declared, "The example of the senior officers contending among themselves, is pregnant with the most baneful effects. It poisons the very fountain of discipline, and never fails

2 J. Fenimore Cooper, *History of the Navy of the United States,* I, xxv. It is not easy to generalize as to the character of senior officers during this period. They were apparently a very independent lot, especially when on the high seas. Maury asserted that the difficulty of bringing officers of rank to trial had passed into a proverb (*Southern Literary Messenger,* VII, 12). On the other hand they indulged in courts-martial for junior officers "for the most petty and trivial offences." Captain George C. Reed was found guilty and suspended for one year on charges brought by a midshipman for conduct unbecoming an officer, oppression, cruelty, scandalous conduct, and violation of Article 30 of the Naval Regulations (*Niles Register,* XLVIII, 361, July 25, 1835). Naval captains had, so Maury charged, been using naval vessels to transport funds on private account with a perquisite running as high as $50,000 a trip (*Southern Literary Messenger,* VII, 14).

3 *North American Review,* XXX (1830), 376.

to bring forth insubordination—letting loose among the crew those refractory and evil spirits, which discipline alone can chain down." [4] Fletcher Pratt recorded the absurd comparison of papers whenever two American warships met to determine which officer was entitled to salute by seniority.[5] The indignity of being required to yield precedence to commanding officers of naval forces of other countries, both on the high seas and at social functions ashore, was, however, perhaps the most grievous wound. Democratic disdain for titles smacking of monarchy nevertheless prevailed, and naval officers had to nurse their frustrations as best they could.[6]

The line and staff officers waged war over the issue of assimilated rank. The staff officers—surgeons, pursers, engineers, chaplains, and professors of mathematics—ardently desired rank; the line officers from captain down to midshipman stoutly defended their monopoly. Paullin wrote:

> . . . . To the naval man the nature of this incorporeal hereditament is very clear and real. In naval and official life, and especially in the society aboard ship, rank confers precedence, social rights and privileges, and the esteem of your fellows. It determines the apartment in which an officer sleeps, the position of his chair at the table when eating, his relative position on entering or leaving the ship, his place of promenade on deck, and the fashion and decorations of his clothes. The official worth of a man on board ship is read by his fellow-officers from the buttons and gold bullion on his coat, and he is esteemed accordingly. To be without rank is to be penniless of the current coin of the naval realm.[7]

This source of controversy was gradually eliminated. Secretary Bancroft granted assimilated rank to the surgeons in 1846, Mason to the pursers in 1847, and in 1854 Congress gave legislative approval. The engineers finally won rank in 1859.[8]

Controversy between marine corps officers and navy officers

[4] *Southern Literary Messenger,* VI (1840), 235.

[5] Fletcher Pratt, *The Navy: a History* (New York: Doubleday, Doran, 1938), pp. 235–36.

[6] For one among repeated recommendations for the rank of admiral, vice admiral, and rear admiral, see Upshur's annual report for 1842. House Doc. 2, 27th Cong., 3d sess., p. 543 (Dec. 1842).

[7] Charles Oscar Paullin, "Naval Administration, 1842–1861," U.S. Naval Institute, *Proceedings,* XXXIII (1907), 1466–67.

[8] *Ibid.,* XXXIII, 1468.

on board ship was so warm and so protracted that Mackenzie considered the abolition of the marine corps "absolutely necessary." "The marines," he wrote, "carry on a continual contest of conflicting privileges. . . ."[9] Personal quarrels were frequent. In 1829 Niles wrote, "We have reason to apprehend that there has been much discord among the officers, as well on the Mediterranean, as on the Brazil station."[10] Many ships were said to be hotbeds of wrangling and bitter animosities. "The Perry party hated the Elliott party; and the Barron faction was at swords' points with the anti-Barron faction."[11] Secretary of the Navy Mahlon Dickerson had a violent dispute with Captain Thomas Ap Jones over the command of the South Sea expedition.[12]

Captain Ramsay of the ship *Porpoise* was ordered by the Secretary of the Navy to receive on board his vessel Commodore Woolsey, Captain Claxton, and Captain Shubrick. A controversy developed as to who should command the ship. Ramsay asserted his rights, but at the cost of a court-martial.[13] General Towson and Commander Elliott barely avoided a duel. Towson wrote Elliott that he had taken credit due to others, that a previous letter from Elliott was "a tissue of false statements," and that Elliott was a blusterer.[14] Dueling was officially frowned upon and punished by removal from the service.[15]

Secretary Paulding made a strenuous effort to improve matters. ". . . my great object," he said, "is to restore the discipline of the Navy." On another occasion, he wrote ". . . please God, if I live, and Congress does not counteract me, I will make both high and low young and old know who is their master, before I have done with them."[16] He denounced drunkenness, and ordered officers to keep their men at work, to maintain discipline,

9 *North American Review,* XXX, 386.

10 *Niles Register,* XXXVI, 377 (August 8, 1829).

11 Charles Oscar Paullin, "Naval Administration under the Navy Commissioners, 1815–1842," U.S. Naval Institute, *Proceedings,* XXXIII (1907), 629.

12 *Army and Navy Chronicle,* IV (1837), *passim.*

13 *Niles Register,* LII, 403 (August 26, 1837).

14 *Ibid.,* XLVIII, 434 (August 22, 1835).

15 The President might, under mitigating circumstances, renominate an officer removed for dueling. Cf. the case of Lieutenant William D. Hurst, renominated by Polk (*Diary,* I, 354–55) and confirmed by the Senate, May 7, 1846 (*Senate Executive Journal,* VII, 71).

16 William I. Paulding, *Literary Life of James K. Paulding,* pp. 274–75 (1839).

to curtail leave of absence, and to refrain from sending communications to the newspapers.[17] Congress was not always cooperative, and Paullin was obliged to conclude that Secretary Paulding left the navy much as he found it.[18]

Promotion. Another cause of concern among the higher ranks was the rule governing promotion, which had been fixed traditionally and firmly on ground of seniority. Some members of Congress were also disturbed on this point. In 1842 Senator Richard H. Bayard declared the consequence was that the higher ranks were burdened with officers unfit for duty from age, infirmity, sickness, and other causes. The seniority rule, he added, was defensible only by reason of "the nature of our institutions, and the influences which may be brought to bear on those who administer the Government." [19] Bancroft attacked the seniority rule and convened a board of naval officers in July 1846 to consider a system of promotion by merit. The board was divided, although a majority was brought to agree with Bancroft. The Senate, however, refused to confirm Bancroft's first subsequent list of naval appointments, an adequate sign of Senate disapproval of this administrative innovation.[20] The navy reverted to tradition.

A new attempt was made by Secretary Dobbin. In his annual report for 1853 he informed Congress,

> The great evil in our present system is, that neither merit, nor sea-service, nor gallantry, nor capacity, but *mere seniority of commission, regulates promotion and pay.* The gallant, chivalrous men of the navy feel subdued, dispirited, discouraged; their ardor is chilled; the fire of their young ambition and pride is well nigh extinguished. . . . The officer who encounters all the perils of the deep, wins the admiration of the world for his brilliant achievements, and makes his countrymen prouder than ever of their country, returns to rest awhile from his toils, but to feel mortified in seeing the indolent, the imbecile, who have known no toils, and have never met the enemy, daily promoted over him.[21]

17 Amos L. Herold, *James Kirke Paulding: Versatile American* (New York: Columbia University Press, 1926), p. 129.

18 Paullin, "Naval Administration, 1815–1842," *op. cit.*, XXXIII, 629.

19 Senate Doc. 283, 27th Cong., 2d sess., p. 2 (April 29, 1842).

20 *Niles Register,* LXX, 384 (August 15, 1846).

21 Senate Ex. Doc. 1, 33d Cong., 1st sess., Part III, p. 312 (Dec. 5, 1853).

Congress was not disposed to legislate a rule of merit. Dobbin went as far as he could to scuttle the seniority system. He said flatly that there were "many officers now in the Navy whose names do not adorn the Register. There are those incapable of performing duties from age or affliction." "The magic touch of reform is needed, and if skilfully applied will impart to the now drooping body of our Navy a robust health and a new life." He informed Congress, "I cannot recommend for promotion to higher rank and larger pay, officers who do not merit it, from incapacity, either moral or physical. I do not appreciate the justice or policy of promoting to a higher grade an officer who cannot perform its duties." [22] Congress nevertheless reaffirmed the rule of seniority.[23]

Furlough. So great was the solidarity of the naval officer corps that they succeeded in protecting themselves not only as to promotion prospects, but also as to furlough. Officers were either on duty or off duty. In the latter case they might be awaiting orders, on leave of absence, or on furlough. If on furlough, they were placed on half pay. In 1835 Congress enacted that no officer should be placed on furlough except at his own request.[24] This provision, commented Senator Bayard, was founded in "a jealousy of the probable abuse" of the discretionary power of the Secretary of the Navy but had the effect of depriving him of one of the most important means of preserving the efficiency of the service. It was also expensive, since officers unfit for active service could only be placed in the condition of waiting orders at full pay. An officer could continue in this status for years, "in a state of perfect idleness." [25] Bayard recommended restoration of discretionary authority to the Secretary of the Navy to put naval officers on furlough at reduced pay, and forecast the necessity of a retired list.

Retirement. The problem of superannuation, which underlay many of the discontents of naval officers, was long standing. Secretary John Branch quoted "a distinguished Naval character" in his annual report of 1829 to the effect that any national estab-

22 Senate Ex. Doc. 1, 33d Cong., 2d sess., Part II, pp. 393–94 (Dec. 4, 1854).

23 10 Stat. 616, sec. 2 (Feb. 28, 1855).

24 4 Stat. 755 (March 3, 1835).

25 Senate Doc. 283, 27th Cong., 2d sess., pp. 1–3 (April 29, 1842).

lishment ran the risk of receiving into its ranks some persons not well calculated to uphold its character. "It is now twenty-eight years since a judicious pruning was given to the Navy; a period sufficient to admit some useless suckers to repose under the shade of its virtues and its valor." The "distinguished Naval character" proposed to get rid of the useless and insubordinate portion of the force, thus rendering the management of the remainder "more easy to the Executive Department." [26] Two years later Secretary Woodbury reported that the moral and religious benefits of naval chaplains were lost by reason of the bodily infirmities of a majority of them.[27]

Not until Secretary Dobbin seized upon this problem in 1853 was any progress achieved.[28] In his first report to Congress, this energetic Secretary set out a reformed personnel system in a single sentence: "I entertain the opinion that *a retired list, on reduced pay, for the faithful who have become infirm; the discharge of the inefficient, who have no claim on the bounty of their government for services rendered; promotion regulated by capacity, merit, and not by mere seniority of commission; pay to some extent controlled by sea-service,* are reforms not only demanded by the condition of the service, by considerations of justice, but absolutely necessary to the preservation of efficiency and usefulness." [29] He recommended a retirement board selected by and reporting to the President. To enable the board to act intelligently and impartially in this ticklish task he advised that the Secretary invite, "in the least offensive and most delicate mode," the opinions of the officer corps.

Congress was finally stirred to action. It directed the President to assemble a board of naval officers—five captains, five commanders, and five lieutenants—to report the names of all naval officers "incapable of performing promptly and efficiently all their duty both ashore and afloat." If the cause of inefficiency

26 Senate Doc. 1, 21st Cong., 1st sess., p. 41 (Dec. 1, 1829). Cf. Admiral Alfred T. Mahan's later confirmation of the need for reform, *From Sail to Steam: Recollections of Naval Life* (New York: Harper and Brothers, 1907), pp. 12–19.

27 House Doc. 2, 22d Cong., 1st sess., p. 42 (Dec. 3, 1831).

28 Fillmore had recommended this reform in 1850. Richardson, *Messages,* V, 88–89.

29 Senate Ex. Doc. 1, 33d Cong., 1st sess., Part III, p. 313 (Dec. 5, 1853).

implied "sufficient blame" on the part of the officer, he was to be dropped from the service; otherwise he was to be placed on a reserved list with reduced pay and no right of promotion. Decision rested with the President in each case.[30]

The board met in 1855 and applied the congressional standard "rigorously and with consummate fearlessness." [31] It found 201 officers incapacitated and recommended that 49 be dismissed, that 81 be retired on furlough pay, and that 71 be retired on leave of absence pay.[32] These recommendations were approved by President Pierce and put into effect.

The report created a profound sensation. The legislatures of New Jersey and Virginia protested in behalf of their officer-citizens, memorials were sent to Congress, and newspapers took up the cause of the unfortunate officers.[33] The board was accused of conspiracy, favoritism, and the promotion of its own interests.

In the face of this uproar Congress retreated. In 1857 it offered every officer dropped or retired an opportunity to secure a review before a court of inquiry, and furthermore granted every officer not reinstated a year's salary.[34] Many officers were thus restored to active status, but many who were incapacitated were permanently retired. The reserved list of 1860 contained the names of 19 captains, 16 commanders, and 35 lieutenants.[35]

The objects of the naval efficiency act of 1855 were thus only partly attained. Furthermore the dissension and hostility evoked by the recommendations of the retirement board would beyond doubt have disturbed officer morale for years to come, had not war soon intervened. On the other hand, important gains were realized, both by eliminating deadwood and by giving younger

30 10 Stat. 616 (Feb. 28, 1855).

31 Paullin, "Naval Administration, 1842–1861," *op. cit.*, XXXIII, 1472.

32 Senate Ex. Doc. 1, 34th Cong., 1st sess., Part III, pp. 10–13; 30–44 (Dec. 3, 1855).

33 Paullin, *op. cit.*, XXXIII, 1471. Poor Dobbin was so harassed that he offered to give the faithful wife of a retired officer his resignation if she thought another Secretary would be less hardhearted. Another wife indignantly declared, "What can they mean by unfitness, my husband is six feet two in his stocking feet." Varina Jefferson Davis, *Jefferson Davis: A Memoir* (2 vols., New York: Belford Co., 1890), I, 562–63.

34 11 Stat. 153 (Jan. 16, 1857). Cf. Secretary Toucey's report, Dec. 3, 1857, Senate Ex. Doc. 11, 35th Cong., 1st sess., Part III, p. 583.

35 Paullin, *op. cit.*, XXXIII, 1473.

officers their well-earned promotions. In the long run, the naval officer retirement plan was to be a powerful means of progress. Admiral Mahan many years later wrote, "It would be difficult to exaggerate the benefit of this measure to the nation . . ." [36]

MIDSHIPMEN

The fundamental cause of impaired morale among the midshipmen was the appointment of many more young men than could be put on active duty. Unemployed, on half pay, with no physical connection with ships or yards, frustrated in the hope of sea duty, their morale deteriorated and their skills were impaired.

Since the War of 1812 the number of vessels in commission and the number of officers and men to be employed had been left to executive discretion, subject to the limitations of the appropriation acts. The number of appointments as midshipmen was also left to the President. In 1828 Adams appointed 115 midshipmen, while in other years a mere handful were commissioned.[37] The number needed was in exact proportion to the number and class of vessels in commission or in prospect. Instead of using this formula, midshipmen were appointed during the 1830's at the rate of forty-two a year, of whom thirty-eight were found on the average qualified for promotion. Not more than sixteen were required for active service; the remainder went into inactive status as "Passed Midshipmen." By 1840 there were over two hundred such, whose half pay ran into $150,000 a year, with no services rendered. Maury calculated that a midshipman appointed in 1839 might expect his promotion as lieutenant in 1870 if the then existing system were continued.[38] Bancroft declared, "The navy languishes from the profusion of officers." [39]

The evil was early recognized, but a remedy was slow in forthcoming. In 1830 Secretary John Branch spoke plainly about deterioration among the younger officers.

36 Mahan, *From Sail to Steam,* p. 23.

37 Maury, "Scraps from the Lucky Bag," *Southern Literary Messenger,* VII (1841), 3.

38 *Ibid.,* VI (1840), 319.

39 House Doc. 188, 29th Cong., 1st sess., p. 3 (April 23, 1846).

. . . to keep in the pay of the Government a greater number of these officers than can be usefully employed, is not only a prodigal waste of the public money, but a prodigal abuse of the character of the youth of the country. When thus appointed to the Navy, and taken from the guardianship of their natural friends, and thrown, without restraint or occupation, upon society, it can rarely happen that they escape the dissolute and enervating habits incident to a life of idleness and indulgence.

Every day's experience gives confirmation to the opinion, that the worst effects to the moral and professional characters of the Midshipmen of the Navy result from this state of emancipation from parental guardianship, unrestrained by the active discipline of the service to which they nominally belong.

Should the exigencies of the nation demand a sudden increase of the corps, it would be far safer to resort to appointments made for the occasion than to rely upon supernumeraries thus become negligent and insubordinate, and who, if brought into service, would rather tend to weaken than to augment its strength.[40]

In apparent contradiction, Lieutenant Maury testified in 1841 to the good moral character of the midshipmen. "The tone of morals among officers in the Navy was never better, or at a higher pitch than it now is." Maury was perhaps thinking of the men on active duty. This satisfactory moral level he ascribed to the introduction of examinations for midshipmen in 1819, the requirement of credentials, and a probationary cruise.[41] Secretary Upshur, however, in 1842 supported Branch: "It is a notorious fact," said Upshur, "that wayward and incorrigible boys, whom even parental authority can not control, are often sent to the navy as a mere school of discipline. . . ." [42]

The midshipmen who were actually assigned sea duty were forced to remain too long in this rank. Their status was not yet that of an officer. They messed with the crew and in many cases gradually lost what capacity for command they may have possessed. "Their powers of initiative and decision were atrophied by nonuse; their approach to life was that of the lower deck—they existed in easy vice in port and unintelligent stoicism at sea, regarded the higher command with a kind of sullen resent-

40 Senate Doc. 1, 21st Cong., 2d sess., pp. 49–50 (Dec. 6, 1830).
41 *Southern Literary Messenger*, VII, 21.
42 Senate Doc. 1, 27th Cong., 3d sess., p. 545.

ment as a state to which they could never hope to reach. 'Drunk as a naval officer' was a simile of the period." [43]

The naval appropriation act of 1842 recognized this problem by providing that the number of officers and midshipmen then in service should not be increased until further order of Congress.[44] This "freeze" was far from a satisfactory solution of the problem. Secretary Upshur told Congress at once that such a policy would prove "extremely unfortunate in its action." There were not enough medical officers then in the service, and the proportion of different grades of officers necessarily had to fluctuate with the class of ships on active duty. It would be impossible, Upshur concluded, "to furnish the proper officers . . . supposing any considerable number of our captains and commanders to be employed." [45]

Maury urged the regular recruitment of only enough officers to meet anticipated needs, the number to be fixed by law in accordance with the number and class of vessels in active employment. This would have been a rational and effective solution in the long run. Secretary Paulding offered another solution by proposing to keep in service a number of vessels sufficient to employ the number of officers available for service.[46] Neither Maury's plan nor Paulding's astonishing project was endorsed by Congress.

SEAMEN

The reputation of the navy among the mariners of the country was low. The quality of seamen who were enlisted for naval cruises was poor, despite many competent men who sailed under the flag. During most of the thirty years from 1830 to 1860 there were complaints about the reluctance of mariners to enlist for naval cruises, and derogatory descriptions of those who did.

The navy was in direct competition with the merchant marine for the service of sailors, and its success in recruitment varied with the state of demand on the open labor market. In 1831 and 1832 Levi Woodbury reported that the navy had found no diffi-

[43] Fletcher Pratt, *The Navy*, p. 236.

[44] 5 Stat. 500 (August 4, 1842).

[45] Senate Doc. 1, 27th Cong., 3d sess., p. 545 (Dec. 1842).

[46] Senate Doc. 1, 25th Cong., 3d sess., p. 598 (Nov. 30, 1838).

culty in assembling crews,[47] but more frequently the reports were less encouraging. In 1841 Secretary Upshur reported that great difficulty was experienced in the enlistment of seamen.[48] In 1853 Secretary Dobbin stated that the difficulty of enlisting young Americans was seriously embarrassing the efforts of the department in maintaining the small naval force allowed by law. "Hundreds of merchant vessels," he wrote, "are almost daily darting forth from our busy marts readily filled with cheerful seamen, courting danger upon the element on which they love to live, while our ships-of-war are lingering in port until the recruiting officers, by hard effort, can manage, by the aid of the exacting landlord of the sailor-tavern and a small bounty, to procure tardy enlistments." [49]

To a considerable degree, indeed, the navy had to depend upon seamen of other countries. Lieutenant Mackenzie declared that the better class of American seamen would not enter the naval service under existing systems of discipline. The navy, he wrote, "was compelled to supply itself from among the less scrupulous; out of whom and the foreigners, who entered extensively, a class was formed and perpetuated of degraded individuals, who have rendered the name of man-of-war's men a stigma. . . ." [50] The *Norfolk Beacon* declared in 1839, "If there was ever a class of men deemed incapable of amendment, they were those, who . . . shipped on board a man-of-war. Such men seemed unassailable by the ordinary means of moral attack; they were given over in despair." [51]

This was not mere newspaper exaggeration. Navy instructor Enoch C. Wines confirmed these derogatory comments after ample opportunity to judge man-of-war mariners both afloat and ashore. In his memoirs he sketched their qualities, good and bad.

> . . . . Generosity; a sort of grumbling contentment; susceptibility to kindness; a mixture of credulity and scepticism; a superstitious

47 House Doc. 2, 22d Cong., 1st sess., p. 42 (Dec. 3, 1831); House Doc. 2, 22d Cong., 2d sess., p. 47 (Dec. 3, 1832).

48 Senate Doc. 1, 27th Cong., 2d sess., p. 373 (Dec. 4, 1841).

49 Senate Ex. Doc. 1, 33d Cong., 1st sess., Part III, p. 314 (Dec. 5, 1853).

50 *North American Review*, XXX (1830), 387–88. *The Army and Navy Chronicle* supported this derogatory opinion, I, 135 (April 23, 1835).

51 Reprinted in *Niles Register*, LVI, 278 (June 29, 1839).

dread of imaginary, and a contempt of real dangers; a strong love of the marvelous; a rough, open-hearted simplicity of manners and language; gross sensuality; shocking profaneness; imperturbable effrontery in lying; and an insatiable thirst for strong drink,—will generally be found to be the constituent parts of a sailor's character when carefully analyzed. On the whole, the bad qualities preponderate, and the character of our seamen as a body is very low in the scale of moral excellence.[52]

This judgment was confirmed by the returns from commanders of ships showing offenses committed. On the ship *United States* from August 18 to November 18, 1848, seventy-two members of the crew were visited with twelve lashes each for such offenses as being drunk and abusing the captain, chasing the captain's cook and beating him, being drunk and fighting ashore, insolence and disrespect, gambling, fighting, and insubordination.[53] A corresponding record reported from other ships produced a dismal view of the quality and character of the men before the mast.

A sailor was hung on board the U.S. sloop of war *John Adams* at sea off Naples in 1836. Niles recorded that the sailor had confessed to the murder of a fellow seaman "in a drunken frolic at Mahon." He was tried by a court-martial. "The event," wrote Niles, "produced a melancholy sensation on board the ship." [54] Mutinies on naval vessels were not unknown.[55] Such dark events must be kept in balance with "the large and meritorious class of mariners" who were also found on American ships-of-war. It is, however, a reasonable conclusion that the conditions of naval employment were not such as to induce the most reliable and competent seamen to enter the public service.

A number of handicaps embarrassed the naval service. Cruises of naval vessels were long, usually of three years; ships were on the Mediterranean, the Brazilian, or other stations, or anchored in foreign ports. The merchant ship on the other hand normally made short cruises and brought its sailors back to home port at frequent intervals.

The quality of American naval vessels was not such as to at-

52 Enoch Cobb Wines, *Two Years and a Half in the American Navy* (2 vols., London: Richard Bentley, 1833), II, 158.

53 House Ex. Doc. 26, 31st Cong., 1st sess., p. 2 (Jan. 15, 1850).

54 *Niles Register,* LI, 32 (Sept. 10, 1836).

55 *Ibid.,* XLI, 104 (Oct. 8, 1831).

tract the best seamen. Naval design had failed to keep up with the fine lines of the merchant marine. "A quick ship for smart officers, and a dull ship for lubbers" was an ocean proverb in good standing. Lieutenant Maury wrote eloquently on the virtue of a good vessel.

. . . . A fast ship on a beautiful model is the pride of a sailor's heart—she bends gracefully to the breeze; and, bounding over the deep, bears him safely and swiftly along; she rides out the gale like a duck on the water—and in the storm she behaves like a thing of life, dashing the foam from her bows and leaping over the waves; or stopping to buffet some threatening billow, she rises, trembling from the shock, as though she were conscious of her danger. On board such a ship, duty is a pleasure, and is always performed with alacrity. . . .

. . . . But your slow ship, Sir; she is "an old *droger*"—a mere log in the water. Dull herself, her officers become habitually so; the crew suiting their actions to her's move lazily along,—and thus her character is impressed upon those who serve in her. Awkward and uncomely in appearance, every thing looks lubberly. There is no pride of ship about her to excite and give energy—nothing to combine pleasure with duty, or give zest to exertion. . . .[56]

Maury called the navy ships "a nest of tubs" and with some bitterness compared the models constructed by Eckerford for private owners with the models "reconstructed" by the Board of Navy Commissioners from Eckerford's drawings.

The principal handicap preventing the recruitment of "smart" mariners was, however, the traditional navy practice of flogging.[57] John Randolph had been so shocked by scenes on the U.S.S. *Concord* which in 1830 was bearing him to Russia that he resolved never again to take passage on a vessel of war. "The odious spectacle," he wrote Jackson, surprised and shocked even his negro slaves.[58]

The temper of the American people was rising against flogging, but the navy resisted any reform. Secretary John Y. Mason informed the House of Representatives that corporal punishment could be inflicted only on order of the commanding officer;

56 *Southern Literary Messenger,* VII, 21.

57 Flogging was known also in the merchant marine. *Niles Register,* LI, 288 (Dec. 31, 1836).

58 Jackson, *Correspondence,* IV, 364 (Oct. 24, 1831).

that he could impose only twelve lashes for a single offense; that a naval court-martial could not impose more than one hundred lashes; and that a quarterly report of offenses and punishments was required from every ship. Mason held that flogging could not be dispensed with on shipboard, "without injury to the discipline of the service, endangering the safety of our ships of war, and making necessary a system of punishment far more oppressive and cruel. . . ."[59]

Congress nevertheless responded to public sentiment and in 1850 abolished flogging both in the navy and the merchant marine.[60] The navy remained unconvinced. Secretary Kennedy reported to Congress in 1852 that all the evidence tended to show "a most unsatisfactory result." He cited evidence "in the history of almost every cruise, of acts of insubordination . . . that threaten to lead to extensive and uncontrollable mutinies," and noted the "invention of new penalties of the most revolting kind" that he feared would raise a hostile sentiment in the public mind.[61] Secretary James C. Dobbin, however, spoke against the restoration of capital punishment and proposed affirmative steps to improve naval morale.[62]

The basis of Dobbin's reforms was to build up a body of seamen permanently attached to the navy. Traditionally seamen had always been shipped for a single cruise, at the end of which they were discharged with no expectation of further service. A new crew would be found for the next cruise. Dobbin proposed to make seamen, like officers, a permanent part of the navy. To this end he suggested, and Congress accepted, a plan by which meritorious seamen, on completing a cruise, would receive an honorable discharge which would be converted into a leave of absence with pay if the sailor reenlisted within a specified time.[63] Congress also accepted a recommendation to increase the pay of seamen from twelve to fifteen dollars a month, the minimum competitive rate.

Secretary Dobbin proposed an ingenious scheme of rewards

59 House Doc. 157, 28th Cong., 2d sess., p. 2 (Feb. 25, 1845).

60 9 Stat. 515 (Sept. 28, 1850).

61 John P. Kennedy, *Political and Official Papers* (New York: G. P. Putnam and Sons, 1872), pp. 525–26.

62 Senate Ex. Doc. 1, 33d Cong., 1st sess., Part III, pp. 316–17 (Dec. 5, 1853).

63 *Ibid.*, p. 315.

and punishments which he thought would greatly improve morale. An indolent mariner could no longer be flogged. Dobbin recommended that he forfeit his pay, and that this sum be divided among the men who faithfully performed their duty. Likewise a deserter's pay was forfeited to the crew. To reduce complaints against the single judgment of the commanding officer, Dobbin proposed a minor court of some of the ship's officers to recommend these pay deductions, the decision to be made by the commander. Such a fund, it was argued, "would constitute a prize sufficient to stimulate the crew to win a share by fidelity to the end," as well as a means of diminishing offenses.[64]

The objectives that Dobbin set, so far as seamen were concerned, were a model of intelligent personnel practice. He proposed, "to *reward* the meritorious, to elevate the character of our seamen, to give more respectability to their pursuit, to cause them to become identified with, incorporated into, and a part of, the navy itself; to pay them better, to encourage them to love the flag under which they sail; and when they walk the deck of the man-of-war in a foreign port, and compare their condition with the sailors of other governments, to feel some pride in being American sailors, under American colors."[65] By 1856 Dobbin could see an improvement in the character of naval seamen—but "the wonderful increase of commerce and demand for sailors" rendered it no easy matter to meet the needs of the navy.[66]

An interesting experiment to assist both the navy and the merchant marine was launched in 1837.[67] Boys between the age of thirteen and eighteen were enlisted to serve until they were twenty-one, with prospects of promotion to petty officer ranks. Four school ships were established and the boys were also taken on cruise.[68] An observer in Norfolk was struck by the appearance of a navy boat whose crew looked "like sailors in miniature"; they were young apprentices from the training ship *Java*. By

64 *Ibid.*, p. 317.

65 *Ibid.*, p. 315.

66 Senate Ex. Doc. 5, 34th Cong., 3d sess., Part II, p. 415 (Dec. 1, 1856).

67 5 Stat. 153 (March 2, 1837).

68 Paullin, "Naval Administration, 1815–42," *op. cit.*, XXXIII, 636–37. Regulations governing this service were reprinted in *Niles Register*, LV, 24 (Sept. 8, 1838).

1841 about a thousand apprentices had been enlisted, but the system lasted only five or six years. The boys found they were not likely to be promoted to petty officer rank, and left the navy. Secretary Dobbin revived the plan in 1855 "as the surest means of making a *radical improvement*" in the character and quality of navy seamen, as well as training sailors for the merchant marine.[69] The system was not destined to secure these admirable results.

In other particulars, however, the lot of the seaman was improved. The quality of clothing and provisions was raised by a new system of inspection. Medicines were no longer "spurious drugs bought up in haste in the shops," but were prepared under the direct supervision of the bureau of medicine and surgery.[70] More comfortable berths were provided. The term of cruises was reduced from three years to two.[71]

THE NAVAL ACADEMY

For three decades and more the navy had envied the army the advantages of West Point, originally planned by Alexander Hamilton for both branches of the armed services. Repeatedly Secretaries of the Navy had recommended an academy for midshipmen, but for years Congress had been indifferent. The West was not interested; an ever present economy bloc was opposed; and good democrats feared the education of rich men's sons or political favorites at public expense. West Point was criticized on this ground, although without justification. Moreover the surplusage of midshipmen during the 1830's did not suggest the need of an academy to train more officers to become redundant.

In 1842 Secretary Upshur renewed the navy's plea for an academy, stating again the case that had so often been made. "Through a long course of years," he told Congress, "the young midshipmen were left to educate themselves and one another."

69 Senate Ex. Doc. 5, 34th Cong., 3d sess., Part II, p. 416 (Dec. 1, 1856).

70 Senate Ex. Doc. 1, 33d Cong., 2d sess., Part II, p. 403 (Dec. 4, 1854).

71 Senate Ex. Doc. 5, 34th Cong., 3d sess., Part II, pp. 414, 416 (Dec. 1, 1856). Paulding had caused a small library to be placed on ships in active service. In addition to technical works, he included Marshall's *Life of Washington,* Gibbon's *Decline and Fall of the Roman Empire,* the *Encyclopedia Britannica,* Plutarch's *Lives,* Kent's *Commentaries,* the *Bible* and *Prayer Book,* the *Federalist Papers,* and some of Cooper's and Irving's novels. Amos L. Herold, *James Kirke Paulding,* p. 130.

He proposed to take over one or more old forts on the seaboard and establish a faculty drawn from officers in active service. No boy should receive an acting appointment as midshipman until he had attended the school and earned a certificate of good conduct, capacity, physical ability, and general fitness. This appointment would be confirmed after a year at sea. After five more years at sea, he would be eligible to take an examination for passed midshipman.[72] Senator James Buchanan helped to frustrate Upshur's hopes; "we were a nation of magnificent ideas," he declared, "but, unfortunately, we had not the money to carry them out." [73]

Pending a naval academy, makeshift arrangements were resorted to. Three small naval schools were maintained at the navy yards in Boston, New York, and Norfolk, and a few schoolmasters were put on board vessels at sea.[74] In 1838 another school was established at the naval asylum for aged seamen in Philadelphia. None of these means of education was satisfactory. Secretary Branch was not able to persuade Congress to recognize them, beyond tolerating contingency funds for their use; and he himself spoke of "the very limited range of instruction afforded by them." [75]

George Bancroft finally presented Congress with a *fait accompli*. He found that he had power to send midshipmen to specified places to await orders, and to direct the sea-going instructors to attend them. During the summer of 1845 Bancroft was acting Secretary of War during Marcy's absence, and in his dual capacity he transferred Fort Severn at Annapolis from the army to the navy. As ships came in during the summer he ordered the midshipmen to Annapolis. Eighteen of the twenty-

72 Senate Doc. 1, 27th Cong., 3d sess., p. 546.

73 Buchanan, *Works,* V, 334 (August 8, 1842).

74 The sea-borne faculty (and educational facilities) were less than successful. Lieutenant Maury's first instructor was qualified and well disposed to teach navigation, but he lacked both a schoolroom and authority: "from him, therefore, we learned nothing"; his second was a Spaniard—after a week the midshipmen voted teacher and grammar a bore, heaved overboard their books and took their stand with Byron:

> " 'Tis pleasant to be taught in a strange tongue
> By female lips and eyes."

His third instructor was far gone in consumption; his fourth spent his time writing a book. *Southern Literary Messenger,* VI (1840), 315.

75 Senate Doc. 1, 21st Cong., 1st sess., pp. 38–39 (Dec. 1, 1829).

five instructors then in the naval service were dispensed with, at a saving of $30,000. Four of the remainder were installed at Annapolis, and a lieutenant to teach steam and gunnery. Commander Franklin Buchanan, "a hard-driving, liquor-hating sea-dog with thirty years in the Navy behind him," became the first superintendent, and immediately began to instill some new ideas of discipline. Within six months he had dismissed two midshipmen for insubordination, four for drunkenness, and one for an extreme case of delirium tremens.[76] When Congress met the Naval Academy was in operation. Congress yielded and began appropriations for the new institution.

Good results were soon apparent. In 1853 Secretary Dobbin reported that the academy was rapidly supplying the navy "with numbers of educated and accomplished young men. . . . The beneficial results already witnessed, demonstrate satisfactorily that it is now sustaining the same relations to the navy that West Point Academy bears to the army." [77] Thus was laid the foundation for the professional navy career man. As sails gave way to steam, formal education and training replaced the salt-sea school of experience. In the midst of many evidences of deterioration, the Naval Academy and Navy Department reorganization spoke hopefully of the future.

76 Russel B. Nye, *George Bancroft,* p. 145.

77 Senate Ex. Doc. 1, 33d Cong., 1st sess., Part III, p. 303 (Dec. 5, 1853). There are several secondary works on the Naval Academy, including Captain W. D. Puleston, *Annapolis: Gangway to the Quarterdeck* (New York: Appleton-Century, 1942); and Alfred T. Mahan, *From Sail to Steam,* ch. 3.

CHAPTER THIRTEEN

Decline of the Post Office

The management of the post office had reached a high peak of efficiency under the dynamic energy of John McLean, Postmaster General from 1823 to 1829. It was destined to fall to one of its lowest points under McLean's successor, William T. Barry, and to be rescued after six years of mismanagement by Amos Kendall.

Barry was a lawyer by profession and a politician by avocation. Three times elected to the Kentucky House of Representatives, he was then sent in 1815 to the U.S. Senate but resigned at the close of the first session to devote himself to the political affairs of his adopted state. He sat in the Kentucky Senate from 1817 to 1821, was lieutenant governor from 1821 to 1825, and in 1828 was defeated for governor by Henry Clay's man. This was enough to recommend him to Jackson, and in 1829 Barry became Postmaster General.

Jackson had been warned by his friend, former Senator John Pope, that Barry was not an administrative genius. "He is not fit," wrote Pope, "for any station which requires great intellectual force or moral firmness but he is a gentleman in his deportment and amiable in his private relations. He is nearly insolvent. . . . I would . . . give him the attorneyship for this District if vacant or make him governor of arkansa and public sentiment might bear his being sent to some of the south american states." [1] As it turned out the Post Office Department needed moral firmness, if not intellectual power. After six years Barry's successor, Amos Kendall, wrote, "Perhaps none believed that the head of the Department had been corrupt, but his best friends

1 Jackson, *Correspondence,* IV, 8 (Feb. 19, 1829).

who knew his amiable disposition and his want of business habits, could readily comprehend how he might have been misled by corrupt men about him." [2]

That the mail service was deteriorating under Barry's management was evidenced by more than the usual volume of complaints. Hezekiah Niles, publisher of *Niles' Weekly Register,* warned against partisanship in the Post Office in the summer of 1829. "And if postmasters are appointed as partizans, it must be presumed that they will act as partizans. . . . This must be expected. Who can calculate the consequences, or limit the effects of such appointments; who do away with the unhappy precedent . . . ?" [3] He became indignant as service continued to grow worse. In 1832 he wrote, "We receive a multitude of complaints of the failure of the REGISTER. . . . 'It's of no use to grumble'—*until after the election!* . . . hundreds of postmasters are in attendance on conventions and committees, or engaged in political correspondences." [4] In the spring of 1833 he declared, "We are exceedingly harassed, and much injured, by the long-enduring irregularity of the mails, and the excessive carelessness or gross ignorance, or something worse, in a good many of the post offices." [5]

The *Mobile Advertiser* of April 17, 1833, complained that no mail had arrived from New York since March 28th, although five were due, and that even from nearby New Orleans five deliveries were in arrears.[6] In the face of "innumerable complaints," Niles echoed what must have been a general opinion: "the concerns of the post office department are wretchedly managed—as every thinking man feared they would be, when party politics were suffered to have influence over the appointment of deputy postmasters, and in the selection of mail-contractors." [7]

More was at fault in the Post Office Department than could

2 Kendall, *Autobiography,* p. 337.

3 *Niles Register,* XXXVI, 329 (July 18, 1829).

4 *Ibid.,* XLIII, 97 (Oct. 13, 1832).

5 *Ibid.,* XLIV, 49 (March 23, 1833).

6 Quoted in *ibid.,* XLIV, 178 (May 18, 1833).

7 *Ibid.,* XLIV, 81 (April 6, 1833). Clay and Webster did not trust the post office for their private correspondence. Clay to Webster, June 7, 1830, "To guard against the treachery of the post-office, if you write me, put your letters under cover to James Harper, Lexington. To whom should I address mine?" Webster, *Writings and Speeches* (National ed.), XVII, 505.

be ascribed to party politics, although its influence was hardly constructive. One of the central problems was management, and the central aspect of the management relationship concerned the contracts for carrying the mail, the unscrupulous character of the contractors, and the incompetence of the department in dealing with them. Involved in the derangement caused by laxity in dealing with the mail contractors was a reckless course of departmental finance, concealment of facts, personal interest in contracts by well-placed subordinates in Barry's organization, extravagance in printing costs, and many minor abuses.

The evidence on post office mismanagement came to light in 1834 and 1835, when committees in both the Senate and House made voluminous reports. The Senate committee, with a Whig majority and an able Whig chairman, Thomas Ewing of Ohio, made two reports.[8] The House committee, with a Democratic majority and a Democratic chairman, Henry W. Connor, made one voluminous report, including evidence and testimony.[9] While the various reports were affected by the political leanings of committee members, the undisputed evidence led even the political friends of the Postmaster General to a severe condemnation of his operations.

CONTRACTS AND CONTRACTORS

From the earliest days Congress had been sensitive to the possibilities of favoritism and monopoly in the award of contracts for carrying the mails. In the first general postal law of 1792 the Postmaster General was required to give at least six weeks public notice of intent to make a contract, describing specifically the service to be performed; and he was also required to lodge the contract, with all bids, with the comptroller of the Treasury. Congress intended competition and publicity concerning these transactions.[10] The postal law revision of 1825 con-

8 Senate Doc. 422, 23d Cong., 1st sess. (June 9, 1834). Majority findings (Whig), pp. 31–33; minority findings (Democrat), pp. 274–75, *hereafter cited as Senate Doc. 422 (1834)*; Senate Doc. 86, 23d Cong., 2d sess. (Jan. 27, 1835). Majority findings (Whig), pp. 88–89; minority findings (Democrat), pp. 115–16.

9 House Report 103, 23d Cong., 2d sess. (Feb. 13, 1835), *hereafter cited as House Report 103 (1835)*. Majority findings (Democrat), pp. 50–51; minority findings (Whig), pp. 218–19.

10 1 Stat. 232, sec. 6 (Feb. 20, 1792).

tinued these provisions, now requiring twelve weeks publication in Washington and in one or more newspapers published in the appropriate state or territory.[11]

Mail contracts were lucrative and attracted large-scale operators on the lines of the "great mails." Until 1829 the contracts were generally let with strict reference to the nature of the bids. There were, indeed, some illustrations of bitter political enemies who were allowed to renew their contracts as the lowest responsible bidders, for example, Isaac Hill of New Hampshire. After 1829 the big contractors found ways and means not only to hold their contracts but to feather their nests by collusion with high-ranking post office employees. Some of their methods are described in the following paragraphs.

Private understandings. When Amos Kendall took over as Postmaster General in 1835, he found it remarkable that the most important mail contracts had been consistently awarded to the same men. The reason was soon evident. One of them called privately at Kendall's residence to ask whether he intended to secure the contracts "to the old and faithful contractors," as his predecessor had done. Kendall asked how this could be managed. The contractor informed him that "it had been done through private understandings, prior to the lettings, between the contractors and the Department." [12]

Straw bids. The House and Senate investigating committees found other ways by which competition was discouraged and favoritism given play. Straw bids became frequent. Irresponsible persons would be engaged to put in fictitious bids below the advantageous figure submitted by the "old and faithful" contractor. These low bidders, as Kendall put it, "turned out to be vagabonds, who could give no security," and the former contractor was then awarded the contract. If a bona fide bidder appeared below the old contractor, some straw bidder could be found able to give security at a still lower offer, but his contract was soon assigned to the old contractors, the bid being high enough at least to secure a profit, if not an exorbitant one.[13] Or the straw bidder would promptly be forced to abandon the

11 4 Stat. 102, sec. 10 (March 3, 1825).

12 Kendall, *Autobiography*, p. 343.

13 *Ibid.*, p. 344.

contract awarded him; the department then made a substitute contract without readvertising. This type of collusive bidding was reported by the Whig minority of the House committee to have been common.[14]

Combined bids. Another means of securing contracts to favored bidders was to receive offers for a number of routes, separately advertised but combined by contractors into a single proposal. The Democratic majority of the House committee condemned this practice, which made it impractical to compare one bid with another. "It follows, of consequence, that the great end and object of advertising contracts, an honest and fair competition, is essentially impaired, if not totally defeated, by bids of this character." [15] The large contractors generally held a considerable number of adjoining routes, and were the only ones in a position to combine bids on several lines.

Improved bids. One of the great abuses was to enter a double bid, one for the services as advertised, and one in the form of an "improved bid," proposing better service at an enhanced price. The improved offer of course eliminated all competition. The department was severely criticized for even receiving such bids. When joined with bids for combined routes (which the large contractors could readily make) they came in the most objectionable form. ". . . the advertisement is, therefore, rendered perfectly nugatory, and might, in such instances, as well be dispensed with." [16] This form of abuse was rendered much more dangerous by allowing improvements and extra allowances *after* the contract had been let, a practice noted below.

Secrecy of bids. A change in practice introduced by Barry in the handling of bids attracted sharp criticism from all quarters, although no corruption could be directly ascertained. Under former administrations, no bids were opened until after the closing date for their receipt. Barry directed that they be opened as they were received. Even Barry's political friends on the House committee could not "forbear to express their conviction that the practice introduced was, in every respect, injudicious. It exposed the subordinates in the department to temptations to vio-

14 House Report 103 (1835), p. 75.

15 *Ibid.*, p. 14.

16 *Ibid.*, p. 15.

late their duty, and it was sure to bring down censure and suspicion upon the department itself." [17] Barry had himself gone back to the old practice after three years (1830–31–32) of this innovation.

Extra allowances. Avoidance of competition in bidding was often achieved by another pernicious practice, the subsequent alteration of the terms of the contract. Extra allowances for improvements in service after the letting of the contract had rested entirely in the discretion of the Postmaster General until 1825 when the law was amended "to bring this discretion into some practical and safe limit." [18] The amendment provided that no additional allowance should be made unless additional service was required; "and then no additional compensation shall be allowed to exceed the exact proportion of the original amount to the additional duties required." [19] Waiving the difficulty of computation, this enactment did set up a standard for the Postmaster General. The House investigating committee found that the law had been "overlooked" by Barry, and further that many improvements had been made quite unauthorized under the limitations of the act of 1825. "Horse routes, at once or twice a week, are sometimes improved into post coach routes. Contracts are made, binding the department to pay a *gross* sum for services, differing in their character on different routes, as, for instance, one a horse route, another a post coach route, and another a conveyance by steamboat. In these, and similar instances, compensation for 'additional service' on a part of these routes cannot by any possibility, be graduated by the contract price for the original service on the whole number of routes." [20]

The House committee majority emphasized the point by reference to cases, notably two Pennsylvania routes held by a prominent contractor, James Reeside. They were let in 1831 as weekly horse routes at $275 per annum. Within six months, an "improvement" was authorized for tri-weekly post coaches at a compensation of $4,500. Within another year the cost of transportation was pushed up nearly $3,000 more. In October 1834 (while

17 *Ibid.*, p. 18.
18 *Ibid.*, p. 12.
19 4 Stat. 102, sec. 43 (March 3, 1825).
20 House Report 103 (1835), p. 12.

the congressional investigation was on foot), the routes were brought back to horse mails at $505 a year. The committee declared that no plausible reason for the improvements could be found. The whole amount of annual postage on these routes was less than $600; the annual expenditure nearly $7,500.[21]

The case of James Reeside's bid on a route from Hagerstown to McConnellsburg hinted at more than laxity, despite Reeside's claim to innocence. He bid $40 for the route, or $99 for improved service. His nearest competitor bid $180 for carriage on horseback. Reeside got the contract, and subsequently claimed that a clerk had misread his figures, which were intended to be $1,400, or $1,999 for improved service. Barry accepted this claim and paid Reeside at the "corrected" rate, which was more than twice the bid of his *highest* competitor. Moreover he failed after less than a year to carry the mail in coaches, as required, instead of horseback. "The case," declared the House minority, "shows how little the public treasury, the convenience of the people, or the law of the land, has been regarded, when they conflict with the emoluments or the conscience of a contractor." [22]

Stockton and Neil, another large contractor, made a four-year engagement to carry the mail westward from Washington through Wheeling into Ohio (twenty-two routes) at an annual compensation of $37,000. By reason of extra allowances, the compensation was "rapidly run up to more than 100,000. . . . Additional lines of stages were ordered and paid for; postilions and extra horses, tolls, and ferriages, were all paid for; but upon what ground of reason, propriety, or justice, some of these allowances were made, the committee do not perceive." [23] These were the comments of House Democrats.

The amount of extra allowances was prodigious. In a period of four years Barry managed to authorize over $1,500,000 above the contract stipulations.[24] Niles printed a table showing the distribution of allowances by states. Virginia led the list with $315,000; Alabama followed with $186,000; Pennsylvania with $158,000; Georgia with $144,000. Massachusetts and Missouri

21 *Ibid.*, pp. 32–33.
22 *Ibid.*, pp. 142–47.
23 *Ibid.*, pp. 42–43.
24 *Niles Register*, XLVI, 101 (April 12, 1834).

contractors were favored with $4,000 extra allowances; Mississippi and Connecticut with $3,000. Niles was hinting at electoral considerations.

The problem of competition. Congressional policy in favor of competition as the great regulator of rates for carriage of the mails was undermined by the bidding customs that flourished under the weak leadership of Major Barry. Most of them could be traced in part to misleading or inadequate advertising by the Post Office Department, and much evidence of abuses was produced in the investigations of 1834 and 1835.

The Post Office Department defended the inadequacy of route advertisements by alleging lack of time to study the needs of the various routes, the number of which ran over 1,500. A considerable proportion of the advertisements were consequently merely copied from previous ones. The House committee declared this was "a very unsatisfactory explanation," and what was worse, they discovered advertisements on major lines that were deliberately deceptive. "To advertise in this way, was to trifle with the subject. . . ." [25]

It was evident that the design of Congress to secure competition, an open field, and no monopoly was being subverted. "The advertisement," said the House majority, "is a thing of substance, not of mere form," and "should, in no event, be departed from lightly, or without causes of a cogent character." [26] The Senate Whigs reported ". . . in these and many similar cases of favored contractors . . . competition is absolutely put down, and the notices published pursuant to law, inviting competition, and the public biddings, are but mere masks to cover their secret transactions." [27]

On the lines of the "great mails" competition was limited by reason of the large investment in coaches, horses, equipment, and in the provision of drivers. Under Barry's administration these natural advantages were doubled as the large contractors began to find ways and means of stifling competition along their lines from "independent" operators. Stockton and Stokes held a contract from Baltimore to Hagerstown, thence to McCon-

25 House Report 103 (1835), pp. 23, 34.
26 *Ibid.*, p. 11.
27 Senate Doc. 422 (1834), p. 13.

nellsburg and points west: the so-called "old line." An opposition line of coaches was instituted between Baltimore and Hagerstown, one link of which involved a short route held by Andrew Lindsay. But after a few days Lindsay refused any longer to take passengers from the opposition line. It appeared in testimony that Obadiah B. Brown, the chief clerk, had informed Lindsay in writing that this infringement on the prerogative of the "old line" was against the interest of the department, and that Lindsay would lose his own contract if he persisted. Brown could not recall the incident, and the incriminating letter was not to be found in the departmental records.

The House committee Democratic majority did not, however, doubt these facts and stated, ". . . they regard this interference, on the part of the chief clerk, as altogether unjustifiable. The road was as free to the new as to the old line of stages; and any effort by the department to embarrass one or the other, would have been a perversion and abuse of its powers. . . . It was an unauthorized and reprehensible act of his subordinate, not brought home to the knowledge of the head of the department. . . ." [28]

In another case the head of the department was directly involved. Two powerful contractors, the National Road Stage Company and the Pennsylvania Western Stage Company, entered into an agreement fixing rates and services, specifically designed to prevent competition by third parties. The agreement was filed in the office of the Postmaster General and he was authorized to fix the penalty for any violation by either party! Subsequently the contractors fell out between themselves: O. B. Brown offered his services as an arbitrator and eventually worked out an amicable agreement. Against his protestations the contractors pressed between fifty and one hundred dollars on Brown. Under questioning he defended acceptance of this sum as a partial remuneration for his expense and labor. "If there was any thing improper in it, it was on their part, in not paying me as large a sum as in justice I might have been entitled to." [29]

The Senate majority report (Whig) summarized the breakdown of contract procedure in three propositions: (1) that al-

28 House Report 103 (1835), pp. 25, 188–89.
29 Senate Doc. 422 (1834), pp. 69–73.

terations in advertisements and accepted bids prevented all fair competition among persons wishing to make contracts, gave undue advantage to favorites, and were in violation of law; (2) that extra allowances had been granted without any increase of duty or service, and in other cases were unreasonable, extravagant, and out of all proportion to the increase of service; (3) that mail lines were authorized more frequently than once a day, at heavy expense and with no adequate public object.[30]

SUPERVISION OF CONTRACT PERFORMANCE

Once a contract was made the continuing administrative task of supervision of its performance began. The supervisory system was dispersed, elementary, and ineffective. It was the duty of postmasters to enter in a record the exact time of arrival and departure of each mail, and to forward the record to Washington. No means existed to satisfy the department that the record corresponded to the facts, and it may easily be imagined that many postmasters would refrain from becoming informers. The sanction possessed by the General Post Office for reported failures was to impose fines according to a scale usually set out in the contract. The contractors, however, could plead unavoidable cause for delay, and in the discretion of the Postmaster General the fine might be remitted. His discretion was hard pushed by the contractors at all times. McLean finally announced that he would impose a fine for every failure, without regard to cause.

This rule was too rigorous for a weaker Postmaster General, and Barry resumed the right to remit. Rumors of unduly free use of this official discretion got around, and on January 29, 1834, Barry was required to make a special report on fines imposed during December 1833 and January 1834 on the route from Washington to Boston.[31] Thirty-nine failures had occurred in December against which six fines were imposed. In January thirty-four failures were reported against which seventeen fines were assessed. Assuming that Barry had private advance notice of this call for information, the record suggests the nature of

30 *Ibid.*, pp. 32–34. The most extensive presentation of evidence is in House Report 103 (1835).

31 House Report 265, 23d Cong., 1st sess. (Feb. 14, 1834).

the working relations between contractors and the General Post Office.

Another of Barry's innovations pointed to unusual tenderness toward the interests of contractors—advances of funds from the post office before service was rendered. How much of this went on was not revealed, but some examples were discovered by the House committee. Thus Barry offered to advance $20,000 or $25,000 to Edwin Porter, and Porter actually drew $20,000. The transaction was not recorded on the books of the department. It appeared that on January 1, 1833, Richard C. Stockton was indebted to the department in the sum of $70,000, but was entitled to a credit, not on the books, of $141,000. These figures mystified the committee, but the department declined to produce its books to clarify the situation. The House minority declared that the advances were unlawful, and beyond that unbusinesslike. No interest was charged on the advances, and no security was taken.[32]

The House committee also heard, "in various ways, insinuations and suggestions that enormous presents had been made by contractors to some of the subordinate officers in the department, with a view to conciliate their goodwill, and secure their aid in obtaining advantageous contracts." [33] Nothing could be identified, however, beyond a small keg of wine to the chief clerk, and three or four dozen bottles of wine to the senior assistant postmaster general. From other sources there is evidence that contractors pressed free transportation on important public figures (an early equivalent of a railroad pass). The austerity of an earlier generation was beginning to wilt. When Kendall became Postmaster General, he was scarcely warm in his seat before contractors' presents began to come in. "On one occasion a whole deer, just killed, came down from the mountains. . . ." Kendall suspected a proposal for an improved contract would soon follow, and was not disappointed. He shortly discovered and removed a clerk who was "an agent and a spy for certain powerful contractors in the Department." [34]

32 House Report 103 (1835), pp. 186–88.
33 *Ibid.*, pp. 25–26.
34 Kendall, *Autobiography*, p. 463.

The new intimacy between contractors and the General Post Office promised scandal. The investments of Obadiah B. Brown, chief clerk of the department, in a post office contract smelled strongly of corruption in view of Brown's other operations, but neither committee of investigation went beyond verbal condemnation. Brown was a clergyman, turned government clerk, and apparently was a hail-fellow-well-met. Kendall had boarded with him when he was awaiting his initial appointment as fourth auditor, and in his *Autobiography* left a neat thumbnail sketch. "Mr. Brown, though a Baptist preacher, is a cheerful, jolly man, who loves good eating and drinking and delights in a joke. He is scarcely ever serious except at prayers and in the pulpit. He is a clerk in the General Post-Office, and gets a salary of $1,400." [35]

Brown became chief clerk and was responsible in 1831 and 1832 for making and "improving" mail contracts. A contract from New Orleans to Mobile, executed on July 24, 1829, proved to be a losing venture on a triweekly basis. It was canceled by the department and a new one agreed to, without advertising, for a daily mail at an increased compensation. After Brown had assented to the improved arrangement in the south, he took occasion to join with one of the Mobile–New Orleans partners (Sidney Porter) in buying up a line in Virginia held by Stockton and Stokes. The transaction was a private one. Brown eventually decided that it was a dubious venture and altered the investment to a loan to Porter—which at the time of the investigation in 1834 remained unpaid. The Democratic House majority roundly condemned the arrangement. "When Mr. Brown advanced these sums . . . he was superintendent of mail contracts, a place of great trust, and in which his advice could not be otherwise than highly influential in the formation of contracts, and in determining the amount of compensation to be allowed. Thus situated, it was manifestly improper that Mr. Brown, in his own right, or in the character of a trustee for others, should become interested in mail contracts." [36] Brown was also discovered to have been reaping rewards from extra allowances—a situation on which Millard Fillmore, then in the House, commented in a letter to Thurlow Weed: "When lo! it appeared that this faithful

35 *Ibid.*, p. 288.
36 House Report 103 (1835), p. 39.

officer, and sanctified priest had been sharing in the SPOILS by having an interest in some of those extraordinary and corrupting *Extra allowances* which have bankrupted that department." [37]

Proper control of the post office contractors was a difficult but not an impossible task. It required qualities, however, that Barry did not possess. The contractors were among the major entrepreneurs of their day, although their day was doomed to pass as railroads pushed across the countryside. The decline in the morals of business enterprise and speculators as new and glittering opportunities for profit appeared brought heavier pressure on the public service. The post office was affected, but it was not the only agency to have its troubles, and railroads and steamship lines soon proved as grasping as owners of stagecoaches. A history of government contractors would throw much light on the course of administration.

POST OFFICE PRINTING

Expenditures for post office printing were considerable, and under Barry began to grow at a rapid rate. Printing contracts were fought for by some hard-pushing and unscrupulous men against whom the amiable Barry proved to be a weak and pitiable figure.[38]

General Duff Green was Barry's principal villain in the piece. A rough, coarse, red-faced contractor who in 1826 had defied Postmaster General McLean and announced his determination to defeat John Quincy Adams in the 1828 campaign, he had well earned the editorship of the party newspaper in Washington, the *Telegraph,* and an election as printer to Congress. Furthermore he had established a claim to the lucrative post office printing. In anticipation of this contract, the retiring Postmaster General (McLean) accepted a draft on the post office for $1,500 conditioned to be paid at maturity if by then Green should have done printing to that amount. When the draft became due on May 6, 1829, Barry refused to pay because the required printing had not been completed. Green stormed into Barry's office, refused to be pacified by the Postmaster General's explanations, and left abruptly. Phineas Bradley, the assistant postmaster

37 *Fillmore Papers,* II, 158 (Dec. 28, 1834).

38 For a general account of the printing problem, see below, ch. 15.

general, was present at the interview. After Green had left Barry remarked "that Mr. Green was a man of power and standing," and began to consider ways and means to extricate himself from his unpleasant situation. He decided to speed up the performance of Green's printing by advertising post office routes in the *Telegraph* daily as well as weekly, "as the only way to satisfy General Green." Bradley replied that it was contrary to usage, but Barry insisted. The contracts were consequently advertised in the daily, semiweekly, and weekly editions, and Green's draft was soon covered by service rendered. The House committee Democratic majority concluded that a weekly insertion would have been sufficient for all useful purposes, and that economy required such a limitation. The committee minority figured that Barry had paid nearly $9,000 more for contract advertising than a weekly insertion would have required.[39]

The Senate committee majority fell back upon Thomas Jefferson in the course of its condemnation of party misuse of printing funds. In their first report, the committee wrote:

> Mr. Jefferson, in his letter to Nathaniel Macon, of May 14th, 1801, says that "a very early recommendation had been given to the Postmaster General to employ no printer, foreigner, or revolutionary tory, in any of his offices." His reason for the exclusion of the PRINTER from any connection with the Post Office Department is obvious; and if we would preserve the press from corruption, and prevent it from exerting a corrupting influence over the community, that recommendation ought to be esteemed as a precept, and religiously observed in the present and in all future times. But this admonition has passed unnoticed, or is disregarded, by those who now conduct the affairs of this department. Large sums of money appear to have been expended in such a manner that the obvious tendency of the expenditure is to extend the influence of the department over the public press, and through that press over the people.[40]

The committee cited specific examples: William Smith, favored with an extra allowance of $11,129, was proprietor of "an efficient party press" in Virginia; Horatio Hill of New Hampshire, "said to be the conductor of a violent party press," held fifteen mail routes with newspaper privileges, i.e., free carriage of his

39 House Report 103 (1835), pp. 37–38, 197, 206, 304–5.
40 Senate Doc. 422 (1834), p. 25.

own sheet; Bennet of Pennsylvania with an allowance of $500 thereupon purchased an opposition press and converted it into an administration paper.[41]

The Senate committee also traced the political course of printing contracts in Massachusetts, and exposed the efforts of the department to conceal the facts. A resolution of July 14, 1832, required each department to publish in the 1833 edition of the *Official Register* a correct list of all printers *in any way* employed by it from 1831 to 1833, with the compensation allowed to each. The subsequent report, according to the Whig majority, was "precisely adapted to mislead the public in reference to the whole subject."

In the *Official Register,* True and Greene, proprietors and printers of the *Boston Statesman,* were recorded as having received a total compensation of $6,899.25. But the hitherto unreported contingent fund of the Post Office Department now revealed that True and Greene had also received nearly $30,000 for furnishing paper, blanks, and twine to various postmasters in "New York and elsewhere." These sums were paid on certificate of the Boston postmaster, Nathaniel Greene, a brother of Charles Greene of the firm of True and Greene; and Nathaniel was apparently financially interested in the firm. For these contracts paid from the contingent fund there was no competition and no advertisement. The Whig committee majority concluded that the press of the *Boston Statesman* "appears . . . to have been sustained in the year 1832, when the last Presidential election occurred, by the employment of its proprietors in rendering services to the amount of nearly sixteen thousand dollars, which were paid out of the revenues of this department." [42]

DEPARTMENTAL FINANCE

The post office was in principle a self-sustaining agency, paying its expenses from its postal revenues. Except for the necessity from time to time of erasing a deficit, Congress made no appropriation. The funds of the department were available for departmental use at the discretion of the Postmaster General. They were not audited by the Treasury auditors but by the

41 *Ibid.*, p. 25.
42 *Ibid.*, pp. 27–28.

post office accountant, from whose hands they went for a cursory examination by the first comptroller. It was McLean's policy from 1823 to 1829 to plow back surpluses into expanded service, but he took care over the years not to incur a deficit, and left a small surplus on hand for Barry.

The Senate committee reported that the amount of funds sunk by Barry in four years amounted to over $3,300,000.[43] The amount of the deficit in 1834 was in dispute owing to the confusion of post office accounts, but Barry said he needed $450,000 to recover his position. Barry's friends admitted a deficit, the extent of which, they said, "had been a point of sturdy controversy"; they figured it at about $238,000.[44] The Senate majority declared that the department was largely insolvent.

Deficits were not unknown in the earlier history of the department, although on a less spectacular scale. What made this one unique was that Barry had borrowed large sums *on the credit of the post office,* and for a time had tried to conceal these transactions.[45] The loans, made without authority of law, were defended on the general ground that the department "created its own funds" and that the bank loans were a claim only on future postal revenues. These opinions were vigorously denied by the House Whigs and were rebuffed by a unanimous Senate resolution in 1834. The Whigs declared, "The great objection to granting the power to borrow money . . . is its tendency to extravagance and bankruptcy," and implied that the financial position of the post office was sufficient proof of their convictions.[46]

POST OFFICE PATRONAGE

The Whig minority on the House committee took advantage of the occasion to record its condemnation of patronage in the post office, although the House had formally excluded this subject from the investigation. Mere size was the first item in the indictment. McLean had managed with a permanent force of 38 clerks in the first quarter of 1829. Barry had 90 clerks on his

43 *Ibid.*, pp. 4–5.
44 House Report 103 (1835), pp. 1, 9.
45 Senate Doc. 422 (1834), p. 1.
46 House Report 103 (1835), pp. 60–62.

regular staff in 1834. The Whigs declared, "The business of the office cannot have increased since the 1st of April, 1829, in the proportion of 38 to 90." [47] Partisan patronage was, however, the principal complaint. Some excerpts from their report revealed the characteristic position of a political minority.

The immense patronage of the Post Office Department is justly a subject of jealousy. If wielded with a view to acquire or retain political power, it is far more dangerous than that of all the other departments, not even excepting the Treasury. The number of postmasters on the 1st of July last was 10,693. Their compensation for the year ending the 30th of June, 1834, was $896,062.53. The number of contractors, and their *immediate* dependants, was then probably not less than 20,000. The compensation of the contractors for the same year was $1,922,431.11. They are usually intelligent and active; and, if disposed, are able to bring an influence to bear that may determine, in the divided state of parties, the fate of the most important elections. The postmasters, through their franking privilege, may be made the organs of communication of political parties. When organized into a political corps, they can give facilities to the circulation of newspapers, extras, &c. favorable to their views, and throw obstacles in the way of the circulation of those of an opposite character, with a secresy and security almost equal to absolute indemnity.

The Post Office Department, from its organization, in 1789, down to the 4th of March, 1829, was not, in the *partisan* sense of the word, a *political* department. The Postmaster General was not a member of the cabinet, nor were his appointments submitted to the control of any party. Until that date, persons were removed only for negligence or misconduct; for *cause,* and not on account of their political opinions; and when cause was alleged, they were not removed without a hearing. Such were the principles and the practice of this department for the first forty years of its existence.

Since the 4th of March, 1829, the removals of postmasters have not fallen much short of 1,300, and in a great majority of the cases without the assignment of any cause.[48]

These sentiments had much to commend them. Not even the Whigs, however, could sustain them in the face of the clamor for office and reprisals that assailed them when they carried the election of 1840.

47 *Ibid.,* p. 192.
48 *Ibid.,* p. 212.

DEMOCRATS AND WHIGS ON THE STATE OF THE POST OFFICE DEPARTMENT

The most favorable interpretation of the mass of evidence before the congressional committees would be expected from the House Democrats, the party friends of the Postmaster General. It was indeed their duty to defend and support him so far as possible. We may, therefore, present a summary of their views, expressed, as they said, in "a few propositions" which "will be admitted as just corollaries" from the evidence.[49] On financial management, they found that "The finances of this department have hitherto been managed without frugality, system, intelligence, or adequate public utility. The cardinal principles of an enlightened economy have been violated. Ignorance of the real fiscal ability of the department has long prevailed. Expenses have not been kept within the limits of income."

With respect to contracts, the majority reported, "The negligent and unsystematic form of making and preserving mail contracts is such that no human mind can comprehend the whole, and maintain in order so vast and complicated a machine as the General Post Office. The contracts are now, and have . . . been most loosely constructed. It is occasionally impossible to penetrate their obscurity; often difficult to decipher their interlineations and marginal notes; and always to be doubted whether they are so framed and executed as to be available in law. An ocular inspection of the mail contract books can alone convey an adequate idea of the careless and confused state in which they are kept."

On advertising for bids, the Democrats were equally caustic. "The mode of preparing advertisements for mail contracts has practically inverted the ends of the law which enjoined it. The law designed it as a great safeguard against fraud and imposition, by bringing the salutary principle of competition into active and beneficial operation. The usage of the department . . . has frustrated the wisdom of this precaution, and rendered the system of lettings in regard to the more important routes little more than an empty form or a bitter mockery." Improved bids and extra allowances were roundly condemned. The practice,

49 *Ibid.*, p. 50. The following passages are from pages 50–51.

the Democrats agreed, had run into wild excesses at various times and had become the principal source of the department's embarrassment. "It is a puzzling problem to decide whether this discretionary power, throughout its whole existence, has done most mischief in the character of impostor upon the department, or seducer to contractors. It has, doubtless, been an evil doer in both guises."

The Senate Whigs were even more caustic than the House Democrats. They concluded, "On the whole, your committee have found the affairs of the department in a state of utter derangement, resulting, as it is believed, from the uncontrolled discretion exercised by its officers over its contracts and its funds; and their habitual evasion, and, in some instances, their total disregard of the laws which have been provided for their restraint." The Whigs declared, in reminiscent phrase, that "the incidental expenses and secret service money of the department have increased, are increasing, and ought to be diminished." [50]

It was no wonder Andrew Jackson told Amos Kendall that something had to be done.

50 Senate Doc. 422 (1834), pp. 31–33.

CHAPTER FOURTEEN

Postal Renaissance

The House committee investigating the post office made its report on February 13, 1835. Shortly after Jackson approached the fourth auditor, Amos Kendall, saying that a change was necessary in the head of the Post Office Department, and asking whether he would accept the position. Kendall was very reluctant, having already decided to leave the public service and go into private business. Jackson was insistent. "There are many men," he told Kendall, "who would be glad to accept the Department, and I suppose would put everything right there; but *I know you will.*" On grounds of personal loyalty to the President, Kendall made the sacrifice.[1] Barry was appointed minister to Spain, and died in Liverpool on his way to Madrid.[2] Kendall became Postmaster General on May 1, 1835.

AMOS KENDALL

Like many other men high in public life during the Jacksonian period, Kendall's early years gave no hint of his later success apart from the uncompromising moral standards that

1 Amos Kendall, *Autobiography*, pp. 335-36.

2 Kendall offered the following tribute to Barry after his death. "It may be said of him, as the head of this Department, that the reason he had not a better fortune was, that he was too good a man. In other positions, and under other circumstances, he would have been one of the greatest and most useful, as he was one of the best and most highly endowed, of our public men. Having for more than twenty years been acquainted with Mr. Barry, and been honored with his friendship; knowing his private worth, his love of country, and his disinterestedness, and having always had an abiding confidence in his integrity and honor, it would be to the undersigned a source of lasting regret, if any thing said or done by him, in the administration of this Department, should be understood as intended or calculated to depreciate his virtues, or cast a stain upon his memory." Senate Doc. 1, 24th Cong., 1st sess., p. 403 (Dec. 1, 1835).

were well fixed in his boyhood days on a New England farm. Kendall was the youngest son of a pious and hard-working farmer, a deacon of the Congregational church in Dunstable, Massachusetts. Young Amos heard grace before his meals and thanks afterward, listened to morning and evening prayers, went to church regularly, and on Sundays joined in the family reading of the Bible and singing of hymns. Card playing and dancing were forbidden, and Amos became so sober and thoughtful a lad that he was called "the Deacon." After a sketchy country school education and one term at Groton Academy he entered Dartmouth College in 1807, graduating in 1811 first in his class.

The early imprint of his character appeared during these college years. He wrote in his journal that despite his diffidence in his own powers, he had an "ambition to appear among the foremost." He quickly discovered that popularity and excellence of scholarship were seldom connected, and took steps to protect his time from "the fools of dissipation." He once yielded to temptation and played cards for money. He won three dollars and resolved never to play again. He joined a secret society which in his words "comprised the best part of the class both in morals and knowledge. . . . it formed a phalanx which not all the sons of dissipation were able to break or terrify." [3] With these marks of character and a Dartmouth diploma, Kendall left Hanover in 1811 to study law in Groton under the direction of William Merchant Richardson.

At the age of twenty-five Kendall set off for Washington to seek his fortune, with letters of introduction to General Varnum, member of Congress from Massachusetts and former Speaker of the House. With Varnum he attended the President's levee on March second, and wrote in his diary, "I felt no awe, although Mrs. Madison is a noble, dignified person, apparently more able to manage the affairs of the nation than her husband. His personal appearance is very inferior." [4] More important, he met Senator Bledsoe of Kentucky, who offered him $100 a year, board, and the use of his library to tutor the Bledsoe children.

Kendall accepted on the spot, endured a seasick stage journey to Pittsburgh, floated down the Ohio to Cincinnati, and walked

[3] Kendall, *Autobiography,* p. 66.
[4] *Ibid.,* p. 95.

thence to Lexington, only to discover that Bledsoe had no intention of fulfilling his contract. Kendall had, however, a happy knack of meeting important people. On the stage to Pittsburgh was Lewis Cass, then governor of Michigan Territory and later Secretary of War. Floating down the Ohio Kendall joined the family of Major William T. Barry, whom one day he was to succeed as Postmaster General. More immediately to the point, he now met Mrs. Henry Clay, and became tutor to her five children at $300 a year, board, and the use of Mr. Clay's library. The prudent Kendall hoped also to profit by Mr. Clay's advice when he returned from Europe. The Clay boys, aged twelve and thirteen, had ungovernable tempers, and Kendall earned all the advice he secured from their father.

The sequence of events by which this young and well-moraled tutor became a public servant and an intimate associate of President Andrew Jackson well illustrates the play of chance in human affairs. His early months in Lexington were full of air castles as he tried to imagine his future, a prospect that he never guessed. "This day," he wrote on September 7, 1814, "I have been one hour a liberal-minded merchant calculating gains, promoting science and literature, and extending my connections for trade and knowledge to every part of the country; the next, an eloquent lawyer defending the cause of innocence, basking in the sunshine of popularity, getting rich, and then thundering with Ciceronian eloquence in the Congress of the United States. On the whole, I think the latter course most brilliant, and best adapted to my knowledge, talents, and ambition." [5]

Pursuing this dream, he went to Frankfort in October 1814 and got a license to practice law before the Court of Appeals. Again his capacity for meeting the right people intervened. Colonel Richard M. Johnson, an active Kentucky politician and later Vice President of the United States, persuaded the young lawyer in 1815 to buy the printing establishment at Georgetown, Kentucky, publish the local newspaper, *The Minerva*, and write the editorials. Thus it was that Kendall abandoned teaching, law, and Ciceronian eloquence for the life of an editor. By a wholly unexpected sequence of events, exactly one year later (September 30, 1816), he found himself part owner and editor

5 *Ibid.*, p. 125.

of the *Argus of Western America,* published in Frankfort, the state capital. Here, as a Kentucky editor, he was to labor in the cause of democracy, religion, and the common school system, and against the United States Bank, for over a decade. Such a record, strengthened by his break with Clay in 1826 and his strong support of Andrew Jackson in the 1828 election, was the bridge over which he walked to his public service career.

Kendall's early success in his first appointment as fourth auditor, his skill in writing, and his complete reliability on such crucial matters as the Bank brought him into Jackson's inner circle, the Kitchen Cabinet. He helped write many of Jackson's state papers, he was Jackson's right-hand man in the Bank negotiations, and was generally understood to be one of the President's most confidential advisers. Harriet Martineau caught a glimpse of "the invisible Amos Kendall, one of the most remarkable men in America," and had this to say about him.

> He is supposed to be the moving spring of the whole administration; the thinker, planner, and doer; but it is all in the dark. Documents are issued of an excellence which prevents their being attributed to persons who take the responsibility of them; a correspondence is kept up all over the country for which no one seems to be answerable; work is done, of goblin extent and with goblin speed, which makes men look about them with a superstitious wonder; and the invisible Amos Kendall has the credit of it all.[6]

Mrs. Martineau would have been contradicted by the political enemies of the administration, to whom Kendall was an evil genie. ". . . it is generally believed in Washington," said one of them, "that . . . the wretch of a printer, Amos Kendall, fourth Auditor of the Navy has more influence with the President than any other man, he puts up and puts down." [7] Philip Hone, conservative New York businessman, later called Kendall the "head devil of the Administration, the actor of all dirty work, at once the tyrant and the slave of Mr. Van Buren, as he was of his 'illustrious predecessor.' " [8] That there might have been a

6 Harriet Martineau, *Retrospect of Western Travel* (2 vols., London: Saunders and Otley, 1838), I, 155.

7 Charles H. Ambler, *The Life and Diary of John Floyd* (Richmond, 1918), p. 133 (March 26, 1831).

8 Philip Hone, *Diary* (Nevins ed.), p. 482 (May 16, 1840).

touch of hypocrisy in his character could have been suspected by editor Niles, who printed in parallel columns two of Kendall's letters. The first, written on March 24, 1829, spoke loudly against partisan feelings in the auditor's office and flatly renounced "the whole business of *electioneering*"; the second, written from the same office early in Jackson's campaign for reelection, begged for subscriptions to the *Globe*, the Jackson newspaper.[9]

With the Horatio Alger story of Kendall's later life, we are not concerned. In passing we may record that after leaving the government in 1840 he became the business agent of the inventor, S. F. B. Morse, and accumulated a fortune in this relationship, as advantageous for Morse as for Kendall. He maintained a close and lively interest in public affairs, and a wide acquaintance with public men. Professor Frank M. Anderson has written a convincing demonstration that Kendall was the mysterious author of *The Diary of a Public Man*—an important historical source for the early years of Lincoln's administration.[10]

Kendall never returned to public life. The qualities of character that make it relevant to think of him as the conscience of Jackson's administration carried through to the end of his life, as he devoted his later years and a generous part of his fortune to charity and to religion. He brought no experience to qualify him as an auditor of naval expenditures, or as Postmaster General. He had the assets of a broad education, training in law, interest in political movements, and character and integrity. These, coupled with energy and a shrewd perception of the relation of means to ends, enabled him to put the post office again on solid foundations and to elevate its ethical standards.

POST OFFICE REFORM

Kendall's first obligation as Postmaster General was to rescue the department from the financial confusion in which he found it. ". . . the unsatisfied demands of contractors from every quarter of the country were daily accumulating; . . . there was a debt of near $300,000 due to banks; . . . the outstanding acceptances of the treasurer exceeded $390,000; . . . a consider-

[9] *Niles Register*, XLIX, 43 (Sept. 19, 1835).

[10] Frank Maloy Anderson, *The Mystery of "A Public Man"* (Minneapolis: University of Minnesota Press, 1948).

able portion of the revenue of some of the large offices for the present calendar year [1835] had been anticipated by drafts discounted in banks, which they had been instructed to pay at maturity . . . the Department was subjected to continual embarrassment in devising ways and means to meet its engagements." [11] At the same time, although the accounts were in confusion it was generally believed that the department was solvent and that current revenue exceeded expenditure.

Kendall took energetic measures. He declared a moratorium on all payments upon obligations incurred before the current quarter. Current income was assigned to pay promptly current expenditures, any surplus being used to pay off preexisting claims. All recent "extra allowances" were forthwith suspended. No drafts drawn on department funds were accepted except by special arrangement. The immediate consequences were gratifying. By mid-August 1835, all the debts of the immediately preceding quarter had been paid and a considerable surplus had accumulated. "From that moment the Department was disembarrassed." By September 30, 1835, a surplus of over $100,000 in current operations had been secured, the bank debt was in course of payment, no deficit appropriation (estimated by Barry at $450,000) appeared necessary, and a clear surplus for new mail routes appeared probable during 1836.[12]

Solvency having been thus dramatically achieved, Kendall turned to the financial records and accounting system. Records of the General Post Office were inexcusably bad. Decisions involving thousands of dollars had been recorded only on slips of paper, without dates. Kendall found that the practice of omitting dates, and sometimes giving false dates, pervaded all branches of the department. He issued instructions to correct this evil, and introduced journals in which to record the decisions of each day.[13] The books had not been balanced for twenty years. They were now closed and a new set of books opened on July 1, 1835. In them a form of accounting analysis was introduced to show both the sources of revenue and the principal objects of expenditure. From them the condition of the depart-

11 Senate Doc. 1, 24th Cong., 1st sess., p. 389 (Dec. 1, 1835).

12 *Ibid.*, pp. 391–92.

13 Kendall, *Autobiography*, p. 343.

ment at the end of each quarter could be quickly ascertained.

Kendall was also instrumental in a radical alteration of the procedures for auditing and settling post office accounts. In his first annual report he laid down the proposition that public officers who had an agency in originating accounts should have none in their settlement. Except for the post office this had always been the rule. The investigating committees had commented on this fault of post office organization, and in the act of 1836, written by Kendall and noted below, a thorough change was introduced.

CONTROL OF THE CONTRACTORS AND POSTMASTERS

Kendall began reform in the Post Office Department in characteristic fashion. "In the outset, I superintended the operations of the system myself, and carried on a large portion of the correspondence." A leading principle of the department, he said, "was to make postmasters and contractors feel that its eye was constantly upon them, not only collectively, but individually." [14] He began his duties by getting acquainted with all the officers and clerks and their respective assignments, visiting their rooms, examining their books and asking questions. He devised an ingenious scheme to make the contractors report on postmasters, as well as postmasters on contractors. The latter practice was of long standing. Now, for 9,000 smaller offices the contractors were told to collect three-fourths of their quarterly compensation from the postmasters on their routes and "to report forthwith every postmaster who fails to pay." The remaining fourth was withheld until the contractors had collected from every postmaster or reported the delinquents, and had proved that they had used due diligence and were not themselves at fault.[15] Timely notice was thus served, in principle, against untrustworthy postmasters, while gaining some guarantee of good conduct by the contractors.

The postmasters themselves, excepting a few of the largest offices, were required to render their quarterly accounts within two days from the close of each quarter. Nearby office accounts were due in Washington within ten days, others at specified in-

14 *Ibid.*, pp. 340–41.

15 Senate Doc. 1, 24th Cong., 1st sess., p. 390.

tervals, and it became the duty of a headquarters clerk to deal promptly with all delinquents.

These innovations were in accord with Kendall's principle that the "efficiency of a department, with so many thousand agents in its employment, essentially depends on the vigilance and energy of the directing and supervising power."[16] Kendall institutionalized the supervisory function by establishing in 1836 an inspection office, at the head of which was placed the new third assistant postmaster general. In its origin it was a classic example of a central supervisory office controlling field operations. Its duties were to enforce the keeping of postmasters' registers of the arrival and departure of the mails; to note all failures by contractors and prepare the cases for action by the Postmaster General; to check on the postmasters' quarterly reports; and to do "all other things which may be necessary to secure a faithful and exact performance" on the part of contractors and postmasters.[17] In Kendall's words, its chief object was to exercise a rigid supervision over the rendition of postmasters' accounts, and the performance of contractors.[18]

The office was made effective by the work of special agents in the field, inspecting, observing, and making reports. Occasional special agents had been employed on *ad hoc* assignments in earlier days. By 1853 the special agents numbered eighteen, of whom one was assigned to California, one to Oregon, and one to Texas. Three were appointed at large, working out of New York, Louisville, and Washington.[19]

These agents also served as investigators of mail depredations, and with the passage of time their energies were nearly exhausted in pursuing mail robbers.[20] The function of inspection and supervision of postmasters and contractors withered away. By 1853 it frequently happened that when an agent was needed for

16 *Ibid.*, p. 393.

17 House Doc. 2, 24th Cong., 2d sess., p. 520.

18 *Ibid.*, p. 513 (Dec. 5, 1836).

19 Senate Ex. Doc. 1, 33d Cong., 1st sess., Part III, pp. 706–7 (Dec. 1, 1853).

20 James Holbrook, *Ten Years Among the Mail Bags: or Notes from the Diary of a Special Agent of the Post-Office Department* (Philadelphia: H. Cowperthwait and Company, 1855), pp. 397–402. Holbrook's volume, the first autobiographical account of a humble government employee that has come to notice, is principally concerned with the story of his success in apprehending mail robbers, and with moral lessons upon the folly of sin.

inspection of mail transportation, he was far away "attending to depredations." The process of specialization was invoked as the administrative remedy: dividing the agents into two classes, one assigned to supervise the transportation of the mails, and one to deal with mail depredations.[21]

To return to Kendall: the system of inspection that he developed and the respective checks and balances between postmasters and contractors brought much needed improvement. Years afterward he met a postmaster in Pennsylvania who had failed to pay a contractor his quarterly stipend. "He informed me," wrote Kendall in his *Autobiography,* "that he was surprised at receiving a letter in my own handwriting asking why he had not paid, and on replying that he was not at home when the contractor called, received another letter from me informing him that such an excuse . . . would not be deemed sufficient thereafter. . . ."[22]

The contractors gave Kendall much anxiety, especially in the controversy that came to a head in *Kendall* v. *Stokes.* The constitutional point involved in this case has already been noted, but not the personal consequences for the head of the Post Office Department. Kendall had been forced to pay the balance of what he firmly believed to be a fraudulent claim amounting to $160,000. But this was not all. Stokes sued Kendall for damages arising out of the delay in payment of the award and for his costs of court. A jury, composed, as Kendall noted, of eleven Whigs and one Democrat, found malice in his conduct and awarded damages for about $12,000. His counsel secured a new trial, on which the allegation of malice was dropped, but Kendall was nevertheless again found liable. Pending appeal to the Supreme Court, the former Postmaster General (Kendall had retired in 1840 to manage Van Buren's campaign for reelection) took advantage of an act hastily passed by Congress to allow him the privilege of prison limits, that is, confinement to the city rather than to jail. The Supreme Court eventually reversed the lower courts and Stokes had to pay his own costs. Kendall's triumph

21 These are the beginnings of the Post Office inspection service, formally organized as such in 1905. Lloyd Milton Short, *The Development of National Administrative Organization in the United States* (Baltimore: Johns Hopkins Press, 1923), p. 352.

22 Kendall, *Autobiography,* pp. 340–41.

was finally sealed when Congress, without a dissenting voice, passed an act to pay his counsel's fees, his costs, and other expenses which, as he said, "had been brought upon me by the honest performance of my public duties." [23]

For more than five years Kendall had been in the courts over this affair, in a sequence of events that strongly suggested to him corruption in Congress as well as strange errors on the part of the solicitor of the Treasury. The Supreme Court had before it no evidence on this aspect of the situation. In retrospect Kendall reflected that the case had at least established his reputation as "an honest man, and a pure, faithful, and inflexible public officer." [24] His confinement to prison limits, moreover, undoubtedly saved his life, for otherwise he would have been standing by the "big gun" that exploded on the ship *Princeton.* By an ironic turn of events, the solicitor of the Treasury, who had supported Stokes' claim, was one of those killed in this catastrophe.

POST OFFICE REORGANIZATION

With finances in order and close supervision over postmasters and contractors reestablished, Kendall turned to a reorganization of the General Post Office. The system that had grown up over the years was based on three major specializations: *appointments,* in charge of the first assistant postmaster general; *finance,* in the hands of the second assistant; and *contracts* and supervision of contractors, under the direction of a superintendent.[25]

Postmaster General Barry continued this arrangement until 1833. He then reorganized the department on new foundations, dividing the business of the post office into two grand geographical divisions, northern and southern. Each division included an office of appointments and an office of contracts. Finance was retained as a single office in a third division under the chief clerk. The principal basis of organization was, however, geographical.[26]

After brief experience Kendall scrapped Barry's organization by area. "This arrangement," he declared, "by burdening the assistants' minds with duties entirely dissimilar in their nature,

23 *Ibid.,* p. 357.

24 *Ibid.,* p. 359.

25 *American State Papers: Post Office,* pp. 222–23; House Report 122, 21st Cong., 1st sess. (Jan. 26, 1830).

26 House Report 103, 23d Cong., 2d sess., pp. 858 ff. (March 4, 1835).

did not seem to me conducive to promptitude or uniformity in the administration of the Department." He returned to the historic pattern of organization by function: appointments and supervision of post offices to the first assistant (*the appointment office*); contracts and mail routes to the second assistant (*the contract office*); the performance of mail service under a third assistant (*the inspection office*). Finance was assigned to the chief clerk under Kendall's immediate direction.[27]

Fiscal reorganization required action by Congress. With the close cooperation of Kendall, a new post office act was put on the books in 1836, incorporating both the recommendations of the House and Senate investigating committees and such of Kendall's reforms as needed congressional support. The act of 1836 was a masterpiece of the art of plugging loopholes. Some provision was made for every phase of mismanagement that had been exposed in 1834 and 1835, but the most substantial change occurred in responsibility for post office finance.[28]

The handling of post office revenue, expenditure, and accounts was now, after nearly a half century, brought into conformity with standard practice in other departments. The financial autonomy of the post office was terminated, and the substantially unchecked fiscal responsibility of the Postmaster General came to an end.[29] Henceforward the revenues collected by the department were paid into the Treasury, expenditures were estimated annually by the Postmaster General, and an annual appropriation was made by Congress from the postal revenue, supplemented when necessary from general funds.

The settlement of post office accounts became the duty of an additional auditor (later known as the sixth auditor), appointed by the President with the advice and consent of the Senate. This independent officer, who replaced the post office accountant, was instructed to close the departmental accounts quarterly, and to

27 Kendall, *Autobiography*, p. 342.

28 Neither House nor Senate debates discussed the record of Postmaster General William T. Barry, nor was there disagreement on the essential features of the bill. The principal point of debate was over a simplification of postal rates recommended by Kendall, an obvious administrative improvement that was finally excluded in deference to the anxious concern of Congressmen for their constituents' supposed interests.

29 5 Stat. 80 (July 2, 1836); cf. Kendall, *Autobiography*, p. 344.

direct suits for the collection of delinquent debts. He also served in a capacity analogous to the register of the Treasury, keeping a register of warrants covering funds received and expended. The one-time responsibility of the Postmaster General for directing expenditure, settling accounts, and payment of money was thus reduced to the management of the department and authorization of expenditure.

To remedy the various abuses of Barry's administration, Congress resorted to the rule of publicity and to a series of specific prohibitions and penalties. To insure that the operations of the department would be known, Congress required the Postmaster General to report annually on all contracts, new routes, extra allowances, fines imposed on contractors and whether remitted, and incidental expenses for wrapping paper, office furniture, advertising, mail bags, blanks, mail locks, keys and stamps, mail depredations and special agents, clerks for offices, and miscellaneous. This meticulous enumeration was founded in the derogatory evidence of the House and Senate investigations. In addition Congress required a full report on finance.

To keep contractors under control and the department in order, Congress forbade consolidated or combined bids; severely restricted extra allowances; required the correct date to be affixed to every contract or obligation; and required readvertising for contracts altered or given up during the year. The difficult issue of awards to other than the lowest bidder, involving straw bids and irresponsible bidders, was dealt with by the following formula: "contracts in all cases shall be awarded to the lowest bidder, except when his bid is not more than five per centum below that of the last contractor, on the route bid for, who shall have faithfully performed his contract." The Postmaster General, however, was not required to accept bids from previous contractors who had wilfully or negligently failed to execute their contracts.

Congress put its finger on other bidding abuses. It required bids to remain sealed until after the closing date, and directed that all bids should be entered in well-bound books and the originals preserved. To prevent straw bids, it required every bid to be accompanied by a written guaranty of one or more responsible persons that the bidder would perform the service offered. No contract was allowed with any person who entered a combination to prevent others from bidding, or who offered anything to another to induce him not to bid. All advance payments to contractors were prohibited. Congress enacted one final precaution, with Obadiah Brown in mind. Persons employed in the department and postmasters were forbidden to have an interest in contracts or to act as agents for contractors, whether with or without compensation.

In addition to these remedial sections of the act of 1836, there were others bearing on organization. The duties of the Postmaster General were spelled out, making clear his responsibility for management. A third assistant postmaster general was established, but Congress did not specify his duties, thus allowing operating freedom to the Postmaster General. Postmasters whose commissions equaled $1,000 per annum became presidential officers, appointed by the Chief Executive with the approval of the Senate for four-year terms—an innovation extending the coverage of the Tenure of Office Act of 1820, which had been anathema to Thomas Jefferson.[30] The Postmaster General was authorized to employ city letter carriers.

Thus was introduced the normal pattern of administrative checks and balances, recognized explicitly in the Senate committee majority report of 1835. Senator Ewing and his Whig colleagues contended that the current abuses could "be principally traced to the absolute and unchecked power which a single individual holds over the resources and disbursements, and all the vast machinery of this department. The checks of various inferior officers upon each other are of no value, when all are guided and controlled in their acts by one dominant will." [31] The office of sixth auditor was designed to provide an independent check at a crucial point.

Apart from the financial and accounting reforms, Congress still left the organization of the department in the discretion of the Postmaster General. It expressed no preference for organization by area according to Barry, or by function according to

30 All incumbent postmasters except Samuel L. Gouverneur in New York were nominated and confirmed. *Niles Register*, L, 313 (July 9, 1836).

31 Senate Doc. 86, 23d Cong., 2d sess., pp. 88–89 (Jan. 27, 1835).

Kendall, and left the door open for any subsequent variations that might appeal to the genius of successive Postmasters General. In fact Kendall's organization remained substantially intact throughout the Jacksonian era.[32]

32 Subsequent changes in detail are described in Short, *Development of National Administrative Organization,* pp. 182–84.

CHAPTER FIFTEEN

The Administration Press and the Public Printing

The rise of the mass-supported political party gave new importance to the daily newspapers, and to Presidents of both parties this phenomenon appeared to require the publication in Washington of a sheet faithfully supporting the administration in power. As Fish remarked, "Newspaper men were still the most important single class of party workers. . . ." [1] The appearance of an administration organ preceded the Jacksonians, but the institution came into full flower after 1829.[2]

An active *party* press had always existed, North, South, and West. An *administration* press falls in a different class, i.e., one or more newspapers sponsored by the President and his advisers, usually published in Washington, edited by persons enjoying the President's confidence and at times named by him, with special access to official circles, and with financial support from perquisites and profits controlled by the government. The distinction is at times blurred but the test of quasi-official status and sponsorship will usually be a sufficient criterion of judgment.

Thus John Fenno received some public printing and a $2,000 loan arranged by Hamilton during Washington's administration while publishing the Federalist *Gazette of the United States,* and Philip Freneau held a $250 clerkship in the State Department while publishing the rival newspaper, the *National Gazette.*

1 Carl R. Fish, *Civil Service and the Patronage,* pp. 148–49.

2 See Frank Luther Mott, *American Journalism: A History of Newspapers in the United States through 260 Years, 1690 to 1950* (revised ed., New York: Macmillan Co., 1950); and James E. Pollard, *The Presidents and the Press* (New York: Macmillan, 1947).

Washington had no connection with Fenno, and the *Gazette of the United States* is properly considered a party newspaper, not an administration press.

Thomas Jefferson took an active part in the establishment of the *National Intelligencer* in 1800, and personally secured the services of its first editor, Samuel Harrison Smith. Pollard states that Jefferson was "the first President to have an administration organ of his own choosing." [3] This famous newspaper later became the spokesman of the Whig party, and after 1819 it enjoyed substantial profits from government printing. It was eventually acquired by Joseph Gales, Jr., reporter of the House debates, and his brother-in-law, W. W. Seaton, long mayor of Washington. John Quincy Adams had close connections with Peter Force, editor and publisher of the *National Journal* and printer of the *American Archives*,[4] but Adams was not a man to support an administration paper with government patronage.

The full import of an administration press became apparent with the election of Andrew Jackson. As the years passed, evil consequences arose in pressure upon government employees for subscriptions, and in extravagant public printing costs that were diverted to the administration organ and to electioneering expenses in ways that approached corruption.

THE ADMINISTRATION PRESS

Jackson's victory brought into existence a new government organ published by Duff Green, the *United States Telegraph*. Green made the mistake of thinking he could secure the election of Calhoun to succeed Jackson in the 1832 campaign, and as soon as this became apparent, the fate of the *Telegraph* was sealed. Amos Kendall was instrumental in making the transition to a different newspaper, with the avowed object of reelecting Jackson and ending successfully the war with the Bank. He was willing to leave Duff Green the Senate printing "should he remain faithful," but was not content to rely on the *Telegraph* as the mouthpiece of the administration.[5] The result was the estab-

[3] *Ibid.*, p. 70.

[4] John Spencer Bassett, *The Middle Group of American Historians* (New York: Macmillan, 1917), pp. 233–39.

[5] Kendall, *Autobiography*, pp. 370–74.

lishment of a new sheet, the *Globe,* and the introduction to Washington (from Kendall's Kentucky paper, the *Western Argus*) of a man destined to play an important part in national affairs for a generation, Francis P. Blair.[6] Green failed to remain faithful, eventually lost the Senate printing, and the *Telegraph* expired.

The *Globe* was the organ of both the Jackson and Van Buren administrations. Blair was on intimate personal terms with Jackson, submitted articles to the President for approval, regularly had inside information on executive plans and policy, and served as the recognized agency of the Jackson administration for public announcements and trial balloons.[7] Niles thought that Kendall was the "real editor" of the *Globe,* and it is certain that he was actively associated with it.[8] The firm of Blair and Rives secured contracts for executive printing, and from 1837 to 1845 participated in House and Senate printing.

The *National Intelligencer,* although not Jackson's party sheet, continued to be read in official circles by virtue of the excellence of its pages. It was, however, the victim of partisan spite at the hands of Secretary of State John Forsyth, who in 1837 abruptly terminated sixteen subscriptions for the legations abroad. Gales and Seaton promptly announced that they would send the *National Intelligencer* to every minister, chargé d'affaires, and consul general abroad, "determined," as they declared, "that the public interest shall not, as far as we can prevent it, suffer by keeping them in ignorance (except as officially advised) of what is going on at home, or, what is as bad, giving them one-sided views of public affairs. . . ." [9]

6 William Ernest Smith, *The Francis Preston Blair Family in Politics* (2 vols., New York: Macmillan, 1933).

7 Sumner probably overstated the case in his vivid description of the *Globe.* "In the hands of Blair the 'Globe' came to be a terrible power. Every office-holder signed his allegiance by taking the 'Globe.' In it both friend and foe found daily utterances from the White House *a propos* of every topic of political interest. The suggestions, innuendoes, queries, quips, and sarcasms of the 'Globe' were scanned by the men who desired to recommend themselves by the zeal which anticipates a command, and the subserviency which can even dispense with it. The editorials scarcely veiled their inspiration and authorization." William Graham Sumner, *Andrew Jackson* (Boston: Houghton Mifflin and Co., 1882, revised ed., 1899), pp. 325–26.

8 *Niles Register,* XL, 73 (April 2, 1831).

9 *Ibid.,* LI, 404 (Feb. 25, 1837).

Tyler depended upon the *Madisonian,* edited by Thomas Allen, who received the printing of the Senate. After Tyler broke with the Whigs, the party returned to the *National Intelligencer.*

The selection of an "official" organ by the returning Democrats under Polk was a delicate matter and well illustrated the issues involved in the status of such a newspaper.[10] Blair was still publishing the *Globe,* expected to resume his old station as the administration sheet, and was vigorously supported by the aged but strong-minded Jackson. But Polk remembered that Blair had not been politically friendly to him, believed that Blair was secretly committed to Senator Benton, and knew that he was out of favor with some sections of the Democratic party. The President told Jackson all this, and added, "There is at present no paper here which sustains my administration for its own sake. . . . I feel that my administration is at this moment defenceless so far as the public press here is concerned." [11] Blair also was writing Jackson for advice, and at one point Jackson informed Polk that refusal to accept Blair would involve the destruction of the Democratic party.[12]

Polk extricated himself from an awkward position by direct and friendly conversations with Blair, emphasizing the necessity of a united party, and offering the post of editor of the government organ to Major Andrew Jackson Donelson. Blair agreed to sell the *Globe,* Donelson declined to come in, and the control of the newspaper was arranged by the administration to fall to the editor of the *Richmond Enquirer,* Thomas Ritchie, and the former editor of the *Nashville Union,* John P. Heiss. The firm of Ritchie and Heiss was to become nearly as famous as Blair and Rives.

Ritchie had long been powerful in Democratic circles in Virginia and now through the *Union,* as the *Globe* was rechristened, occupied a similar position in national affairs. Polk and Ritchie were on intimate terms, although the latter's "leaks" occasionally annoyed the President. In utmost secrecy Polk gave the *Union* an advance copy of his first annual message; he saw that Ritchie

10 See Senator Benton's account of the transaction, Thomas Hart Benton, *Thirty Years' View,* II, 650–55.

11 Jackson, *Correspondence,* VI, 382–83 (March 17, 1845).

12 *Ibid.,* VI, 394 (April 4, 1845).

had first notice of messages from the front during the Mexican War; he kept Ritchie closely informed, and on a few occasions even outlined articles to appear in Ritchie's paper.[13]

The *Union* continued during the Taylor-Fillmore administration as an important but private publication. Its Democratic affilications were continued after 1849 by Edmund Burke, coming in as associate editor. Burke was a New Hampshire editor and lawyer who served in Congress from 1839 to 1845, and who was commissioner of patents under Polk and later a lobbyist. Taylor depended upon the *Republic,* owned in part by A. C. Bullitt, who came to Washington at Taylor's personal request.[14] The Whig *National Intelligencer* was thought to be more friendly to Clay and Webster than to the Chief Executive.

President Pierce had the same problem that had perplexed Polk. The *Union* was at hand ready to resume its place as the administration organ, but Pierce did not have confidence in Ritchie's successors. He managed a satisfactory arrangement by insisting upon the connection with the *Union* of A. O. P. Nicholson and Major Donelson. Nicholson was public printer to the House and Senate during most of Pierce's administration.[15]

Meanwhile a strong, energetic and independent press was being established in New York, notably the *New York Herald* under James Gordon Bennett, and the *New York Tribune,* edited by Horace Greeley. The position of a "captive" organ became less tenable and less important. Buchanan finally terminated the whole institution of an official paper in 1857, giving the editor of the *Union* a collectorship and announcing that no paper would succeed to the position the *Union* had occupied.[16]

13 Polk, *Diary,* I, 108–9 (Dec. 1, 1845); II, 468–69 (April 10, 1847); I, 351–52 (April 24, 1846).

14 Brainerd Dyer, *Zachary Taylor* (Baton Rouge: Louisiana State University Press, 1946), p. 332.

15 Alfred Osborne Pope Nicholson was an active politician-editor from Tennessee. Educated both as a physician and as a lawyer, he became interested in banks and railroads, served both in the Tennessee House and Senate and from 1840 to 1842 served the remainder of Grundy's term in the U.S. Senate. In 1845 he became editor of Polk's organ in Tennessee, the *Nashville Union.* He declined Pierce's offer of a Cabinet post, but accepted election as public printer and editor of the *Union.* Elected to the Senate in 1859, he joined the Confederacy. From 1870 to 1876 he was chief justice of the Tennessee Supreme Court. *Dictionary of American Biography,* XIII, 498.

16 Fish, *Civil Service and the Patronage,* p. 167.

In 1860 Buchanan had to take a more decisive step. Writing to William M. Brown, editor of the *Constitution* (successor to the *Union*), he said:

I have read with deep mortification your editorial this morning in which you take open ground against my message on the right of secession. I have defended you as long as I can against numerous complaints. You have a perfect right to be in favor of secession, and for this I have no just reason to complain. The difficulty is that the "Constitution" is considered my organ, and its articles subject me to the charge of insincerity and double dealing. I am deeply sorry to say that I must in some authentic form declare that the "Constitution" is not the organ of the administration.[17]

Thus terminated thirty years' active experience with an administration organ, located in Washington and speaking with a certified voice for the party in power. Every President from Jackson to Buchanan thought it necessary to secure one important newspaper, solidly devoted to his personal support as well as the program of the party. Factionalism in New York and Pennsylvania and an often irresponsible press throughout the country urged Presidents on this course. But they discovered that this was not a means of subduing factions or controlling fabricated stories against the party in power.

The party out of power often complained bitterly about the increased executive power that came from the "official" organ, and demanded that the press be free from the corruption of executive patronage. This was largely a party war cry and ignored another disturbing aspect of the government organ: the source of its financial support. Here emerged a problem of deep moral significance, since it involved the use of public money for party success, or even for factional domination.[18]

17 Buchanan, *Works,* XI, 75 (Dec. 25, 1860).

18 A party press appeared also in some of the state capitals, notably New York and Philadelphia—the political capital of Pennsylvania at this time. For Weed and the *Albany Journal,* see Glyndon G. Van Deusen, *Thurlow Weed: Wizard of the Lobby* (Boston: Little, Brown and Co., 1947), pp. 73–74. Weed's office as public printer to the state of New York was estimated to be worth $30,000 a year. *Ibid.,* p. 108. For Franklin Pierce's attempt to control the upstate New York press, see Stewart Mitchell, *Horatio Seymour of New York* (Cambridge, Mass.: Harvard University Press, 1938), p. 149. See also Mott, *American Journalism,* and Pollard, *Presidents and the Press.*

THE PUBLIC PRINTING

The first statutory notice of public printing occurred in 1794 in an appropriation item amounting to $10,000 for the expenses of "firewood, stationery, and printing work, and all other contingent expenses of the two Houses of Congress." The expenditure of this sum was vested in the secretary of the Senate and the clerk of the House. In 1804 Congress required these functionaries to advertise for bids and to award the contract to the lowest bidder. This first simple contract system lasted until 1819.[19]

Dissatisfaction with the service of the master printers who secured the awards for the congressional printing induced an investigation in 1818 and a recommendation for an official government printing office.[20] Congress refused to go into the printing business and thus postponed the establishment of the government printing office for forty years. Instead it embarked upon a new and extravagant procedure by authorizing the election of a public printer for each House, and specifying the rates at which congressional printing should be done.[21] The initial contract system was thus abandoned in favor of a fixed price set in statute and the election of one (or two) public printers for each succeeding Congress. This legislation did not affect the printing required by the *executive* establishments, the arrangements for which are described in later paragraphs.

The printing firm of Gales and Seaton, publishers of the *National Intelligencer,* was promptly elected public printer by both the House and Senate in 1819, and reelected by the 17th, 18th, and 19th Congresses. Jackson's friends controlled the Senate in the 20th Congress (Adams' second) and in 1827 Duff Green, a Jackson man, was elected printer to the Senate. Gales and Seaton were continued by the House.

Green was not a printer, but a mail contractor. His award of the Senate printing was part of a deal by which Green undertook to establish the *United States Telegraph,* to be financed

19 Laurence F. Schmeckebier, *The Government Printing Office: Its History, Activities and Organization* (Baltimore: Johns Hopkins Press, 1925), pp. 2–4.

20 Senate Doc. 99, 15th Cong., 2d sess. (Feb. 19, 1819).

21 3 Stat. 538 (March 3, 1819).

by the profits of the Senate printing.[22] A Senate committee later summarized the transaction. "This cemented the alliance between the congressional printing and partisan presses." The *Telegraph* was supplanted, as already observed, by the *Globe*. This newspaper was established under a contract with a practical printer, "who was to receive certain 'patronage,' one third of the profits resulting from which was to be retained by him, while the remaining two-thirds were to be given to the editor, who was not required to furnish a dollar of capital." [23]

The connection between the administration organ and party newspapers outside Washington, on the one hand, and the profits of the public printing on the other became more and more entangled as the years marched on, until a situation approaching scandal developed in the 1850's. The Whigs endeavored to stop party diversion of printing contracts in 1831 and 1833 by means of publicity, requiring the departments to make an annual statement listing all printers in any way employed and the compensation allowed to each.[24] In 1835 they sought to exclude from official printing all persons concerned with any public journal or newspaper, but the Democrats repelled such a "proscription, by law, of a particular profession of men from a particular kind of public employment." This, they declared, was a startling principle, contrary to the genius of free government.[25] The Whigs were not convinced, but later when they needed the support of the public printing for their party press, they forgot their scruples.

The election of the public printers consequently became a strictly party affair, and within the party an often bitter struggle. The eclipse of Duff Green, as already noted, brought to Washington the firm of Blair and Rives, publishers of the *Globe*. They soon acquired a substantial share of the executive printing, with Jackson's blessing: "It would be mortifying," he said, "to see his establishment [i.e. Blair's] again embarrassed for the want of that support which the work of the Departments afford." [26]

22 His printing contract with the Post Office Department has already been described in chapter 13.

23 Senate Report 247, 40th Cong., 3d sess., p. 7 (Feb. 19, 1869).

24 Senate Doc. 422, 23d Cong., 1st sess., pp. 27–29 (June 9, 1834).

25 House Report 138, 23d Cong., 2d sess., pp. 1–2 (March 2, 1835).

26 Jackson, *Correspondence*, IV, 465 (July 21, 1832).

In 1837 Blair and Rives became printers to the Senate, and with the play of politics they held both House and Senate printing from time to time. In 1840 Van Buren wrote Jackson, "You will see that those really honest men Blair and Rives have at last been appointed Printers to Congress, after the fiercest opposition that was ever made on a similar occasion." [27]

Thoughtful men in Congress became concerned about the implications of the connection between the public printing and the press.[28] In 1840 a House committee minority renewed the idea of a government printing plant as the only solution for a bad situation. "The intrigues, compromises, and imputations of improper and corrupt purposes and motives, are enough to sicken the heart of a patriot. . . . Of the persons elected printers to either House of Congress since 1819, none have been practical printers except Messrs Gales & Seaton. All have been political partisans; and it is quite probable that the political opinions and services of those gentlemen have always had more influence than the fact of their being practically qualified for the station." [29] The biennial election of the printer, declared the Senate Committee on Printing in 1842, "presents the humiliating spectacle of eagerly contending conductors of party newspapers, claiming the prize as a reward for party services." [30] The committee protested against favoritism to the party press, "for, in this, there would be danger that the great and paramount purpose would degenerate into the unworthy object of ministering to the cupidity of mere party men, and to the extension of a vast corrupting patronage with the funds of the nation." [31]

Such criticism led in 1846 to the abandonment of the public printer system and a return to the competitive contract plan under the direction of the Senate and House clerks that had prevailed to 1819.[32] To encourage out-of-town bidding by small contractors, the congressional printing was divided into five

27 *Ibid.*, VI, 48 (Feb. 2, 1840).

28 For example, House Report 298, 26th Cong., 1st sess. (March 26, 1840); Senate Doc. 332, 27th Cong., 2d sess. (June 17, 1842).

29 House Report 425, 26th Cong., 1st sess., p. 6 (April 14, 1840); reprinted in Senate Doc. 332, 27th Cong., 2d sess., pp. 13–14.

30 Senate Doc. 332, 27th Cong., 2d sess., p. 2 (June 17, 1842).

31 *Ibid.*, p. 1.

32 9 Stat. 113, Joint Resolution of August 3, 1846; House Report 754, 29th Cong., 1st sess. (July 6, 1846).

classes, a device that failed to produce the anticipated results. A Joint Committee on Printing was established with authority to adopt measures to remedy any neglect or delay on the part of the contractors, to refuse unsatisfactory work, and to audit printing accounts. In 1852 the Whigs tried to safeguard the contract system still further by establishing the new office of superintendent of public printing. This officer was appointed by the President and Senate for each Congress, was required to be a practical printer, and was directed to supervise the execution of the public printing, including that offered by the executive branch. The Joint Committee on Printing was continued, with added authority to arbitrate disputes between the superintendent of public printing and the successful contractors.[33]

Results continued to be extremely unsatisfactory and in 1860 a third and final solution of the problem was agreed upon, the government printing office. Proposed in 1819 and on later occasions, it had been rejected in 1846 in favor of the contract system for reasons stated and unstated. Officially it was alleged that "all government establishments are prone to become the source of unnecessary, not to say profligate expenditure. That sagacity and vigilance which contribute so much to the success of individual enterprises is, to a great extent, wanting in its operations when the government becomes jobber." [34] Behind this opinion was the unstated intention of politicians of both parties to keep control of printing profits for party advantage.

The amounts involved were substantial. The rates fixed by Congress in 1819 were such as to allow a profit of about 55 per cent.[35] Expenditures for congressional printing quickly rose from about $17,000 to about $29,000 per session.[36] The investigation of 1842 showed that the aggregate printing bill for the Senate, the House, and the executive departments averaged (for the seven years 1834 to 1840 inclusive) $166,951. On this figure the Senate Committee on Printing estimated conservatively an an-

33 10 Stat. 30 (August 26, 1852).

34 House Report 754, 29th Cong., 1st sess., p. 49 (July 6, 1846). It was also argued that a government printing office "would constitute a formidable electioneering machine of the majority of Congress."

35 Excessive costs were evident at an early date, and were publicly stated in 1840. House Report 425, 26th Cong., 1st sess., pp. 4–5 (April 14, 1840).

36 Schmeckebier, *Government Printing Office*, p. 5.

nual profit of over $66,000. In addition the committee estimated an annual profit of nearly $20,000 on binding, and of nearly $7,000 on engraving and lithographing.[37]

These figures grew steadily. The cost of Senate and House printing for the period 1853–59 was nearly $3.5 million; the cost of executive printing about $375,000; congressional binding over $825,000; executive binding $115,000. Profits were estimated by the printer, Cornelius Wendell, as averaging at least 50 per cent.[38] Just before establishing the Government Printing Office, Congress required the superintendent of public printing to award the printing of the post office blanks to the bidder who offered the greatest per cent deduction from the price fixed by law.[39] The cost of printing this item promptly went down from $45,000 a year to $3,000.[40] The master printer who held the post office contracts for some years before 1852, under subcontract with the printer designated by the President, agreed to do the work by direct contract for 7 per cent of the old price. Presumably he included an adequate profit for himself.[41] Senator Simon Cameron, a printer by trade, declared that the actual cost of printing was not more than 20 per cent of the price paid.[42]

Where did these handsome profits go? In substantial part they went into the party war chest, or into the support of party newspapers both in Washington and in the field. "The dominant party," wrote Schmeckebier, "elected the printer with a positive understanding that he would devote specified sums out of his profits for partisan purposes.[43] The record shows that much

37 Senate Doc. 332, 27th Cong., 2d sess., pp. 16–17 (June 17, 1842).

38 House Report 249, 36th Cong., 1st sess., pp. 5–8 (March 26, 1860).

39 12 Stat. 1, sec. 5 (Feb. 15, 1860).

40 House Report 249, 36th Cong., 1st sess., p. 18 (March 26, 1860). For evidence of collusive bidding, see House Misc. Doc. 55, 31st Cong., 1st sess. (Sept. 30, 1850); and Senate Report 247, 40th Cong., 3d sess., pp. 9–11 (Feb. 19, 1869).

41 *Ibid.*, p. 11.

42 Lee F. Crippen, *Simon Cameron: Ante-Bellum Years* (Oxford, Ohio: Mississippi Valley Press, 1942), p. 198.

43 This statement was confirmed by John D. Defrees, unsuccessful Republican candidate for House printer in 1860, who testified that he authorized a member of Congress to inform the Republican caucus he would devote one-half the profits to the good of the party. House Report 249, 36th Cong., 1st sess., pp. 153–54 (March 26, 1860). The Republicans voted solidly for Defrees with the single exception of Charles Francis Adams, son of the late President. The loss of Adams' vote was decisive. Senate Report 205, 36th Cong., 1st sess., pp. 12–13 (May 31, 1860).

of the printing of the executive departments was given out secretly and at extravagant figures. In some cases six times a fair rate was paid for certain jobs, and the plunder thus secured was systematically distributed for partisan purposes." [44] Some printers elected by the House of Representatives used part of their profits, indeed, to help elect representatives who might aid them in their future election as public printers.[45]

The transfer of printing profits into party press and electioneering expenses was exposed in the testimony of Cornelius Wendell before the House and Senate committees in 1859 and 1860. Wendell had succeeded to the ownership of the *Union,* one of the two establishments in Washington capable of executing the extensive government printing.[46] He not only did a large amount of official printing and binding as printer to the Senate (1857–59) and on subcontract from the public printers or successful prime contractors, but also acted as agent for printing houses in other cities who were interested in contracts from the executive departments or in subcontracts for the congressional printing. In addition, he was active politically in the Democratic party, and was one of the principal figures involved in diverting printing profits to party purposes. He was an intimate of President Buchanan, and during the congressional elections of 1858 saw the President almost daily.

Much of the evidence on printing operations appeared in the hearings of the Covode Committee, a select committee established by the House of Representatives on March 5, 1860, on motion of Congressman John Covode.[47] The committee was motivated by partisan hostility to Buchanan, and was indeed directed to inquire whether he had sought by money, patronage, or other improper means to influence Congress. The President made a solemn protest against the charge of the committee.[48] The sworn testimony may nevertheless be generally accepted as trustworthy evidence.

Wendell testified before the Covode Committee in 1860 that

44 Schmeckebier, *Government Printing Office,* p. 7.

45 *Ibid.,* p. 8.

46 The other was the printing office of the *National Intelligencer.*

47 House Report 648, 36th Cong., 1st sess. (June 16, 1860), contains the voluminous report of the committee and its hearings.

48 Richardson, *Messages,* V, 614 (March 28, 1860).

he had almost the whole of the executive printing in 1858 (on subcontract) and that from 1856 to 1860 he had contributed over $100,000 for party purposes in New York, New Jersey, Connecticut, Ohio, Maine, and particularly in Pennsylvania.[49] According to Schmeckebier he also paid $200,000 to the printers of the Senate and House for the right to subcontract with them, and loaned $150,000 to political friends on insufficient security.[50] Wendell was doing business in the amount of nearly one million dollars a year.[51] When asked if he would have contributed as freely to the party if he had not had the public printing, he replied, "I would not have been able to contribute so much. It was the profit I made out of the public printing that enabled me to contribute these amounts of money. The fact that I was in a public position known to be remunerative induced frequent calls upon me, to which I responded." [52] On another occasion he testified that the amounts he contributed to the election of Congressmen ran from $250 to $2,250 per district.

Wendell fought a losing battle to retain his profits during the election of 1858. The Democrats had lost the Philadelphia patronage, and the editor of Buchanan's "house organ," the *Pennsylvanian* (William Rice, editor), claimed a part of the printing to sustain his journal. Wendell objected strenuously but in vain, and was "induced" to make as good a deal with Rice as he could. Rice wanted fifty cents in the dollar, but Wendell finally got him down to forty-three cents, and actually paid him between $11,000 and $12,000 in the course of 1858. Meanwhile another publisher, Severns of the *Argus,* demanded a cut, and Wendell had to pay him about $7,000. Wendell found he was losing money, became disgusted with the pressure brought to bear on him, and sold out the *Union* to A. O. P. Nicholson. According to Wendell all these transactions were done after close consultation with Buchanan, although not at his specific direction.[53]

Wendell had sources of income as the agent of out-of-town printers that were also turned back in part to electioneering purposes, income that would hardly have stood the scrutiny of the

49 House Report 648, 36th Cong., 1st sess., p. 459 (June 16, 1860).
50 Schmeckebier, *Government Printing Office,* p. 8.
51 House Report 189, 35th Cong., 2d sess., p. 249 (Feb. 28, 1859).
52 House Report 249, 36th Cong., 1st sess., p. 14 (March 26, 1860).
53 House Report 648, 36th Cong., 1st sess., pp. 462, 506 (June 16, 1860).

old Jeffersonians. He stoutly defended his commissions as strictly business transactions. "Gentlemen," he said, "would come to me and ask my assistance. I would do what I could for them, make what I could out of it, pocket the affront [*sic*], and use it as I pleased thereafter. If a gentleman offered me a thousand dollars to aid him, and I could do it in an honest way, I was willing to do it, and I was pretty successful in it too, sir." [54] He described his services as helping printers to get contracts, collecting their bills, and sometimes advancing them money. He denied that he had ever split his commissions with any other party.[55] On the other hand he stated that he had expended for party purposes twice the amount of the commissions he had collected.[56]

PRINTING, POLITICS, AND REFORM

These disclosures involved primarily the control of congressional printing. Control of executive printing was vested by law in the heads of the departments, but it gravitated in fact into the hands of the President and was often assigned to the House and Senate printers. A Senate report of 1858 disclosed that for the previous five years A. O. P. Nicholson had received departmental printing amounting to over $175,000; Gales and Seaton over $54,000; and Robert Armstrong over $33,000. Much of this, indeed most of it, was contracted out to Cornelius Wendell who, in the same five years, held direct contracts amounting to only $392.23.[57] One consequence of these operations was to strengthen the Chief Executive as the head of the party which had elected him.

This trend of events remains obscure in its details, but it had come to full fruition in Buchanan's administration. The position was described by Wendell in 1860, and is best given in his own words.

> . . . . The editor of the organ is generally supposed to command the patronage of the President. There is a good deal of this work at

54 House Report 189, 35th Cong., 2d sess., p. 249 (Feb. 28, 1859).

55 *Ibid.*, p. 252.

56 *Ibid.*, p. 344. More information of the same general tenor was disclosed before the Committee on Public Expenditures in 1860. House Report 249, 36th Cong., 1st sess. (March 26, 1860), *passim*.

57 Senate Ex. Doc. 50, 35th Cong., 1st sess., p. 9 (April 19, 1858).

the disposal of the President—say an aggregate of one hundred thousand dollars per year, more or less.

Q. At the disposal of the President?

A. Yes, sir. That patronage the organ has commanded for years, it being impossible to keep a paper up here without government support.

Q. Is this one hundred thousand dollars worth of patronage you speak of at the disposal of the President personally?

A. The law provides that it shall be under the control of the heads of the departments; but if the President signifies to his Cabinet that he would be pleased to see A, B, or C get it, as a matter of course they will obey his wishes. It has been a matter of custom for the President to dispose of it. Mr. Buchanan has done it, and his predecessor, Mr. Pierce, did it. I never had any intercourse with the Cabinet in the matter; my intercourse has been direct with Mr. Buchanan, and was so with Mr. Pierce. . . .

Q. Was there ever any understanding with you while you had that printing that a portion of the profits should be used towards sustaining the organ?

A. Yes, sir; it was given for the purpose of sustaining the organ.[58]

There is no doubt that Buchanan was cognizant of the diversion of some of Wendell's profits to the *Pennsylvanian* and elsewhere, although Wendell denied in a "card" published in the *Union* that the President had ordered him to make the split. Wendell, who had a high idea of his own capacity, told the Covode Committee, however, that he had seen enough "to take a hint." [59] The Committee on Public Expenditures declared in 1860 that Congress, "in voting much larger sums for the public printing than had been required to do the work, has placed in the hands of the President an immense patronage," and asserted that from the beginning of Buchanan's administration he had tried to use it for "a centralization of power." [60] The intimate relations between Wendell and Buchanan tended to confirm this view.

Forty years' experience had thus demonstrated the incapacity of Congress to secure economy, efficiency, or even honesty in

58 House Report 249, 36th Cong., 1st sess., p. 28 (March 26, 1860).

59 House Report 648, 36th Cong., 1st sess., pp. 580–81, 582 (June 16, 1860). The card was suggested to Wendell by an intermediary; Wendell signed as written.

60 House Report 249, 36th Cong., 1st sess., p. 18 (March 26, 1860).

the execution of its own printing. Neither the contract system, presumably safeguarded by the superintendent of public printing, nor the public printer system, had proved reliable. The pressure for profit and for party advantage had been too great.

The House Select Committee on Printing was well justified in declaring in 1858 that "a very large amount of money is annually paid to politicians and speculators through contracts for printing, binding, engraving, &c., and that the mode by which the public work is now done not only presents opportunities for fraud upon the treasury, but invites and stimulates an unnatural competition among parties who are willing to risk their reputation in a business promising such large gains. . . . It contributes very largely to lower Congress in the estimation of the public, and thus it inflicts a serious wound upon our institutions."[61] Congress reluctantly turned to a government printing establishment in 1860.[62]

By this reforming legislation, full responsibility for congressional, executive, and judicial printing was vested in the superintendent of public printing, who was directed to secure the necessary plant and equipment for a government printing establishment. He was also authorized to purchase paper and to employ staff, but with the proviso that he should employ no more hands than "the absolute necessities" of the work required, the number to be reported to Congress. The Joint Standing Committee on Printing was continued and retained the duty of settling disputes between the superintendent and contractors for supplying paper. The status of the Government Printing Office as a bureau was confirmed by the requirement that it should make annual estimates through the Secretary of the Treasury.

Thus was closed, in the words of the Committee on Public Expenditures, the Pandora box that had tempted every party in power.[63] The act establishing the Government Printing Office and the act requiring examinations for clerks were among the first to modify the long trend toward spoils, and to prevent the diversion of public money to partisan purposes.

61 House Report 350, 35th Cong., 1st sess., p. 11 (April 21, 1858).
62 12 Stat. 117 (June 23, 1860).
63 House Report 249, 36th Cong., 1st sess., p. 1 (March 26, 1860).

CHAPTER SIXTEEN

Theory and Practice of Rotation

Forty years of substantially steady practice prior to 1829 had established a tradition of permanence and stability in the public service of the federal government. Washington and Adams, Jefferson after a couple years of adjustment, Madison, Monroe, and John Quincy Adams all assumed that no man was subject to discharge for difference in political opinion or for a free expression of his political views. Appointments to fill vacancies, caused most often by death of an incumbent, were regularly taken from the ranks of Republicans after 1801, but many Federalists quietly held office without disturbance; and both Republicans and Federalists were gentlemen. Adams had resolutely refused to allow the Tenure of Office Act to be used for political purposes and had steadfastly reappointed both friend and foe as commissions expired. If one could discount the patronage ferment in New York and Pennsylvania, one might have concluded in 1828 that the tradition of permanence and stability was as well established as the two-term tradition of the presidency.

Events subsequent to 1829 exploded such a comfortable assumption. Many circumstances combined to shake, but not wholly to destroy, the old tradition. Much more was involved than the will of one man, or the animosity that existed between the two wings of the Republican party, or even the ardor for office that boiled up during those years. A new sense of democracy was brewing, and a belief that self-government required wide participation by citizens, not only in legislative halls but in executive offices. In the state and local governments this belief was effectuated by the direct election of most officeholders. In the federal government this solution was impossible, short of constitutional amendment. Rotation was an alternative.

Quite apart from theory and disquisition, which are noted at the end of this chapter, the old stability in officeholding was threatened by the voice of the people themselves. The demand for appointments grew apace, and local politicians did not hesitate to tell their successful partisans in places of authority what they expected. Rotation was imposed because it was demanded from below, not merely because it was advocated from above.

THE VOICE OF THE PEOPLE

Office had always been an object of interest to Americans, but Federalist and Republican leaders alike had done nothing to stir up a latent storm. Jefferson had warned about the "rottenness" that begins in a man's conduct when he casts a longing eye on office. John Quincy Adams thought the passion for public office one that required "great moderation, self-management and control." From Washington through the administration of the younger Adams, the expectation of federal office was held down by the scarcity of vacancies in a stable service, by choice from among those holding a "respectable" station in social life, by presidential success in holding off congressional interference, and by the failure of the Federalists to maintain an effective party organization after 1800.

The deferential and circumspect attitude of office seekers characteristic of Federalist years had, nevertheless, gradually passed away, and in the turmoil of New York and Pennsylvania politics a strident, pushing, and insistent type of office seeker took the place of the respectable sons of Federalist or Republican families. Likewise the crowds of people who swarmed about the streets of Washington in March 1829 spoke of a new world of public life, a difference, as Fish observed, "not in numbers of candidates alone, though that was marked, but still more decidedly in character. The trimly dressed gentlemen of the old régime, with their high stocks and good breeding, were jostled by hack politicians from New York and country editors and farmers from the West." [1]

1 Carl R. Fish, *Civil Service and the Patronage,* p. 109.

The newcomers instructed Presidents and department heads in no uncertain terms. Jesse Hoyt, an active New York politician who one day became collector of the port of New York, told Van Buren exactly what was expected of him in the national capital in the early days of Jackson's administration.

. . . . I take it for granted that all who do not support the present administration you will not consider your friends, and of course will lose your confidence. I have said from the commencement of the contest that I would not support any administration who would support men in power that had contributed to overthrow the democratic party in this State. I have preached this doctrine too long, and it has taken too [strong] a footing here, to be easily got rid of. This is not only the doctrine in theory, but we require it to be reduced to practice by the servants of the people to whom we have temporarily delegated the trust. I speak now the universal sentiments of the democracy of this city, and you may rely upon it no man can be sustained who aids or abets in the disappointment of the just expectations of the people on this subject—and all personal considerations and private friendships must yield to *political justice*. . . . In calling upon our friends, to act in this matter, we shall, as we have always done, repudiate the doctrine of neutrality. We shall expect every man to take sides one way or the other, *either for or against removals*. The old maxim of "those not for us are against us," you have so often recognized that its authority cannot be denied.[2]

Van Buren, driving down by stage from New York to become Secretary of State, arrived late at night in a state of exhaustion. He was immediately surrounded by a crowd of applicants for office, who followed him into his hotel room where he lay on a sofa while they pleaded their cause.[3] Amos Kendall went to Washington hoping for a clerkship or, if Fortune smiled, an auditorship. He met a Kentucky friend who, with an unusual sense of delicacy, said, "Mr. Kendall, I am ashamed of myself, for I feel as if every man I meet knew what I came for." To which Kendall replied, "Don't distress yourself, for every man you meet is on the same business." [4] President Jackson wrote his

2 William L. Mackenzie, *The Lives and Opinions of Benj'n Franklin Butler . . . and Jesse Hoyt* (Boston: Cook and Co., 1845), pp. 51–52 (March 21, 1829).

3 Van Buren, *Autobiography*, pp. 231–32.

4 Kendall, *Autobiography*, p. 307.

friend, John Coffee, that there was not more than one office for five hundred applicants.[5]

Pressure for appointment to such vacancies as occurred during the later years of Jackson's administration was unremitting. In 1834 Niles reported, "The desire to feed at the 'public crib' is excessive. It is truly astonishing with what eagerness offices are sought that yield a less annual amount than a respectable mechanic earns by his daily labor. The great inducement, perhaps, is laziness—a mortal hatred of work. In the new organization of the marine corps, eight or ten new lieutenants were to be appointed. It is said that there were *four hundred* applicants!"[6] It was not surprising that Daniel Webster was moved to remark, "No candid man can deny that a great, a very great change has taken place, within a few years, in the practice of the executive government, which has produced a corresponding change in our political condition. No one can deny that office, of every kind, is now sought with extraordinary avidity. . . ."[7]

The defeat of the Democrats in 1840 started a new march on the White House. Hordes of Whigs "rushed pell-mell to Washington, every man with a raccoon's tail in his hat. . . ."[8] A Whig editor attending the inauguration wrote privately that "the rush of Whigs for office is beyond any thing you could have imagined—even disgraceful."[9] John Quincy Adams called them the "wolves of the antechamber, prowling for offices."[10] John J. Crittenden, soon to become Attorney General, predicted in January that "Old Tip" would "bring along with him such a storm as old Aeolus could hardly raise."[11] He was correct in his forecast.

5 Jackson, *Correspondence,* IV, 14 (March 22, 1829).

6 *Niles Register,* XLVII, 147 (Nov. 8, 1834).

7 Webster, *Writings and Speeches* (National ed.), VII, 181 (Feb. 16, 1835).

8 Henry A. Wise, *Seven Decades of the Union* (Philadelphia: J. B. Lippincott, 1872), p. 179.

9 Joseph Howard Parks, *John Bell of Tennessee* (Baton Rouge: Louisiana State University Press, 1950), p. 179, quoting a letter of William G. Brownlow, March 8, 1841.

10 Adams, *Memoirs,* XI, 156 (May 19, 1842).

11 Ann M. B. Coleman, ed., *Life of Crittenden,* I, 139, letter of January 17, 1841. Cf. Adams' account of the annoyance caused him by General Joseph G. Swift, "one of the numberless office-hunters blockading the President's house and all the Executive departments of the Government—famished for place." Adams, *Memoirs,* X, 447–48 (March 19, 1841).

Harrison was besieged and taken prisoner in the White House itself by a crowd of office seekers. General Hunter, the marshal of Washington, calling at the White House a few days after the inauguration, found it full of people.

. . . . The President wanted to have a meeting of his cabinet but could not go into a room where he was not pressed by the crowd. Hunter expostulated but in vain. He prepared to rally a force to drive out the intruders, but suggested to the president first to make a speech to them, stating his conditions. This he did, told them it was impossible to attend to their claims upon him then as public business imperiously required his time. The Spoils men, however, refused to quit unless he would *then,* receive their papers and pledge himself to attend to them. He capitulated, and first all his pockets were filled with papers, then his hat, then his arms, and finally Hunter was loaded; and both marched up stairs with as much as they could carry. It was with difficulty then that the House was cleared.[12]

Congressman Millard Fillmore wrote that the Whigs were in danger of being utterly and forever disgraced by the detestable scramble for office. "Heaven save general Harrison from such friends and this country from such officers. I insist that such men are neither patriots nor whigs and that the whig press ought to come out universally and administer such a rebuke to these selfish, *spoil hunting* parasites as will drive them back to the party to which they belong. They have no rights here and we are in danger not only of being utterly disgraced, but utterly ruined by their association." [13]

The Democratic contingent of office seekers came back to the capital with Polk in 1845 and for four years he suffered importunities which in deference to democratic sentiment he endured publicly but condemned privately in no uncertain terms. On the first anniversary of his inauguration, he wrote, "I am ready to exclaim, will the pressure for office never cease! It is one year today since I entered on the duties of my office, and still the pressure for office has not abated. I most sincerely wish I had no offices to bestow." [14] In 1847 he predicted that no President would

12 Jackson, *Correspondence,* VI, 97–98 (April 4, 1841).

13 *Fillmore Papers,* II, 215 (Dec. 20, 1840).

14 Polk, *Diary,* I, 261 (March 4, 1846). The insistence of applicants was sometimes almost overbearing. One H. K. Smith sought the Buffalo collectorship, using Marcy as his intermediary. The appointment, he told Marcy, was "absolutely essen-

ever again be reelected. "The reason is that the patronage of the Government will destroy the popularity of any President, however well he may administer the Government. The office seekers have become so numerous that they hold the balance of power between the two great parties of the country." [15] His growing impatience with the men caused them to send their wives to intercede for them.[16]

After a few months in office President Taylor was reported to have said that matters had come to such a pass that if he did not kick a man downstairs, he went away believing he had a promise of office.[17] Pierce and his Cabinet were pursued from dawn until dark by an estimated thirty thousand office seekers who crowded into Washington. The *National Intelligencer* reported that the President and department heads "had to assume *roundabouts* to enable them to pass *from their offices to their boarding houses.*" [18]

Not all requests were from the impecunious or the mediocre. Significant of other drives was the desire of Philip Hone, the prominent New York merchant, for a customhouse appointment

---

tial" to him, to clear up old debts. "Now my dear Sir *everything depends on you.* . . . I feel confident that if you take your coat off—& go to work for me, I shall succeed. . . ." (Library of Congress, Marcy Papers, Vol. 10, No. 34, 417, April 15, 1845.) A month later another needy applicant, Thomas N. Carr, wrote Marcy, "it would be almost impossible, for me to give you an idea of my distresses. To the last farthing, *all is gone;* and my only hope is in Washington." (*Ibid.*, Vol. 10, No. 34, 442, May 14, 1845.) A week later he wrote again. "Should it be *decided against me,* God only knows what I am to do! I hope you will favourably overlook my importunities; *necessity, absolute necessity* is my only plea." (*Ibid.*, Vol. 10, No. 34, 458, May 23, 1845.) Carr got the consulship at Morocco. One innocent asked his friend, Judge Mason, for help. When the Judge asked what office was desired, the hopeful statesman said he thought he would be a good hand at making treaties and would therefore like to be a minister abroad. (Polk, *Diary,* III, 422–23, April 10, 1848.)

15 *Ibid.*, II, 313–14 (Jan. 7, 1847).

16 *Ibid.*, III, 136 (August 23, 1847).

17 Coleman, *Life of Crittenden,* I, 344 (July 11, 1849).

18 *National Intelligencer,* April 28, 1853. Pierce had received an amusing offer of support during the campaign from a New Hampshire Democrat. "As you are the Nominee of the Democratic Party for the Presidency of these United States . . . I propose to help you Provided you will help me. Now sir I will turn in all my forces, and help you in the Presidential Chair Provided you will give or appoint me Collector of United States Customs of Champlain District Northern New York for the next four years following your election." New Hampshire Historical Society, Pierce Papers. Letter dated July 2, 1852.

at a low point in his fortune. Significant of new forces also was the request of the Dupont family of Delaware for an appointment as purser for one of its younger members. The matter was handled by former Senator John M. Clayton of Delaware, who wrote his friend Crittenden (then Attorney General) a long letter praising the Dupont family and concluding with these paragraphs.

Now, my dear Crittenden, these Duponts have spent a fortune for the Whig party, and have never received a favor from it, for they never desired any,—they have been the chief prop and support of our party ever since its origin; they did more to build it up, originally, than any other family in the State, and but for their powerful influence we should have sent two Locofoco senators to Congress for the last twenty years.

Charles has now set his heart upon the appointment of his son as a purser, and he is sustained in this application not only by the just influence of his relatives and personal friends, but by all the Whigs of the State and the friends of the administration, who feel that they owe more and have paid less to these Duponts than to any other family.

I think I am boring you with some things as well known to you as to me; let me, therefore, cut my letter short by begging you, as soon as you have read this letter, to go down and see the President, and tell him he would do more to gratify his friends by this little appointment than he could by a full mission abroad. Take a glass of Bourbon whisky before you start; call on Graham, and get him to go along with you, and do not leave the President until you get a promise that young Dupont shall have the first vacancy. This little appointment will do more to enable us to redeem the State at the next election than anything else the President could do for us.[19]

In short the voice of the people was loud, brazen, and insistent, and the words of its "betters" were only a happy echo. Quite irrespective of the theoretical doctrine of rotation, it is doubtful whether such pressures could have been resisted. Doctrine never-

19 Coleman, *Life of Crittenden,* II, 11 (Oct. 8, 1851). In 1857 one hundred and thirty-one Democratic citizens of New York caucused in Willard's Hotel and elected a slate to present to James Buchanan for the nine principal federal offices in New York City, after which the company adjourned to the refreshment room "in the confident expectation that the result of their proceedings will be adopted by the President." *National Intelligencer,* March 21, 1857. Buchanan accepted only three.

theless whetted appetites and combined with interest to launch a sequence of events of vast importance.

THE COURSE OF EVENTS

The breeze that Daniel Webster had prophesied began to blow in the spring of 1829. In anticipation of being displaced, anxiety and apprehension mounted among the government clerks and agents. In his diary of May 1, 1829, John Quincy Adams wrote, "Every one is in breathless expectation, trembling at heart, and afraid to speak. Some of the dismissions are deserved: from age, from incapacity, from intemperance, from irregularities of private life; and these are made the pretext for justifying all the removals. The persons appointed are of equally various characters—some good, the greater part very indifferent, some notoriously bad—on the average, much less respectable than those dismissed." [20]

James Parton described the psychological upheaval in vivid terms. "Terror, meanwhile, reigned in Washington. . . . The great body of officials awaited their fate in silent horror, glad when the office hours expired at having escaped another day. . . . No man deemed it safe and prudent to trust his neighbor, and the interior of the department presented a fearful scene of guarded silence, secret intrigue, espionage, and tale-bearing." [21]

"A clerk in the War Office, named Henshaw," Adams wrote in his diary, "who was a strong partisan for Jackson's election, three days since cut his throat from ear to ear, from the mere terror of being dismissed. Linneus Smith, of the Department of State, one of the best clerks under the Government, has gone raving distracted, and others are said to be threatened with the same calamity." [22]

The shock was undoubtedly great, but the statistics show that the number of removals, although unprecedented, was small in terms of percentage. An early reckoning of gains and losses, which is generally accepted as the most reliable indication of the number of removals during the months when they were in full swing, was published in the Washington *Telegraph* on Sep-

20 Adams, *Memoirs,* VIII, 149.

21 James Parton, *Life of Andrew Jackson,* III, 212.

22 Adams, *Memoirs,* VIII, 144 (April 25, 1829).

tember 27, 1830. The editor declared that the list had been compiled "with the most sedulous care, and authenticated by a reference, in each individual case, to the Public Departments." It was reprinted in 1832 by the *Globe,* then the administration paper, with a statement that the general accuracy of the list had never been questioned.[23] These figures showed a total of 919 removals out of 10,093 officeholders or somewhat less than 10 per cent.

They represent the situation as of early autumn 1830, after about eighteen months of the new administration. They indicate the magnitude of the "proscription," for subsequent changes were made principally as vacancies occurred by death, resignation, lapse of commission at the end of a four-year term, or on ground of proved delinquency. Eriksson was not able to present figures for the rest of Jackson's administration, but concluded that less than 20 per cent of all officeholders were removed, and that probably the figure was nearer 10 per cent.[24]

The evidence of the figures published in the *Telegraph* and the careful study by Eriksson show that the "reform" was far from a clean sweep. Many officeholders who saw Jackson inaugurated on March 4, 1829, were of course his partisans. The proportion is now impossible to calculate. Among the clerks in the Post Office Department in Washington, Abraham Bradley reported that 17 were Jackson men, 21 were Adams men, and 5 were neutral.[25] Many other clerks and agents who, in accordance with old tradition, had remained neutral during the campaign of 1828 were left in peace. John Quincy Adams, who would rate as a credible witness on this point, wrote in his diary at the end of 1830 that Samuel Swartwout, the new collector at the port of New York, had refused to remove any of the Adams men in the customhouse, and had been attacked on this ground by Van Buren's paper, the *New York Courier and Enquirer.*[26] Such re-

23 Erik McKinley Eriksson, "The Federal Civil Service under President Jackson," *Mississippi Valley Historical Review,* XIII (1926–27), 527–28.

24 Another view of Jackson's record on removals arises from considering the presidential offices only. Fish discovered that of an approximate total of 612 such officers, 252 were removed during his two terms. *Civil Service and the Patronage,* p. 125.

25 Senate Doc. 73, 21st Cong., 2d sess., p. 89 (Feb. 19, 1831).

26 Adams, *Memoirs,* VIII, 259 (Dec. 30, 1830).

straint was not long to endure, however, in these green pastures.

The abandonment of old ideas of tenure during good behavior was well illustrated in Postmaster General Barry's letter to Nathaniel Mitchell, postmaster at Portland, Maine, announcing his removal.

> As your official conduct had met with my decided approbation, not only in reference to the discharge of your ordinary duties, but also in respect to the performance of a difficult service that had devolved on you as the special agent of the department, and which you had attended to with commendable zeal and fidelity, I have all along cherished the hope that the circumstances of the case would be such as would justify your retention. But it is obvious that the public sentiment in Maine demands a change in the office. . . .[27]

The situation of Martin Van Buren when he entered the White House in 1837 as successor to Andrew Jackson did not suggest the virtue of rotating Jackson's friends out of office, and relatively few removals were made. In 1837 he removed only one presidential postmaster; in 1838 only two.[28] His Postmaster General, Amos Kendall, announced in 1837 that he would not remove postmasters, whatever their political opinions, if they were good, faithful, and quiet. "All the support I ask for the administration from postmasters is a faithful, polite, and obliging performance of their duties, contenting themselves with the exercise of their own rights without attempting to proselyte others." [29] At the end of two years he had removed 364 postmasters; there were then about 12,000 post offices.[30] Van Buren's removals in 1839 and 1840, when he was looking forward to a second term, suggested, however, that a new rule of personal allegiance, as well as party membership, was to be required of officeholders.

The crucial test would be the behavior of the Whigs, who carried the election of 1840 after a campaign in which, if any issue could be discovered, it was reform—reform in the sense of the old Republican tradition. Not much was known of Harri-

27 *Niles Register*, XLVII, 186 (Nov. 22, 1834). Mitchell had been appointed by Barry himself on April 9, 1829.

28 House Doc. 132, 26th Cong., 1st sess., p. 23 (March 13, 1840).

29 Kendall, *Autobiography*, pp. 433–34.

30 Senate Doc. 292, 25th Cong., 3d sess. (Feb. 27, 1839).

son's views, but in a letter written prior to the election of 1836 he declared that executive power was granted for the public interest and "not to requite personal favors or gratify personal animosities." [31] According to the Washington *Madisonian* (March 22, 1841), Harrison warmly refused to yield to the importunities of "three or four leading Whigs" who were urging the immediate discharge of Democratic officeholders.[32] Around the Cabinet table sat Daniel Webster and Thomas Ewing, who had taken a conspicuous part in the great debate of 1835 against the theory of rotation; and the Vice President, John Tyler, was a stern old Republican from Virginia. Would now the tide sweeping the country to corruption and despotism be turned? Would now the public service become again an institution serving the country irrespective of the party in power? Would the invincible power of the Executive, buttressed by a corps of one hundred thousand dependents, be cropped? These were the questions the Whigs had raised against Jackson, and their day of reckoning was at hand.

Whatever the personal repugnance of the chief actors, the Cabinet decided during March 1841 to make an extensive change of personnel throughout the service. Ewing found justification in the actions of the departing Van Buren Democrats. "It had been the policy of the party just thrust from power," he wrote in his diary, "to retain in office none but their *active* political adherents, those who would go for them thorough in all things; and the performance of official duty, was far less requisite to a tenure of office, than electioneering services. Hence the offices had become for the most part filled with brawling offensive political partisans, of a very low moral standard—their official duties performed by substitutes, or not performed at all." [33] Henry Clay was no help; he asked for removals in order to place his personal friends,[34] and Postmaster General Francis Granger

31 Freeman Cleaves, *Old Tippecanoe: William Henry Harrison and His Time* (New York: Charles Scribner's Sons, 1939), p. 296, from *Richmond Whig*, Oct. 30, 1835.

32 Cleaves, *op. cit.*, p. 341, n. 49.

33 "Diary of Thomas Ewing, August and September, 1841," *American Historical Review*, XVIII (1912–13), p. 98. Evidence presented in a following chapter suggests that Ewing overlooked the continuance in office of a substantial proportion of competent career clerks and agents.

34 Cleaves, *op. cit.*, p. 338.

was active in changing the party complexion of the postal establishment. In the six months he held office he removed 39 of the 133 presidential postmasters, and by September 1841 almost 2,500 postmasters had been appointed in the lesser offices to vacancies most of which were caused by removals.[35] Granger later boasted that he had removed 1,700 postmasters and had he remained two or three weeks longer, would have removed 3,000 more.[36]

John Tyler, succeeding Harrison almost immediately, took high ground in his inaugural address to Congress, declaring that he would make no removals of faithful and honest incumbents except those guilty of active partisanship.[37] But in 1842 he ordered the removal of some thirty measurers and weighers in the Philadelphia customhouse to make room for his men.[38] Fish concluded his study of the Harrison-Tyler administration by declaring that the Whigs adopted all the characteristic practices of the spoils system. "Their leaders were indifferent; either willingly or perforce they permitted a repetition of the deeds which they had so violently condemned." [39]

Unlike Tyler, Polk had never made any professions that would stand in the way of clearing out the Whigs and Tyler men whom he found in office. Polk's Secretary of War, Marcy, wrote his friend General Wetmore, "The President has ordered a thorough investigation in regard to the clerks in all the Departments and there is to be quite a sweep—I am altogether the most moderate man in the concern." [40] By April 1845 the task had begun, and the publisher, Joseph Gales, told old John Quincy Adams that for the first time rotation was openly avowed as a motive for making removals.[41] It was unnecessary as a rule for orders to issue from the White House to create vacancies for partisans, but Polk descended to this level. He called in the Secretary of the Treasury, Walker, "to show him a list of very ob-

35 Dorothy G. Fowler, *Cabinet Politician,* p. 46.

36 *Congressional Globe,* 27th Cong., 2d sess., p. 701.

37 Richardson, *Messages,* IV, 38 (April 9, 1841).

38 Philip Hone, *Diary* (Nevins ed.), p. 621 (Sept. 17, 1842).

39 Fish, *Civil Service and the Patronage,* p. 151.

40 Library of Congress, Marcy Papers, Vol. 10, No. 34, 482 (July 23, 1845).

41 Adams, *Memoirs,* XII, 190 (April 1, 1845). See a valuable article by Norman A. Graebner, "James K. Polk: A Study in Federal Patronage," *Mississippi Valley Historical Review,* XXXVIII (1951–52), 613–32.

noxious Whig clerks which had been furnished to me, who are now employed in his department. I informed him that members of Congress were daily complaining to me that so many bitter Whigs were retained in the offices here, whilst worthy and competent Democrats who desired the places were excluded." Polk made it clear that he expected action, and furthermore told Walker that his brother-in-law, chargé d'affaires to Denmark, "was exceedingly obnoxious to the Democracy of Western Pennsylvania." [42] During Polk's four years more than 13,500 postmasters were appointed to vacancies caused by removal in 1,600 cases and by resignation in nearly 10,000. Some of these may have been induced by low salary or other reasons, nonpolitical in nature. The total number of post offices at the end of Polk's administration was about 16,000.[43]

The Whigs had a second chance to return to principle when Taylor was inaugurated in 1849. Thurlow Weed recorded that the President assured him he did not think it wise or just to kick away the ladder by which he ascended to the presidency—"colonels, majors, captains, lieutenants, sergeants, and corporals are just as necessary to success in politics as they are to the discipline and efficiency of an army." Weed also related that he and Taylor walked over to the Treasury Department where the President said to the Secretary, "I came over, Mr. Meredith, to inquire whether you think our friends are getting their share of the offices?" He went on to remind Meredith that there were plenty of Whigs "just as capable and honest, and quite as deserving of office, as the Democrats. . . . Rotation in office, provided good men are appointed, is sound republican doctrine." Weed took this directive with Taylor's authorization to the Postmaster General, Judge Collamer, "who lost no time in appointing meritorious Whig Postmasters throughout the Union." [44] When Fillmore succeeded Taylor he gave directions that the dissident wing of the Whigs should be turned out in favor of "real" Whigs: ". . . I wished he [Secretary Corwin] would turn out Loco focos and put good competent Whigs in their

42 Polk, *Diary,* I, 345–46 (April 22, 1846).

43 Fowler, *Cabinet Politician,* p. 63.

44 Thurlow Weed Barnes, *Memoir of Thurlow Weed* (Boston: Houghton, Mifflin, 1884), pp. 175–76.

places wherever it could be done without prejudice to the public service. . . ."[45] Whig denunciation of the Democratic rule of rotation in the 1830's had faded from memory.

The details and the approximate number of removals as Polk succeeded Tyler, himself to give way to Taylor, and as Pierce and Buchanan carried the Democrats into office for two consecutive terms need not detain us.[46] Both Whig and Democratic administrations followed the practice of Jackson. The full application of the theory of rotation came with Buchanan. The Pierce officeholders had worked for Pierce's renomination—but they were Democrats and presumably had supported Buchanan in his successful contest against the Republican candidate, Frémont. Were they now to be spared, as Democrats, or decapitated, as Pierce men? Buchanan stood squarely on the doctrine of rotation and announced that no one would receive reappointment after his commission expired, unless under exceptional circumstances. To his friend, John Y. Mason, he wrote after his election was assured, "They say, and that, too, with considerable force, that if the officers under a preceding Democratic administration shall be continued by a succeeding administration of the same political character, this must necessarily destroy the party. This, perhaps, ought not to be so, but we cannot change human nature."[47] Marcy wrote on March 27, 1857, "Strange things have been enacted here during the last three weeks. Pierce men are hunted down like wild beasts."[48] The theory of rotation had finally been perfected. The triumph of the new system was complete in civilian circles. No one thought to remember the days of the old Republicans nor the care with which they had preserved the character of the public service above faction and party.

45 *Fillmore Papers,* I, 341 (April 16, 1851).

46 The meanness of partisan temper in the 1850's is suggested by the following extract from the Democratic paper, *New Hampshire Patriot and State Gazette* (March 23, 1853). "We begin to hear the howlings of the whig press over the removals of their friends from office, and as more removals are made their complaints will doubtless become louder and more violent. This is at once foolish and contemptible. . . . How childish and contemptible it is then, for these fellows to whine about being removed from office, after having staked their offices upon the issue, and lost."

47 Curtis, *Life of Buchanan,* II, 185–86 (Dec. 29, 1856).

48 "Diary and Memoranda of William L. Marcy, 1857," *American Historical Review,* XXIV (1918–19), 647.

Democrats and Whigs condemned this cannibalistic application of the rule of rotation. Marcy declared, "How the notion of such a rule could get into the mind of a sound thinking man is to me utterly inconceivable." "This feature of his [Buchanan's] policy deserves . . . a more severe rebuke than I am now willing to administer. . . . What its effect will be upon the party, remains to be seen. That it will be mischievous no sound thinking man doubts. . . ." [49] It was at this time that Marcy repudiated the doctrine of seizing the spoils of victory so far as mere factional opponents were concerned. The *New York Herald* on March 23, 1857, carried the following editorial: "It is said that that sarcastic old statesman W. L. Marcy, on hearing that the policy of rotation in office had been resolved upon by the new administration, dryly remarked, 'Well, they have it that I am the author of the office seeker's doctrine, that "to the victors belong the spoils," but I certainly should never recommend the policy of pillaging my own camp.' " [50]

The *National Intelligencer* rebelled against the doctrine of rotation "when it is made to hold the same language and awards the same doom to ancient friends as to inveterate enemies." It quoted from *The South* of Richmond the following passage: "This policy of 'rotation in office,' as applied to individuals in the same party, is abhorrent to every generous sentiment and repugnant to every sense of justice. It is proper enough, when one Administration is replaced by another of a different party and principles. . . . But, when there is no such succession of opposite parties . . . it is idle to justify 'rotation in office' on any other principle except on the atrocious maxim that to the victors belong the spoils." *The South* predicted the early and miserable demise of the party, "and, while it lives, [it] will wear the hideous aspect of the portress of hell, with a womb torn by the cries and curses of its own canine brood." [51] These protests were prophetic, but they did not change Buchanan's policy.

In retrospect, it might have been thought in 1840 that the old tradition could reassert itself. The turmoil was noticeably slight

49 *Ibid.*, XXIV, 644, 652 (1857).

50 *Ibid.*, XXIV, 642, n.

51 *National Intelligencer,* May 14, 1857. So also many men were disturbed, including Chief Justice Taney. "Some Papers of Franklin Pierce, 1852–1862" (P. O. Ray, ed.), *American Historical Review,* X (1904–5), 359 (August 29, 1857).

in the South; the new system had slowed down after a year and a half, and was not generally pursued thereafter by Jackson or his department heads; he did not, significantly, apply the theory of rotation to his party friends when he entered upon his second term; the process of arbitrary removal had proved personally painful to more than one engaged in the task; Jackson and others in high place were disgusted by the office seekers; Jackson's successor in the White House was his own protégé who inherited a full complement of Jackson's and his own friends; and the Whigs had fully committed themselves in principle to return to the old system at the first opportunity.

The years immediately succeeding the departure of Andrew Jackson from Washington were, therefore, crucial. A long period of political stability might have reproduced the Jeffersonian tradition. This happy circumstance was not to occur. The Whigs carried the 1840 election; the Democrats returned in 1844 only to be thrown out again in the election of 1848. The Whigs lost in 1852 and it was not until then that the Democrats were able to remain in office for two consecutive terms. They were defeated in 1860 by a new national party that had never held the presidency. No sequence of events could have been more conducive to coerce party leaders to apply the doctrine of rotation.[52]

Nevertheless, despite these untoward circumstances and in defiance of the rule of rotation, the old Federalist-Republican practice of a permanent service persisted in some measure. A dual system was in operation from 1829 to 1861, one sector partisan, rotating its personnel; the other, based in part on examinations and in part on custom, neutral and permanent. The evidence on this matter is presented in a succeeding chapter.

Moreover the practice of rotation did not affect the armed forces on sea or on land, nor the revenue cutter service, although it made heavy inroads on the civilian employees in the navy shore installations. Some efforts have been noted by Congressmen to secure early promotion or favored assignments for officer personnel in these services, but they were met by strict observ-

52 The system was a "shocking revelation" to young Carl Schurz, fresh from the undemocratic but renowned Prussian officialdom, famous for "the severest kind of official honor." Then and there, upon his first contact with it in 1854, he became a civil service reformer. See an illuminating passage in *The Reminiscences of Carl Schurz* (2 vols., New York: Doubleday, Page, 1913), II, 23–28.

ance of the established regulations in which seniority was the controlling factor. Jefferson Davis was particularly strict in these matters while Secretary of War. The Democratic Committee in Philadelphia sought to lay an assessment on War Department clerks stationed in that city. Davis wrote the local commandant, "It is my desire to keep the military branch of the government free from political influences—and your employees need have no apprehension that they will suffer in my estimation from unfriendly reports of their conduct in failing to comply with the requisition of political committees."[53] This statement corroborated an earlier one by Secretary of the Navy Badger in 1841.

> . . . . It is my earnest desire that no person in the service shall be either the better or the worse off in consequence of his political opinions—merely that he shall feel himself at perfect liberty to exercise the elective franchise according to the dictates of his own judgment and conscience, and that no agent of the Government shall be allowed to impose any restraint upon him for any party or political purpose, and that it be made manifest that as the Navy belongs to the nation, so its stations are established, their officers appointed, their laborers employed and their whole operation directed solely for the honorable and efficient service of the country.[54]

THE THEORY OF ROTATION: DEFENSE AND ATTACK

The removal of honest men long in the service of their country to make way for inexperienced but willing fellow citizens caused a storm of argument, the echoes of which were to sound indefinitely. There were stout defenders of the rule of rotation, although Buchanan's application of it to men of his own party found few admirers. There were also violent critics, both within Jackson's party and among the Whigs. The great debate over the removal power in 1789 had involved constitutional questions and related to the executive power. The new debate that opened in 1829 over the removal power was primarily concerned with

[53] Davis, *Letters, Papers and Speeches,* II, 275 (Oct. 17, 1853). Cf. the effort by Senator Slidell to compel the political allegiance of 300 laborers working on public buildings in New Orleans under army direction. Louis Martin Sears, *John Slidell* (Durham: Duke University Press, 1925), p. 167.

[54] Peter M. Wilson, "George Edmund Badger," *North Carolina Booklet,* XV (1915–16), 146.

the political and administrative consequences of its use to reward party workers.

The theoretical defense of rotation was based upon attachment to democracy; practical men defended it by virtue of its value in winning elections. Among the first group Edward Everett, then a young Massachusetts Republican with political ambitions, was one of the most persuasive. He based his argument, which was worked out in an extraordinary correspondence in 1828 with John McLean, Postmaster General, on human nature and the character of party struggle.[55] "What then," he asked McLean, "binds the mass of the parties together. . . . Indubitably the hope of office, and its honors and emoluments. The consequence is, that the moment any Administration is formed, every man out of office, and desirous of getting in, is arrayed against it. If the Administration then discard the principle of bestowing patronage on their political friends, they turn against themselves not only the expectants but the incumbents. . . . For an Administration then to bestow its patronage, without distinction of party, is to court its own destruction." [56] Recognizing that John Quincy Adams had followed an opposite rule, he said, "I know he adopted and has pursued the policy from pure motives: but the People will not sustain it. They cannot; it is not in human nature." [57] Comparing the British patronage pattern with American, Everett argued, "But office here is family, rank, heredity, fortune, in short everything, out of the range of private life. This links its possession with innate principles of our nation; and truly incredible are the efforts men are willing to make, the humilations they will endure, to get it. . . . while office is so passionately coveted, no party will sit still and see themselves postponed to their opponents in politics." [58]

The formal and official defense of rotation was stated by Andrew Jackson in his first annual message. This oft-quoted passage is so important, in the light of the subsequent hold patronage took on the country, that its familiar words must be repeated at this point.

55 Massachusetts Historical Society, *Proceedings,* 3d series, I (1907–8), 360–93.
56 *Ibid.,* p. 361.
57 *Ibid.,* p. 372.
58 *Ibid.,* p. 376.

There are, perhaps, few men who can for any great length of time enjoy office and power without being more or less under the influence of feelings unfavorable to the faithful discharge of their public duties. Their integrity may be proof against improper considerations immediately addressed to themselves, but they are apt to acquire a habit of looking with indifference upon the public interests and of tolerating conduct from which an unpracticed man would revolt. Office is considered as a species of property, and government rather as a means of promoting individual interests than as an instrument created solely for the service of the people. Corruption in some and in others a perversion of correct feelings and principles divert government from its legitimate ends and make it an engine for the support of the few at the expense of the many. The duties of all public officers are, or at least admit of being made, so plain and simple that men of intelligence may readily qualify themselves for their performance; and I can not but believe that more is lost by the long continuance of men in office than is generally to be gained by their experience. I submit, therefore, to your consideration whether the efficiency of the Government would not be promoted and official industry and integrity better secured by a general extension of the law which limits appointments to four years.

In a country where offices are created solely for the benefit of the people no one man has any more intrinsic right to official station than another. Offices were not established to give support to particular men at the public expense. No individual wrong is, therefore, done by removal, since neither appointment to nor continuance in office is matter of right. The incumbent became an officer with a view to public benefits, and when these require his removal they are not to be sacrificed to private interests. It is the people, and they alone, who have a right to complain when a bad officer is substituted for a good one. He who is removed has the same means of obtaining a living that are enjoyed by the millions who never held office. The proposed limitation would destroy the idea of property now so generally connected with official station, and although individual distress may be sometimes produced, it would, by promoting that rotation which constitutes a leading principle in the republican creed, give healthful action to the system.[59]

This is probably the most important defense of rotation in office that has ever been made by an American. Jackson made no reference to the party advantage that rotation would induce, nor

[59] Richardson, *Messages,* II, 448–49 (Dec. 8, 1829).

to its effect upon executive power. He made no defense of the abuses that might follow from the theory of rotation and he would certainly have denounced them could he have foreseen them, for Jackson was a man of rigid integrity. He struck out at tendencies which had already caused concern among his contemporaries in all factions of the Republican party. The idea of property in office *was* uncongenial to American ideas, and the not uncommon succession of son to father in office, the rise of official families, and the tendency to nepotism suggested both a property right in office and the support of the few at the expense of the many. The idea of wide participation by citizens in office *was* clearly in accordance with republican creed and devotion to the art of self-government. Long continuance in office *had* created a genuine problem of superannuation, in which private interests of officeholders seemed in conflict with the general interest in the energetic performance of public duties. Officious attitudes *are* always unpopular.

Moreover Jackson stated some simple but undoubted facts. Office *is* created for the benefit of the people, not for the support of the incumbent. Millions had never held office. And, at that time, the duties of most public offices were so plain and simple that men of intelligence could perform them. Jackson sincerely believed he was about to introduce reform, and he could make a case for it; but he did not foresee the subsequent consequences of his program.

The men who surrounded Jackson and supported him in Congress spoke in more immediate and practical terms. They defended rotation because it brought results, and they were not ashamed to say so. The Postmaster General, William T. Barry, declared, ". . . it is right and politic to encourage and reward friends. . . . Public employments must necessarily and ought to be upon the principle of rotation in office. . . . Those who prefer the calm of perpetuity in office, would certainly be better pleased that the Executive head be made permanent. This will not suit a Republic. . . ."[60] Senator Felix Grundy, Jackson's leader in the upper House, saw no impropriety, after some lucky persons had enjoyed office for a reasonable time, in bestowing

60 William T. Barry, "Letters," *American Historical Review,* XVI (1910–11), 333 (June 11, 1829).

their places on others equally meritorious and as well qualified.[61] Senator Isaac Hill, who as post office contractor in New Hampshire had been a sharp thorn in John Q. Adams' side, added the opinion that, "the idea of dependence on the emoluments of office is degrading to a republican freeman; and it has degraded many who have spent their whole lives as clerks in the Departments, and died leaving destitute families." [62]

Senator Shepley of Maine opposed the repeal of the Tenure of Office Act, since the effect would be to create a privileged class in the community, "divided off from the people by distinguishable lines." "But, sir," he went on, "I go further, and I will say plainly that I hold to 'rotation in office.' I would not necessarily require any positive fault in an officer in order to remove him from office. . . . Others are equally entitled, with himself, at all times, and he has no just cause of complaint if he is required to share either honors or emoluments with others. It is just, and proper, and useful, without regard to party, or party favors, to change public officers. It is in accordance with our system of Government, which holds out equal rights and equal privileges to all." [63]

Senator Marcy had already uttered the words that were to cause him to be remembered by later generations. "It may be, sir, that the politicians of the United States are not so fastidious as some gentlemen are, as to disclosing the principles on which they act. They boldly preach what they practice. When they are contending for victory, they avow their intention of enjoying the fruits of it. If they are defeated, they expect to retire from office. If they are successful, they claim, as a matter of right, the advantages of success. They see nothing wrong in the rule, that to the victor belong the spoils of the enemy." [64]

Thoughtful men in both parties, however, were appalled at the breach made in old tradition and the consequences they foresaw in the new ideas. The elderly Madison privately condemned the practice of rotation as the reward of those who supported

61 *Register of Debates,* 23d Cong., 2d sess., p. 531 (Feb. 18, 1835).

62 *Ibid.,* p. 569 (Feb. 20, 1835).

63 *Ibid.,* p. 453.

64 *Ibid.,* 22d Cong., 1st sess., p. 1325 (Jan. 24, 1832). See also *Niles Register,* XXXVII, 101 (Oct. 10, 1829), for corresponding views of Jackson's collector of the port of Boston, David Henshaw.

and the punishment of those who did not support the party in power. ". . . the principle," he declared, "if avowed without the practice, or practised without the avowal, could not fail to degrade any Administration; both together, completely so." [65]

Postmaster General McLean, in his correspondence with Edward Everett, had stated his opposition to indiscriminate removals for party purposes in language reminiscent of the great Federalists. He wrote Everett, "Patronage is a sacred trust, committed by the people, to the hands of their agents, to be used for the public benefit. It was never designed for the personal gratification of the individual holding it. . . . I would found an Administration upon a totally different basis. It should rest on the virtue and intelligence of the people. The motives of its supporters should arise from pure patriotism and high moral principle." [66] These ideas would hardly have been recognized by the pushing, crowding horde of office seekers who filled the boarding houses and hotels of the capital city in March 1829.

After Jackson had left the White House, Major William B. Lewis, his friend and confidential adviser, spoke his mind freely. ". . . in relation to this principle of rotation," he wrote Jackson, "I embrace this occasion to enter my solemn protest against it as a *general rule*—not on account of my office, but because I hold it to be fraught with the greatest mischief to the country; If ever it shall be carried out, *in extenso,* the days of this Republic will, in my opinion, have been numbered, for whenever the impression shall become general that the Government is only valuable on account of its *offices,* the great and paramount interest of the country will be lost sight of and the Government itself ultimately destroyed." [67]

Some old-fashioned Jeffersonian Republicans, including John Tyler and editor Thomas Ritchie of the *Richmond Enquirer,* both from Virginia, joined in these opinions. Ritchie caught the drift of events instantly and wrote to Van Buren in 1829:

65 *The Writings of James Madison* (Gaillard Hunt, ed., 9 vols., New York: G. P. Putnam's Sons, 1900–10), IX, 539–40 (August 29, 1834).

66 Massachusetts Historical Society, *Proceedings,* 3d series, I, 366.

67 Jackson, *Correspondence,* VI, 23 (August 30, 1839). When Lewis fell out with Van Buren in 1839, Jackson declined to intervene. ". . . ours is a Government based upon public opinion, and that opinion is for reform and rotation in office. . . ." *Ibid.,* VI, 36 (Oct. 19, 1839).

. . . I go for reform, but what is reform? Is it to turn out of office all those who voted against him, or who decently preferred Mr. Adams? Or is it not rather those, who are incapable of discharging their duties; the drunken, the ignorant, the embezzler, the man who has abused his official facilities to keep Gen. Jackson out, or, who are so wedded to the corruptions of Office, as to set their faces against all Reform? Is it not to abolish all unnecessary Offices, and to curtail all unnecessary Expences? It surely is not to put out a good and experienced officer, because he was a decent friend of J. Q. Adams, *in order* to put in a heated partizan of the election of Gen. Jackson. . . . I trust that such a spirit of Reform will not come near to us in Virginia.[68]

To these views we may add the sage comments of the young de Tocqueville. He wrote:

I shall not remark that the universal and inordinate desire for place is a great social evil; that it destroys the spirit of independence in the citizen, and diffuses a venal and servile humor throughout the frame of society; that it stifles the manlier virtues: nor shall I be at the pains to demonstrate that this kind of traffic only creates an unproductive activity, which agitates the country without adding to its resources: all these things are obvious. But I would observe, that a government which encourages this tendency risks its own tranquility, and places its very existence in great jeopardy.[69]

The sweep of officeholders that took place after 1829 and the justification put forward by the administration could not fail to arouse apprehension and resistance. Anti-Jackson men, eventually brought together in the Whig party, seized upon "abuse" of the removal power as one means of attacking the party in control. The conflict of men and principles eventually rose to high pitch, involving not merely the power to remove but the nature of the executive power, the relations of the President to Congress, and the fate of the United States Bank, to say nothing of the personal fortunes of persons in the highest ranks of political preference.

The vain struggle of the Whigs to restrain the removal power has already been dealt with.[70] Webster had described the mis-

68 *Ibid.*, IV, 18, n. (March 27, 1829).

69 De Tocqueville, *Democracy in America* (1863 ed.), II, 306.

70 See ch. 2.

chievous results of rotation in statesmanlike terms, pointing out that men in office had begun to think of themselves as mere agents and servants of the appointing power and not as agents of the government or the country. "The army," said Webster, "is the army of the country; the navy is the navy of the country; neither of them is either the mere instrument of the administration for the time being, or of him who is at the head of it. The Post Office, the Land Office, the Custom-house, are in like manner, institutions of the country, established for the good of the people; and it may well alarm the lovers of free institutions, when all the offices in these several departments are spoken of, in high places, as being but the 'spoils of victory.' . . ." [71] Calhoun had made common cause with Clay and Webster on this issue.

The Whigs never advanced beyond the remedies they espoused in 1835: an assertion of the power of Congress to prescribe the tenure of officeholders and to protect them against the unrestricted power of the President to remove; and a proposal to require the President to give the Senate his reasons for removal of presidential officers. They attacked the patronage system again in 1842, declaring in a House report that "The practice of treating all the offices of this great Government as 'the spoils of victory,' and, with the rise and fall of contending parties, the ejection of a large multitude of experienced, honest, and capable incumbents, to make room for needy mercenaries, who entered the political conflict without any principle or love of country, but impelled wholly by a hope of plunder, is the greatest and most threatening abuse that has ever invaded our system." [72] The chairman of the committee, Garrett Davis, would have cheerfully impeached John C. Spencer, the Secretary of War, for the summary removal of a pension office clerk on complaint of Daniel Webster, except that he had been in some degree excused by previous similar abuses.

The last effort of the Whigs for reform took place in the summer of 1844, just before the presidential election. Senator James T. Morehead offered the most elaborate report that had been prepared on the evils of patronage—more elaborate by far than

71 *Register of Debates,* 23d Cong., 2d sess., pp. 460–61 (Feb. 16, 1835).

72 House Report 945, 27th Cong., 2d sess., p. 6 (1842).

Senator Benton's Report of 1826 but quite as partisan in character. Morehead's proposals for reform followed Clay's attempt to require reasons for removals, but recommended a statutory declaration of the causes sufficient to authorize the removal of either presidential or inferior officers in lieu of requiring a particular statement of reasons.[73] None of these recommendations were pressed.

The Whigs failed, both in their opposition to rotation and by their eventual desertion of the cause they had so eloquently upheld. They nevertheless worked out a reasoned statement of the case for the traditional system of permanent employment and against Jackson's "reform." They condemned the theory of rotation because it dangerously magnified executive power, because it corrupted public and private morals, and because it lowered the competence and impartiality of the public service, reducing it to a mere party agency instead of preserving a status like that of the armed forces—the common servant of the people.

[73] Senate Doc. 399, 28th Cong., 1st sess., p. 55 (June 15, 1844).

CHAPTER SEVENTEEN

The Consequences of Rotation

As the years passed the effects of rotation upon public life gradually became apparent. Some had been predicted, others had not been imagined, some that had been feared did not materialize. It was an open question whether executive power had been dangerously increased as the Whigs had expected; President Polk denied it, and the record of elections did not sustain it. The liberty of the people seemed to be no less; indeed many would argue that it was much greater than in the days when an office-holding class seemed to be established. The country, as Garrett Davis had reported in 1842,[1] heaved and tossed in wild commotion at every presidential election as a result of the hope of office, but it cheerfully accepted the popular verdict and became quiet on the day after the result was known.

The effect of rotation on the American party system is beyond the scope of this study. It was profound, and caused much anxiety among farseeing men. Thomas W. Gilmer wrote in 1842:

> . . . . The election ceases to be a fair and calm expression of the popular judgment on the principles and policy of Government, and becomes a tumultuous scramble for place and power. It is not merely a contest between the candidates for the highest prize in the lottery, but between the incumbent of each subordinate office in the Government and all those who have their eyes on his place. The distribution of the minor stations often excites more interest than the election itself. Who shall dispense the patronage? is the absorbing question, not only with those who expect favors themselves, but with those who, in the various relations of society, are connected and interested

1 House Report 945, 27th Cong., 2d sess., p. 16 (July 27, 1842).

with them. When the election has ended, nothing is decided more than when it commenced, except that one set of men are to go out and another set are to come in. The victors practice the abuses for which they condemned the vanquished. . . .[2]

Certain it was that patronage greatly increased the power of the local party organizations, in a vicious circle that gave them constantly greater standing to demand more and more in return for services rendered. Both parties, unable to take clear-cut positions on the greater issues of the time, tended to sink into the status of organizations existing for the control of office and power. Much of this was epitomized in a despairing letter of Congressman John Bell, soon to become Secretary of War. "I am growing pretty sick already of this thing of *office* in my own case, and the increasing tide of application from new quarters that daily beats against my ears gives me spasms. In truth, I begin to fear that we are, at last, or rather that our leading politicians in the several States are, chiefly swayed by the thirst for power and plunder. Would you think that Senator Talmadge is willing to descend from the Senate to the New York custom-house? This is yet a secret, but it is true! God help us all and keep us, I pray. I fear to speak of the list of congressional applicants." [3]

The broad-ranging effect of rotation on executive power was frequently debated during Jackson's administration. The issue was stated by Senator George Poindexter.

. . . . It cannot be disguised . . . that the question is now distinctly presented to the American people, of the importance of which they seem to be but little aware, whether power is to be perpetuated in the hands of a dominant party by the influence of patronage and the public money; and whether, by the use of these means, the incumbent of the executive chair shall be enabled to transfer the power which he now wields to some favorite successor; or whether that high office is, as heretofore, under the practical operation of our system, to be freely conferred by the unbought suffrages of the people. It is a question of grave import, in which the office-holders and their dependents are ranged on the one side, and the friends of popular rights and free suffrage on the other.[4]

2 House Report 741, 27th Cong., 2d sess., p. 4 (May 23, 1842).

3 Ann M. B. Coleman, ed., *Life of John J. Crittenden*, I, 136–37 (Jan. 13, 1841).

4 *Register of Debates*, 23d Cong., 2d sess., p. 362 (Feb. 9, 1835).

This phase of the matter was hard pushed by the Whigs, but they failed to convince the country. Poindexter's question, however, was to disturb other generations than his.

Among the varied consequences of rotation for the public service, three are dealt with in the following pages: the loss in efficiency, the lowering of prestige, and the imposition of political obligations and duties upon government employees. There were mitigating factors that softened the blow, notably the retention of many career employees, and the preference of both Democrats and Whigs for competent and trustworthy members of their own party.

LOSS OF EFFICIENCY

That the competence of the public service would suffer as a consequence of the rule of rotation and political preference was a foregone conclusion. Much evidence to support this expectation has already appeared, notably the deterioration in the Post Office Department and in the navy yards. The army found it necessary to refuse to appoint civilians as superintendents of the armories, owing to the impossibility of getting enforcement of even the most salutary regulations. "This," said Secretary Bell, "is the inevitable result of the nature of the interests and influences, in no manner connected with the objects of those establishments, which too often control the conduct of the superintendents. For these reasons, it is deemed of great importance that the armories should be separated, as far as possible, from all connexion with the party politics of the day." [5] Bell's successor, John C. Spencer, removed the Reverend John Robb from the head of the Springfield armory for these reasons, waiving the question of the qualifications of a minister of the Gospel for this warlike occupation.[6]

The House Committee on Retrenchment reported in 1842 that great practical inconvenience resulted "from the habit of filling the most important clerkships and bureaus with persons who have had no previous experience as to their duties . . . it very often happens that individuals are brought from a distance, perfect strangers to the duties and details of their offices, installed

5 Senate Doc. 1, 27th Cong., 1st sess., p. 38 (May 31, 1841).
6 Senate Doc. 345, 27th Cong., 2d sess. (June 27, 1842).

in bureaus or clerkships with which they never become familiar until in their turn they have to give place to others equally ignorant with themselves." [7] The committee asserted that a substantial reduction in staff could be produced if political considerations in appointment could be removed. The rising Democratic politician, George Bancroft, one day to become Secretary of the Navy, gave unwitting testimony to confirm this fact when he wrote in 1831, "Talk of reform! The departments are full of the laziest clerks, and men are paid large salaries for neglecting the public business." [8] John A. Dix, appointed by Buchanan to clean up the New York City post office after Postmaster Fowler's peculations, found a common practice "of quartering on the office gentlemen whose services were not needed." One of these came in one day a week, copied a list of letters for a few hours, and drew $800 a year, while many of his fellow clerks worked the year around for less. Dix promptly removed this supernumerary but at the cost of trouble with an unnamed Senator.[9]

William L. Marcy noted that Secretary Ewing had removed men in the Interior Department who were acquainted with the course of business and the nature of unfounded claims against the government. The result was that many rejected claims were reviewed and admitted and "old ones awaked from the slumber of years." [10] The third auditor reported that from April to June 1853, "there was considerable confusion naturally consequent upon a change of administration of the head of the office: numerous changes took place by removals, new appointments, and resignations. . . . This caused almost a suspension of effective work. . . ." [11]

Appointment of illiterate clerks as a reward for party services did not advance the competence of the public service. Charles W. Clement was a clerk in the naval storekeeper's office in the Philadelphia Navy Yard, keeping books. He was asked if he was acquainted with business of that kind, and replied, "Not much."

7 House Report 741, 27th Cong., 2d sess., p. 19 (May 23, 1842).

8 M. A. De Wolfe Howe, *Life and Letters of George Bancroft,* I, 197 (Dec. 27, 1831).

9 Morgan Dix, compiler, *Memoirs of John Adams Dix* (2 vols., New York: Harper and Brothers, 1883), II, 214 (June 21, 1860).

10 William L. Marcy, "Diary," *American Historical Review,* XXIV, 461.

11 Senate Ex. Doc. 2, 33d Cong., 1st sess., p. 125 (Oct. 31, 1853).

He was invited to spell "crucifix" but failed in this test: "My memory is poor, and it is a long time since I went to school. I do not suppose I could spell it." [12] He was a bricklayer by trade.[13] This unhappy clerk corroborated the prediction of Governor George R. Gilmer of Georgia. "I certainly do believe," he wrote his cousin, Thomas W. Gilmer, "that it is better to put honest, capable men into office than insolent, dependent knaves. But now that the spoils belong to the victors, those who stand in most need of a share and will fight the hardest for it are most apt to procure public appointments." [14]

Henry J. Alvord, a clerk in the Detroit post office, admitted under examination that he performed his official duties in about one hour a day.[15] He was also a reporter for a Detroit newspaper. George W. Baker was a brother of the collector of the port of Philadelphia, and had the good fortune also to marry a niece of President Buchanan. He was appointed assistant disbursing clerk at $1,200 a year in the Philadelphia customhouse, but admitted he acted instead as a confidential clerk to his brother. The Covode Committee could discover no official work that he performed.[16] He was editor of the *Pennsylvanian,* Buchanan's state journal.

In short, the efficiency of the public service fell as men were placed on the pay roll because they had influential political connections, or worked for a partisan newspaper, or distinguished themselves in local politics. The decline was cumulative because they were soon displaced by others with the same lack of qualifications. The burden of administrative work was carried on by a nucleus of permanent clerks who knew what had to be done.

LOSS OF PRESTIGE

The prestige of the public service suffered as the rule of rotation took hold. The psychological devastation caused by ruthless partisan removals was severe, destroying the personal inde-

12 House Report 648, 36th Cong., 1st sess., p. 404 (June 16, 1860). This report will be cited hereafter as the Covode Committee Report.

13 *Ibid.*, p. 348.

14 Lyon G. Tyler, *The Letters and Times of the Tylers* (3 vols., Richmond: Whittet and Shepperson, 1884–96), II, 295, n. (Jan. 28, 1839).

15 Covode Committee Report, p. 640.

16 *Ibid.*, pp. 328–32.

pendence upon which Americans so justly prided themselves.

Within a week after Jackson's inauguration Henry Clay wrote a friend, "Among the official corps here there is the greatest solicitude and apprehension. The members of it feel something like the inhabitants of Cairo when the plague breaks out; no one knows who is next to encounter the stroke of death; or which, with many of them is the same thing, to be dismissed from office. You have no conception of the moral tyranny which prevails over those in employment." [17]

Nathaniel Hawthorne spoke for the dispossessed in his description of his own discharge in 1845 by the Democrats.

> . . . . It is essential, in order to a complete estimate of the advantages of official life, to view the incumbent at the incoming of a hostile administration. His position is then one of the most singularly irksome, and, in every contingency disagreeable, that a wretched mortal can possibly occupy; with seldom an alternative of good, on either hand, although what presents itself to him as the worst event may very probably be the best. But it is a strange experience, to a man of pride and sensibility, to know that his interests are within the control of individuals who neither love nor understand him, and by whom, since one or the other must need happen, he would rather be injured than obliged. Strange, too, for one who has kept his calmness throughout the contest, to observe the blood thirstiness that is developed in the hour of triumph, and to be conscious that he is himself among its objects! There are few uglier traits of human nature than this tendency—which I now witnessed in men no worse than their neighbors—to grow cruel, merely because they possessed the power of inflicting harm. If the guillotine, as applied to office holders, were a literal fact instead of one of the most apt of metaphors, it is my sincere belief that the active members of the victorious party were sufficiently excited to have chopped off all our heads, and have thanked Heaven for the opportunity! [18]

The editor of *Harper's New Monthly Magazine* recorded with sorrow a not untypical case: "the scant figure of an old gentleman of sixty, who, by courtesy and attention, had managed to retain place through three successive administrations—who had reared his family through a dozen of years upon the small income be-

17 Henry Clay, *Works,* IV, 225 (March 12, 1829).

18 Nathaniel Hawthorne, "The Custom House." Introductory to *The Scarlet Letter* (1949 ed.), p. 37.

longing to his post—saving nothing, and yielding much of independence in his endeavor to retain the place that gave bread to his household; and, at the opening of the fourth administration, when his head was white with labors, and his hand and brain cramped to his tread-mill offices, turned carelessly adrift, an aimless and almost hopeless wreck of a man. We can imagine no position more disconsolate, or more full of harassment. . . ." [19]

The advice of many public men to their young friends turned against a public service career. Buchanan declared in 1841 that private employment was "a much more honorable & independent vocation than to be hanging around the public offices here as a subordinate clerk." [20] It was with some justification that Jefferson Davis declared that there were very few American citizens who were not better off without than with an office,[21] or that a correspondent of the *New York Journal of Commerce* wrote, "If a friend in need ever asks you to help him to obtain a Government office, deny him with all your might, and advise him with all your energy to abandon the pursuit." [22] Secretary Corwin flatly advised a young man persistent in his desire for a clerkship to

> go to the North-west, buy 160 acres of Government land . . . and live like a freeman—your own master, with no one to give you orders, and without dependence upon any body. Do that and you will be honored, respected, influential, and rich. But accept a clerkship here, and you sink, at once, all independence; your energies become relaxed, and you are unfitted in a few years for any other and more independent position. I may give you a place to-day, and I can kick you out to-morrow; and there is another man over there at the White House, who can kick me out, and the people by-and-by can kick him out; and so we go. But if you own an acre of land, it is your kingdom, and your cabin is your castle—you are a sovereign, and you will feel it in every throbbing of your pulse, and every day of your life will assure me of your thanks for having thus advised you.[23]

A new sense of envy also seemed to enter the discussion of public office, even in the mind of so well balanced a person as

19 *Harper's New Monthly Magazine,* VI (1852–53), 420.

20 Buchanan, *Works,* V, 72 (Sept. 5, 1841).

21 Davis, *Letters, Papers and Speeches,* II, 236–37 (July 15, 1853).

22 Reprinted in *National Intelligencer,* July 12, 1853.

23 A. P. Russell, *Thomas Corwin: A Sketch* (Cincinnati: Robert Clarke, 1881), pp. 48–49.

Hezekiah Niles. Early in the Jacksonian years he wrote, "And it must be admitted, that it is a 'snug' thing to have an office, worth more than two or three thousand dollars a year (including the 'candle-ends and cheese-parings'), without any necessity of being present to perform its duties ten times in a year, except to sign some *official* paper, which 'Uncle Sam' pays a clerk to make out. . . ." [24] A year later, calling for a 33 per cent reduction of public salaries, he wrote, "We do not see why these should be set aside as a *privileged class, a peculiar people,* rioting on the distress of the farmers and mechanics and other *honest* men, and insulting honorable labor in the 'spoils' made upon it." [25]

These were not the sentiments that had prevailed among either the Federalists or the Jeffersonians. Rotation had in large measure replaced security, and distrust was replacing confidence.

POLITICAL OBLIGATIONS OF OFFICEHOLDERS

Before 1829 few federal officeholders had been required to discharge any obligation to the party or faction in power, although Philadelphia and New York City were moving in this direction. After 1829 they were progressively brought under the dominion of the local party machine and subjected to various party requirements as a condition of continuing their employment. Among these were obligations to pay party assessments, to do party work at election time, and to "vote right."

Party assessments. There were substantial reasons why assessment of federal officeholders stationed in the various states should not have developed before 1829. There were no national party organizations in the sense in which they had come into existence by 1836. There had been no national contest involving voters in the *nomination* of a candidate for the presidency, since the congressional caucus had taken care of this matter. Moreover incumbent Presidents seeking renomination had made no campaign, and would have thought it corrupt to influence the decision by asking for contributions of money from officeholders to support their ambitions. John Quincy Adams was both surprised and annoyed when one of his partisans asked him to contribute

24 *Niles Register,* XLIV, 323 (July 13, 1833).
25 *Ibid.,* XLVI, 99 (April 12, 1834).

$5,000 to help elect a friendly governor and legislature in Kentucky in the 1828 campaign. He indignantly refused to take any such steps.[26]

James Buchanan refused a similar request to support the Pennsylvania state campaign in 1858, but hardly for reasons of principle. The fact appeared in the following interrogation of Cornelius Wendell by the Covode Committee.[27]

Q. You do not wish it to be supposed that the President furnished any of the money?
A. No, sir, not a red; he did not bleed as I thought he ought to.

The character of party organization and party warfare changed rapidly after the election of 1828. Large masses of new voters were enrolled as old suffrage limitations were abandoned. Urban population was growing rapidly and the prizes of municipal government in the form of contracts for new facilities and improvements were more and more worth fighting for. But above all, the voters were now called upon, in their respective parties, to elect delegates to city conventions, to state conventions, and every four years (indirectly) to the national convention that named the candidates for the presidency. The party organization, therefore, had to be dealt with; and the means of action too clearly included the offices in the public service. Carl R. Fish observed that assessment of official salaries for party purposes appeared in national politics simultaneously with the spoils system.[28] It would perhaps be more accurate to assert that both came with the change in the composition of the electorate and the character of the party system.

An early form of assessment was to invite subscriptions to a party newspaper. Thus Jackson's appointees to offices in Boston were asked in 1830 to help pay the debts of the *Statesman*, contracted during the 1828 campaign.[29] Amos Kendall, whose record on assessments was better than many of his contemporaries, nevertheless sent out a circular to 20,000 postmasters on May 20, 1840, asking them to obtain subscriptions to a campaign

26 Adams, *Memoirs*, VII, 469 (March 8, 1828).

27 Covode Committee Report, p. 470.

28 Fish, *Civil Service and the Patronage*, p. 180.

29 *Ibid.*, p. 180.

sheet, the *Extra Globe,* and promising "to take care" of those who helped the cause.[30]

The practice of assessing officeholders on their salaries for party expenditures took form during the 1830's. The custom had become so well known by 1834 that Senator Daniel Webster went out of his way to condemn it—"since nothing can be a greater abuse of official station, or greater misuse of the money paid for public services." [31] This warning had no effect.

Testimony brought out in the investigation of Samuel Swartwout proved that assessments were regularly made in the New York customhouse for some years before 1837. David S. Lyon, first deputy collector from 1829 to 1837, declared that he had been frequently called on to make political contributions, in amounts from twenty to one hundred dollars. "The tax was *pro rata,* according to salary. It bore a proportion of from one to six per cent. . . . I believe that nearly *all* of the officers of the custom-house, indoors and out, and the clerks, were similarly taxed, and generally paid what they were assessed. . . . The collector of the general committee [i.e., Democratic central committee of New York] has an alphabetical book, which contains the names of persons taxed, and the amount each individual is required to pay." [32]

The committee investigating the affairs of Swartwout were scathing in their denunciation of this innovation. ". . . of its direct tendency to reduce public office to the degraded character of merchandise, to be bought and sold to subordinates by a regulated annual stipend, and to demoralize and prepare the mind of incumbents of office for acts of peculation and plunder upon the public revenues, there is no doubt remaining in the judgment of the committee." [33] An investigation of Swartwout's successor as collector of the port of New York revealed no improvement. Under Jesse Hoyt assessments grew into "a regular system"—in the spring for the city election and in the fall for

30 Noted in Dorothy G. Fowler, *Cabinet Politician,* pp. 34–35; Kendall edited the *Globe* during the 1840 campaign after resigning as Postmaster General.

31 Senate Doc. 435, 23d Cong., 1st sess., p. 1 (June 12, 1834).

32 House Report 313, 25th Cong., 3d sess., p. 250, and pp. 511–12; testimony given on Feb. 7, 1839.

33 *Ibid.,* p. 249. Cf. another severe condemnation by a House committee in 1850, *Congressional Globe, Appendix,* 31st Cong., 1st sess., pp. 1319–20 (Sept. 30, 1850).

the state and national elections. The system was said to have produced between twenty and thirty thousand dollars a year.[34] In 1845 Collector Van Ness received between $1,000 and $1,500 from customs employees for the city election and spent the money under his own direction.[35] In 1853 two "collectors" for Tammany Hall appeared on the scene at the close of business on the monthly pay day, October 31, and made an assessment on the following scale:

19	weighers, $25 each	$ 475.00
15	measurers, $25 each	375.00
7	gaugers, $25 each	175.00
195	inspectors, $15 each	2,925.00
184	clerks, $10 each	1,840.00
137	night watchmen, $7.50 each	1,027.50
	Total	$6,817.50

"All this took place in the custom-house, and in the most public manner," commented the *New York Express*.[36] In the campaign of 1856 the party collector complained that it was very hard "to bring a heterogeneous mass of men—officeholders though they be—to a proper sense of duty on occasions like these." [37]

The Covode Committee investigation of 1860 gathered sworn testimony which demonstrated the prevalence of political assessments in Washington and some of the big field establishments in return for such favors as office and government printing. Cornelius Wendell testified that from 1856 to 1860 he had contributed over one hundred thousand dollars for party purposes.[38] He added that there was a continual struggle to get more and that the collector of the port of Philadelphia, Joseph Baker, was very importunate: "like Oliver Twist, he was always crying for more." [39] From these large sums, the collections ran down to small individual payments, described by a former night watchman in the Philadelphia customhouse, George Downey.[40]

34 House Doc. 212, 27th Cong., 2d sess., pp. 66–67 (April 30, 1842).
35 Library of Congress, Marcy Papers, Vol. 10, No. 34,411 (April 10, 1845).
36 Reprinted in *National Intelligencer,* November 10, 1853.
37 Fowler, *Cabinet Politician,* p. 86.
38 Covode Committee Report, p. 459.
39 *Ibid.,* p. 463.
40 *Ibid.,* p. 367.

Q. I want you to explain the mode of making collections for political purposes. . . .
A. Our captain comes there and tells us that we are assessed so much; that comes from headquarters. The amount that we have to pay is put down; it is seven dollars and a half at a presidential election, that is the highest; for a State election it is about five dollars.

. . . .

Q. Was it obligatory on you to pay this?
A. We need not pay it that I know of; but I never saw it refused.
Q. What did you understand would be the consequence of refusing?
A. That I cannot tell you. It might be that the man would have his head cut off; but I have never seen any refusal to pay the assessment.

In New York the superintendent of the assay office defended his "habit of giving money to very nearly all the congressional districts in and about the city of New York" because he thought the success of the Democratic party essential to the good government of the country.[41] The postmaster of the New York City office subscribed $1,000 to a party fund, and agreed readily that money had been contributed regularly by post office employees for political purposes. He insisted, however, that he had had nothing to do with the collections—"it is a matter between them and the organization of the party." [42] J. L. Cramer, a clerk in the General Land Office in Washington, admitted asking for political contributions in 1856 and 1858 at the request of the commissioner, to whom he paid his collections.[43]

Only an occasional effort was made to protect employees against such assessments. Shortly after his inauguration President Harrison issued a circular to heads of departments declaring that the payment of a contribution or assessment by officeholders would be regarded as cause for dismissal.[44] He was unable, however, to prohibit party managers from requiring such contributions. John A. Dix, former U.S. Senator, temporarily in charge of the New York City post office, flatly refused to allow the party collectors on the premises, although making a personal contribution and allowing the clerks to make voluntary contributions

41 *Ibid.*, p. 485.
42 *Ibid.*, p. 525.
43 *Ibid.*, pp. 560–61.
44 Senate Doc. 26, 27th Cong., 1st sess. (March 20, 1841).

if they chose. He wrote the party committee: "I know nothing more degrading to our public offices, and those who fill them, than the practice which has existed of sending political tax-gatherers to the doors of the pay-room, to levy contributions on the clerks as they emerge with their hard-earned stipends. I cannot allow this office to be so dishonored." [45]

The evidence drawn from official reports was based for the most part on practice in three principal centers, Boston, New York and Philadelphia, and it is uncertain to what extent the party was collecting from officeholders elsewhere. Other evidence makes it appear likely that the same development was occurring generally in the northern cities. It was slower to develop in the South. In any event, the warm declarations condemning it were wasted. Congress took no action, and executive warnings were unobserved. The party had fastened upon a lucrative and dependable source of income and did not intend to forego its advantage. So far as the law was concerned, party assessments were perfectly legal until reform began its course after the Civil War.

Political activity. The course of events encouraged officeholders to throw themselves into the congressional and presidential campaigns on a scale and with an energy hitherto unknown. Thus emerged a perplexing problem of statecraft that was vigorously debated during the 1830's and that was to be dealt with effectively only in a later age. Practice settled the issue during the Jacksonian years in favor of democratic freedom to engage in political activity, but the opposite doctrine was widely held.

Felix Grundy, himself an ardent Jackson man, took a conservative view of the duties of officeholders. Their right to vote freely and independently was accepted, but, said Grundy, "when they become partisans in elections, and attempt to control the elective franchise in others, they should be dismissed from public employment. . . ." [46] Niles was indignant at the party activities of officeholders, declaring that persons "feeding at the public crib . . . should absent themselves from popular assemblies for political purposes." [47] In 1836 and later, bills were introduced to

[45] Dix, *Memoirs of John A. Dix*, II, 217 (Oct. 15, 1860).
[46] *Register of Debates*, 23d Cong., 1st sess., p. 433 (Jan. 30, 1834).
[47] *Niles Register*, XLV, 409 (Feb. 15, 1834).

prevent officials from endeavoring to persuade citizens how to vote for President, but they secured slender support.

In a very thoughtful letter to Senator Samuel McKean of Pennsylvania, Postmaster General Kendall noted the difficulty in drawing the line between the rights of the citizen and the political activity of the officeholder, and confessed his inability to form any well-defined rule. His advice to postmasters and agents was "to keep as clear from the excitement of political strife as possible—to shun mere political meetings, or if present to avoid taking any part in their proceedings. To decline acting as members of political committees or conventions . . . and to take especial care to treat all men alike in their official intercourse." [48]

President Harrison issued a strict order to all officers and agents of the public service against interference in popular elections and receipt of compensation for party purposes. He declared that federal employees "are not expected to take an active or officious part in attempts to influence the minds or votes of others, such conduct being deemed inconsistent with the spirit of the Constitution and the duties of public agents acting under it. . . ." [49] Despite contrary practice, this view was officially repeated from time to time, and was admirably stated by Secretary of the Treasury Howell Cobb in 1857.

> . . . I do not think that a citizen loses his political identity or independence by accepting office under the Government. He does, however, commit himself to the service of the country, to the utmost extent required for a faithful discharge of the duties of his position. His political associates ought not to expect of him any service to his party at the expense of his duty to the Government. Holding, as you do, an office of great pecuniary responsibility, and one requiring your constant personal attention, I cannot sanction the propriety of your absence from your post for the purpose of an active engagement in the approaching election of your State.
>
> No one regards with more interest than I do the success of the national Democratic party at this important period in our history. But that success must not be purchased at the expense of the public interest, which might be the case if those holding high and important

48 *Ibid.*, LI, 138 (Oct. 29, 1836).

49 Senate Doc. 26, 27th Cong., 1st sess., p. 2 (March 20, 1841).

offices should absent themselves from their posts to conduct the canvass. Regarding your letter in the light of an application for leave of absence, I have withheld my approval for the foregoing reasons.[50]

Official orders and instructions were too feeble to withstand the pressure from the party machines, and officeholders, especially in the large cities, became both the leaders of tens and hundreds and filled the rank and file. The abundant evidence can be epitomized by a few examples.

The Hoyt investigation in 1841–42 showed that the collector's chief function was to return a Democratic majority in New York City. A former customs inspector stated, "I have myself been absent attending the polls all day, and for two or three days in succession, on some occasions, and also absent at other times for several days, for objects connected with elections. . . . other inspectors have also been absent for similar purposes. . . . On these occasions I was absent without leave from any superior officer of customs. I judged for myself as to my services being required, by my official duties, and was never concerned for such absence." [51] Gideon G. Westcott, an appraiser in the Philadelphia customhouse, 1853–57, and subsequently postmaster of Philadelphia, admitted in 1860 that he had been absent from his official duties from June to November 1856 to serve on the State Democratic Central Committee, meanwhile drawing his government pay upon a sworn statement that he had performed his duty in the customhouse.[52] Postmaster General James Campbell, in an effort to switch his political allegiance from Pierce to Buchanan, the successful Democratic nominee in 1856, wrote the latter that he would be glad to visit quietly any part of Pennsylvania and would esteem it a favor to be told what was to be done. Earlier Campbell had been active in trying to organize the Pennsylvania state convention for Pierce, but without success. He also had sent post office agents into New York to help reelect Governor Seymour, who was supporting Pierce.[53]

More humble workers were involved in election day work.

50 *National Intelligencer,* April 7, 1857.
51 House Doc. 212, 27th Cong., 2d sess., pp. 487–88 (April 30, 1842).
52 Covode Committee Report, pp. 414 ff.
53 Fowler, *Cabinet Politician,* pp. 85–87.

James O'Reilly was appointed in the public stores division of the Philadelphia customhouse, worked for a part of one day, and was then excused. His testimony follows.

Q. What were you excused to do?
A. I believe for the purpose of going out to do what I possibly could for Gen. Ward.
Q. Are you a working politician? an active politician?
A. They say I am middling smart in that way. . . .

O'Reilly was not very smart on this occasion, for he was discharged after five days and only reinstated for a short time after threatening to expose the whole affair. Meanwhile he had lost his regular job in private employment.[54]

Another aspect of the political activity problem involved double officeholding in the public service and in the party organization. The party thus established a sort of personal union with the government, a union which at once raised difficult questions about primary loyalty and obligation.

On a small scale postmasters had helped manage the party machinery, primarily local in character, before 1829, and collectors and other customs officers in the large cities were sometimes active in the local party organizations. The postmasters of the large cities gravitated toward the state central committee under the Jackson administration and for the next two decades tended to become important members of the party organization. At the first Democratic national convention there were sixteen postmasters in attendance out of a total of 344 delegates. At the New York State Whig convention of 1850 former Postmaster General Francis Granger presided; Hugh Maxwell, the collector of the port of New York, was on hand with several of his subordinates; and the United States subtreasurer appeared in order to influence the delegates toward the Fillmore administration.[55]

Duality of officeholding in the public service and the party organization had become common by the decade 1850–60. By way of further illustration we may note the case of John H. George, United States district attorney for New Hampshire and chairman of the state Democratic organization during Pierce's

54 Covode Committee Report, p. 496.
55 Barnes, *Memoir of Thurlow Weed,* p. 186.

administration;[56] George Plitt, clerk of the United States Circuit Court in Philadelphia in 1856 and also treasurer of the Democratic state central committee;[57] Thomas J. McCamant, pay clerk in the sixth auditor's office and secretary of the Pennsylvania Club—an organization assessing federal officeholders—during the campaigns of 1856 and 1858;[58] Isaac V. Fowler, the postmaster of New York in 1856, a Grand Sachem of Tammany Hall and a delegate to the Democratic national convention of 1856.[59]

The climax of this duality was reached in 1860 when it appeared that President James Buchanan was actively directing the party organization and was using the federal patronage to secure his own renomination.[60] The one-time district attorney for Pennsylvania described his personal relations with Buchanan in these words: "Your conversations with me, as well as your letters to me on this subject [i. e., his relations with the collector of customs in Philadelphia], have invariably referred to the subject in its political aspects, and as affecting the management of internal party politics. . . . in our last conversation . . . your only request of me at that time was that I would not interfere with the collector in his management of the then approaching campaign to elect delegates to our State convention, called for the purpose of nominating a governor and sending delegates to the Charleston national convention."[61]

A corollary of this union of local machines and important federal officeholders was the tendency to subordinate local combinations to national political interests. James C. Van Dyke was removed from the office of federal district attorney in 1860 for failure to cooperate with the Philadelphia collector at the port. Van Dyke declared that lack of cooperation occurred only in local political maneuvers, the effect of which would have been to reduce the local party organization to Buchanan's wishes. In the course of his interrogation before the Covode Committee the following colloquy took place:

56 Jefferson Davis, *Letters, Papers and Speeches,* III, 129.
57 Covode Committee Report, p. 546.
58 *Ibid.,* p. 578.
59 Fowler, *Cabinet Politician,* pp. 85–86.
60 Covode Committee Report, *passim.*
61 *Ibid.,* p. 344.

Q. Do you know of any effort made on the part of federal officers to control state politics?

A. In my opinion there has been in the city of Philadelphia a general combination among all the federal officers, with very few exceptions, to control the internal politics of that city. . . . that influence has been attempted by the federal officers to be extended beyond the city of Philadelphia.[62]

Van Dyke plainly told President Buchanan that he regarded these efforts "as in conflict with the doctrine of State rights as interpreted by the democratic party." [63] In this position he was able to support his view by appealing to the often expressed judgments of Buchanan himself when he was an aspirant for high office.

Loss of independent vote. Where party warfare was heaviest and the stakes greatest, pressure on subordinate officeholders reached the point in some cases of compelling employees to vote as they were told. The penalty for refusal was immediate discharge for political insubordination.

Francis McCormick was an employee of the Philadelphia customhouse from 1853 to 1858. He was directed to vote for the collector's choice to the state convention to nominate candidates for the Supreme Court of Pennsylvania, but declined, telling the collector that his friends were committed the other way. After the election of delegates he found "his head off" politically, although the collector admitted that he was "one of the first officers in the department" and although no charges had been made against him as a man or as a Democrat. He lost his job nevertheless.[64]

An inspector of customs in New York testified, "It was well understood, generally, by persons employed in the collection of customs under the late collector, Mr. Hoyt, that no person could consider himself safe, in regard to retaining his place, unless he was orthodox in his politics, according to the locofoco creed." [65] The investigating commission, an executive body appointed by President Tyler, was indignant at this state of affairs. "The direct and obvious tendency of this practice," it was noted, "is to de-

62 *Ibid.*, pp. 332–33.

63 *Ibid.*, p. 344.

64 *Ibid.*, p. 361.

65 House Doc. 212, 27th Cong., 2d sess., p. 482 (April 30, 1842).

grade the subordinate officers—reducing them to a state of abject dependence upon their superiors, in regard to a subject on which every man should be independent; to establish a different and adverse criterion of official qualification from the true one, '*Is he honest? Is he capable?*' and, as a natural result, to fill these important stations with a set of party hacks, whose principal qualification is political subserviency, and who think it no sin to cheat the public if they support the party." [66] The issue was overshadowed by far more dramatic ones arising out of the misdeeds of Swartwout and Hoyt, and won little attention against the silent but effective opposition of the party managers.

Political activity by federal officeholders, high and low, was most intense in the large cities, but became common elsewhere. Indeed the proposal to restrict their political activity encountered objections of a fundamental nature that were one day to divide the Supreme Court itself. Senator James Buchanan denied both the constitutional power of Congress to abridge this aspect of freedom of speech and also the wisdom of such a policy in a democratic form of government.[67] He carried Congress with him. Customhouse employees, told by the government that it was wrong to attempt to influence the political opinions of their fellow citizens, and told by the local party leaders that it would go hard with them if they did not, bowed to the nearer and greater power.

BRAKES ON DETERIORATION

It would be easy to draw conclusions from facts such as those contained in the preceding pages that would be far removed from reality. The consequences of rotation on the public service were unfortunate as a whole, but they were balanced in part by democratic gains, and because both Whigs and Democrats looked for character and competence among their partisans, and often found these qualities.

Thus it was an advantage, in a democratic society, to have destroyed the concept of a personal property right in office, so far as it prevailed. Postmaster General Kendall notified his clerks that no "personal claims to office or promotion" were recognized.

66 *Ibid.*, pp. 66–67.
67 Buchanan, *Works,* IV, 54 ff. (Feb. 14, 1839).

"The offices are the property of the people, and the officeholders their hirelings. . . . Each clerk . . . in relation to any higher or more lucrative station which may become vacant, stands on the same footing as the citizens out of office."[68] There were gains as well as losses in securing actual experience in the art of government for many citizens. There was value in the sense of union between common folk on the one hand and their public officers on the other.

Moreover, neither party welcomed scoundrels or irresponsibles in public office. Democrats and Whigs alike preferred men of integrity and skill and steadily sought for them among the ranks of their party friends. Jackson wrote that he "determined to hear with caution, examine well, and grant offices to none but such as was honest and capable. . . ."[69] Kendall declared that ability, integrity, and fidelity to republican institutions were necessary qualifications for appointment to office.[70] Polk expressed satisfaction in appointing as secretary of legation a man of experience, in command of the Spanish and French languages, and "an educated gentleman, qualifications which eminently fit him for the Station."[71] In his private correspondence Daniel Webster gave his support to a hostile officeholder because he was an "honest man, faithful, capable, fit to be trusted; and as one, who gives general satisfaction."[72] On another occasion he asked a correspondent for "the name of a man, the fittest, within your knowledge, to be Naval Officer. He must be a firm and energetic friend to the present Administration; not too old, altogether trustworthy, and enjoying public confidence."[73] These men made mistakes, and many more errors of judgment were committed in their names; they were sometimes driven from their principles; but they were not hypocrites.[74]

68 *Niles Register,* L, 330 (July 16, 1836).

69 Jackson, *Correspondence,* VI, 504 (1831).

70 Kendall, *Autobiography,* p. 432.

71 Polk, *Diary,* III, 382 (March 13, 1848).

72 Webster, *Writings and Speeches* (National ed.), XVI, 531 (Jan. 27, 1850).

73 *Ibid.,* XVI, 615–16 (June 9, 1851).

74 Examination of many letters of recommendation in the files of the National Archives reveals that character and competence as well as party regularity were also accepted by the influential public as prerequisites to appointment, particularly for responsible officers such as collectors. See Treasury Section, National Archives, Collectors of Customs Applications, *passim.*

Conversely, bad habits were generally deemed a bar to consideration for office. Marcy wrote General Wetmore concerning a pending nomination, "I have heard that his moral character is bad. If that fact could be charged upon him in an authoritative way, it would settle the question. Yet it is a delicate as well as a difficult matter to handle." [75] Jackson directed the Postmaster General to look into the behavior of three of his clerks reported to be of dissipated habits, one "intoxicated on the cow-field, and *all* in the streets." The President proposed to prevent "such disgraceful conduct" by promptly removing the offenders.[76] The Secretary of the Treasury had already issued a warning to the customs service about intoxication: "It appears to me that officers whose habits are not positively sober, cannot be vigilant; that they cannot exercise their skill with effect, and that an indulgence in one vice, mean, in itself, too naturally removes repugnance, to others." He asked the collectors to report offenders for the attention of the President.[77] Van Buren expressly followed the same rule.[78]

Jackson required the removal of any officer who contracted a debt under his administration and subsequently took advantage of the insolvent debtors act.[79] Former officeholders who had defaulted in their obligations were not usually considered for a second appointment. Jackson had to withdraw two nominations after discovering that each person had been delinquent,[80] and it was standing practice for Senate committees to ask for a report on this point.[81]

Mere benevolence played its part, too, amidst the corners of a complex pattern. General Harrison, one day to become President, had been rescued from his financial burdens by an appointment as clerk of the county court of common pleas in

75 Library of Congress, Marcy Papers, Vol. 10, No. 34,471 (June 9, 1845).

76 Jackson, *Correspondence,* V, 351–52 (May 21, 1835).

77 *Niles Register,* XLV, 53 (Sept. 21, 1833).

78 National Archives, Treasury Department, Miscellaneous Letters to the President, Set A, p. 141 (Jan. 30, 1840).

79 Jackson, *Correspondence,* IV, 323 (August 1, 1831); Richardson, *Messages,* II, 544 (August 6, 1831).

80 Richardson, *Messages,* II, 474 (Feb. 20, 1830), and *ibid.,* II, 477 (May 1, 1830).

81 National Archives, Treasury Department, Letters to Cabinet and Bureaus, Set B, No. 1, p. 75 (March 24, 1834).

Cincinnati.[82] Major A. J. Donelson, Jackson's ward, had a severe attack of sickness and, said Jackson to Polk, "wishes to be sent where health is promised. Spain, would suit his views, Brazil or Mexico. . . ." [83] He was appointed to Prussia. Jackson also looked around for a clerkship for Thomas J. Donelson—to enable Mrs. Donelson and her three little children to live with her mother in Philadelphia.[84] A lad of fifteen became a pension office clerk, his work being done by his compassionate elders in the office, to provide support for his widowed mother. The commissioner of pensions declared in defense that "such arrangements had been frequently made in the various Departments, and in the particular case referred to it was dictated solely by considerations of humanity and justice." [85] Jacksonians were warm in their sympathies for the distressed even if indifferent to the sufferings of their political opponents.

The experience of officeholding under the Jacksonians was consequently various. The tone and character of this period were set by the rule of rotation, and this rule brought deterioration in its wake. The public service was seized upon by the party system and made to support it in large measure. The politically neutral quality of the service generally sustained from 1789 to 1829 was impaired and in some quarters destroyed. The appetite of the office-seeking class was augmented and became more obnoxious. The efficiency of the public service was diminished and its prestige damaged. These were losses that had to be set off against the wholesome objects sought by the friends of rotation. By the time of James Buchanan there could be little doubt that the losses were great.

This conviction, indeed, became so clear that Congress itself took remedial steps by introducing in 1853 a system of examinations for the departmental clerks. This reform implied tenure for a career service which in fact had not been destroyed by the party aggressions of these years. This career service and the examination system form the subject of the next succeeding chapters.

82 Freeman Cleaves, *Old Tippecanoe*, p. 291.

83 Jackson, *Correspondence*, VI, 369 (Feb. 15, 1845).

84 *Ibid.*, VI, 344 (Dec. 18, 1844).

85 *National Intelligencer*, March 1, 1853; *Congressional Globe*, 32d Cong., 2d sess., p. 882 (Feb. 26, 1853).

CHAPTER EIGHTEEN

The Career Service

The conduct of government in a democracy requires a judicious combination of politics and administration, and the cooperation of men within the executive departments devoted to each branch of the public service. This cooperation had been relatively easy and effective under Federalists and Jeffersonians, since both groups were drawn from the broad class of gentlemen, and could work in the relative freedom of a society in which organized mass parties and pressure groups were negligible.

Where to draw the line between the two sectors of the public service had never been precisely defined, and fluctuated from time to time. From 1789 to 1829 the political sector comprised hardly more than the four department heads: State, Treasury, War, and Navy. The Post Office was politically neutral, the chief accounting officers were career men, and the heads of such agencies as the General Land Office, the Patent Office, the Indian office, the Pension Office, and the mint were concerned with executive duties, not with elections.

After 1829 the line was drawn differently, although the change was not abrupt. Heads of departments became more obviously political personalities, in the sense of participating actively in elections. The commissioners in charge of a number of the important offices were more frequently chosen on the basis of political considerations. Thus in the General Land Office there were eleven commissioners from 1829 to 1860, of whom only one (John Wilson) was a career man. The Patent Office showed a similar trend. There were eight commissioners of patents from 1836 to 1861, of whom only the first, Henry L. Ellsworth, survived the administration to which he owed his office. Philip F.

Thomas, the last to hold the position under Buchanan, had been collector of the port of Baltimore under Pierce. The commissioner of pensions was nonpolitical until 1850, but there were four commissioners in the next decade. The commissioner of Indian affairs was a political choice throughout the Jacksonian period. The director of the mint at Philadelphia was a political figure after 1850. There were ten Treasury solicitors from 1829 to 1861.

In the field service, the collectors of customs in a few of the larger ports had been suspected of political activity during the 1820's. After 1829 the collectorships generally became political plums. Beginning in 1836, the heads of the large post offices were subjected to Senate confirmation and generally went over to the political sector. There were exceptions; thus, John McRae resigned the postmastership of Fayetteville, North Carolina, in 1853 after seventeen years as clerk to his father and thirty-five years as postmaster, a continuous service of fifty-two years.[1] The smaller offices continued to be filled by the Postmaster General without confirmation, but he tended to pick fellow partisans. Again the rule was not universal, for Abraham Lincoln, a Clay man and an Illinois Whig, was appointed postmaster of New Salem in 1833 and served as such for three years. United States district attorneys and marshals generally became political officers. The trend was clearly to extend the rule of political reliability to positions at the second level of administration, and to the important field offices. The principle was correctly stated by Polk, referring to the removal of a Whig U.S. attorney in New York. "I did so upon the general principle that the important subordinate public offices should be filled by persons who agreed in opinion with the President as to the policy to be pursued by the Government, and who would cooperate with the President in carrying out that policy." [2] This trend was not necessarily based on mere partisanship, since the duties of commissioners and other high officials had direct relationship to policy. More than one influence was at work at these levels.

The loss of tenure status, however, was not confined to important officials. Humble clerks, customhouse weighers and meas-

1 *National Intelligencer,* April 2, 1853.

2 Polk, *Diary,* IV, 114 (Sept. 1, 1848).

urers, Indian agents, messengers suffered the same fate, for somewhat different reasons. Nevertheless the permanent service that had distinguished the first forty years of the Republic was not completely destroyed. It was restricted in scope, and it often suffered from the pressure and interference of the political wing. It was saved, however, by the hard necessities of administration, by the sheer need to get things done. Department heads did not have the grasp on daily business, on routine and procedures, and above all on precedent that would enable them to handle departmental business without the aid of men who knew the precedents, who were familiar with the flow of work, and who could be counted on to avoid the errors and misjudgments of novices.[3] Amidst the clamor for removals and partisan appointments to resulting vacancies, a hard core of experienced men consequently remained steadily at work. The evidence concerning their existence has been overlooked and as a result the evils of the rotation system, bad as they were, have been overemphasized. The actual conduct of the public business remained after 1829 as before largely in the hands of old-timers who "knew the ropes." The employment record of the accounting officers, the chief clerks, and many rank-and-file clerks, is convincing testimony of the fact.[4]

It will not be assumed by the reader that the new men who filled accounting and clerical offices from time to time were necessarily incompetent or undesirable. Many of them possessed high talent and were well suited to the work for which they became responsible. The case may be illustrated by John Appleton, a Maine lawyer who became editor of a Democratic newspaper,

3 The point is perfectly illustrated by reference to a simple clerical error in a Treasury financial statement of 1847. John D. Barclay, the clerk involved in the error, had been an employee of the register's office for over forty years and had prepared this annual statement for a long period of time. He was described by the Acting Secretary of the Treasury as a "gentleman of the most exemplary character . . . [who] has never before made any known mistake or omission," and who discovered and promptly reported his error. It was due to pressure of work, day and night, for several months. The Acting Secretary absolved him from all fault, and declared that the confidence of the department and all its officers remained unshaken (as well it might), in his "high moral worth and great experience, accuracy, and knowledge of the financial operations of this department." House Ex. Doc. 6, 30th Cong., 1st sess., pp. 172–73 (Jan. 19, 1848).

4 Unless otherwise indicated the following data are derived from the successive editions of the *Official Register of the United States.*

the *Daily Eastern Argus,* and who was appointed chief clerk of the Navy Department by Bancroft in 1845. Subsequently he became chief clerk of the State Department and chargé d'affaires in Bolivia. In 1850 he was elected to Congress and in 1857 became assistant secretary of State, where he contributed effectively to the diplomatic correspondence of the time.

The term "career service" was not used either before or after 1829, nor were the advantages and handicaps of such an institution praised or criticized. Young men did not prepare for the civil service as a career, although they did for both the army and the navy officer corps. Clerks became government employees with the same expectations that alternatively would have induced them to become countinghouse clerks. In either case there was reasonable hope of continued employment for faithful service. In neither case was there a career in the sense of opportunity to rise to higher, more responsible and better paid positions reaching into what a later age would call middle-management, except for the very few who became chief clerks. A career as a clerk in the government service meant, before 1829, the prospect of continued employment, with infrequent change of assignment, and with the possibility of salary advancement as better paid clerical positions became vacant. *Mutatis mutandis,* the same comments applied to such higher officers as the comptrollers and auditors, who enjoyed stable tenure. Careers were not part of a planned system conducive to the efficient conduct of government. They were originally based on the proper code of a gentleman toward his fellow workers, and later on the minimum necessities of handling the public business.

THE CAREER SERVICE: COMPTROLLERS AND AUDITORS

The Jeffersonian tradition had favored almost a judicial tenure for the principal accounting officers, the number of whom had been increased by the reforms of 1816. Joseph Anderson had been first comptroller from 1815 to 1836, when he was persuaded to resign. From 1829 to 1861 the office of first comptroller, which had special duties connected with customs administration, was occupied at times by professional accounting officers and at others by men who had been active in public affairs in various capacities. The most notable of the latter type was the able

Elisha Whittlesey, a Connecticut Yankee who sat in the House of Representatives from 1823 to 1838, served as sixth auditor from 1841 to 1843, and as first comptroller under Taylor, Fillmore, and Pierce from 1849 to 1857. Removed by Buchanan, he was reappointed by Lincoln and died in office in 1863.

The office of second comptroller was more definitely a tenure position. It was held from 1836 to 1850 by a former judge of the Supreme Court of Maine, Albion K. Parris. He was followed briefly by a former judge of the Vermont Supreme Court, and later governor of the state, Hiland Hall; and then by a Vermont lawyer who was one day to become Kent Professor of Law at Yale and U.S. minister to Great Britain, Edward J. Phelps. His successor, John M. Brodhead, was an auditing clerk with literary interests who had entered this office in 1829 and had served five years as chief clerk. Buchanan removed him, but appointed another career man, James Madison Cutts, son of the former comptroller, Richard Cutts, and a clerk in the comptroller's office since 1821.

The auditors were drawn primarily from the permanent service. Here toiled Peter Hagner, third auditor, who had been advised by James Madison to enter the public service in 1793 as a clerk in the accounting division of the War Department, who became chief clerk in 1799, and third auditor in 1817, in which office he died in 1849. Another such figure was the fifth auditor, Stephen Pleasanton, who held this office from 1817 until his death in 1855. Of him James Buchanan said in 1849, "He is an excellent old gentleman and a faithful officer. With him and with his family I am on terms of more intimate friendship than with any other persons in this City." [5] Illustrating the less frequent political type was a short-term fourth auditor, James C. Pickett (1836–38), an army officer, lawyer, and politician who served in the Kentucky State legislature, was secretary of state in Kentucky, secretary of the U.S. legation at Colombo, and for a few months superintendent of the Patent Office before he became fourth auditor; and who afterward was chargé d'affaires to Peru, and editor of the *Daily Globe* from 1848 to 1853. Pickett, First Auditor William Collins, First Comptroller James McCulloh, and some others were responsible for allowing political

5 Buchanan, *Works*, XI, 485 (Feb. 18, 1849).

assessments of the auditing clerks. Typically, however, the auditors and their clerks were career men, outside the range of politics, well versed in the mystery of settling accounts.

THE CAREER SERVICE: THE CHIEF CLERKS

The pivot on which daily business turned both before and after the Civil War was the office of chief clerk. The office existed both at the departmental level (in the Secretary's office), at the bureau or commission level, and in the accounting services. The chief clerks were the principal reliance of department heads, commissioners, comptrollers, and accountants, and the military and naval officers at the head of the bureaus in the armed services. The concern of the chief clerks was administration, and for the most part they were career men who rose to these posts on the basis of long experience in lower grades.

The Treasury Department. Almost all chief clerks in the Treasury became such after service as clerks, and most of them remained in their posts from administration to administration. In the office of the Secretary of the Treasury, Asbury Dickins was chief clerk from 1829 to 1833, having already been twelve years a clerk in the department; in 1833 he became chief clerk of the State Department, and later clerk of the House of Representatives. He was succeeded in the Treasury by McClintock Young, who remained in the office until 1849 under Whig and Democratic Secretaries alike. He in turn was followed by John McGinnis, originally appointed a Treasury clerk in 1829; his two successors to 1861 were also experienced men.

In the office of the treasurer of the United States from 1829 to 1861 there were only two chief clerks, both of them permanent employees: Peter Grayson Washington (1829–36) and William B. Randolph (1836–68). Randolph began his career in 1816 as a Treasury clerk and ended it fifty-two years later. Much the same situation prevailed in the office of register of the Treasury, where Michael Nourse (of the Nourse family that provided so many members of the early public service) was chief clerk from 1820 to 1853. Nourse began his public service as a clerk in this office in 1795.

The chief clerks in the accounting offices required a fund of special knowledge that was acquired only by long training.

Without entering upon detail, it may be stated that the chief clerkship of both the first and second comptrollers' offices was uniformly nonpartisan in character, and held regularly by clerks who had been promoted after long experience in the accounting offices. With rare exceptions, the chief clerks in all the six auditors' offices were also drawn from the permanent service. William Mechlin was a genuine "old-timer," serving as clerk from 1817 to 1849, and as chief clerk of the second auditor's office from 1849 to 1861. His career was paralleled by that of James Thompson, War Department accounting clerk from 1811 to 1817 and chief clerk of the office of third auditor from 1817 to 1853. This office had only two chief clerks during the Jacksonian period; Thompson was followed by Samuel S. Rind, who began his clerical life in 1831 in this office and finished it as chief clerk from 1853 to 1861. The chief clerks in the auditors' offices, indeed, furnish the most dramatic evidence of the carry-over from preceding administrations of experienced men. The following list indicates the permanent character of these officeholders:

William Parker, chief clerk, first auditor's office,	1818–1837
James Eakin, chief clerk, second auditor's office,	1817–1845
James Thompson, chief clerk, third auditor's office,	1817–1853
Thomas H. H. Gillis, chief clerk, fourth auditor's office,	1816–1850
Thomas Mustin, chief clerk, fifth auditor's office,	1822–1855
Peter Grayson Washington, chief clerk, sixth auditor's office,	1836–1845

War Department. In the office of the Secretary of War there were fourteen chief clerks from 1829 to 1861, of whom six were definitely career men, serving the government in one capacity or another both before and after their appointments as chief clerk.

The major bureaus of the War Department were characteristically served by chief clerks having permanent connections with the department. The heads of the War Department bureaus were army officers; the chief clerks were civilians. It was at this point that military and civil administration touched each other, a boundary having its own special problems. That they were well met is suggested from the employment records of the chief clerks in these bureaus from 1829 to 1861.

Brooke Williams became chief clerk of the adjutant general's office in 1814 and died there in 1843. He was succeeded by John M. Hepburn, who had been a clerk in the office since 1812, and who served until 1850. In the next decade there were only two chief clerks, each one taken from the department, one with twenty years' earlier experience, the other with five.

The chief clerk of the quartermaster general's office, William A. Gordon, was appointed by Monroe in 1824 and was still in office when Lincoln became President. The chief clerk of the office of commissary general of purchases had been appointed by Madison in 1812; in 1840 he was replaced at age 67; his successor was not disturbed until Lincoln's administration. In another army supply office, the commissary of subsistence, Jackson continued Charles G. Wilcox, appointed by Monroe in 1820. He was succeeded in 1839 by Richard Gott, who served until Lincoln's administration opened in 1861. The chief clerk in the paymaster's office, appointed by Jefferson in 1808, served in this post until 1853, when he was "demoted" to a clerk; his successor served until 1861. The engineer department had only two chief clerks from 1829 to 1861, the first having been appointed under Monroe. The ordnance department had only one chief clerk from the initial appointment in 1842 to the outbreak of the Civil War.

Navy Department. The Navy Department represented a similar pattern of organization: naval officers at the head of the bureaus established by the act of 1842, chief clerks serving immediately under them. The bureau of navy yards and docks had two chief clerks from 1842 to 1861; the bureau of construction, equipment, and repair had three, the first of whom served only a short time. John Lenthal, appointed chief clerk in 1855, was serving as naval constructor in 1869.

THE CAREER SYSTEM: THE CLERKS

The effect of rotation was most pronounced among the clerks, and more extensive among the clerks in the large field establishments than in the departmental offices in Washington. Yet even among the rank and file, whose positions could presumably be most easily occupied by "unpracticed men" and whose jobs were ardently sought, there remained a substantial proportion of men seasoned in their respective specialties. Some of them have been noticed in preceding pages, as they rose to the chief clerk level.

The persistence of this corps of permanent clerks, despite the inroads of patronage, could be evidenced by the records of almost any office. In 1836 a special report was required by Congress giving the names and dates of original appointment of the clerks then employed in the several departments. This record disclosed a permanent corps of clerks in the different agencies during the turmoil of the Jackson administration. A few examples follow. In the office of the Secretary of the Treasury in 1836 twelve clerks were employed, of whom three were appointed before 1829, one in 1807 and two in 1816 respectively.[6] The register of the Treasury, the venerable Joseph Nourse, had been promptly removed by Jackson, but the rest of the office was undisturbed, including the principal clerk, Michael Nourse. There were twenty clerks, including Nourse, at work in 1836. Two had been appointed under Washington, three under Jefferson, one by Madison, five by Monroe, three by John Quincy Adams, and six by Jackson, the latter ranging from 1829 to 1835. The clerical staff of this office was thus practically untouched by the theory of rotation.[7]

In the office of the third auditor twenty clerks were employed in 1836. Of them, one had been appointed under John Adams, five by Madison, five by Monroe, and nine by Jackson—of the latter, none until 1831. This office was thus in the hands of the old Republican clerks in 1836, even toward the close of Jackson's two terms.[8] The fourth auditor had thirteen clerks, six of whom had been appointed before Jackson.[9] In the Pension Office, on the contrary, only three old-timers survived in an office of eighteen clerks.[10] The State Department and the General Post

6 House Doc. 251, 24th Cong., 1st sess. (May 6, 1836).

7 House Doc. 216, 24th Cong., 1st sess., pp. 2–3 (April 15, 1836).

8 House Doc. 217, 24th Cong., 1st sess., p. 2 (April 15, 1836).

9 House Doc. 227, 24th Cong., 1st sess. (April 16, 1836).

10 House Doc. 223, 24th Cong., 1st sess. (April 15, 1836).

Office also showed only a small contingent from the years before Jackson.

These examples indicate that when the 1829–31 storm of removals had subsided, a nucleus of experienced clerks remained on duty in the respective government offices. In some they were a substantial majority, in others a minority. These figures must be read, of course, in the light of the normal turnover due to death, voluntary resignation, or removal for delinquency which would in any event bring some change. They demonstrate the persistence of the old system at the clerical level, as well as in middle management.

The erosion of patronage among the rank and file became progressively greater, and the proportion of tenure men among the departmental clerks tended to diminish. They persisted, nevertheless, and nearly twenty years after the 1836 data had been gathered, new evidence came to light at the beginning of the Democratic Pierce administration. A list of clerks in the second comptroller's office, March 9, 1853, included one appointed by Monroe, two by Jackson, two by Tyler, six by Polk, and seven by Taylor and Fillmore.[11] A report from the office of the first auditor revealed, among a total staff of seventeen, one clerk appointed by John Quincy Adams, two by Jackson, three by Tyler, three by Polk, and eight by Taylor and Fillmore.[12] A report from the office of the treasurer showed much the same distribution; in this case the oldest clerk had been appointed by Jefferson.[13] James Guthrie, Secretary of the Treasury, reported in 1854 that in most cases he had retained the best of the clerks whom he found in office.[14] From time to time the *National Intelligencer* reported the retirement of old-time clerks who had weathered the storms. Thus in 1853 it recorded the resignation of William G. Eliot, "who has for the last thirty-three years filled important positions in the accounting departments of the

11 National Archives, Second Comptroller Correspondence, 1836–1861; statement of March 9, 1853.

12 National Archives, First Auditor Reports and Correspondence, 1834–1877; report dated March 9, 1853.

13 National Archives, Treasurer Correspondence, 1818–1866 (1853).

14 Senate Ex. Doc. 2, 33d Cong., 2d sess., p. 20 (Dec. 4, 1854). An evidence of continuity is discovered in the existence of the Provident Association of Clerks in 1860 (12 Stat. 17), founded in 1819.

General Post Office with the strictest fidelity, and with that excellent deportment which won from all having official business with him the esteem which he enjoyed in the community. . . ." [15]

THE SCIENTIFIC OFFICES

The scientific and professional agencies of the general government were recognized as tenure offices throughout the Jacksonian period, within which, indeed, some of them were established. The Coast Survey was administered alternately by the Treasury and the Navy, but in either case its personnel was drawn principally from among naval officers. A single effort to displace its distinguished head, Alexander Dallas Bache, met with a storm of disapproval from scientific societies not only in the United States, but also, more discreetly, in Great Britain and Europe. The small staff of the Naval Observatory was strictly professional. The Smithsonian Institution was not disturbed by the theory or practice of rotation.

The professional and nonpolitical character of the army and navy medical corps was also fully recognized by the Jacksonians. As will be noted below, both the army and the navy extended the examination system for medical officers that had been originated earlier, and the politicians did not interfere with the professional character of these services. The two departments, indeed, repeatedly praised the steady improvement in the quality of medical service under the regime of examinations. By common consent, these were areas not suitable for the rotation of "unpracticed men."

The regular army and navy officers corps also stood outside the play of partisanship, so far as permanence of tenure and personal progress was concerned. Both groups were professionally trained, and although generally nominated in the first instance for West Point or Annapolis by Congressmen, they stood on their own feet thereafter. Advancement in the service was by strict rule of seniority, a rule which the officer corps insisted upon. The two major career systems, indeed, in the United States were those of the army and navy. Less could be said of the volunteer forces called in to help fight the Mexican War, and much

15 *National Intelligencer,* April 16, 1853.

less of the state militia, over which both Congress and the federal executive had little influence.

LITERARY FIGURES IN THE PUBLIC SERVICE

The prestige of the public service during the Jacksonian years may have been depressed by the invasion of small politicians, but it was also enhanced by the appointment of many literary men of great and lesser stature. The first appointment of George Bancroft was owing to his success as a politician rather than as a historian, but eventually his literary fame far outweighed his political significance.

Washington Irving, trained for the law but destined for authorship, had already established his literary reputation when he became secretary of the legation at London under Louis McLane in 1829. Returning to the United States in 1832 he continued his career as a man of letters until he was appointed minister to Spain (1842–46). His novel, *The Alhambra,* and his travels in Spain as well as his literary reputation and his capacity for official work made him an appropriate choice.[16]

A government post was an economic lifesaver for Nathaniel Hawthorne, but a trial to his spirit. Bancroft appointed him a weigher and gauger in the Boston customhouse, where he toiled for two years—truly an incongruous occupation, "measuring coal all day on board of a black little British schooner, in a dismal dock at the north end of the city." After a year he declared, "I do detest all offices,—all, at least, that are held on a political tenure. And I want nothing to do with politicians. Their hearts wither away and die out of their bodies." [17] From 1846 to 1849 he was surveyor of the port of Salem, an appointment instigated by Charles Sumner through Mrs. George Bancroft. Sumner had heard of Hawthorne's poverty and asked for "some post-office, some custom house, something, that will yield daily bread" for the hard-pressed author.[18] Hawthorne lost this post when the Whigs triumphed in 1849, but his Democratic friends gave him

16 Stanley T. Williams, *The Life of Washington Irving* (New York: Oxford University Press, 1935).

17 Nathaniel Hawthorne, *Passages from the American Note-Books,* pp. 214, 215–16.

18 Howe, *Life and Letters of George Bancroft,* I, 264–65 (Jan. 9, 1846).

the consulship at Liverpool when they returned to power in 1853. To the Salem surveyorship we owe the charming essay, "The Custom House." [19]

Bancroft, Irving, and Hawthorne were the great men of the literary world who for one reason or another graced the public service during these years. Two heads of the Navy Department bore good literary reputations in their day. James K. Paulding, Van Buren's Secretary of the Navy, published *Letters from the South* (1817), a Jeffersonian tract praising the values of country life, and wrote many novels and humorous works for the next forty years.[20] In Vernon Parrington's phrase, he was "an amusing amateur" in the literary field, but too casual in his work and too undisciplined in the craft of writing.[21] John P. Kennedy, Fillmore's Secretary of the Navy, was trained for the law, but devoted himself to higher education (as provost of the University of Maryland), to literature, and to politics. His two best known works are *Quodlibet,* a satire on Jacksonian democracy (1840), and the *Life of William Wirt* (1849).[22] Kennedy and Paulding were both close friends of Washington Irving, and Paulding collaborated with Irving in some of his early writings.

Lesser historians than Bancroft held important government positions. John Milton Niles, for a short period Postmaster General, wrote the *Life of Oliver Hazard Perry,* and a *History of South America and Mexico.* Hiland Hall, second comptroller under Taylor and governor of Vermont, wrote a history of that state. John R. Brodhead, naval officer of the port of New York, was by instinct and long experience a professional historian. Trained in law, he served two years as attaché to the United States legation at The Hague and spent the next four years collecting material from the European archives relating to the history of New York. From 1846 to 1849 he was secretary of the

19 Nathaniel Hawthorne, "The Custom House," Introductory to *The Scarlet Letter* (1850).

20 Oscar Wegelin, "A Bibliography of the Separate Publications of James Kirke Paulding, Poet, Novelist, Humorist, Statesman," in Bibliographical Society of America, *Papers,* XII (1918), 34–40.

21 Vernon Louis Parrington, *Main Currents in American Thought* (3 vols., New York: Harcourt Brace, 1927–1930), II, 221.

22 *Ibid.,* II, 46–56. Parrington identified *Quodlibet* as "the most vivacious criticism of Jacksonianism in our political library, one of our few distinguished political satires. . . ."

legation in London with Bancroft. Returning to New York and to history, he published the first volume of his *History of the State of New York* in 1853, the second in 1871. He was a thorough, accurate, and conscientious scholar.[23]

The minor poets, dramatists, and essayists were also represented. James Nelson Barker was one of the leading playwrights of his time, and also one of the important Pennsylvania politicians. His first successful play was produced in 1807, and in 1808 appeared one of his greatest successes, *The Indian Princess*, a work that reached the London stage. In 1817 he was elected alderman of Philadelphia, in 1819, mayor; and in 1824 he produced his finest drama, *Superstition*. From 1829 to 1838 he was collector of customs for the port of Philadelphia, and from 1838 to 1841 first comptroller. His later years were spent as a Treasury clerk. His writing days were over.[24]

Prosper Montgomery Wetmore of New York was a soldier, merchant, politician, regent of the University of New York, secretary of the New York Chamber of Commerce, president of the American Art Union, navy agent at the port of New York from 1845 to 1849, friend and intimate correspondent of Secretary of War Marcy, and also a poet. He began to write for magazines at the age of 17, and in 1830 published a collection of his works, entitled *Lexington, with Other Fugitive Poems*. His correspondence with Marcy, both official and personal, is full of interest.[25]

Charles Lanman, departmental librarian and private secretary to Daniel Webster, was also an author, editor, amateur explorer, and artist. His official career included duties as librarian of the War Department (1849), secretary to Webster (1850), librarian of the Interior Department (1855), librarian of the House of Representatives (1861), and after the Civil War, American secretary to the Japanese legation in Washington (1871–82) and assistant assessor of the District of Columbia. He was the author of over thirty works including *Letters from a Landscape Painter*, *Adventures in the Wilds of the United States and British Ameri-*

23 *Dictionary of American Biography*, III, 63; not to be confused with John M. Brodhead, second comptroller for many years.

24 *Ibid.*, I, 603.

25 *Appleton's Cyclopaedia of American Biography*, VI, 445.

can Provinces, the Private Life of Daniel Webster, and the still useful *Biographical Annals of the Civil Government of the United States.*[26]

Certainly one of the most irresponsible officials was John Howard Payne, dramatist, actor, and author of *Home, Sweet Home.* Shortly after his first play in New York in 1806 he sailed for Europe where he spent the next twenty years, constantly harassed by creditors. Returning to the United States, he finally secured a temporary clerkship in the War Department through the intervention of friends. This task at an end, Payne's friends, in Secretary Webster's absence, persuaded his son, Fletcher Webster, who was acting as Secretary of State, to appoint Payne consul to Tunis. He insisted upon being conveyed to his post of duty in a vessel of war, and while this weighty issue was being debated in Washington, he spent his advance payment for outfit and all his own money in New York "in every sort of extravagant folly." His friends contributed money to pay his passage to Paris. He arrived destitute, but was lucky enough to secure funds from an acquaintance sufficient to transport him to Tunis. Here he settled down in a large palace with a retinue of servants none of whom could speak any of the languages at his command. "If he needed any thing, he blew a silver whistle, and there filed in at least a dozen tall Arabs, who placed themselves in a semicircle around him, as silent as graven images. . . ."[27]

A number of men in public stations also were publishing scholarly works about the fields in which they worked. The navy was prolific in this respect. Commander David Porter published in 1835 his journal of an earlier cruise in the Pacific Ocean. Lieutenant A. S. Mackenzie wrote a life of Commodore Perry and of John Paul Jones. The writing of Lieutenant Matthew F. Maury criticizing the naval system has already been noted; his scientific work is referred to in a later chapter. James Fenimore Cooper, once a midshipman, wrote his *History of the Navy,* published in 1839, as well as many sea stories less well known than *The Last of the Mohicans.* William H. Trescot, secretary of legation at London (1852–54) and assistant secretary of State under Bu-

26 *Dictionary of American Biography,* X, 606.

27 T. N. Parmelee, "Recollections of an Old Stager," *Harper's New Monthly Magazine,* XLVI (1872–73), pp. 96–97.

chanan, was an authority in the field of international law. He published in 1852 *The Diplomacy of the Revolution: An Historical Study;* and in 1857, *Diplomatic History of the Administrations of Washington and Adams.* After the close of the Civil War he held a number of important diplomatic posts.[28]

No one, in or out of government, wrote about the art of administration.

A DUAL SYSTEM

From 1789 to 1829 a single type of public service had existed that may properly be designated a career system. Without any formal method of selection and with no guarantees other than custom, the system stood unchallenged for forty years. Young men began as clerks, and most of them continued to toil as clerks in the office in which they entered, except for the few who became principal clerks or chief clerks. They had the assets of correct habits, complete knowledge of their small world, and official reliability.

After 1829 this simple, single system bifurcated under the influence of the theory of rotation. It was not, however, destroyed. Old-time clerks remained at their desks; "party" clerks came and went. The toughness of administrative systems was again exemplified as the career system continued despite the handicaps to which it was exposed and the sudden blows it received every four years from 1840 to 1860.

Two personnel systems were thus in operation in the public service. The patronage system held the public attention, but it was primarily the career system that enabled the government to maintain its armed forces, to collect its revenue, to operate its land system, to keep its accounts and audit its expenditures. The patronage system had a fatal defect, because it possessed a double loyalty—one to the executive branch, the other to the political party. It also had a unique asset, because it enabled many citizens to participate in the business of government. The adjustment of the two systems remained even a century later an object of concern.

28 "Narrative and Letter of William Henry Trescot . . . ," *American Historical Review,* XIII (1907–8), 528–56.

CHAPTER NINETEEN

The Rise of Examinations

During the latter years of the Jeffersonians a simple system of examinations had been put into operation by departmental regulation for army surgeons (1814), for navy surgeons (1824), for West Point cadets (1818), and for midshipmen (1819). The practice of rotation was never applied to these officers, and the Jacksonians did not interrupt these examination procedures. Not only did they sustain their predecessors; a Democratic Congress in 1834 put the army medical examinations on a permanent statutory base.

PROFESSIONAL EXAMINATIONS IN THE ARMY AND THE NAVY

The original army surgeon examination was required only for gentlemen who did not possess a medical school diploma. In 1833, Secretary of War Lewis Cass set up a board of able and experienced surgeons who examined the incumbent medical corps and who were charged with the duty of "rigid scrutiny" of the "pretensions of medical gentlemen seeking appointments in the army." [1] The next year Congress required by law that no initial appointment as assistant surgeon could be made prior to examination by an army medical board, and further that no assistant surgeon could be promoted to the rank of surgeon without at least five years' service and examination by a medical board.[2]

Good results were immediately forthcoming. Surgeon General Joseph Lovell reported in 1835, the first year of statutory opera-

1 Senate Doc. 1, 23d Cong., 1st sess., p. 19 (Nov. 29, 1833).

2 4 Stat. 714 (June 30, 1834).

tions, "Of 121 applicants, who had been recommended as qualified for appointment, and who were authorized to present themselves for examination, 50 have failed to attend, and, of the remainder, but 44, or somewhat over one-third of the whole number, have been found qualified for the commission applied for." [3] Year after year the surgeon general reported official satisfaction with the results of the examination system. The proportion of successful applicants was sometimes as low as one-sixth of the the whole number, and usually less than one-third. In 1838 the surgeon general declared, "In truth, we have now an efficient corps of talented and experienced medical officers; and as . . . the bar to admission into the service without merit is, through the action of the medical boards, complete, we may reasonably calculate on introducing into the army, in each succeeding year, a portion of the very *élite* of the profession." [4]

The system of examinations for entrance into and promotion within the naval medical service had been put on a statutory base in 1828.[5] The Jacksonians accepted this system also, and the navy by regulation extended it into new fields. The examinations for promotion from assistant surgeon to surgeon attracted much attention, the results being publicly announced and widely reported. Two years' service at sea was prerequisite for appearance before the naval medical boards. The navy put additional emphasis upon the examination, which was oral, by ranking successful candidates in order of merit.[6]

Midshipmen were regularly required to pass an examination before promotion to the rank of lieutenant. In 1835 an examination was established to fill the position of professor of mathematics assigned to the training of midshipmen.[7] In 1846 Secretary Bancroft required an entrance examination for naval constructors, boatswains, gunners, carpenters, and sailmakers, and tried to impose a system of examinations for the promotion of

[3] Senate Doc. 1, 24th Cong., 1st sess., p. 99 (Nov. 21, 1835). These figures were larger than the normal class of applicants. For the record in an illustrative later year, see Senate Ex. Doc. 11, 35th Cong., 1st sess., p. 167 (Nov. 10, 1857).

[4] Senate Doc. 1, 25th Cong., 3d sess., p. 146 (Nov. 10, 1838).

[5] 4 Stat. 313 (May 24, 1828).

[6] For examples, see *Niles Register,* LI, 163 (Nov. 12, 1836); *National Intelligencer,* March 1, 1853.

[7] Senate Doc. 1, 24th Cong., 1st sess., p. 331 (Dec. 5, 1835).

line officers.[8] In 1852, Secretary Kennedy required navy yard apprentices to take an examination twice a year, and the best of them were offered a more rigorous examination that Kennedy hoped might open the doors of Annapolis to them. In this he was disappointed.[9]

With the advent of steam warships an engineer service was introduced into the navy, a graded service including the engineer in chief, chief engineers, and first, second, and third assistant engineers.[10] Examinations of a technical order were the means of securing admission into and promotion within this corps.[11] In 1843 the revenue cutter service introduced an examination system for its junior officers as they became candidates for the rank of first lieutenant.[12] An examination system was thus firmly planted in the Jacksonian era, flourishing side by side with the theory of rotation and appointment for partisan and personal considerations.

EXAMINATIONS FOR CLERKS

The advantages of competence and tenure and the mounting evils of patronage led to an effort in the early 1850's, headed by Senator Robert M. T. Hunter of Virginia, to install an examination system for the departmental clerks. Unexpectedly Congress agreed to this proposal almost, it would seem, in a fit of absent-mindedness. The reform was modest, but that there should be reform at all at this point was hard to be imagined. With the somewhat lame support of the heads of departments, it slipped through the Senate with bare notice, and through the House with almost none.

The case for selecting clerks by examination had been first stated by the Gilmer Committee in 1842. After referring to the examinations in the military services, the committee declared:

> . . . the application of the same principle in the original appointment of clerks would be attended with beneficial results. For this pur-

[8] Charles Oscar Paullin, "Naval Administration, 1842–1861," U.S. Naval Institute, *Proceedings,* XXXIII (1907), 1457.

[9] Senate Ex. Doc. 1, 32d Cong., 2d sess., Part II, pp. 310–11 (Dec. 4, 1852).

[10] 5 Stat. 577 (August 31, 1842).

[11] For a sample report of an examining board see *National Intelligencer,* Dec. 29, 1853.

[12] House Doc. 45, 28th Cong., 1st sess., p. 6 (Jan. 9, 1844).

pose, a board of examination might be instituted in the Departments, to consist of six members, one to be designated annually by each head of a department; three at least to be heads of offices or bureaus, and the residue principal clerks. The board might hold regular sessions semi-annually or quarterly, and special sessions as often as required. The members should be sworn to act impartially, and they should examine the candidates designated by the heads of Departments, as to character, moral habits, knowledge of accounts, penmanship, capacity to write good business letters, &c.; and the heads of Departments should be limited in their appointments to the lowest grade of clerks to such applicants as had satisfactorily passed their examination. The secretary of the board should probably be a permanent officer, and keep a minute of the proceedings, or record them. He might be selected from one of the offices, and receive a compensation of a few hundred dollars per annum for this additional duty.

Such a plan, the committee declared, would diminish the number of applicants, protect the heads of departments, and insure justice "by rendering the appointment of the most worthy at least probable." [13] No such reform ensued for a decade.

On March 7, 1851, the six Secretaries of departments were directed by a Senate resolution to report a plan for classifying clerks, adjusting their salaries, and providing for "a fair and impartial examination of the qualifications of clerks, and for promoting them from one grade to another upon a due regard to qualifications and services." [14] On May 3, 1852, the "Plan of the Five Secretaries" (Webster declining to join) was submitted to the Senate and was substantially enacted into law in 1853 as part of the civil and diplomatic appropriation act for 1853–54.[15]

The act was not as far-reaching as either Senator Hunter or the Secretaries had proposed. In his communication to the six Secretaries, Hunter envisaged an entrance class limited to young men under eighteen who would be paid a training-grade salary and who would supply the manpower for promotion to all the higher clerical grades. Each such grade would be filled by promotion from the grade below. This was a genuine closed career system, and Hunter emphasized this fact by proposing annual salary

13 House Report 741, 27th Cong., 2d sess., p. 24 (May 23, 1842).

14 *Senate Journal,* 31st Cong., 2d sess., p. 288 (March 7, 1851).

15 Senate Ex. Doc. 69, 32d Cong., 1st sess.; 10 Stat. 189, sec. 3 (March 3, 1853).

increments within each grade up to the minimum pay of the next higher level.[16]

The five Secretaries introduced their plan with an endorsement of "the importance of securing, more uniformly, a high grade of qualifications, and a more permanent tenure to the clerkships in the several departments. . . ." They recommended departmental boards to examine candidates nominated by the head of the department as to their health and physical energy, education, skill, and other qualifications. No person was to be eligible for appointment without a certificate from the board of examination, nor to be eligible for promotion without examination and a certificate that he was "fully qualified." Exceptionally the door was left open for independent appointments to the higher grades before examining all the lower grade clerks, but the cause for such unusual appointments had to be entered on the records of the agency. The five Secretaries were not too confident about the soundness of such an innovation; several entertained doubts in regard to the practicability or utility of the plan, but they agreed "with some hesitation . . . to unite in reporting it as worthy of trial. . . ." [17]

Daniel Webster, Secretary of State, refused to try the plan and did not sign the report. He thought examinations inexpedient for either original appointment or promotion, preferring to rely on the opinions of "the more experienced clerks." Webster noted that State Department clerks were more than "mere penmen and copyists . . . they should understand the modern languages, especially the French and Spanish; be persons of literary attainments, and should possess a good knowledge of geography and statistics and the laws and history of their own country, and a quick capacity for learning." Webster, however, stood strongly for permanence of tenure: "Few things are more prejudicial to the public service than the removal from office of experienced and faithful clerks of proved ability and industry. This is a general truth verified by all experience both in courts of law and in public office." [18]

This is a convenient point to notice a few other objections.

16 Reprinted in Senate Ex. Doc. 7, 32d Cong., 2d sess., pp. 16–17.

17 Senate Ex. Doc. 69, 32d Cong., 1st sess., pp. 1–2 (May 1, 1852).

18 Webster, *Writings and Speeches* (National ed.), XIV, 552–53 (June 30, 1852).

The most thoughtful was made by the treasurer of the United States, John Sloane. He pointed out that the real evil was not failure to secure competent clerks but lay in the fact that no degree of merit could insure retention in office. He argued that there was only one effective remedy: to organize the clerical force "as a permanent corps," after the manner of the army and navy. These branches, he declared, "are regarded as scientific, and the power of removal . . . is by that system of organization done away with, much to the peace and harmony of the members, and eminently to the great interest of the nation." [19] The first auditor raised another objection, that an examination board would be ineffective since only the department head and chief clerk would have adequate knowledge of the qualifications of employees.[20] Senator John Pettit criticized vesting in the hands of a board "of three men already in office the power to say who shall . . . come in and who shall stay out. Necessarily it will produce a system of favoritism." [21] The basic objection, that the plan would curtail the power of political managers, was not voiced. To the contrary, James Buchanan wrote, "The new law is excellent, provided it be executed according to its spirit. . . ." [22]

Webster was the principal executive dissenter whose views were reported in the public documents. The quality of departmental opinion supporting reform was impressive and may be judged by the views spread on the record by the Postmaster General, Nathan K. Hall.[23] After stressing the importance of a probationary trial on the job, he continued:

> I take leave to suggest, in conclusion, that probably no observing or thoughtful man has ever been long in charge of an Executive De-

[19] National Archives, Treasurer Correspondence 1818–1866, letter of Sept. 13, 1851.

[20] National Archives, First Auditor Reports and Correspondence, 1834–1877, letter of March 7, 1851.

[21] *Congressional Globe,* 32d Cong., 2d sess., p. 897 (Feb. 28, 1853).

[22] National Archives, Fifth Auditor Correspondence, 1834–1866, letter of March 30, 1853.

[23] Senate Ex. Doc. 69, 32d Cong., 1st sess., pp. 12–18 (March 3, 1852). Hall was a law partner of President Fillmore and was made Postmaster General less than two weeks after Fillmore succeeded General Taylor in the White House. Fillmore was anxious for renomination and Hall was active in his preconvention campaign. His views as executive head of a large agency clashed with his obligations as a political supporter of his chief.

partment or Bureau, without becoming satisfied that the proper standard of clerical qualification and performance will not be established in them, and the public business performed in the best manner until the clerk can reasonably entertain a confident expectation of continued employment. If his continuance in office and his promotion be made to depend on his good behaviour and assiduity in the performance of his duties, a motive is offered him which uniformly produces improvement and excellence in all the other employments of life, and could not fail to do so in this.

Men originally qualified to perform properly the duties of a clerk become, with each years' experience, more competent and useful. Those of them, therefore, who by devotion and assiduity render their services valuable to the country, certainly should, if possible, be protected from arbitrary and capricious removal. This would, in my opinion, more than any other measure, tend to elevate the character of the force employed in the public offices, and facilitate the business devolving on them.

I am unable to recommend any plan likely to accomplish this object more effectually than to secure by preliminary examination and sufficient trial, under a temporary appointment, the employment of men whose acquirements, physical endowments and business capacity shall be fully equal to their position. When to these qualifications—with two or three year's experience—are added *industry and faithfulness,* the services of such a clerk will be found so necessary, not only to the proper despatch of business, but to the comfort and convenience of the head of the department or office in which he is employed, that the probability of his removal, except for cause, will be greatly diminished.

Thus relieved from the apprehension of removal from political reasons merely, the clerk will have no motive for becoming a political partizan; but on the contrary will labor with devotion and zeal to promote the public good without reference to party divisions, or to the hopes and fears which are often connected with them.

. . . I believe it to be important, in every point of view, that the clerks employed in the several departments of the government should be withdrawn from active participation in the political struggles which so frequently agitate the country. . . .[24]

The accounting officers were also warmly in favor of the proposed clerical career service. The second comptroller, Edward J. Phelps, reported to the Secretary of the Treasury:

24 *Ibid.,* pp. 17–18.

I take the liberty to add a word in regard to the propriety of the reorganization suggested in the resolution. I think it is imperatively demanded by the public interest. Whatever may be the character and efficiency of heads of departments and of offices, it is upon the industry, fidelity, and capacity of their clerks that reliance must necessarily be placed for that correct administration of the details of business on which the prosperity of the government so largely depends. It is idle to expect these qualities, as a general rule, from men whose tenure of office is that of caprice, whose salaries are insufficient, and to whom no prospect of promotion or advancement is open. All human experience is to the contrary. And where honorable exceptions are found to exist (and they are many) they only add to the justice of the proposed reform, without detracting from its general necessity.

Regular grades of clerkships ought to be established, to the lowest of which all new appointments should be made. Promotions should take place from one grade to another, as nearly in the order of seniority as the merits of incumbents would justify. The tenure of office should be practically permanent, except where cause for removal exists; and the salaries of the higher classes should be such as to offer an inducement for usefulness and improvement. Such a system could be readily established; would diminish the expenses of the departments; would do justice to many deserving men; and would, in my judgment, go further to promote economy, efficiency, and despatch in the management of public business, than any measure that has ever been adopted.[25]

Views such as these were expressed by Secretary of the Interior Alexander H. H. Stuart,[26] Secretary of the Treasury Thomas Corwin,[27] the register of the Treasury,[28] the acting treasurer,[29] and others. Nearly everyone in the administrative service approved the main features of the system—examination, tenure, graded pay, and systematic promotion. The chief criticism was with regard to the age limitation of eighteen years on original appointment to class one. This requirement was not included in the legislation.

By the terms of the act of 1853 the clerks in the respective de-

25 Senate Ex. Doc. 7, 32d Cong., 2d sess., p. 13 (Sept. 13, 1852).

26 Senate Ex. Doc. 3, 32d Cong., 2d sess., p. 3 (Dec. 7, 1852).

27 Senate Ex. Doc. 7, 32d Cong., 2d sess., p. 2 (Dec. 21, 1852).

28 *Ibid.*, p. 6. The register complained particularly about the evil consequences of appointing new clerks over the heads of the older men.

29 *Ibid.*, p. 10.

partments (State excepted) were arranged in four classes, identified by their respective pay scales.[30] The number in each class in each office was expressly stated in the statute, and was specifically declared to be "the whole of the permanent clerical force" of the respective agencies. The head of the department was allowed to alter the distribution of clerks among his bureaus, but not to exceed the number of each class fixed by law. The provisions with respect to examinations follow. "No clerk shall be appointed in either of the four classes until after he has been examined and qualified by a Board, to consist of three examiners, one of them to be the Chief of the Bureau or office into which he is to be appointed, and the two others to be selected by the head of the Department to which the said clerk will be assigned." This language required all incumbent clerks as well as applicants to meet the examination before being assimilated in the new clerical classes. The first set of examinations was held in June 1853.

The act applied to just under seven hundred clerks in the departmental offices in Washington, of which the three largest groups were the General Land Office (106), the office of the auditor for the Post Office (101), and the Postmaster General's office (78). Postmasters and their clerks were not affected, nor were the mass of clerks in customhouses, Indian offices, land offices, and other field establishments. Chief clerks were not included. The act did not establish the rule of open competition for applicants for original appointment; only those persons were examined who were nominated by the head of the department or office. The examination merely attested qualification, not superior qualification. The act did not specify the subjects of examination, and did not organize a standing board of examiners, even for each department. It brought no new restraining influence on the *nominating* power. It did not prescribe a system of promotions. It did, however, assume minimum standards that would have to be met by partisans, and to bureau chiefs and clerks it also connoted permanent tenure.

30 10 Stat. 189, sec. 3. The compensation features of the act are dealt with elsewhere. In addition to the State Department were also excluded the Attorney General's office, the census office, the Coast Survey, the Observatory, the offices of the superintendent of public printing, the commissioner of public buildings, the archi-

THE FIRST CLERICAL EXAMINATIONS

In accordance with the requirements of the act of March 3, 1853, *incumbent* clerks were required to stand examination before July 1 of that year. Study of the manuscript departmental records in the National Archives reveals that during the month of June the Secretaries appointed examining boards which by July 1 had made their reports as to all incumbent clerks. Secretary of the Treasury James Guthrie appointed eleven examining boards for the Treasury offices, and instructed them to ascertain whether each clerk was adequate to the "fit, prompt and proper performance" of his duties. The examination appears to have been conducted orally, although in the office of the commissioner of customs questions were sent to each clerk to be answered in his own handwriting before the oral examination.

With few exceptions the incumbent staff was found qualified. In the quaint language of the examining board in the fifth auditor's office, it was reported that "Mr. Houston is entirely master of the business under his charge & fully qualified for his public duties"; and that Mr. Devlin was also entirely master of his business, "with a cast of mind peculiarly qualified for his duties." An occasional clerk was found slow, and others burdened by ill health; and in one or two cases the examining boards found an unhappy clerk wholly unqualified.[31]

The act of 1853 contemplated that every applicant for clerical appointment in the agencies covered by it would also be subject to examination, after nomination by the head of the department. There is evidence that in the accounting offices this practice was followed until the passage of the Pendleton Act in 1883. The sixth auditor, William F. Phillips, reported in 1854 that the board of examiners in his office required applicants to be able to write an ordinary business letter in a fair and legible hand, to use the first four rules of arithmetic with ordinary celerity, and to evince some knowledge of the principles of accounting.[32]

---

tect and superintendent of the Capitol extension. Most of these offices had small clerical staffs. *National Intelligencer,* April 16, 1853.

31 National Archives, Fifth Auditor Correspondence, 1834–1866, report of June 25, 1853.

32 Senate Ex. Doc. 2, 33d Cong., 2d sess., p. 98 (Nov. 21, 1854).

In 1855 he reported that during the two years preceding, eighty-six applicants had been examined and twenty-five rejected.[33] Scattered data in the files of the auditors' offices refer to the examinations of individual clerks thereafter. A Treasury department form letter has been seen which was used in 1865 and presumably earlier that testifies to the continuance of the examinations. In the following copy the italicized words were written by hand.

> By direction of the Secretary, you will receive herewith a designation to a First Class Clerkship in *the Office of the Fifth Auditor of the Treasury.*
>
> This designation is for examination by a Board of Departmental Officers. It is indispensable to the satisfactory transaction of the public business that the entire competency of gentlemen to be employed in it should be thus ascertained, and the examination must necessarily be strict. Should you pass it to the satisfaction of the Board, you will receive an appointment as a First Class Clerk.
>
> Unconditional loyalty, as well as competency, is of course a condition of appointment.[34]

To pursue the matter briefly, a House report of 1868 demonstrated that clerks were appointed throughout the Treasury Department by examination, except "female clerks" who were exempt. Thus the commissioner of customs stated that he conducted the examinations himself or by delegation under his supervision. The examination dealt particularly with arithmetic and bookkeeping, but also history, grammar, and geography. The fourth auditor included these subjects and spelling and composition.[35] In 1882 the Senate Committee on Civil Service and Retrenchment (Senator George H. Pendleton, chairman) recorded the continuance of these examinations, although arguing that they were inadequate. The language of his report indicated they were given throughout the departmental service: "The examinations provided for . . . are still made, in form at least, as a condition for appointment in those departments." [36]

[33] Senate Ex. Doc. 2, 34th Cong., 1st sess., p. 165 (Nov. 20, 1855).

[34] National Archives, Fifth Auditor Correspondence, 1834–1866, letter of May 9, 1865.

[35] House Report 47, 40th Cong., 2d sess., pp. 16 ff. (May 25, 1868).

[36] Senate Report 576, 47th Cong., 1st sess., pp. iv–v (May 15, 1882).

RESULTS

To return to the 1850's and the early years of the examination system, it may be noted that the Treasury was well satisfied with the results. Secretary Guthrie found that there had been a great improvement in the clerical force, that the examinations had secured more capable men for the first class, and that promotions had been governed by capacity and efficiency. ". . . there exists commendable industry, capacity, efficiency, and, it is believed, integrity in the corps employed." [37] Auditor William F. Phillips stated that the efficiency, general character, and deportment of his clerks had been materially improved as a result of the "rigid system of *examination*," and that he could report "a spirit of emulation to secure promotion, not by political or personal favor, but by that moral, intellectual and clerical improvement and qualification, of which it is the appropriate official acknowledgment and reward." [38] Phillips repeated his satisfaction with the new system in 1854, noting an improved morale among his clerks, protected "from the apprehension of being supplanted or overslaughed by untried and inexperienced men. . . ." [39] Other officials made similar declarations of approval.

The spirit of reform also raised its head briefly but feebly in the consular service. In 1856 at the suggestion of Secretary of State Marcy, Congress authorized the appointment of twenty-five consular pupils, and required each of them to furnish the Secretary of State with satisfactory evidence "by examination or otherwise" of his fitness for office.[40] Before any such qualified pupils could be appointed, Congress repealed this statute.[41] Consular appointments continued on the basis of party preference.

The impetus for reform by examination was not great. It was not, as it later became, a public issue. Neither the Democratic nor Whig parties had advocated an examination system, and there had been practically no prior discussion or agitation in the country, or in the leading journals of opinion. No particular

37 Senate Ex. Doc. 2, 33d Cong., 2d sess., p. 20 (Dec. 4, 1854).

38 Senate Ex. Doc. 2, 33d Cong., 1st sess., p. 138 (Nov. 19, 1853).

39 Senate Ex. Doc. 2, 33d Cong., 2d sess., p. 98 (Nov. 21, 1854).

40 11 Stat. 52, sec. 7 (August 18, 1856).

41 11 Stat. 159 (Feb. 7, 1857). This episode is described by Henry Brooks Adams, "Civil-Service Reform," in *North American Review*, CIX (1869), 461–65.

scandal immediately preceded the enactment of 1853. It was, however, in the main stream of historic development, reaching back to the tradition of the Federalists and the Jeffersonians, and fortified by the successful experience of the army and navy medical corps. The corollary of the examination system stated by Treasurer John Sloane, that the public service should be recognized as belonging to the country, not the party, was not yet ready for acceptance. The career system that continued to exist was overshadowed by the partisan system that encroached upon it. It is remarkable, in the light of the attitudes that generally prevailed during the middle years of the nineteenth century, that Senator Hunter's reforms continued until the Civil Service Act of 1883.

CHAPTER TWENTY

Theory and Practice of Compensation

The responsibility for establishing rates of pay for all classes of government officers and employees, excluding day laborers, was jealously guarded by Congress. The characteristic attitudes of Congressmen in favor of economy and strict limits on the number of employees developed at an early date and flourished during the Jacksonian era, with some recognition on the part of a few leaders that economy could be pressed too far. On the other hand there emerged the characteristic attitudes of top executives in favor of liberal payment for faithful service and for a staff numerous enough to cope with the steadily increasing volume of business. These differing opinions gave rise to a continuous struggle between the legislative and executive branches. Now also appeared a third, if still minor force in the conflict, the organized activity of employees, petitioning Congress for improvements in pay, and discovering endless subterfuges for "extra allowances" to mitigate the parsimony of Congress.[1]

The general base for clerical salaries in force when Jackson became President was contained in the act of 1818. It established five pay rates for clerks ranging from $800 to $1,600 a year, and two for chief clerks, $1,700 and $2,000. There were no pay scales. Two general revisions of these rates were made in 1836 and 1853 respectively.[2]

1 This chapter does not deal with the compensation and allowances of army and navy officers. There was constant complaint about their inadequacy and a considerable volume of legislation.

2 3 Stat. 445 (April 20, 1818); 5 Stat. 80, secs. 43–44 (July 2, 1836); 10 Stat. 189, sec. 3 (March 3, 1853).

The settlement of 1836 established three basic annual rates for clerks, $1,000, $1,200, and $1,400; a rate of $1,600 for principal clerks; and a figure of $2,000 for chief clerks. The improvement in compensation was not substantial but the lowest figure of the 1818 enactment was dropped and a somewhat larger proportion of employees in the middle rate for clerks ($1,200) was authorized.

The settlement of 1853 established four basic annual clerical rates, reintroducing a "training-grade" figure of $900, and increasing the other rates to $1,200, $1,500, and $1,800 respectively. Chief clerks in the lesser agencies also received $1,800, but in the six departments were raised to $2,200. There was consequently a moderate tendency for pay levels to rise during these thirty years, but against much reluctance on the part of Congress.

CONGRESSIONAL AND EXECUTIVE ATTITUDES

Congress. The traditional position of Congress on pay rates was stated by Senator John Davis in 1836 for the Committee on Post Offices and Post Roads. "The committee are for adhering to the old republican doctrine of economy in the expenditure of public money. They are for preserving something like an equality between the State and Federal Governments. . . ." Davis thought the influence of high salaries "in all respects pernicious," by creating expectations among those paid less, and by attracting well-qualified persons from the state governments. "They are," he declared, "literally bought out of State service, for very subordinate stations, by the salaries given." [3] Millard Fillmore had developed the same argument two years earlier, with apt illustrations from the state of New York, already known as the Empire State. High salaries in the federal government, he declared, were in effect "offering a bribe for every man of talents and enterprise to abandon the service for the State Governments and obtain an office in the General Government." He recommended to Congress the same rule "that every man adopted in his own business; to pay that amount which would command the services of a person of competent talents, skill, integrity, and qualifications, to discharge the duties of the office, and no more." [4]

3 *Register of Debates*, 24th Cong., 1st sess., pp. 1772–73 (June 14, 1836).
4 *Fillmore Papers*, I, 96 (April 17, 1834).

Representative Francis Smith of Maine, speaking for the Committee on Ways and Means, put the issue on more philosophical grounds. "Every Government, like every individual, has a moral being superior to its physical composition; and its moral being, like that of an individual, is susceptible of acquiring habits of lavish expenditure and extravagance in its operations . . . all political history concurs in bearing testimony, that *every* Government has a tendency to such habits, and, therefore, requires constant watching to preserve its own purity." [5] And on another occasion Senator William Allen of Ohio remarked, "Sir, there are two things that never go back: one the increase of officers, the other the increase of their salaries. We never decrease officers; we never decrease salaries." [6]

In the course of the 1852 debate on the compensation and classification act of 1853, Congressman Orin Fowler of Massachusetts strenuously opposed any improvement in salaries that, he said, were "high enough now." "If the clerks, and other employees of the Government, are not satisfied with their present positions, there are thousands upon thousands who would rejoice to take their places, and even to pay a handsome percentage for the privilege." [7] Congressman Charles Skelton of New Jersey echoed these opinions: "I cannot forget," he declared, "that I represent the mechanics, and working men, and farmers of a State where there is not one man in a thousand who can make $500 a year; and it is their money that you now call upon me to take out of their pockets to increase the salaries of these men who get $1,000 a year. . . . They tell us that they cannot live here. Well, let them leave, and live as people do in other portions of the country. We can find plenty of men to fill their places . . . and be glad of the job." [8]

In the 1852 debate also appeared a tendency to do more for the less well-paid clerks than for their supervisors. Labor had become politically significant. Congressman Andrew Johnson of Tennessee moved to increase the pay of mechanics and laborers by 20 per cent. Johnson was eloquent in his claim. "The man

5 House Report 297, 24th Cong., 1st sess., pp. 1–2 (Feb. 10, 1836).
6 *Congressional Globe,* 30th Cong., 2d sess., p. 670 (March 3, 1849).
7 *Ibid.,* 32d Cong., 1st sess., p. 2165 (August 10, 1852).
8 *Ibid.,* p. 2167.

who wears the dinge of the shop or dust of the field upon his garments is never thought of or cared for by this House, except upon occasions when the Government needs taxes. . . . I should like to know why the men who work in your navy-yards and forge your anchors . . . men who wield the broad-axe, chisel, and hammer, not only five hours in the day, but ten hours, at $1.50 and $2 a day, should not have twenty per cent also added to their days' wages?" [9]

Reluctance to increase salaries or the number of employees was balanced to some extent by the bare necessity of getting business done and of protecting the government against dishonesty induced by insufficient pay. Senator James Buchanan asserted that he was as anxious for economy as any of his colleagues, "yet he would be sorry to introduce the spirit of economy to such an extreme as would induce the collectors of the revenue to become dishonest." [10] Jackson's friend, Cave Johnson, speaking for the House Committee on Ways and Means, also took a statesmanlike view of the problem, arguing that the principle of economy was not inconsistent with but in fact demanded "a fair remuneration" for public services.[11] The House Committee on Commerce declared in 1836 that "inadequate compensation is inconsistent with the true interests of the country." [12] Responsible Congressmen like Gentry of Tennessee concurred in the opinion that it was "a wise economy to give a fair compensation for the governmental employees." [13] Such statements left open the decision as to what constituted a fair compensation.

The executive. The views of department heads emphasized their official needs rather than economy and the reduction of expenditures. Postmaster General Amos Kendall sent in a sensible report to Congress in 1836 based on the knowledge that clerical salaries were then so inadequate "that a large proportion, probably a considerable majority of the clerks of this Department, are hopeless insolvents, and many of them are put to great

9 *Ibid.*, p. 2166.

10 Buchanan, *Works*, II, 413 (Feb. 10, 1835).

11 House Report 641, 24th Cong., 1st sess., p. 8 (May 10, 1836). Johnson made in this document an early if not the first analysis of the elements that are to be considered in fixing pay levels.

12 House Report 480, 24th Cong., 1st sess., p. 1 (March 24, 1836).

13 *Congressional Globe*, 32d Cong., 1st sess., p. 2164 (August 10, 1852).

straits even to subsist themselves and families on their present compensation." He laid down the following general rule: "It seems but right that men of talents and great business qualifications, who voluntarily relinquish all high aspirations, and content themselves with the distinction which is to be gained within the walls of the Executive Departments, should be paid by their country a compensation so liberal that they will not be obliged to raise their children in ignorance, and leave their families in want."[14]

Secretary of War Jefferson Davis made some analogous statements with special reference to the compensation of army officers that had general applicability and that well reflected executive attitudes. ". . . a policy," he wrote in his annual report for 1854, "which confines so large a body of intelligent and instructed men to a rate of compensation below that given in the ordinary avocations of life, must tend to drive from the military service its more active and efficient officers."[15] Two years later he wrote, "There is surely no economy in a practice which must, in the end, drive the more active and intellectual from a service which they adorn . . . to seek a competent support in some other pursuit."[16]

Both Congressmen and heads of departments were aware of the desirability of graduating pay according to the value of services performed, but no adequate procedures to achieve the rule of equal pay for equal work were invented. In 1838 five heads of departments and twenty-two other officials signed an address to Congress advocating an increase in pay and compensation graduated according to the services required.[17] In 1852 Postmaster General Nathan K. Hall stated the rule which was to be progressively achieved in a later age: that salaries should be "in proportion to the amount, responsibility, importance, and value of the service rendered."[18]

14 Senate Doc. 362, 24th Cong., 1st sess., p. 4 (May 9, 1836).

15 Davis, *Letters, Papers and Speeches,* II, 397 (Dec. 4, 1854).

16 *Ibid.,* III, 75 (Dec. 1, 1856).

17 Senate Doc. 239, 25th Cong., 2d sess., p. 1 (Feb. 19, 1838).

18 Senate Ex. Doc. 69, 32d Cong., 1st sess., p. 13 (March 3, 1852).

ADEQUACY OF COMPENSATION

During the middle years of the 1830's the cost of living rose substantially. The index, calculated at 58 in 1829, dropped briefly, and then rose to 60 in 1835, 68 in 1836, and 72 in 1837.[19] The clerks and other employees felt the pinch and began to petition Congress for redress. No less distinguished a sponsor than John Quincy Adams introduced the first petition in 1834—as Adams suspected, to discharge a service believed by members of Jackson's Cabinet "not likely to be very popular." [20] A second general petition was presented in 1836; [21] and a number of requests from special groups appeared during 1836 and 1837. A parallel situation developed in the early 1850's following the price dislocation subsequent to the discovery of gold in California. The cost of living index stood at 54 in 1850, but shot up to 67 in 1855, and to 70 in 1857. The public service again faced a compensation crisis.

Before recording congressional action it is convenient to survey briefly the adequacy of prevailing compensation in the 1830's. Waiving the opinion of the petitioning clerks, we may note some official statements of their executive officers. Postmaster General Kendall reported that he employed in 1836 six clerks at $800, twenty-three at $1,000, and eight at salaries up to $1,400. He recommended higher rates and told Congress, "A salary of $900 will support a single man in this city, and if he be prudent, afford him a moderate income. A married man without children can barely subsist upon it." Even the rates he proposed, he said, would afford little more than subsistence.[22] At almost the same time Cave Johnson reported for the House Committee on Ways and Means that a salary of $1,000 or less was "wholly inadequate for a family of ordinary size." [23]

Families of ordinary size were not always the rule—at least according to later standards! The second comptroller reported, among others, the case of his chief clerk, John Moulder, salary

19 *Historical Statistics of the United States,* p. 235.

20 Adams, *Memoirs,* IX, 66–67 (Jan. 3, 1834).

21 House Doc. 196, 24th Cong., 1st sess. (April 1, 1836).

22 Senate Doc. 362, 24th Cong., 1st sess., pp. 1–3 (May 9, 1836).

23 House Report 641, 24th Cong., 1st sess., p. 3 (May 10, 1836).

$1,700, with a wife and eleven children; Jonathan Seaver, salary $1,400, with a wife and five children; John Davis, salary $1,400, supporting a family consisting of his wife and seven children; J. L. Cathcart, salary $1,150, with a wife and nine children. Four other clerks were less blessed, but the messenger with a salary of $700 had to provide for a wife and six children.[24]

Quartermaster General Jesup complained of the "entire inadequacy" of the salaries of the civilian clerks in the quartermaster corps.[25] The acting surgeon general declared that no class of persons in the government service was so badly underpaid as the hospital stewards, who had to make up and administer the physicians' prescriptions. ". . . it is necessary," said Benjamin King, "they should be intelligent, honest, and sober"; and he declared he could not secure such minimum standards at prevailing rates of compensation.[26] Other executives in the 1830's added their corroboration of the inadequacy of the settlement of 1818.[27]

Convincing evidence was also produced from the account book of Jonathan Seaver, described by the second comptroller as "a gentleman in my office, who keeps a regular diary of his expenses, and who is proverbial for economy and correctness. . . ."[28] Seaver had a family of three grown persons, five children, and two servants (part-time); his children had been taught at home in their early years and thus caused no expense for education; he paid neither house rent nor pew rent; he served neither wine nor spirituous liquor; and he gave no dinners. His expenses for 1833 were $1,323.61; for 1834, $1,120.72; and for 1835 (set out in fascinating detail), $1,447.96.[29] House rent would have added another substantial amount.

Customs employees were able to secure endorsement of their claims to better pay from merchants and importers. One hundred and twenty-two citizens of Boston stated their opinion that

24 Senate Doc. 355, 24th Cong., 1st sess., pp. 2–3 (April 29, 1836).

25 Senate Doc. 1, 24th Cong., 1st sess., p. 79 (Nov. 6, 1835).

26 Senate Doc. 1, 25th Cong., 2d sess., p. 265 (Nov. 29, 1837).

27 See for detail Senate Doc. 355, 24th Cong., 1st sess., *passim* (May 4, 1836). In 1851 Fillmore had nothing but declinations for the office of commissioner to China at $6,000 a year, but without outfit. He also had great difficulty in finding anyone willing to take the office of private land claims commissioner in California at $6,000 a year. Richardson, *Messages,* V, 122, 126–27 (Dec. 2, 1851).

28 Senate Doc. 355, 24th Cong., 1st sess., p. 2 (April 29, 1836).

29 *Ibid.,* pp. 3–12.

the compensation of customs officers was not an equivalent for their services nor sufficient to meet the ordinary expense of a family. Sixty-six merchants of New Orleans gave figures to demonstrate the inadequacy of salaries for customs employees in that port.[30]

The relation of government compensation rates to corresponding rates in private employment is difficult to establish. It was frequently asserted that army engineers were seriously underpaid in comparison with salaries available for employees of railroads or canals. In 1859 Senator Jefferson Davis, recently Secretary of War, reported that the best army officers were constantly tempted by better paid civilian opportunities, especially in railroads.[31] Secretary of War Cass declared in 1835 that civilian engineers could not be hired at government rates for short-time service.[32] A post office cartographer was appointed under the designation of a clerk in 1836 at a clerk's salary of $1,200, but, said Kendall, "We cannot expect to keep him long at that salary, because his skill and talents will soon enable him to command better wages elsewhere." [33]

Resignation to accept business opportunities was a new phenomenon, still exceptional but more and more frequent. Charles S. West in Treasury resigned to engage in commercial pursuits, for which, said the *National Intelligencer,* "by his long and varied experience, he is eminently qualified." [34] Resignation followed by private practice as claims attorney was also frequent. Horatio King, long an important figure in the General Post Office, became an attorney before the executive departments and international commissions after 1861.[35] Peter Grayson Washington followed the same course after retiring as assistant secretary of the Treasury in 1857. Charles Lanman, Webster's private secretary in the State Department, resigned in 1853 from the copyright bureau "to devote himself hereafter exclusively to the pen and pencil." [36]

30 House Report 480, 24th Cong., 1st sess., pp. 12, 29 (March 24, 1836).
31 Jefferson Davis, *Letters, Papers and Speeches,* III, 559–60.
32 Senate Doc. 1, 24th Cong., 1st sess., p. 44 (Nov. 30, 1835).
33 House Doc. 153, 24th Cong., 2d sess., p. 1 (Feb. 7, 1837).
34 *National Intelligencer,* Nov. 3, 1853.
35 Horatio King, *Turning on the Light,* p. 15.
36 *National Intelligencer,* Oct. 1, 1853.

Advocates of more liberal rates of compensation were embarrassed by the undoubted fact that clerkships were eagerly sought by hundreds of applicants in good times and bad. Kendall had one explanation for this seeming inconsistency, i.e., that these applicants were "almost exclusively young unmarried men—men in desperate circumstances, or men who are incompetent to make a living elsewhere. . . ." [37] Another explanation, in part, might have been found in the expectation of enjoying various perquisites of office that supplemented many an official salary.

EXTRA ALLOWANCES

From an early date great ingenuity had been employed by clerks and some of their betters for earning extra allowances. Congress frowned upon such evasions and in the compensation act of 1818 had, it was supposed, legislated them out of existence with the flat declaration that "no higher or other allowance shall be made to any clerk . . . than is authorized by this act." [38] Jackson's executive heads found widespread evasion of the letter and spirit of this prohibition, both in the armed forces and in the civilian service. With respect to navy officers, Amos Kendall, then fourth auditor in charge of navy accounts, told Congress, "The minds of officers, instead of being devoted to the interests and glory of the Navy, are employed upon the means of persuading the Secretary or accounting officers to eke out their emoluments by additional allowances." [39]

Law enforcement officials were apparently among the most persistent claimants for extra compensation. By way of illustration, the district attorney for Maryland requested an extra fee of $100 for the arrest of a mail robber; [40] the marshal of Missouri asked extra compensation for the arrest of a counterfeiter; [41] another district attorney, Hogg, claimed (and was allowed) extra compensation for attending a state court on federal business; [42]

37 Senate Doc. 362, 24th Cong., 1st sess., pp. 3–4 (May 9, 1836).

38 3 Stat. 445, sec. 9 (April 20, 1818).

39 Senate Doc. 1, 21st Cong., 1st sess., pp. 271–72 (Nov. 30, 1829).

40 National Archives, Treasury Department, Miscellaneous Letters to the President, Set A, p. 24 (Nov. 28, 1834).

41 National Archives, Treasury Department, Letters to Cabinet and Bureaus, Set B, No. 1, p. 90 (May 20, 1834).

42 *Ibid.*, p. 192 (Feb. 24, 1835).

and Jared Ingersoll, one-time district attorney for Pennsylvania, recovered a sum due from a person indebted to the United States, charged a fee of $1,000 for his legal services, and retained the balance of the recovery to pay himself for an earlier claim in his favor that the auditor had disallowed.[43]

The treasurer of the United States and the register of the Treasury Department allowed themselves one cent each for signing Treasury notes. When this was discovered, Congress prohibited the practice, but a year later they still continued to receive this extra allowance by reason of a barefaced evasion of the spirit, although not the letter, of the prohibition.[44] The law did not enforce itself.

The collector, naval officer, and surveyor of the port of New York retained for themselves one-half the fines and penalties for violation of the revenue acts which, for the year ending June 30, 1853, amounted to almost $20,000. The Treasury had acquiesced in this practice despite an act of Congress in 1841 that purported to prevent it.[45] Collectors of customs had been given an extra allowance since the earliest days for serving as superintendents of lighthouses, and a few of them earned an allowance as agents for the marine hospitals. Press of work in the Philadelphia customhouse brought extra compensation to deputy collectors and deputy naval officers who took clerical work home after hours—"at an expense of rest, light, and fuel." The Secretary of the Treasury thought the arrangement a dubious one, but the House Committee on Commerce endorsed it.[46] Master workmen in the navy yards received an extra compensation for instructing the apprentices.[47]

Payment of invalid and revolutionary pensioners had been an uncompensated duty of the Second Bank of the United States. The termination of relations with the Bank forced the government to find other agents, and Congress required the state banks holding government deposits, or one of their officers, to perform this service, also without compensation. The initial reaction of

43 The incident was alluded to in House Report 276, 23d Cong., 1st sess., p. 9 (Feb. 21, 1834).

44 Jefferson Davis, *Letters, Papers and Speeches,* III, 224 (May 13, 1858).

45 Senate Ex. Doc. 2, 33d Cong., 1st sess., p. 12 (Dec. 6, 1853).

46 House Report 257, 24th Cong., 2d sess., pp. 1–2 (Feb. 3, 1837).

47 Senate Ex. Doc. 13, 36th Cong., 2d sess., p. 1 (March 2, 1861).

these agents was to refuse the assignment,[48] but a satisfactory arrangement was invented that was disclosed by Daniel Webster in 1838. The Treasury advanced the necessary funds six months before they were needed; the pension agent consequently had the use of half the whole amount of pensions paid annually at his office; and for the Boston agency Webster calculated this perquisite was worth more than $9,000 per annum.[49] Webster thought this mode of compensation, "the worst in the world, as it keeps the funds of the government always at hazard."

Clerks were also busy improving their stated salaries. A small annual appropriation was regularly made for Mediterranean passports and sea letters; it was applied as extra compensation to the Treasury clerk who transmitted them to the collectors.[50] Secretary of the Treasury Louis McLane somewhat naïvely reported to Congress in 1832, "It will be perceived that the salaries of the [customs] clerks are generally low, and it has consequently been usual to distribute out of the surplus emoluments of the custom-house, at the end of each year, amongst those officers, such further sum as may be deemed adequate to afford them a reasonable compensation for their services." [51] As late as 1860 the New York post office clerks handling foreign mail retained the postage collected by them on the wharf immediately before the departure of the mail, a sum amounting to about $1,500 a year.[52]

These and other examples that could be produced demonstrate how difficult it was for Congress to find a formula that would put an end to extra allowances. The pressure on lowly paid clerks, customs employees, and other agents was too great, and a sympathetic executive winked at practices that could hardly be squared with the law. Congress nevertheless did not intend clerks to evade the compensation standards it deemed appro-

48 For example, see Senate Doc. 404, 25th Cong., 2d sess., p. 59 (letter of Feb. 9, 1836); and *ibid.*, pp. 59–60 (letter of May 5, 1836).

49 Webster, *Writings and Speeches* (National ed.), VIII, 124–25, remarks in the Senate on the Commonwealth Bank, Boston, Feb. 6, 1838.

50 National Archives, Treasury Department, Letters to Cabinet and Bureaus, Set B, No. 1, p. 175 (Jan. 9, 1834).

51 House Doc. 202, 22d Cong., 1st sess., pp. 1–2 (April 9, 1832). The report showed that this practice was generally confined to New York under Samuel Swartwout.

52 House Ex. Doc. 91, 36th Cong., 1st sess., p. 17 (May 25, 1860).

priate, or to allow imposition upon the public with which government agents had to deal, and enacted many rules to plug up one gap after another. In 1835 naval officers were given improved remuneration, extra rations were eliminated, and allowances of all kinds were terminated—including servants, clothing and rations for servants, rent of quarters and furniture, light and fuel, and transportation of baggage.[53] A parallel enactment applying to army officers was construed by the Attorney General to prevent no less than sixteen forms of extra allowances then recognized, including an extra payment to the officer acting as professor of chemistry at West Point.[54]

In 1837 clerks were denied pay for extra services; [55] in 1839 extra compensation for the disbursement of public money was outlawed, doubtless as a consequence of Joseph Nourse's dramatic success in collecting a large fee for such activity from 1789 to 1829; [56] in 1842 congressional employees were denied extra pay from the contingency fund; [57] in the same year the clerks lost another means of stretching their official income when Congress denied extra compensation for the performance of duties belonging to another clerk, or for carrying the office mail; [58] and in 1844 corresponding rules were laid down for customhouse inspectors.[59] Congress thus sought to protect its own enactments, and to implement the recommendations of Amos Kendall in 1829: "It is more important that Congress should give us a *system* of pay and emoluments, because discretionary allowances by the Executive tend to injustice, corruption, and endless jealousies. . . . The supple and corrupt may monopolize the favors of the Government, while the independent and honest are kept in obscurity, or driven from the public service." [60]

Carl Schurz could not understand why Americans were so hungry for office, but a New York friend gave some answers: "Partly the distinction and influence which official position con-

53 4 Stat. 757 (March 3, 1835).

54 Adjutant General's Office, Order No. 14 of March 14, 1835, reprinted in *Niles Register*, XLVIII, 65–66 (March 28, 1835).

55 5 Stat. 176 (March 3, 1837).

56 5 Stat. 349 (March 3, 1839); White, *The Jeffersonians*, pp. 408–9.

57 5 Stat. 475 (May 18, 1842).

58 5 Stat. 475, 487 (May 18, 1842).

59 5 Stat. 681, sec. 7 (June 17, 1844).

60 Senate Doc. 1, 21st Cong., 1st sess., p. 271 (Nov. 30, 1829).

fers, and partly the pecuniary emoluments." Schurz remonstrated that the salaries were low. "Well," said his mentor, "but there are the pickings."[61]

FEE OFFICERS

One additional problem requires notice before turning to the classification and compensation act of 1853, viz., the situation of the fee officers. The Federalists had relied heavily upon fees for compensation of the great mass of field agents, and this practice had continued through the years. With the passage of time the fee system became less and less practical. Compensation varied unpredictably; subordinates sometimes collected more than their superiors; the amount differed in many instances from state to state for the same service; control was difficult; and the amounts collected for some services were exorbitant. Two or three cases will illustrate the problem.

The law enforcement officers—district attorneys, clerks, marshals, and commissioners—were compensated principally by fees, the amount of which had been fixed by Congress in 1789 by prescribing the fees set in each state for its corresponding law officers. The consequences were a baffling variety and complexity, a strong inducement to charge unnecessary fees for legal actions that had become pure fiction, difficulties in the settlement of accounts, overpayment and underpayment for services actually performed, and annoyance on all sides. Congress considered a uniform fee bill in 1833, but gave up in despair.[62] President Fillmore informed Congress in 1851 that the lack of a uniform fee bill was still the cause of much vexation, injustice, and complaint.[63] Congress finally responded by enacting a comprehensive uniform fee bill for these classes in 1853, thus terminating reliance upon the fees established by the several states.[64]

A different situation was presented by the Navy Department pursers, an office described by the Senate Committee on Naval Affairs as requiring "great industry, care, and experience." It

61 Carl Schurz, *Reminiscences,* II, 26 (1854).

62 See the excellent report of the Treasury solicitor, Virgil Maxcy, House Doc. 148, 22d Cong., 2d sess., *passim* (Feb. 26, 1833). See also Senate Doc. 1, 25th Cong., 2d sess., p. 169 (Nov. 28, 1837).

63 Richardson, *Messages,* V, 130 (Dec. 2, 1851).

64 10 Stat. 161 (Feb. 26, 1853).

was also an office greatly sought for, because its emoluments were supposed to be great, and in any event were not subject to inspection and audit. The compensation of a purser was fixed at $40 a month, 2 rations per day, and a percentage upon articles sold to seamen. The profit upon these articles was a private transaction and constituted the principal compensation of these trader-officers.

Apart from the easy possibility of imposition and of earnings far beyond service rendered, there were other objections well summarized in 1838: there was no good reason for taxing seamen to support pursers; there were constant complaints about huge profits; and the system was conducive to teasing seamen to buy articles they did not need.[65] The Senate Committee on Naval Affairs proposed to end this system by cutting off the pursers from any personal interest in the purchase and sale of seamen's supplies, and by placing them on a stated salary.[66] Four years later Congress approved this reform.[67] Pursers were also forbidden to advance or loan money, public or private, or to extend credit to naval officers, "under any pretence whatever." [68]

The fee problem in the customs service was primarily due to fluctuation in income, depending on the value of imports and the rate of duty, each subject to change with tariff policy and the economic cycle. The House Committee on Commerce reported in 1838 that, in addition to fluctuations, there was disparity from port to port, that in numerous instances subordinates had taken more in fees than their superior officers, and that the actual compensation was not a true measure of the value of the services rendered. The committee recommended the abandonment of the fee system in favor of fixed salaries.[69] Congress did not accept this proposal, although it had long sought to prevent enrichment by specifying maximum amounts that could be retained. Some evasion was possible and some loopholes nevertheless existed. An economy drive in 1841 and 1842 induced a series of addi-

65 Senate Doc. 443, 25th Cong., 2d sess., pp. 1–2 (May 15, 1838).

66 *Ibid.*, p. 3.

67 5 Stat. 535 (August 26, 1842).

68 *Ibid.*, sec. 6.

69 House Report 472, 25th Cong., 2d sess. (Jan. 25, 1838). A severe indictment of the fee system in consular offices was written by Secretary Livingston in 1833. Senate Doc. 83, 22d Cong., 2d sess. (March 2, 1833).

tional ceilings on fee earnings for postmasters,[70] law enforcement officers,[71] and new ceilings for the principal customs men.[72] Subordinate customs officers had already been dealt with in 1837.[73]

The big cities offered the greatest opportunities for large rewards. Samuel Swartwout made from $5,000 to $15,000 annually on charges to New York importers for storing their goods in the public warehouses. Philip Hone alleged in 1841 that Nathan Sanford had made $100,000 a year out of the fees of the office of district attorney for the southern district of New York, and estimated that Sanford's successor, Benjamin F. Butler, was making at least one-third as much.[74] The public records did not contain such figures.

Perhaps the best evidence on the actual value of the important field offices is a private letter from William L. Stone to General Solomon Van Rensselaer in 1841 concerning the principal offices in New York City, to any one of which the General was an aspirant. The letter follows.

The Marshal's office, on an average, is worth about fifteen thousand dollars a year. It is a very genteel office, and the duties are nearly all discharged by a Deputy. The profits have been as high as Eighteen thousand Dollars. But there is some talk in Congress of cutting down the fees to five thousand. If the fees should not be reduced, this is the most desirable office in the city. The regular proceeds of the Collector's office in ordinary times, and when administered more with a view to the public good than to private Emolument, I believe is rated at an average of Twelve Thousand. But as I said to you, the income can be largely increased by the *Storage System,* as it has been practiced by Mr. Hoyt. He has also been in the practice of making many Seizures. In consequence of these additions—it is believed that Hoyt's income has been from 17,000 to 20,000 Dollars per Annum. But under the new order of things it will probably fall down to Twelve Thousand. The office of Collector is very arduous, requiring the whole time of the Collector, and is brought into continual contact with the merchants, every day, upon nice legal points, and a thousand vexatious questions. The next important Office is the Post Office —I have taken great pains to ascertain all about this office, and so has

70 5 Stat. 421, 430 (March 3, 1841).
71 5 Stat. 475, 483 (May 18, 1842).
72 5 Stat. 421, 432 (March 3, 1841).
73 5 Stat. 163, 175 (March 3, 1837).
74 Hone, *Diary* (Nevins ed.), p. 526 (Feb. 23, 1841).

my partner—Mr. Hall—who is also your friend. Mr. Hall, you know, has, all his life, had a great deal to do with the Post Office. And as it is now conducted, both Mr. Hall and myself think it the very best office in the City. The boxes now produce *Eight Thousand Dollars* per annum. The Salary is *Two Thousand Dollars.* The City Letters produce an average of *One Thousand Dollars* a year. This makes the clear income *Eleven Thousand Dollars per Annum.* But this is not the best part of it. There are *two Post Offices.* The lower Post Office costs the Post Master fourteen hundred Dollars a year, and its clear income is more than *ten Thousand Dollars,* as I am informed. This, then, is the best office in the City. With its duties you are perfectly familiar. The labor can in a great measure be done by Deputy. It is a far better office than the Collectors, with not a hundredth part of the labor and responsibility.[75]

Stone was a long-time resident of New York City and a leading journalist, who at this time was editor of the *New York Commercial Advertiser.* He was well placed to know the facts.

THE CLASSIFICATION AND PAY ACT OF 1853

Congress, as already noted, had long since established a simple compensation plan for the clerks. The general idea that employees doing the same kind of work at similar levels of difficulty ought to receive the same pay could be recognized in the remarks of Congressmen during the Federalist period. The compensation acts of 1818 and 1836 were based on this principle. Standard rates were fixed for the compensation of land office agents, for Indian agents, and for other classes of field employees not compensated by fees.[76] The classification and compensation settlement of 1853, contained in the civil and diplomatic appropriation act, had therefore substantial precedent and was built on prevailing practice.[77]

By means of the act of 1853 Congress sought (1) to grant an increase of compensation, (2) to secure pay uniformity among the departmental clerks,[78] (3) to control the size of the permanent clerical staff, and (4) to allow administrative discretion in assign-

75 Catharina V. R. Bonney, compiler, *A Legacy of Historical Gleanings* (2d ed., 2 vols., Albany: J. Munsell, 1875), II, 149 (Jan. 23, 1841).

76 For examples, see 5 Stat. 107, sec. 10 (July 4, 1836), General Land Office clerks; 5 Stat. 147 (Feb. 13, 1837), branch mint at New Orleans.

77 10 Stat. 189, sec. 3 (March 3, 1853).

78 The principle of uniform compensation rates was formally endorsed by the

ing clerks but no discretion as to their compensation or numbers. In all this there was nothing new in principle.

The classification and compensation act assumed that there was work of varying difficulty and importance, properly recognized by pay rates ranging from $900 to $1,800. No means were thought of to insure that the clerks performing the hard work secured the higher pay; a duties classification was a technical refinement far over the horizon. The act did not require any judgments as to the relative efficiency of clerks doing the same work, or permit any variation in pay according to production.[79] Nor did the act establish a system of promotion from one class to another although this was common practice. Vacancies in any of the three higher classes might be filled by an original appointment or the reassignment of an incumbent clerk from the next lower grade. The act did not apply to the field service, nor to other categories than clerks. They, as heretofore, were dealt with by legislation restricted to each group. Despite these limitations the classification and pay act of 1853 was an excellent arrangement as of its time. It continued and strengthened an established system; it was simple, orderly, and intelligent as far as it went. More could hardly have been expected of any legislative body in the 1850's.

The attainment of consistency and equity within this system depended on administrative discretion and wisdom. Little evidence of complaint has been observed on the part of dissatisfied clerks, but in a decade when rotation and insecurity had reached their height, complaints were hardly to be expected. The influence of politics in pay matters was recorded by Postmaster General Nathan K. Hall. "It cannot be denied," he wrote, "that much inequality exists in the apportionment of salaries and duties among the clerkships in the several departments and offices of the government, and also among those of the same department, and that such inequalities are often invidious and unjust. They arise principally from errors made in the assignment of salaries

heads of departments in 1852. Senate Ex. Doc. 69, 32d Cong., 1st sess., p. 2 (May 3, 1852).

79 A piecework system was introduced in 1838 for clerks and draftsmen in the field offices of the surveyors general in the General Land Office. The beneficial results were reported as having "surpassed the most sanguine expectations." Senate Doc. 17, 25th Cong., 3d sess., p. 5 (Dec. 17, 1838).

on the original appointment of clerks; generally upon the recommendation of influential friends of the appointee, who have formed a wrong estimate of his qualifications for the place sought." [80]

A general view of experience in compensation policy and its administration during these thirty years leaves one with a sense of the gulf between operating needs and the willingness of Congress to meet them. Congressmen were sensitive to the sentiments of their constituents who, in rural areas particularly, did not command cash incomes even approaching those that clerks asserted were starvation wages in Washington. The interests of agency heads were the same as those of the clerks, and they supported the clerks in the two cost-of-living crises in 1835–36, and in the early 1850's.

Although Congress was slow to move and reluctant to appropriate handsome salaries, the members did make two general settlements, each representing a modest improvement in pay rates. Congress, moreover, was committed to the rule of uniformity across departmental lines, and the system established in 1853, reflecting past practice, was sound as far as it went. Congress also was determined to protect the integrity of its system by uprooting every sort of extra allowance that came to its attention and by insisting that clerks and other employees should receive no other compensation than that specified by statute. Legislation put ceilings on the fee officers, but the sound principle supporting these maximum earnings was not infrequently subverted by ingenious subterfuge. In short, a sort of guerrilla warfare smoldered during the Jacksonian years between those who made appropriations and those who received salaries, fees, and perquisites. For most employees the net consequence was well and tersely put by a staunch New York Federalist, John Pintard, for many years secretary to the Mutual Insurance Company. "No situation or office in our economical government," he wrote, "affords a salary or income beyond immediate support, if it does that." [81] Government compensation rates remained close to the subsistence level.

80 Senate Doc. 69, 32d Cong., 1st sess., p. 12 (March 3, 1852).

81 John Pintard, *Letters from John Pintard to his Daughter, 1816–1833* (4 vols., New York: New York Historical Society, 1940–41), IV, 162 (June 16, 1833).

CHAPTER TWENTY-ONE

The Personnel System

A personnel system may be thought of as the aggregate of laws, rules, regulations, judicial decisions, and customary practices that prevail in any jurisdiction. Some kind of arrangement necessarily prevails, whether embryonic or fully developed, whether resting wholly on custom or partly on law. The system under the Federalists was largely customary; gradually formal rules and statutes established a legal framework. Custom, nevertheless, remained an important ingredient of the system.

The theory and practice of rotation and the consequences that flowed from these innovations were based on custom, although the Tenure of Office Act of 1820 and the Post Office Act of 1836 provided some statutory foundations. The permanent service that withstood the tide of rotation was protected only by custom, not by law. The working relationships between auditors and comptrollers, and between chief clerks and their subordinates, were mostly unwritten. The changing standards of ethics were affected by custom, not by statute.

The personnel system of 1860 was more complex and in some respects more fully rounded out than in earlier years. A number of its special aspects have already been explored, notably the selection of medical officers, army cadets and navy midshipmen, clerks, and others by examination; the classification of clerks into four grades; the establishment of fixed pay scales for each grade; the prohibitions against extra allowances; the navy superannuation plan; and the gradual extension of the policy level downward in the administrative structure, a trend probably independent of the rule of rotation.

A formal definition of the policy level was offered in 1842 by the Gilmer Committee in differentiating the political and the "mere ministerial" officers. The former were described as those who stood in the confidential relation of advisers to the President, who "under the laws, have a discretion which may be employed to aid or to defeat the political policy of an administration." [1] The ministerial level remained undefined and indeed undescribed.

Other aspects of the personnel system as it grew during these years deserve attention. The apportionment rule for departmental clerks was introduced in 1853, and the authority for field appointments was clarified. Some attention was given to the need for supervision of clerks, but none to their training. Hours were fixed by Congress, but no rules against nepotism were made. Promotion tended to favor the most competent clerks so far as the chief clerks had a voice, but competence often failed to secure its just due, and a promotion system did not exist. Some experiments with efficiency ratings were made, but the idea of retirement of ancient clerks on a pension was summarily dismissed. On the other hand, removal for cause casting a cloud on the character of the dispossessed clerk was usually attended by notice and hearing. The government had no labor policy for its work force other than that stated in the rule of hire and fire, except for the ten-hour day. There were, nevertheless, intimations of labor problems yet to arise.

APPOINTMENT AUTHORITY AND THE APPORTIONMENT RULE

Formal authority to appoint *inferior* officers and clerks was usually vested in the heads of departments. In the Treasury records, for example, there were many letters from the Secretary to the comptrollers, auditors, commissioners of the General Land Office, and others approving the nominations of clerks, agents, draftsmen, and messengers sent up for clearance.[2] Occasionally the Secretary would act directly, as for example when Secretary of War Marcy searched for "the right sort of person for chaplain" at West Point—a delicate and as it turned out an embarrassing affair.[3]

1 House Report 741, 27th Cong., 2d sess., pp. 3–4 (May 23, 1842).

2 National Archives, Treasury Department, Letters to Cabinet and Bureaus, Set B, *passim*.

3 Library of Congress, William L. Marcy, Private Letter Book, 1845–49, p. 57 (Dec. 25, 1846).

A customary practice to consult the President existed so far as the more important appointments were concerned, such as chief clerks; and the major field officers were regularly cleared with the President and sometimes dictated by him. Subordinate field officers and employees were usually nominated by the head of the local office—for example, the collector of customs or the postmaster in large towns—and after approval by the head of the department were formally appointed by the responsible field officer. A Treasury circular spelled out Jacksonian practice.

> . . . no subordinate officers of the customs can be removed or appointed without the approbation of the secretary of the treasury previously obtained. . . .
>
> When additional officers are thought necessary, the collector will report fully to the secretary, the grounds of such necessity, and the rate of such compensation proper to be allowed. After he has received the secretary's approval of the proposed increase, he will nominate the person whom he desires to employ. . . .[4]

Congress fixed the number of authorized clerks in the appropriation acts. Since this number was chronically less than enough to do the work, the departments usually received a fund for extra clerk hire, and sometimes were forced to use their contingent funds for this purpose. The body of clerks therefore fell into two divisions: those authorized by law, and the extra clerks. The latter often were regularly employed for long periods of time and were frequently absorbed into the body of authorized clerks as Congress increased their number. A permanent clerk (to use a phrase employed by Secretary Woodbury in 1837) was allowed to find a substitute in case of temporary disability or absence.[5]

The apportionment of departmental clerks among the states became settled practice during this period. Locality had always been an important consideration for federal field offices operating within states or smaller districts. It was formally enacted into legislation in 1836 for postmasters.[6] The claims of states and territories became more insistent. Jackson lost a "born

4 *Niles Register,* XXXVII, 7 (August 29, 1829).

5 National Archives, Treasury, Letters to Cabinet and Bureaus, Set B, No. 2, p. 13 (Oct. 12, 1837).

6 5 Stat. 80, sec. 33 (July 2, 1836).

Democrat" because, it was said, he filled all federal offices in Mississippi "with carpetbaggers from Tennessee." [7] The Senate, in its great battle with Jackson, resolved that it was "inexpedient to appoint a citizen of one State to an office which may be vacated or become vacant in any other State of the Union within which such citizen does not reside, without some evident necessity for such appointment," [8] but this was an indication of bad temper against Jackson as much as devotion to local liberty.

Polk recorded in his private correspondence that the "locality of the applicants and geographical considerations are constantly urged." [9] States claimed and were recognized as having rights to appointments as states. Fillmore felt bound to give the Keystone State the diplomatic mission to Russia in 1851. "Pennsylvania is a large State, and she gave her entire vote for the whig candidates at the late election, she has no member of the cabinet, no foreign mission, no highly honorable appointment held by any of her citizens." [10] The list of army officers to be appointed to new regiments during Jefferson Davis' administration of the War Department, originally selected purely on their military record, was modified at the direction of President Pierce to recognize geographical distribution.[11]

The climax to this trend came under Pierce. Pressure had already been apparent in Congress for an apportionment rule for the departmental clerks. A former Methodist preacher, Samuel Brenton, who had suffered a paralytic stroke and been appointed register of the land office in Fort Wayne, Indiana, and who later became a member of the thirty-second Congress, formally proposed the rule of apportionment by states in 1852.[12] Members figured to benefit by an average of three or four clerks for each congressional district. The consequences for the clerks resident in the District of Columbia (220 out of about 800) promised disaster, and the *National Intelligencer* made a strong

7 Percy L. Rainwater, ed., "The Autobiography of Benjamin Grubb Humphreys," *Mississippi Valley Historical Review,* XXI (1934–35), 231–55, at 238.

8 Resolution of Feb. 3, 1831, cited in Richardson, *Messages,* II, 636.

9 Polk-Nicholson Letters, in *Tennessee Historical Quarterly,* III (1944), 78 (April 2, 1846).

10 Webster, *Writings and Speeches* (National ed.), XVI, 607 (April 7, 1851).

11 Varina J. Davis, *Jefferson Davis,* I, 520.

12 *Congressional Globe,* 32d Cong., 1st sess., p. 2189 (August 11, 1852).

protest. This theory of "reform" was declared "a great error, fraught with alarming evils, and will in practice work more fatally for the interests of Government than any scheme out of the multitudes that the spirit of reform has at different times engendered." [13]

Nevertheless, in May 1853, Secretary of the Interior Robert McClelland announced that clerkships would be distributed among the states in proportion to their representation in Congress. The new idea took hold. In August, McClelland wrote to his colleagues in Treasury, War, Navy, and the General Post Office (but excluding State) as follows: "In order to [get] a proper distribution, among the several States, of the appointments in my Department, I have the honor to request that you will furnish me a statement, showing the number of Clerks, from each State, in your Department, and their salaries, similar to the one which I have caused to be prepared in reference to this Department. . . ." [14] The *Baltimore Sun* gave away the inside situation. "All officers," it declared, "are, in fact, at the disposition of members of Congress, and they cannot retain the control of them as well by a general scramble as by a fair distribution. They have insisted upon the establishment of the rule that the clerkships shall be distributed among the States in proportion to their federal numbers." [15] The rule of apportionment settled into a permanent feature of the personnel system.

NEPOTISM

The growing lack of delicacy among persons holding the highest offices with respect to the appointment of their relatives was one symbol of the decline of public service ethics. Jackson was "sound" against his relatives, but other Presidents were weaker. Tyler placed his son Robert in the General Land Office, a son-in-law became a navy purser, and Robert's father-in-law became a military storekeeper under aggravated circumstances that cast no credit on the President.[16]

13 *National Intelligencer,* May 24, 1853.

14 National Archives, Department of the Interior, Letter Book, Miscellaneous, No. 1, p. 180 (August 27, 1853).

15 Reprinted in the *National Intelligencer,* May 24, 1853.

16 Chitwood, *John Tyler,* p. 391; House Report 932, 27th Cong., 2d sess., pp. 1–2 (July 21, 1842).

A nephew of President Polk was appointed cadet at West Point; and the President appointed his brother chargé d'affaires at Naples and later commissioned him a major in the army.[17] President Taylor at first declined to satisfy his relatives, but eventually appointed a nephew as a navy purser, a nephew by marriage as postmaster at Louisville, Kentucky, and a grandson as cadet at West Point.[18] Vice President Fillmore forwarded a petition from his brother, Cyrus, for appointment as receiver of the land office at Fort Wayne, Indiana, and added, "Being a brother it seems improper that I should express any opinion as to the propriety of the appointment." [19] This delicacy was hardly necessary. Buchanan, according to his secretary, disliked nepotism.[20]

The attitudes of department heads on the appointment of relatives differed from case to case. Daniel Webster's solicitude for his son Fletcher was extreme. When Webster became Secretary of State he promptly made Fletcher chief clerk, a post which he lost when his father retired. As soon as Taylor was in the White House, Webster sought Fletcher's appointment as U.S. district attorney for Massachusetts but, despite his insistence, failed in the effort. As a substitute, Taylor proposed the office of U.S. marshal for Massachusetts. Webster wrote his son, "Let us secure the Marshalsea. That will be a great office for you. Its duties may be performed, very much by Deputy. You can practice in the State Courts, & so keep your hand in, in the Law." Fletcher was reluctant, and was finally appointed surveyor of the port of Boston where he served from 1850 until removed by President Lincoln in 1861.[21]

With such precedents in high quarters, it is not surprising to discover the toplofty Philip Hone beginning his duties as naval officer of the port of New York in 1849 by discharging deputy naval officers in order to appoint his son Robert and his nephew Isaac to the vacancies.[22]

17 Polk, *Diary,* I, 371 (April 30, 1846); *ibid.,* III, 153–54 (August 30, 1847).

18 Hamilton, *Taylor: Soldier in the White House,* pp. 140–41; pp. 207–8.

19 *Fillmore Papers,* II, 286–87 (April 10, 1849).

20 Curtis, *Life of Buchanan,* II, 237–38.

21 Claude Moore Fuess, *Daniel Webster* (2 vols., Boston: Little, Brown and Co., 1930), II, 195–96. Cf. Webster's letters on this affair, Webster, *Writings and Speeches* (National ed.), XVI, 503–4, 515, 519, 520; XVIII, 352, 356.

22 Philip Hone, *Diary* (Nevins ed.), p. 874 (April 25, 1849).

SUPERVISION AND MANAGEMENT

Hours. By congressional order in 1836 all public offices were required to be open for public business at least eight hours from October first to April first, and at least ten hours during the spring and summer seasons.[23] This rule did not assume that all clerks would work during these hours. Their day normally began at 9 a.m. and ended at 3 p.m. but the Treasury regulation required four hours more work in the summer and two in the winter, if the public business demanded. Early morning and late afternoon attendance was rotated among the clerks, alphabetically.[24] Apparently a luncheon hour was exceptional, for a Treasury memorandum to the sixth auditor gave permission "for a respite near the middle of the day on making up the lost time in the after portion of it." [25]

Training. Clerks and other employees, once authorized and appointed, were assigned their respective tasks by the chief clerks. The duty of each clerk tended to be the same year after year. He became responsible for the particular duties of his "desk," which might range from one involving much discretion and a wide knowledge of law and precedent to the "humble but yet important situation" held by the clerk of the Norfolk Navy Yard for twenty-two years in succession.[26]

Training, fully recognized in the armed forces, was unknown in the civil departments. The novice clerk sat down to his desk and learned by doing, under the eye of the chief clerk and with the advice of his elders. The case for some attention to the training of clerks was made in 1852—the earliest statement that has come to attention. William B. Randolph, acting treasurer, reported:

> The principle (for it may be called one) of educating men for the discharge of special duties, is recognised as important, and even necessary, in the military and naval service of the United States, and in all the social occupations of civilized communities; but it has not ob-

23 5 Stat. 107, sec. 12 (July 4, 1836).

24 National Archives, Treasury Department, Letters to Cabinet and Bureaus, Set B, No. 1, p. 391, Circular of July 8, 1836.

25 *Ibid.*, p. 409 (Sept. 8, 1836).

26 House Report 247, 27th Cong., 2d sess., p. 1 (Feb. 18, 1842).

tained, and seems to have been deemed unnecessary in the civil service of our government.

. . . . One or more youths, of sufficient education, of good character and habits of industry and application—being, withal, good penmen—might be employed in each bureau as copyists, with a view to their being qualified for the discharge of higher and more important duties.[27]

Nothing came of this suggestion. Nor did the plan for consular students fare any better. Training came by practice and experience on the job.

Supervision. Supervision of the small office staffs was the duty of the chief clerks and principal clerks. This duty was formally recognized by statute in 1842,[28] in terms indicating clearly that Congress wanted better supervision in the interests both of efficiency and of fairness in the distribution of work. Chief clerks and principal clerks were directed "to supervise . . . the duties of other clerks . . . to see that their duties are faithfully executed, and . . . distributed with equality and uniformity"; to redistribute work to prevent "undue accumulation or reduction . . . whether arising from individual negligence or incapacity" or variations in the volume of business; and to make a monthly report of any existing defect in the arrangement or dispatch of business.[29]

The need for supervision was obviously greater than in the Jeffersonian period, when a few "gentlemen" worked together year after year on the same tasks under the guidance of another

27 Senate Ex. Doc. 7, 32d Cong., 2d sess., p. 9 (Nov. 23, 1852).

28 5 Stat. 523, sec. 13 (August 26, 1842). So far as we know this is the first statutory recognition of the function of supervision.

29 The duties of a chief clerk were multifarious. A study of the office and some of its noted incumbents would be rewarding. The duties of the chief clerk of the War Department in 1836 were stated in the following passage. "Receives and opens letters addressed to the Secretary of War, lays such of them as are important before him, and gives the proper direction to the others; distributes the business among the clerks, superintends, receives, and examines the work prepared by them, and lays it before the Secretary; is the organ of oral communications from the Secretary to the bureaux of the Department, disburses the funds appropriated for the contingencies of the office, and for books, maps, plans, &c.; is charged by law with the care of the books and papers when the Secretary is absent; assists in preparing reports to Congress, and in the execution of such other duties as may be assigned to him, or as may be necessary, and has, generally, the supervision, under the direction of the Secretary, of the details of the office." House Doc. 223, 24th Cong., 1st sess., p. 2 (April 16, 1836).

gentleman who had the responsibility of the office. Although many such continued in office under the Jacksonians, there was also a shifting group of clerks who had earned their place by political preferment and who soon lost it by the same token. Elisha Whittlesey, first comptroller, urged that his clerks be assembled in a large room accommodating up to fifty, working under the eye of the principal clerk in charge. "The plan," he said, "would effectually put an end to the reading of newspapers, and other printed matter not connected with official duty, and absence from the office during office hours. It would relieve clerks from company that is frequently annoying, when not required to give or receive information." [30]

Promotion. The formal recognition of four grades of departmental clerks in 1853 raised the question of promotion from one to the next higher. Practice varied greatly. In some offices it was customary to select a clerk paid at a lower salary to fill a vacancy in a clerkship paid at a higher rate. The procedure described by the very competent sixth auditor, William F. Phillips, illustrates the case. "In recommending Clerks for promotion in this office," he wrote, "I have looked to the claims of all below the vacancy to be filled, and have taken into consideration—first, the official merits of each, his fidelity, capacity & good habits; 2d, the length of time he had been employed in the office; and 3d, the number of white persons dependent on him for support. . . ." [31] This practice, however, was limited as the appointment of outsiders for party reasons multiplied, and in any event the opportunity for promotion was not great.[32] Transfer from office to office was not unknown but it was exceptional.

The Gilmer Committee urged a regular scheme of promotion in 1842. "If those who have acquired accurate knowledge, from service in the Departments, could be promoted to the heads of bureaus, the committee believe that the office of chief clerk for bureaus could in many instances, if not altogether, be dispensed

30 Senate Ex. Doc. 2, 33d Cong., 2d sess., p. 103 (Nov. 13, 1854).

31 National Archives, Sixth Auditor Correspondence, 1834–1869 (March 27, 1857). Phillips was an independent character who would not lower the standards of his office to please even the head of the Treasury Department. Secretary Guthrie passed to him one Bemis, as a clerk. Phillips reported after a few weeks that Bemis was diligent but could not do one quarter's work in three. Letters of Sept. 30, 1856, and Jan. 6, 1857.

32 See data in House Docs. 216–251, 24th Cong., 1st sess. (1836).

with. This would moreover, have a happy effect on the clerks, of every grade. The hope of promotion is the most powerful encouragement to official fidelity and skill." [33] An effort was made in 1854 to require all promotions in the classes established in 1853 to be made from the next lower class. It was defeated both on policy and constitutional grounds.[34]

Efficiency records. It became increasingly obvious that the efficiency of clerks varied greatly, and that the public service would be improved if records could be kept both as a means of stimulating exertion and of removing the lazy or incompetent. In 1842 Congress took the first step toward a system of efficiency records by requiring an annual report from the heads of departments, stating among other things whether each clerk had been usefully employed and whether the removal of some to permit the appointment of others would lead to a better dispatch of the public business.[35] In 1845 Polk required these reports to be sent to him before they were submitted to Congress. It was unjust, he declared, "that the meritorious and faithful should have to perform the duties of such as may be found to be negligent, idle, or incompetent." [36]

In 1853 Secretary of the Interior McClelland wrote an amusing but pointed letter to the four commissioners in his department, bearing on the efficiency of the clerks.

> It is customary, at the beginning of a New Year, to post up one's books and take a new start. New Year's day is likewise a fitting occasion for the correction of any abuses or irregularities which may exist, and with this in view, I have to request that you will direct the Chief Clerk of your Office, in making the monthly reports required by law, to state whether the absences, so often noted, are from inattention or indisposition, or from any other cause whatsoever, and whether they have been satisfactorily explained to you, and to report the name of every clerk whose work does not come up to the standard of the Office, or whose habits are exceptionable, and who from any cause neglects his duties.[37]

33 House Report 741, 27th Cong., 2d sess., pp. 19–20 (May 23, 1842).

34 *Congressional Globe,* 33d Cong., 1st sess., pp. 933–34 (April 18, 1854).

35 5 Stat. 523, sec. 11 (August 26, 1842).

36 National Archives, Treasury Department, Letters from Executive Officers, AB, No. 4 (April 11, 1845).

37 National Archives, Department of the Interior, Letter Book, Miscellaneous, No. 1 (Dec. 28, 1853).

During the 1850's a simple form of efficiency record was used in some offices. The standard form included statements as to competence, faithfulness, and attention. In some instances the replies were perfunctory, as the response of James Madison Cutts, the second comptroller. Speaking of his clerks, he reported: "I regard their competency, faithfulness, and attention, one and all, as fully equal to the average obtainment by the Government of these necessary qualities. . . ."[38]

From other offices came more subtle variations: "competent, and recently faithful and more attentive"; "faithful when able to attend to his duties but in consequence of ill health his duties are performed by a substitute"; "faithful but not very attentive during office hours"; "competent, faithful, and attentive but very slow"; and the like.[39] Illness and affliction were treated tenderly in the efficiency reports. Thus the treasurer reported in 1858 that he had a good copying clerk but he was so much afflicted with disease as to be unable to attend regularly. Another, employed on light duty, was competent "and as faithful & attentive as his personal infirmities will permit."[40] Other cases of this character appeared in the departmental correspondence. These reports were not used, so far as has been ascertained, in deciding upon the selection of clerks for retention or promotion. The choice remained a discretionary one, initiated by the bureau head and confirmed by the Secretary of the department.

Superannuation. The problem of superannuation, that had become conspicuous at the close of the Jeffersonian period, quickly reappeared—an indication that rotation was not a universal remedy for an aging bureaucracy. A civil retirement system, however, was even less congenial to the Jacksonians than to their predecessors. The very competent Gilmer Committee reflected contemporary opinion in its 1842 report, declaring against "establishing, what is justly obnoxious to disapprobation, a system of civil pensions. The Government exacts service from none of its civil servants by compulsion, nor without ade-

[38] National Archives, Second Comptroller Correspondence, 1836–1861 (July 29, 1858).

[39] National Archives, Sixth Auditor Correspondence, 1834–1869, *passim.*

[40] National Archives, Treasurer Correspondence, 1818–1866 (June 28, 1858).

quate and often liberal (sometimes extravagant) compensation. The man who has grown old, therefore, in the public service has received from his country what he and the Government, at the time when he accepted office, deemed a fair compensation; and he has no more right to complain of indigence than those private citizens, who, by misfortune or improvidence, have to share his lot." [41]

Removal. Authority to remove subordinate personnel was unregulated either by law or by presidential order. No officer or employee had protection against the arbitrary exercise of the removal power,[42] and the influence of rotation and partisanship made the act of removal a common practice. Statutory removal for cause, or for the good of the service, or for reasons stated, was still beyond the horizon. The rule of unrestrained executive responsibility prevailed.

When, however, removal was for cause reflecting upon the character of the employee, heads of departments were mindful of the rules of fair play that had hitherto prevailed. Abraham Bradley, a long-time post office employee, testified in 1831 that "it was uniformly the practice to give notice to the person accused of the charges, if they implicated his character. . . ." [43] A few years later Secretary of the Treasury Woodbury wrote that it was "not the custom of this Department to remove any officer, unless he shall, upon full investigation, be found incompetent & unworthy of his place." [44] Removal on grounds of mere partisanship was one thing—abrupt and no reasons given; but removal on grounds of delinquency or incompetency continued to be restrained by a sense of order and fairness to the employee.

Removal for incompetence was probably relatively uncommon, whether among the permanent or the politically appointed staff. The record of auditor William F. Phillips shines as an ex-

41 House Report 741, 27th Cong., 2d sess., pp. 20–21 (May 23, 1842).

42 The status of subordinate customs officers appointed by the collector was declared by the U.S. Circuit Court for the Massachusetts district in 1815 to be merely during the pleasure of the collector, and terminated automatically upon his death, removal, or resignation. 2 Gallison 361 (1815). The case is reprinted in Senate Doc. 430, 24th Cong., 1st sess., p. 34.

43 Senate Doc. 73, 21st Cong., 2d sess., p. 89 (Feb. 19, 1831).

44 National Archives, Treasury Department, Letters and Reports to Congress, Series E, Vol. 8, p. 312 (Feb. 24, 1835).

ample of official duty in an unpleasant task. In his annual report for 1854, he wrote,

> In so large an office as this, composed of men of every variety of character and education, and coming from every section of the country, it could scarcely be expected that none of them should fall into habits of dissipation and unfaithfulness to duty. During the year it has been my painful duty to report several such persons to you, as useless to the office, and they have been thereupon invariably removed from office. Though free to confess that reporting even the most unworthy for removal is altogether the most disagreeable duty which has been required of the present head of this office, I shall not shrink from its performance when the character and interests of the public service demand it. I have pleasure in stating that the correct moral deportment and business habits of the gentlemen at present employed in the office are, so far as I am advised, entirely unexceptionable. . . .[45]

GOVERNMENT LABOR POLICY

The position taken by Congress and by the executive branch with reference to the early movements of organized labor, and with respect to the blue-collar government worker, makes one realize that these were years in which laissez faire philosophy was dominant—emphasized by an atmosphere of official superiority and sometimes repression. It need hardly be recorded that the federal government had no policy and no administrative agencies to deal with private labor disputes. It had only fragments of a policy and no special official agency to deal with its own workmen who, by 1857, numbered over 7,000 in the navy yards alone. So far as Congress was concerned, its policy was to leave the hiring and firing of craftsmen and laborers to the unregulated discretion of executive officers.[46] So far as the latter were concerned, they operated on the theory that they were like any other employers, and could hire and fire as circumstances dictated. The concept of a permanent labor force was urged by Commodore John Rodgers,[47] but the policy of the

45 House Ex. Doc. 3, 33d Cong., 2d sess., p. 98 (Nov. 21, 1854).

46 Cf. statement by Secretary of the Navy Toucey: "With but few exceptions, there is no law fixing the compensation of master workmen, or of workmen; but it is left entirely to the regulation of the department." Senate Ex. Doc. 13, 36th Cong., 2d sess., p. 2 (March 2, 1861).

47 Senate Doc. 1, 21st Cong., 1st sess., p. 226 (Oct. 19, 1829).

navy-yard commanders was forced by the political machines into other patterns. Indeed, the most significant aspect of public employment at this level was its domination by the local political machines and its use for electioneering purposes.[48]

For a short time during the 1830's it appeared that organized labor might become politically active and influential. The role of labor in the Jackson campaigns has been fully developed by Arthur M. Schlesinger, Jr.[49] A workingmen's convention was held in Boston in 1833 which declared its members would vote for no person "but such as are known to be openly and decidedly favorable to a system of general education, by means of manual labor schools, supported at public expense, and open alike to the children of the poor as well as to the rich—the abolition of all chartered monopolies—the revision or abolition of the present militia system—the abolition of imprisonment for debt—an effective lien law for laborers on buildings—a less expensive law system—and equal taxation on property."[50] A smart political instinct appeared among the Philadelphia mechanics who protested a salary increase for naval officers as a "gross infraction on the rights of the poor," unless something were done for the "subordinate officers, sailors, and marines, who perform all the labor."[51] The political importance of labor soon evaporated, however, and laissez faire reigned in the employment field.

Five hundred navy mechanics at the Philadelphia Navy Yard, laid off in December 1837, petitioned Congress to direct immediate work to repair the frigate *Raritan*. Senator James Buchanan supported their petition but it was received unsympathetically, as tending toward a general system of pauperism: "it was extraordinary," exclaimed Senator William C. Preston of South Carolina, "that the government should be called on to find them employment!"[52] He could, he said, use this argument to support a "general system of pauperism." Two years

48 See above, ch. 11.

49 Arthur M. Schlesinger, Jr., *The Age of Jackson* (Boston: Little, Brown, 1945); John R. Commons and Associates, *History of Labour in the United States* (4 vols., New York: Macmillan, 1918–35), I, 386 ff.

50 Reported in *Niles Register*, XLV, 147 (Nov. 2, 1833).

51 House Doc. 108, 23d Cong., 2d sess. (Jan. 28, 1835).

52 Buchanan, *Works*, III, 339–41 (Jan. 2, 1838).

later the navy funds ran low during the winter season, and the Brooklyn Navy Yard mechanics now petitioned Congress for relief in the form of an early appropriation to support repair and construction work. They declared that "the winter has commenced with unusual severity, that fuel and provisions are dear; that the works of private enterprise are generally suspended; that it is in consequence difficult to procure employment; and that their discharge from the navy yard must be productive of serious embarrassments, if not of absolute distress." [53] It was nearly a century before their philosophy of the duty of government was to command respect.

The climate of the times was friendly to the employer. Hezekiah Niles condemned a combination of laborers seeking higher wages on the Pennsylvania canals, employed by private contractors, and announced his own principles: "It is lawful for every man to make his own bargain for his labor, and whoever forcibly interferes to prevent it, should be punished. Employers have rights, as well as the employed." [54]

A petition of the Trades Union of Baltimore in favor of the ten-hour day was laid on the table in the House of Representatives after comment by Congressman Thomas L. Hamer. ". . . there were some politicians in this country," he said, "who seemed to think that every thing ought to be regulated by law. Now, he was against that doctrine. Every man should be left free, being prevented from encroaching on the rights of his fellow-man, and ought to be left free to manage his affairs in his own way, with this restriction. . . . We might just as well prescribe by law what sort of clothes a man should wear, or at what time he should eat his dinner! A man who is free should be left to make his own contract." [55] The House Committee on Public Buildings took the same line in 1838. The laborers on the public buildings wanted a reduction in their hours. The committee asserted that the petitioners were all freemen who had voluntarily sought their employment on terms set by the government, and declared that the regulation of the

53 House Doc. 62, 26th Cong., 1st sess., p. 1 (Feb. 5, 1840).
54 *Niles Register*, XXXVI, 101 (April 11, 1829).
55 *Register of Debates*, 24th Cong., 1st sess., pp. 2891–92 (March 21, 1836).

time and price of labor was not a suitable matter for legislation.[56]

The single departure from this standard was the order of President Van Buren in 1840 establishing a ten-hour day for laborers and mechanics employed on public works.[57] An initial victory for the ten-hour day had been won in 1835 from the Philadelphia Common Council for municipally employed workmen, a "revolution" that marked the turning point from the "sun to sun" agricultural system to the "six to six" industrial system.[58] A campaign of petitions finally brought favorable action at the hands of the President.

The government had, however, never heard of the doctrine of the model employer. It followed prevailing practice and undertook no responsibility for improving the lot of workmen. Complaints were generally dismissed as "factious and troublesome." An amusing incident occurring in Polk's day illustrates the point. Thirty journeymen painters called at the White House to present their grievance—that they were not paid for wet days on which they did not work. Polk listened to them impatiently, telling the workmen that he "could not go to the Capitol & superintend the work in person." He suspected the painters of being Whigs anxious to make an issue that might carry Baltimore and Alexandria in the imminent election.[59]

A different problem arose in 1853 when the bricklayers at work on the Capitol extension decided to impose the closed shop rule. Jefferson Davis put an end to such subversion. "The Department," he declared to the superintendent of the work, "feels it a duty to resist a movement so improper in itself, and so injurious to the public interests. If, therefore, the society, after due notice, persists in its resolutions, you will employ none of its members in any capacity, on the works under your charge, but take prompt measures to procure competent mechanics from other places, if enough cannot be found here. . . ." [60]

Turbulence among some of the newborn unions in the 1830's

56 House Report 886, 25th Cong., 2d sess. (May 11, 1838).

57 Richardson, *Messages,* III, 602 (March 31, 1840).

58 John R. Commons, *History of Labour in the United States,* I, 391–93.

59 Polk, *Diary,* IV, 172–74 (Oct. 30, 1848).

60 Davis, *Letters, Papers and Speeches,* II, 251–52 (July 22, 1853).

was rarely repeated among government workers, but in 1835 Niles reported a "strike" at the Washington Navy Yard. About one hundred and fifty mechanics marched to the office of the Secretary of the Navy, praying for redress of grievances. The commandant had issued an order which they considered an undeserved reflection upon their integrity.[61] A year later he reported a rumor of a strike among the Washington clerks, who were then agitating for a pay raise.[62]

These matters were, after all, mere flashes illuminating the future but not characteristic of their time. The controlling fact in government labor policy was its domination by considerations of partisan advantage. These have already been noted. It is enough to add that neither the efforts of Secretaries as competent as Bancroft or Dobbin nor the resistance of naval commandants availed to protect the navy mechanics and workmen from abject dependence upon the local party organization in the big cities. The efficiency of labor diminished and its costs increased, but the electioneering needs of Democrats and Whigs alike were satisfied.

A public personnel system develops in accordance with the preferences and prejudices of its time. The federal system in 1860 faithfully reflected the general atmosphere of the Jacksonian years. There was little legislation beyond that fixing hours of work, requiring a simple examination system, arranging clerks into four pay classes and controlling their number, and requiring chief and principal clerks to supervise.

The management of the public offices was recognized by Congress to be an executive function. The executive officers imposed no restrictions on their own authority to hire (only their nominees could take the pass examinations), to assign to duty, to favor or disfavor, and to remove at will. Within a system highly discretionary in nature, the individual clerk had almost no rights but many obligations. This situation was in full agreement with the status of employees everywhere. Not until some protection of tenure had been achieved could the personnel system develop its more creative aspects.

61 *Niles Register*, XLVIII, 395 (August 8, 1835).
62 *Ibid.*, L, 33 (March 19, 1836).

CHAPTER TWENTY-TWO

Public Service Ethics

That traditional standards of public service morality were in decline could not be denied at the close of Andrew Jackson's administration. The decline continued, with variations and exceptions, through the years ending with the dreary term of James Buchanan. The standards of official conduct in 1860 were consequently regrettably inferior to those which had been nurtured and protected by Federalists and Republicans alike.

Nevertheless it is impossible to draw a blanket indictment of the Jacksonian period. Against the undoubted current of general deterioration, there were eddies and countercurrents, and deep reaches that were hardly touched by surface movements. During the years made conspicuous by the unparalleled embezzlements of Samuel Swartwout, collector of the port of New York; his successor, Jesse Hoyt; and Isaac V. Fowler, postmaster of New York City, the public service was adorned by such men of character and talent as Amos Kendall, Postmaster General; George Bancroft, Secretary of the Navy; and Jefferson Davis, Secretary of War. During these years also a code of public service ethics was reduced to writing, the examination system was extended with the intent of establishing a stable and reliable civilian career service, and department heads strove to protect their agencies from corrupting influences that beat upon them from a restless and careless world outside.[1]

1 There is no general history of morals in American society, a gap in the understanding of American life greatly to be deplored. Likewise there is no general account of the trends in business morals, which have been so important in forming American character. Perhaps needless to say, there is also no history of public service morals; the materials in the author's *The Federalists*, *The Jeffersonians*, and in this volume merely open the subject. Much can be learned from the major

DECLINE IN MORALITY

Deterioration in official circles was not an isolated phenomenon. Indeed, it was parallel with and consequent upon a decline in business ethics that affected society generally. The trend was recorded by editor Freeman Hunt after it had already run a long course. "A great and growing evil," he wrote in an editorial headed Commercial Integrity, "and we may say the great evil of the times, is the lack of integrity among business people—tradesmen and mechanics—in regard to business transactions, especially the payment of bills, notes, drafts, &c." [2]

Face-to-face personal transactions among neighbors and well-known business associates were giving way to impersonal dealings with banks and corporations, and with men in distant cities and of unknown character. The normal remedy for fraud or wrongdoing that was adequate in a less complicated age, i.e., recourse to the courts, became less and less adequate as corporations increased in power and multiplied their means of evasion. Moreover, the temptations to ruthless and unscrupulous operations in the business world were constantly greater as rich prizes in railroad construction, shipping, and manufacturing took shape. The spirit of speculation that swept through public land transactions in the 1830's took possession of business generally as expansion of territory, population, and resources marked each decade of the middle years, and was carried to new heights by the discovery of gold in California in 1849.

The decline in morals was accelerated by the impersonal life of city dwellers, as traditional village and small-town existence gave way to the anonymity of urban life in Boston, New York, Philadelphia, and other communities that were rapidly expanding with the industrial revolution. The increase in immigration also brought various standards of morality into conflict and competition with each other.

The consequences for business morality were disastrous. The evidence was spread on the record in the bank investigations

---

biographies and autobiographies, and from such monographs as Carl R. Fish, *The Civil Service and the Patronage,* and Dorothy Ganfield Fowler, *The Cabinet Politician.* The raw material for a general study is available in the published letters of public men and in the long series of congressional investigations.

2 *Hunt's Merchants' Magazine,* XXVIII (1853), 776.

in Massachusetts in 1837–38; in railroad corruption in New York during the 1850's; and in the unscrupulous management of insurance companies whose agents misrepresented their benefits to a confused and innocent public.[3] From such impositions was gradually to develop administrative regulation by the states of banks, insurance companies, and railroads.

Citizens became more ready to impose upon their government, notably in connection with pensions. A House committee reported in 1835, "Men in the highest walks of life, of the most honorable pretensions, and in whom the greatest confidence was reposed, are among those who have largely participated in drawing money from the Treasury, by means of false papers, the grossest acts of forgery, and the most wilful and corrupt perjury." [4] Magistrates conspired with their clerks of court to issue false certificates to claimants for pensions. The number of "disabled veterans" multiplied; an agent sent out from Washington found seventy able-bodied men on the pension rolls of Illinois in a total of about ninety.[5] The fraudulent contracts with post office contractors have already been noted, and contractors elsewhere seemed ready to deceive the government for their own profit. The first comptroller declared in 1854, "The accounting officers might fill volumes, if their detections of fraud were made public." [6]

All this was recognized by sensitive persons who saw the decline and sought to understand its causes. Henry T. Tuckerman touched on them in an article on "American Society."

> With the great increase of travel there has been a diminution in that local and family attachment which is the best guarantee of public spirit; as the population of our cities has enlarged, municipal negligence and corruption have been developed; as the area of the national territory has spread, enterprise has manifested itself in a reckless disregard of both economical and honest principles; with the advance of material prosperity, culpable indifference to life and to legitimate industry is displayed . . . and in the ratio of our mechanical triumphs has been the decline of our moral superiority.[7]

3 Leonard D. White, "The Origin of Utility Commissions in Massachusetts," *Journal of Political Economy,* XXIX (1921), 177–97.

4 House Report 37, 23d Cong., 2d sess., p. 2 (Jan. 8, 1835).

5 *National Intelligencer,* Feb. 12, 1853.

6 Senate Ex. Doc. 2, 33d Cong., 2d sess., p. 104 (Nov. 13, 1854).

7 *North American Review,* LXXXI (1855), 30.

DECLINE OF POLITICAL MORALITY

The quality of public life in the states and cities and in Washington, in congressional and administrative circles alike, was adversely affected by these trends. John A. Dix, able and honest leader in New York Democratic politics, wrote Van Buren in 1836 about the situation in Albany. "The legislation of the whole winter has been a matter of bargain and sale; and if we cannot get a different class of men into the Legislature, the sooner we go into a minority the better. We have been betrayed by the inordinate spirit of speculation which is abroad. It has taken possession of too many of our own political friends; and it is not to be disguised that their conduct is more under the regulation of pecuniary considerations than motives of a higher origin and character." [8]

The decline of congressional morality has already been noted.[9] The devotion of Congressmen to local rather than national interests was perhaps less an indication of low ethical standards than of irresponsibility. However this may be, rivers and harbors bills came to be dramatic evidence of a concern with "pork." By 1837 the evil had progressed so far as to cause a House committee to declare, "the system is expensive, and yet feeble; flattering, and yet uncertain, in all its operations and results, unless it be viewed only with reference to its fitness, to the purposes of the individual wealth and profit of the agents and contractors immediately concerned." The annual rivers and harbors appropriation had risen from $129,000 in 1829 to $1,786,000 in 1836.[10] In 1847 Polk vetoed a bill for national improvements that began its legislative course with an appropriation of six thousand dollars for the improvement of Milwaukee harbor, and was loaded down with thirty-eight other river and harbor items running over half a million dollars.[11] River and harbor bills continued nevertheless to flourish.

The decline of political morality has been illustrated to some extent in previous pages devoted to the War Department, the

8 Morgan Dix, *Memoirs of John A. Dix,* I, 147 (June 4, 1836).
9 See ch. 2.
10 House Report 175, 24th Cong., 2d sess., pp. 1, 2 (Jan. 31, 1837).
11 Richardson, *Messages,* IV, 610 (Dec. 15, 1847).

Navy, and the Post Office—pages that contain evidence both of honor and contamination in the executive branch. The trend may be further illustrated by observations concerning the lobby and claims agents.

The lobby. In the contemporary sense of the term a lobby hardly existed before the railroad age, although the tariff question had induced efforts by northern manufacturers to persuade Congress to recognize their interests. By 1850 there were at least three major lobbies concerned respectively with the tariff, steamship subsidies, and railroad land grants, as well as a number of "specialty" lobbies such as the one involved in the Colt revolver patent renewal. The activity of these lobbies was in part legitimate, but at times their influence was harmful and conducive to the destruction of sound standards of public life.[12]

President Polk took notice of the lobby that was fighting his tariff reduction bill in 1846. "The most tremendous efforts," he wrote, "I understand are being made by the Capitalists who are engaged in manufacturies to defeat the Bill of the House now before the Senate to reduce and modify the duties imposed by the tariff act of 1842. Scores of them I understand are flocking to Washington for that purpose." [13] And a few days later, "The City is swarming with manufacturers who are making tremendous exertions to defeat it. The truth is that such a struggle has rarely been witnessed in Congress. . . ." [14]

12 Lobbyists early fell into disrepute. Secretary of War Marcy wrote his friend General Wetmore on March 31, 1845, with reference to an applicant for office: "He has been here much of the time during the session of Congress for the last four or five years without any generally known ostensible occasion for such attendance—Some put him down in the category of idle hangers on or lobby members—This employment has a tendency to *lower* a man . . . & it operates adversely to his claim for a high & responsible office." Library of Congress, William L. Marcy Papers, Vol. 10, No. 34,394. The great lobbyist of the Jacksonian era was the New York Whig, Thurlow Weed. He operated in Washington as well as in Albany, and had useful connections with both political parties. See Glyndon G. Van Deusen, *Thurlow Weed: Wizard of the Lobby,* and *Autobiography of Thurlow Weed* (Harriet A. Weed, ed., Boston: Houghton, Mifflin, 1883). He was followed by Sam Ward, "King of the Lobby," son of a wealthy New York banker and brother of Mrs. Julia Ward Howe, who enjoyed the literary and social life of the wealthy and leisure class until he lost his fortune in the late 1840's. This disaster was recouped by adventures in the California gold rush. *Dictionary of American Biography,* XIX, 439.

13 Polk, *Diary,* II, 27–28 (July 15, 1846).

14 *Ibid.,* II, 53–54 (July 28, 1846).

The attempt to reinstate the patent on the Colt revolver gave rise to a House investigation in 1854 that was largely defeated by the refusal of Colonel Samuel Colt and his Washington agents to answer questions on the ground that the committee had no right to inquire into their "private business." The committee could not establish bribery of members of the House despite much talk thereof. It did find that money had been liberally used to facilitate passage of bills, specifically in giving presents and "costly and extravagant entertainments," [15] and condemned the suspicious behavior of Colonel Colt.

Some idea of the terms demanded by a successful lobbyist is gained in the correspondence of Edmund Burke, one-time commissioner of patents. He agreed to oppose the extension of a patent on a planing machine for his traveling expenses and board in Washington, a per diem of eight dollars a day while absent from home, and one thousand dollars contingent upon success. To his correspondent he observed that the chairman of the Senate Committee on Patents came from his state "and the majority are my political friends." [16]

The impact on public morals of such operations deeply disturbed responsible statesmen. James Buchanan wrote Franklin Pierce at the opening of the 1852 campaign, "The Federal Government for some years past has been rapidly becoming more & more extravagant in its expenditures. The hosts of contractors, speculators, stock jobbers, & lobby members which haunt the halls of Congress, all desirous per fas aut nefas and on any & every pretext to get their arms into the public Treasury, are sufficient to alarm every friend of his Country. Their progress must be arrested, or our Government will soon become as corrupt as that of Great Britain." [17] Jefferson Davis exclaimed in 1859, "I hold it to be a curse in legislation, that such things as lobby men can ever be tolerated about either of the two Houses of Congress." [18] These sentiments failed to impress his fellow Senators. Regulation of the lobby was still far in the future.

15 House Report 353, 33d Cong., 1st sess., p. 4 (August 3, 1854); House Report 132, 33d Cong., 2d sess. (Feb. 23, 1855).

16 *New Hampshire Patriot and State Gazette,* July 6, 1853. Letter dated Dec. 25, 1851.

17 Buchanan, *Works,* VIII, 453 (June 21, 1852).

18 Davis, *Letters, Papers and Speeches,* III, 534 (Feb. 7, 1859).

The claims agents. Related to the lobby and influential also in depressing public morals was the class of claims agents that grew up in Washington. Repressive measures had been taken in 1818 to prevent government clerks from acting as agents for private persons, and they were generally responsive to this prohibition. Nothing had been done, however, to regulate the conduct of private citizens as claims agents, and by 1837 they had become the cause of official condemnation. Pension agents were described by the commissioner of pensions as "unprincipled men" who deceived both the government and the honest pensioner, to their own profit.[19] Amos Kendall, in economic straits in 1843, was driven to become a claims agent in partnership with his nephew—a business, it was noted by the editor of his autobiography, "to him always irksome and repugnant to his feelings. Necessity alone reconciled him to it." [20] Private claims were pressed upon Congress for an almost endless variety of objects and the "lobby" of the professional claims agents became so great a nuisance that a Senate committee had to be established in 1852 to seek reform.

The committee made a blistering report on this "class of persons who are not only useless in their vocation to society, making no contribution to its welfare, but who hang like parasites upon its industry, and tend, by their daily practices, to poison the very sources of its prosperity." [21] Among the most dangerous were the representatives of the press, then allowed the freedom of the floor, who did not scruple to lobby for claims and benefits for others. The committee demanded the end of the agency system, leaving the prosecution of claims to "lawyers and attorneys who would stand upon the respectable footing established by the salutary rules which govern the practice in our judicial tribunals." [22]

An ominous aspect of the claims agent problem arose because some members of Congress also acted in this capacity. John Quincy Adams noted a disturbing case in which Senator William D. Merrick had secured favorable action in a single day on

19 Senate Doc. 1, 25th Cong., 2d sess., p. 674 (Nov. 11, 1837).
20 Kendall, *Autobiography*, pp. 507, 525.
21 Senate Report 1, 33d Cong., Special Session, p. 29 (March 22, 1853).
22 *Ibid.*, p. 35.

a claim of one of Adams' constituents. Adams had sought in vain to get a favorable settlement. Merrick visited Tyler on his last day of office, persuaded him of the justice of the claim, and got a written order from the President to the accounting officers. For this service Merrick was paid five hundred dollars.[23]

A less disturbing aspect involved former members of Congress and former officials who engaged in legal practice before the departments. Thus Thomas J. D. Fuller, Representative from Maine (1849–57), and then second auditor (1857–61), practiced before the Court of Claims thereafter. Michael Nourse, for many years chief clerk in the register's office, established a "Home and Foreign Patent and General Agency" in 1853 across the street from the Patent Office at Eighth and E Streets. R. H. Gillett, one-time solicitor of the Treasury, set up a law office for the prosecution of claims in the same year.[24]

Partial remedies were enacted in 1853, directed against the claims agents. No assignment of a claim was permitted henceforth before it had been allowed and the amount determined, and then only in the presence of two witnesses. This rule was to prevent misrepresentation in the prosecution of claims. The old rule against executive officers acting as claims agents was restated and extended to members of Congress. Bribe givers as well as bribe receivers were condemned. Penalties were established for the destruction of records or fraudulently withdrawing them.[25] In addition the Senate sought to bar unauthorized persons, including representatives of the press, from the floor.[26]

DECLINE OF PUBLIC SERVICE ETHICS

The decline in business and political morals that became apparent during the 1830's and continued to the outbreak of the Civil War furnishes a necessary background to the trend in the public service. Little evidence has been observed to suggest any sudden or marked change in the habits of clerks and their superior officers in the departmental service in Washington, and it is probable that older standards of rectitude gen-

23 Adams, *Memoirs,* XII, 179, 180 (March 5, 7, 1845).
24 *National Intelligencer,* Nov. 22, 1853.
25 10 Stat. 170 (Feb. 26, 1853).
26 Senate Report 1, 33d Cong., Special Session, p. 33 (March 22, 1853).

erally prevailed among the great majority of the rank and file. Many of them were lifetime employees despite political fluctuations; they were under close scrutiny in their official work; and the heads of departments, with rare exceptions, steadily required honest and faithful performance of duty.[27] Individual failures occurred inevitably, but the standard of conduct generally was commendable; no clerical or auditing scandal occurred in the Washington offices during the Jacksonian period.

Less can be said with respect to the field service where temptation was often great, supervision lax, and community standards less exacting than in the capital city. Circumstances were at work that were bound to undercut older canons of correct official behavior, whether in Washington or in the field, and to some of them it is useful to advert before noting a series of incidents and tendencies that illustrate the general drift of the times.

One consequence of the election of 1828 was to terminate the quasi-monopoly of officeholding enjoyed by the class of gentlemen who had been called to official position since the foundation of the Republic. Officeholders tended now to be drawn from the ranks of active politicians, a class that had its own merit in some important respects, but one that did not serve to elevate public morality. Secretary of the Navy John P. Kennedy regretted the change in a letter to his uncle: "Do you remark," he wrote, "how lamentably destitute the country is of men in public station of whom we may speak with any pride? . . . How completely has the conception and estimate of a *gentleman* been obliterated from the popular mind! Whatever of that character we have seems almost banished from the stage." [28]

27 Three of Taylor's Cabinet members were involved in the settlement of the Galphin claim, which cast a cloud on the reputation of Secretary of War George W. Crawford. See William P. Brandon, "The Galphin Claim," *Georgia Historical Quarterly*, XV (1931), 113–41. The financial irregularities of Buchanan's Secretary of War, John B. Floyd, have been both defended and condemned. See William Norwood Brigance, *Jeremiah Sullivan Black* (Philadelphia: University of Pennsylvania Press, 1934), p. 93, for one of several summary accounts. See also *The Diary of Edward Bates, 1859–1866* (Howard K. Beale, ed.), American Historical Association, *Annual Report, 1930,* IV, 160 (Nov. 29, 1860), for other damaging allegations concerning Floyd's honor.

28 Henry T. Tuckerman, *Life of John Pendleton Kennedy,* p. 187. The change was even more apparent in political life. John A. Dix commented on the "Log Cabin and Hard Cider Campaign" of 1840 in these terms: "This appears to be

The effect of rotation in office was to confirm the consequences of the decline of the class of gentleman in official station. Persons interested in a merely transitory appointment brought to office a set of expectations far different from those who intended a lifetime service. The conditions that predisposed to care and circumspection in the latter group were often absent from the former. What could be gained by birds of passage had to be garnered quickly. The corporate influences that for forty years had molded newcomers into the character of a government clerk were weakened, although not destroyed, as old-timers were surrounded by incoming party appointees, now Democrat, now Whig. Office morale suffered as these newcomers often took the best places, while the old-timers were confined to the lower clerical classes.

In the field service government employees were exposed to the full force of the new democracy, especially where employment was most numerous, viz., in the larger cities. This was exactly where the political machines first developed and where they indulged in their most violent operations. The long pay rolls of customhouses and post offices were easy prey to these machines, particularly, as already noted, because the collectors and the postmasters tended more and more to be among the leading members of the organization. Some of the evidence of deterioration will be presented below in dealing with the careers of Swartwout, Hoyt, and Fowler. Here it is sufficient to record the decline of the gentleman class, the consequences of rotation, and the aggression of the big city machines as among the general conditions that were adversely affecting the ethical foundations of official behavior. Here also it is proper to observe that three of the foundations of the old traditional code of official ethics were progressively withdrawn: care in the initial selection for office, stability in officeholding, and relative absence of external pressure upon the public service.

---

the first time in our history in which a direct appeal was made to the lower classes by exciting their curiosity, feeding the desire for amusement, and presenting what is low and vulgar as an inducement for support. Since that day the thing has been carried farther, until it is actually a disadvantage to be of good stock and to have inherited 'the grand old name of gentleman.' " Dix, *Memoirs of John A. Dix,* I, 165.

THE LAND OFFICE

Perhaps the greatest temptations in the field service arose in the scattered land offices. Opportunities for collusion were frequent; pressure by speculators was great; and agents of the land offices were almost irresistibly drawn into speculation themselves—sometimes with government funds.[29]

Confirmation of much adverse rumor came in 1835 in the report of the Senate Committee on Public Land, Senator George Poindexter, chairman.[30] Despite widespread refusal to testify on the part of important witnesses, the committee found speculation and fraud on a large scale in Alabama, Mississippi, and Louisiana. "All these things have occurred for the last three or four years in districts where the most atrocious and outrageous frauds have been committed. . . ." [31] The greatest offender was Samuel Gwin, register of the Mount Salus land office, and subsequently in the Chocchuma district, the person over whom the Senate and President Jackson had fought bitterly. Poindexter now put responsibility for this situation directly on the President, alleging "the undue confidence often reposed in a political favorite or personal friend by the Chief Magistrate [who] too frequently protects officers who violate the laws from punishment. . . ." [32] The committee declared that the laws were adequate, and that the trouble in the land offices was due to maladministration.

In 1839 a further report exposed abuses among the receivers of public money in the land offices.[33] This report disclosed 75 receivers in trouble with the government over arrearages in accounts, of whom 23 antedated the Jackson administration. In some cases the sums involved were small, and in some the difficulty was an accounting problem rather than a shortage. In

[29] Thus *Niles Register* reported in 1837 that great excitement had been produced in Kalamazoo, Michigan, when some land agents were exposed who had entered fictitiously several hundred of the choicest lots and sent persons east to sell them. *Niles Register,* LI, 384 (Feb. 11, 1837).

[30] Senate Doc. 151, 23d Cong., 2d sess. (March 3, 1835).

[31] *Ibid.,* p. 3.

[32] *Ibid.,* pp. 2–3. Poindexter declared in 1837 that the whole power and patronage of the federal government had been subsequently employed to destroy both his public and private character. *Niles Register,* LII, 140 (April 29, 1837).

[33] House Report 313, 25th Cong., 3d sess., pp. 142–246 (Feb. 27, 1839).

other cases the sums were large and the discrepancies due to official misbehavior.

Two cases will illustrate a common practice of neglecting to deposit money collected for the sale of land, money declared by the investigating committee to have been used for private speculation. William Linn, receiver at Vandalia, Illinois, was a brother of Senator Linn, and was appointed to this office in 1830. Correspondence between Linn and the Secretary of the Treasury ran as follows. On June 23, 1834, Linn was ordered to deposit his collections. He paid no attention, and on October 23, 1834, a new demand was made, with a threat of removal. Linn asked for time. On December 4, 1834, a third order was issued against him, to which he made sufficient excuses so that Jackson renominated him for a second term. On February 12, 1835, the Treasury ordered him "once for all" to deposit his funds. In May Linn replied that he could not do so because the roads were impassable. The Treasury apparently gave up for a while at this point. At the end of the year Linn informed Washington that circumstances beyond his control prevented closing his accounts. On three occasions during 1836 the Treasury repeated its orders to remit, to no effect. When the pressure became great, Linn referred Secretary Levi Woodbury to "his friends" in Washington. On January 26, 1838, Linn resigned with an outstanding balance against him of over $55,000.[34]

General Wiley P. Harris, receiver at Columbus, Mississippi, who had a similar correspondence with Secretary Woodbury, asked his friends in Mississippi to intercede for him. Representative John F. H. Claiborne did so, without concealment. He wrote directly to Jackson, declaring that a more honorable man than Harris did not live, and adding that he was "one of the main pillars of the democratic cause, and one of the earliest and most distinguished friends of the administration in Mississippi. His family and connexions are extremely influential. . . . They are true democrats; and the bank, nullifying, and White parties would shout 'victory' at any blow aimed at them. . . . We are now in the midst of an electioneering campaign. . . . It will be a close contest." [35]

34 *Ibid.*, pp. 159–66.

35 *Ibid.*, pp. 174–75 (Sept. 15, 1835). The reference is to Hugh Lawson White, a political enemy of Jackson at this time.

With this endorsement Jackson agreed to give Harris a month to make his returns and deposit his funds. The days of grace stretched out for nine months, at the end of which Harris wrote Jackson, "I regret to say that I still find there is a deficit against me, which as yet I am unable to account for." [36] The balance due was $109,178.08. Harris tendered his resignation and recommended a "warm personal friend," Colonel Gordon D. Boyd, as his successor. Jackson refused to accept Harris's resignation and ordered him suspended or removed. He did, nevertheless, appoint Harris's "warm personal friend."

By June 1837 the friend was in arrears over $55,000. The land examiner sent to investigate made an oft-quoted report, advising against his removal.

> . . . . The man seems really penitent; and I am inclined to think, in common with his friends, that he is honest, and has been led away from his duty, by the example of his predecessor, and a certain looseness in the code of morality, which here does not move in so limited a circle as it does with us at home. Another receiver would probably follow in the footsteps of the two. You will not, therefore, be surprised if I recommend his being retained, in preference to another appointment; for he has his hands full now, and will not be disposed to speculate any more. . . . Lenity towards him, therefore, might stimulate him to exertions, which severity might, perhaps, paralyze.[37]

The tolerance of the Treasury Department must indeed have given encouragement to the receivers, one of whom had reminded Woodbury of the maxim, "a gentle hand will lead an elephant with a hair." [38]

The report of the committee from which this evidence is drawn, nevertheless, concluded, "The practice . . . of retaining men in office after gross and repeated violations of law . . . too clearly point to the inference that such officers were retained in place because they possessed extensive political influence, and were useful and active partisans." [39] The Democratic minority did not dispute this finding.

It must be added that some receivers in trouble paid up their arrearages, at times by selling their extensive holdings of land.

36 *Ibid.*, p. 181 (August 27, 1836).
37 *Ibid.*, p. 189 (June 14, 1837).
38 *Ibid.*, p. 158.
39 *Ibid.*, p. 143 (Feb. 27, 1839).

Often, too, they had legitimate excuses: press of business left them no time to make their reports; they or their families or their clerks were ill; their instructions were misunderstood; the mail was irregular and subject to delay. These were normal aspects of administrative operations in a frontier community. But also on the edge of civilization, morality did not move in so limited a circle as in the metropolis, and the standards of many receivers fell below the expectations of the capital city. In 1841 Congress sought to strengthen official morality by legislation imposing penalties upon any official converting public money to his private use, investing it in property, or lending it with or without interest. Neglect or refusal to pay over public money on demand was declared prima facie evidence of conversion.[40]

THE NEW YORK CUSTOMHOUSE AND POST OFFICE

The big cities were the seat of recurrent trouble, and among them New York had some spectacular lapses. The most astounding of these was the case of Samuel Swartwout, collector of the port of New York from 1829 to 1838.

Swartwout, a descendant of one of the earliest Dutch families to emigrate to the New World, was born in Poughkeepsie, New York, in 1783. He and his brothers, John and Robert, were all active in the public affairs of their day. Samuel became one of Aaron Burr's messengers, was arrested by General Wilkinson in New Orleans as the bearer of secret code messages, subsequently tried and acquitted, and testified against Burr at his trial in Richmond.[41] Afterward he challenged Wilkinson to a duel, and posted the General as a coward when he declined. This event aroused the admiration of General Andrew Jackson. Later Swartwout transferred his political allegiance to Jackson and worked without success to swing the New York vote in his favor in 1824.

Among the crowds that attended Jackson's inauguration on March 4, 1829, Samuel Swartwout was present and actively occupied. He wrote his friend, Jesse Hoyt, on March 14, 1829, "*. . . no d—d rascal who made use of his office or its profits*

40 5 Stat. 439 (August 13, 1841).

41 *Dictionary of American Biography*, XVIII, 238.

for the purpose of keeping Mr. Adams in, and General Jackson out of power, *is entitled to the least lenity or mercy, save that of hanging*. . . . Whether or not, I shall get any thing in the general scramble for plunder, remains to be proven; but I rather *guess* I shall. . . . The great goers are the new men; the old troopers being all spavined and ringboned from previous hard travel." [42] Swartwout guessed right. He became collector of the port of New York, where entered nearly two-thirds of all imports into the United States.

The appointment astonished and dismayed Van Buren. He had taken the initiative to warn the merchants of New York and to put the two New York Senators on guard. To Jackson he wrote, "It is my clear and decided opinion (and a firmer or better grounded conviction I never entertained in my life) that the appointment of Mr. Swartwout to the office of Collector of the Port of New York would not be in accordance with public sentiment, the interests of the Country or to the credit of the administration. . . . I feel it my duty to add that his selection would in my judgment be a measure that would in the end be deeply lamented by every sincere and intelligent friend of your administration throughout the Union." [43]

Jackson disregarded this well-informed advice and on the following day wrote Van Buren, "Respecting Mr. Swartwout all agree, and many have spoken, that he is a warm hearted, zealous and generous man, strictly honest and correct in all his dealings and conduct; none have impugned his integrity or honor. He is reputed to be poor, but as an honest man is 'the noblest work of God,' I cannot recognise this as an objection to any man." [44] Jackson's judgment was never more completely confused.

At the end of his first four-year term there was some suspicion that all was not well in the New York customhouse, but after personal explanations Swartwout was confirmed by a Whig Sen-

42 This letter was first published in a political book by William L. Mackenzie, *The Lives and Opinions of Benj'n Franklin Butler . . . and Jesse Hoyt*, pp. 50–51.

43 Van Buren, *Autobiography*, pp. 262–64 (April 23, 1829). Van Buren was not alone in these early apprehensions. Representative C. C. Cambreleng, in private life a New York merchant, wrote Van Buren on April 28, 1829, ". . . mark me—if our Collector is not a defaulter in four years, I'll swallow the Treasury if it was all coined in coppers." *Ibid.*, p. 268.

44 *Ibid.*, pp. 264–65 (April 24, 1829).

ate for a second term that expired March 29, 1838. Van Buren did not nominate him for further service. In August 1838, he sailed from New York for England. On November 13, 1838, the Attorney General, Felix Grundy, wrote Jackson, "You will be surprised to hear, what is a secret here as yet, but will be public in a few days, General Saml Swartwout, late collector at the port of Newyork is a defaulter to the amount of a million and a quarter dollars. . . ." [45] The secret was soon disclosed to an astounded public, and was followed by the departure for Europe of the New York district attorney, William M. Price, an accomplice who had embezzled customhouse funds on his own account as well as cooperating with Swartwout.[46]

The amount finally ascertained to have been stolen by Swartwout was $1,225,705.69.[47] All previous losses sank into insignificance and relative oblivion. Philip Hone wrote in his diary, "it is the most appalling account of delinquency ever exhibited in this country. . . ." [48] There followed an investigation by the Treasury Department and by a select committee of the House of Representatives. The reports of these two inquiries presented an intimate picture of lax administration and outright corruption.[49]

Swartwout found several methods of hoodwinking a somnolent Treasury. He collected fines and forfeitures, reported them quarterly, but retained the proceeds. He withheld from deposit large sums paid by importers under protest, awaiting a final determination of their liability. He also withheld large sums paid by importers on duty "not yet ascertained." The merchants got their goods, and Swartwout received the money, in both cases reporting faithfully the sums held. He took bonds from import-

45 Jackson, *Correspondence*, V, 569–70 (Nov. 13, 1838).

46 The customhouse auditor had discovered a part of the shortage in August 1838. Swartwout appeared surprised and asked the auditor to make a reexamination, during which he went off to England. Apparently all this did not become known in Washington until early November.

47 House Doc. 13, 25th Cong., 3d sess., p. 25 (Dec. 10, 1838).

48 Hone, *Diary* (Nevins ed.), p. 375 (Dec. 26, 1838).

49 The Treasury investigation was conducted by the first comptroller and solicitor and is found in House Document 13, 25th Cong., 3d sess. (Dec. 10, 1838). The House committee report is found in House Report 313, 25th Cong., 3d sess. (Feb. 27, 1839), including the findings of the Whig majority and the Democratic minority as well as the journal, with a verbatim record of evidence and testimony. This document will be cited hereafter as House Report 313; the Treasury investigation as House Doc. 13.

ers to secure payment of duties, and when the bonds were paid, neglected to report payment or to deposit the amount. This was his greatest source of "revenue," and the last one to which he resorted. About one million dollars of his embezzlement occurred in these four operations.[50]

What could have permitted such a "flagrant breach of morality"? The first cause was obviously the error in assessing the true characters of Swartwout and Price. They came to Washington armed with their letters and record of service to Jackson. Had the President inquired, he might have discovered that among those who knew Swartwout's reputation in 1829 his character as a man of pecuniary responsibility was "decidedly bad," and that Price had "as little reputation for pecuniary responsibility as any man you could find." [51]

Negligence or connivance among key members of the customhouse staff was a contributing factor. The naval officer apparently failed to examine the cash and bond accounts and merely certified the figures that were supplied to him. As an independent internal check, he was useless.[52] The behavior of the cashier, Henry Ogden, and the assistant cashier, Joshua Phillips, was much worse. As soon as the first comptroller and solicitor arrived on the scene from Washington to begin the Treasury investigation, Ogden met them and revealed that he had known about the shortages from the beginning.[53] Phillips also was aware of the embezzlements.[54] When asked why he concealed Swartwout's deficiencies, he replied, "I was Mr. Swartwout's clerk, and would not betray the secrets of my employer." [55] Nathaniel Schultz, one-time auditor of the New York customhouse, confirmed this extraordinary sense of personal responsibility. Schultz, who retired on July 1, 1836, after thirty-seven years of service as auditor and who was privy to Swartwout's transactions, was asked why he did not inform the Treasury Department. He replied, "I did not, *because I did not think it my duty* . . . we clerks of the custom-house consider ourselves *as in the service of the collector, and not in the*

50 House Doc. 13, p. 29.
51 House Report 313, pp. 31–32, 102, 104.
52 House Doc. 13, p. 97.
53 *Ibid.*, p. 19.
54 *Ibid.*, p. 47.
55 House Report 313, p. 362.

service of the United States."[56] Swartwout was the prince of adventurers, a sanguine speculator who to the last expected to win and who no doubt intended to repay his "loans" from the customhouse.

The sequel of Swartwout's defalcations was in its way as amazing as the case itself. It was reasonable to suppose that at least the barn door would have been securely locked against any more thievery, but Swartwout's successor, Jesse Hoyt, outdid his predecessor in everything but the amount embezzled. Van Buren's judgment was sound with respect to Swartwout, but grievously wrong with regard to Hoyt. He fled the collector's office in 1841, a defaulter in the admitted sum of over $150,000 and probably in the sum of $200,000 more.

Hoyt not only stole customs revenue freely for stock speculation. He corrupted the whole New York customhouse, defied the Secretary of the Treasury, and entered into fraudulent relations with American importers seeking to kill the trade of foreign competitors. Almost every aspect of corruption was revealed after he fled the scene. Purchasing was full of graft, favoritism, and extravagance; appointments were based entirely on party affiliation; subordinates were inattentive and absent from duty; the evil practice of taking private fees from importers flourished; the accounting system was defective and encouraged Hoyt's reckless course; political assessments were levied against all and sundry; employees who testified against the system were discharged from their offices; excessive fees were collected and pocketed; and illegal seizures were made to swell the collector's profits.[57] A more complete scene of demoralization would be difficult to imagine.[58]

[56] *Ibid.*, p. 265. At least four high-ranking officials thus admitted knowledge of Swartwout's affairs: Price, the district attorney; Ogden, the cashier; Phillips, the assistant cashier; and Schultz, the one-time auditor of the customhouse.

[57] *Niles Register*, LV, 357 (Feb. 2, 1839).

[58] The evidence on this situation is set out at length in the report of the three commissioners appointed by President Tyler to investigate Hoyt's stealings. The majority report (William M. Steuart and Alfred Kelley) set out the facts that have been summarized here; an independent report by George Poindexter concurred for the most part but added a severe condemnation of the Whig incumbent who had succeeded Hoyt, Edward Curtis. The system was obviously deeply entrenched in both the Whig and Democratic New York machines. House Doc. 212, 27th Cong., 2d sess. (April 30, 1842). The Poindexter report was also separately

The decline of standards in the New York customhouse was illustrated by the sinister practice of extorting private fees from merchants. Secretary of the Treasury Duane condemned this practice in the strongest terms and ordered the removal of any person proved to have taken private compensation. "One abuse of this kind will lead to others; and at last there will be a laxity of moral feeling utterly inconsistent with the character of the country, and the honor of its government. It is altogether a mistake that the receipt of private compensation is, *as one of your officers supposes,* a private affair between the officer and the merchant. . . ." [59]

How ineffective letter writing by the Treasury Department to the New York collectors was as a means of administrative control was soon revealed. In 1842 it was demonstrated that "the practice of *taking more than legal fees* . . . and the practice of receiving from importers and consignees, or their clerks, *donations either in money or goods,* as a compensation for the prompt performance of official or extra-official duties by others, had become so general in the New York custom-house as no longer to call forth censure or excite surprise, and scarcely even to attract notice." [60] This form of bribery was not confined to clerks, but prevailed also among the assistant appraisers and the inspectors.

The New York City post office fell into the hands of another political adventurer during the 1850's, Isaac V. Fowler. Fowler had been an active Democratic politician in New York, and held his first appointment as postmaster in 1853 from President Pierce. Buchanan gave him a recess appointment in 1857 and he was nominated and confirmed on May 17, 1858. His embezzlements had already been running for over two years and continued until his flight to Mexico in 1860, leaving arrearages of over $150,000.[61] The circumstances surrounding the case were curiously reminiscent of the exploits of Samuel Swartwout.

---

printed in House Report 669, 27th Cong., 2d sess. (April 28, 1842). For incidental data, including the defense of some of the implicated merchants, see House Doc. 213, 27th Cong., 2d sess. (May 10, 1842); and House Doc. 230, 27th Cong., 2d sess. (May 20, 1842).

59 *Niles Register,* XLIV, 417 (August 24, 1833).

60 House Doc. 212, 27th Cong., 2d sess., p. 61 (April 30, 1842).

61 House Ex. Doc. 91, 36th Cong., 1st sess. (June 5, 1860).

Fowler's regular reports showed deficits on their face, but the sixth auditor seemed unable to grasp their significance and failed to comply with his clear obligation to report the arrearages to the Postmaster General. Fowler long delayed executing his bond under his second appointment; the department did nothing but write repeated letters on the subject—an extraordinary leniency based on Fowler's presumed character as a gentleman possessed of an ample fortune. The assistant postmaster in the New York office readily admitted that he knew about Fowler's defalcation from 1857 onward, and excused his silence by declaring, "as the appointed and confidential clerk of the postmaster, he did not feel at liberty to communicate to the department information of the fact." [62] He in turn was short $1,190 in his accounts, a sum that he had advanced to Fowler.

Such individual stealings as these do not condemn a whole service, and it must be recognized that the great mass of officials accountable for public money performed their duty faithfully. At the close of President Tyler's administration he reported that during the preceding four years only two cases of embezzlement had occurred.[63] A history of fraud in government office from 1829 to 1861 would disclose much more than these pages record,[64] but it would also disclose honest performance of duty by the large majority of public officials.

JACKSONIAN IDEALS

The frauds and perversions that occurred from 1829 to 1861 were condemned by responsible members of both Houses and by the heads of the executive departments. The ideals of most men in public life, indeed, were not different from those that had prevailed during the years of the Federalists and the Jeffersonians. The pressures and temptations were greater, and a minority, both in Congress and in the executive branch, betrayed the standards that the majority set for themselves.

62 *Ibid.*, p. 15.

63 Richardson, *Messages*, IV, 365 (Feb. 21, 1845).

64 The history of public contracting remains to be written and would produce much evidence of graft and corruption in supplies and construction. See for one example the investigation of corrupt practices in building the Capitol extension during the 1850's. Senate Report 1, 33d Cong., Special Session, pp. 10–24, and supporting evidence (March 22, 1853).

Congress found it particularly difficult to discipline or control its members. A high standard of conduct was, nevertheless, formulated for Congressmen by the House committee investigating the Colt revolver case, set out in the following passage.

The character of the representative of a free people, especially in its highest halls of legislation, should not only be pure, but it should be beyond the reach even of suspicion. It should be frank, manly, incorruptible in all respects, and unapproachable by those who are interested in the results of his action. . . . Any departure from this high standard fixed by the people, and reflected in the institutions under which we live, shocks the moral sentiment of the country, and inflicts a mortal stab upon the influence, power, and permanency of the government. The highest standard of moral propriety should exhibit itself in every act connected with the public trust with which he has been clothed. Such being the only standard which the representative should be willing to recognise, his life and conduct should be such as to be a standing advertisement to the world, that to approach him in any other than an honorable cause, or to seek his services in any other than the advancement of honest and just schemes and measures strictly within the bounds of the constitution and laws of the land, would be an outrage of so grave a character as to merit and receive the sternest rebuke and the severest punishment.[65]

Men high in public station were usually sensitive to the moral requirements of their position. "It is a safe rule," said Lewis Cass, "for a public officer, never to do an act, which he would not be willing should be disclosed to the whole world." [66] Amos Kendall found much abuse of the franking privilege by persons holding high station and in his 1836 report as Postmaster General condemned this laxness. Local postmasters were subject to removal for this offense, but "public officers of higher dignity, though more criminal" who franked the letters of their friends and neighbors could not be reached.[67] Kendall declined to frank even his wife's letters, a departure from ordinary practice that brought him some "sarcastic" remarks from his colleagues.

Harriet Lane, Buchanan's niece and mistress of the White House, took advantage of her position to use the public vessel named in her honor for personal trips, much to the annoyance

65 House Report 353, 33d Cong., 1st sess., p. 2 (August 3, 1854).

66 Frank B. Woodford, *Lewis Cass,* p. 150.

67 Senate Doc. 1, 24th Cong., 2d sess., p. 543 (Dec. 5, 1836).

of the President. "The practice," he told his niece, "of employing national vessels on pleasure excursions, to gratify any class of people, is a fair subject of public criticism." He undertook to issue a general order through the Treasury and Navy Departments to end this privilege.[68] Jefferson Davis scolded his wife because she asked the departmental messenger to carry a parcel for her to a shop—a strictness of conduct that was in remarkable contrast to general practice.[69]

Repeated instructions from the Secretaries of departments enjoined proper standards of official behavior. Kendall summarized his circular to the clerks of the fourth auditor's office by declaring, "It is important to guard against the slightest violation of principle. . . . Not only the public interest, but the reputation of our government and country require the practice of rigid morality by those engaged in public business." [70] The Pension Office issued instructions in 1833 and again in 1836 to prevent fraudulent practices.[71] The collectors of customs were instructed to use "every possible diligence to check and expose any attempted fraud" on the part of those claiming fishery bounties.[72]

Department heads were also vigilant to protect the reputations of their clerks, unjustly accused. An irresponsible member of the House made allegations against an Interior Department clerk in 1850, and when he refused to substantiate the charges, Secretary Ewing demanded their withdrawal "on the floor of Congress" as publicly as they were made.[73]

Public men, then as later, were embarrassed by receiving unsolicited gifts. President Jackson was annoyed by receiving a present of a lion and two horses from the Emperor of Morocco. He had to ask Congress what to do with these animals, and meanwhile instructed all foreign agents not to receive presents

68 George T. Curtis, *Life of Buchanan,* II, 243 (June 10, 1859).

69 Varina J. Davis, *Jefferson Davis,* I, 571–72.

70 Kendall, *Autobiography,* p. 318.

71 Senate Doc. 404, 25th Cong., 2d sess., p. 45 and p. 51 (Nov. 27, 1833, and September 1836).

72 National Archives, Treasury Department, Circulars to Collectors and Others, 1850–1862, New Series, No. 58 (August 30, 1851).

73 National Archives, Department of the Interior, Letter Book, Miscellaneous, No. 1, pp. 19a, 21 (March 25, and April 16, 1850).

under any circumstances.[74] An acquaintance in the New York customhouse sent Secretary of the Treasury Taney two boxes of his favorite cigars. The Secretary insisted on paying for them, writing to his friend, "You will, perhaps, smile at what you may think my fastidiousness about such a trifle as your cigars. But I have thought it the true rule for a public man, and that it ought to be inflexibly adhered to in every case. . . ." [75] President Polk would accept nothing of greater value than a book or a cane, a rule applied also to Mrs. Polk.[76] Buchanan made it an invariable rule as President to accept no gifts of any value even from his intimate friends.[77]

John Quincy Adams received a gift of soap from a manufacturer exhibiting at a Washington fair. His inclination was to decline the present but his wife, as he put it, shamed him out of that fancy. "My principle has always been," he wrote in his diary, "to refuse all presents offered to me as a public man; but, where the value is very small, I thought it would be ridiculous to make a point upon it. It has not always been easy for me to draw the line of distinction." [78] More alarming was the practice discovered by Amos Kendall by which pursers and navy agents made valuable presents to the clerks who examined their accounts. He promptly forbade such transactions on pain of instant removal.[79]

Despite much contemporary aspersion, Amos Kendall, fourth auditor and Postmaster General from 1829 to 1840, might well be remembered as the defender of traditional standards of public morality. To him is due the first code of official ethics that has come to attention. In an 1829 circular addressed to his

74 Richardson, *Messages*, III, 37 (Jan. 6, 1834).

75 Carl Brent Swisher, *Roger B. Taney* (New York: Macmillan, 1935), pp. 289–90.

76 Eugene Irving McCormac, *James K. Polk: a Political Biography* (Berkeley: University of California Press, 1922), p. 331.

77 Curtis, *Life of Buchanan*, II, 239.

78 Adams, *Memoirs*, XII, 267 (June 2, 1846). See Senate Doc. 49, 23d Cong., 1st sess. (Jan. 22, 1834), for an account of presents given to foreign agents of the United States. The efforts of stage-line contractors to give free transportation to important persons and Kendall's account of presents from contractors have also been noted.

79 Kendall, *Autobiography*, p. 463.

clerks he preached a little sermon on the duties of public officers and laid down a series of rules of conduct. He told his clerks that it would give the office a bad name if they were seen traversing the city or country during office hours, that they must not spend the hours of business reading newspapers, or use quills and stationery for private purposes. The reputation of the government, he said, requires "the practice of rigid morality by those engaged in public business. Gambling, intemperance, and extravagance ought not to be tolerated in the agents of the people. An habitual gambler can scarcely be a man of integrity. . . . The intemperate man, if not led into other vices by his indulgencies, is no better than a lunatic. A madman ought as soon to be trusted in office. Extravagant habits of any kind, leading to expenditures beyond our income, ought not to be tolerated in a public officer." [80] The rules of behavior followed these admonitions.

1. Every clerk will be in his room, ready to commence business, at nine o'clock A.M., and will apply himself with diligence to the public service until three o'clock P.M.

2. Every clerk will hold himself in readiness to discharge any duty which may be required of him in office hours or out, and in no case where by laboring a short time after office hours an account can be closed or a citizen released from attendance at this city, must he refrain from continuing his labors after three o'clock.

3. Newspapers or books must not be read in the office unless connected directly with the business in hand, nor must conversation be held with visitors or loungers except upon business which they may have with the office.

4. Gambling, drunkenness, and irregular and immoral habits will subject any clerk to instant removal.

5. The acceptance of any present or gratuity by any clerk from any person who has business with the office, or suffering such acceptance by any member of his family, will subject any clerk to instant removal.

6. The disclosure to any person out of the office of any investigation going on, or any facts ascertained in the office, affecting the reputation of any citizen, is strictly prohibited without leave of the Auditor.

7. No person will be employed as a clerk in this office who is engaged in other business. Except the attention which the families of

80 *Ibid.*, pp. 318–19.

clerks require, it is expected that all their time, thoughts, and energies will be devoted to the public service.

8. Strict economy will be required in the use of the public stationery or other property. No clerk will take paper, quills, or anything else belonging to the government from the office for the use of himself, family, or friends.[81]

Governor William C. Lane of the Territory of New Mexico, and superintendent of Indian affairs ex officio, issued a set of rules for his Indian agents that were as exacting as those of Kendall. His order follows.

1. Sinecures are abolished.
2. The public service is to be the great end and aim of all agents, interpreters, and other persons who may be employed in the Department, and every possible exertion must be made to advance the public interest.
3. Private business must not interfere with the discharge of public duties.
4. The expenditures of agents must be confined to the narrowest possible limits which may be consistent with a proper discharge of public duty; and a careful discrimination must be made between private and public expenditures of agents.
5. The residence of the agent must be within the limits of the tribe to which he is assigned, or as near thereto as practicable.
6. All orders from superiors must be promptly obeyed, or satisfactory reasons given for the failure to obey.
7. *The expressions "I can't," "I couldn't," or "I don't know," are inadmissable phrases in reports to this superintendency.*
8. All officers who may disregard or fail to observe these rules will be deemed to be *"out of health,"* and will be relieved temporarily from duty; and should not satisfactory assurance be given that the *"health"* of the officer is likely to amend, his unhappy case will be reported to Washington.[82]

Not all department heads were as strait-laced as Kendall and Lane, but most of them intended to maintain high standards of integrity and morality in their establishments. Their efforts met with both success and failure. The failures were due primarily to the brevity of their own tenure in office and to the incessant

81 *Ibid.*, pp. 319–20.

82 *National Intelligencer,* Jan. 20, 1853. Cf. the rules established by Secretary Guthrie in the Treasury in 1853, noted in chapter 9.

pressure from outside—from Congressmen, from claimants, from lobbyists, from party henchmen, from the young but powerful interests that emerged with the rise of manufacturing and cities. The public service from 1829 to 1861 was engaged in a ceaseless struggle to protect its old standards against heavy odds and a tireless army of miners and sappers.

There were weaklings inside the ramparts, of course, and lack of determination sometimes at the crucial bridgehead, the post held by the Cabinet member who had to mediate between the world outside and the official world within. The outcome was not total defeat for the ideals of the Federalists and the Jeffersonians, but the net result was retreat from the high ground once occupied.

CHAPTER TWENTY-THREE

Government and the Public Economy

During the years of the Jacksonians, the voice of John Quincy Adams was the last to be raised to urge improvement of the national estate by the general government. Federalist doctrine favoring implied powers and broad construction had gone out of fashion, and Jefferson was remembered as the apostle of strict construction, not as the purchaser of Louisiana nor as the architect of the embargo. The Supreme Court had amply demonstrated its willingness to allow Congress a wide latitude of action, but Congress turned its back on Marshall's interpretation. The American system devised by Henry Clay as his road to the White House steadily declined; Jackson destroyed the Bank; his veto blocked the development of internal improvements at national expense; and South Carolina turned the tide on protective tariffs.

In the face of a body of opinion adverse to governmental activity and especially to federal operations, the general government would hardly be expected to multiply its good works for the benefit of citizens. The facts supported such a deduction. The federal government did very little in 1860 that it had not undertaken before 1830. Its only large public service was the post office. The disposition of the public lands was in principle a once-for-all operation, quite different from supporting agricultural education. The federal government withdrew from the controversial area of internal improvements, leaving the interior system of communication to the states and their subdivisions, and to private businessmen building railroads. John Quincy Adams was prophetically right when he wrote in 1837 that with his defeat in 1828 fell, "certainly never to rise again in my day, the system of internal improvement by means of national energies." [1]

During the thirty-two years from Adams to Lincoln the federal government did not, however, stand motionless. It established some lifesaving stations on the Atlantic coast, developed the collection of commercial statistics and in a very small way agricultural statistics, and allowed the distribution of free seeds. Beyond these services to citizens, it was forced into the regulation of steam vessels and imported drugs. It originated a system of subsidies to railroads and to ocean mail carriers. It fought some battles with private manufacturers over military supplies and with the railroads over compensation for the carriage of the mail. It was tempted to take over Samuel F. B. Morse's electromagnetic telegraph as a part of the postal system, but withdrew from this venture. Although the federal government was dominated by laissez faire ideas, it could not stand entirely aloof from the rapidly expanding economy.

The increase in the size of the public service from 1830 to 1860, in round figures from 20,000 to 50,000 federal employees,[2] was due, however, primarily to the growth of population and territory, not to the establishment of new functions. The increase was almost in exact proportion to the growth of population.

NEW SERVICES TO CITIZENS

Lifesaving stations. Federal aid for shipwrecked sailors and property began in 1848 with an appropriation to establish lifesaving stations along the Long Island and New Jersey coasts leading into New York harbor. Within the next few years twenty-seven such stations were set up. At the outset no provision was made for placing these stations in charge of an employee paid for the purpose. As a consequence, Secretary Guthrie reported in 1854 that they had fallen into a dilapidated state. In 1853 the Treasury took initial steps to secure supervision and care of equipment by requiring, where no government officer was available, the services of a person living on the spot

1 White, *The Jeffersonians,* p. 483.
2 *Historical Statistics of the United States, 1789–1945,* p. 294.

and bonded in the sum of $500 to preserve the boats and supplies, to see to their proper use, and to make quarterly reports.

A more perfect system was established by law in 1854. Congress authorized additional stations, and directed the Secretary of the Treasury to appoint a keeper at each one, and a superintendent for the coast of Long Island and of New Jersey. The Secretary also acquired authority to give instructions, thus securing some uniformity and definite responsibility. This was the beginning of the Lifesaving Service, created as such in 1878.[3]

Aid to agriculture. The persistent reluctance of Congress to assist agriculture is surprising, in view of its importance in the American economy. President Fillmore reminded the legislative branch in 1850 that more than three-fourths of the population was engaged in the cultivation of the soil, and that agriculture was accordingly the most important interest of the nation.[4] The House Committee on Agriculture was nevertheless in a state of perpetual frustration. "Agriculture, manufactures, and commerce," the committee told the House in 1838, "have been considered the three great interests of the country; yet it is a strange and singular fact, that whilst millions upon millions of the public treasure, drawn in a great measure from the agricultural portion of the community, have been expended to protect, preserve, and promote the interests vested in manufactures and commerce, scarcely a dollar has been appropriated, either directly or indirectly, to advance the interest of agriculture. . . ."[5]

This was a subject matter, however, that strict constructionists held to be beyond the range of the federal government. When Washington proposed in 1796 an agricultural board to collect and disburse information, Thomas Jefferson objected on constitutional grounds. When in 1859 an agricultural college was recommended to Congress, Jefferson Davis denied the right of the federal government to act. The record of Congress in the field of agriculture was one of repeated refusal to follow presidential recommendations, and of niggardly appropriations for such incidental activities as the distribution of seeds.

3 10 Stat. 597 (Dec. 14, 1854); House Ex. Doc. 44, 33d Cong., 2d sess. (Jan. 24, 1855); 20 Stat. 163 (June 18, 1878).

4 Richardson, *Messages,* V, 85–86 (Dec. 2, 1850).

5 House Report 655, 25th Cong., 2d sess., p. 1 (March 7, 1838).

An important venture was launched in 1827 that forecast the future, however uncongenial it was to the times. The navy had long been concerned about a supply of live oak for naval vessels, having been caught in a competitive price situation in the middle 1790's.[6] In 1799 the Federalists had caused two oak-covered islands off the Georgia coast to be purchased for public purposes. Both Louisiana and Florida contained considerable live-oak forests, but it proved impossible to protect them against depredation.[7] In 1827 Samuel L. Southard, Secretary of the Navy, recommended four lines of action: purchase of particularly valuable tracts in private hands; reservation from sale of timberland in Florida and Louisiana; reforestation of lands already owned by the government; and stockpiling by purchase of timber held for sale by private parties. He was prepared to stockpile enough oak to rebuild the entire navy, to the amount of over 900,000 cubic feet.[8] This was administrative planning of a high order.

Congress approved these plans and authorized five hundred thousand dollars a year, for six years, for the procurement of timber, for reservation of timberland, and for the preservation of live-oak timber growing on the public lands.[9] A forest reservation was organized at Santa Rosa, adjacent to Pensacola; a director, Henry M. Brackenridge, was appointed, with an assistant, and the task of reforestation began. Brackenridge was hardly trained for his task; professionally he was a lawyer, with a taste for literature, and an ambition for diplomatic and public life. He was then serving as a judge of the Florida Territory.[10] He may, however, be regarded as the first United States forester, and was the author of a pamphlet, *On the Cultivation of Live Oak*.

The experiment was short-lived. The new Jackson administration was not interested in a nursery for live oaks ready for use

6 *American State Papers: Naval Affairs,* I, 38.

7 House Doc. 114, 19th Cong., 2d sess. (Jan. 29, 1827); see also House Report 102, 21st Cong., 2d sess. (Feb. 26, 1831).

8 House Doc. 114, 19th Cong., 2d sess., pp. 7–8.

9 4 Stat. 242 (March 3, 1827). Out of this sum the navy had also to construct two dry docks, a marine railway, and to prepare plans for navy yard improvement. See House Doc. 178, 22d Cong., 1st sess. (March 19, 1832). This document exhibits the names and payment of all agents appointed in connection with the live-oak program from 1817 to 1832.

10 *Dictionary of American Biography,* II, 543.

fifty years hence. The reforestation project withered on the soil, much to Adams' disgust.[11] "It was, indeed, a magnificent conception, but it was many, many years ahead of its time." [12] The conservation of forests hardly seemed an object of interest, although in 1837 John Chipman Gray commented on the shortage of firewood and the probable disappearance of the best timber within fifty years. His remedy was private not public effort to conserve forest resources.[13]

Beginning in 1839 Congress appropriated $1,000 for the collection of agricultural statistics. The figures were justified by the commissioner of patents as a safeguard against monopoly or exorbitant prices. In 1854 Congress legitimatized the purchase of seeds for distribution. But when the commissioner of patents called an agricultural conference in Washington in 1858, Congress promptly reduced his appropriation and forbade its use for any such purpose.[14]

While Congress was thus demonstrating its lack of interest in agriculture, the executive branch was doing what it could, with doubtful authorization and with meager resources. The collection of seeds, cuttings, and animals had been an incidental duty of our foreign agents and commanders of naval ships since the days of the Federalists. Merino sheep were introduced into the United States in 1810 by an American consul in Spain. In 1819 Secretary William H. Crawford circularized American consuls on the subject of procuring seeds, plants, and inventions. The collection of seeds abroad became the special care of the Patent Office, an activity organized in 1836 under the vigorous leadership of Henry L. Ellsworth of the Connecticut Ellsworth family. By 1840 he was distributing 30,000 packages of seeds; in 1847, 60,000. The annual reports of the Patent Office, in the section dealing with agriculture, began to carry papers of a scientific character in the early 1840's. In 1838 Congress made

11 Adams, *Memoirs,* VIII, 322–23 (Feb. 20, 1831).

12 Jenks Cameron, *The Development of Governmental Forest Control in the United States* (Baltimore: Johns Hopkins Press, 1928), p. 40.

13 *North American Review,* XLIV (1837), 357.

14 10 Stat. 292 (May 31, 1854); 11 Stat. 427 (March 3, 1859). See on this topic Alfred Charles True, *A History of Agricultural Experimentation and Research in the United States, 1607–1925* (Washington: U. S. Department of Agriculture, Mis. Pub. No. 251, 1937).

a gesture toward encouraging the introduction of tropical plants.

All this was on a relatively minor scale. The annual appropriations for the benefit of agriculture were only $5,500 in 1851. By 1860 the agricultural division of the Patent Office included a superintendent, four clerks, and a curator. The establishment of a Department of Agriculture, foreshadowed in 1789 by John Vining in his proposed Department of Home Affairs, was not to occur until 1862.[15] The improvement of agriculture before the Civil War remained a responsibility of the states and of flourishing private agricultural societies.

THE REGULATION OF PRIVATE ENTERPRISE

Steamships. Although the railroads escaped federal regulation during the Jacksonian era, steamboat owners were, from their point of view, less fortunate. Government regulation of railroad rates and services was not even discussed, but the loss of life and property by explosions of boilers, often caused by negligence or bravado, became a scandal that forced Congress to intervene.

Congress had considered action in 1824–25 to prevent such accidents, but at that time laissez faire doctrines had prevailed. A sequence of shocking accidents finally persuaded Congress to abandon theory in favor of government regulation. It took five years to secure enactment of legislation even after the death of Senator Josiah S. Johnston of Louisiana in an explosion on the steamboat *Lioness* on the Red River in 1833.[16]

The situation was truly serious. Niles reported in 1830 that 1,500 persons had been killed by explosions of steamboat boilers.[17] The *Talisman* was destroyed by fire at St. Louis in 1832, without loss of life "though one lady had to jump over-board." [18] President Jackson directed Andrew Jackson, Jr., to ship no cotton except on board a ship with an experienced engineer and a careful captain.[19] The government lost a substantial sum of money on board the *Black Hawk,* sunk by an explosion on the

15 *Ibid.*, pp. 34–40.
16 *Niles Register,* XLIV, 255, 260–61 (June 15, 1833).
17 *Ibid.*, XXXIX, 222 (Nov. 27, 1830).
18 *Ibid.*, XLII, 201 (May 12, 1832).
19 Jackson, *Correspondence,* V, 227 (Nov. 25, 1833).

Mississippi; the funds were not insured on account of high rates.[20]

The causes of repeated disasters involving serious loss of life and property were mostly due to the human factor. Captains, pilots, and engineers were often reckless and irresponsible. Daniel Webster accused them of criminal negligence, especially in the common practice of steamboat racing which, he said, was "a wanton, intentional, and reckless exposure of human life." [21] A Louisiana statute provided severe penalties for any accident that occurred while the captain, pilot, or engineer was engaged in gambling, or attending to any game of chance or hazard, a commentary on the habits of these persons.[22] James M. Higbee almost despaired of effective control because the boatmen were "so numerous, form so powerful a class in all the river towns, and have so long lived uncontrolled. . . ." In addition to the hazard of careless, ignorant, or intemperate engineers was the difficulty (growing out of the great demand for labor of all kinds) of securing captains of suitable age and experience, and of enforcing discipline upon the crew.[23]

Congress first stirred itself by setting up an inquiry under the Secretary of the Treasury. The results were slight, owing to the unwillingness of owners and masters to cooperate.[24] Secretary Louis McLane then sent out a twenty-three point questionnaire to any who would reply,[25] but without useful results. Senator Johnston's death in the spring of 1833 prompted Jackson to recommend "precautionary and penal legislation" in his fifth annual message.[26] Action was finally forthcoming in 1838.

The legislation, requiring inspection of boilers and hulls, was a weak beginning of a development that led in course of time to the United States Steamboat Inspection Service. Author-

20 *Calendar of Joel R. Poinsett Papers in the Henry D. Gilpin Collection* (Grace E. Heilman and Bernard S. Levin, eds., Philadelphia: Historical Society of Pennsylvania, 1941), p. 69, Letter No. 207 (Jan. 3, 1838).

21 Webster, *Writings and Speeches* (National ed.), XIV, 173 (Dec. 23, 1833).

22 Louisiana Laws, 1833–34, p. 55 (March 6, 1834).

23 *North American Review,* L (1840), 36, 37.

24 House Doc. 131, 21st Cong., 2d sess. (March 3, 1831).

25 Printed in *Niles Register,* XLI, 198–99 (Nov. 5, 1831).

26 Richardson, *Messages,* III, 34 (Dec. 3, 1833).

ity was vested in the hands of the several district judges, each of whom was authorized to appoint one or more persons to be inspectors of hulls, and inspectors of boilers and machinery. No standards of judgment as to safety were specified nor any qualifications of experience or suitability of inspectors.[27] So far as the vessels were concerned, the inspector was merely to certify that in his opinion the vessel was seaworthy and fit to be used. Inspectors of boilers and machinery, after an examination satisfactory to them, certified that the boilers were "sound and fit for use." The owners and masters were required to employ "a competent number of experienced and skilful engineers," but no standards were set and no inspection was required at this point. Failure to employ such engineers, if proved, made the owners and masters liable for damages caused by explosion; and in case of loss of life, every captain or employee was deemed guilty of manslaughter if the accident was caused by misconduct, negligence, or inattention to duties.[28]

Experience proved the necessity of more stringent regulations than those accepted by Congress in 1838, and a much more highly developed system of regulation was enacted in 1852.[29] Responsibility was now transferred from the district judges to the Treasury Department. The center of the new system lay in nine supervising inspectors, appointed by the President with the advice and consent of the Senate, who met annually to prescribe rules and regulations, who acted individually as an appellate authority in their respective areas, and who were directed to watch over the local inspectors, reporting any delinquency to the Secretary of the Treasury. In each inspection district, organized around a major port, two inspectors—one for hulls and one for boilers and machinery—were appointed by an *ad hoc* board of three, consisting of the collector, the supervising inspector, and the district judge, with the approval of the Secretary of the Treasury. The business of steamboat inspection was thus re-

27 The *Commercial Advertiser* spoke with approval of two inspectors appointed in New York. "Captain Bunker has been long known to the public for superior judgment and prudence in the construction and management of steamboats." Inspector Clark "had attained a high character for skill, sound judgment, and prudence." Quoted in *Niles Register,* LV, 32 (Sept. 8, 1838).

28 5 Stat. 304 (July 7, 1838).

29 10 Stat. 61 (August 30, 1852).

moved from the nominal supervision of the district judges and anchored, if not too firmly, in the Treasury.

This statute was more explicit in prescribing the duties of inspectors and the obligations of owners and masters. Specific provisions were written into the statute against fire hazards, a special license was required to carry gunpowder and inflammable materials, the boilers were tested beyond their allowable pressure, the quality of their construction was prescribed, and pilots and engineers were required to take an annual license after proof of competence. Laissez faire thus gave way to public control in the interest of safety of persons and property.[30]

The inspectors promptly went to work, although the roving Treasury agent, William M. Gouge, thought they were too timid at the outset. Their reports for the year ending September 30, 1855, showed that certificates had been granted to 1,042 steam vessels and that 16 had been reported for violations of the rules, while 50 had been found with defective boilers. Over 2,000 pilots and over 2,500 engineers had been licensed. Seventy-four applicants had been refused a license, and fifty-eight licenses had been revoked.[31]

Early experience cast much light on the regulatory process. Owners and captains tended at first to resist, claiming that the regulations were unnecessary in their case, that they were put to heavy expense, that they had as much right to carry on their trade without government interference as a tailor or a shoemaker, that the wages of pilots and engineers would rise with the restriction of their number by licensing requirements, and that the regulations requiring life preservers were useless—passengers could keep afloat, it was said, by taking cabin doors off their hinges and using them as one-man rafts. The engineers were reported to be forming associations to control the local inspectors, and the masters argued that boilers did not explode from excess pressure but from lack of water.[32]

30 This statute was of much technical interest in its provisions for appeal and in the range of discretion vested in the inspectors. For references to supplemental legislation, see Lloyd M. Short, *Steamboat-Inspection Service: Its History, Activities and Organization* (New York: D. Appleton and Co., 1922), ch. 1.

31 Senate Ex. Doc. 2, 34th Cong., 1st sess., p. 433.

32 Report of William M. Gouge, "clerk having charge of correspondence in relation to the steamboat law of 1852," August 29, 1854, Senate Ex. Doc. 2, 33d Cong., 2d sess., pp. 399–404.

Interference with free enterprise was a delicate point, and the obviously competent Treasury clerk, William M. Gouge, who traveled the steamboats for the Secretary, had some revealing comments to make. He agreed that in most matters of buying and selling "the interference of government must necessarily do harm," but in buying passage on a steamboat the traveler was unjustly forced to trust his life to blind chance. With reference to the power to refuse or to revoke a license, he admitted, "This is a monstrous power; but it is a monstrous evil it is intended to avert." [33]

The inadequacy of the administrative organization, much improved as it was in 1852, remained obvious. The Secretary of the Treasury appeared to be responsible, but his powers were severely limited. He had little control over policy as it emerged in the rules and regulations; the supervising inspectors did not report to him as a body; he had no authority to issue instructions (as in the lifesaving service) or to supervise the work of the inspectors. Gouge put the matter boldly. "The system is at present without an efficient head. The president of the board of supervising inspectors is, from the necessity of the case, little more than a moderator of debates at their annual meetings. The powers that the law confers on the Secretary of the Treasury are very limited. A body without a head is a monster: and so likewise is a body with nine heads." [34] This nine-headed monster continued to operate, nevertheless, until a single head was provided by the organic act of 1871.[35]

Minimum standards for passenger vessels. The tide of European immigration had set in during the 1840's. Overcrowding, lack of ventilation, indifference to elementary requirements of health forced some regulation of passenger vessels plying the Atlantic. The first enactment, in 1847, specified the maximum number of passengers according to the ship's tonnage, and the minimum space allowed to each. No enforcing agency was specified; presumably the U.S. district attorney acted on information to recover fines imposed on the master.[36]

[33] Senate Ex. Doc. 2, 34th Cong., 1st sess., pp. 424, 425 (Nov. 6, 1855).

[34] *Ibid.*, p. 427.

[35] 16 Stat. 440 (Feb. 28, 1871).

[36] 9 Stat. 127 (Feb. 27, 1847).

A more effective statute requiring ventilation and health regulations on shipboard was passed a year later. Minimum ventilation apparatus was specified, a minimum stock of provisions for passengers was required, the captain was responsible for regulations to preserve health and had to furnish "one safe, convenient privy, or water closet for the exclusive use of every one hundred passengers." Enforcement of these necessities was made the duty of the collector of customs, who appointed an inspector for the purpose.[37] These provisions were extended to the Pacific in 1849, at the beginning of the gold rush.[38]

Pilots. The regulation of pilots had traditionally been a concern of each American colony, and the first Congress allowed its constitutional authority over the subject to rest without use. The respective states continued to license and control pilots without congressional intervention until 1837.[39]

Two disastrous shipwrecks in New York harbor in 1837 were believed by many to have been caused by fault of the pilots, although they were subsequently acquitted of blame. In the excitement of the moment, it was discovered that New Yorkers held a monopoly in this port, preventing neighboring New Jersey pilots from offering their services. The merchants, shipowners, masters, marine insurance companies, and the Chamber of Commerce of New York seized the occasion to cure what they alleged to be indifferent service, by petitioning Congress for relief.[40] Congressional action swiftly followed. The episode illustrates one aspect of administrative dualism as well as contemporary attitudes on competition and on the value of laissez faire.

The House Committee on Commerce found that in the laws of New York State the "leading defect is the monopoly. To carry on the navigation of one of the first ports in the world, but sixty pilots are enabled to act. The true principle is, to throw the whole business open to competition." [41] It also appeared that agreements had been formed among the New York pilots to apportion the pilotage and the profits in such a manner as to

37 9 Stat. 220 (May 17, 1848).

38 9 Stat. 399 (March 3, 1849); 10 Stat. 715 (March 3, 1855).

39 The various state systems are summarized in House Report 263, 24th Cong., 2d sess. (Feb. 22, 1837).

40 House Report 390, 25th Cong., 2d sess. (Jan. 12, 1838).

41 House Report 263, 24th Cong., 2d sess., p. 4 (Feb. 22, 1837).

destroy competition among themselves. The specter of monopoly was a spur to legislation, and Congress authorized a master entering or leaving a harbor whose waters touched on two states to employ pilots from either.[42] The New Jersey pilots were thus called in to destroy the New York monopoly.

Congress, however, declined to take any further responsibility for the regulation of pilotage. It concurred fully with the declaration of the House Committee on Commerce: "In an industry unshackled by legislation lies the best guaranty of the prosperity of a country. If the door is thrown open to every competent man, the public wants will be attended to." [43] Indeed it was said that within a year pilots were scouring the sea twenty to eighty miles distant from port to offer their services.[44]

Meanwhile in 1837 New York had established a board of commissioners to license pilots, the number of whom was increased; careful regulations were imposed in respect to training and licensing, and free competition between individual pilots was encouraged.[45] The New York pilots were now at a disadvantage in relation to their unregulated New Jersey competitors, and in 1845 induced the New York Assembly to repeal the licensing act of 1837. Senator John A. Dix asked Congress in 1847 to restore the status quo ante by repealing the federal law of 1837, presumably on the hypothesis that New York would then be free to regulate its pilots in the public interest without the handicap of New Jersey competition. Congress declined to follow this program, but did not itself enter the field of pilot regulation. Its single brief enactment required no administrative action whatever.

Regulation of imported adulterated drugs. Restrictions on the importation of adulterated drugs and medicines in European countries had caused the United States to "become the grand mart and receptacle of all the refuse merchandise of that description." [46] The College of Pharmacy of New York had led

[42] 5 Stat. 153 (March 2, 1837).

[43] House Report 263, 24th Cong., 2d sess., p. 5.

[44] House Report 390, 25th Cong., 2d sess., p. 2 (Jan. 12, 1838).

[45] New York Acts, 1837, ch. 184 (April 12, 1837). This is an important licensing act.

[46] From the able report of a House select committee, House Report 664, 30th Cong., 1st sess., p. 3 (June 2, 1848).

agitation for protection against this evil, and in 1848 Congress responded by requiring inspection of all imported drugs, medicines, and chemical preparations used as medicines.[47]

The legislation required a standard of purity equal to that found in the pharmacopoeias of the United States, Edinburgh, London, France, or Germany, and prescribed correct labeling with the name of the manufacturer and the place of preparation. Special examiners were appointed in the ports of Boston, New York, Philadelphia, Baltimore, Charleston, and New Orleans. Unsatisfactory imports were either reexported or destroyed.

The regulation of drugs and medicines stirred hot opposition from many importers and manufacturers. According to Dr. Thomas O. Edwards, the chairman of the House select committee, "No bill ever met with more decided opposition. . . . A large number of honest importers were fearful that great injustice and injury would result to business. Many commission houses and drug brokers attacked it, with a violence unexpected by its friends; while one or more leading commercial journals in New York . . . resorted to abuse of its authors and friends." [48] The House committee was sensitive to the charge of governmental interference with business, but reminded Congress that it had recently barred the importation of obscene prints and pictures and argued that this was a parallel case.[49]

> . . . . The paternal supervision of all good governments is not only needed to protect the morals of the people, but is justly demanded in all that pertains to their health and physical well being.
>
> A suggestion against the bill is, that it interferes with trade, and restricts commerce; and that all men should be allowed to purchase what either comports with their tastes or interests, without restriction. The most zealous advocate of these doctrines admit they are but general rules, and to them there are obvious exceptions. We deem that articles used as medicine come under the exception.[50]

Dr. Edwards, successful in his bill, was defeated in the election of 1848, and was promptly appointed by the Treasury to make a report on the operation of the new law. He found that early

47 9 Stat. 237 (June 26, 1848).

48 House Ex. Doc. 43, 30th Cong., 2d sess., p. 2 (Dec. 26, 1848).

49 5 Stat. 548, sec. 28 (August 30, 1842). On the same theory Congress penalized the seduction of female passengers on vessels, 12 Stat. 3 (March 24, 1860).

50 House Report 664, 30th Cong., 1st sess., p. 19.

prejudices were rapidly passing away, that the medical profession was vocal in its support, that the standards of judgment were clear and adequate, and that the examiners were "good selections, and are diligent, faithful, and capable." Substantively he reported that there had been an elevation in the quality and purity of imported drugs and medicines, an entire prevention of the importation of adulterated and deteriorated drugs, no embarrassment to the honest importer and dealer, increased revenue, and protection to the medical profession and the community.[51] He urged the states to follow the same course, since "the general government has done all in its power." [52] The possibilities of the interstate commerce clause were still obscure.

SUBSIDIES

The novel policy of subsidies to private companies operating steamships that carried mail abroad was designed to secure steam vessels that could readily be converted to use by the navy in case of emergency, a plan that had already been adopted by Great Britain.[53] The report on the subject by the House Committee on Naval Affairs in 1846 also spoke of the desirability of bringing "American energy, enterprise, and skill, into successful competition with British sagacity and capital." [54] The Cunard line was favored with a British subsidy. This policy had been pressed upon Congress by persons interested in steamship lines, was endorsed by President Tyler in 1844, and accepted by Congress in 1847.[55]

The initial act authorizing contracts with steamship owners for carrying the trans-Atlantic mail carried no promise of a subsidy.[56] The proposals offered by Edward K. Collins in 1846, however, required a subsidy, which Congress authorized in 1847. One million dollars was appropriated toward the cost of four seagoing steamships, to be constructed under the inspection of an official naval constructor. Collins secured an annual

51 House Ex. Doc. 43, 30th Cong., 2d sess., p. 11.

52 *Ibid.*, p. 8.

53 House Report 685, 29th Cong., 1st sess. (June 12, 1846).

54 *Ibid.*, p. 4.

55 Richardson, *Messages*, IV, 350 (Dec. 3, 1844); 9 Stat. 187 (March 3, 1847); Harold and Margaret Sprout, *Rise of American Naval Power*, pp. 133–35.

56 5 Stat. 748 (March 3, 1845).

operating subsidy of $385,000, built four vessels surpassing any of their kind, and opened service in 1850. In 1852 the subsidy was increased to $858,000 annually.[57] The Collins line never paid dividends and came to an untimely end with the loss at sea of two of its ships, the *Arctic* and the *Pacific*. In 1857 the post office contract was terminated in favor of a better bargain proposed by Cornelius Vanderbilt.[58] The policy of subsidy was continued.

Subsidies were also invoked to expedite the construction of railroads. The grant of public land to the states for use as a right of way for publicly owned canals in 1822 and 1824 was a helpful precedent. Such grants to Ohio and Illinois were made available for the construction of railroads in 1831 and 1833 respectively. Beginning in 1835 grants of right of way to railroads through public lands became frequent, but efforts to secure subsidy by land grants beyond the right of way failed until 1850.

In this year policy changed. Public lands in the amount of over 2,500,000 acres were granted to the state of Illinois for the construction of the Illinois Central Railroad and over 1,100,000 acres to Mississippi and Alabama for its extension to Mobile on the Mobile and Ohio line.[59] This grant was followed in 1852 by a general law allowing a one hundred foot right of way to any railroad corporation passing through public lands. Despite the resistance of President Pierce, huge grants were made to about forty-five different railroad companies in 1856 and 1857. They were all made in form to a state, which then disposed of the land to finance the construction of the railroad. In 1862 the first grant beyond the right of way was made directly to a railroad, the Union Pacific. The last one was authorized in 1871.[60]

57 10 Stat. 21 (July 21, 1852).

58 11 Stat. 102 (August 18, 1856); *Congressional Globe,* 34th Cong., 1st sess., pp. 2162–66; 2219–22 (August 15, 16, 1856).

59 9 Stat. 466 (Sept. 20, 1850).

60 This topic is discussed in the standard works dealing with land policy. See Matthias Nordberg Orfield, *Federal Land Grants to the States with Special Reference to Minnesota* (Minneapolis: Bulletin of the University of Minnesota, 1915), pp. 102–11; Roy M. Robbins, *Our Landed Heritage: the Public Domain, 1776–1936* (Princeton: Princeton University Press, 1942), pp. 159–68. See also John Bell Sanborn, *Congressional Grants of Land in Aid of Railways* (Madison: Bulletin of the University of Wisconsin, 1899), and Lewis Henry Haney, *A Congressional History of Railways in the United States to 1850* (Madison: Bulletin of the University of Wisconsin, 1908).

Neither the subsidies to steamships nor land grants to states for railroads required new administrative agencies. The Postmaster General handled the first, the General Land Office the second.

CONFLICT WITH PRIVATE ENTERPRISE

At two points the government came into conflict with private enterprise, involving in one case the problem of public or private production of military supplies, in the other the control of a new monopoly, the railroads, in the carriage of the mail. These were to become persistent and complicated problems.

Production of war materiel. Both the army and navy required the construction or manufacture of large quantities of implements of war. Contracts for the supply of these objects were in big amounts and were eagerly sought by private firms. One school of thought held that it was sound public policy to depend principally or wholly on private enterprise in this area, allowing nevertheless that there were no constitutional objections to government manufacture or production. Neither the army nor the navy, however, was content to allow control to fall exclusively into the hands of business firms.

In 1853 Congress directed Secretary of War Jefferson Davis to state his opinion whether it would not be "more economical, proper, and advisable, to cause all the arms of the United States to be made by contract"—a broad hint that some Congressmen inclined in this direction. Davis disputed this view in an able report declaring that arms could be made more cheaply by government manufacture than by contract, that government manufacture gave a standard to determine proper contract terms, and that reliance on private production would tend to delay improvement in models since every change would require abandonment or modification of tools and machinery. He recommended continuation of the existing plan by which arms were made both in the government arsenals and by contract—the latter having importance in case of emergency.[61] Cannon both for the army and navy were made by private firms. A House select committee entered a strong report favoring a national

61 Davis, *Letters, Papers and Speeches*, II, 326–29 (Dec. 1, 1853).

foundry in 1839,[62] and Secretary Davis renewed the recommendation in his first annual report in 1853, but to no avail.

The construction of naval ships induced the same kind of tug of war between private shipbuilders and the government navy yards. The House Committee on Naval Affairs advocated the claims of private shipbuilders in 1846 on the ground of superior economy and efficiency. Navy yard deterioration caused by political interference, already noted, gave some ground for this opinion.[63] When, however, Congress authorized six new steam frigates in 1854 and left the decision to Secretary Dobbin, he directed them to be built in the navy yards.[64]

Four of five steam sloops-of-war authorized in 1857 were also built in government yards, one in New York by contract. Thus an element of competition was placed upon the navy yards. As Secretary Toucey put it, "The object is to open the way to improvement, by summoning the skill and genius of the country to contest the palm of superiority with the navy yards in the endeavor to give the government the best sloop-of-war that can be built." [65] Main reliance, however, was put on the government yards.

The navy could not get authority and facilities to build or repair steam engines and machinery except in the single yard at Washington. This lack annoyed the department, especially by reason of the inadequate performance of repair work by private firms. Repeated recommendations for the establishment of machine shops in connection with the navy yards brought some improvement, but Congress was evidently influenced by the conviction that too much money was being spent on repairs. Moreover the contracts for the construction of steam engines, involving substantial sums, fell under the influence of Congressmen whose districts included marine establishments.[66] In 1861 there were fifty-seven private firms capable of constructing and repairing machinery for war vessels.[67]

Compensation for the carriage of the mails. Railroads were

[62] House Report 168, 25th Cong., 3d sess. (Jan. 12, 1839).
[63] House Report 681, 29th Cong., 1st sess., pp. 4–6 (May 20, 1846).
[64] Senate Ex. Doc. 1, 33d Cong., 2d sess., Part II, p. 392 (Dec. 4, 1854).
[65] Senate Ex. Doc. 11, 35th Cong., 1st sess., Part III, p. 584 (Dec. 3, 1857).
[66] Notably J. Glancy Jones of Pennsylvania.
[67] Senate Ex. Doc. 4, 36th Cong., 2d sess., pp. 58–59 (Jan. 15, 1861).

subject to no administrative regulation by the federal government during the Jacksonian era. Indeed the first state railroad commission was not established until after the Civil War. As the legislative authority for the District of Columbia, however, Congress imposed certain statutory requirements on the Baltimore and Ohio Railroad as a condition of entry into Washington, D.C.

A sharp conflict arose between the Post Office Department and the railroads in respect to rates for carrying the mails. The increased speed and safety secured by rail carriage rendered the stagecoach obsolete. The railroads were in a very favorable position; they had no real competitor and believed with some justification they could set the mail rates themselves. Their concept of a just compensation was far different from that held by the government. Negotiations during 1835 disclosed that the railroads expected to receive from $250 to $320 a mile for a single mail, annually. Members of Congress had been considering $75 a mile. Kendall was indignant and declared that he would put coaches back on the roads rather than submit to the railroads' demands.[68] A temporary deadlock ensued.

Some persons thought only a root-and-branch change could meet the situation. They proposed government construction and operation of railroads under the war and the postal powers. It was clear that the mail had to be carried on the railroads and that it was "not in the power of the Postmaster General to raise up competition with them." [69] The Senate Committee on Post Offices and Post Roads, however, reported against such a breathtaking proposal, advising that it would be better to leave to the states and private companies "the expense and trouble of making them and keeping them in repair." The Cumberland Road was still fresh in men's minds! The committee proposed on its part "a contract, in effect perpetual," with provision for government purchase in case of failure to perform the required mail service.[70]

In this dilemma, Jackson found another occasion to attack monopoly, for such was the situation that the government faced. The old established system of competitive bids for mail routes vanished as rapidly as a stretch of railroad went into operation.

68 Senate Doc. 1, 24th Cong., 1st sess., pp. 395–97 (Dec. 1, 1835).
69 Senate Doc. 291, 24th Cong., 1st sess. (April 7, 1836).
70 *Ibid.*, pp. 3, 5.

"Already," said the President, "does the spirit of monopoly begin to exhibit its natural propensities in attempts to exact from the public . . . the most extravagant compensation." Hinting at more drastic measures, he proposed as an immediate step that Congress fix the mail rate by law.[71] This proposal was in fact the initial solution. In 1838 all railroads were declared post roads,[72] and in 1839 maximum rates for the carriage of the mail were established by Congress.[73] The railroads were successful, however, in the struggle over compensation, for Congress set a maximum of $300 a mile for the conveyance of one or more daily mails.

In 1841 President Tyler complained again about the "heavy and unreasonable charges" imposed by the railroads on the basis of their "complete monopoly," [74] but it was not until 1845 that Congress found a different solution to the problem,[75] a solution that called into play the discretion of the Postmaster General. Railroads were divided into three classes, according to the size of the mail, speed of conveyance, and the importance of the service. Maximum rates were fixed for each class, viz., $300, $100, and $50 a mile. But if half the mail service on a railroad was performed "in the night season," an increment of 25 per cent was allowed; and if more than two mails daily, such additional increment as the Postmaster General deemed just and reasonable. If, however, the Postmaster General could not secure a bid at these figures, or such lesser amounts as he deemed reasonable, he was authorized to reintroduce competition for letter mail by a horse express. It may be noted that the Postmaster General was not required henceforth to advertise for bids for railroad conveyance of the mails, nor for the competitive carriage by horse express. The whole foundation of competitive bids was in fact being swept away.

Here the matter rested. The fear of competition by a horse express was hardly a handicap to the bargaining power of the railroad monopolies. The Postmaster General could do little but accept the maximum rates fixed by law—at about the figure the railroads desired.

71 Richardson, *Messages,* III, 174 (Dec. 7, 1835).
72 5 Stat. 271, sec. 2 (July 7, 1838).
73 5 Stat. 314 (Jan. 25, 1839).
74 Richardson, *Messages,* IV, 88 (Dec. 7, 1841).
75 5 Stat. 732, sec. 19 (March 3, 1845).

THE GOVERNMENT AND THE TELEGRAPH SYSTEM

The invention of the electromagnetic telegraph put a difficult issue before the government, much discussed for nearly a decade before a final decision was reached.[76] Everyone recognized that this invention, the "last and most wondrous birth of this wonder-teeming age," [77] would have a profound influence upon both public and private affairs. The control of the telegraph in the public interest was a perplexing matter to an age deeply committed to the doctrine of the less government the better and to primary reliance on the states for what regulation seemed unavoidable. Despite this predisposition, a strong sentiment developed for public ownership and operation of the telegraph as a part of the post office system or for regulation by law under the general government.

Samuel F. B. Morse conceived the idea of the electromagnetic telegraph in 1832 while returning from Europe. In 1837 the House directed the Treasury Department to gather information on the various systems of telegraph then in use—all of the manual semaphore type. Secretary Levi Woodbury took occasion to make the first executive statement of policy, recommending government operation under the Post Office Department, but not committing himself to the electromagnetic system as against semaphores.[78]

Van Buren and Congress alike were so preoccupied by the depression and by the banking system that no attention was paid to the matter until a subsequent report by the House Committee on Commerce in 1842 which, impressed by Morse's successful demonstration in Washington, urged that the government should "seize the present opportunity of securing to itself the regulation of a system which, if monopolized by a private company, might be used to the serious injury of the Post Office Department . . . your committee . . . earnestly recommend the adoption of it by the Government of the United States." [79]

76 Robert Luther Thompson, *Wiring a Continent: The History of the Telegraph Industry in the United States, 1832–1866* (Princeton: Princeton University Press, 1947), chs. 1–2.

77 House Report 187, 28th Cong., 2d sess., p. 3 (March 3, 1845).

78 House Doc. 15, 25th Cong., 2d sess., p. 1 (Dec. 6, 1837).

79 House Report 17, 27th Cong., 3d sess., p. 3 (Dec. 30, 1842).

Congress responded by appropriating $30,000 to construct an experimental line between Baltimore and Washington.[80] The connection was completed in 1844 in time to convey news of both Whig and Democratic conventions to the capital city. The practicability of the invention was now demonstrated beyond argument. The question remained, what was to be the relation of the federal government to this new force in American life?

Morse proposed government ownership and offered to dispose of his patent rights.[81] The House Committee on Ways and Means, despite some trepidation over the already alarming power exercised by the Post Office, believed the evils of private monopoly even greater, and recommended government operation under the Post Office Department.[82] The Postmaster General, Cave Johnson, who in 1843 as a member of the House of Representatives had ridiculed the telegraph, now recommended either government ownership or public regulation. "The use of an instrument so powerful for good or for evil cannot with safety to the people be left in the hands of private individuals uncontrolled by law." [83] He repeated this view in 1846. ". . . the public interest, as well as the safety of the citizen, requires that the government should get the exclusive control of it, by purchase, or that its use should be subjected to the restraints of law." [84]

Meanwhile events seemed to be moving in this direction. During 1844 the operation of the line from Washington to Baltimore was under the general direction of the Treasury, and the actual management of Samuel Morse. In 1845, the responsibility was transferred to the Post Office Department, and the line was opened for commercial use as a branch of the postal establishment.[85] Morse was continued as superintendent with a staff of four, rates were set, hours of operation prescribed, and the secrecy of messages insured.[86] But at the end of 1846, with the consent of Congress, the line passed into private ownership.[87]

80 5 Stat. 618 (March 3, 1843).

81 House Doc. 24, 28th Cong., 2d sess., p. 9 (Dec. 12, 1844).

82 House Report 187, 28th Cong., 2d sess., pp. 2, 5–6 (March 3, 1845).

83 Senate Doc. 1, 29th Cong., 1st sess., p. 861 (Dec. 1, 1845).

84 Senate Doc. 1, 29th Cong. 2d sess., p. 689 (Dec. 7, 1846).

85 Under authority of appropriation language, 5 Stat. 752 (March 3, 1845), at 757.

86 Senate Doc. 1, 29th Cong., 1st sess., p. 892 (March 29, 1845).

87 9 Stat. 19 (June 19, 1846).

The experiment of government operation of a telegraph line was thus short-lived. Laissez faire triumphed. Congress not only would not buy the patent rights, it was indifferent to the regulation of the telegraph system. Both the "safety of the citizen" and the threat of disastrous competition to the post office by a private monopoly yielded to the predisposition of the times.

TRIUMPH OF LAISSEZ FAIRE

Jeffersonian doctrines of strict construction of national power and of freedom of the individual from government control to the widest extent were so congenial to Americans before the Civil War that the federal government made few advances in its services or activities. Democrats and Whigs left businessmen, merchants, farmers, and craftsmen to follow their fortunes free from government supervision. At some points the government conferred benefits and subsidies, ostensibly for public and national reasons—the tariff, mail subsidies to steamship lines, land grants to railroads, and a long-established bonus to the cod-fisheries. At two or three points the government imposed slight regulations on private enterprise—notably in the inspection of boilers and hulls of steamboats, the requirement of minimum facilities for comfort and health on trans-Atlantic passenger vessels, and the inspection of imported drugs.

To perform these minor regulatory functions no new agency was required, except in the case of boiler inspection. The steady expansion of the government pay roll was due to an increase in the volume of business, not to the discovery of new ways of aiding citizens or restraining them in the pursuit of their affairs. The expansion of public business during these years took place not in Washington, but in the states and cities. The federal government, hampered by the doctrine of strict construction and divided by controversy over the nature of the Union and the future of slavery, drifted through thirty years. Inspector Gouge expressed the sentiments of the time when he wrote in an official report, "In most matters of buying and selling, and of negotiation between man and man, the interference of government must necessarily do harm. . . ." [88]

88 Senate Ex. Doc. 2, 34th Cong., 1st sess., p. 424 (Nov. 6, 1855).

CHAPTER TWENTY-FOUR

The Banks and the Canal Companies

The political struggle between Andrew Jackson and the Second Bank of the United States, the destruction of the Bank, and the long controversy over the proper means of managing public funds have obscured the less dramatic administrative relations between both the First and Second Banks and the government. These have an interest in themselves, since the Banks provided an eminently successful service to the general government for forty years, and since their relations with the government provided the first American experience with mixed public-private corporations.[1]

The Constitution was silent on the question of banks; the Convention of 1787, indeed, had rejected a proposal to authorize Congress to establish them. The monetary power given Congress was to coin money, to regulate its value, and to pro-

1 Much has been written about the two Banks, especially the second one, but very little about their corporate nature or about the means of public supervision of their management. See for the principal account, Ralph C. H. Catterall, *The Second Bank of the United States* (Chicago: University of Chicago Press, 1903); John Thom Holdsworth and Davis R. Dewey, *The First and Second Banks of the United States,* Senate Doc. 571, 61st Cong., 2d sess. (1910); and for the general setting and financial development, Arthur M. Schlesinger, Jr., *The Age of Jackson;* William J. Shultz and M. R. Caine, *Financial Development of the United States* (New York: Prentice-Hall, 1937); Bray Hammond, "Jackson, Biddle, and the Bank of the United States," *Journal of Economic History,* VII (1947), 1–23. The most recent study is by Walter Buckingham Smith, *Economic Aspects of the Second Bank of the United States* (Cambridge: Harvard University Press, 1953). See also for important source material *The Correspondence of Nicholas Biddle dealing with National Affairs, 1807–1844* (Reginald C. McGrane, ed.). The principal contemporary public documents are noted below.

vide penalties against counterfeiting. The Constitution was silent also on the capacity of Congress to issue paper money, or to charter a bank that could issue paper money. The constitutional issue was settled in the first instance by Hamilton's *Opinion* supporting the constitutionality of the First Bank of the United States, and conclusively by Chief Justice Marshall in *McCulloch* v. *Maryland.* The Jackson wing of the Democratic party, however, was not convinced by either Hamilton or Marshall and continued to doubt the authority of Congress in the premises.

Apart from constitutional authority was the question of the relation of the Bank to the government. There were almost no precedents in the states, but such as they were they gave little backing for public supervision. For decades the states chartered banks by special acts of incorporation, prescribed their powers and obligations in each special act or by reference to a previous charter, assumed that they would be subject to suit at common law for failure to meet their obligations, and required periodic reports, but with no means to check their accuracy.

THE FORMS OF PUBLIC CONTROL

The charter of the First Bank of the United States, granted by Congress in 1791, followed this general model, but recognized its *public* function, gave it governmental support, and imposed certain obligations. The preamble to the act of incorporation declared that the Bank would be "very conducive to the successful conducting of the national finances; will tend to give facility to the obtaining of loans, for the use of the government, in sudden emergencies; and will be productive of considerable advantages to trade and industry generally. . . ." [2] Its primary function was thus stated to be public, not private.

The Bank was the beneficiary of government support in several particulars. The Treasury subscribed $2,000,000 of the capital stock of $10,000,000. Its bills or notes, payable on demand in gold or silver, were accepted in all payments to the United States. No other bank was to be established by the federal government during the life of this institution. The President of the United States appointed persons to accept the initial stock subscriptions and to call the first election of the Board of

2 1 Stat. 191 (Feb. 25, 1791).

Directors. Although the government intended to deposit its funds in the Bank, there was no legal obligation to do so.

In its capacity as an agent of the government, the Bank had certain duties and responsibilities and was placed under some supervision, including a few government directors. The principal safeguards to good banking practice were not, however, found in executive inspection, but in the fifteen fundamental rules to which it was subject by law. Among them were regulations against loaning the United States more than $100,000, any state more than $50,000, or making any loan to a foreign prince or state unless authorized by law.

Apart from these fifteen fundamental rules government supervision of the Bank was very slight. The Secretary of the Treasury was authorized to require bank statements not oftener than once a week, showing the amount of capital stock and debts due, the money on deposit, the notes in circulation, and the cash on hand. In addition he had the right to inspect general accounts relating to these matters, but had no authority to inspect the account of any individual.[3] He had no means to test the soundness of loans or discounts or the accuracy of the returns.

The principal reliance for correct banking practice was the assumption that the requirements laid down in the charter, and especially in the fundamental rules, would be observed by the Bank directors, and would per se guarantee the stability of the Bank. Conservative business judgment within the range of these rules was taken for granted. The remedy pointed out either to the government or to persons having private transactions with the Bank for violation of charter or loss of funds was a charge of 12 per cent interest on any obligation of the Bank not met on demand. The ordinary capacity of an injured person to sue the Bank for damages on the basis of the common law was considered to be protection enough. For twenty years these assumptions proved adequate.

Public control of the Second Bank of the United States was somewhat more extensive.[4] Five of its twenty-five directors were appointed by the President, with Senate confirmation. The government thereby presumably had full means of information and

3 *Ibid.*, sec. 16.

4 3 Stat. 266 (April 10, 1816).

a direct channel of communication with the Bank, as well as some voice in its policy. In addition Congress reserved authority to investigate its affairs in case of suspected violation of its charter, and both the President and Congress were enabled to secure judicial writ to force the Bank to show cause why its charter should not be forfeited for charter violation. Revocation was possible, however, only by court decision, with a jury trial on the facts and an appeal to the Supreme Court. Substantially the same fundamental rules of management were continued from the First Bank; and the Secretary of the Treasury had the same power to call for statements. He also obtained authority to approve state banks selected as agents of the Bank of the United States. The government subscribed seven million dollars of the capital stock of thirty-five million.

The special status and privileges of the First Bank were continued in the new institution. Bills and notes of the Second Bank were made legal tender for payments to the United States; Congress guaranteed its monopoly position for twenty years; and it now undertook the obligation to deposit with the Bank all public money wherever it maintained branches—"unless the Secretary of the Treasury shall at any time otherwise order and direct; in which case the Secretary of the Treasury shall immediately lay before Congress . . . the reasons for such order or direction." [5] This was the crucial section that later caused the deadlock between Secretary Duane and President Jackson, and his summary removal by the President.

Both Banks performed important duties for the government that otherwise would have had to be done either directly by Treasury agents, or through other instrumentalities. These included (1) loans to the government, and not merely in "sudden emergencies"; (2) transfer of public funds from place to place; (3) the custody of such funds; (4) payment to creditors of the government, including pensioners; (5) serving as loan commissioners. As a matter of convenience the Banks also made advances to government agencies and to members of Congress for salaries and mileage in anticipation of appropriations.[6] In addition the Banks provided another service of benefit to the gov-

5 *Ibid.*, sec. 16.

6 House Report 460, 22d Cong., 1st sess., pp. 567, 569.

ernment and to citizens alike by furnishing a sound circulating medium acceptable throughout the Union. Beyond this, the availability of notes of both Banks of the United States had a considerable influence in driving out of the market state bank notes of uncertain value and of primarily local circulation. This was a national advantage, although disliked by the state banks and by speculators.

The services of the First and Second Banks of the United States to the government were well performed. They provided a perfectly safe depository of public funds. The transfer of funds was regularly carried out, although the Second Bank required sufficient advance notice in case of large sums. Notice and transfer became routine, and at substantial saving to the government over other means. The Banks not only paid pensioners and holders of the public debt but assumed the risks of error or defalcation in handling these sums. Loans were made through the Banks on favorable terms. Catterall calculated that on the whole the government made a direct profit of over $8,000,000 on the agency transactions of the Second Bank.[7] In turn the Banks enjoyed a profitable relationship with the government.

Albert Gallatin had repeatedly praised the services performed by the First Bank for the government. Secretary of the Treasury Richard Rush gave official commendation to the services of the Second Bank in his annual report for 1828. "The Department," he wrote, "feels an obligation of duty to bear its testimony, founded on constant experience . . . to the useful instrumentality of this institution, in all the most important fiscal operations of the nation." [8]

Complaints against either the First or Second Banks of the United States had relatively little to do with their competence in discharging the functions they performed for the government. The tide of hostility to the Second Bank in the early 1830's was in part deliberately stimulated, but it fed on the complaints of some state banks, on the belief that the Bank was draining the West to the advantage of the eastern money market, and on the

7 Catterall, *Second Bank of the United States,* pp. 464–65.

8 House Doc. 9, 20th Cong., 2d sess., pp. 8–10 (Dec. 6, 1828). This statement, incidentally, had been the subject of correspondence between Rush and Biddle. Nicholas Biddle, *Correspondence,* p. 55 (Nov. 19, 1828); p. 56 (Nov. 25, 1828); p. 59 (Dec. 10, 1828).

charge that it was a monopoly. From the special point of view of this study, the underlying problem was the lack of effective governmental control over the financial power of the Bank, and the inherent conflict between the economic power of the Bank, personified in Nicholas Biddle, and the political power of the government, personified by Andrew Jackson.[9]

THE BANK AND THE GOVERNMENT

Before examining the specific means reserved by the government to affect the operation of the Bank, it is necessary to consider the problem of the Bank and governmental relationships from a broader perspective. The facilities of the Bank were such as to make them advantageous to persons with political influence; and conversely the favor of the government was sufficiently important to the Bank as not to be overlooked. Moreover, the influence and facilities of the Bank, through its branches, might affect the success or failure of politicians or of parties. There were consequently possibilities of grave import in the relation of the Bank to the course of public affairs.

None, however, arose after Nicholas Biddle became president of the Bank in 1823 until Jackson entered the White House. The government during these years was in the hands of James Monroe and John Quincy Adams, neither of whom would have countenanced any improper use of banking facilities. Biddle also was conscious of the necessity of keeping the Bank out of politics. The relation of the government to the selection of directors and branch directors, however, was a delicate one, and delicately handled by Biddle.

[9] The principal public documents, excluding presidential messages, bearing on the relations of the Second Bank to the government are these: (1) Report of the Committee to Inspect . . . the Bank, House Report 92, 15th Cong., 2d sess. (Jan. 16, 1819); (2) McDuffie Report on Jackson's Recommendations concerning the Bank, House Report 358, 21st Cong., 1st sess. (April 13, 1830); (3) Report of the Select Committee on the Bank (Clayton, McDuffie, Adams), House Report 460, 22d Cong., 1st sess. (April 30, 1832); (4) Letter from the Secretary of the Treasury concerning removal of the public deposits, and containing the 1833 reports of the government directors, House Doc. 2, 23d Cong., 1st sess. (Dec. 3, 1833); (5) Memorial of the government directors, House Doc. 12, 23d Cong., 1st sess. (Dec. 9, 1833); (6) Letter from the Secretary of the Treasury, transmitting correspondence between Jackson and the government directors, House Doc. 45, 23d Cong., 2d sess. (Dec. 29, 1834).

Before he became president, Biddle stated his idea of the relation of the head of the Bank to the government.

He should be known to, & stand well with the Govt—not an active partizan—not even a party man—but a man in whom the govt would confide. I am far from thinking that the govt should have any direct or indirect influence over the Bank—on the contrary the less of it which exists the better for both. But the govt is a great stockholder and a great customer—and as the govt Directors cannot exercise the same degree of concert & previous communication as the rest of the Directors & stockholders do. It would be not unwise to consult to a certain extent the feelings of the govt where the great interests of the Bank may depend so much on its countenance & protection.[10]

Biddle thus struck a balance between independence and a prudent realization of the value of official confidence in the Bank's management.

He was determined, however, to keep Bank affairs both out of Congress and out of politics. In 1826 he consulted Webster as to a minor charter alteration and remarked, "I have been for three years past so anxious to keep the Bank out of view in the political world & bring it down to its true business character as a Counting House, that I have been very reluctant to apply to Congress for anything. . . . if our purpose can be obtained without bringing on two weeks debate upon the constitutionality of the Bank, the usurpations of the Supreme Court, & omni scibile & quibusdem aliis, it would be a great satisfaction. . . ."[11]

The Bank's record on political neutrality, at least to 1832, seems beyond dispute. Biddle repeatedly stated his determination to keep the Bank, its branches, and all their officers out of politics. In connection with an inquiry relating to the election of 1828, he denied any political interference, and declared, "There is no one principle better understood by every officer in the Bank, than that, he must abstain from politics. . . . We believe that the prosperity of the Bank & its usefulness to the country depend on its being entirely free from the control of the Officers of the Govt, control fatal to every Bank, which it ever influenced. In order to preserve that independence it must never

10 Biddle, *Correspondence*, pp. 27–28 (Oct. 29, 1822).
11 *Ibid.*, p. 39 (Feb. 16, 1826).

connect itself with any administration—& never become a partizan of any set of politicians." [12] In 1831, when relations with the administration were already strained, he wrote to the cashier of the Lexington, Kentucky, branch, "I believe it to be a fundamental principle in the administration of the Bank that its officers should abstain from any connexion with what are called politics, to abstain not in appearance merely, but entirely, candidly and honestly." [13]

The Democrats denied the truth of this oft-repeated declaration. Jackson had long been known as unfriendly to banks, and was later to tell Biddle that he was no more opposed to the Bank of the United States than to all banks. He might easily have believed that necessarily the Bank of the United States and its branches would have preferred the reelection of John Quincy Adams and would have quietly worked to this end. In any event, the Democrats believed that the branch banks were in the hands of their political opponents, and asserted that in Kentucky at least there was political favoritism in making loans and discounts.[14] A similar charge was made against Jeremiah Mason, president of the Portsmouth, New Hampshire, branch by Isaac Hill, who played a stormy role in the politics of succeeding years. Secretary of the Treasury Samuel D. Ingham intimated to Biddle his intention of keeping an eye on the Bank in view of its relation to the currency, the credit, and the political affairs of the country.[15]

In a letter to the cashier of the Lexington, Kentucky, branch Biddle made known his attitude on these matters. "Politics," he wrote, "should be rigorously excluded from the administration of the Bank. In selecting Directors, the first considerations [should be] integrity, independence, & knowledge of the busi-

12 *Ibid.*, pp. 62–63 (Dec. 29, 1828). After Biddle had lost the battle, he asserted that the attack on the Bank was due to its refusal to yield to political pressure. ". . . they began in 1829 with an effort to remove an obnoxious President of one of the Branches. . . . This experiment failed, owing to the firmness of the Directors. . . . From that moment they . . . have been intent on breaking it down to substitute some machinery more flexible." *Ibid.*, p. 209 (May 6, 1833).

13 Quoted in Catterall, *Second Bank of the United States,* p. 251 (May 10, 1831).

14 Biddle, *Correspondence,* p. 64 (Jan. 5, 1829); the charge was denied by a Jackson man, a director of the Lexington branch, *ibid.*, p. 74 (August 14, 1829).

15 John Spencer Bassett, *The Life of Andrew Jackson* (New ed., New York: Macmillan, 1931), p. 594.

ness. No man should be shunned, & no man should be sought on account of his political opinions merely. Nevertheless in a community where broad political divisions prevail, we must not be wholly insensible to them—we must not exclude, nor even seem to exclude, any one particular denomination of politicians. . . . But still the first question is, their qualifications, distinct from their political opinions." [16] The Bank received intimations from Washington favoring the appointment of branch directors from Jackson's friends, but Biddle stoutly declared that they were given no particular attention: "Nor would the influence of the President and all the Departments put together be sufficient to appoint a single Director who was not qualified for his trust." [17] The record discloses two individual loan applications that strongly support Biddle's contention of neutrality —refusal of a loan to Joseph Gales, the Washington printer and an Adams man; [18] and a grant of a loan to Duff Green, an active not to say offensive partisan of Jackson.[19] The charge of favoritism was not, however, easily put down, and it is probable that branch banks were not always responsive to Biddle's admonitions.

It is difficult to assess the significance of the Bank's relations to individuals important in government circles, but there is evidence that it was not unaware of the value of well-placed friends. Webster was given a retaining fee as counsel, and had no compunction in 1833 in asking the Bank to send him "the usual retainers." [20] In the same year Biddle offered a directorship to Samuel Swartwout, an appointment that might have been defended in view of his knowledge of merchants' accounts.[21] Swartwout, then collector of the port of New York, had an unenviable financial reputation that could not have been unknown to Biddle.

Asbury Dickins, chief clerk of the Treasury Department, was

16 Biddle, *Correspondence,* pp. 67–68 (Jan. 9, 1829).

17 *Ibid.,* p. 72 (June 23, 1829). In November 1829, Major William B. Lewis, Jackson's confidential adviser, asked Biddle to use his influence to assist Jackson's candidate for clerk of the House! *Ibid.,* pp. 85–86 (Nov. 15, 1829).

18 *Ibid.,* pp. 58–59 (Dec. 2, 1828); pp. 95–96 (Jan. 9, 1830).

19 *Ibid.,* p. 124 (Feb. 10, 1831).

20 *Ibid.,* p. 218 (Dec. 21, 1833).

21 *Ibid.,* p. 217 (Nov. 23, 1833).

pressed to reduce his accommodations from the Bank in 1828. He was in considerable straits, and the cashier of the Washington branch asked Biddle to make him an additional loan on the security of his future salary payments. The cashier referred to other considerations, "of a delicate nature," bearing on the case; that Mr. Dickins filled a confidential station in the Treasury "which has the management of the Bank accounts"; that he had evinced the most friendly disposition toward the Bank; that he had rendered important services—all in strict accordance with his duty to the Treasury.[22] These individual relationships do not suggest in any way corruption, but they do hint at a shrewd prudence in choosing friends of the Bank.

The Bank was eventually faced with a difficult policy problem. Should it, under attack from the administration, remain silent, leaving its defense to its friends in Congress, among the press, and elsewhere, or should it take positive steps to defend itself and its claim for a new charter? Biddle decided on the latter course, but at heavy cost to the Bank. His most effectual resistance, he wrote to William B. Lawrence, was "the dissemination of useful knowledge among the people." To do this the newspapers were to be used, "not for their influence, but merely as channels of communication with the people." He offered Lawrence one thousand dollars for causing the insertion in newspapers of articles that he would supply, and added, "There is as you perceive nothing in this communication which I should care to conceal, but as it might be misconstrued, I inclose your letter to me & request that you will have the goodness to return what I have written to you." [23]

The country, according to Jackson's friends, was flooded with Bank propaganda. Jackson construed this appeal to the public as a flagrant misuse of Bank funds, and as a political challenge to his own survival. Biddle may or may not have seen this consequence, but his Whig friends, Webster and Clay, were well aware of it, and were fully prepared to make the Bank the political issue of the campaign of 1832. Jackson was willing, too, and both sides were confident of victory.

Despite Biddle's consistent record of neutrality in politics,

22 *Ibid.*, pp. 53–54 (Sept. 22, 1828).
23 *Ibid.*, pp. 123–24 (Feb. 8, 1831).

he could not be neutral on the issue of the very existence of the Bank itself. Early in 1832 he wrote Charles J. Ingersoll, referring to Jackson, "Long may he live to enjoy all possible blessings, but if he means to wage war upon the Bank—if he pursues us till we turn & stand at bay, why then—he may perhaps awaken a spirit which has hitherto been checked and reined in—and which it is wisest not to force into offensive defence. Ponder over these things. . . ." [24] Biddle was in politics to protect the Bank, but events proved him much more competent as a banker than as a political prophet.

The ensuing controversy over the recharter of the Bank was a political, not an administrative issue. It is sufficient to record that Congress approved a new charter in 1832, that Jackson vetoed the bill, that he was sustained in his view by the election of 1832, that in 1833 he withdrew the government deposits from the Bank after a struggle which has already been described, and that the charter expired in 1836. The Bank continued to do business as a private institution under a Pennsylvania charter.

We may now turn to the less dramatic means that were available to the government to deal with the Second Bank from 1816 to 1836—the power to investigate, to appoint five government directors, and to have recourse to judicial proceedings to annul the charter.

GOVERNMENT SUPERVISION OF THE SECOND BANK

Investigating committees. The affairs of the Second Bank fell into a desperate state within less than two years of its establishment, but its recovery was not due to the safeguards that Congress had erected.[25] These were put in motion, however, by the appointment in 1818 of a House committee to examine the Bank and report on the causes of its embarrassments.[26]

The committee found that the Bank had embarked upon a reckless policy of loans and discounts in excessive amounts at a time when it was steadily losing specie from its vaults. The disparity between loans and reserves was exaggerated by the even

24 *Ibid.*, p. 181 (Feb. 11, 1832).
25 Catterall, *The Second Bank of the United States*, chs. 2–4.
26 *American State Papers: Finance*, III, 306–91 (Jan. 16, 1819).

more reckless policy of its western and southern branches, which not only loaned upon poor security but eventually refused to obey the orders of the central office in Philadelphia to curtail. The president and directors of the Bank were found ignorant of the true state of affairs. To make matters worse, some of the directors and others gambled in Bank stock and pushed its quotations into fictitious levels. In addition the officers of the Baltimore branch engaged in fraudulent operations that alone resulted in a loss of over $1,600,000.

These were among the matters that the House committee disclosed. Their report censured the officers of the Bank for mismanagement, speculation, and charter violations which opened the door to legal action to close the institution. A minority report, friendly to the Bank, minimized the charter violations, and the criminal operations of the Baltimore group had not yet been disclosed. The minority argued that correction of abuses, not destruction of the Bank, was called for.

The House concurred. It defeated a motion to sue out a *scire facias* to repeal the charter, and declined to impose less stringent remedies. It did pass an act curbing proxy voting for Bank directors.[27] The Senate was equally complaisant, declining to require the Bank to secure state consent for branch establishments or to make public its accounts with individuals. "The Bank was saved and the people were ruined," it was said.[28] The distress caused by Bank mismanagement and by the restrictive policies that restored the Bank's solvency under Langdon Cheves nevertheless left a heritage of popular resentment that was to reappear in Jackson's day.

The experience of 1818–19 did not suggest that congressional investigating committees were likely to become an effective means of banking control. Catterall described the House report as "exceedingly weak, being constructed hastily and imperfectly, contradictory in its charges, and in places incomprehensible." [29]

One other House committee was set up to report on the Bank at the height of the debate over the renewal of its charter in

27 3 Stat. 508 (March 3, 1819).
28 Catterall, *op. cit.*, pp. 60, 61.
29 *Ibid.*, p. 58.

1832. This committee split on political lines. The anti-Bank majority reported that the charter ought not to be renewed at that time, but was vague on allegations of charter violation. The minority recommended immediate favorable action on renewal, and John Quincy Adams also made a strong personal report as a minority of one sustaining the Bank.[30] Since the object of this report was not primarily to examine the conduct or affairs of the Bank, which were above suspicion and in a prosperous state, but to set the lines for or against renewal of the charter, its work throws little light on the value of committee investigation as a means of correction or regulation.

The government directors. The institution of government directors was in principle admirably designed to exert a continuous influence on the affairs of the Bank. These directors enjoyed at least the same status as other directors, and presumably afforded an immediate means of contact between the government and the Bank. Experience demonstrated that their usefulness was not so great as might have been expected.

The first group of five government directors, appointed by Madison, were all Republicans.[31] Subsequent appointments were also generally drawn from Republican sympathizers; Federalists, indeed, were a disappearing sect. Nicholas Biddle himself was originally appointed in 1819 as a government director, and continued to serve in this capacity, with the exception of 1822, through 1832. In 1829, 1830, 1831, and 1832 he was both a government director and a stockholders' director, holding two seats on the board of twenty-five. The stockholders elected ten Republicans and ten Federalists at the first election in 1816. This policy of political balance was continued under Presidents Jones and Cheves, but Biddle supported a policy of "complete estrangement from politics." [32]

The five government directors apparently did not function independently as safeguards of the public interest until called

30 House Report 460, 22d Cong., 1st sess. (April 30, 1832). The majority report concludes at page 29; the minority report at page 314; and Mr. Adams' report at page 410.

31 A complete list of directors for government and stockholders, 1816–32 inclusive, is found in *ibid.*, pp. 285–90.

32 Catterall, *Second Bank of the United States,* p. 244, n. 3, letter of Feb. 5, 1829.

into action by Jackson in 1833. They made no regular annual reports and no notice of any separate action by them has come to attention. Although their number was only a small fraction of the Board, they could have exerted considerable influence as a minority block. They seem to have had no weight in checking the reckless policy of President William Jones in 1818–19; Langdon Cheves dominated the Bank during his presidency (1819–22) which was devoted to retrenchment and conservative banking policy; and the government men were shelved for practical purposes by the operation of an Exchange Committee, in effect an executive committee acting for the full Board, appointed after 1828 by Biddle. The whole Board, indeed, fell under Biddle's domination. Attendance of the twenty-five directors at the two weekly meetings was irregular and slender; eight was noted as an unusual number.[33]

The government directors suddenly became important in the conflict between Jackson and the Bank during 1833. By this time Jackson had vetoed the act granting a new charter. The 1832 election was construed by the administration as a mandate supporting the veto and declaring against the Bank; but it was nevertheless fighting desperately to reverse this adverse trend. The government directors were therefore no longer accepted by their private colleagues as friends, and steps were taken to exclude them from Bank affairs. In particular, none of them were allowed on the central Exchange Committee during this crucial year.[34]

In early April 1833, Jackson requested information from the government directors. In reply they recorded their opposition at Board meetings to the method of doing business through the Exchange Committee, and called attention to apparent favors to Gales and Seaton.[35] In August Jackson asked them for information on the Bank's expense account, which was suspected of concealing payments to printers for electioneering purposes. The Board refused to make a full statement, and passed a resolution expressing confidence in the wisdom and integrity of Nicho-

33 *Ibid.*, pp. 279–83.

34 House Doc. 2, 23d Cong., 1st sess., p. 13 (Dec. 3, 1833).

35 *Ibid.*, pp. 23–27.

las Biddle.[36] These actions were not conducive to good relations with the government directors or with Jackson.

When Congress met in December 1833, the government directors sent in a long memorial defending their conduct and assailing their exclusion from effective contact with Bank business. They stated that they had been met with "an organized system of opposition," that their efforts had been thwarted and their rights denied.[37] ". . . from the moment we took our seats at the Board, a systematic policy has been pursued of so conducting the affairs of the institution, as to exclude the directors appointed on the part of the United States from a participation in or knowledge of its most important transactions."[38]

Jackson promptly renominated them as directors for 1834. They were rejected by the Senate on February 27, 1834. Jackson renominated them in a special message alleging that the only ground for senatorial dissent was the submission of the two reports to him in the preceding April and August. John Tyler for the Senate retorted that the reasons for the rejection were not a subject for discussion, and the Senate again rejected the nominations, now by a substantially larger majority (11–30). Jackson yielded and nominated others, acceptable to the opposition majority.

Relations between the government directors and their colleagues on the Bank Board did not improve. In October 1834 Jackson asked them to secure a statement of the profits made on the public stock of the Bank and the charges deducted from these profits.[39] Two of the government directors demanded the proper books from the cashier. He refused them. The directors thereupon took possession of one of the books and worked on it during the day at the Bank. When they returned for more data the cashier was absent, the second assistant cashier had locked the book in the vault and refused to deliver the key.[40] The government directors never again saw even the book that they had previously seized.

36 *Ibid.*, pp. 29–33.

37 House Doc. 12, 23d Cong., 1st sess., p. 2 (Dec. 13, 1833).

38 *Ibid.*, p. 18.

39 House Doc. 45, 23d Cong., 2d sess., pp. 1–2 (Oct. 14, 1834).

40 *Ibid.*, p. 3.

The Bank took the position that the government directors had no status different from that of those elected by other stockholders. Documentary evidence clearly demonstrated that this was not and had not been the view of the executive branch. The special function of the government directors had been clearly stated by Secretary of the Treasury Alexander J. Dallas in 1815. He informed Congress:

> . . . The National Bank ought not to be regarded simply as a commercial bank. It will not operate upon the funds of the stockholders alone, but much more upon the funds of the nation. Its conduct, good or bad, will not affect the corporate credit and resources alone, but much more the credit and resources of the Government. In fine, it is not an institution created for the purposes of commerce and profit alone, but much more for the purposes of national policy, as an auxiliary in the exercise of some of the highest powers of the Government. Under such circumstances the public interests cannot be too cautiously guarded, and the guards proposed can never be injurious to the commercial interests of the institution. The right to inspect the general accounts of the bank may be employed to detect the evils of a mal-administration; but an interior agency in the direction of its affairs will best serve to prevent them.[41]

This opinion was reasserted by Jackson in 1834. "The directors appointed by the United States," he declared, "can not be regarded in the light of the ordinary directors of a bank. . . . They are public officers. They are placed at the board not merely to represent the stock held by the United States, but to observe the conduct of the corporation and to watch over the public interests . . . it was . . . deemed necessary as a measure of precaution to place at the board watchful sentinels. . . ." [42]

Until the crisis of 1833–34 there is no evidence that these

[41] Letter from the Secretary of the Treasury, Dec. 24, 1815, *Annals,* 14th Cong., 1st sess. (1815–16), p. 508. The desirability of government directors had been stubbornly resisted in the course of debate. The section providing them had been stricken from a pending bill on November 22, 1814 (*ibid.,* 13th Cong., 3d sess., p. 632). It was renewed in the fourteenth Congress and fought by Daniel Webster, among others (*ibid.,* 14th Cong., 1st sess., p. 1213). A new attempt to strike out this section was defeated by a vote of 54 for, 91 against (*ibid.,* 14th Cong., 1st sess., p. 1210). The arguments on both sides were summarized by the House reporter (*ibid.,* 14th Cong., 1st sess., p. 1137).

[42] Richardson, *Messages,* III, 43 (March 11, 1834).

watchful sentinels were alert to their special responsibilities; and in the crisis they were successfully immobilized as an obstructive minority—from Mr. Biddle's point of view.

Judicial proceedings. The ultimate authority of the government over the Bank, apart from refusal to renew its charter at the end of twenty years, was to petition the circuit court for a writ of *scire facias,* leading to judicial annulment of the charter for violation of its provisions. Jackson thought of proceeding in this direction, but the success of his veto of the charter renewal prompted him instead to wait for its expiration on March 3, 1836, meanwhile withdrawing the government deposits. The battle over withdrawal, involving the relations of the President to the Secretary of the Treasury, and of both to Congress, has been dealt with elsewhere.[43]

A review of the record leaves one with no doubt that the public interest required public control over the Bank of the United States because of its potential and actual economic power. However, the means included in the charter—periodical statements, power of congressional investigation, five government directors, and authority vested both in Congress and in the President to institute judicial proceedings to forfeit the charter for violation of its provisions—were inadequate to the end in view. The government could protect its immediate interest in the safety of its deposits by action on the part of the Secretary of the Treasury; but this was not a normal means of regulating the conduct of the institution.

In fact neither the state nor federal governments had yet discovered the only effective means of controlling the corporate affairs of banks, viz., regular inspection in detail of the operations by official agents skilled in understanding and evaluating banking practice, and with power to act. The discovery was made, in principle, by Massachusetts in establishing the first Bank Commission in 1838.[44]

THE CUSTODY OF PUBLIC FUNDS

This is a convenient place to note the various means by which the government provided for the custody of its funds, a house-

[43] See above, ch. 2.

[44] Laws of the Commonwealth of Massachusetts, 1838, ch. 14 (Feb. 23, 1838).

keeping function that commenced in 1789 when the collectors of customs began to receive money from importers. For an interim period the four existing state banks were used where it was convenient. Otherwise agents who received public money generally held it until instructed to make direct disbursements to government creditors. Post office funds were long managed on this basis.[45]

The incorporation of the First Bank of the United States, with its branches, provided a convenient and safe depository, and from 1791 to 1811 it was the principal custodian. State banks were also employed where the Bank of the United States had no branch. From 1811 to 1817 state banks again were the principal custodians, with disastrous consequences both for the convenience of the government and the safety of its money. When they suspended in 1814, they held $9,000,000 of government money. Much of this sum was eventually recovered although the government was caused great embarrassment. In addition the government suffered heavy losses in being obliged to accept state bank notes of depreciated value.[46]

By charter stipulation the Second Bank of the United States became the depository of public funds, and acted in this capacity until 1833. It replaced eighty-nine depository state banks.[47] The Second Bank, with Treasury approval, authorized some state banks as its agents; they thus became custodians of government funds. By 1818 a few state banks also were independently selected as depositories, where the Bank of the United States had no facilities. Thirteen such were employed in 1822, with deposits of $900,000 held without payment of interest in return for receiving and transferring public funds. Six of them eventually failed, holding over $500,000, of which a large por-

45 This topic has been extensively dealt with by John Burton Phillips, "Methods of Keeping the Public Money of the United States," *Publications of the Michigan Political Science Association,* IV (1900–1902). See also William J. Shultz and M. R. Caine, *Financial Development of the United States, passim.* The present account follows Phillips. In 1837 Secretary of the Treasury Levi Woodbury submitted an official account of methods of keeping public funds, House Doc. 29, 25th Cong., 1st sess. (Sept. 22, 1837).

46 Phillips, *op. cit.,* pp. 20, 23. Cf. Van Buren's special session message, Richardson, *Messages,* III, 331 ff. (Sept. 4, 1837).

47 Phillips, *op. cit.,* p. 29.

tion was lost.[48] Experience with the state banks as custodians was consequently not encouraging.

With the passing of the depression of 1819–22, the custody of funds presented no problem, held as they were for the most part by the Bank of the United States. No question of the safety of government deposits in its custody was ever raised. Money was flowing in from over 9,000 government agents, of whom 8,000 were postmasters and 343 collectors of customs.[49] Receipt, acknowledgment, accounting, and disbursement went forward smoothly. The government earned no interest on its deposits, which fluctuated considerably from less than $3,000,000 in some years to more than $10,000,000 in others, and the fluctuations were sometimes sudden.[50] The interest earnings were reckoned broadly as a part of the payment to the Bank for transfer of funds and other services performed without commission.

Removal of deposits from the Second Bank in 1833 threw the government back again upon the state banks, the selection of which was governed in some measure by political considerations.[51] Eighty-seven were authorized to hold public money in 1837, when with four exceptions the banks suspended.[52] They held, collectively, about $26,000,000 on deposit, most of which was eventually recovered.[53] The Treasury, however, again suffered great inconvenience.

In 1836 Congress had provided that government funds should not be placed with state banks which failed to redeem their notes in specie.[54] Emergency measures were consequently dictated in

48 *Ibid.*, p. 39.

49 *Ibid.*, p. 47.

50 House Report 460, 22d Cong., 1st sess. (April 30, 1832), pp. 279–80.

51 Cf. a letter from Webster to his son, Fletcher, "I have reason to think some very meddlesome people, in Portsmouth, N. Hamp. are interfering with the Navy Agent, at that place, in regard to his selection of a Bank for the deposite of public funds, entrusted to him. . . . say to the Secretary of the Navy that Genl. Upham, the Navy Agent, is entirely trust-worthy, & discreet; & I should regret that any change, in the arrangements made by him, should be thought advisable. . . ." Webster, *Writings and Speeches* (National ed.), XVI, 360 (Oct. 25, 1841).

52 The failure of the state banks, acting as federal depositories, raised the problem of federal regulation, although no steps were taken in this direction. Senate Doc. 2, 25th Cong., 2d sess., pp. 13–14 (Dec. 5, 1837).

53 Phillips, *op. cit.*, pp. 80, 92, n.

54 5 Stat. 52 (June 23, 1836).

1837. Receivers of public money were instructed to keep their funds in their own possession; the Secretary of the Treasury reverted to the primitive system of drawing drafts on these scattered pockets of specie to the order of government creditors. Until the establishment of the independent treasury system in 1846, state banks remained the principal custodians of federal funds as rapidly as they were able to restore specie payments, although considerable sums also continued to be held and disbursed by receivers of public money. The Secretary of the Treasury protected the government deposits in the state banks by requiring collateral security, and reserved the right to make an examination of the banks' books and accounts.[55]

The Independent Treasury Act of 1846 in principle terminated the employment of state banks for the custody of federal funds.[56] Government money was now deposited in the Treasury and in other designated subtreasuries such as the mint and government offices in conveniently located cities. Assistant treasurers were appointed as custodians at these places. The transition to the new system was gradual, and the banks continued to be used until 1850 as agents for the transfer of funds.[57]

Government agents in remote parts of the country who had to act as custodians of public money were hard put to it in many cases. Some simply deposited the government money in a bank to their account as public officers. For a long time adequate safeguards against fire and theft were lacking. In 1854, special agent William M. Gouge reported to the Secretary of the Treasury that in the whole Ohio valley the government had no building or vault "in which to deposite a dollar or a paper." [58]

An amusing case was discovered in Jeffersonville, Indiana, across the Ohio River from Louisville. A room adjoining the bar in the chief tavern in the town was judged to afford the greatest available security. The entrance was through a back passage under a stairway, so low that a person entering had to stoop until he was almost double. Inside were wooden boxes holding the silver, partly concealed by a wooden casing "somewhat resem-

55 Phillips, *op. cit.*, p. 113.

56 9 Stat. 59 (August 6, 1846).

57 Phillips, *op. cit.*, pp. 128, 130.

58 Senate Ex. Doc. 2, 33d Cong., 2d sess., p. 256 (Nov. 27, 1854).

bling in form a giant coffin." Here also was an iron safe, holding the gold. Around the room was a low gallery from which the receiver could throw down upon any intruder stone bottles, of which an ample supply was kept in stock. The agent slept in this room with guns, pistols, and pikes. "In this fantastical fortification was kept, for years in succession, hundreds of thousands of dollars of the United States money, simply because Congress had made no appropriation to provide anything better." [59]

The independent treasury system continued until replaced in the twentieth century by the Federal Reserve System, although the government made some use of national banks after 1863. The safety of government deposits ceased to be a serious problem after 1846, although secondary inconveniences in the transfer of funds were slow in being removed.

THE CANAL COMPANIES: ANOTHER EXPERIMENT WITH MIXED CORPORATIONS

During J. Q. Adams' administration it seemed likely that the government would become a partner in private canal companies on a substantial scale. The precedent had been established on the last day of Monroe's second term, when he signed an act directing the Secretary of the Treasury to subscribe for 1,500 shares of the Chesapeake and Delaware Canal Company out of funds due the government upon their stock in the Bank of the United States. The Secretary of the Treasury was instructed to vote for the president and directors of the company in proportion to the number of government shares, and to receive the proper proportion of earnings.[60]

Adams was willing to accept this form of government support for internal improvements if nothing better could be secured. Other government subscriptions, on the same pattern as that of the Chesapeake and Delaware Company, were made to the Louisville and Portland Canal Company,[61] the Dismal Swamp Canal Company,[62] and the Chesapeake and Ohio Canal Com-

59 *Ibid.*, p. 257.

60 4 Stat. 124 (March 3, 1825); 4 Stat. 350 (March 2, 1829).

61 4 Stat. 162 (May 13, 1826); 4 Stat. 353 (March 2, 1829).

62 4 Stat. 169 (May 18, 1826); 4 Stat. 350 (March 2, 1829).

pany.[63] Land grants to states for expediting canal construction were also made, but they involved no government relations with private corporations. A Treasury report in 1838 showed a total investment of $3,533,490. Dividends from these sums had amounted over a decade to only $77,854, and it was doubtful whether the government stock could be converted into money at any price, excepting only that of the Louisville and Portland Canal Company.[64] The policy of purchase of stock in such private companies came to an end when Jackson entered the White House. He tried to get out of existing commitments by the sale of government stock in the canals, but Congress declined to approve his recommendation.

Contrary to the provisions of the charters of the First and Second Banks of the United States, the government retained no means of supervising the canal corporations. With the exception of the Dismal Swamp Company, they were not required to submit their construction plans or costs for inspection or approval. The Secretary of the Treasury voted for president and directors in proportion to the government investment, but he had no status different from that of a private stockholder. The companies were not required to make annual reports; their books were not subject to inspection; their tolls were not placed under any control. The government provided capital funds, on the theory that these were works of national importance. The brief experience with canal companies proved little about the usefulness of the mixed corporation. The issue was settled for the time being by political considerations, and was to remain settled for many decades.

Experience with the canal companies and with the Second Bank of the United States nevertheless confirmed old ideas that the government ought to stay out of business. The money subscribed to the canal companies vanished, partly by reason of railroad competition that could hardly have been foreseen when the investment was made. The money invested in the Second Bank justified the appointment of government directors, but neither they nor other means of supervision provided by law were strong enough to secure the degree of control needed.

63 4 Stat. 293 (May 24, 1828).
64 Senate Doc. 371, 25th Cong., 2d sess. (April 11, 1838).

The power of the Bank frightened many of its contemporaries, and Jackson finally determined that the public interest could be secured only by its termination, not by regulation. The destruction of the Bank solved one problem, created others, and did nothing to advance the art of public regulation of fiscal or other corporations. This art was to be worked out in the states, as they struggled with banks, insurance companies, and railroads, and was to take form in the regulatory commissions.

CHAPTER TWENTY-FIVE

Government and Science

The first and last of the Republican Presidents were men with a strong taste for science. Thomas Jefferson was widely acquainted with the science of his day, kept meteorological observations, experimented with plants, and for many years was president of the American Philosophical Society. John Quincy Adams was fascinated with the inventions on display in the Patent Office and sighed for time to become more familiar with them. Jefferson founded the University of Virginia and Adams renewed the plea of George Washington for a national university in the capital city. None of their Jacksonian successors in the White House had a scientific bent.

A parsimonious Congress was slow to make appropriations for scientific purposes, unless an obvious and practical objective was in view, such as the Coast Survey. There were members of Congress distinguished for their scientific and professional attainments but they were unable to sway majorities on these matters. The arts, philosophy, science, the professions, higher education, all these were the undisputed domain of private citizens, or of state and municipal governments. So far as science and invention were concerned, Washington was disinterested, apart from the patent and copyright law. Eli Whitney put together his cotton gin in his Connecticut shop without benefit of government subsidy, or official scientific publications. It would, indeed, have been surprising, given the temper of the Jeffersonian and the Jacksonian world, if government had gone beyond the close confines of necessary expenditures.[1] The age was not one

1 Congress occasionally appropriated small sums to test the feasibility of inventions that promised to have application in government operations. See, for ex-

that looked to government for initiative; it was not expected to perform more than the historic tasks of maintaining order, protecting property, providing defense against external aggression, and raising the necessary revenue for these elementary duties.

In 1825 John Quincy Adams had reminded Congress that one of the duties of a civilized nation was to make its proportionate contribution to knowledge. In 1843 he had to complain, privately, that "the people of this country do not sufficiently estimate the importance of patronizing and promoting science as a principle of political action. . . ." [2] Scientists nevertheless commanded the respect of many men in public life. A House committee, recommending the claims of some scientists on the Wilkes expedition, had this to say: "Men who devote themselves to the advancement of science and knowledge, and the honor and improvement of their country, establish claims to public gratitude. . . . The very nature of their pursuits excludes this class of men from those fields of adventure where the enterprising, sagacious, and prudent, make fortunes. The primary object of their pursuit is useful knowledge, and its application to the wants of mankind. Wealth with them is a secondary consideration. We, who are acting in this behalf, for a just people, should not fail to guard the rights of those who render valuable service." [3]

These admirable views were tempered in other quarters by a certain skepticism as to the practical value of scientific effort. Thus Edward Bates, soon to become Lincoln's Attorney General, entered a comment in his diary concerning the scientists who went out with the surveying parties to locate a rail route to the Pacific. Their publications, he wrote, "contain very little about the road, but are filled up mainly with a mass of learning on the great national subjects of *Geology, Ornithology,* and *ichthyology,* and many beautiful pictures of rocks, beasts, birds and fishes!" [4] Science was nevertheless on the march, although the basic concept of evolution was still ahead and the germ theory of disease was yet to be announced. A general view of the state

ample, 4 Stat. 728 (June 30, 1834) for testing a steam boiler; and 5 Stat. 667 (June 15, 1844) to test the utility of a submarine telescope.

2 Adams, *Memoirs,* XI, 441 (Nov. 24, 1843).

3 House Report 832, 27th Cong., 2d sess., p. 2 (May 25, 1842).

4 Edward Bates, *Diary,* p. 98 (Feb. 4, 1860).

and trends of scientific research and discovery is beyond the scope of this book but it is relevant to note how the conduct of public business was affected by science and invention, and the ways in which the general government participated in scientific work. Since this topic has not been dealt with in *The Federalists* and *The Jeffersonians,* some attention will be given to early experience and attitudes.

INFLUENCE OF INVENTION UPON ADMINISTRATION

The course of life and society was profoundly affected by the inventions of the first half of the nineteenth century. The cotton gin, the application of steam to ships, to manufactures, and to railroads, the electromagnetic telegraph and other inventions were to bring fundamental changes in the economy. Americans lived in a state of excited wonder and admiration as a new world opened before their eyes.

In 1823 a traveler could pass by steamboat and stage from New York to Boston in twenty-five and a half hours, with "a whole night's sleep, in a comfortable bed, on the way! If any one, 30 years ago, had said that such a thing was possible, he would have been thought of as nearly insane." [5] "Do all that we can," exclaimed Hezekiah Niles, "it is impossible to keep pace with the progress of knowledge, march of science and growth of useful speculation. . . . we may well ask ourselves, in astonishment, where is the end of all this, whereat shall we stop?" [6]

The marvels of the steamboat were eclipsed by the extraordinary possibilities held out by the steam locomotive. Niles himself had already asked, "DISTANCE—*what is it?*" and had answered his own question in a remarkable prophecy. "We shall soon have *Oliver Evans'* ideas of steam wagons realized, when a trip to Pittsburg will be only a little excursion—the mighty ridges of the Alleganies being sunk by the pressure of scientific power! Over the water and over the earth—when shall we travel in the air, as we will it? By steam?—we know not; but dare not say what is impossible in respect to it." [7]

It was indeed in the field of communications that the greatest

5 *Niles Register,* XXV, 160 (Nov. 8, 1823).
6 *Ibid.,* XXVIII, 113 (April 23, 1825).
7 *Ibid.,* XXIII, 130 (Nov. 2, 1822).

progress was being made. Since the dawn of civilization man had traveled in nothing more pretentious than horse-drawn vehicles and sailing vessels. Now he was to embark on board steam vessels that defied the wind, and to climb into carriages drawn by steam locomotives that swiftly surmounted hills and rivers. The *Clermont* left New York on its first run to Albany in 1807. By 1830 hundreds of steamboats were plying in American rivers and a House committee could declare, with literary pride, "The Ohio river, which presented an obstructed and dangerous navigation, is now resorted to by the intelligent traveller from the banks of the Thames, the Seine, and the Danube, as an object of anxious research, and of picturesque beauty." [8]

The consequences of Robert Fulton's invention upon the fortunes of the nation were endless and profound. Speed and ease of navigation permitted the settlement of the west in a generation. The Mississippi Valley became an integral part of the nation. The wealth and prosperity of the community were multiplied, and the value of the public lands was increased. In 1830 the same House committee recorded that a voyage from New York to Albany occupied about as many hours as it formerly required days. "Thirty years have scarcely elapsed," the committee recalled, "since the canoe of the savage gave place to the scarcely more perfect flat-boat of the emigrant; and that, in its turn, was made to yield to the unprotected and open keel-boat of the Western trader, or the flat-roofed ark of the Mississippi; and a voyage was then the laborious employment of a year." [9]

The steamboat was first put to use in the public business in 1813 when the Postmaster General was authorized to contract for carrying the mails in steamboats, *provided* they could "secure the regular transportation of the mail throughout each year." [10] The army, curiously enough, took to steamboat transportation more readily than the navy. By 1820 steamboats were used, where available, to transport troops, but the army maintained no such vessels itself. Its experience was none too encouraging. The delay and embarrassments of the Yellowstone expedition in 1820 were due in part to the steamboats on which the contractor re-

8 House Report 267, 21st Cong., 1st sess., p. 2 (March 30, 1830).

9 *Ibid.*, p. 2.

10 2 Stat. 805 (Feb. 27, 1813).

lied, later described as "broken, feeble, and subject to constant decay." [11] The army, however, like citizens everywhere, found the steamboat had no competitor for transporting supplies and men.

The railroads were employed for official use almost from the beginning. Mail *had* to go by the "steam cars" wherever they moved. They were also available for the transport of government officials and supplies and for the use of the armed forces. No special problem arose except the controversy over rates for the carriage of the mail, already noted. The government reserved certain special privileges, particularly with respect to the free transportation of troops, but in many instances were merely a purchaser of services, like any person or corporation.

The potential value to the government of the electromagnetic telegraph (a term then in common use to distinguish it from the semaphores in use in Europe and also in the United States) was pointed out by its inventor, Samuel F. B. Morse.[12] "The importance generally, to the government and to the country, of a *perfect* telegraphic system, can scarcely be estimated by the short distance already established between Baltimore and Washington. But when all that transpires of public interest at New Orleans, at St. Louis, at Pittsburg, at Cincinnati, at Buffalo . . . and at all desired intermediate points, shall be *simultaneously* known in each and all these places together,—when all the agents of the government, in every part of the country, are in instantaneous communication with headquarters,—when the several departments can at once learn the actual existing condition of their remotest agencies, and transmit at the moment their necessary orders to meet any exigency,—then will some estimate be formed both of the powers and advantages of the magnetic telegraph." [13]

The government promptly began to use this new marvel, this "strange and wonderful discovery, which has made 'swift-winged lightning' man's messenger, annihilated all space, and tied the two ends of a continent in a knot." [14] It became an invaluable

11 House Report 70, 16th Cong., 2d sess., p. 5 (March 1, 1821).

12 The semaphore system is described in Senate Doc. 107, 24th Cong., 2d sess. (Jan. 26, 1837).

13 House Doc. 24, 28th Cong., 2d sess., p. 9 (Dec. 12, 1844).

14 Philip Hone, *Diary* (Nevins ed.), p. 773 (Sept. 26, 1846).

military asset during the Mexican War. Secretary Marcy kept in touch with New York by telegram; [15] the *New York Sun* sent Buchanan its latest information "by wire"; [16] the *Baltimore Sun* occasionally sent war news to Polk in the same way.[17] The telegraph was used to summon important persons to Washington for consultation.[18] President Taylor wired former Congressman Abraham Lincoln on September 25, 1849, "Is Mr. Lincoln in Springfield? The President wishes to hear from him immediately." [19] Soon the new wonder was being used for ordinary departmental business that required dispatch. By 1860 the General Land Office was sending telegrams as a matter of routine to receivers five days delinquent.[20] The New York City police department installed a telegraph system between headquarters and the ward offices, on the Berlin plan, in 1853.[21]

The laying of underwater cables began in Europe in 1850, only six years after the Morse system had been demonstrated on land. The first attempts to lay a trans-Atlantic cable (1857 and 1858) failed, but Morse lived to see cable communication in full operation at the end of the Civil War. The State Department was then as close to its ministers and consuls as was the General Land Office to its agents.

The capacity of government to direct and control its agents was obviously vastly increased by the revolution in the means of communication. Relations between headquarters and field no longer depended wholly upon a lengthy correspondence consuming weeks or months. Where the telegraph went, field information could get to Washington in an instant and instructions be dispatched on the same day. The foundations were laid in these inventions for a level of administrative performance that would have been impossible in the days of Thomas Jefferson. The words of man, as Andrew Preston Peabody so eloquently

15 Library of Congress, William L. Marcy Papers, Vol. 12, No. 34,800 (Sept. 27, 1846).

16 Buchanan, *Works,* VII, 129 (Dec. 5, 1846).

17 Polk, *Diary,* II, 465 (April 10, 1847); cf. *ibid.,* III, 17 (May 7, 1847).

18 *Ibid.,* IV, 108 (August 29, 1848).

19 National Archives, Department of the Interior, Letter Book, Miscellaneous, No. 1, p. 11.

20 Senate Ex. Doc. 1, 36th Cong., 2d sess., p. 76.

21 *National Intelligencer,* March 1, 1853.

put it, could "emulate the speed of light, and anticipate the flight of the hours." [22]

Numerous inventions were improving the instruments of warfare, apart from those that facilitated communication and transportation. Fulton invented the submarine and the torpedo, but they were not brought into use.[23] Commander John Rodgers invented a marine railway, to be worked under a vessel for the purpose of pulling it to land for repairs.[24] A carpenter foreman at the Norfolk Navy Yard invented means of working under water on the side of a ship without the necessity of "heaving down." Congress granted him an award of $1,000.[25] Guncotton had surprised James K. Polk with its explosive powers,[26] but it was not until later that it replaced powder. Samuel Colt invented the repeating revolver; the government could not buy his patent at a reasonable figure and the Secretary of War was obliged to contract for 2,000 of them.[27] Just before the Civil War rifled cannon were brought into production, with improvements in shooting that surpassed anything known before.

The effect of invention upon the conduct of government business before 1829 was limited principally to speeding up the mails and facilitating the movement of army personnel and supplies by means of the steamboat. During the Jacksonian period government business was expedited and control made more firm as railroads and the telegraph bound together center and circumference. Technology was also beginning to change the arts of war. The office inventions that were to transform the tasks of clerks were, however, still over the horizon.

SCIENTIFIC AGENCIES AND ACTIVITIES

During the Jacksonian era the federal government maintained three scientific agencies, the Coast Survey, the Naval Observatory, and the Smithsonian Institution. The oldest of these was

22 *North American Review,* LXXXVII (1858), 538.

23 *American State Papers: Naval Affairs,* I, 211–27 (1810); *ibid.,* I, 234 (1811); Bernard Brodie, *Sea Power in the Machine Age* (Princeton: Princeton University Press, 1941), pp. 261–68.

24 *American State Papers: Naval Affairs,* III, 576.

25 6 Stat. 336 (March 3, 1825).

26 Polk, *Diary,* II, 230 (Nov. 10, 1846).

27 Richardson, *Messages,* IV, 580–81 (April 13, 1848).

the Coast Survey. The Observatory was nursed into existence over a decade by a mere handful of naval officers, under cloak of an immediate practical purpose; the Smithsonian was a pure windfall in the shape of a handsome bequest from an Englishman. The army and navy, in the course of their respective explorations, did some scientific work as well.

The Coast Survey. The Coast Survey was primarily a vast operation in applied science, but in its course much original scientific work was performed. The survey itself invented new procedures and came to be recognized as a pioneer and perfectionist institution.

Authorization for a complete survey of the coasts had been made in 1807 in the combined interest of navigation and national defense.[28] An able but somewhat difficult Swiss geodesist and mathematician, Ferdinand R. Hassler, was appointed to secure the necessary instruments in London. He finally returned from Europe in 1815 with the apparatus and became the first superintendent of the Coast Survey in 1816. After two years he was peremptorily removed and the work transferred to the army and navy.[29] Here it languished for twenty years. Hassler became a New York farmer, a customhouse gauger, and a teacher of mathematics.[30]

Jackson reappointed him in 1836 to the Coast Survey and until his death in 1843 he pushed on the work, quarreling successively with his official superiors in Washington and with the auditors who revised his accounts. John Quincy Adams, at Hassler's request, introduced him to the newly appointed Secretary of the Treasury, John C. Spencer, and dryly recorded in his diary the qualities that made Hassler so troublesome. "Hassler . . . said that the work, being scientific, must be conducted on scientific principles. The Potentate answered in a subdued tone of voice, but with the trenchant stubbornness of authority, the laws must be obeyed. The pride of science clashed with the pride of place, and I left them together." [31]

Hassler's scientific work was sound, but the Coast Survey first

28 2 Stat. 413 (Feb. 10, 1807).
29 3 Stat. 425 (April 14, 1818).
30 *Dictionary of American Biography,* VIII, 385.
31 Adams, *Memoirs,* XI, 335–36 (March 10, 1843).

came into its own with the appointment of his successor, Alexander Dallas Bache, great grandson of Benjamin Franklin and grandson of Alexander James Dallas, Secretary of the Treasury under Madison. Bache was both a brilliant scientist and a capable organizer. A graduate of West Point, he had become professor of natural philosophy and chemistry at the University of Pennsylvania, and the first president of Girard College, while carrying on his own experiments in terrestrial magnetism.[32] Despite much opposition from inland Congressmen and others, Bache carried the survey steadily forward for nearly a quarter century. By 1854 the chain of triangulation extended with a single short break from Maine to North Carolina, and thence with some breaks to Key West, and around the Gulf coast to the Mexican border.[33] The precision of the work was remarkable. The immense triangulation from Maine to Florida was completed with an error of only eighteen inches, which was found in a mistake that had occurred near Cape Hatteras.[34]

The range and variety of scientific work under Bache were impressive. He tapped the scientific resources of the country by securing noted men for special assignments or for consultation. Louis Agassiz was put to work on the study of Florida coral reefs, and discovered that the peninsula had been formed by a succession of coral reefs, from north to south. The electric telegraph was utilized to determine longitude, photography for chart reproduction, and an electric process for multiplying copperplate engravings.[35] Self-registering tide gauges were installed. In February 1855 they recorded singular curves along the west coast, which were soon related to a disastrous earthquake in Japan. Bache then computed the rate of motion of the earthquake wave, the length of the wave, and the average depth of the Pacific on the San Francisco path. Thus the tide gauge became a new and valuable seismometer.[36]

[32] *Dictionary of American Biography,* I, 461; Merle M. Odgers, *Alexander Dallas Bache: Scientist and Educator, 1806–67* (Philadelphia: University of Pennsylvania Press, 1947); Benjamin Apthorp Gould, "Alexander Dallas Bache," American Association for the Advancement of Science, *Proceedings,* XVII (1868), 1–56.

[33] Senate Ex. Doc. 10, 33d Cong., 2d sess. (Nov. 22, 1854), pp. 4–5.

[34] Odgers, *op. cit.,* pp. 154–55.

[35] *Ibid.,* pp. 154–55.

[36] *North American Review,* XC (1860), 449–60.

During these years the Coast Survey developed into a world-renowned scientific agency, doubtless producing the best known of all the scientific work sustained by the government. The president of the Royal Geographical Society of London praised it in 1852 as "one of the most perfect exemplifications of applied science of modern times." Six years later, in presenting Bache with the Society's gold medal, the president said, "Whether we regard the science, skill and zeal of the operators, the perfection of their instruments, the able manner in which the Superintendent has enlisted all modern improvements into his service, the care taken to have the observations accurately registered, his modest and unpretending demeanor, or the noble liberality of the Government, tempered with prudent economy, all unprejudiced persons must agree that the trigonometrical Survey of the United States of America stands without a superior." [37]

The Naval Observatory. An observatory had been one of John Quincy Adams' warmest aspirations, but a skeptical and politically hostile Congress had ridiculed his plan for "a light house of the skies." [38] The successive steps by which the Naval Observatory came into existence well illustrate the origin of institutions. In 1830 the Navy Department established in Washington a depot of charts and instruments, renting a small building for this purpose. To correct ship chronometers, simple meridian observations were necessary. Three years later a new building for the purpose, designed as an observatory, was erected on Capitol Hill at the private expense of the officer then in charge of charts and instruments, Lieutenant Charles Wilkes. In 1836 Lieutenant James M. Gilliss, a young naval officer with an intense interest in astronomy, was detailed to the depot and when Wilkes sailed off for the Antarctic in 1838, Gilliss took his place. From 1838 to 1842 he made astronomical observations of so remarkable a character that Paullin described them "as a lasting monument to the great energy, indefatigable industry, scientific

37 Gould, *op. cit.*, p. 41.

38 Joseph E. Nourse, "Memoir of the Founding and Progress of the United States Naval Observatory," Appendix IV in U.S. Naval Observatory, *Astronomical and Meteorological Observations, 1871* (Washington: Government Printing Office, 1873); Charles O. Paullin, "Early Movements for a National Observatory, 1802–1842," Columbia Historical Society, *Records,* XXV (1923), 36–56; Gustavus A. Weber, *The Naval Observatory* (Baltimore: Johns Hopkins Press, 1926).

ardor, and consummate skill as an observer, of this young naval lieutenant." [39]

The makeshift observatory put up by Wilkes was far from adequate, and so frail that twice during the season of 1841–42 its doors were blown from their hinges by winter gales. Gilliss persuaded the Board of Navy Commissioners to recommend a permanent building for charts and instruments. Inertia in the House Naval Committee was overcome at a crucial moment when a reluctant member heard that it was Gilliss who had just discovered the Encke's comet. It was not, however, until the last hour of the session of 1841–42 that the House voted approval of the new structure—for charts and instruments. Nothing was said in the act about astronomy, science, or research. The building was completed in 1844, and the depot of charts and instruments soon became the United States Naval Observatory. With some satisfaction, John Quincy Adams observed on the floor of the House that an astronomical observatory "had been smuggled into the number of institutions of the country, under the mask of a small depot for charts." [40]

The Observatory performed a number of practical operations, such as proving nautical instruments, checking chronometers, and preparing charts. In 1846 the Secretary of the Navy cautiously suggested that the Observatory could produce an American nautical ephemeris, "for which we are now dependent on foreign nations, and without which our ships that are abroad could not find their way home, nor those at home venture out of sight of our shores." [41] The first ephemeris was published in 1852. Thus inconspicuously was launched one of the great scientific enterprises of the federal government. No longer did John Quincy Adams need to feel chagrin because "the earth revolves in perpetual darkness to our unsearching eyes." [42]

The Smithsonian Institution. James Smithson, the natural son of the Duke of Northumberland and Elizabeth Keate Macie, a lineal descendant of King Henry VIII, died in 1829, after a life spent in scientific investigation. He left his estate to a

39 Paullin, "Early Movements for a National Observatory," *op. cit.*, pp. 50–51.
40 *Congressional Globe*, 29th Cong., 1st sess., p. 738 (April 28, 1846).
41 Senate Doc. 1, 29th Cong., 2d sess., p. 385 (Dec. 5, 1846).
42 Richardson, *Messages*, II, 314 (Dec. 6, 1825).

nephew, with the provision that if he died without issue it should go to the United States, to found at Washington an establishment for the increase and diffusion of knowledge among men. The nephew died six years later and in due course of time the sum of $550,000 was deposited in the U.S. Mint.

The best method of using this large sum perplexed the members of Congress. Adams stubbornly sought to found an observatory, others a library, others a university. The establishment of the Naval Observatory avoided Adams' opposition to other programs, and in 1846 the act creating the Smithsonian Institution was approved.[43] The "establishment" comprised the President of the United States, the heads of departments, the commissioner of the Patent Office, and the mayor of Washington. The general direction of the Institution was committed to a Board of Regents, including the Chief Justice, members of the Senate and House, and six citizens. The active head was a secretary. Congress made no appropriation for its support, but prescribed that its accrued funds should be used for the purposes of its founder.

The first secretary, Joseph Henry, a noted professor of physics at Princeton University, served in this office from 1846 to 1878.[44] A wide-ranging program of research and publication in the field of science immediately got under way. The Institution began collections of fauna and flora, and the study of the language and customs of the Indian tribes. The range and variety of its interests are revealed in the subjects of some of the early monographs published under its auspices: the physical geography of North America, the archaeology of the United States, the classification of insects (by Agassiz), fluctuation of lake levels, winds of the northern hemisphere, tidal and magnetic observations in the Arctic seas, and a catalogue of North American reptiles.

One of its early contributions was in meteorology. Weather observations by government agents began in 1817, when Josiah Meigs, commissioner of the General Land Office, sent out instructions to the twenty local registers of land offices requiring them to submit regular daily reports on temperature, wind, and

[43] 9 Stat. 102 (August 10, 1846); George Brown Goode, ed., *The Smithsonian Institution, 1846–1896* (Washington: de Vinne Press, 1897); Webster P. True, *The First Hundred Years of the Smithsonian Institution, 1846–1946* (Washington: Smithsonian Institution, 1946).

[44] *Dictionary of American Biography*, VIII, 550.

weather. In addition he asked for miscellaneous observations, under fourteen heads, including such items as the life history of plants, the migration of birds and fishes, droughts, storms, distempers, meteors, and topography. Meigs concluded his circular by remarking, "My only object being the increase of *our physical* knowledge of our country, I flatter myself you will not think my request unreasonable." [45]

About 1819 Surgeon General Lovell ordered army surgeons to keep detailed day-by-day weather records at all posts. These records were compiled in 1839 by Dr. Samuel Dorry of the medical corps. They constituted the basic data for the first scientific study of meteorology in the United States. The Smithsonian Institution became the center for subsequent meteorological reports. In 1849 weather reports were brought together by telegraph, and by 1856 daily weather maps were on display. These were the origins of the Weather Bureau.

SCIENTIFIC CONTRIBUTIONS OF NONSCIENTIFIC AGENCIES

Considerable scientific work was also carried on by agencies whose primary mission was in the field of operations, particularly the army and the navy. The peculiar assets possessed by both the army and the navy for the advancement of science were financial resources, a body of technically trained officers, equipment and manpower that often had no immediate use and could be put at the disposal of exploration or research without specific authorization by Congress and without much additional expense. The civilian agencies had none of these assets. Exploration in a broad sense of the term was a continuing preoccupation of the army, to the Oregon country, the West, and the Southwest; and of the navy, around Cape Horn, to the polar regions, and to the China Sea.[46] The exploits of discovery on land and on sea filled Americans with pride, and justified in the public mind the expenditure of time, money, and effort.

Land exploration. On the continent, the march of Lewis and Clark across the Rocky Mountains to Oregon (1804–06) was in

45 The circular is reprinted in *Niles Register,* XII, 167–68 (May 10, 1817).

46 An excellent general view of western exploration is found in Edmund W. Gilbert, *The Exploration of Western America, 1800–1850* (Cambridge, England: University Press, 1933). Note especially his bibliography, pp. 208–20.

some ways the most spectacular enterprise. It was also the first major publicly supported exploration. Jefferson had long been intent on securing knowledge of the country across the Mississippi, and the House Committee on Commerce and Manufacture came promptly to his aid after the acquisition of Louisiana.

> It is highly desirable that this extensive region should be visited, in some parts at least, by intelligent men. Important additions might thereby be made to the science of geography. Various materials might thence be derived to augment our knowledge of natural history. . . . individuals of research and curiosity would receive ample gratification as to the works of art and productions of nature which exist in those boundless tracts.
>
> . . . . The masses of virgin silver and gold that glitter in the veins of the rocks which underlay the Arkansas itself . . . and offer themselves to the hand of him who will gather, refine, and convert them to use, are no less uncommon and wonderful.[47]

Two months after this glowing prospectus, Lewis and Clark left St. Louis on their famous expedition up the Missouri, across the mountains, and down the Columbia to the Pacific Ocean. The company reappeared at St. Louis on September 23, 1806, and in the winter of 1807 Lewis was in Washington telling the eager Jefferson about the vast territory he had added to the United States. Meanwhile Captain Zebulon Pike had ascended the Mississippi River to its source in the Lake of the Woods, producing information that the President believed "highly interesting in a political, geographical, and historical view." [48] Pike also explored the Red River well into Spanish territory in what is now New Mexico. Long climbed the peak named in his honor.

Numerous expeditions into the Rocky Mountain area were rounded out by the explorations of John Charles Frémont, whose marriage to Senator Thomas H. Benton's daughter combined

[47] *American State Papers: Miscellaneous,* I, 390–91 (March 8, 1804). The lure of the unknown west did not abate. In 1827 Thomas L. McKenney, then head of the Indian office, wrote the Secretary of War, "the mountains of this immense region, so barren in other places, combine with the prairies and fertile table lands to make the whole country one vast storehouse of wealth." House Doc. 277, 20th Cong., 1st sess., p. 11 (Sept. 17, 1827).

[48] *American State Papers: Miscellaneous,* I, 719; Elliott Coues, ed., *The Expeditions of Zebulon Montgomery Pike* (3 vols., New York: F. P. Harper, 1895).

with a dashing career to make him the Republican candidate for President in 1856. His first expedition in 1842 took him from St. Louis into the Wyoming region. His second, 1843–44, took him along the Oregon trail to Ft. Vancouver in Oregon, thence southward, east of the Sierras to Lake Tahoe, southward west of the Sierras through California to the neighborhood of Los Angeles and thence eastward to the intermountain region and the Mississippi Valley.[49] In 1848–49 he made another journey through the southwest to Los Angeles.

The acquisition of California and the southwest from Mexico in 1848 led to the establishment of the overland mail in 1849, and to agitation for a rail connection across the continent. Competition for the route, whether north or south, delayed action beyond the work of surveying parties. The continent, nevertheless, was rapidly becoming known, as immigrants poured into Oregon and as '49ers toiled across the southwest deserts to the California gold fields.

Indeed the normal operations of government were themselves steadily contributing to geographical knowledge. Indian agents penetrated steadily westward beyond the settlements, and factors followed in their footsteps. Army posts pushed far across the Mississippi, and regular lines of communication along the river courses were established. Post roads, at first no more than trails or traces, connected distant settlements, and post riders gained familiarity with unknown regions. Surveyors of the public lands steadily ate their way into the open country which had never known the transit and the chain. In short, government agents of many kinds were involuntary explorers and geographers, along with the trappers and traders who pushed ahead even of the most distant agents of the government. Circumstances compelled exploration by public authority even though it was exceptional to find Congress adding the weight of its influence in this field.

Naval exploration. Maritime interests meanwhile were pressing upon the general government for greater knowledge of the southern seas and of the Pacific. The fur trade with China and the whaling industry in the northern Pacific were two of the

49 J. C. Frémont, *Report of the Exploring Expedition. . . .* Senate Doc. 174, 28th Cong., 2d sess. (March 1845); Allan Nevins, *Frémont, Pathmaker of the West* (New York: Appleton-Century, 1939).

larger far-eastern enterprises. While President, John Quincy Adams had warmly supported the use of naval vessels for purposes of exploration and science, but he was not successful in converting a dubious Congress. First fruit of agitation for support for the shipping and trading interest in the Pacific[50] was the appointment of a commercial factor, Edmund Roberts, as special agent of the government and the detail of two ships, the *Peacock* and the *Enterprise,* to make treaties with far-eastern potentates. Roberts sailed in 1832 and returned in 1836, having concluded treaties with the Sultan of Muscat and the King of Siam.[51]

One of the most renowned undertakings was the South Sea Exploring Expedition under Lieutenant Charles Wilkes. This famous expedition, authorized by Congress in 1836,[52] included six small ships and a dozen scientists. It sailed about 85,000 miles, surveyed 280 islands, explored 1,500 miles of the Antarctic continent, 800 miles of the Oregon coast and rivers, and circumnavigated the globe to reach New York in 1842, after an absence of four years. The scientific results of the expedition were substantial, not merely in the field of geography.[53] Materials were collected relating to zoology, botany, geology, ethnography, philology, and hydrography. Nineteen quarto volumes were published, including three on zoology by James D. Dana and one on botany by Asa Gray.

Oceanography. Perhaps the greatest single scientific achievement of the navy, however, was the work of Lieutenant Matthew Fontaine Maury on winds and currents. This outstanding naval officer spent most of nine years at sea, 1825 to 1834, and then took leave of absence to prepare his first publication on the theory and practice of navigation.[54] From 1840 to 1841 he published a series of critical articles on naval mismanagement that have already been noted. In 1842 he became superintendent of

50 See, for example, House Report 94, 23d Cong., 2d sess. (Feb. 7, 1835).

51 Edmund Roberts, *Embassy to the Eastern Courts. . . .* (New York: Harper and Brothers, 1837).

52 Naval Appropriation Act, 5 Stat. 27, sec. 2 (May 14, 1836).

53 Charles Wilkes, *Narrative of the United States Exploring Expedition. . . .* (5 vols., Philadelphia: Lea and Blanchard, 1845).

54 M. F. Maury, *A New Theoretical and Practical Treatise on Navigation. . . .* (Philadelphia: Key and Biddle, 1836).

the depot of charts and instruments and began his researches on winds and currents. Five years later he published his Wind and Current Chart of the North Atlantic.[55] World-wide interest in these investigations led to an International Congress in Brussels in 1853 of which Maury was the central figure. Here a uniform method of recording oceanographic data was established. The consequences of the wind and current observations were immediate, substantial, and practical. Sailing time from New York to Rio de Janeiro was cut by ten to fifteen days, and from New York to San Francisco by 45 to 50 days, with savings amounting to millions of dollars annually. In 1855 Maury published the first textbook of modern oceanography.[56] In short, he earned a reputation as the greatest scientist who had adorned the navy rolls since its establishment, brilliantly fulfilling the function that John Quincy Adams had proposed for it.[57]

Secretary of the Navy James C. Dobbin confessed his pride in the science and genius of the navy in his annual report for 1856. "These deep-sea soundings—this study of the winds and currents and temperature of the ocean—these gradual approaches to greater familiarity with the wonders of the great deep, are pregnant with incalculable usefulness to those who conduct mighty navies, as well as to all who 'go down to the sea in ships.' "[58]

Geology. The expeditions within the American land area produced considerable elementary information about geological formations, but geological science was not directly recognized in congressional appropriations. Indeed in 1852 Congress specified that no new geological surveys be undertaken unless au-

55 M. F. Maury, *Wind and Current Chart of the North Atlantic* (1847). This was followed by his *Explanations and Sailing Directions to Accompany the Wind and Current Charts* (Washington: C. Alexander, 1851).

56 M. F. Maury, *The Physical Geography of the Sea* (New York: Harper and Brothers, 1855).

57 Maury's life has been written by three authors: Charles Lee Lewis, *Matthew Fontaine Maury, the Pathfinder of the Seas* (Annapolis: U. S. Naval Institute, 1927); Jaqueline Ambler Caskie, *Life and Letters of Matthew Fontaine Maury* (Richmond: Richmond Press, 1928); John Walter Wayland, *The Pathfinder of the Seas: the Life of Matthew Fontaine Maury* (Richmond: Garrett and Massie, 1930). See also Ralph Minthorne Brown, *Bibliography of Commander Matthew Fontaine Maury* (Blacksburg, Va.: Virginia Polytechnic Institute, 1944).

58 Senate Ex. Doc. 5, 34th Cong., 3d sess., Part II, p. 410 (Dec. 1, 1856). Perry's famous expedition to Japan was for diplomatic rather than for scientific purposes.

thorized by law.[59] The executive departments had given some support for research in this area. Lewis Cass, while Secretary of War under Jackson, became interested in an English traveler and geologist, George William Featherstonhaugh. *The Monthly American Journal of Geology and Natural Science,* founded by him in Philadelphia in 1831, survived only a year due, as Cass reported, "to the limited number of its votaries." [60] Cass suggested a professorship of geology at West Point for his English friend, but Congress was disinterested. In 1834 Featherstonhaugh accompanied an army column operating west of the Mississippi, and in 1835 presented a learned report on the science of geology which must have cooled any congressional ardor for the public support of this science.[61]

Subsequent geological work was undertaken in connection with the sale of mineral lands—the upper Mississippi in 1839 by David Dale Owen, the Lake Superior region in 1851 by Owen, now signing his report as U.S. geologist for Wisconsin, and the far west in connection with exploration and railroad surveys. The most systematic work of this kind was being done on the smaller scale of the states, notably in Massachusetts.[62]

PUBLIC HEALTH

The Jacksonians, like their predecessors, were baffled and frustrated by the occurrence of disease. The key to many health problems, the germ theory, was not discovered until years later, and speculations as to the cause of disease were far wide of the mark. Advances were made in the art of medicine, such notably as the use of anesthetics and the discovery by Dr. Oliver Wendell Holmes of the contagious character of puerperal fever. These,

59 10 Stat. 15, at 21 (July 21, 1852).

60 Senate Doc. 35, 22d Cong., 2d sess., p. 1 (Jan. 17, 1833).

61 Senate Doc. 153, 23d Cong., 2d sess. (Feb. 17, 1835). *Geological Report of . . . the Elevated Country between the Missouri and the Red Rivers* (Washington: Gales and Seaton, 1835). See also *Geological Reconnoissance in 1835 from Green Bay to Coteau de Prairie* (1836).

62 George Otis Smith, "A Century of Government Geological Surveys," in Edward S. Dana and others, *A Century of Science in America* (New Haven: Yale University Press, 1918); *North American Review,* XLII (1836), 428; Dirk J. Struik, *Yankee Science in the Making* (Boston: Little, Brown, 1948), pp. 183–89. George Watterston, librarian of the Library of Congress, had started a collection of minerals on the basis of voluntary contributions in 1825. *Niles Register,* XXVIII, 38 (March 19, 1825).

however, gave practitioners no principles on which a science could be erected.[63]

Although the cause of disease was unknown, the belief that it was associated with filth, uncleanliness, and unwholesome air became well established. Public interest in sanitation was greatly stimulated in 1850 by the report of the Massachusetts Commissioners for a State Sanitary Survey.[64] This document, hailed by the *North American Review* as marking "a new epoch in cis-Atlantic sanitary legislation," [65] was followed in 1857 by the first National Quarantine and Sanitary Convention, whose annual meetings became the center of professional discussion of public health problems. Congressional legislation regulating ocean passenger traffic was based on the doctrine of this still elementary sanitary science. The first national quarantine law was not passed until 1878, and the marine hospitals did not come under central direction until 1870, thus providing an overhead organization that was one day to become the United States Public Health Service.[66]

Army and Navy Medical Corps. The first and immediate responsibility of the government in the health field was with respect to its armed forces. The office of surgeon general, established in 1818 and marking the initial recognition of the army medical corps, was first held by the distinguished Joseph Lovell. The navy lagged in securing the benefit of central organization and direction, but the reorganization of 1842 established the bureau of medicine and surgery. Thus came to an end the independent—and isolated—status of the medical officer on shipboard or at naval stations. A medical service, with a head, some

63 See especially Henry Burnell Shafer, *The American Medical Profession, 1783 to 1850* (New York: Columbia University Press, 1936).

64 *Report of a General Plan for the Promotion of Public and Personal Health* (Boston: Dutton and Wentworth, 1850).

65 *North American Review*, LXXIII (1851), 134.

66 20 Stat. 37 (April 29, 1878); 16 Stat. 169 (June 29, 1870). See Laurence F. Schmeckebier, *The Public Health Service: its History, Activities and Organization* (Baltimore: Johns Hopkins Press, 1923); Ralph Chester Williams, *The United States Public Health Service, 1798–1950* (Washington: Commissioned Officers Association of the United States Public Health Service, 1951); Franz Goldmann, *Public Medical Care: Principles and Problems* (New York: Columbia University Press, 1945).

capacity for supervision, and a basis for planning, came into existence.[67]

The mere organization of a medical corps was not enough to guarantee the health of the armed forces. The American armies were seriously handicapped by sickness in the northern campaigns of the War of 1812. Jackson's force at New Orleans suffered more from disease than from the enemy, and a detachment under General Wilkinson was incapacitated by fevers and dysentery. Experience during the Mexican War again revealed an alarming morbidity and mortality rate. The fault lay not merely, perhaps not primarily, with the medical corps officers but in part to the indiscipline of the individual volunteer, in part to lack of medical supplies, in part to poor judgment of commanding officers.

Hospitals. A second direct responsibility of the general government was the maintenance of three groups of hospitals: army, navy, and merchant marine. The War of 1812 required the erection of hospitals or the conversion of buildings to hospital uses for wounded soldiers.[68] They were closed at the end of the war. Subsequently the army erected small hospitals at army posts.[69]

Naval hospitals were established at navy yards and in 1859 numbered five. The medical and nursing staffs were small. The New York hospital, the largest, required one surgeon, two assistant surgeons, and four nurses. The Navy Asylum at Philadelphia had no doctors or nurses. In none of these institutions did medical research or inquiry form any part of the duty of the professional staff.[70]

The so-called marine hospitals rounded out the federal health establishment. These were institutions for the short-time care of sick or disabled seamen, financed by monthly contributions of 20 cents deducted by the collectors of customs. The first of

67 Congress had been asked for such a system for at least a decade. See comments of Secretary of the Navy Woodbury in Senate Doc. 1, 23d Cong., 1st sess., p. 26 (Nov. 30, 1833); and a petition from the navy surgeons, Senate Doc. 176, 24th Cong., 2d sess. (Feb. 15, 1837).

68 P. M. Ashburn, *A History of the Medical Department of the United States Army* (Boston: Houghton Mifflin, 1929), p. 33.

69 5 Stat. 29 (May 14, 1836) at 30–31.

70 The government also maintained a hospital for army and navy insane in Washington, D.C.

these hospitals was erected at Chelsea, Massachusetts, overlooking Boston Harbor.[71] By 1850 only six were in operation, but the needs of sailors on the Great Lakes and on the Mississippi water courses were to lead to rapid expansion in numbers. By 1860 twenty-three such hospitals were available for seamen, fourteen of which were on inland waters.[72] The hospital at Charleston, South Carolina, was a joint responsibility of the city and the federal government.[73]

The condition of these hospitals was influenced considerably by the character of the collector of customs, under whose administrative direction they fell. Each hospital was a separate unit, having no relation with the others and no common superior in Washington. They came under the Treasury merely because the collector of customs was their fiscal agent. By 1848 they had succumbed to the spoils system. A report by Navy Surgeon Ruschenburger declared, "the physicians of marine hospitals . . . are generally changed with every administration of the general government in Washington. They serve no apprenticeship in the system. . . . The arrangement of appointments and contracting out for hospital supplies places considerable patronage at the disposal of the Treasury Department and of Collectors, if they be pleased to avail themselves of it for political purposes." [74]

Vaccination. The experience of the federal government with vaccination was symptomatic of its reluctance to go far in health matters. Protection against smallpox by vaccination was discovered by Jenner in 1798. Congress first came to the aid of civilians in this connection in 1813, authorizing the President to appoint an agent to preserve the genuine vaccine matter and to furnish it to any citizen through the post office, with the benefit of the postal frank.[75] The agency was established in Baltimore; its head, Dr. James Smith, furnished vaccine for nearly

71 Senate Ex. Doc. 14, 31st Cong., 2d sess. (Jan. 20, 1851), *passim.*

72 Senate Ex. Doc. 27, 36th Cong., 1st sess., pp. 2–6 (March 22, 1860).

73 2 Stat. 357 (March 28, 1806); House Report 83, 20th Cong., 1st sess. (Jan. 16, 1828); 6 Stat. 419 (May 20, 1830).

74 W. S. E. Ruschenburger, *Remarks on the Condition of the Marine Hospital Fund of the United States* (1848), quoted in Robert D. Leigh, *Federal Health Administration in the United States* (New York: Harper and Brothers, 1927), p. 83.

75 2 Stat. 806 (Feb. 27, 1813).

ten years. Then occurred an unfortunate accident. The agency sent out to Tarboro, North Carolina, a culture of smallpox instead of "cowpox," causing an outbreak of the disease in that community. Congress investigated the error and in 1822 repealed the act of 1813.[76]

The reasoning leading to this reversal turned wholly on administrative, not medical considerations. The House committee declared its unshaken confidence in vaccination but expressed the opinion that the responsibility was one more appropriate to the state and local governments. ". . . it is doubted," reported the committee, "whether Congress can, in any instance, devise a system which will not be more liable to abuses in its operations, and less subject to a prompt and salutary control, than such as may be adopted by the local authorities." Heavy demand for vaccine concentrated upon a single agency, the committee thought, would put the hard dilemma of "either relinquishing the proferred fee, or of transmitting matter of doubtful character." Careless or incompetent assistants, "guided more by cupidity than intelligence," might make the fatal error of disseminating a pestilence rather than a prophylactic. The matter was, therefore, turned over altogether to the local authorities, "who, with the aid of professional men, will be more competent to the successful management of it and to whom they believe it properly belongs." [77] This consequence of a single official error reveals the underlying predispositions of the period.

The army and navy, however, took no chances with smallpox. Both services vaccinated their recruits immediately upon arrival at their posts. From 1818 to 1826 only two deaths from smallpox were reported in the army, and in the navy "only one is mentioned as having taken place for a long time." [78] In 1832 Congress authorized Indian agents and army physicians to vaccinate the Indians, with their consent.[79]

Localities, of course, had been active in the matter of vaccination, as well as private physicians. In 1816 the city of Philadelphia secured the services of Dr. Joseph G. Nancrede as vaccine

[76] 3 Stat. 677 (May 4, 1822).

[77] House Report 93, 17th Cong., 1st sess., p. 2 (April 13, 1822).

[78] *Niles Register*, XXX, 36 (March 18, 1826).

[79] 4 Stat. 514 (May 5, 1832); House Doc. 82, 22d Cong., 2d sess., p. 5 (May 10, 1832).

physician. In 1827 he reported to Congress, in supporting his petition for a new federal vaccine institution in Philadelphia, that he vaccinated annually about one thousand persons.[80] The city of Washington had a municipal health board, under authority of Congress, which maintained an isolation hospital for smallpox cases and encouraged "very general vaccination." [81] A health officer had been appointed in 1819 to demonstrate "the salubrity of our situation" and to correct "many gross misrepresentations often industriously circulated by weak and designing men." [82] In 1820 a health board consisting of one physician and one citizen in each of the six wards replaced the health officer.[83] Thus early the layman and the expert joined forces.

Neither Congress nor the executive branch recognized much responsibility for public health matters beyond the needs of the military forces. Medical research was almost unknown everywhere. The regulation of the medical profession was in the hands of the states. Medical schools were private institutions. The simple task of the medical men in the employ of the federal government was to give relief to sick or wounded soldiers and sailors, and to the mariners of the merchant service. The science and art of public health were being developed in a few states and large cities, but not by the general government.

SCIENCE—A RESPECTABLE STEPCHILD

The Naval Observatory, the Smithsonian Institution, the Coast Survey; exploration by land and sea with considerable related activity in the biological sciences and geology; meteorological observations; and quite incidental contributions to the improvement of public health, these comprise the roster of scientific activities maintained by the general government from 1829 to 1860. They were not extensive, and they often suffered from congressional indifference, but they did nevertheless lay foundations on which future work within government was to proceed. The pioneering studies of Matthew Fontaine Maury were almost accidental, so far as naval or public policy was concerned,

80 House Doc. 66, 20th Cong., 1st sess. (Dec. 18, 1827).

81 House Report 215, 20th Cong., 1st sess. (March 27, 1828).

82 Quoted in Wilhelmus Bogart Bryan, *A History of the National Capital* (2 vols., New York: Macmillan, 1914–16), II, 11–12.

83 Authorized in 3 Stat. 583, sec. 7 (May 15, 1820).

although the navy became increasingly cooperative as the value of his research emerged. So also the brilliant investigations of Army Surgeon William Beaumont on the process of digestion, as viewed in the stomach of an unfortunate Canadian voyageur.[84]

While government hardly made a commitment to science as such, its two professional schools, West Point and Annapolis, were training men in the sciences, and the more energetic of them pursued their scientific training. Although the number of scientists in government employ was small, it included some very distinguished names. Joseph Henry, first secretary of the Smithsonian Institution, Alexander Dallas Bache, second head of the Coast Survey, James M. Gilliss of the Naval Observatory, and Matthew Fontaine Maury were great scientific figures in their generation. It is worth noting that all of them spent most of their mature lifetime in the public service, and that the theory of rotation did not disturb their tenure of office. A sound tradition was thus established in this branch of the public service, while older standards were being undermined elsewhere.

84 *William Beaumont's Formative Years: Two Early Notebooks, 1811–1821* (New York: Henry Schuman, 1946); Jesse S. Myer, *Life and Letters of Dr. William Beaumont* (St. Louis: C. V. Mosby Co., 1912, reprinted 1939).

CHAPTER TWENTY-SIX

Administrative Dualism

The general pattern of administrative relations between the federal government and the states was not altered during the years from 1829 to the Civil War. These were the decades of the great debate over the nature of the Union, the place of the states in the general government, the location of sovereignty, and the right of a state to nullify a federal law that it deemed unconstitutional. Beneath the tumultuous level of political and constitutional debate, the original decisions on administrative relations were undisturbed and at most points unquestioned.

These decisions had established two administrative systems, as well as two judicial systems, over the same citizens. The administrative systems were autonomous and each was complete in itself. The initial effort to lay upon state officials the task of collecting the federal revenue and upon state courts the duty of deciding federal cases in the first instance had failed. The general government had its own officials to do its business, and the states continued to maintain their officials to carry on their business.

The occasion for cooperation had arisen at an early date, and mutually advantageous arrangements easily came into existence. The states allowed the federal marshals to use state and county jails for federal prisoners; the federal customs officers helped enforce the state quarantine laws in ports of entry. For the convenience of citizens, small federal causes were allowed to be heard in nearby state tribunals.

At one point the states and the general government were required by the Constitution to cooperate, and at this point effective relations were never established: i.e., the management of the militia. The states were jealous of their militia rights, citizens feared a standing army, and no President had been able to persuade Congress to set minimum standards for militia companies. The War of 1812 proved how necessary such standards were, but still they were not forthcoming.

The regulation of immigration, a subject matter of mutual interest and joint constitutional authority, was left almost exclusively in the hands of the states. Congress limited itself to the single requirement that the master of an incoming ship deliver to the collector a list of passengers showing among other things the country to which they "belonged." [1] The states were faced with the problem of protecting themselves against paupers, criminals, and persons of unsound mind whose emigration was facilitated by their governing authorities.[2] New York took the lead by requiring lists of passengers, by exacting bond from the master of the ship against the dependency of the immigrant for a two-year period, and by exacting a head tax from the immigrant, from the proceeds of which relief was available in case of dependency. The head tax was later declared unconstitutional as a regulation of foreign commerce.[3] Despite mounting sentiment against foreign immigration, the states sought to do no more by way of regulation than to protect themselves against the cost of pauper support. Congress left the field to them.

Democrats were consistent in their support of the state governments as the principal public agency of the American people, and Whigs fell in line with an almost universal climate of opinion. Francis Bowen, writing in the *North American Review* in 1850, observed, "In the distribution of authority between the National and the State Governments, so much power is reserved to the latter, so many subjects fall exclusively within their control, that if the former, in its legislative capacity, should suddenly cease to act, if it should fall asleep, or remain in a comatose state, for a year or two no great harm would result." [4]

The extravagant bias against action by the federal government was revealed in the debate on the bill to create the Department of the Interior in 1849. The bill merely brought together

1 3 Stat. 488 (March 2, 1819).

2 Evidence on this nefarious practice is found in House Report 1040, 25th Cong., 2d sess. (July 2, 1838).

3 7 Howard 282 (1849).

4 *North American Review,* LXXI (1850), 221–22.

well-established activities under a new head, adding nothing to functions long accepted. Gloomy forecasts were made, nevertheless, concerning its tendency. Senator Mason of Virginia asserted that the new agency would "absorb hereafter as much power as those who hold the reins of Government shall see fit to place in their hands." [5] Senator Calhoun was overcome with apprehension. "Mr. President, there is something ominous in the expression, 'The Secretary of the Interior.' . . . Everything upon the face of God's earth will go into the Home-Department. . . . This is a monstrous bill. It is ominous. It will turn over the whole interior affairs of the country to this department; and it is one of the greatest steps that has ever been made in my time to absorb all the remaining powers of the States." [6] Senator Mason was full of trepidation: "But, sir, I fear this unknown 'Department of the Interior.' Sir, there is a dark cloud now lowering over this Capitol—" Here Senator John M. Berrien took a cue, and pointing to the galleries filled with ladies, gallantly said, "I deny it, Sir." [7] Polk signed the bill with reluctance, suspecting its consolidating tendency.[8]

The doctrine of strict construction was repeated again and again by Democratic and Whig Presidents. In his first annual message Jackson warned Congress against all encroachments upon the states: "The great mass of legislation relating to our internal affairs was intended to be left where the Federal Convention found it—in the State governments." [9] Toward the close of his first term he told Congress that the strength of the Union consisted "in leaving individuals and States as much as possible to themselves . . . not in binding the States more closely to the center, but leaving each to move unobstructed in its proper orbit." [10] In his farewell address he repeated these sentiments.[11]

At the end of his administration, Van Buren echoed these views, praising "a total abstinence from the exercise of all doubt-

[5] *Congressional Globe,* 30th Cong., 2d sess., p. 672 (March 3, 1849).
[6] *Ibid.,* p. 673.
[7] *Ibid.,* p. 677.
[8] Polk, *Diary,* IV, 371–72 (Nov. 2, 1849).
[9] Richardson, *Messages,* II, 452 (Dec. 8, 1829).
[10] *Ibid.,* II, 590 (July 10, 1832).
[11] *Ibid.,* III, 298 (March 4, 1837).

ful powers on the part of the Federal Government." [12] President Harrison made no personal pronouncement on the issue before his early death; Tyler, his successor, was a stern states' rights man.[13] Polk stood squarely with Jackson against transforming "a plain, cheap, and simple confederation of States . . . into a consolidated empire." [14] Whig President Fillmore agreed: ". . . it is," he said, "at all times an especial duty to guard against any infringement on the just rights of the States." [15] Pierce and Buchanan continued the traditional Democratic position.

Calhoun's theoretical exposition of the priority of the states was confirmed as practical issues such as the establishment of the Interior Department came up for settlement. Jefferson Davis was his firm supporter. He opposed federal acceptance of the Smithsonian Institution; [16] he helped defeat a bill to grant land for the support of the indigent insane; [17] and he fought an appropriation to establish an agricultural college.[18]

Despite the vitality of states' rights theory, laissez faire doctrine, and the relative absence of new federal functions, the balance between the central government and the state governments was beginning to tilt toward Washington. The dramatic issues of war and peace were determined there. Business was already drawn into the central vortex, especially on matters of tariff and military contracts. Establishment of the Department of the Interior did reveal, as Calhoun remarked, a new trend of opinion. The scale of federal expenditure far exceeded that of any single state although the thrifty Yankee, Levi Woodbury, tried to reduce it. Such a reduction, he urged, would be "the great safeguard against a too splendid central government, which would constantly threaten to overshadow all State independence, and attract the ambition of most of the friends of State rights from humbler paths of frugality and principle into the dazzling vortex of higher patronage, honors, and emoluments." [19] Ambitious

12 *Ibid.*, III, 614 (Dec. 5, 1840).
13 Cf. his veto of a rivers and harbors bill, *ibid.*, IV, 330 (June 11, 1844).
14 *Ibid.*, IV, 658 (Dec. 15, 1848).
15 *Ibid.*, V, 79 (Dec. 2, 1850).
16 Davis, *Letters, Papers and Speeches,* II, 15 (Jan. 30, 1851).
17 *Ibid.*, II, 18 (Feb. 11, 1851).
18 *Ibid.*, III, 518 (Feb. 1, 1859).
19 House Doc. 3, 26th Cong., 2d sess., p. 16 (Dec. 7, 1840).

men sought federal rather than state distinction. The party press dealt with both state and national politics, but the latter came to seem more important.

The effect of the new party system was to emphasize the importance of the nation-wide struggle for the presidency recurring every four years. States' rights men such as Abel P. Upshur of Virginia were worried about this trend as early as 1840. To his friend, Henry A. Wise, he wrote, "Federal politics absorb all other considerations. The Federal Govt. is regarded as all that is good and all that is evil in our condition; the states are overlooked; the beneficent action of their governments upon our rights, our interests and our daily comforts, is forgotten; they sink to nothing in the scale of public importance, and their dignity, their rights, and their powers perish under the neglect of their own people. To such an extreme has this error been carried, that we can not elect a single State officer, from the constable of a village to the Governor of a State, without reference to Federal politics." [20] Another Virginian, Thomas W. Gilmer, confirmed this opinion. "The presidential election," he declared, "becomes, in fact, the question which influences and determines all other questions of State and Federal policy." [21]

The quiet transfer of prestige that was going on was observed also by Gideon Welles, who wrote President-elect Pierce, "The power of the federal government is derived from the whole of the States, and consequently the addition of every new state adds to its powers. . . . Every year the federal government more and more overshadows the States, and the people are more and more inclined to look to it as *the government,* and to regard the States as mere subordinate corporations. I am almost every day surprised at the erroneous opinions on this subject even by men of tolerable intelligence and professing to be Democrats. And we have now a large foreign element in our population who cannot well understand our system. . . ." [22]

A new aspect of federal-state relations now appeared, destined

20 Lyon G. Tyler, *Letters and Times of the Tylers,* III, 78 (March 23, 1840).

21 House Report 741, 27th Cong., 2d sess., p. 4 (May 23, 1842). Judge Grimke held the same view. *The Works of Frederick Grimke* (2 vols. in one; Columbus: Columbus Printing Co., 1871), I, 559–60.

22 Quoted in Allan Nevins, *Ordeal of the Union,* I, 157–58. Letter dated Dec. 16, 1852.

to be of much importance in later years—the drain of official manpower from the states to the federal government. The cause was supposed to be the higher salary levels prevailing in the latter. "This inequality," the Gilmer Committee reported in 1842, "has had an injurious influence, it is believed, on the character and interests of the State Governments, by inducing too general a preference for the service of the Federal Government. The offices of the States, even the first of them, are too often regarded as mere means of obtaining inferior situations under the United States." [23] Congressman Millard Fillmore had already complained about this unfair competition. "Was it not grossly unjust," he asked, "that the same amount should be allowed by this Government to a mere copyist, a scrivener, whose occupation required neither learning nor talents" as the state of New York allowed to the chancellor, sitting as the head of the single court of chancery for that commonwealth? [24] Fillmore and Gilmer both proposed to terminate this drain on the states by reducing federal salaries, but this was not a realistic remedy. The *National Intelligencer* observed in 1853 that "in the general rush for Federal offices, the highest officers of the State Governments, to say nothing of men prominent in professional life, are foremost. Any subordinate office under the Federal Government is preferred to the highest office under a State Government. . . ." [25] Thus, by way of example, Governor Daniel Dunklin of Missouri resigned to become a land surveyor under the General Land Office.[26]

Evidence of this nature suggests a tilting of the federal-state balance, but not a substantial alteration. It was still true, as de Tocqueville observed in 1831, that America was preeminently the country of state and municipal government.[27] Nearly twenty years later this was also the theme of Francis Bowen.

. . . . The President has one postmaster in every little village; but the inhabitants of that village choose their own selectmen, their own

23 House Report 741, 27th Cong., 2d sess., p. 21 (May 23, 1842).

24 *Fillmore Papers,* I, 91 (April 17, 1834).

25 *National Intelligencer,* April 7, 1853.

26 *Niles Register,* LI, 144 (Oct. 29, 1836).

27 De Tocqueville, *Democracy in America* (1863 ed.), I, 537. Indeed he thought that the government of the Union was destined to grow progressively weaker. *Ibid.,* I, 534.

assessors of taxes, their own school-committee, their own overseers of the poor, their own surveyors of highways, and the incumbents of half a dozen other little offices corresponding to those which, in bureaucratic governments, are filled by the appointment of the sovereign. In all these posts, which are really important public trusts, the villagers are trained to the management of affairs, and acquire a comprehensiveness of view, a practical administrative talent, and a knowledge of business, which are, or ought to be, among the chief objects of every system of education. And this training is very general; for owing to our republican liking for rotation in office, the incumbents of these humble posts are changed every year or two, till every decent man in the place has had his turn.[28]

The weight of the general government was still well balanced by such local institutions.

On three occasions during these thirty years the limited administrative relations of the two sets of governments were severely strained. The nullification controversy barely avoided a head-on collision between the collectors of customs in South Carolina and the state sheriffs and courts. The attempt of northern abolitionists to flood the South with antislavery literature through the post office produced a successful *de facto* resistance in many southern communities to the delivery of such incendiary material. The attempt of the federal authorities to assist southern slaveholders to secure the return of their fugitive slaves from the North met increasing and often successful resistance from the state governments and local peace officers as well as citizens.

These events reflected a subtle but important change in the character of the relations between the states and the general government. For forty years they had been administratively separate and autonomous, but they had been cooperative. Now the states, both North and South, tended to assume attitudes of official hostility that denied the comity of mutual assistance which had long characterized traditional relations.

NULLIFICATION

James R. Pringle was appointed collector of customs at Charleston, South Carolina, in 1820 by President James Mon-

28 *North American Review,* LXXI (1850), 502.

roe. He could never have guessed that twelve years later in this same office he would become the very center of the struggle between the government of the United States and that of South Carolina. For, reduced to its *administrative* terms, the great constitutional and political contest over nullification in 1832 and 1833 might be put in the simple question, could James R. Pringle perform his official duty to collect the customs duties in the port of Charleston on and after February 1, 1833? South Carolina had taken every step that her leaders could devise to prevent Pringle from collecting the customs; Andrew Jackson and the Treasury Department had taken measures to insure that he would be able to execute his duty. By a narrow margin the issue was not then put to the final test, but the preparatory administrative and judicial measures almost shattered the quiet and settled pattern of federal-state administrative relations, as well as introducing new ideas of law enforcement.

The constitutional and political aspects of the nullification controversy are well known. The "Tariff of Abominations" of 1828 had set import duties at levels far above customary standards, was alleged by the South to injure the southern economy for the benefit of northern manufacturers, and was construed by southern leaders as an unconstitutional exercise of power. The Tariff of 1832, designed to mollify the South, failed to do so. To the contrary, many southerners came to the conclusion that no relief could be expected from Jackson or the Democratic party, and that no recourse was left but to prevent the collection of the tariff in their ports.

That South Carolina was determined to stop Collector Pringle could not be doubted. The Nullification Ordinance, approved on November 24, 1832, declared flatly that the tariff acts of 1828 and 1832 were null, void, and no law, and were not binding upon the state, its officers, or citizens. The ordinance made unlawful any attempt by either state or federal officials to collect the customs and directed the legislature to enforce its declarations. South Carolina protected the legal validity of its ordinance by refusing to permit any court record to be taken for an appeal to the United States Supreme Court, and put in contempt of court any person seeking such an appeal. It required all state officers and jurors to take a special oath to obey and execute the ordinance and the supplementary statutes.[29]

Governor James Hamilton charged the ensuing special session of the state legislature to "render it utterly impossible to collect, within our limits, the duties imposed by the protective tariffs thus nullified." [30] The legislature responded (1) by authorizing importers to secure their imports by writ of replevin in the state courts, notwithstanding failure to pay the proper duty; (2) by allowing recovery of damages from the collector for detaining the imports, and by authorizing the county sheriff to seize the collector's personal property, as a guarantee of payment of such damages; (3) by protecting an importer arrested for failure to pay duties by extending to him the writ of habeas corpus, giving him a right to sue for unlawful arrest, and barring any sale of his property to satisfy a judgment in the federal court; (4) by allowing any person paying duties to recover the amount in any court of competent jurisdiction; (5) by directing the sheriff to prevent recapture of goods delivered on replevin; and (6) by imposing heavy fines and imprisonment for resisting any of these processes, and by forbidding jailers to receive or detain any person arrested for failure to pay duties. Obviously Collector Pringle was in danger of being thrown in jail for any attempt to collect the customs, while merchants were freed of all responsibility for defying him.[31]

Jackson prepared to meet South Carolina at every point. Foreseeing an armed collision he ordered the Charleston garrison to be purged of any disloyal elements and the officers to be on guard against a surprise.[32] He issued confidential instructions to the

29 The ordinance, supplementary legislation, and other documents were printed in Senate Doc. 30, 22d Cong., 2d sess. (Jan. 16, 1833).

30 *Ibid.*, p. 64.

31 *Ibid.*, pp. 70–73. These means of enforcement were framed on the assumption that the federal collectors and district attorneys would perform their respective duties. Another possibility had already appeared in the summer of 1831. The district attorney for South Carolina, Edward Frost, refused to bring suit on a defaulted importer's bond on the ground that, in his opinion, the tariff was unconstitutional. Frost resigned his office, and there was no further indication that the tariff would be voided by refusal of the federal agents to act. Jackson, *Correspondence,* IV, 316 (July 23, 1831).

32 The military and naval orders are printed in Senate Doc. 71, 22d Cong., 2d sess. (Feb. 12, 1833); see also Jackson, *Correspondence,* IV, 481 (Oct. 16, 1832), and IV, 483 (Oct. 29, 1832).

collectors.[33] He sent a confidential emissary to report on the loyalty of customs personnel and on the attitudes of other federal officeholders and employees in Charleston.[34] In his special message of January 16, 1833, he outlined the precautions that Congress was soon to embody in the "Force Bill." [35]

This act, "to provide for the collection of duties on imports," was drafted in the light of the South Carolina scheme for resistance. The President was authorized in case of unlawful obstruction to remove the customhouse to any secure place within the district, either upon land or on board any vessel—for instance, a ship of war. Any process other than an order of a federal court designed to take a vessel or cargo from the collector, such as an action of replevin, was forbidden, and all property detained under the revenue law was declared irreplevable—thus striking at the fundamental instrument of the state. Any person seeking to dispossess property held by the collector—for example, a sheriff—was made guilty of a misdemeanor. Any action against a revenue officer in a state court—such as a suit for damage—was declared removable to the federal courts; if no record could be obtained from the state court, the case could be commenced *de novo;* and any person held by the state authorities—for example, a collector—could be freed from custody by the federal marshal using the writ of habeas corpus, and refusal to obey the writ was heavily penalized. If local jails were not available, the marshal was authorized to use other convenient places for persons in his custody. Finally the act authorized the President to use land or naval forces or the militia.[36]

This imposing battery of powers and authorizations confronted the equally impressive array of prohibitions and obligations established by the legislature of South Carolina. They came to sharp focus in the persons of the collector of customs of the port of Charleston and the sheriff of Charleston County, with prosecuting officers and courts back of each of them and, close behind, the state militia on the one hand and the armed forces of the general government on the other. Two administrative sys-

33 Senate Doc. 30, 22d Cong., 2d sess., pp. 92–97 (Nov. 6, 1832).

34 Jackson, *Correspondence,* IV, 484 (Nov. 7, 1832).

35 Richardson, *Messages,* II, 629–30.

36 4 Stat. 632 (March 2, 1833).

tems, as well as two theories of the nature of the Union and two economic systems, were in deadlock.

The play of administrative power was not put in motion; the resolution of the deadlock took place elsewhere by political negotiation rather than by judicial intervention or executive power. Henry Clay joined with John C. Calhoun to work out a new tariff act providing for a ten-year reduction of duties to the level of a tariff for revenue only; the Force Bill was enacted to insure the supremacy of the federal system; and South Carolina repealed the Ordinance of Nullification. Men breathed easier. The issue was dramatic, indeed terrifying, and the compromise was recognized as much less than a permanent solution. Even before the crisis of 1833 John Quincy Adams gave up his faith that "this federative Union was to last for ages. I now disbelieve its duration for twenty years, and doubt its continuance for five. It is falling into the sere and yellow leaf." [37]

ABOLITION AND THE USE OF THE MAILS

Another conflict between the federal government and the states came to a head in the post office. In 1835 the American Anti-Slavery Society launched a pamphlet campaign against the evils of slavery, and during the years from 1836 to 1840 placed hundreds of thousands of pamphlets in the mail to be delivered to leaders of opinion, North and South. Southern citizens and officials believed the result of the campaign would be a slave revolt and the ultimate destruction of this form of property. To them the papers were incendiary and dangerous in the extreme, a view also held by many northerners.[38]

The southerners intended to protect themselves and their institutions. In July 1835 the mail steamer to Charleston, South Carolina, brought in packages of antislavery publications. Local citizens forced open the post office, seized the packages, and burned them publicly on July 30. A mass meeting expressed

[37] Adams, *Memoirs,* VIII, 479 (Feb. 22, 1832).

[38] On this topic see Russel B. Nye, *Fettered Freedom: Civil Liberties and the Slavery Controversy, 1830–1860* (East Lansing: Michigan State College Press, 1949); William Sherman Savage, *The Controversy over the Distribution of Abolition Literature, 1830–1860* (Association for the Study of Negro Life and History, Inc., 1938); Clement Eaton, "Censorship of the Southern Mails," *American Historical Review,* XLVIII (1942–43), 266–80.

horror and detestation at the attempt to introduce antislavery literature, and appointed a committee headed by former governor Robert Y. Hayne to inspect the mails in cooperation with the postmaster and to burn any objectionable matter.[39]

Such a violation of the mail was, of course, a grave breach of the law, but the circumstances were unique. Postmaster Alfred Huger immediately wrote to the Postmaster General, Amos Kendall, for instructions, and to the New York postmaster, Samuel L. Gouverneur, begging him to detain any future shipments of abolitionist papers until Kendall could make a ruling. The plain administrative issue was whether a state could forbid or prevent, within its own borders, the delivery of mail entrusted to the United States Post Office. Involved in it was the constitutional question whether even Congress could abridge the liberty of freedom of speech declared in the First Amendment. This issue also raised an important problem of policy, as to whether any restriction on the use of the mails was desirable, considering the far-reaching implications of the precedent. Back of these controversial problems, arising so soon after the nullification dispute had been disposed of, stood the specter of slavery.

Postmaster Huger was concerned primarily with his duty to the department. He had a right to expect guidance from its head. He was disappointed. Kendall gave him no rule or direction and left him to his own discretion. The terms of his letter to Huger follow.

SIR: In your letter of the 29th ult. just received, you inform me that by the steamboat mail from New York your office had been filled with pamphlets and tracts upon slavery; that the public mind was highly excited upon the subject; that you doubted the safety of the mail itself out of your possession; that you had determined, as the wisest course, to detain these papers; and you now ask instructions from the department.

Upon a careful examination of the law, I am satisfied that the postmaster general has no legal authority to exclude newspapers from the mail, nor prohibit their carriage or delivery on account of their character or tendency, real or supposed. Probably, it was not thought safe to confer on the head of an executive department a power over the press, which might be perverted and abused.

39 Nye, *op. cit.*, pp. 55–56.

But I am not prepared to direct you to forward or deliver the papers of which you speak. The post office department was created to serve the people of *each* and *all* of the *United States,* and not to be used as the instrument of their *destruction.* None of the papers detained have been forwarded to me, and I cannot judge for myself of their character and tendency; but you inform me, that they are, in character, "the most inflammatory and incendiary—and insurrectionary in the highest degree."

By no act, or direction of mine, official or private, could I be induced to aid, knowingly, in giving circulation to papers of this description, directly or indirectly. We owe an obligation to the laws, but a higher one to the communities in which we live, and if the *former* be perverted to destroy the *latter,* it is patriotism to disregard them. Entertaining these views, I cannot sanction, and will not condemn the step you have taken.

Your justification must be looked for in the character of the papers detained, and the circumstances by which you are surrounded.[40]

Kendall, it must be admitted, was in a difficult position. The issue was a novel one; it was obviously charged with the most alarming potential consequences; it appeared as though nullification might be thrust again into the hot center of debate at this new point; election year was just ahead; Kendall was holding an interim appointment as Postmaster General, had expected that the Senate would reject him, and was not in fact confirmed until March 15, 1836. Granting all these circumstances, it must nevertheless be stated that he dodged the question and raised new controversy in his appeal to the "higher law." As the Attorney General was later to declare, it seemed hard "to throw upon a deputy postmaster the whole responsibility of deciding for himself, and at his peril, the graver questions of official duty, when the lighter ones are habitually determined for him by the Department." [41]

Events took a course that gave no promise of a solution. Many southern communities passed resolutions directing postmasters to detain and destroy abolition papers. Vigilance committees were occasionally instituted to see that the postmaster observed

40 *Niles Register,* XLVIII, 448 (August 22, 1835). Cf. Kendall's discussion in his annual report for 1835, Senate Doc. 1, 24th Cong., 1st sess. (Dec. 1, 1835), pp. 397–98, in which he stated that the United States had no right by delivering "incendiary" material through the post office to foment insurrection.

41 8 *Opinions of the Attorneys General* 489, 492 (March 2, 1857).

local sentiments. A movement took form in favor of state laws prohibiting the delivery of "incendiary" papers. The issue took on major proportions, as Congress awaited Jackson's proposals in December 1835 for federal action.

Jackson left no doubt about his views. He condemned the "unconstitutional and wicked attempts" of misguided persons to circulate inflammatory appeals "calculated . . . to produce all the horrors of a servile war," and recommended legislation to prohibit the circulation in the southern states of "incendiary publications intended to instigate the slaves to insurrection." [42]

This relatively simple and direct solution was deceptively easy. One basic disagreement lay in the question whether the delivery of the mail should be controlled by the federal government, as Jackson proposed, or by the states, as Calhoun demanded. He introduced a bill providing that no postmaster should receive or transmit any material touching the subject of slavery addressed to any person in a state, territory, or district whose laws forbade such material or to deliver such to anyone except those entitled by state law to receive it.[43] To allow Congress to legislate on the subject of exclusion from the mail was to grant a power that Calhoun denied on constitutional grounds and opposed for practical reasons.

Another disagreement arose on the issue of civil rights. Exclusion from the mails was a type of censorship, it was argued, that was as abhorrent as censorship of the press. The Dayton, Ohio, *Republican* declared, "The next step will be to stop the circulation of all anti-masonic papers, then those that are opposed to the administration." [44] The New York *Evening Post* denied that either the states or the federal government possessed authority to prohibit the movement of abolition tracts in the mail. "If the government," wrote William Leggett, "once begins to discriminate as to what is orthodox and what heterodox in opinion, what is safe and what unsafe in tendency, farewell, a long farewell to our freedom." [45] The abolitionists warned that the prin-

[42] Richardson, *Messages*, III, 175–76 (Dec. 7, 1835).

[43] Senate Doc. 118, 24th Cong., 1st sess. (Feb. 4, 1836); Nye, *Fettered Freedom*, p. 63.

[44] Quoted in Nye, *op. cit.*, p. 65.

[45] Allan Nevins, *The Evening Post: A Century of Journalism* (New York: Boni and Liveright, 1922), p. 148 (1835).

ciple of censorship by exclusion could be directed against the opinions of any group as well as theirs.

The difficulty, if not impossibility, of defining what was incendiary was obvious. Jackson would at least have furnished an opportunity for a single effort at definition through departmental instructions to postmasters. Calhoun's bill would have secured as many different definitions as there were states that made the attempt. The task of a northern postmaster would have become indeed impossible.

In the end, neither Jackson's bill nor Calhoun's became law.[46] The problem was left to the interpretation, or application, of section 32 of the Post Office Act of 1836, in the drafting of which Kendall had had an important part. This section on its face enforced federal responsibility and left no room for state interference. Postmasters were forbidden to detain any postal matter with intent to prevent its delivery or to give preference to any letters or pamphlets.[47] In terms, the law merely stated the duty of postmasters to deliver the mail; in implication, it appeared to deny any ground for interference with delivery, including "incendiary" abolition pamphlets.

This provision of the act of 1836 was in fact a dead letter from its passage, so far as forcing the delivery of abolition pamphlets in the South. In this region it was construed to mean that federal power over mail ceased at the reception point. Violations of the letter and spirit of section 32 were common, and considerable state legislation flatly contradicted its apparent meaning. The Virginia law of 1836 was a cunning example. This enactment provided that *if* a postmaster should notify a justice of the peace that abolitionist or antislavery writing had been received at his office, it became the duty of the justice of the peace to examine the literature. If he found that it was writing of this character, he was directed to have it burned in his presence, and to arrest the person to whom it was addressed, if he subscribed with intent

46 Neither the Postmaster General nor the local citizens were sustained by Attorney General Caleb Cushing. He held that a postmaster was not required to deliver mail which had the tendency to promote insurrection in a slave state, but that only a court of the state or the federal government could determine the character of the mail matter in question. 8 *Opinions of the Attorneys General* 489-502 (March 2, 1857), Yazoo City Post Office Case.

47 5 Stat. 80, sec. 32 (July 2, 1836).

to further the abolition cause. The law prescribed a fine for any postmaster who knowingly violated these provisions.[48] Virginia thus refrained from imposing a specific duty upon the postmaster, a federal official, while making it clear that he was expected to yield to local sentiment. Other states passed corresponding laws. Their constitutionality was never contested by the federal government in the courts.

Indeed, the states succeeded at this point in controlling the operation of the post office, insofar as they cared to do so. Their official interference was buttressed from time to time by the action of groups, often "respectable" in social standing, who simply took abolition literature from the custody of the postmaster and destroyed it. The mob that seized the abolition pamphlets in Charleston in 1835 was pursued neither by post office agents nor by the United States district attorney. The federal authorities did not assert their responsibility for delivering this kind of mail. Nor did many northerners demand the enforcement of the postal law in the South in this particular.

In his annual report for 1835, Kendall declared in substance that the state laws against the circulation of incendiary material should be obeyed by the postmasters. Jackson never went so far; failing to get legislation to permit exclusion of such matter from the mail, he would have depended on exposure of the names of those who received it and social pressure to compel conformity to local sentiment.[49]

The nonassertion policy of Amos Kendall prevailed to the outbreak of the Civil War. An effort was made in 1856 by the Postmaster General to follow the plain intent of section 32 of the act of 1836 by instructing the postmaster of Yazoo City, Mississippi, to deliver a copy of the *Cincinnati Gazette,* an abolition sheet. Local sentiment was forcibly expressed in a letter to Jefferson Davis. "The question then arises," it was said, "who is to be judge of the character of documents, transmitted through the mail? We reply unhesitatingly the Post Master: And he must judge at his peril. . . . the Post Master cannot shelter himself beneath an official appointment, and recklessly spurn and

48 Virginia, Acts of the General Assembly, 1835–36, ch. 66.

49 Jackson, *Correspondence,* V, 360–61 (August 9, 1835).

defy the laws of the State. A felon's penalty, confinement in the Penitentiary, would be the reward of his temerity." [50]

At this point of conflict, therefore, between state and federal agencies, the former prevailed. The operation of the post office was controlled in the South by the official action of the states and by the unofficial interference of citizens. The federal government continued to recognize the right of abolitionists to deliver their propaganda to the post office, and their right to have it carried to its destination. At the same time the government tolerated the state's assertion of power to prevent its delivery. Postmasters, who were local residents and presumably usually in sympathy with local sentiments, thus escaped the fate that at one moment seemed to impend over Collector Pringle.

THE FUGITIVE SLAVE ACT

The federal government and the northern states came into collision over the recovery of fugitive slaves, a conflict rendered almost beyond solution by the moral indignation that was generated in the North over the slavery issue. The administrative problem was a deep-seated one, running back many years before the Fugitive Slave Act of 1850.[51]

The duty to secure the return of runaway slaves was recognized in the Northwest Ordinance, which prohibited slavery in the Northwest Territory. It was also recognized in the Constitution (Article IV, section 2) which provided that persons held to service or labor in one state escaping into another should be delivered up on claim of the party to whom the service was due. The constitutional injunction was enforced by the act of 1793, providing both for the return of fugitives from justice (extradition) and from labor.[52] This was the statute under which fugitive slaves were rendered until the act of 1850.

The act of 1793 provided that a slave owner or his agent could seize a fugitive slave in another state or territory and bring him

50 Davis, *Letters, Papers and Speeches,* III, 104 (Dec. 21, 1856).

51 The most useful references dealing with the Fugitive Slave Act from the point of view of this study are Marion Gleason McDougall, *Fugitive Slaves, 1619–1865* (Boston: Ginn and Co., 1891); Russel B. Nye, *Fettered Freedom,* ch. 7; Senate Report 143, 30th Cong., 1st sess. (May 3, 1848); Senate Report 24, 38th Cong., 1st sess. (Feb. 29, 1864).

52 1 Stat. 302 (Feb. 12, 1793).

before any federal judge or any local magistrate. Upon proof of servitude, the judge or magistrate was required to give a certificate authorizing the removal of the fugitive. Any person obstructing the claimant, rescuing the slave, or concealing him was subject to a fine of $500. Since the number of federal judges was small and access to them often difficult merely by reason of distance, reliance for the certificate was normally upon a local magistrate. Congress did not intend in 1793 to establish a national police force or to expand its judicial establishment for the purpose of apprehending fugitive slaves.

The judicial duty to assist slave owners thus was a dual responsibility. The states became less and less inclined to cooperate as anti-slavery sentiment grew, and as individual cases of the return of slaves or the kidnapping of free colored persons aroused northern feelings. The effectiveness of the act of 1793 was greatly weakened by the decision of the Supreme Court in the Prigg case of 1842.[53] A slave woman who had fled into Pennsylvania was arrested and sent back to Maryland in disregard of the procedure required by Pennsylvania law. Prigg, the attorney who engineered the return, was convicted of an offense against the state, and appealed to the United States Supreme Court, alleging that the state law was unconstitutional. The Supreme Court unanimously held that the Pennsylvania law was unconstitutional since the power of Congress over fugitive slaves was exclusive. The majority opinion went further and held that any state statute dealing with fugitive slaves, whether in aid of or in conflict with federal legislation, was invalid.

The majority opinion declared, however, that state legislatures might relieve their magistrates from the duty of returning slaves under the federal act of 1793. Many states promptly followed this lead by forbidding their officials from taking any steps to grant certificates or otherwise to facilitate the return of fugitive slaves. Vermont was one of the earliest. It provided in 1843 that no court of record, justice of the peace, or other magistrate should grant a certificate for the return of fugitive slaves; that no sheriff or other peace officer should arrest or detain any fugitive slave; and that no officer or citizen should remove any fugitive slave to any other place within or without

[53] 16 Peters 539.

the state. To avoid outright conflict of duty on the part of Vermonters, the law exempted citizens of the state acting as federal judges or marshals or persons acting under their authority.[54] Massachusetts, stirred deeply by the case of George Latimer, who had been seized without a warrant in Boston, passed a similar statute in 1843,[55] and within a short period of time, so-called personal liberty laws of this nature were enacted in Pennsylvania and Rhode Island.

The effect of these statutes was to terminate the administrative dualism that had been instituted in 1793. In states enacting such laws, the federal government became the only agency by means of which fugitive slaves could be restored to their masters. Events during the 1840's gave signs that the states were moving in the direction of active opposition to the agents of the federal government, as well as to the slave hunters. Massachusetts and Vermont offered fugitives the right of trial by jury which would have made it nearly impossible to return a fugitive to slavery. Slave owners were consequently insistent that more effective means be established by the federal government to enforce their claims.

The Fugitive Slave Act of 1850, a part of the slavery compromise of that year, was the answer to their demand. Its general purpose was to enlarge the facilities of the federal courts for southern claimants, and to protect them against force and violence. Federal courts had long been authorized to appoint commissioners with powers of local magistrates to act with reference to offenders against the United States. The courts were now directed to increase the number of commissioners "with a view to afford reasonable facilities to reclaim fugitives from labor." Each commissioner was vested with authority to grant certificates to take and remove fugitives, and to appoint persons to execute their orders or to call bystanders to their aid. It became the specific duty of federal marshals and their deputies to execute such warrants, and the marshal was held personally responsible for the full value of any fugitive who might escape from his custody. With a certificate from a commissioner, a claimant to a fugitive was authorized to use such reasonable force and re-

54 Vermont, Acts of 1843, No. 15.

55 Massachusetts, Acts and Resolves, 1843, ch. 69.

straint as might be necessary to remove the slave; no testimony from the fugitive was allowed at the hearing; and the certificates were declared conclusive against process issued by any court or magistrate. Heavy fines and imprisonment were imposed upon any person convicted of obstructing claimants, rescuing or attempting to rescue fugitives, or concealing them. The commissioners earned a fee of ten dollars for each certificate granted, but only five dollars where a certificate was denied.[56] Howell Cobb, a moderate southerner, said of this enactment, "it was prepared by one of the most extreme advocates of Southern rights in Congress. It contains every provision that was demanded by the South. . . ."[57]

Immediately the question arose whether the law could be enforced. Jefferson Davis, who had fought the Compromise of 1850, was not optimistic. "I did not expect," he stated in 1851, "that the law would effect everything which would be desired. I could not with the evidences around me expect that it would be faithfully observed."[58] Trouble broke out at once, and President Millard Fillmore was faced with a new form of nullification, more difficult to grapple with than the problem of collecting the tariff in South Carolina in 1832 and 1833.

Another wave of personal liberty laws swept over the North.[59] They repeated the provisions of earlier statutes denying the use of state jails in fugitive cases, forbidding state officers from issuing certificates or assisting claimants, and punishing the seizure of free persons. A person seized under the act of 1850 who appealed to a state court was protected by requiring proof of identity by two persons, or by recourse to habeas corpus, or by a jury trial. The alleged fugitive was required to be defended by an attorney, often the state or county attorney. The purpose of these enactments was to defeat the execution of the federal statute.

The temper of the North quickly became evident, not only in legislation but in direct action obstructing the seizure and removal of fugitives. An escaped Negro slave, living in Boston

56 9 Stat. 462 (Sept. 18, 1850).

57 Ulrich B. Phillips, ed., *Correspondence of Toombs, Stephens, and Cobb*, American Historical Association, *Annual Report, 1911*, II, 250 (August 12, 1851).

58 Davis, *Letters, Papers and Speeches*, II, 98 (Sept. 25, 1851).

59 Marion G. McDougall, *Fugitive Slaves*, pp. 66–67.

under the name of Shadrach, was arrested under warrant in 1851 and taken to the courthouse for hearing by the U.S. commissioner. A crowd gathered and at an opportune moment it rushed into the courthouse, rescued Shadrach, and sent him off to Canada. Several persons were subsequently prosecuted for taking part in the rescue, but no convictions were secured.

Meanwhile intense excitement prevailed not only in Boston but throughout the country. What would the government do in the face of such unlawful and tumultuous acts? President Fillmore was faced with a relatively simple problem, since it was an unlawful assembly of citizens, not an official action of the state, which brought about the rescue, but the refusal of the state of Massachusetts to aid in the prosecution of its citizens complicated the situation. In his private correspondence Fillmore had already affirmed his intention to enforce the Fugitive Slave Act. Two Cabinet meetings were held in October 1850, at which the decision was reached to use military force if necessary. "I mean at all hazards," the President wrote Webster, "to do my part toward executing this law. I admit no right of nullification North or South." [60] Jefferson Davis, on the contrary, declared that if Massachusetts had cast off her obligations under the Constitution as a member of the Union, "then she is, of her own free will and sovereign act, virtually out of it. I, for one, will never give a dollar to coerce her back. . . . I deny the power of Massachusetts to nullify the law and remain in the Union. But I concede to her the right . . . to retire from the Union. . . ." [61] Fillmore was on impregnable constitutional ground, but the enforcement of the Fugitive Slave Act was a political and administrative, not a legal, problem.

The reluctance of federal agents to act either against their own conscience or the overwhelming sentiment of the community came into play again, as it had earlier in 1808 during the embargo. Daniel Webster, Secretary of State, was in Boston during the escape of William and Ellen Crafts, and made a report to Fillmore. "The District Attorney here [George Lunt]

60 *Fillmore Papers,* I, 336 (Oct. 28, 1850).

61 Davis, *Letters, Papers and Speeches,* II, 41 (Feb. 24, 1851). Later however, as Secretary of War, he authorized use of the regular army to support the marshal in Massachusetts in returning a fugitive slave. *Ibid.,* II, 360–61 (May 31, 1854).

has no talent, no fitness for his place, & no very good disposition. The Claimant, in this Craft case called on him for assistance or advice, which he declined to render. . . . Mr. Lunt associates with him in nearly all his business a young lawyer, by the name of Sanger. This Mr. Sanger . . . is a professed & active free soil man. . . . The Marshall, Mr. Devens, is, as I believe very well disposed, but I fear not entirely efficient. . . . I am sorry to be obliged to say that the *general weight* of U.S. officers in this District is *against* the execution of the Fugitive Slave Law. I hear this when I go into the Streets from every sound Whig, and every Union man I meet. Mr. Greeley, the Collector, is more than indifferent. . . ." [62] The alleged owner of the Crafts complained directly to Fillmore that his agents had been arrested as kidnappers, unreasonable bail demanded, and that his own warrants lay dead in the marshal's office.[63] The degree to which federal attorneys and marshals proved to be reluctant varied from case to case, and many of them did their duty, however obnoxious it may have been to them.

Another handicap was the refusal of juries to convict persons for obstructing the return of slaves. As Webster observed to Fillmore, "we need one thing further, viz: the conviction and punishment of some of the rescuers. After that shall have taken place, it will be no more difficult to arrest a fugitive slave in Boston, than to arrest any other person." [64] Convictions in communities where antislavery sentiment was strong were, however, difficult to secure, and penalties were generally light. Elizur Wright was prosecuted for assisting at the rescue of Shadrach. The jury could not agree, and at the second trial Wright was acquitted. The Reverend Samuel Williams was tried for giving timely notice to a slave named Gorsuch, in an affair that led to "the battle of Christiana." He was acquitted in a Pennsylvania court. The rescue of Jerry McHenry in Syracuse, New York, led to the indictment of eighteen persons. The jury failed to convict any one of them for violating the Fugitive Slave Act. The agent of the supposed owner was arrested but died before he

62 Webster, *Writings and Speeches* (National ed.), XVI, 576–77 (Nov. 15, 1850).

63 *Fillmore Papers,* II, 301 (Nov. 19, 1850). Cf. a parallel case reported in Senate Report 143, 30th Cong., 1st sess. (May 3, 1848), occurring in Michigan in 1847.

64 Webster, *Writings and Speeches* (National ed.), XVI, 606 (April 13, 1851).

came to trial. A deputy marshal was indicted for kidnapping, but was eventually acquitted.[65]

Two Kentuckians seized a slave in Oberlin. The slave was promptly rescued and dispatched to Canada. The federal authorities secured indictments against thirty-seven of the rescuers. Meanwhile the grand jury indicted the Kentuckians under state law as kidnappers. When they came to trial their counsel feared heavy terms and arranged a compromise by which both proceedings were dropped. The hazard of arrest and conviction of a slave agent on a charge of kidnapping was indeed an impediment to southern slave owners. Such cases came before the state courts, and here evidence could be introduced to prove that the alleged fugitive was in fact a free Negro. There was no doubt in many communities where the sympathy of the jury would lie. A charge of kidnapping could be brought against a federal officer as well as a slave agent.

The conflict went beyond juries to the high courts in one notable case. A Wisconsin abolitionist editor, Sherman M. Booth, was taken into custody by the U.S. marshal for violating the Fugitive Slave Act. He was promptly freed on a writ of habeas corpus, and the discharge sustained by the Wisconsin Supreme Court. Booth then was indicted and tried before the U.S. District Court, found guilty, and remanded to the custody of the marshal. The Wisconsin Supreme Court again granted habeas corpus. The case eventually came to the Supreme Court of the United States, which in an able opinion sustained the marshal and declared the subordination of the state supreme court in cases falling under the federal judicial power.[66]

Many of the northern states thus sought to obstruct and defeat the operation of the Fugitive Slave Law within their borders. They withdrew from the mutual responsibility which they had accepted under the old act of 1793. They forbade their officials, executive and judicial, to assist in the execution of the act of 1850. They directed their county attorneys to defend a fugitive. They closed their jails to federal agents. They secured indictments against slave agents for kidnapping Negroes. They protected alleged fugitives by offering them jury trial. Their courts

65 American and Foreign Anti-Slavery Society, *Annual Report, 1853*, pp. 30–36.
66 *Ableman* v. *Booth*, 21 Howard 506 (1858).

failed to convict citizens guilty of obstructing slave agents or concealing slaves. These were all actions taken by the public authorities of the state. They were emphasized by speeches, mass meetings, demonstrations, and forcible rescues of fugitives from federal custody on the part of citizens.

The normal pattern of federal-state cooperation, which had begun with the foundation of the government in the use of state and county jails for federal prisoners, thus broke down in the case of fugitive slaves in many states and communities. The breakdown, as Fillmore observed, was a form of nullification aimed not against a particular law as inconsistent with the Constitution, but against the Constitution itself.[67] The parallel with the problem of delivery of incendiary material through the post office in the South is obvious. In both cases, local sentiment defeated federal authority in substantial measure by means both legal and extralegal.

Nullification, abolition tracts, and the Fugitive Slave Act raised in each case sharp issues concerning the effective authority of the federal government when moral conviction was measured against legal duty. Although states might be invited to cooperate with the general government, they could not be compelled to do so. They could formally withdraw, as they did in the fugitive slave cases, or they might merely sabotage in obedience to the consciences of their officials or to community sentiment. The experience of these years demonstrated how wisely the first Congress had acted when it decided not to save money by employing state officers to execute federal law.

The use of armed force, such as had occurred in the Whiskey Rebellion, was avoided, thanks to the genius of Henry Clay for compromise. It could have been used, and would have been in the controversy over the tariff, had not a *modus vivendi* been agreed upon. It is an open question whether armed force would have been feasible either in the case of delivery of the mails in the South, or in the case of rendition of fugitives from labor in the North. Here resistance was dispersed, and the withdrawal of the states in the latter case was merely a symbol of the will of the people to resist. No reliable means of securing compliance has been found under such circumstances in a democratic society.

67 Richardson, *Messages*, V, 137–38 (Dec. 2, 1851).

CHAPTER TWENTY-SEVEN

The State of the Administrative Art

The development of the art of administration during the early years of the Republic was slow and unattended. Experience added something here, something there; and the example of gifted executives such as Albert Gallatin, the young Calhoun, and Amos Kendall established standards and traditions that bore good fruit, although often obscured by influences hostile to good administration. Since change was gradual and under the Jeffersonians relatively slight, it will be convenient now to observe the improvements in the administrative art from 1801 to 1860. The experience of a half century and more brought both gains and losses in the art as it had been understood and practiced by the Federalists.

THE INFLUENCE OF ENVIRONMENT

The basic forces that played upon the public business and affected its conduct were primarily three: magnitude, facility of communication, and democracy. The public services of 1800 were extensive for their day, but they were confined to the Atlantic seaboard, apart from a few Indian agents and military posts across the Alleghenies. The public services of 1860 covered the continent, but with a huge unoccupied area cutting off the Pacific coast from the settled regions of the Mississippi Valley. A few diplomatic posts were maintained in Europe in 1801; by 1860 they had girdled the globe to the Far East and reached into the southern hemisphere. The American fleet had stations on both coasts, in the Mediterranean, off Africa, in the South

Pacific, and in the Far East. Geographically speaking, the public service had reached the outer limits of its growth, although many areas remained to be filled in.

Magnitude was also obvious in the size of the public service. Excluding the armed forces, the public service required in 1800 about 3,000 employees. In 1860 the number was about 50,000.[1] Some departments required more employees than were needed by the whole public service in 1800. There were over 800 officials and agents of the federal government on the Pacific Coast in 1860. The management task of 1860 was, in fact, so different in magnitude from that of 1800 as to seem almost unrelated to its infant days. In subject matter, however, it was much the same. The execution of the public business on this enlarged scale was greatly facilitated by the improvements that had occurred in the field of transportation and communication. In 1861 Washington could send messages on Professor Morse's invention, the telegraph, directly to such distant points as San Francisco.

The impact of democratic ideas and party spirit upon the administrative system has already been disclosed. The consequences were to break down whatever sense of separation may have existed between the public service and the people, and to open up to all adult male citizens the possibility of direct experience in the duties and responsibilities of public office. These tendencies were salutary. Partisanship brought other consequences in the lowering of official standards of rectitude and in the waste of resources that were harmful. Wherever the balance may lie, there is no doubt that the tide of democracy that ran so strongly during the middle years of the nineteenth century was a major influence conditioning the administrative system.

The public service was also affected by borrowing from European experience in ways and means of carrying on the King's business. English forms and procedures had always been significant, and the system set up by the Federalists was based heavily on English precedents, notably in the customs service. Now both Congress and the executive branch began to make specific investigations of foreign experience as a guide to administrative and technical improvement.

[1] *Historical Statistics of the United States,* p. 294.

A few illustrations will suggest the range of information sought from overseas. In 1839 a report was rendered from American consuls on the methods of collecting, keeping, and disbursing public money; [2] in 1840 the regulations of France, Holland, and Belgium for safety of steam navigation were before the Senate Committee on Commerce; [3] in 1842 the British warehouse system was studied and in 1847 examined on the spot by two Treasury agents sent abroad for this purpose.[4] It became the model for a reorganization of American customhouse stores.[5] In 1842 British and French experience in the construction and maintenance of lighthouses was considered,[6] and in 1845 two naval lieutenants were sent abroad to study foreign lighthouse systems.[7] Their report was the basis for a reorganization of the American lighthouse system.

In 1846 British experience was cited as support for the construction of war vessels by contract rather than by government yards.[8] British and French naval programs were regularly observed by the Navy Department, and their shift to steam-propelled warships much emphasized in the campaign to equip the American navy in similar fashion.[9] Secretary of War Poinsett was especially alert to the military advances made in Europe, and in 1839 secured permission for three cadets to study for a year in the French cavalry school at Saumur. One of these was Philip Kearny, later commander of the force that proceeded overland to California during the Mexican War. In 1855 a military commission was sent abroad to examine the principal military systems of Europe.[10]

A special agent was sent abroad in 1840 to study the British penny post plan and the mail establishments of other European countries, "as might conduce to the improvement of our own

2 Senate Doc. 113, 25th Cong., 3d sess. (Jan. 7, 1839).

3 Senate Doc. 241, 26th Cong., 1st sess. (March 2, 1840).

4 House Ex. Doc. 6, 30th Cong., 1st sess., pp. 140–43 (July 29, 1847).

5 Senate Ex. Doc. 32, 30th Cong., 2d sess., p. 16 (Feb. 22, 1849); 9 Stat. 53 (August 6, 1846).

6 House Report 811, 27th Cong., 2d sess. (May 25, 1842).

7 Senate Doc. 488, 29th Cong., 1st sess. (August 5, 1846).

8 House Report 681, 29th Cong., 1st sess., p. 6 (May 20, 1846).

9 House Report 685, 29th Cong., 1st sess., pp. 1–3 (June 12, 1846).

10 Davis, *Letters, Papers and Speeches,* II, 446 (April 2, 1855).

system."[11] Postage stamps were introduced in 1847 as a direct result of the British innovation.[12] British methods of managing the public printing were cited in the long struggle to improve the congressional system.

These cases indicate that executive officers were not only anxious to improve the operations of their respective departments but were ready to borrow from the politically despised monarchies of Europe. The administrative process began to appear, almost intuitively, as something in part at least independent of constitutional structure and adaptable from an undemocratic to a democratic environment.

As one decade followed another, changes large and small were introduced both by act of Congress and by executive direction. Many of them have already been recorded, as they were initiated in the Treasury, War Department, Navy Department, and Post Office. They were innovations designed to solve immediate problems, but through them ran at times a common pattern that revealed underlying trends in the art of administration, as it responded to common pressures and needs.

DEVELOPMENTS IN ADMINISTRATIVE ORGANIZATION

The structure of the executive departments in 1860 was much more complex than in 1800; they were not merely larger, they had patterns of organization consistent with original principles but substantially more complex and more highly developed. The difference may be stated, with some exaggeration, by asserting that in 1800 a department consisted of the Secretary, clerks, and a field establishment, while in 1860 a department consisted of the Secretary, a group of bureaus handling the mass of routine business usually without the intervention or even knowledge of the Secretary, and a field service that, in the larger establishments, exceeded in size the parent departments of an earlier day.

The need for devolution. The necessity of providing aid to Presidents and department heads has already been remarked. The Chief Executive suffered from a burdensome mass of triviali-

11 House Doc. 2, 26th Cong., 2d sess., p. 482 (Dec. 5, 1840).

12 House Report 731, 30th Cong., 1st sess. (June 23, 1848).

ties, and secured only moderate relief by the act setting up the President's household in 1857. The Postmaster General, whose establishment was the most numerous, was the first civilian executive to obtain the advantage of assistant heads; State and Treasury followed later. The pressure of business remained unremitting; help came too slowly to match need. Department heads were not provided with personal staff assistance to facilitate control of their agencies. The office of the Secretary was a clerical office, and on a relatively small scale. Thus the Interior estimates for the fiscal year ending June 30, 1852, showed a figure for "the Department proper," of $28,000, including the Secretary's salary of $8,000, while the Land Office required over $800,000.[13] The Secretary managed with a chief clerk, eleven clerks, and three messengers.[14]

Relief was to come by the effective organization of the bureau system, the elements of which went back to earlier years. Bureau responsibility for routine work was a genuine means of preventing administrative bottlenecks, but it brought its own problems. Nevertheless the course of administration was to pivot on the bureaus and the rule of delegation.

The bureau system. With the passage of time, the steady increase in the volume of work, the constantly more persuasive authority of the special knowledge possessed by subordinates, and the preoccupation of their short-lived superiors, clerks tended to become in fact, although not at first in law, the responsible agents for the transaction of their particular business —so long as it was well enough done to escape attention. The conclusion of this trend was the formation, by law, of a bureau, the elevation of the principal clerk to the rank of bureau chief or commissioner, and the delegation to him of statutory authority for the performance of his work under only the general supervision of the head of the department. Direct relations might be set up with the Treasury accounting officers, by-passing the head of the department. The semiautonomy of the bureau was often symbolized by a special seal of office for the authentication of records.

This tendency could have been observed during the Jeffer-

13 House Ex. Doc. 1, 31st Cong., 2d sess., p. 20.
14 *Official Register, 1853,* p. 131.

sonian era, but it seldom reached the dignity of legislative authorization. The Patent Office is in point. In 1802 Jefferson appointed Dr. William Thornton a clerk in the State Department in charge of patents. So far as Congress was concerned he was merely a clerk; the grant of a patent was still a personal act of the President on advice of the Secretary of State.[15] Thornton, on his own motion, assumed the title of superintendent of patents. Early in 1830 Van Buren reported to Congress, "*A Clerk of this Department is* charged with the duty of superintending the preparation of patents for new inventions. . . ." [16] Congress then authorized the title of superintendent with no different status.[17] Thus the matter stood until 1836, when Congress established the office of commissioner of patents in the State Department.[18] The commissioner was now appointed by the President with the consent of the Senate: he was vested with authority to superintend and perform all acts concerned with the granting of patents; and the office had its own seal. The final validation of a patent was brought down one step in the official hierarchy, the signature of the President being omitted in favor of the signatures of the commissioner and the Secretary of State. The one-time clerk in charge of patents thus became a commissioner, with a chief clerk and subordinate examiners and clerks of his own.

A corresponding development took place with respect to military pensions. Where to place final authority to grant a pension to disabled members of the armed forces greatly puzzled both Federalist and Republican Congresses. Failing in an attempt to saddle the job on the courts, Congressmen undertook to decide each individual case themselves, on recommendation of the Secretary of War.[19] With the exception of three years, this was the method of administration for the Revolutionary army pension fund from 1793 to 1818. A pension clerk in the office of the Secretary of War prepared cases for the Secretary, who then forwarded them to Congress. After 1818 pension business became

15 Leonard D. White, *The Federalists: A Study in Administrative History* (New York: Macmillan, 1948), pp. 136–39; *The Jeffersonians,* pp. 205–10.

16 House Doc. 85, 21st Cong., 1st sess., p. 4 (March 4, 1830).

17 4 Stat. 396 (April 23, 1830).

18 5 Stat. 117 (March 3, 1836).

19 1 Stat. 324 (Feb. 28, 1793).

excessively heavy, but Secretary of War Calhoun had no one to assist him except clerks and no one upon whom to devolve this mass of detail.

By 1826 a "pension office" had been established in the War Department by departmental order and was making reports under that designation, although unrecognized by law.[20] Concerning the individual at the head of this office, Secretary of War Cass stated in 1833, "His duties are not defined by law, nor are his acts recognized by law. While, in fact, controlling the disbursement of near $2,500,000 annually, he is still known upon the statute book as a clerk only, with a compensation attached to that situation, and without the slightest allusion to the powers and duties he actually exercises." [21] Congress could be persuaded only to provide temporarily for a commissioner of pensions to act under the direction of the Secretary of War.[22] It was clearly impossible to revert, however, to a clerkship; new duties were added in subsequent years; and Congress finally recognized the office as a permanent establishment in 1849.[23]

A parallel trend was in motion in the State Department, changing the status of clerks dealing with specified geographical areas into the professional area officers of a later day. In 1846 Secretary of State Buchanan complained to Congress about his need of assistance. "Of the persons belonging to the Department," he informed Congress, "not one, except its head, has authority to sign a single paper, or to decide upon any question, however trivial." Even the miscellaneous business, not relating to foreign affairs, came to his desk: "all of it, in its minutest details, must undergo the personal supervision of the Secretary. . . ." [24] The department had, of course, its various branches, diplomatic, consular, claims, fiscal, and others, but none of these had statutory recognition and none could do more than *prepare* matters for the Secretary's signature.

Buchanan asked for the appointment of three additional clerks (note the tenacity of terminology) in the diplomatic branch: "men of intellect and information, competent to prepare a des-

20 Senate Doc. 1, 19th Cong., 2d sess., p. 510 (Oct. 12, 1826).

21 House Doc. 34, 22d Cong., 2d sess., pp. 1–3 (Jan. 7, 1833).

22 4 Stat. 619 at 622 (March 2, 1833).

23 9 Stat. 341 (Jan. 19, 1849).

24 Buchanan, *Works,* VI, 412–13 (March 16, 1846).

patch upon any subject arising in the ordinary course of business and involving only principles which have been clearly settled by the action of our Government. Their first duty would be to devote themselves to a careful perusal and study of all the correspondence from the beginning, between this government and the foreign governments with which their duties may be connected; so that they might be able, always, without delay, to furnish to the head of the Department any information or documents which he may require." [25] Obviously such persons of "intellect and information" hardly corresponded to the usual concept of clerk. They were intended to be professional aides to the Secretary of State.[26]

The emergence of the bureau system was due primarily to the great increase in volume rather than in variety of the public business. The system was not imposed to foster the advantages of specialization, for they were being achieved automatically in the face of sheer convenience and necessity. The great gain was relief to the head of the agency from immediate responsibility for each and every transaction. Responsibility for operations, under direction, could be delegated.

The point was clearly recognized by scholarly George Bancroft, Secretary of the Navy. Writing to the Speaker of the House, he stated, "The chiefs of the bureau have powers of direction. Their act is esteemed as the act of the Secretary. They have power to originate, authorize, and sanction expenditures. On their activity, vigilance, scrupulous supervision of expenditures, and hearty co-operation, success in administering the department must depend." [27]

Consequences of the bureau system. The establishment of bureaus also served the cause of administration by strengthening headquarters control of the field service. The case is well illustrated by events in the revenue cutter service (also known as the revenue marine service). Secretary of the Treasury John C. Spencer found upon entering his office in March 1843 that no efficient control could be exercised at Washington over the service or

25 *Ibid.*, VI, 414–15.

26 For the establishment of the bureau system in the War Department, see White, *The Jeffersonians,* pp. 236–40; in the Navy Department, ch. 11 of this work.

27 House Doc. 188, 29th Cong., 1st sess., p. 2 (April 23, 1846).

its finances. "The clerks could not be expected to be seafaring men. . . ." He consequently selected a captain of the revenue cutter service, brought him to Washington with a lieutenant as his assistant, and directed him "to take charge of the business."

The results of professional supervision of the service were good. "Order and system," Spencer reported, "have been established. Economy in expenditures and efficiency in service have been greatly promoted. . . . And, above all, the department now knows what is done and what is neglected. . . ." [28] Captain Alexander V. Fraser, the new bureau chief, confirmed these views. Control of purchasing for the revenue cutters was removed from the collectors and concentrated in Washington; officers were rotated from station to station; the journals of each vessel were submitted monthly for inspection, "and no case of remissness in discharge of the duties, or want of diligence, is suffered to escape." Great care was taken in the selection of officers of junior rank.[29]

This advance in the form of organization was attended by a new problem, barely sensed during the Jacksonian period but destined to become serious in later years: control of bureaus that tended to become autonomous principalities, pursuing their own policy with support drawn from beyond the boundaries of the department to which they belonged. The bureaus of the War Department were foremost in this trend, but the bureaus of the Navy Department were also to become notorious offenders. The bureaus of the Interior Department, each with an already long history of its own and none closely related to the others, and directed by a succession of short-term Secretaries, were favorably placed to maintain their operating independence. Indeed, in the debate on the Interior Department bill, Senator John M. Niles declared that they were already "substantially independent of the departments" to which they were then severally attached. "All the detail of the ordinary business of the bureau may be considered as independent of the department." [30] The issue was not to attract much attention during these years, but it was

28 House Doc. 45, 28th Cong., 1st sess., p. 1 (Jan. 10, 1844).
29 *Ibid.*, pp. 3–6.
30 *Congressional Globe,* 30th Cong., 2d sess., p. 671 (March 3, 1849).

to become serious during the era of congressional government after the Civil War.

The formation of bureaus was regularly resisted by Congress, not on account of the administrative implications (which attracted neither interest nor attention) but because a bureau meant additional expenditure. Even the moderate and intelligent Gilmer Select Committee on Retrenchment revealed hostility against bureaus. "Some of the bureaus," the report declared, "are rapidly growing into Departments. . . . The Patent Office is considered an appendage to the Department of State; but it has all the external arrangements and appearances of a Department itself. From a mere depository of models, seeds, &c., it is making rapid strides to rank among the Departments. . . ." [31] In 1843 Senator Buchanan had to defend a small appropriation for meteorological observations by denying that a new bureau would be established.[32] When in 1856 Secretary of the Navy Dobbin asked for the establishment of the office of judge advocate general, he began his request by declaring that he, too, was "much opposed to multiplying Bureaux and Officers." [33]

The specialization of effort and devolution of responsibility encouraged by the bureau system were, nevertheless, essential to prevent delay in departmental operations. In 1846 Colonel J. J. Abert, head of the topographical engineer corps, remarked on the value of the bureau system installed by Calhoun: "The reflection is not generally made, that, by the organization of the War Department into distinct bureaus, all the immense correspondence, and the detail duties of that department, have now to be performed by the several bureaus, which contain and preserve the records of the War Department on all the several subjects assigned to each bureau. The order, economy, promptness, and responsibility, which have attended this arrangement . . . are essential to the despatch and efficiency of the duties of that department." [34] Before its reorganization in 1842 the Navy De-

31 House Report 741, 27th Cong., 2d sess., p. 17 (May 23, 1842).

32 Buchanan, *Works,* V, 419–20 (Feb. 10, 1843).

33 Senate Ex. Doc. 5, 34th Cong., 3d sess., Part II, p. 418 (Dec. 1, 1856).

34 House Doc. 70, 29th Cong., 2d sess., p. 6 (Dec. 16, 1846).

partment envied its neighbor this form of organization; the House Naval Affairs Committee said that since Calhoun's time "the War Department has been well said 'to work itself.' "[35]

The inspection system. Another development in administrative organization was the extension of field inspection as a means of preventing fraud and corruption, and of securing consistency of action. In some cases the inspection system was also conceived as a means of increasing the efficiency of operations, but this object was secondary.

The normal method of headquarters control of the field service from earliest times had consisted in the issuance of instructions and the making of reports, chiefly on financial matters. Supplementary requirements were an oath of office, bonds and securities, and penalties to be recovered in court for misfeasance. The instructions were assumed to be self-enforcing. If financial reports came in promptly and on their face showed no irregularity, most field agents were undisturbed by Washington. The forms of central control of distant agents were thus elementary and often ineffective.

The system of inspection slowly supplemented older methods, but reliance on personal integrity was still deemed normally to be sufficient and peculiarly appropriate. "The only safeguard for the public security against fraud and embezzlement, upon which *entire reliance* can be placed," declared the first comptroller in 1837, "is to be found in the heart and conscience of the individual intrusted with the receipt and disbursement of the public funds, and his high sense of the value of a character for unyielding integrity and moral rectitude."[36] All this was correct enough so far as it went, but men of character might be anything but competent and effective agents, and not all agents could qualify as men of character.

The first scheme of field inspection of civilian operations had been inaugurated in 1816 with respect to the land offices.[37] It was moderately successful but apparently never developed into a regular periodic inspection of each and every land office. Many

[35] House Report 157, 27th Cong., 2d sess., p. 2 (Feb. 12, 1842).

[36] Senate Doc. 1, 25th Cong., 2d sess., p. 165 (Nov. 9, 1837).

[37] White, *The Jeffersonians,* pp. 523–26. The military inspection staff is a relevant parallel, the study of which is much needed.

irregularities and frauds were uncovered in the 1830's, but usually too late to protect the interest of the government.[38] Inspectors were appointed *ad hoc,* and the value of experience was consequently lost.[39] Commissioner James Whitcomb recommended the regular appointment of examiners drawn from the clerks or officers of the General Land Office, but without success.[40] In 1853 the *National Intelligencer* made the sensible suggestion that the Interior Department would "find it to the public interest to keep some one of the thoroughly competent employés of the Land Office bureau travelling and inspecting the books and operations of the various land offices over the country." [41] An inspection of the surveyors' offices was made in 1841 to inquire "into the facts and circumstances . . . of long standing and of great embarrassment." [42] For many years the surveyors had been independent principalities.

A second system of inspection was instituted in 1836 by Amos Kendall in the post office. In his annual report he informed Congress, "The duties of the inspection office are rapidly extending. . . . Its chief object is a rigid supervision over the rendition of postmasters' accounts and the performance of contractors. Conducted with system and energy, it will soon be felt on our thousands of mail routes whenever a delinquency occurs." [43] The special agents found, however, that their energies were drained off in hunting down mail robbers and dishonest postmasters.[44] The concept of inspection as a means of securing consistency and legality, to say nothing of efficiency, was thereby impaired. The central function of an inspection system, however, was recorded by an able special agent, George Plitt. He recommended at least one intelligent and experienced agent for each of the larger states to visit every post office in his district, to instruct postmasters, to give advice on the location of new post offices and the discontinuance of those not required, to recom-

38 For example, see Senate Doc. 439, 23d Cong., 1st sess. (June 12, 1834).

39 For sample instructions to one such, see House Doc. 142, 24th Cong., 2d sess., pp. 14–17 (July 16, 1836).

40 House Doc. 46, 25th Cong., 3d sess., pp. 4–5 (Dec. 26, 1838).

41 *National Intelligencer,* August 4, 1853.

42 Senate Doc. 22, 27th Cong., 2d sess., p. 7 (Dec. 24, 1841).

43 Senate Doc. 1, 24th Cong., 2d sess., p. 546 (Dec. 5, 1836). See above, ch. 14, for information on the operation of this system.

44 House Doc. 51, 26th Cong., 2d sess., p. 1 (Jan. 5, 1841).

mend removal of unworthy postmasters, and to keep a vigilant eye upon all the operations of the department within his territory.[45]

The revelation of the embezzlements of Collector Samuel Swartwout would presumably have inaugurated a stringent system of field inspection in the Treasury Department. Indeed the first comptroller went so far as to suggest that the "system of frequent and rigid examination of the land offices, as heretofore practised, might be extended with advantage to the collectors of customs in all the districts where the receipts exceed the expenditure." [46] No such system emerged, due perhaps in part to the political importance of collectors of customs and of the customhouse patronage. In 1853 a reforming Secretary of the Treasury, James Guthrie, sent out inspectors to examine the books and operations of the collection districts, but this appears to have been a single investigation.[47]

In 1846 the Independent Treasury Act directed the Secretary of the Treasury to appoint special agents to examine the books and accounts of the several depositories, "to the end that uniformity and accuracy in the accounts, as well as safety to the public moneys may be secured thereby." [48] The instructions to William M. Gouge, appointed special agent for this purpose in 1854, required him not only to verify books and accounts, but also to observe whether safeguards against fire, thieves, and burglars were adequate, what could be done to meet the convenience of fiscal officers, whether the transfer of funds could be facilitated, and whether all the different requirements of law were observed. "On all these points you will converse fully and freely with the officers of the different depositories. . . ." [49] The report rendered by Inspector Gouge gave gratifying evidence of the proper operation of the independent treasury system.

[45] House Doc. 2, 26th Cong., 2d sess., p. 529 (November 1840).

[46] Senate Doc. 1, 25th Cong., 2d sess., p. 165 (Nov. 9, 1837).

[47] Senate Ex. Doc. 2, 33d Cong., 1st sess., p. 12 (Dec. 6, 1853).

[48] 9 Stat. 59, sec. 11 (August 6, 1846). The annual reports of the Secretary of the Treasury for 1847 (House Ex. Doc. 6, 30th Cong., 1st sess., Dec. 9, 1847) and for 1848 (House Ex. Doc. 7, 30th Cong., 2d sess., Dec. 11, 1848) have been examined; they do not mention the inspection system.

[49] Senate Ex. Doc. 2, 33d Cong., 2d sess., p. 255 (May 26, 1854).

After hearing severe criticism of the management of the lighthouse system by the fifth auditor, Congress established a Lighthouse Board in the Treasury Department in 1852 and set up a statutory scheme of inspection. To each of twelve districts the President assigned an army or navy officer to act as lighthouse inspector under the orders of the Lighthouse Board.[50]

Another type of inspection was brought into the spotlight in 1847 when the House demanded a report on secret Treasury agents or inspectors of the customs. According to Secretary Walker, they were intended to detect smugglers, and had been appointed in accordance with uniform long-standing practice. Walker demurred against revealing their names, and thus destroying their usefulness. They were obviously available for any service desired by the Treasury,[51] and, as already noted, had become patronage offices.

These examples indicate that gradually but surely the means of headquarters control of the field services were being developed. It was evident enough that mere written instructions and reports from field agents were insufficient with the new practice of rotation among politically active, short-term incumbents.[52] Regular inspection by an experienced force of qualified men gained ground, however, but slowly. Congress in its customary state of penny-pinching was reluctant; politicians in Congress and in the field were presumably equally reluctant; and the oft-expressed desires of the departments were delayed in achievement.

LIBRARIES AND RECORDS MANAGEMENT

Governmental offices with responsibility for reaching decisions on points of law felt a progressive need for their own law collections. Elijah Hayward, commissioner of the Land Office, appealed to Congress in 1833 for $2,500 to collect the statutes and supreme court decisions of the several states—works, he said, absolutely necessary to correct action on land cases in his agency.[53] No record has been noted that Congress heeded his

50 10 Stat. 112, secs. 8, 12 (August 31, 1852).

51 House Doc. 80, 29th Cong., 2d sess. (Feb. 8, 1847).

52 Foreign service inspectors, called consular superintendents, were recommended in 1842. *Hunt's Merchants' Magazine,* VI (1842), 305.

53 Senate Doc. 9, 23d Cong., 1st sess., p. 53 (Nov. 30, 1833).

request, perhaps because only the year before a special law library had been set up in the Library of Congress.[54]

A lively debate occurred in 1835 over an item of $3,000 to purchase books for the Attorney General. John Quincy Adams opposed the appropriation, and Representative Benjamin Hardin argued against departmental libraries on principle. The Attorney General was warmly defended on the ground that he needed tools to work with, and that he had "to study much at night, when the Congress library was closed and inaccessible." [55] The House allowed $2,000 by a vote which clearly supported the principle of departmental libraries. In 1836 Congress appropriated $1,500 out of the patent fund, supported by fees from inventors, to found the library of the Patent Office.[56] This was a single appropriation.

Meanwhile the departmental libraries, already well established, continued to use their special appropriations or contingent funds to maintain their collections. The State Department library, fostered earlier by Secretary John Quincy Adams, was the most extensive. Annual expenditures from 1830 to 1834 inclusive averaged about $9,000—a figure that may be compared with the annual appropriation to the Library of Congress at that time of $5,000. Treasury spent less than $2,000 in an average year for its library, War a little over $1,000, and Navy and Post Office negligible amounts.[57]

There was, therefore, in some executive departments an emerging appreciation of the value of a library as a tool of administration. Congress was not unfriendly but was characteristically parsimonious. State was the only department reasonably well equipped in this respect.

Records management. As records accumulated, offices became glutted with old papers, important chiefly on account of the precedents that may have been established by them. The care and custody of these papers and the preparation of indexes to make them available for reference became more and more a cause of concern. They were in a deplorable state by the 1830's,

54 4 Stat. 579 (July 14, 1832).

55 *Register of Debates,* 23d Cong., 2d sess., p. 1020 (Jan. 20, 1835); for Hardin's remarks, see *ibid.*, p. 1125 (Jan. 28, 1835).

56 5 Stat. 117, sec. 19 (July 4, 1836).

57 Senate Doc. 11, 24th Cong., 1st sess., pp. 16–74 (Dec. 10, 1835).

and little progress in securing order and control was made during the Jacksonian period.

The volume and condition of the records are suggested by a report in 1832 showing in the Navy Department 135 volumes of records with a name index; 52 volumes with no index; 504 volumes of letters received, with a name index; 25 volumes of the same with no index; and 546 cases of courts of inquiry and courts-martial with a name index.[58] Land Office private claim records had never been copied or organized from the inception of the system to 1836. They were described by the principal clerk in charge in these terms: "These originals, which are now upon every kind of paper, from the largest size wrapping paper to letter paper, should, therefore, be most carefully and neatly copied into well-bound and durable volumes. . . ." [59] Two tons of General Land Office records were found in 1833 "deposited in the attic story of the [Treasury] building, immediately under the roof, in the utmost confusion, in bundles arranged neither in chronological order, nor in the order of consecutive numbers." [60] Conditions in the field offices were generally worse. The original field notes of the land survey in Illinois were represented in 1834 as "fast decaying . . . . in numerous instances, nearly illegible, on account of the indifference of the ink and papers." [61] The quality of ink and paper used in the departmental offices, however, was excellent, and these records remain today in near perfect condition.

Fireproof storage was urgently demanded from Congress during the 1830's, a drive stimulated by disastrous conflagrations

58 National Archives, Senate Committee on Finance, 22d Cong., 1st sess., letter dated Feb. 9, 1832. This is a convenient point to indicate, by way of example, the volume of daily correspondence in the office of the Secretary of the Treasury. An estimate of the number *received* daily, including Sunday, as of October 1834 showed 6 single letters, 25 double, 20 triple, 9 quadruple, and one packet; those *sent* daily, 2 single letters, 22 double letters, 4 triple letters, 5 quadruple letters, and one packet. National Archives, Treasury Department, Letters to Cabinet and Bureaus, Set B, No. 1, p. 150.

59 Senate Doc. 216, 24th Cong., 1st sess., p. 13 (February 1836).

60 Senate Doc. 9, 23d Cong., 1st sess., p. 52 (Nov. 30, 1833). The embryonic character of the filing system is suggested by directions to diplomatic officers requiring papers "to be carefully filed, endorsed with a short note of the contents, and an index formed of the contents of each bundle, package, or box in which they are contained." House Doc. 94, 22d Cong., 2d sess., p. 8 (Feb. 24, 1832).

61 House Report 20, 23d Cong., 2d sess., p. 1 (Dec. 30, 1834).

in the Treasury building in 1833 and in the building housing the General Post Office and the Patent Office in 1836.[62] It was gradually secured for the most important current records, but old papers had to be stored wherever space was available, often in garrets or basements. A few customhouses had fireproof safes, but most field records had no protection against loss or destruction.

Indexing was another problem. Without a satisfactory index, papers quickly passed beyond effective use. With few exceptions, the only index to the bound volumes of correspondence was by name of the writer, and this index often did no more than bring together all the names beginning with a single letter, with no further alphabetization. Subject matter indexes were rare.

Secretary of War Lewis Cass asked help in 1832 from the Senate Finance Committee to prepare an index to the War Department papers, a measure, he asserted, "indispensable to the prompt and correct performance of the Department." The existing alphabetical indexes to the letter books were inadequate. "What is wanted," he wrote, "is a 'catalogue raisonne,' which shall exhibit at once every document on file, arranged in such a way that any one can be found by reference to the subject matter, as well as to the names of the persons concerned." [63] The first comptroller reported in 1836 that "no regular index" to the decisions under the tariff laws had been made since 1819, and that great inconvenience and trouble had resulted. ". . . the uniformity and harmony of decision, the convenience of the

62 Both fires were disastrous. Congress delayed authorization of fireproof buildings despite the lessons of the Treasury conflagration. In Jackson's last annual message, December 5, 1836, he begged Congress for a new fireproof building for the Post Office Department (Richardson, *Messages,* III, 258). In the early morning of December 15, 1836, ten days later, the old building went up in smoke: "the whole building was a heap of ruins" (Adams, *Memoirs,* IX, 326–27). Everything belonging to the Patent Office was destroyed: 168 large folio volumes of records; 26 large portfolios, containing 9,000 drawings; all the original descriptions and specifications of about 10,000 inventions; about 7,000 models, said to be "the largest and most interesting collection of models in the world"; and a small library—all lost "by the improvidence which exposed so many memorials and evidences of the superiority of American genius to the destruction which has overtaken them." Senate Doc. 58, 24th Cong., 2d sess., pp. 1–2 (Jan. 9, 1837). In 1853 the War Department was still occupying a building defective in its construction and not fireproof. Jefferson Davis, *Letters, Papers and Speeches,* II, 332 (Dec. 1, 1853).

63 National Archives, Senate Committee on Finance, 22d Cong., 1st sess. (Feb. 9, 1832).

department, the despatch of the public business, as well as the public interest and security, require that such a work should be forthwith commenced, and, as soon as practicable perfected." [64] The indifference to good indexing was suggested by the fact that the old index up to 1819 had been done out-of-hours as extra work—not as a necessary part of office procedure.[65] The solution of the indexing problem was partly, as Lewis Cass told Congress, to discover talent to suggest and mature the best plan; for the rest, extra clerk money.[66] Neither was generally forthcoming, and proper indexing remained a problem for the future.

Private possession of public papers became an object of concern. Secretary of State Edward Livingston reminded diplomatic agents that their letters and papers were not private property but were required to be delivered to their successors, a requirement "in many instances, but imperfectly executed, and in others totally disregarded." [67] President Pierce recommended legislation requiring records and papers of a public character to be left by outgoing officers. The issue became urgent because four collectors had gone off with their records, concealing frauds amounting to $198,000.[68] Congress had recently imposed severe penalties upon either private persons or officials who willfully took away or destroyed public papers.[69]

Private access to public papers in the Treasury Department was regulated in 1830 by the rule that copies of accounts or other papers were to be furnished only to individuals having a personal interest in them.[70] Corresponding regulations were issued later to protect customhouse papers, ostensibly to expedite merchants' business with customs clerks but obviously with other purposes also in mind. In a circular of 1851 Secretary Corwin directed that inspection of customhouse papers and records be permitted only on written application and special permission of the collector who, in case of doubt, was required to submit the

64 House Doc. 55, 24th Cong., 2d sess., pp. 1–2 (Dec. 27, 1836).

65 *Ibid.*, p. 2.

66 National Archives, Senate Committee on Finance, 22d Cong., 1st sess. (Feb. 9, 1832).

67 House Doc. 94, 22d Cong., 2d sess., pp. 7–8 (Feb. 24, 1832).

68 Richardson, *Messages*, V, 285–86 (Dec. 4, 1854).

69 10 Stat. 170 (Feb. 26, 1853). See Senate Ex. Doc. 2, 33d Cong., 2d sess., p. 20 (Dec. 4, 1854) for Secretary Guthrie's further recommendations.

70 House Report 449, 22d Cong., 1st sess., pp. 11–12 (Oct. 20, 1830).

matter to Washington. Corwin added that he would expect a rigid and literal compliance with this order and threatened discharge to any clerks who gave information to private individuals.[71]

OFFICE MANAGEMENT

Although the public service expanded, methods of office management failed to keep pace with the problems that magnitude imposed. Government business was carried on in about the same way in 1860 as in 1800. A government office would have looked much the same in the days of President James Buchanan as in the time of Albert Gallatin. Wooden desks, tables, paper and pen, pigeonholes, ledgers, huge volumes into which outgoing letters were copied, other volumes in which incoming letters were eventually bound, bundles of papers tied with red tape mounting ever higher as cases were closed—all this would have seemed perfectly familiar to a clerk who toiled in the 1820's, could he have entered his old office again in 1860. Typewriters had been invented but had not been sufficiently perfected to interest government offices. Secretary of the Interior Ewing penned a polite refusal to consider the offer of a *typographer* "designed to substitute printing for writing in copying and recording documents. . . ."[72]

The office skills that were required in 1860 were about the same as those needed in 1800 or 1830. At the lowest level, diligence and a good copying hand; at a somewhat higher level, knowledge of routine forms and reports and of the duties of officers and citizens that were recorded thereon; at still another, methods of bookkeeping and principles of accounting which, apart from copying, were the most nearly universal phases of office work; and at the highest levels, specialist knowledge of law, decisions, rules, precedents, and practice peculiar to each office. This skill was acquired exclusively by experience.

The tasks that had to be performed were also nearly identical with those of early days. They were broadly clerical in character

71 National Archives, Treasury Department, Circulars to Collectors and Others, 1850–1862, New Series, No. 63 (Nov. 22, 1851).

72 National Archives, Department of the Interior, Letter Book, Miscellaneous, No. 1, p. 14 (Nov. 29, 1849).

in the midcentury use of the term that included the keeping of accounts and their settlement by auditors and comptrollers. "Clerk" was still the nearly universal designation of government employees, although "agent" was common. Both terms covered a wide variety of occupation and some differentiation of title was taking shape, but the fact remained that most government work was paper work, performed by persons designated as clerks.

There was much evidence of faithful and diligent labor by the clerical forces. After a year's service as Postmaster General, Amos Kendall reported that "more faithful, devoted, and efficient public officers" than his three assistants could not be found, and that "the clerks generally partake of their spirit." [73] Secretary of the Navy Mahlon Dickerson expressed his "entire satisfaction in the faithfulness and diligence with which the duties of all the clerks in my Department are performed." [74] Land Commissioner Richard M. Young recorded that he had been aided "by intelligence and talent of no ordinary character . . . a sense of duty demands of me the pleasing task of bearing testimony to the exemplary deportment of the gentlemen employed in this office, and to the ability and zeal with which each, as a general rule, has faithfully performed his duty." [75]

A constant complaint from the field service was the failure of Congress to authorize expenses for office rent, equipment, and operating costs. The State Department circularized the diplomatic officers abroad in 1845, reminding them that the following charges were inadmissible and would not be allowed: "office rent; messenger's wages; fuel and candles for office, except to the legations at London and Paris; office furniture, with the exception of cases for the preservation of the archives, &c, of the Legation; repairs of office; printing, with the exception of blanks for passports; printed books; maps; clerk hire; copying or translating, except for copies or translations made by order of the Department; donations or contributions to charitable objects; and carriage hire." [76]

Collectors of customs furnished their offices at their own ex-

73 Senate Doc. 1, 25th Cong., 2d sess., p. 797 (Dec. 4, 1837).
74 Senate Doc. 366, 24th Cong., 1st sess., p. 2 (May 7, 1836).
75 Senate Ex. Doc. 2, 30th Cong., 2d sess., p. 35 (Nov. 30, 1848).
76 Printed in Buchanan, *Works,* VI, 208 (July 25, 1845).

pense,[77] and surveyors general of the public lands had to provide office rent and fuel from their own funds. This bore hard on the surveyors, one of whom reminded the General Land Office that the salary of his office was the same in 1836 as when first created forty years before, despite the increase in office expenses and the duties of the office.[78] The General Land Office was sympathetic enough, but Congress was indifferent. In 1837 it appropriated a single sum of $300 to the surveyor general of Arkansas for office rent and fuel, but this item was discontinued thereafter.[79] The registers and receivers of the land offices were notified in 1831 that the only articles of stationery allowed were paper, quills, sealing wax, ink, pencils, wafers, tape or twine; they were expected to buy a year's supply at a time; and they were notified that a "rigid regard to economy must be observed *in the use* as well as in the *purchase*" of these items.[80]

The consequences of throwing the cost of office equipment upon the field agents were precisely those that could have been anticipated. The surveyor stationed at Washington, Mississippi, informed the General Land Office that nowhere in his district were suitable houses and necessary office furniture procured. ". . . there is not half sufficient furniture here for the safekeeping of the papers. The mice, roaches, and crickets all have free access to them; and the mice may and do make beds out of old field notes. Roaches are very destructive to papers, and cannot be kept out without close cases . . . the papers are thrown into old boxes and put out of the way: the roof leaks, perhaps, and injures the books and papers, and at last the Government is the looser [*sic*] for too much economy. . . . I have often heard persons express their surprise at the penurious mistaken economy of the Government in relation to public offices." [81]

STAGNATION IN ADMINISTRATIVE THEORY

The predominance of political and constitutional issues and tension between North and South helps to account for the ab-

77 Senate Doc. 151, 25th Cong., 2d sess., p. 2 (Jan. 26, 1838).
78 Senate Doc. 3, 24th Cong., 2d sess., p. 21 (Sept. 21, 1836).
79 5 Stat. 163, at 167 (March 3, 1837).
80 Senate Doc. 37, 25th Cong., 2d sess., p. 9 (May 25, 1831).
81 Senate Doc. 54, 22d Cong., 1st sess., pp. 4–5 (Nov. 9, 1831).

sence of interest in and writing about the art of administration in terms other than current problems of particular agencies. The dearth of writing about government is nevertheless surprising, if the subject matter of constitutional law is set aside. In the controversy between Democrats and Whigs much was uttered about the proper field of government in human affairs, about the doctrine of strict construction, and the nature of federal executive power. But discussion of the most effective way of organizing an administrative system, of the most suitable means of conducting it, and of the best means of coordinating and controlling its operations was notably absent.

The Jacksonians depended on experience, not on theory, and were confident of the capacity of the people to administer their common affairs. They faced problems, but they dealt with them as practical men on the basis of common sense. It may be argued, indeed, that such a procedure was enough for its time. At any rate, the Jacksonians had nothing to guide them beyond what Hamilton had said in the *Federalist Papers,* and Hamilton was not likely to be acknowledged as the fountainhead of their administrative wisdom.

The administrative art was, in fact, obscured by the art of politics. The two complemented each other, but they also were at war with each other. Victory on the whole was won during these years by the politicians, and their interests seemed to demand sacrifices from the administrative system.

There were nevertheless advances. Science and invention were expediting the course of government business, the bureau system took form, better central control was made possible by the inspection system, and the foundations of the examination system were well laid in the army and navy. The art of management had to be practiced, even if by an "unpracticed man," in Jackson's phrase. Although Hamilton's teaching was lost from sight and no new Hamilton or Gallatin appeared on the scene, the underlying necessities of these expanding years wrought their changes and brought both gain and loss to the administrative art.

CHAPTER TWENTY-EIGHT

Democracy and Administration

William B. Randolph of Virginia, appointed a Treasury clerk in 1816 and chief clerk in the office of the treasurer in 1836, held this post until his death in 1868. His personal experience thus comprehended the transition from the Jeffersonian era to the Jacksonian years, and the full length of the period with which this volume is concerned. As an old man looking back over his official career, he could have recalled both much continuity and much change in the administrative system of which he had so long been a member.

Continuity was imposed by virtue of the essential soundness of the organization established by the Federalists and accepted by the Jeffersonians. It is an arresting fact that the system stood intact from 1789 to the Civil War, and indeed far beyond, adaptable to the emergencies of war and the needs of peace, capable of indefinite expansion in substance, in area, and in means of operation without the necessity of departure from the original foundations on which it was set. Continuity was imposed also by the inherent toughness of any established administrative system, a resistance to change itself based on the stability of law and precedent, on the power of custom, and on the habits of a large number of persons used to fixed ways of working together over the years.

Change was imposed from without, and in large measure can be traced to the impact of democracy on a public service that had become routine and somewhat ingrown in character. The rising spirit of democracy did not require organizational changes in the public service. It simply took possession of the system through the instrumentality of the political party, and by the rule of rotation "restored" the public service to the common man. It was *democracy* in America, not the executive power or the bureaucratic structure, that so forcibly struck the attention of the young Alexis de Tocqueville when he made his journey to the states in 1831.

During these years the administrative system was progressively falling under the influence of pressures and forces external to itself. On the one hand Congress, and individual Congressmen, were making demands upon the government offices. They harassed the departments with requests for information. They were in and out of the public offices on constituents' business. They hunted for places for their political friends. They gave advice on pending claims, and some were not averse to using their influence for the award of contracts. Only when Congress had adjourned could the regular routine of business be resumed.

It was not only Congress and Congressmen who pressed in upon the administrative services. The party organizations in the great cities, and elsewhere to a lesser extent, bore down hard on the field establishments, demanding partisan conformity, political work at election time, and assessments for party funds. Randolph would have heard also of the pressure brought to bear by business lobbies, primarily on Congress, but occasionally on some public offices as well. The protected, insulated service in which he began his official career in 1816 had become exposed to a harsher environment for many years before he retired.

There had nevertheless been no break in the administrative system. The inauguration of Andrew Jackson had many political and some administrative consequences, but the change was not a break in the system. There were no constitutional amendments; the body of administrative law was substantially untouched; the courts continued to mark the legal limits of administrative action. The formal structure and organization of the system were substantially the same in 1860 as in 1830.

The primacy of the Chief Executive in matters of administration stood intact, as Washington and Hamilton and Jefferson had established it. Jackson had roundly confirmed this aspect of Federalist doctrine, Polk had supported it, and lesser Presidents accepted it. No one, not even Duane, challenged it. Likewise the concentration of authority in the respective Secretaries was denied by no one; and Congress took care to attach all parts of the administrative machine to one or another department. There were no more loose ends in 1860 than when Jackson took the oath of office in 1829.

The concept of executive responsibility to the legislative branch of government had been much disputed, and Congress had made dramatic efforts to assert itself. There was no institutional change. The pitched battles that occurred while Jackson was President left the executive power at the moment stronger rather than weaker. The emergence of a new type of party system and the play of rotation and patronage made each branch more dependent on the other, but the net effect was not to weaken the position of the Chief Executive. There had been strong Presidents and weak ones, and the weight of the office had varied with the character of its incumbent. The nature of executive responsibility was not changed by these circumstances, although the effectiveness of executive leadership waxed and waned.

Moral standards and office efficiency both declined during the Jacksonian years. Government business was affected by the same adverse influences that caused deterioration in private business, and that induced many scandals in banking, insurance, and railroad operations. At the same time that vast opportunities for making money were opened up to energetic men, new ideas about democracy, citizen participation, the competence of the untrained but intelligent American, and the character of party warfare were driving forward. The country was full of energy, but it seemed increasingly indifferent to ways and means, so long as they met with success. The contrast between the austere administration of John Quincy Adams and the patronage and contract-dispensing administration of James Buchanan was too vivid to be misunderstood.

DEMOCRATIC THEORY AND ADMINISTRATIVE PRACTICE

It was rare good fortune indeed that brought an intelligent and perceptive Frenchman, Alexis de Tocqueville, from the aristocratic France of his time to the United States to study its penal institutions, and to record the nature of the strange democracy that so fascinated him. Democracy was native to the Americans he met; they boasted about it but could not easily understand it or grasp its significance. Its meaning and interpretation were the contributions that de Tocqueville made in explaining America to his fellow citizens abroad. "In America," he wrote, "the aristocratic element has always been feeble from its birth; and if at the present day it is not actually destroyed, it is at any rate so completely disabled, that we can scarcely assign to it any degree of influence on the course of affairs. The democratic principle, on the contrary, has gained so much strength by time, by events, and by legislation, as to have become not only predominant, but all-powerful." [1]

Democracy rested, de Tocqueville declared, on the economic, social, and educational equality of the people. "The more I advanced in the study of American society," he declared, "the more I perceived that this equality of condition is the fundamental fact from which all others seem to be derived, and the central point at which all my observations constantly terminated." [2] And again, "America, then, exhibits in her social state an extraordinary phenomenon. Men are there seen on a greater equality in point of fortune and intellect, or, in other words, more equal in their strength, than in any other country of the world, or in any age of which history has preserved the remembrance." [3]

The sensitivity of Americans to the democratic quality of their society and government was manifest on every hand. Hezekiah Niles took advantage of remarks by a contemporary about President Jackson traveling "unarmed and unattended, but by his household," to write an indignant editorial.

> The remark is well—and proper. But the servile stupidity is in reference to it as something *extraordinary*. . . . None but a grovelling slave—a fit subject for the sultan of Turkey, would imagine a *president* of the United States travelling otherwise—for so all our presidents have travelled, and, we trust in heaven! always will do. We have seen *president* Adams taking care of his own baggage in a steamboat—and sitting down at the common table, like any other passenger—and thus, we hope, that it ever will be. . . . We saw *general* WASHINGTON thus proceeding to New York, to take his first oath

1 De Tocqueville, *Democracy in America* (1863 ed.), I, 66–67.

2 *Ibid.*, I, 1.

3 *Ibid.*, I, 67.

as president—and have seen *president* WASHINGTON on his return to Mount Vernon—"unarmed and unattended, but by his own household;" and beheld a negro, doff his three cornered *revolutionary* hat, and heartily shake hands with him who was "first in war, first in peace, and first in the hearts of his countrymen"—whose "name and fame" will outlive the pyramids of Egypt, and be more cherished as time shall hallow their adamant. It is the glory of our country that such things always have been; and to suppose that they can be otherwise is—"moral treason." [4]

Candidates for office boasted of their humble origin. Thomas Ewing wrote his constituents in 1836, "If wealthy parentage, tender nurture, and youth spent in ease, in indulgence or luxury, be essential to qualify a man for office in a republic, then am I not qualified, for I have none of those advantages. My father was poor, and lived a life of hardship and privation. . . . With my mental and physical powers as my only inheritance, I was brought up a workingman, or, rather, a workingboy—among the people, and truly one of them. . . ." [5] A log cabin became the passport to political fortune.

This democratic power, which de Tocqueville found somewhat wild, but at least robust, had no place for an officeholding class. Rotation and democracy, as understood in the 1830's, were perfect corollaries.

Public officers in the United States are confounded with the crowd of citizens; they have neither palaces, nor guards, nor ceremonial customs. This simple exterior of persons in authority is connected, not only with the peculiarities of the American character, but with the fundamental principles of society. . . . A public officer in the United States is uniformly simple in his manners, accessible to all the world, attentive to all requests, and obliging in his replies. I was pleased by these characteristics of a democratic government; I admired the manly independence which respects the office more than the officer, and thinks less of the emblems of authority than of the man who bears them.[6]

4 *Niles Register,* XLIV, 353 (July 27, 1833).

5 *Ibid.,* LI, 123 (Oct. 22, 1836).

6 DeTocqueville, *op. cit.,* I, 262–63. He added that the entire absence of unpaid offices was one of the most prominent signs "of the absolute dominion which democracy exercises in that country. All public services . . . are paid; so that every one has not merely a right, but also the means of performing them." *Ibid.,* I, 264.

Francis Bowen repeated the same opinions in an article contrasting American and continental public services. In England and the United States, he declared, public officials "do not constitute a class by themselves, bound together by a semi-military discipline, and responsible only to the head of the government. The feelings and preferences of the people are respected in the selection of them, and they are usually appointed from the vicinity where their services are needed. Men are not educated for office, as for a distinct profession, in which they are to continue through life; but they accept and resign posts of public service, or are turned out of them, as circumstances may require, and consequently are not distinguishable from the body of the people." [7] It was this characteristic of America that so deeply impressed the young Carl Schurz on his first walk around New York after his arrival from Europe in 1852: "no military sentinels at public buildings; no soldiers on the streets; no liveried coachmen or servants; no uniformed officials except the police." [8]

It was the sense of obligation to the people that induced Polk to meet all and sundry who came to the White House, whether friend or foe, office seeker or beggar, visitor from abroad or mere idle citizen. Democracy was visibly present at the presidential mansion, both before and after Polk, even though Commodore Jesse Duncan Elliott had to complain that his pocket was picked "in the president's parlour." [9]

One of the American spokesmen defending democracy and clarifying its philosophy was Judge Frederick Grimke, a South Carolinian who removed to Ohio and served on the State Supreme Court until his retirement in 1842 to devote his time to writing *The Nature and Tendency of Free Institutions.*[10] Grimke examined one by one the allegations against the influence of democracy in officeholding, and refuted them by describing the benefits which popular participation produced.

And first, as to the corrupting influence of office, Grimke

7 *North American Review,* LXXI (1850), 500.

8 Carl Schurz, *Reminiscences,* II, 6.

9 Jackson, *Correspondence,* VI, 381 (March 13, 1845).

10 Frederick Grimke, *The Works of Frederick Grimke* (2 vols. in one, Columbus: Columbus Printing Co., 1871). Volume I contains the third edition of *The Nature and Tendency of Free Institutions,* pp. 1–733, first published in 1848.

argued that office could have a directly opposite effect. He cited the cases of men who seemed to be deficient in intelligence, industry, and sobriety of demeanor transformed by the responsibility of office into men of singleness of purpose and indefatigable industry as if they had discovered an inexhaustible source of enjoyment. In most countries, he pointed out, these individuals would have been wholly cut off from office; and their transformation illustrated, in his view, the automatic correction which representative government imparts to the population.[11]

It was true, Grimke agreed, that the emoluments and influence of office might outweigh the officeholders' sense of the public interest. The remedy for this evil was simple: to distribute power as widely as possible, to assign moderate salaries, and to limit the duration of office.[12] Moderate salaries, neither high nor low, Grimke maintained, enlisted in the service of the state persons in the middle walks of life, raising solid usefulness from obscurity.[13]

Political parties, an essential aspect of a democratic polity, might seem to be merely a struggle between the ins and the outs. But in a republic, parties take the place of the old system of checks and balances. "The latter," wrote Grimke, "balance the government only, the former balance society itself." [14] He stoutly defended the system of rotation.

> Frequent changes are a consequence of these vicissitudes among parties. But it is of the greatest importance, in a country where the electoral franchise is extensively enjoyed, that as large a number of citizens as practicable should be initiated into the mode of conducting public affairs, and there is no way by which this can be so well effected as by a rotation in office. . . . public office, of even an inferior grade, is a species of discipline of no unimportant character. It extends the views of men, trains them to the performance of justice, and makes them act for others as well as for themselves. It thus builds together the parts of society by the firmest of all bonds, and makes it tend constantly to a state of order and tranquillity, in the midst of the greatest apparent disorder.[15]

11 *Ibid.*, I, 130–31.
12 *Ibid.*, I, 131.
13 *Ibid.*, I, 148.
14 *Ibid.*, I, 178.
15 *Ibid.*, I, 178.

"There is," he declared, "no possible way of making free institutions succeed, but by training the popular mind to habits of self government; to make it feel and realize the consequences which ensue from any mistake in the management of public business." [16] He consequently proposed that postmasters should be elected by the votes of the citizens whom they served, although subject to the control of the Post Office Department.[17]

Few were the voices raised against the cult of democracy, either with respect to suffrage and elections or with regard to officeholding, tenure, and rotation in the public service. An occasional aristocratic lament was heard. The biographer of Edward Livingston asserted that the worst of "present evils" was the progress in bridging the gulf which once generally separated low manners from high positions. "How far the effrontery of ill-bred ignorance and incapacity will carry itself towards monopolizing places of dignity, power, and trust, is truly a question of moment." [18]

A scion of an old New England merchant family, James Handasyd Perkins, disagreed completely with Judge Grimke, arguing among other matters against the democratic doctrine of instruction by constituents of their Senators or Representatives. "The idea that the law maker is to obey orders," declared Perkins, "causes us to send blockheads to our legislatures; and having blockheads, instruction, indeed, becomes needful. Could we return to the doctrine of those who wrote the Federalist; could we make our public men leaders, instead of servants, of the people, we should have more heroes, and fewer demagogues and flunkies, among the Honorables of the land." [19]

Francis Bowen denied that rotation was essential to democratic government. On the contrary, he asserted,

> . . . . Frequent change of the incumbents of office is a willful sacrifice of all the tact, skill, and knowledge which may be gained from experience. . . . It is idle to say, that the peculiar principles of our government require this sacrifice of the national interest, or that

16 *Ibid.*, I, 572.

17 *Ibid.*, I, 571–73.

18 Charles Havens Hunt, *Life of Edward Livingston* (New York: Appleton, 1864), p. 13.

19 *North American Review*, LXIX (1849), 452–53. His views corresponded to those of the New York merchant, Philip Hone. See his *Diary* (Nevins ed.), *passim*.

frequent rotation in office is consonant with the genius of democratic institutions. It is not so; true democracy regards the public officer as a public servant, as appointed not because he has any personal claim to the office, not because the appointment itself is a reward, but because it is for the public interest that he should sustain the burden of the station.[20]

The doctrine of popular election of federal officeholders was not accepted in practice, the Constitution standing in the way of Judge Grimke's proposal. It swept the states and local governments, however, to the astonishment of more observers from overseas than de Tocqueville. In the United States, he declared, "society governs itself for itself. . . . The people reign in the American political world as the Deity does in the universe." [21] Even in the states, this phase of democracy caused some concern. The New York city election was described as "making every body vote for every body." "It is the height of folly," said the *New York Express*, "to be making a whole State vote for Inspectors of State Prisons, for example. What do we here know about them, about the management of them, or the proper men to manage them?" [22]

These were voices crying in the wilderness. Americans were committed to democracy and pushed their preference to the limit. The first consequence was the extension of the suffrage, the multiplication of the number of elective officers, abbreviated terms, and the doctrine of instruction of representatives. The administrative system was captured by democratic rotation and the common man—busy with matters political. The structure of the federal system stood intact; its spirit and its customs were deeply affected.

DEMOCRATIC AND WHIG DOCTRINES ON ADMINISTRATION

It would be gratifying if the historian could record that Federalist theories of administration were taken over bodily by the Whigs, and that Jeffersonian doctrines were carried forward intact by the Democrats for another thirty years. Unfortunately for simple exposition, the administrative and political scene

20 *North American Review,* LXXVI (1853), 496.
21 De Tocqueville, *Democracy in America* (1863 ed.), I, 72.
22 Quoted in the *National Intelligencer,* Nov. 24, 1853.

was much too complex to allow such an easy generalization. The Whigs were called Federalists as a term of derogation by the Democrats, but they did not always qualify. The Democrats were the lineal descendants of Jefferson and his Republican party, but Jefferson would have disavowed some of the Democratic doctrine. The great issues of organizational theory and of administrative practice that had divided Hamilton and Jefferson remained the same, but the exigencies of party position shifted alignments of Whigs and Democrats alike.

The most consistent and most precise body of administrative doctrine had been that of the Federalists. Inspired by Hamilton, they preached and practiced the ideas of energy in the executive branch, sustained by the unity of its parts in subordination to the Chief Executive; ample funds; stability; and adequate powers. They recognized the necessity of executive responsibility, both to Congress and the people, but they emphasized power rather than accountability. They insisted upon a fully organized federal administrative system independent of the states, and in conformity with their general theory of loose construction were willing to give it ample authority to do its work. They were friends of administrative discretion, but sought to concentrate it so far as possible in the hands of the President and heads of departments. They drew their public service from the well-to-do classes, and as a matter of course endowed it with permanent tenure. Upon it they impressed the high ethical standards common to gentlemen of the time, north and south. This administrative organization was designed to be intelligent and capable, since the Federalists foresaw great works for it to accomplish in building the national economy.

The Federalists represented the business and mercantile interests, and their policy was designed to foster these classes. They consequently established the First United States Bank; they sought to aid manufacturing, shipping, and merchants; and they created the navy. To insure internal order and external security, they tried, without success, to gain federal leadership of the state militia and to set up a military academy. The Federalists did not hesitate to use force to put down resistance in western Pennsylvania to the payment of the excise tax on whiskey.

The Republicans, in opposition, had also developed a consistent view of the nature and relationships of the administrative system. They were not, however, successful in operating consistently with their initial stock of ideas, and two schools of Democratic thought developed. The old Republicans, to whom Jefferson gave his ideological support, if not his practice as a statesman, and of whom Gallatin was the member most distinguished for consistency, believed that the doctrine of energy was the doctrine of tyranny. They accepted the idea of the unity of executive power, but they had no intention of allowing it to escape a narrow responsibility to Congress. They disliked executive discretion, even in high circles, and sought to limit rather than extend administrative authority. They could do this the more readily since they had no large programs for the general government to carry forward, and they were bound, in theory, by the doctrine of strict construction. The floundering of Congress in 1801 and 1802 quickly brought Jefferson to the practical conclusion, at variance with his theory, that he, as President, would have to take the lead in the direction of both Houses; and the enforcement of the embargo led him to the application of executive power on a truly Hamiltonian scale.

The old Republicans allowed the Bank of the United States to expire in 1812, and only reluctantly established the Second Bank in 1816. They curtailed the army and nearly extinguished the navy, and allowed West Point to languish among the hills up the Hudson. They drastically reduced federal expenditures, set out to liquidate the federal debt, and declined to allow federal authority to be used for internal improvements. Their attachment was to the agricultural interest, and their policy was consistent with their attachment.

The new Republicans, Clay, the young Calhoun, John Quincy Adams, and others, were less cautious in their views on the function of the federal government. Impressed by the urgency of internal improvements they could find room even within the accepted tradition of strict construction for roads and canals built directly by the general government, and John Quincy Adams in this respect was as Federalist as his father. This wing of the Republican party favored energy as well as unity in the executive branch; they did not hesitate to exert executive influence on Congress; and they were not worried by the exercise of administrative discretion.

The Federalist party had disappeared by the election of 1820. The Republican party broke up after the election of 1828. Out of the reshuffling that followed, the Whig and Democratic parties had been formed by the election of 1836, following some years of controversy between groups sufficiently described as Jackson men and Adams men.

At some points Democrats and Whigs were in substantial agreement on doctrine. Neither party pursued any constitutional reforms affecting administration, although Jackson recommended an amendment to allow only a single term for the President, and the Whigs talked about an amendment to establish an independent Treasury. Both parties were reluctant to use federal power to regulate private affairs. They agreed to require the inspection of boilers on steamships, certainly a bold departure from laissez faire, but the issue was a practical, not a theoretical one. The prevailing temper of the times was to leave men free to pursue their own business, and both Whigs and Democrats acceded to it.

Likewise there were no party differences concerning the *administrative* relations between the federal government and the states, despite the great debates on the constitutional issue. The independent dual system of administration, with occasional cooperation where mutually advantageous, was universally accepted. The problems that arose over the mails and the rendition of fugitive slaves were sectional, not administrative, disputes.

It was common ground that the executive branch was responsible to Congress and there was no diminution of the ways and means by which this responsibility was achieved. Indeed, excepting Jackson and Polk, Congress tended to be the aggressive partner under any administration.

Both parties accepted the original pattern of organization and methods of carrying on the public business. These were not years of innovation or experiment, although many improvements were made within the established framework. Administrative stability as to form and structure contrasted with the instability of personnel.

Despite some common ground there were substantial differences in position on basic questions affecting the nature of the administrative system. The Democrats tended to be strict constructionists of federal power and the Whigs, particularly the Clay and Adams men, to favor liberal construction. Had the Whigs been able to support effective national leadership, this distinction might have had considerable influence upon the subject matter assigned to federal agencies.

There was a genuine difference between Democratic and Whig theory of the nature and status of the executive power. Here the Democrats joined the Federalists, while the Whigs shrank even from the cautious theory of the old Republicans. Jackson's energetic exercise of the powers of the President during his warfare with Clay had terminated in his dramatic victory over Congress. The Democratic party thus became committed to a theory of the executive power that was Federalist in character, but that exceeded Federalist pretensions by asserting that the President was as directly a representative of the people as Congress. Jackson and Polk—the only other Democratic President before 1861 to leave an impress upon the office—also drew from Federalist sources in sustaining the unity of executive authority and in using its powers with energy and decision. Both—particularly Polk—were Hamiltonian in their willingness to tell Congress what to do, to use influence to see that its task was done, and to veto actions of Congress they did not like. Jefferson had operated in this way (apart from the veto), but in contradiction to his principles; but his disciples, Madison and Monroe, had faithfully followed his principles.

The Whigs were driven into an incongruous position on the nature and extent of executive power because they had to offer political opposition to the bold exercise of executive authority by Jackson. As a consequence of their minority position from 1829 to 1841, they proposed to restrict the veto. They turned away from executive leadership of Congress. They refuted the doctrine of direct representation. They sought to separate the Treasury from the President. They denied that the President could control the discretion of a department head in the performance of a statutory duty. They denied that the executive power included authority to remove an officer appointed with the consent of the Senate without its concurrence. They sought thus to weaken the presidency, in complete conflict with Federalist doctrine. When Harrison became their first President, they apparently even sought to destroy the unity of the executive by subordinating the President to a majority vote of the Cabinet. Taylor also pursued a policy of abnegation in 1849. The Whigs thus went beyond even the strictest old Republican theory, which had never asserted that the heads of departments were other than subordinate assistants to the Chief Executive.

Implied in these differences in the reading of executive power was a difference in attitude toward Congress. The Whigs tended, in theory, to be more deferential to the legislative branch; but some Democratic Presidents, Van Buren and Pierce for example, worked within the Whig tradition in practice. At this point the Whigs abandoned what might have been thought their proper Federalist inheritance.

There were party differences in theory, but not in practice, with respect to rotation in office and the limitation of tenure. The Whigs argued violently against this departure from both Federalist and Republican theory and practice, but joined company with the Democrats at the first opportunity they had to desert their professions. Both parties came to require partisan loyalty from the bulk of the public service.

The line of doctrinal descent, therefore, was not clear-cut. The Democrats adopted old Republican ideas of strict construction but rejected their views on the limitation of executive power. They accepted the idea of economy and parsimony in government, but abandoned Republican standards in rewarding their friends with office and contracts. They denied the virtue of both Federalist and Republican attachment to a permanent body of clerks and agents and declared efficiency was less important than democracy in administration, to be secured by rotation of officeholders.

The Whigs were also unable to follow the tradition from which they drew their ideas. They were Federalist in their broad view of national authority but old-line Republican in their denial of executive leadership. They were Federalist in their professions about the iniquity of rotation in office, but not in their practice. They were strong in their support of high standards of official conduct, and the loss in this respect in fact occurred under Democratic administrations. The same destructive influences, however, were at work in both parties, as well as resistance on the part of leaders of both, and it is unjust to draw a theoretical difference between them on this point.

These were not years, indeed, in which administrative doctrine was an object of attention. Constitutional and democratic theory absorbed speculative minds. Political partisans were an unlikely source of administrative generalization. Their contribution to theory was made in the heat of controversy and flowed from actions of defense or offense or from calculations of gain or loss taken with respect to particular issues. There was indeed no body or profession concerned with administration in any way corresponding to the lawyers and judges and professors who debated the meaning of the Constitution.

THE JACKSONIAN BEQUEST

Despite confusion in the lines of doctrinal inheritance, and despite interest in action rather than reflection about the course and nature of administration, there could be no doubt in 1860 that a new force had been introduced into the system established by the Federalists and generally maintained by the Jeffersonians. This new element was democracy. It altered profoundly the character and spirit of the old system, for better and for worse. It was an innovation that deserves to rank in its influence, both in its own time and in succeeding generations, with the original doctrines on which the system was based. Moral reform, science, technology, and management were in due course of time to bring new accretions of a different order, but the democratic character of governmental administration was to persist. This was the great contribution of the Jacksonians. It brought endless sources of vitality into the body administrative directly from the body politic, granting all the confusion and waste that were finally to be corrected by more orderly and systematic methods, themselves democratic in character. The relationship between the people and their administrative system was not again to suggest preference to the well-born and the well-to-do.

It seemed in these years as though the Americans had found

new sources of energy and activity with which the spirit of democracy may well have been associated. Richard Cobden could not withhold his amazement on returning to the New World in 1859 after an absence of nearly twenty-five years. ". . . nobody," he wrote, "who has not twice visited the States can comprehend the vitality, force, & velocity of progress of that people, & their inborn aptitude for self-government." [23] The nation was on its way to fulfill the destiny foreseen by de Tocqueville in 1831.

> The time will therefore come, when one hundred and fifty millions of men will be living in North America, equal in condition, all belonging to one family, owing their origin to the same cause, and preserving the same civilization, the same language, the same religion, the same habits, the same manners, and imbued with the same opinions, propagated under the same forms. The rest is uncertain, but this is certain; and it is a fact new to the world,—a fact which the imagination strives in vain to grasp.[24]

To build an administrative system equal to the needs and aspirations of these one hundred and fifty millions of men, on the foundations laid by the Federalists and reconstructed in part by the Jacksonians, was the task of the generations that were yet to come.

23 Cobden, *American Diaries,* p. 73 (Dec. 4, 1861).

24 De Tocqueville, *Democracy in America* (1863 ed.), I, 558.

List of Important Characters

Adams, John Quincy (1767–1848). Federalist son of a Federalist President who joined the Jeffersonian Republicans in 1808; trained to diplomacy; Secretary of State (1817–25); President of the United States (1825–29); Whig member of the House of Representatives, 1831 until his death in 1848; an erudite nationalist whose political sagacity was hampered by his personal independence but whose vision of the future was prophetic.

Bache, Alexander Dallas (1806–1867). Great grandson of Benjamin Franklin and grandson of Madison's Secretary of the Treasury, A. J. Dallas; graduate of West Point; first president of Girard College; a distinguished scientist and an able administrator whose direction of the Coast Survey won world-wide renown.

Bancroft, George (1800–1891). A Massachusetts Democrat who began life as an unsuccessful clergyman and an unsuccessful schoolmaster, who led rural Democracy to factional success and thereby became collector of the port of Boston on his way to the office of Secretary of the Navy (1845–46) where he founded the Naval Academy; diplomat and historian.

Barry, William T. (1785–1835). A Kentucky gentleman, interested in local politics, who became Jackson's Postmaster General and whose amiable character allowed gross impositions and frauds upon the Post Office (1829–35) which in turn led to Post Office reorganization in 1836.

Benton, Thomas H. (1782–1858). Democratic Senator from Missouri; powerful and willful figure in American politics, ambitious for military command during the Mexican War, and an annoyance to the executive branch by demanding favors for relatives and constituents.

Biddle, Nicholas (1786–1844). A cultivated New Yorker, president of the Bank of the United States (1823–36), who unwisely challenged Andrew Jackson in the election of 1832; his defeat involved the destruction of the Bank and eventually his own loss of fortune and reputation.

Blair, Francis P. (1791–1876). Political editor, a friend of Amos Kendall, who supported Jackson in Kentucky in the 1828 election and became editor of the Jackson organ, *The Globe,* in Washington in 1830, a post from which he denounced the Whigs for fifteen years; founder of a politically famous family.

Brown, Obadiah. Clergyman employee of the General Post Office whose jolly good nature facilitated his rise to be assistant Postmaster General in Jackson's first administration, but whose ethical code was inadequate for his responsibilities.

Buchanan, James (1791–1868). A Pennsylvania Democratic politician, life-long participant in the politics of his state and nation; Secretary of State (1845–49) and aspirant for the presidency which he finally attained, too late, in 1857; his ambitions for a second term facilitated the worst features of the spoils system.

Calhoun, John C. (1782–1850). Brilliantly successful as Secretary of War (1817–25); nationalist in his early career and subsequently defender of the doctrine of nullification and of states' rights; frustrated in his hopes for the presidency, he fought every extension of federal activity and of executive power; a Democrat who at times joined the Whigs in opposition to Andrew Jackson.

Cass, Lewis (1782–1866). Governor of Michigan Territory (1813–31) when the canoe was the best means of travel; successful investor in Detroit real estate; Secretary of War (1831–36); Democratic candidate for the presidency in 1848; Senator; Secretary of State under Buchanan until his resignation in 1860.

Clay, Henry (1777–1852). A man of great and unsatisfied ambitions who, after service in the U.S. Senate, entered the House of Representatives in 1811, immediately seized its leadership, and remained a dominant influence therein until his death; an organizer of the Whig party, a nationalist, and a political enemy of Andrew Jackson; his administrative experience as Secretary of State (1825–29) was overshadowed by his political career and his skill in inventing formulae to solve critical divisions of opinion.

Cobb, Howell (1815–1868). A well-educated and well-to-do Georgian who devoted his life to public affairs; a Union Democrat, Speaker of the House (1849–51), and Secretary of the Treasury under Buchanan (1857–61); a Confederate Army general.

Corwin, Thomas (1794–1865). A self-made Whig politician, Governor of Ohio in 1840 and U.S. Senator (1845–50); Secretary of the Treasury (1850–53).

Crittenden, John J. (1787–1863). A Kentucky Whig, highly respected in state and national circles; Attorney General for a few months under Harrison (1841), and again under Fillmore (1850–53); Governor of Kentucky 1848, 1850; U.S. Senator, 1855–63.

Cushing, Caleb (1800–1879). A Massachusetts judge and politician, Attorney General under Pierce (1853–57); a powerful exponent of executive power.

Davis, Jefferson (1808–1889). Professional military officer, graduate of West Point, planter, Senator and defender of states' rights; Secretary of War (1853–57) in which post he demonstrated both much administrative skill and high standards as well as an oversensitive and quarrelsome character; President of the Confederate States.

Dobbin, James C. (1814–1857). A prosperous North Carolina lawyer and reluctant candidate for the House of Representatives where he served one term under Polk; influential in securing the nomination of Franklin Pierce, he became Secretary of the Navy (1853–57); although unfamiliar with naval matters he made a bold and aggressive attack on abuses and failures; a "big navy" man, an advocate of steam rather than sails, and the founder of the navy officer retired list. He demonstrated the value of high intelligence, courage, and determination in civilian leadership of the armed forces.

Duane, William J. (1780–1865). Son of the pamphleteer, William Duane, who suffered under the Alien and Sedition Acts in 1799; a

Pennsylvania merchant, lawyer, and politician, he was appointed Secretary of the Treasury in 1833 to withdraw government funds from the Bank of the United States; his independence in refusing to follow Jackson's intentions cost him his office after less than four months.

Eaton, John H. (1790–1856). Friend of Andrew Jackson; U.S. Senator from Tennessee; Secretary of War (1829–31), and the unwilling cause of the collapse of Jackson's first Cabinet.

Everett, Edward (1794–1865). Scholar, orator, politician, and diplomat; Governor of Massachusetts (1836–40); Secretary of State (1852–53); Whig defender of the doctrine of rotation and party responsibility.

Fillmore, Millard (1800–1874). A hard-working New York Whig politician and state executive; member of the House of Representatives; elected Vice President in 1848 and succeeded Taylor in the White House in 1850.

Gilmer, Thomas W. (1802–1844). A Virginia Democrat of the Jeffersonian school who, as author of a remarkable House committee report in 1842 advocating economy and reform, earned the title "Retrenchment Gilmer"; Secretary of the Navy (1844) until his death occasioned by an explosion on the *U.S.S. Princeton.*

Gouge, William M. (1796–1863). A student of banking who became a Treasury clerk and who during the 1840's and 1850's was so often relied upon for field investigations in different governmental agencies that he may be justly called the first federal inspector.

Guthrie, James (1792–1869). A Kentucky Democrat active in state politics who turned to railroad, finance, and real estate enterprises; Secretary of the Treasury under Pierce (1853–57), he was a ruthless reformer and a master of faction.

Harrison, William H. (1773–1841). A successful military officer in the War of 1812; unsuccessful in private life, he became clerk of court in Cincinnati; the successful Whig candidate in the election of 1840, he advocated executive submission to the legislative branch, but was resisting Cabinet control of the executive power when he died after one month in office.

Hawthorne, Nathaniel (1804–1864). A distinguished literary figure whose friends found him government employment as a customs officer and as a consular agent while the Democrats were in power; perhaps the most distinguished writer among a number who became public servants during the Jacksonian era.

Henry, Joseph (1797–1878). A distinguished physicist, member of the faculty of Princeton University, first secretary of the Smithsonian Institution (1846–78).

Hill, Isaac (1788–1851). A New Hampshire politician, newspaper publisher, and mail contractor whose nomination by Jackson as second comptroller was defeated in the Senate in 1830 and who in 1831 was elected a member of the body that had denied him his appointment; a violent Democrat.

Hone, Philip (1780–1851). A New York merchant, a Whig with aristocratical leanings who, when his fortunes were at a low ebb, accepted a subordinate post in the New York customhouse, and who there took care of his relatives.

Hoyt, Jesse. Collector of the port of New York (1838–41), a freebooter in the world of politics who exploited the customhouse patronage for the Democratic party and for himself.

Hunter, Robert M. T. (1809–1887). A Virginia statesman, of the Democratic persuasion, Senator (1847–61), and author of the first examination system for the headquarters clerks; Confederate Secretary of State.

Jackson, Andrew (1767–1845). Tennessee planter, soldier, Governor of Florida Territory, Senator, and President of the United States (1829–37); advocate of rotation in office as a defense against bureaucracy; defender of the Union against nullification, and of the executive branch against the Senate.

Kendall, Amos (1789–1869). A Yankee who emigrated to Kentucky, became an editor and advocate in 1828 of Andrew Jackson; fourth auditor (1829–35); Postmaster General (1835–40); an executive of high ideals and much administrative skill touched with hypocrisy, and an intimate political adviser of Presidents Jackson and Van Buren; in his later years an associate of the inventor, Samuel F. B. Morse, and a philanthropist.

King, Horatio (1811–1897). A career man in the Post Office who by diligence and reliability became indispensable to Democratic and Whig Postmasters General alike; assistant Postmaster General and for the last month of Buchanan's term, Postmaster General—the first career man to hold Cabinet post.

Marcy, William L. (1786–1857). A New York politician, one-time Governor of the state, Senator, Secretary of War under President Polk (1845–49) and Secretary of State under Pierce (1853–57); author of the phrase "to the victor belong the spoils of the enemy," who after administrative experience recanted and sought to establish a career consular service.

Maury, Matthew Fontaine (1806–1873). A professional naval officer and scientist who earned world-wide fame by reason of his studies of ocean winds and currents; one of the founders of oceanography and a symbol of an emerging interest of the executive branch in the pursuit of science.

Paulding, James K. (1778–1860). Author and friend of Washington Irving; Secretary of the Navy (1838–41) where he tried unsuccessfully to restore the navy to its high tradition before Jackson.

Pierce, Franklin (1804–1869). New Hampshire Democratic politician and soldier who sat inconspicuously in the Senate (1837–42) and became a successful compromise candidate for the presidency (1853–57); he was personally popular but not an executive success.

Polk, James K. (1795–1849). A Tennessee politician, active in both state and national affairs, influential member of the House of Representatives (1825–39); an unexpectedly vigorous Chief Executive (1845–49) who ran the Mexican War from the White House, successfully led a reluctant Congress, and wore himself out performing the mass of executive duties that he felt under moral obligation to handle personally.

Scott, Winfield (1786–1866). A professional army officer who in his early years made valuable contributions to the military art; commander of the expedition against Mexico City; Democratic candidate for the presidency in the election of 1848; his proud, touchy, and quarrelsome nature progressively became a burden to the government of the day.

Swartwout, Samuel (1783–1856). A New York speculator and politician appointed collector of the port of New York in 1829, an office from which he fled to Europe in 1838 having embezzled about $1,250,000; one of Jackson's most resounding errors.

Taney, Roger B. (1777–1864). A Maryland Democrat and successful member of the bar; Attorney General (1831–33); enemy of the Bank of the United States; Secretary of the Treasury (1833–34); member and Chief Justice, U.S. Supreme Court.

Taylor, Zachary (1784–1850). A professional soldier, although not a West Point graduate, who made his reputation in the Mexican War and was the successful Whig candidate in the election of 1848; although he adopted the Whig theory of executive abnegation he showed capacity for independence before his death in 1850; he yielded to the practice of rotation in office.

Tyler, John (1790–1862). A Virginia Democrat of the old Jeffersonian school, friend of states' rights and opponent of the Bank of the United States; elected Vice President on the Whig ticket in 1840, and succeeded to the presidency in 1841; a critic of rotation in office and defender of high standards; broke with Whigs and not sustained by Democrats; his was a stormy and frustrated administration.

Van Buren, Martin (1782–1862). Wily New York politician who resigned as Governor in 1829 to become Secretary of State (1829–31) and Jackson's principal adviser; the Senate, by Calhoun's vote, rejecting his nomination as minister to Great Britain, he was elected Vice President in 1832, and President in the election of 1836. Undistinguished in executive office.

Walker, Robert J. (1801–1869). A Mississippi planter and speculator, who as Secretary of the Treasury (1845–49) was responsible for financing the Mexican War, and who became a notable exponent of tariff for revenue only.

Webster, Daniel (1782–1852). Orator and statesman whose hope for the presidency was frustrated; a Whig opponent of Andrew Jackson and the executive power; Senator and critic of rotation in office; Secretary of State (1841–43) and again (1850–52).

Weed, Thurlow (1797–1882). A New York Whig, printer to the state of New York when his friends were in control, a lobbyist who exerted influence on state and national affairs for more than two decades, serving the rising business interest of his time.

Woodbury, Levi (1789–1851). New Hampshire Democrat, Senator, Secretary of the Navy (1831–34) and of the Treasury (1834–41); in the latter capacity a friend of congressional influence on federal field appointments.

INDEX